THE SECOND SOVIET REPUBLIC

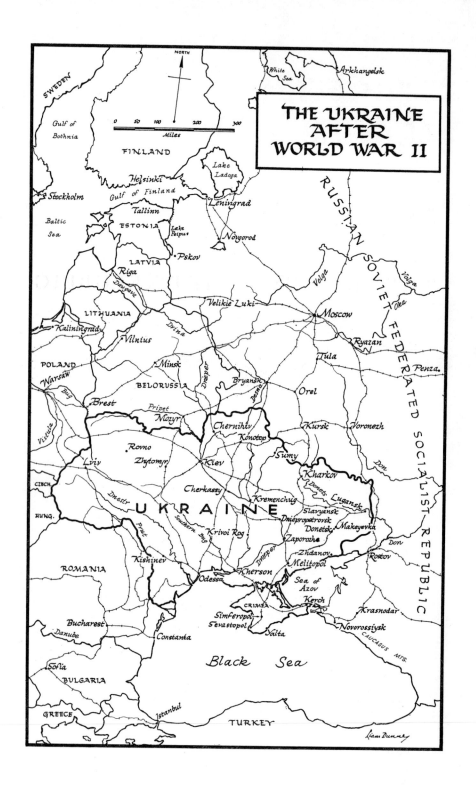

THE UKRAINE
AFTER
WORLD WAR II

THE SECOND SOVIET
REPUBLIC: *The Ukraine*
after World War II · · ·

by

YAROSLAV BILINSKY

RUTGERS UNIVERSITY PRESS
New Brunswick   *New Jersey*

To my mother and the memory of my father

PREFACE

This book has grown out of ten years' study of the Ukraine—half of them as an undergraduate at Harvard College and a graduate student at Princeton University. In essence, it constitutes a substantially revised and updated version of my doctoral dissertation *Ukrainian Nationalism and Soviet Nationality Policy After World War II* (1958). Some of the material goes back to my bachelor's honors thesis on *The Ukrainian National Movement Since 1920* which was written in 1954.

My objective is to shed light on recent political events and processes in the Ukraine, a country which for the past two decades has played a passive but not inconsiderable role in world affairs. When in 1945 the Ukraine was admitted as one of the charter members of the United Nations, this only served to emphasize in the minds of the public what had long been known to experts, that in terms of economic potential and political future she was the second Republic in the Soviet Union.

At the present time, to be sure, the Ukraine is as dependent upon the dictates of the central government in Moscow as are the fourteen other Soviet Republics. The Ukraine's membership in the United Nations ought not to be construed as an indication that the country is sovereign, except in the special meaning of Soviet constitutional law. But it is not difficult to envisage that in the long run a people of forty million will not remain content with their present subordinate position. The Ukraine occupies a strategic location in the south of the USSR. Known of old as the breadbasket of Europe, she has now reached or even surpassed West European standards in the spread of higher education and the production of the basic industrial commodities: coal, iron, and steel.

Since Stalin's death in 1953, the Ukrainian people have shown a political assertiveness unequalled except during the relatively liberal 1920's. A French diplomatic maxim—which ought to serve as a motto for political science as well—stresses that *prévoir est prévenir* (to foresee is to forearm). It explains in part why I have undertaken this study. It is my belief that the role of the Ukraine in East European and world affairs is bound to grow with time, and that it is none too early to analyze the politics of that country in her present severely restricted state.

The reader may also want to know the basic values with which I have approached the subject. I am convinced that in the long view the Ukraine would benefit from a loosening of her bonds with Russia and a closer association with other countries of Europe. But I am not sanguine about the prospects for such a realignment in the near future. In any case the decisions will be made by the Ukrainian people themselves, and their friends abroad can help only by clarifying the issues.

Many persons and institutions have helped me in the task of writing this book. It will be my pleasant duty to express my gratitude in a separate section. To conclude the preface, the reader's attention is invited to some technical matters.

The bibliographical references furnished in the main text and the notes are sufficiently complete to identify the sources without ambiguity, but they are not exhaustive. Thus, most of the titles of articles in Russian and Ukrainian have not been transliterated, but directly translated into English. To alert the reader that those are not the original titles, they have been put in brackets in the case of journal articles. Nor have the publishers been indicated in Soviet materials, only the place and the year of publication. The missing information will be found in the bibliography at the end. Furthermore, it will be noticed that lengthy notes on particular topics have all been put into the appendix. Finally, a few words on the transliteration of Russian and Ukrainian words.

There is no standard system of transliteration which would please the professional linguist and the nonspecialist alike. The author's aim has been to give the latter a reasonably accurate rendition of the original, while shying away from diacritical marks and other subtleties which linguists may regard as necessary for their own purposes. In this book there has been used a simplified version of the system employed in the Slavonic Division of the New York Public Library as well as by the former Research Program on the USSR. (It is outlined in Jurij Lawrynenko's bibliography of *Ukrainian Communism and Soviet Russian Policy toward the Ukraine* [New York: Research Program on the USSR, 1953], pp. 417–18.) The main characteristic of our version is that, unlike the Library of Congress system, it uses the English "y" instead of the "i" to render both the Russian and Ukrainian "short i" (й). The English "y" has also been used to transliterate the Russian "ы" and the Ukrainian "и." Whenever a "short i" in the two languages (й) immediately follows an "ы" or an "и," the awkward combination of "yy" has been contracted to a single "y." The Ukrainian "i diphthong" (ï), which has no equivalent in Russian, has been rendered in English as "yi," as in *Ukrayina* (Ukraine). The same word transliterated from Russian would be *Ukraina*.

Wilmington, Delaware   YAROSLAV BILINSKY
May, 1964

ACKNOWLEDGMENTS

It is an honor and a pleasure to express my indebtedness to the following institutions and persons:

In the spring of 1956 the University of Pennsylvania awarded me a Penfield Traveling Scholarship in Diplomacy, International Affairs, and Belles Lettres, which enabled me to undertake postgraduate training in Soviet affairs at the Harvard Graduate School of Arts and Sciences in 1956–57, and to conduct interviews in this country and in Western Europe.

The Russian Research Center of Harvard University appointed me an Associate in September 1956, opening to me its excellent technical facilities and enabling me to learn from the quality of its staff. I was associated with the Center until 1958.

In 1962 the University of Delaware awarded me a Summer Faculty Fellowship toward the revision of the manuscript for publication.

Furthermore, I should like to acknowledge the kind help which the following institutions and organizations have given me with materials and with personal contacts: The American Committee for Liberation, of New York; the Association of Ukrainians in Great Britain (S.U.B.), in London; the Central Union of Political Emigrants (Ts.O.P.E.), the Executive of the Ukrainian National Council, and the Institute for the Study of the USSR—all three in Munich; the Yivo Institute for Jewish Research, the Prolog Research and Publishing Association—both of New York; the Shevchenko Scientific Society, in Paris; the Ukrainian Academy of Arts and Sciences in the United States, of New York; the Ukrainian Free University, of Munich; and the Ukrainian Congress Committee of America, in New York.

Professor Merle Fainsod of Harvard University had encouraged me to undertake the first venture in this field. His incisive criticism of my honors bachelor's thesis proved useful in all of my subsequent work. Professors Gabriel A. Almond, Cyril E. Black, William Ebenstein, and Dankwart A. Rustow, then all of Princeton University, read my dissertation. Subsequently, the following scholars read the manuscript with a

ix

view toward publication and offered many valuable suggestions: Mr. Vsevolod Holubnychy; Dr. Myroslav Prokop, of the Prolog Research and Publications Association; Professor John S. Reshetar, Jr., of the University of Washington; and Professor Roman Smal-Stocki, of Marquette University.

The following persons have kindly helped me with advice and materials, or have consented to be interviewed at length:

Father Volodymyr Gavlich, Ph.D.; the Right Reverend Vicar General Msgr. Peter Holynskyj, Ph.D.; the Right Reverend Vicar General Msgr. Myron Hornykevycz, Ph.D.; Father Iwan Leskowycz;

Professor John A. Armstrong, Professor I. Bakalo, Mrs. Vera Beke, Mr. Bentsal', Mr. Andrij Bilinskyj, Prof. Dr. phil. Jurij Boyko, Dr. Randolph L. Braham, Professor Zbigniew K. Brzezinski, Mr. Fedir Bulbenko, Professor Nicholas Chubaty, the late Mr. Yaroslav J. Chyz, Mr. M. Czekanskyj, Mrs. Catharine de Bary Dupuy, Professor Nicholas De Witt, Col. Jaromir Diakow (ret.), Mr. Michael Dobriansky, the late Professor Volodymyr Doroshenko, Mr. Spyrydon Dovhal', Mr. Iwan Dubrowskyj;

Professor Rupert Emerson, Dr. Bohdan Fedenko, Professor Panas Fedenko, Miss Nina Fedorenko, Professor Robert Feldmesser, the late Dr. Philip Friedman, Professor Carl J. Friedrich, Professor Eugene Glowinsky, Mr. Sergius I. Golbov, Professor Erich Goldhagen, the late Gen. Michael Grekov (ret.), Mr. Fred Holling, Dr. Oleksa Horbatsch, Professor Vasyl Hryshko;

Professor Alex Inkeles, the late Professor Michael Karpovich, Mr. Volodymyr Kasianchuk, Dr. Khrobak, Col. Arkhyp Kmeta (ret.), the late Dr. Anthony Knyazhynsky, Professor H. Kolodij, Professor Nestor Korol, Professor Ivan Krylov, Professor Volodymyr Kubijovyč, Mr. Jurij Lawrynenko, Mr. Mykola Lebed', Mr. Eugen Lewitzky, Mr. Borys Lewytzkyj, Dr. Joseph L. Lichten, Mr. Mykola Livitsky, Mr. and Mrs. Omel'yan Logush;

Mr. Iwan Majstrenko, the late Dr. Arnold D. Margolin, Professor Vasyl Markus, the late Professor Ivan Mirchuk, M. Wasile Mychaltchouc, Professor Petro Odarchenko, Professor Jacob Ornstein, the late Dr. Lyubomyr Ortynsky, Dr. Jaan Pennar, Professor Alexander Philipov, Mr. Fedir Pigido, Professor Richard E. Pipes, Professor Oleksa Powstenko;

The late Professor Leo Rebet, Professor Alvin Z. Rubinstein, Mrs. Milena Rudnycka, Professor John L. Rudnytsky, Col. Vladimir Rudolf; Joseph Scholmer, M.D.; Mr. George Semenko, the late Mr. John Senko, Professor Leo Shankowsky, Professor Yury G. Shevelov, Dr. Matthew Stakhiv, Mr. Volodymyr Stakhiv, Mr. Michael Sushko, Prince Basil Swiatopolk-Mirski;

Mr. George Tarkovych, Mr. Michael Terpak, M. Georges Turkewicz, Mrs. Olena Usenko, the late Professor Michael Vetukhiv, Mr. Michael

Verbytsky, Mrs. Valentina Vorobay, Dr. Morris Watnick, Professor John B. Whitton, Professor I. Zamsha, Mr. Vladimir Zhukovsky, Mrs. Osyp Zinkevych.

I am grateful also to a number of persons, including a former staff officer of the Soviet Army, who have chosen to remain anonymous.

As usual, acknowledgment does not imply that any of the above mentioned institutions and persons would agree with everything I have said; I have not always been able to accept their advice. I am deeply grateful for their help and take upon myself any errors of fact or judgment which I may have committed.

I have greatly benefited from the courteous assistance of the Staffs of the Harvard University Libraries: Widener, Lamont, and that of the Russian Research Center; the Columbia University Libraries; the Libraries of Congress and of the Department of State; the Library of the Institute for the Study of the USSR, in Munich; the New York Public Library; the *Svoboda* editorial library, in Jersey City; the Memorial Library of the University of Delaware.

The editorial staff of Rutgers University Press patiently endured long delays and then subjected the manuscript to a painstakingly careful scrutiny. I have learned from them a great deal, and the book is the better for it.

The lion's share of the dissertation was financed from the proceeds of the Penfield Traveling Scholarship of the University of Pennsylvania. The Harvard Russian Research Center supported a linguistic study based on the data of the Harvard Project on the Soviet Social System. The book itself has been supported by a faculty fellowship from the University of Delaware, a grant from the Ukrainian American Association of University Professors, and a sales guarantee by the Prolog Research and Publishing Association.

The following publishers, institutions and persons have given permission to use the copyrighted material indicated in parentheses:

His Excellency Msgr. Ivan Buchko, Apostolic Visitator of Ukrainians in Western Europe (*First Victims of Communism: White Book on the Religious Persecution in the Ukraine;* 1953); George Allen & Unwin Ltd (*The Soviet Economy: An Introduction,* by Alec Nove; 1961); the Associated Press (one despatch); A. S. Barnes & Co. (*Star in Eclipse: Russian Jewry Revisited,* by Joseph B. Schechtman; 1961); Blaisdell Publishing Co. (*Constitutional Government and Democracy,* by Carl J. Friedrich; 1946); Columbia University Press (*Ukrainian Nationalism, 1939–1945,* by John A. Armstrong; 1955); Duell, Sloan & Pearce (*Why I Escaped,* by Peter Pirogov; 1950); Farrar, Straus & Co. (*Eastern Exposure,* by Marvin L. Kalb; 1958); Harper & Row (*Roosevelt and Hopkins,* by Robert E. Sherwood; 1948); the Harvard Russian Research Center (unpublished material of the Harvard Project on the Soviet Social System); Harvard University Press (*How Russia Is Ruled,* by Merle Fainsod; 1st ed., 1953; and *How the Soviet System Works,* by Raymond A. Bauer, A. Inkeles, and C. Kluckhohn; 1956); *International Organization* (an article by Rupert Emerson and Inis L. Claude); International Publishers (*Marxism and Linguistics,* by I. V. Stalin); Joint Committee on Slavic Studies, appointed by the American Council of Learned Societies and the Social Science Research Council (several items from the *Current Digest of the Soviet Press,* published at Columbia University, and from *Current Soviet Policies II* [1957] and *Current Soviet Policies IV* [1962]); The Macmillan Company (*The Idea of Nationalism,* by Hans Kohn; 1946); St. Martin's Press, Inc., and Macmillan & Co. Ltd. (*German Rule in Russia, 1941–45,* by Alexander Dallin; 1957); the Massachusetts Institute of Technology Press (*Nationalism and Social Communication,* by Karl W. Deutsch; 1953); *The New York Times* (three items); Oxford University Press (*Nationalism,* 1939; and *America, Britain and Russia,* by William H. McNeill; 1953— books published under the auspices of the Royal Institute of International Affairs); Frederick A. Praeger, Inc. (*The Soviet Bureaucratic Elite,* by John A. Armstrong [1959], and *Russia Under Khrushchev,* ed. by Abraham Brumberg [1962]); Prentice Hall, Inc. (*Russia's Soviet Economy,* by Harry Schwartz; 1950); Mr. Solomon M. Schwarz (his *Antisemitizm v Sovetskom Soyuze,* 1952); The Stettinius Fund, Inc., and Doubleday & Company, Inc. (*Roosevelt and the Russians,* by Edward R. Stettinius, Jr.; 1949); Syracuse University Press (*The Jews in the Soviet Union,* by Solomon M. Schwarz; 1951); the Ukrainian Academy of Arts and Sciences in the U.S., Inc. (articles by Petro Odarchenko, Vyacheslav Prokopovych, John S. Reshetar, and A. Yakovliv published in their *Annals*); United States Information Agency (an article by Erich Goldhagen, which appeared in the *Problems of Communism*); University of Pittsburgh Press (*Khrushchev and the Central Committee Speak on Education,* by George S. Counts; 1959); Viking Press Inc. (*Russia Without Stalin,* by Edward Crankshaw; 1956); Yivo Institute for Jewish Research (an article by Philip Friedman in a *YIVO Annual*). In addition, I would like to thank the editors of *Soviet Studies* and the Ukrainian Academy of Arts and Sciences in the U.S., Inc. (publishers of *The Annals . . .*) for permission to use my articles, which were first published in their journals.

To all those persons and institutions I wish to express my cordial gratitude, but above all to my former teachers at Princeton and Harvard Universities, named and unnamed. The debt which I owe to my mother, Mrs. Natalia Bilinsky, and my wife, Wira Rusaniwskyj Bilinsky, is too great to be adequately described in these pages.

Y. B.

CONTENTS

TABLES

Table No.

CHART

Chapter I

SOVIET POLICY TOWARD THE UKRAINE AFTER WORLD WAR II: AN HISTORICAL SURVEY

When World War II ended in the spring of 1945, millions of Ukrainian citizens had been killed and millions either evacuated or deported; the cities and towns lay in rubble; the countryside had been emptied of all but women, old men, and children; the economy had been desolated and ravaged. Paradoxically, for all the horrendous impact of the war, Ukrainian nationalism—that complex amalgam of a people's aspirations which, in due course, crystallizes into a desire for national independence [1]—was stronger in 1945 than it had been at the end of a similar catastrophe in 1917–18, possibly stronger than it had been ever before in modern Ukrainian history. For the first time since the Middle Ages were the different branches of the Ukrainian people reunited in one state. In Eastern Ukraine, a modern economy had been created, many people had obtained a modern education and become nationally conscious partly owing to, and partly in spite of, Soviet policy. In smaller Western Ukraine, the political and socio-economic struggle with the powers that held the territory between the wars—chiefly Poland—had brought Ukrainian nationalism to the boiling point. It was in those areas that the Ukrainian Insurgent Army offered resistance to the victorious Soviet troops in a desperate guerrilla warfare that was not ended until some five years after the fall of Berlin. The Soviet government that had always paid lip service to the idea of Ukrainian sovereignty within the confines of the USSR, in 1944–45, sponsored the admission of the Soviet Ukrainian Republic—the second Republic of the Soviet Union—to the newly organized United Nations, though the Ukraine had been previously kept out of the League of Nations. The Ukraine still remained a part of the Soviet Union, to be sure; but ravaged and depopulated as she was, her weight in Soviet politics had increased and, albeit under Moscow's strict supervision, she made her first exploratory steps in the world of the dictators, the democracies, and the atom bomb.

This work seeks to unravel that supreme paradox of a nation rising from the ashes of one of the bloodiest wars in the history of mankind— a nation still dependent, but no longer unknown. Relying on its apparatus of control, the Soviet government has attempted to portray the Ukrainian people as desirous of nothing but union with its elder Russian brother. It has almost succeeded in suppressing all *overt* manifestations to the contrary. Unlike a historian of the struggle for independence in 1917–20 or the German occupation of 1941–44, this writer cannot evaluate the actions of Ukrainians at comparative liberty. On the contrary, he is dealing with a people whose freedom of action is severely limited by a totalitarian state. This calls for a broad, perhaps a seemingly unfocussed, analysis of the different aspects which are important in the growth of a modern nation: its demographic and socio-economic base (Chapter II), the problems linked with the integration of new territories (the integration of Western Ukraine in Chapters III–IV), the Ukrainian cultural heritage as manipulated by the regime in power (Chapters V, VI, VII), the question of the rising elite (Chapter VIII), and the possible impact of the admission to the United Nations (Chapter IX). To give the work a measure of cohesion, to help the reader find his path in this array of topical analyses, the first chapter presents a chronological survey of Soviet policy toward Ukrainian nationalism, mainly after World War II; the last chapter presents interview findings on the depth of national feeling among Soviet Ukrainians.

Many of our conclusions about the strength of Ukrainian national feeling will of necessity be tentative, grounded as they are on inferences from the effectiveness of Soviet policy in the Ukraine and from interviews with a small sample of former Soviet citizens. In a sense, the entire book, resting to a large degree on such indirect evidence, is not so much a definite conclusion as a tentative prediction. Only future historians will be able to substantiate whether the rise of the Ukrainian people after World War II is the irreversible growth of a nation or the last desperate struggle of a group of men who are being ground under the wheels of time. The author is not a chronicler of the past, but one who wants to understand the politics of the present and hopes to aid to foresee that of the future. In this chapter he has tried, for the sake of readers who are not familiar with modern Ukrainian history, to give not only an account of postwar Soviet policy in the Ukraine but also some of its background.

In the aftermath of the February Revolution of 1917 and the break-up of the Austro-Hungarian Empire in October, 1918, the Ukrainians tried to set up an independent state. It is common knowledge that they failed and that the Ukrainian-inhabited territories were partitioned among the stronger neighbors: Soviet Russia reconquered the lion's share of the Tsarist patrimony, Poland retained Eastern Galicia and annexed the province of Volhynia, Czechoslovakia incorporated the Transcarpathian Ukraine, and Rumania—Northern Bukovina and Bessarabia. While this is not the place even to sketch what occurred in those years,[2] it might nevertheless be useful to consider what appear to be the most important reasons for the failure to achieve independence.

Analyzing the struggle for independent Ukrainian statehood in 1917–20, one cannot divest oneself of the impression that the whole attempt was premature, at least so far as the Eastern Ukraine is concerned. In other words, a case might be made for the proposition that no matter how hard Ukrainian nationalists [3] may have tried, their efforts were doomed from the beginning. In the first place, the overwhelming majority of the Eastern Ukrainian peasantry, while being conscious of their ethnical distinctness from the Russians and while having an economic stake in Ukrainian autonomy (see below), did not join the nationalist armies in sufficiently large numbers to ensure their victory. They were preoccupied with obtaining land and hoped that whatever regime came to power it would help them divide the large estates in accordance with their liking. Secondly, the cities and towns in the Ukraine that for decades had been the bastions of Russian influence did not turn Ukrainian overnight: the Ukrainian nationalist intelligentsia who were not too numerous in any event, were greatly handicapped by not commanding the allegiance of, for example, the majority of the residents of the Ukrainian capital—Kiev. Third, extensive as the contacts with the national movement in Galicia had become in the first two decades of the twentieth century, the differences in the outlook of the Ukrainian leaders on both sides of the frontier persisted and were bound to erupt into serious policy conflicts at some critical stage of the war for independence.

If one carefully reads the pre-Revolutionary writings of one of the foremost Ukrainian leaders, Symon Petlyura, one is struck by the deep sense of responsibility that prevailed among the most influential Ukrainian nationalists. Petlyura was fully aware of the weaknesses of the movement and in late 1914, for example, advocated for his people no more than political autonomy.[4] The decision to declare Ukrainian independence *de facto* on November 20, 1917 (New Style), and quite openly on January 22, 1918, seems to have been taken not so much in response to the youthful exuberance of the rapidly developing national movement, but on the sober consideration that in the political vacuum following the collapse of the Provisional Government, the representative organs in the Ukraine—the Central *Rada* (Council) and its General Secretariat—simply had to provide for civil order in the territory which they effectively or nominally controlled. The peculiar goals of the Bolshevik government soon made any cooperation between Kiev and Petrograd impossible, and so long as the Bolsheviks remained in power, any plans of collaborating with a democratic Russian movement had to be shelved in favor of complete independence, however risky that latter course might have appeared to all but a group of nationalist firebrands.

The Ukrainian leaders also committed several mistakes which did not improve the situation in the least. Unlike Lenin, who knew how to ride the tides of popular passions whenever this suited his ulterior purposes, Ukrainian nationalists did not dare to endorse the peasants' taking over the land until the Bolsheviks had stolen their thunder. Lacking munitions and drugs, they would rely on the aid of Allies, which, on the whole, was not forthcoming because the Western Powers remained committed to the notion of a one and indivisible "Russia." Ukrainian inability—but not unwillingness, as has sometimes been alleged—to curb anti-Jewish pogroms [5] greatly contributed to ill-feeling abroad and was probably an important factor in the decision of the Allies to support the conservative Russian general Denikin rather than the socially progressive, but unknown Ukrainian leader Petlyura. While it is difficult to say how much Allied matériel would have helped Petlyura, it seems clear in retrospect that a worse choice than that of Denikin could hardly have been made.[6]

While in 1917–20 the hurdles on the road to Ukrainian independence were high, if not altogether insurmountable, one ought not to assume that the movement in that direction was nothing but a rash venture of a few intellectuals, supported by a few thousands of romantic youth. In terms of integrated popular backing the Galicians were furthest advanced on the road to statehood, but there were too few of them to fight off the well-armed Poles who claimed Eastern Galicia as a historically Polish territory.[7] Nor was the movement in the Dnieper Ukraine without popular roots though they proved weaker than those in Galicia. Students as critical of the Ukrainian national movement as E. H. Carr and Richard Pipes have indicated occasions on which the great potential strength of the movement was clearly revealed. As Pipes points out, the Ukrainian peasantry were not interested in sharing their land with the landless Russian peasants from the North—which would have been the likely outcome of an all-Russian land reform—and in the spring of 1917 it was they who pressed the Central *Rada* to demand greater self-rule for the Ukraine.[8] Furthermore, in the election to the Constituent Assembly on November 25, 1917, the Ukrainian peasants gave an overwhelming proportion of their vote to Ukrainian rather than to the corresponding all-Russian parties.[9] Carr draws attention to the fact, which Pipes substantiates at length, that when the unpopular Hetman Skoropadsky fell from power in November, 1918, it was the Ukrainian nationalist Directory rather than the Bolsheviks who assumed authority in Kiev, at least for the time being.[10] Finally, to a limited but none the less significant extent, the Ukrainian leaders were able to enlist the support of certain sections of the non-Ukrainian minorities [11]—a political necessity in a country in which the cities were dominated by minorities.

On balance it would appear that the protracted struggle in 1917–20, however obscure in goals and means, if one views it with the critical eye of an historian,[12] and however unsuccessful in terms of *Realpolitik*, did nevertheless leave a great imprint upon the thinking of its participants, their kin, and a good many uncommitted observers. In the opinion of many Ukrainians it became a valiant attempt to re-establish Ukrainian statehood. If we insist that nationalism involves the existence of or definite aspirations toward political independence, we must admit that while the events of the "Ukrainian revolution" exposed the weaknesses of Ukrainian nationalism, they also served to reinforce it for years to come.

The events after 1920 in the Polish occupied parts of the Ukraine I shall sketch in a later chapter when I come to discuss the problems of integrating the Western Ukraine into the Ukrainian SSR. It may suffice here to point out that the greatest mistake which the Polish government made in regard to its "Eastern borderlands" was virtually to ignore the tremendous impact that the struggle for independence was bound to have upon a minority that was politically, economically, and culturally as well organized as the Galician Ukrainians. The Ukrainian movement grew in strength despite Polish persecution, which became increasingly ruthless by the outbreak of World War II, but was still a far cry from the vastly more effective terror of the Soviets. The repressions frustrated repeated efforts on the part of moderate Ukrainian elements to come to a mutual understanding with Polish authorities. They only played into the hands of nationalist extremists who with the encouragement from circles in Nazi Germany, but not without ample provocation by the Poles, engaged in terroristic activities on a considerable scale. By 1939 the extremists had probably captured the allegiance of the majority of the Ukrainian youth in Galicia.

In the aftermath of the Munich Conference of September, 1938, the Ukrainian inhabited Subcarpathian province of Czechoslovakia came briefly to the fore and achieved something of an international prominence as a possible nucleus for a German sponsored "Greater Ukraine." Members of the Organization of Ukrainian Nationalists, that according to a competent German source had "excellent connections" with the German *Abwehr* (counter-intelligence) under Admiral Canaris,[13] helped local Ukrainian patriots to organize their political life. At once, Poland became alarmed lest her Ukrainian subjects should demand greater freedom (which they did); and at the Eighteenth Party Congress Stalin referred half-jokingly to the "hullabaloo raised by the British, French and American press over the Soviet Ukraine" and to the "few lunatics in Germany" who wanted to attach the Soviet Ukraine to the Carpatho Ukraine, the "elephant" to the "gnat." [14] For reasons on which it is idle to dwell in this context, on March 12, 1939, Hitler withdrew his protection from the Carpatho Ukraine, and within a few days it was occupied by Hungarian troops, that overwhelmed the armed resistance of the Ukrainians.

How did the Ukrainian national movement fare under Soviet occupation? First of all, it should be pointed out that Communist leaders—Lenin in particular—were surprised at the strength of this movement.[15] They recognized it by creating an allegedly sovereign Ukrainian Soviet republic *roughly within the boundaries claimed by the nationalist governments of 1917–20.* The attempts on the part of native Communists to detach from the Ukraine several important provinces in which the Russian minority was particularly strong (an independent Donets-Krivoy Rog area, the Ruhr basin on the Ukraine, and the Odessa, Crimea, and Don Soviet Republics) were endorsed by Lenin and Stalin in December, 1917,[16] but all these projects had to be quietly shelved within two months. Except for Crimea, which was incorporated into the Ukrainian SSR as late as 1954, all these republics were persuaded (respectively ordered) to join the latter in 1918, thus making the Ukraine a viable administrative and, potentially, a viable political unit. Apart from the continuing recognition of Ukrainian "sovereignty," i.e., apart from recognizing the Ukrainians as a distinct group with political traditions, as a nation rather than an ethnographic mass, and apart from the persistent goal to enforce or respectively to win their allegiance to the objectives of the regime, Soviet policy towards the Ukraine has followed the two distinct phases of general domestic policy.

During the period of the New Economic Policy (N.E.P.) the Soviet government embarked on what is known as the policy of *korenizatsiya* (taking roots). It consisted essentially in permitting or encouraging the development of non-Russian languages and cultures—within certain limits, of course—and also in compelling local administrators to learn and to use the native languages. Lenin's and Stalin's motives in pursuing this policy seem to have been the following: A regime like the Soviet that was committed to forcibly reconstructing the existing order rather than to administering it in the manner of the Tsars, had to penetrate more deeply into its multinational fabric than ever before, especially if, in addition, it hoped to provide a model for the impending revolution of all the peoples of the world. Moreover, so long as important sections of the Ukraine remained incorporated into the neighboring countries in the West, the Soviet Union could use its policy toward the Eastern Ukrainians as a means of increasing tension in Eastern Europe, by attracting Ukrainian *irredenta* in Poland, Rumania, and Czechoslovakia. The Fifth World Congress of the Comintern, for example, which was held in 1924, passed a resolution declaring that:

> The Congress . . . considers it necessary for the Communist Parties of Poland, Czechoslovakia and Rumania to launch the general slogan of separation of Ukrainian lands from Poland, Czechoslovakia and Rumania and their union with the Soviet Ukraine and through it with the USSR.[17]

Third, many of the Russian and Russified bureaucrats were likely to be adherents of the *ancien régime,* whereas the emerging *natsionaly* ("nationals," that is, non-Russians) might be expected to support the new order.[18] Fourth, it was politic to placate the national feelings of the minorities during a period when the regime was consolidating its power. Consolidation was, moreover, seriously hampered by the activities of Ukrainian nationalist guerrillas, who were not eliminated until about 1923—a difficulty freely admitted by recent Soviet Ukrainian historians.[19] Finally, the possibility that Lenin's and Stalin's governments were engaged in a large scale political provocation should not be excluded: Many leaders who gained prominence during the period of *korenizatsiya* were liquidated in the 1930's.[20] The disadvantage of such a policy from the government's point of view was that, lacking substantial cadres in the national republics, it was forced to rely on former supporters of the nationalist governments to help it take root. There is evidence that Ukrainian nationalist thinking, which was sometimes couched in Marxist arguments, greatly influenced the pronouncements and actions of leading Ukrainian communist administrators and intellectuals.[21]

During the period of the Five Year Plans, the liberal policy in regard to the nationalities was reversed as was the relatively tolerant attitude toward independent peasants and many others. The collectivization "liquidated the kulaks as a class"—a severe blow to the Ukrainian national movement which in 1917–1920 had apparently relied for its support on independent and relatively prosperous landholders. The attendant famine cost so many Ukrainian lives that in the minds of some nationalists who had lived through it, the collectivization in the Ukraine has come to be regarded as an insidious plot of the Russian-dominated regime to break the backbone of the Ukrainian nation. While this seems to be a rather ethnocentric viewpoint not grounded in fact, but still rather important for the development of national consciousness, it is true that in the process of totalitarian *Gleichschaltung* which culminated in the Great Purge of 1936–38, Ukrainian and other "local nationalisms" were simultaneously being persecuted, while at the same time some of the props of the former Tsarist regime such as Russian cultural and political hegemony were being restored. In any case, the available studies indicate that in the 1930's, on one pretext or another, the regime destroyed in a rather systematic fashion the leading cadres of Ukrainian political and cultural life. At the same time, the results of the *korenizatsiya* were partly undone by reintroducing Russian on a large scale into offices, schools, and universities.[22]

It was during this stage of "total regimentation" [23] that German armies attacked the Soviet Union. In the period between September, 1939, and June, 1941, however, Stalin expanded the boundaries of the Soviet state to include among other things all the Ukrainian-inhabited territories in the West and South West, with the exception of the former Subcarpathian Republic that had caused such a great international excitement in 1938–39.

The German attack in the dawn of June 22, 1941, found the Soviet Union badly prepared for the strain of total warfare. It was not only arms that were lacking; the morale of Soviet citizens had suffered in the mad drive for collectivization and in the widespread purges of 1934–38. In the Ukraine the social transformations of the 1930's had been associated with a campaign against Ukrainian nationalism which claimed many additional victims. The harvest of those years was reaped in Soviet military defeats in 1941–42, and it would not be too far from the truth to assert that only the unwitting cooperation between Stalin and Hitler—the maniacally brutal regime that Nazi satraps imposed in the occupied territories and the pedantically precise extermination policy that was applied to Soviet prisoners of war and forced laborers—enabled the Soviet Union to survive World War II.[24]

That the War put the governmental structure of the country to a severe test has been admitted by none other than Stalin himself. In a rare moment of candor he told a gathering of Red Army officers in the Kremlin, May 24, 1945:

Our government made quite a few mistakes; in 1941–42 there were moments when we faced a desperate situation: our army was in retreat, abandoning our native villages and towns of the Ukraine, Belorussia, Moldavia, the Leningrad province, the Baltic sea coast, the Karelo-Finnish Republic. It abandoned them because there was no other way out. Another people might have told the Government: You have not fulfilled our expectations, get out—we shall set up another government which will conclude peace with Germany and ensure our peace.[25]

The rolling back of Soviet authority by German arms also presented Ukrainian nationalists with a unique opportunity to prove their worth. After analyzing in detail the response of Eastern Ukrainians to the efforts of the predominantly Galician Organization of Ukrainian Nationalists (OUN) to organize Ukrainian cultural and political life under the German occupation (1941–44), John A. Armstrong has come to the conclusion that:

Ukrainian nationalism was the only dynamic anti-Communist movement which was able to carry on extensive propaganda in the East Ukraine under German occupation. It possessed a body of devoted followers to serve as its organizers; it was capable of arousing enthusiasm and exacting sacrifices. Lack of experience and judgment cost its adherents dearly. The movement proved, however, to be flexible enough to adapt its program to the demands for social measures which the Soviet experience had instilled in the East Ukrainian population. It attracted a large proportion of the intellectuals and technicians who comprised the only group capable of reorganizing life after the Soviet evacuation, but it was unable to penetrate the mass of the population to any great extent. *The galvanizing force was present; the cadres which might have transmitted it were half-formed; but the essential mass remained uncommitted.*[26]

Such a case study as this is the most reliable means for testing the strength of Ukrainian nationalism because it deals as a rule with overt manifestations of it and not with assumptions, hypotheses and projections. But like every other case study it analyzes events that occurred under certain irrepeatable historical conditions. It might even be argued that the existing historical circumstances led to an underestimate of the strength of the Ukrainian movement: from late 1941 on, German occupation authorities showed themselves increasingly hostile to Ukrainian nationalism and, the outcome of the war still being undecided, it took unusual courage if not plain recklessness on the part of the Eastern Ukrainian population to support openly the Ukrainian cause. If they did so, they ran the double risk of being liquidated either by the Gestapo or the possibly returning NKVD (Soviet secret police), whereas to remain uncommitted, at least for the time being, seemed the wisest course to take.

However restricted the extent of Ukrainian disaffection may have been, it sufficed to provoke Stalin's wrath. In the "secret speech" at the Twentieth Party Congress, his successor Khrushchev enumerated some of the Soviet nationalities that had been deported during the war for disloyalty to the regime. He said that Stalin would have equally dealt with the Ukrainians except that he did not know how and where to deport a people of forty million.[27]

During the war, Stalin employed all possible means to restore the morale of his unwilling subjects. Religious sentiment was appealed to by official recognition of the Russian Orthodox Church. The Party was ordered to expand its ranks and to enroll "better elements" from the people, especially distinguished combat soldiers. Above all, Stalin appealed to the patriotic sentiment of the population by invoking the heroic figures of Alexander Nevsky, Dmitry Donskoy, Kuz'ma Minin, Dmitry Pozharsky, Alexander Suvorov, and Michael Kutuzov, adding the victorious banner of Lenin for good measure.[28]

Not a single non-Russian appeared in this galaxy of names. Before long, Stalin realized, however, that concessions to the feelings of this group would have to be made, too. November 26, 1941, a number of Ukrainian intellectuals who had been evacuated to Saratov issued a fighting appeal to their compatriots in which among other things they cited "certain heroes from Ukrainian history who had resisted foreign domination." [29] In 1943 a high military decoration was established for Ukrainians—the Order of Bohdan Khmelnytsky—and toward the end of that year Soviet armies were renamed according to the republics in which they were operating: The Southern Fronts came thus to be called "Ukrainian Fronts," central armies were renamed the "Belorussian Fronts," the northern, the "Baltic Fronts." Military units whose soldiers had been recruited primarily from one nationality were employed to a small extent: The constitutional amendment of February 1, 1944, which allowed the Union Republics to set up *supplementary* Defense Ministries of their own, was believed to be a step further in the creation of national units.[30] At the same time, all Republics were given the formal right but not the opportunity of entering into direct relations with foreign powers. At first, only the Ukraine and Belorussia received permission to organize supplementary Foreign Ministries, to enter the United Nations, and to play host to UNRRA relief missions accredited at their Republican capitals. It appears that the law of 1944 was to serve, among other things, as a "concession" to the national feelings in the non-Russian Republics.[31]

All the Government measures, together with the overpowering elation that was born out of the struggle for life or death with a technically well equipped enemy, led to the widespread belief that after the war "things would be different." Moreover, the occupation of Germany brought Soviet soldiers in direct contact with the supposedly decaying West, and what they saw reinforced their yearning for a change. A former Soviet pilot, who later defected to the West, described his feelings in 1945 like this:

The entire atmosphere was charged with the expectation of something new, something magnificent and glorious. None of us doubted the brightness of the future.[32]

The wartime policies have been commented upon at some length because they form a necessary background for the period after 1945. After the reoccupation of the Ukraine the Soviet government was confronted with many specific tasks. Foremost among them was the reconstruction of the badly damaged economy, but political questions had to be solved, too. The nationalist insurgent movement in Western Ukraine was the gravest of them: Several appeals to surrender were issued starting with February, 1944; and on September 27, 1944, the Central Committee of the All-Union Party issued a resolution directed against the "Deficiencies in Political [Party] Work among the Population of the Western Provinces of the Ukrainian SSR." [33] For several years the struggle against the Ukrainian underground and the total integration of Western Ukraine occupied much of the attention of the Communist Party of the Ukraine. A special facet of the integration process was Soviet policy toward the Uniate Church.[34]

While considering these specific policies, we must not, however, lose sight of the general trend. Already in the middle of the war the Party started to reassert its authority against "ideologically incorrect attitudes" both among the Russian and the non-Russian peoples. In January, 1944, the Central Committee reprimanded the Soviet humorist Zoshchenko for publishing amidst the clash of arms what they considered to be a less than heroic piece, the rather intimately autobiographical novel "Before Sunrise." The leitmotiv of the critique was the writer's ignoring the tasks of the present, an escapism into the past of Russia when, once and for all, the past had been "overcome" by victorious Communism.[35]

While the criticism of Zoshchenko could still be interpreted as a narrow-minded, but not unjustified indignation at signs of escapism, a decree passed sometime in September, 1944, clearly indicated the Government's intention to tighten its hold over the non-Russian nationalities. According to the authoritative Party journal *Bol'shevik*, "the resolution of the Central Committee of the All-Union Communist Party 'About the Present Conditions and Ways of Improving Mass Political and Ideological Work in the Tatar Party Organization' [had] a tremendous significance for the raising of ideological political work not only of the Tatar but also of other Party organizations." The Tatar Provincial Committee of the All-Union Party was reprimanded for "badly directing the work of historians, writers, and artistic workers. Hence,—continues the commentary in *Bol'shevik*—[arose] serious deficiencies and mistakes of a nationalist nature in the interpretation of Tatar history." Some Tatar historians and writers had indulged in "an anti-scientific idealization of the role of the Golden Horde"; had regarded the Tatar military leader Ideghey as a progressive though he had destroyed many a Russian village; and had not dwelt sufficiently on the cooperation of Tatars with the Russians, and the socialist transformations in their country.[36]

In interpreting this resolution it should be kept in mind that at the same time Russians were encouraged to venerate Dmitry Donskoy who had achieved his laurels precisely in fighting the Tatars. In other words, as in the 1930's when Pokrovsky's historical school was rejected, the notion of the friendship of Soviet peoples came to be regarded as a cover for the predominance of the Russians.

This predominance was openly acknowledged in Stalin's well-known toast to the health of the Russian people of May 24, 1945, in which the Russians were hailed as "the most outstanding nation, . . . the leading force in the Soviet Union," and commended for their "clear minds, firm character, and patience." [37] Soviet nationality policy from 1944 until Stalin's death can be described as a continued and outspoken effort to impress the notion of Russian predominance upon the minds of the non-Russian peoples of the Soviet Union: It is very characteristic, for example, that virtually every year, from 1946 to 1953, on May 24, the central Ukrainian language newspaper in Kiev would remind its readers of Stalin's toast to the virtues of the Russian people. As a rule there would be an appropriate editorial and several featured articles, sometimes as much as one half of the paper would be devoted to the "friendship of Soviet peoples." [38] In the following paragraphs I should like to sketch in a few landmarks of Stalin's policy and to point out a few of its motivations; then I shall indicate the changes after Stalin's death.

The signal for the tightening of all totalitarian screws was given in Stalin's election speech of February 9, 1946,[39] but it was only in Zhdanov's address of August 14, 1946, that its implications for Soviet arts and letters and ultimately for cultural life as such, were spelled out in detail.[40] The Soviet leaders appeared insecure in the face of the bottled-up aspirations of their own peoples, and baffled as to the course that the West would take at this point: Hence Stalin blatantly asserted the supremacy of the Party by crediting it rather than the armed forces with victory in the war, hence Zhdanov unfurled the ugly banners of ideological vigilance and xenophobia, hence the collective farmers were robbed of any land which they might have acquired during the war for their private use.[41] The only lid that was kept open deliberately as a kind of safety valve was official tolerance of a particularly strident brand of Russian nationalism. Nay, to be more precise, Russian nationalism was deliberately cultivated as an antidote to disillusionment with the regime and admiration for the West.

In the Ukraine this was manifested in numerous lectures on the superiority of all things Russian, and in several Party resolutions against

"bourgeois-nationalist" distortions in scholarship, letters, and arts, which entailed a rewriting of textbooks and the purging of libraries.[42] To obtain the flavor of the propaganda campaign, a summary of an article by L. Klyuchnyk, Secretary of the Zaporozhe Provincial Committee of the Communist Party of Ukraine is particularly useful. (It appeared in *Radyans'ka Ukrayina* of November 25, 1945, p. 2.)

Under the title of "Educating the Love of the Fatherland," he boasts that only in his province 90 lectures were given on subjects such as "The Heroic Past of the Russian People," "The Russian People—The Leading Force of the USSR," "The Friendship of the Peoples of the USSR." Zaporozhe lecturers gave about 500 talks devoted to Russian composers, and propagandists published many articles on great Russian poets and critics.

A series of lectures was also devoted to exposing the "Cain's Face of Ukrainian Nationalists." "During the last months in the factories and on the construction sites of Zaporozhstal 13 lectures were given on the subject 'Ukrainian-German Nationalists Are Heinous Enemies of the Ukrainian People.' " The orders for launching this campaign are disclosed in the phrase "[Stalin's toast of May, 1945] brought forth a particular interest for Russian culture."

How far the Soviet government went in ferreting out Ukrainian "nationalism" may be gauged from the following two examples. A Ukrainian literary historian, Professor Doroshkevych, was attacked by one S. Kovalev in *Kul'tura i zhizn'*, the organ of the Propaganda Section of the Central Committee of the All-Union Party, for comparing the historical novel *Chorna Rada* (Black Council) by the nineteenth century Ukrainian writer P. Kulish to Tolstoy's *War and Peace* and finding the Ukrainian novel superior.[43] The Ukrainian woman writer Varvara Cherednychenko provoked the ire of the official critics because in her wartime diary published under the title "I, the Lucky Valentina," instead of dwelling on the Soviet present she had drawn many fond parallels to the Ukrainian Cossack past. One of her critics objected to the following:

There you will find the Balyky—an ancient burgher stock from Kiev, made famous more than 350 years ago by the village elder Yats'ko [Jimmy] Balyka, and Demyan Hnatovych Mnohohrishny who had been the Cossack Hetman of the Left Bank Ukraine from 1668 to 1672, . . . and the wounded Soviet soldier Jacob who having a fever of 41 degrees centigrade keeps telling anecdotes about the Cossacks, who used to make jokes while they were being impaled.[44]

At the same time the Communist Party of the Ukraine under Khrushchev had its hands full with economic reconstruction. In the summer of 1946 it was criticized by the Central Committee in Moscow for mistakes which it had committed in the placement of leading cadres, especially in the Western provinces.[45] In the fall and winter of 1946–1947 a minor famine broke out in many agricultural regions of the USSR, including the Ukraine, due apparently to the ruthless procurement drive on the part of the regime.[46] In March, 1947, Khrushchev was suddenly relieved of his First Secretaryship in the Ukraine and replaced by Kaganovich. But before long, in December, 1947, Kaganovich went back to Moscow and Khrushchev resumed his old post.[47] In January 1948 the thirtieth anniversary of the Ukrainian SSR was celebrated, and Molotov, who attended the jubilee session of the Ukrainian Supreme Soviet, transmitted Stalin's compliments to the Ukrainian people in general and the Communist Party of Ukraine in particular.[48] If this was an expression of Stalin's confidence in Khrushchev's leadership, more was to follow. After the shake-up in party ranks following Zhdanov's death, in December, 1949, Khrushchev was promoted to the First Secretaryship of the Moscow Province Committee, a post that he had previously held in the middle 1930's and one that would help him to assume the leadership of the entire Party after Stalin's death. Khrushchev's successor in the Ukraine became Leonid G. Melnikov. On the whole, things appeared to have quieted down: By 1950 the Ukrainian economy had been reconstructed to a significant extent and the danger from Ukrainian nationalism had receded, too, except in the Western provinces, where the last major extermination drive against the nationalist underground was begun in the winter of 1949–50.[49]

But the peace was deceptive. On September 21, 1948, Ilya Ehrenburg published in *Pravda* an article denouncing Zionism, the State of Israel, and any common bond uniting the Jews in the world.[50] In February, 1949, this was followed by an attack that was ostensibly directed against "a group of anti-patriotic theater critics." But the fact that most of them had Jewish names raised the suspicion that it was Jews as such who were the real subjects of attack.[51] An increase in international tension in 1949–50 must have persuaded Stalin that a new tightening of the ideological reins was in order, and, as usual, the non-Russian nationalities had to bear a goodly part of the restrictions.

In May, 1950, the appropriate Committee "recommended" to the USSR Council of Ministers to revoke a Stalin Prize that had been awarded for the previous year to a scholarly book on philosophical thought in nineteenth century Azerbaydzhan. Its author, Geydar Guseynov, had distorted history in failing to mention that Shamil, the famous leader of the North Caucasian mountaineers' uprising against Russian rule, was in reality an agent of English capitalism and the Turkish Sultan. Until 1950, he had been regarded by Soviet historiography as a progressive fighter for his people's independence; now he became a reactionary

nationalist.[52] In April of 1951, the Russian playwright K. Finn was attacked for his uncomplimentary presentation of Party officials: his play
Honesty was ordered to be taken off the stage.[53] But it was on July 2,
1951, that *Pravda* fired the broadside in the ideological battle with the
article "Against Ideological Distortions in Literature." Its victim was
the Soviet Ukrainian poet Sosyura, who had written a poem called "Love
the Ukraine." The article illustrates so well Soviet nationality policy
from 1944 to 1953 that it is worth analyzing in some detail.

Volodymyr Sosyura (1898–) is a talented Ukrainian poet whose
political loyalty until 1951 seemed beyond suspicion. He had joined the
Communist Party as early as 1920, after several years' service with the
Red Army.[54] In April 1948, four months after his fiftieth birthday, he
was awarded a First Stalin Prize for his collection of poetry entitled
"That the Woods May Rustle." [55] But among the wider reading public
he is best known for his poem "Love the Ukraine," which had been
written in the patriotic fervor of 1944.[56] From an interview of mine it
would appear that Sosyura's poem was quietly withdrawn from the curricula of Ukrainian schools; [57] it also seems to have been deprived of
official recognition by 1948; [58] but it was reprinted in the Ukraine, and
several translations of it were published in Russian periodicals. It was
one such translation that appeared in No. 5 (1951) of the ill-fated *Star*
of Leningrad that provoked the angry outburst from *Pravda's* editors,
who declared the poem to be an ideologically defective work.[59] Their
reasoning is worth quoting:

To judge by the title of the poem, the author's intention was to give artistic
embodiment to the great idea of Soviet patriotism. . . .

Unfortunately, Sosyura's poem "Love the Ukraine" does not engender such
[lofty patriotic] feelings. What is more, it evokes a feeling of disillusionment
and protest. It is true, in his poem the poet calls for love of the Ukraine. The
question arises: Which Ukraine is in question, of *which* Ukraine is Sosyura
singing? Is he singing of that Ukraine which groaned for centuries under the
exploiters' yoke and whose sorrow and bitterness poured out in Taras Shevchenko's angry lines? . . .

Or does Sosyura's poem refer to the new, prosperous Soviet Ukraine, created
by the will of our people, led by the party of Bolsheviks?

It is sufficient to examine Sosyura's poem to remove any doubt that, contrary
to the true facts, he is singing of some primordial Ukraine, the Ukraine "in
general":

> Love the Ukraine, like sun, like light,
> Like wind and grass and water . . .
> Love the wide open spaces of the ancient Ukraine,
> Be proud of your Ukraine,
> Of her new and eternally living beauty
> And of her nightingale voice.

Out of time, out of historical epoch,—this is the Ukraine in the poet's portrayal. . . .

And the poet's words, grossly distorting the true facts, sound openly nationalistic:

> We are nothing without her,
> Like dust in the field, smoke,
> Eternally driven by the winds.

Even more illuminating is *Pravda's* criticism of various Russian translations of the poem. The *Zvezda* (Star) translation had been made by one of the editors of that magazine, the Russian poet A. Prokofyef. This was his second version, for in 1947 he interpolated into the poem the following passage:

> We are nothing without the Soviet Fatherland . . .
> There is only one Fatherland in the world for us:
> In the verses which flow over the Volga,
> In the Kremlin's stars and the Uzbek gardens,
> Everywhere beat kindred hearts.

Preparing his second translation for the ten days' celebration of Ukrainian culture in Moscow, June 15–25, 1951, Prokofyef either misjudged the current political situation or became ashamed of his previous rendering, or both, for he removed the added passage and together with it a spiteful reference to the "foreigners in green uniforms" (the Germans) which was contained in the original.

But the classical example of intellectual obsequiousness imposed by a totalitarian regime was provided by one Ushakov, who rendered an important sentence differently in each of his three translations of the poem. Here are the variants, which evoked adverse comment from *Pravda:*

> She is behind the wattles in the silence, all in blossom,
> And in the most harmonious songs. (1948)

> She is behind the collective farm wattles, all in blossom,
> And in the most harmonious songs. (1949)

> She is in the wealth, of the collective farm, all in blossom,
> And in the most harmonious songs. (1951)

As in 1946, efforts against Ukrainian "bourgeois nationalism" were stepped up again in 1951,[60] with the significant difference that Jewish "nationalists and cosmopolitans," that is, leaders of Jewish life, were now thrown together with their Ukrainian confrères. Melnikov's report at the Seventeenth Congress of the Communist Party (Bolshevik) of Ukraine, held shortly before the Nineteenth All-Union Congress in the fall of 1952, contains many references against both national groups.[61]

But the execution of eight Jews following the Slansky trial in Czecho-slovakia in November, 1952,[62] and the arrest of Jewish doctors in Moscow in January of the next year,[63] indicated that the regime would not stop at verbal reprimands this time. The political atmosphere in the Soviet Union became threateningly dense, when Stalin died in March, 1953.

In appraising postwar Soviet nationality policy until Stalin's death, two things should be kept in mind. Undoubtedly, it was part of the general policy of tightening ideological controls which were applied to Russians, too. But it bore down more heavily on the patriotic feelings of non-Russians than on those of the Russians. Both for the Russian and the Ukrainian people the Fatherland was said to be not Russia nor the Ukraine, but the USSR. But at the same time, the Fatherland had to have a historical basis going beyond 1917. In the light of Zhdanov's strictures the Russian cultural heritage, too, was distorted to suit the Soviet conception of a heroic, intensely anti-Western people, material-istic to the extreme. But at this price, it was possible to refer to famous events in Russian political and cultural past without humiliating quali-fications.[64] But not so with the non-Russian peoples. The Soviet Ukraine was a subject to praise, but the Ukraine as such was regarded as a pro-foundly nationalistic concept. It was ideologically correct to depict the Ukraine before 1917 as a country groaning "under the exploiters' yoke," but it was unpatriotic to dwell with fondness on the ancient Cossack families, and a wounded Soviet soldier was expected to speak of Stalin, not about his Cossack ancestors. On the other hand, the Tsarist Russian general Kutuzov was celebrated over more than one full page in the Soviet Ukrainian press.[65] Whatever be the reasons for the general policy of tightening ideological controls—wrath over wartime defections, un-certainty over what the West would do, fear that the Soviet peoples were expecting a change from the strict regimentation of the 1930's—as in the late 1930's, the regime felt that it had to fall back on the Russian national heritage to serve as a cementing force, and by 1953 Soviet patri-otism came virtually to be identified with Russian nationalism.[66]

Stalin's death released the forces that had been kept pent up in Soviet society. In *Doctor Zhivago,* the well-known Soviet poet and writer Boris Pasternak characterizes the preceding years as follows:

Though the clarification and freedom they had expected after the war had not come with victory as they had hoped, that did not matter. A foreboding of free-dom was in the air in the years after the war and was their only historical content.[67]

The nationality policy in the Ukraine could not remain unaffected by the general pressure for liberalization.

In what looked like his bid to assume the dictator's seat, Beria may have appealed to the native leadership in non-Russian republics. On June 13, 1953, Leonid G. Melnikov, the First Secretary of the CP of the Ukraine, that is, of the most powerful regional Party organization outside the Russian Republic, was curtly dismissed because among other things he had virtually replaced Ukrainian as the language of instruction in Western Ukrainian higher schools with Russian.[68] His successor was Kirichenko—thus for the first time in the history of the CP of the Ukraine a Ukrainian assumed leadership of its Party organization. The attendant changes in the high command of the Ukrainian MVD (secret police) seemingly point to Beria as the *spiritus movens* behind Melnikov's ouster.[69]

Beria's fall at first did not seem to have reversed the post-Stalinist trend toward granting more freedom of expression to the non-Russian peoples. The regime met their wishes to the extent of relenting its rigid insistence on the superiority of everything Russian: Starting with 1954, the editors of *Radyans'ka Ukrayina* were no longer required to pay their annual tribute to Stalin's toast of May 24, 1945.

In 1954 the 300 year anniversary of the Treaty of Pereyaslav, the "union" of the Ukraine with Russia was celebrated with an unusually loud fanfare throughout the Soviet Union.[70] In February of that year, as a token of the "friendship of peoples" the Russian Republic presented the Ukraine with Crimea, which since the Revolution had been under immediate Russian jurisdiction. During the ceremonies attending the transfer of jurisdictions no mention was made of any historical rights which the Crimean Tatars might have to the territory.[71] The chief celebrations in May were attended by the inner circle of the Party Presidium; units of the Red Army were ordered to parade on the Khreshchatyk, the main thoroughfare in Kiev (May 23) and on the Red Square in Moscow (May 30); Poland sent a parliamentary delegation; an appropriate exhibition was organized in Prague; and editorials on the significance of the Treaty of Pereyaslav appeared in the Chinese press in Peking.[72] In this connection, a slight change in the official propaganda line might be of greater importance than the ceremonial pomp. Writes Reshetar:

. . . Soviet publications dealing with the Tercentenary at times convey the distinct impression of an attempt on the part of the regime to picture the Ukrainians as junior partners of the Russians or as the eldest of the younger brothers. A recurring phrase in various pronouncements was: "the Ukrainian people were the first after the Russian people" to embark on "the path of socialism" or "the glorious road of October." A Kirghiz, one Usembayev, expressed gratitude to the Ukrainians for having taught the Kirghizians so much regarding the cultivation of sugar beets and observed that the [Ukrainian] opera *Natalka Poltavka* was being presented in the Kirghiz language.[73]

It is interesting that the theme of the Ukrainians being the first after the Russian people to have entered the road toward socialism, that is, as the second people in the Soviet Union, is not new: To my knowledge, it had been first used by Molotov in addressing the jubilee session of the Ukrainian Supreme Soviet in 1948 (see above). But until 1954, it remained very much in the background.

The year 1954 was also the start of the ostensibly voluntary emigration of Ukrainian youth to cultivate jointly with Russians the virgin lands in Kazakhstan and Western Siberia, following Khrushchev's appeal in February, 1954.[74] Eighty thousand of such youth had left the Ukraine through 1957.[75]

In 1956 the centenary of the birth of Ivan Franko, the second greatest Ukrainian poet, was celebrated. The ceremonies were much less elaborate, but none the less impressive.[76] As a gesture toward the Ukrainians, the Soviet government ordered the international communist movement to commemorate his anniversary: the World's Peace Council declared it to be a cultural holiday for its adherents,[77] and lectures about Ivan Franko were read as far as in Communist China.[78]

Of greater significance than modifications in the general "ideological" policy toward the Ukraine have been certain changes in the administrative structure of the country. Starting with 1954, the Republics were given increased authority in a number of fields. In the Ukraine were thus established a number of Union-Republican "co-ministries" (Ferrous Metallurgy, Coal, Higher Education, and others). In 1957 greater power was given to the newly established regional economic councils, of which eleven were created in the Ukraine. The implications of those moves will be analyzed later.[79] But already now it is worth noting two facts. The number of enterprises involved in that jurisdictional transfer —whatever the latter meant—was quite considerable. It amounted to about 10,000 enterprises and organizations.[80] In 1953, 64 per cent of the total industrial output of the Ukraine belonged to the immediate jurisdiction of the All-Union Ministries in Moscow. The next year the relationship was reversed: Moscow immediately controlled only 33 per cent of the Ukrainian output; the corresponding figure for 1956 was only 24 per cent.[81]

An important landmark in Soviet nationality policy after the war undoubtedly was the Twentieth All-Union Party Congress of February, 1956. In his anti-Stalin speech which was delivered in closed session, Khrushchev denounced the dead leader not only of decimating the ranks of devoted Party members during the purges and of misconduct during the war, but also—what is not so well-known—of dealing too harshly with several non-Russian peoples.[82] In his open report to the Congress, Khrushchev acknowledged the emergence of qualified non-Russian cadres who were ready and eager to assume greater administrative responsibilities than they had been granted before.[83] Reading the materials of the Congress we find it difficult to escape the conclusion that in 1956 Khrushchev was deliberately courting the support of Party members in the non-Russian Republics. That conclusion is reinforced by the publication, a few months later, of Lenin's so-called testament, documents that have been circulating in the West for a long time but had been suppressed in the Soviet Union ever since 1923. A part of Lenin's testament is directly relevant to our concern: in it Lenin criticizes Stalin's scheme to make the Soviet Republics nothing but autonomous provinces of the Russian Soviet Federated Socialist Republic (RSFSR) and enjoins Communists to show the greatest political tact in dealing with non-Russian nations. In particular, Lenin warns in his note not to suppress non-Russian languages.[84] In commenting on the newly released document, Moscow's *Kommunist,* the most authoritative journal in the Soviet Union, quoted the resolution of the Twentieth Party Congress on the nationality policy:

In its nationalities policy the Party has always proceeded from Lenin's thesis that socialism not only does not eliminate national differences and characteristics but, on the contrary, ensures the all-round development and flowering of the economies and cultures of all nations and nationalities. The Party must continue to consider these characteristics most carefully in all its practical work.[85]

Though the *Kommunist* editorial did also call for a continuing struggle with the remaining "survivals of nationalism," the alert Soviet citizen could not fail to notice that for the first time since the 1930's the emphasis was on combating "the lack of respect and attention to various nations, to the interests of nationalities and their particular features," that is on fighting what in the 1920's was more openly called (Russian) "great-power chauvinism." [86] The regime did indeed increase the powers of local and Republican administrators and, encouraged by the liberalization in the official nationality policy Ukrainian historians and poets, supported by a section of the reading public, pressed for a more respectful treatment of the Ukrainian national heritage, of which more below.

In July, 1957, the disgraced "anti-Party group" of Malenkov, Molotov, Kaganovich, and others were still castigated, among other things, for opposing the expansion of Republican rights in the fields of economic and cultural development and in the field of legislation,[87] but already by that time the attitude of the regime toward the non-Russian peoples had changed—apparently under the impression of the Hungarian up-

rising and the Polish near-revolution of October-November, 1956. The
same issue of *Komunist Ukrayiny* that contained strictures against the
centralist views of Malenkov and his followers, printed a highly significant attack by I. Kravtsev on " 'National Communism'—The Ideological Diversion of Imperialism and Its Agents in the Workers Movement." [88] The bulk of his article deals with nationalist deviations in the
East European Communist parties, but the last three pages are directed
against Ukrainian "bourgeois nationalism," which, too, serves as a tool
of Western imperialists. But it was not until August of the following
year (1958) that the Party chose the Tadzhik scholar B. Gafurov to
announce the change in its nationality policy as defined by the Twentieth Party Congress—little more than two years after its inception.
Gafurov's article in Moscow's *Kommunist* admirably defines current
Soviet policy, and I shall, therefore, analyze it in some detail.[89]

Gafurov begins his article with the assertion that "one of the greatest
achievements of the Soviet Union has been the solution of the nationality problem" (p. 10). As evidence he cites that the more backward
nationalities at the time of the establishment of the Soviet Union have
become nations (p. 12); that the territories inhabited by the various
peoples, for example, the Belorussians and Ukrainians, have been consolidated (p. 13); that there are no more economically and culturally
backward peoples in the USSR (pp. 13–14); and that there is friendship
and cooperation among the nations of the USSR (p. 14). Much more
important than that series of poorly documented assertions is the operative part of the article. Gafurov writes:

> Leading the struggle of the peoples of the USSR for the construction of Com-
> munism, our Party conducts the policy of further developing Soviet "national"
> [i.e., non-Russian—Y.B.] Republics, their economies and their cultures. In con-
> nection with the transition from Socialism to Communism we cannot help being
> interested in the problem of the further rapprochement of the Socialist nations
> in the USSR, and also *the problem of the future fusion of nations and the
> development of a single language.*
>
> *The fusion of nations is an altogether complex and lengthy process.* For its
> achievement is necessary not only the victory of Socialism throughout the world,
> but also the transition from the first, lower phase of Communist formation—
> Socialism—to its second and higher phase—Communism. Under the conditions
> of Socialism, similarly as there are still differences between cities and villages,
> mental and manual labor, national differences will also be preserved, which—
> we must suppose—will still exist for a long time even under Communism. But
> it can hardly be doubted that on the higher levels of Communist society the
> disappearance of national differences and the fusion of nations will be inevita-
> ble. Facts show that as we are advancing toward Communism there is a levelling
> of boundaries not only between classes, but also between Socialist nations. We

observe with our own eyes how the process of their inevitable rapprochement takes place, how gradually the differences in the material conditions of their lives, their morals and their culture disappear. The Socialist mode of production which is common to all Soviet peoples does indeed give rise to and strengthens forms of, social consciousness that are common to all. It would have been very dangerous, however, to visualize the paths to the fusion of nations in an oversimplified manner. That task cannot be solved by any administrative or similar measures whatsoever that are directed toward the weakening of the sovereignty of the national non-Russian Republics and national culture. On the contrary, the recent years in the USSR have been characterized by an expansion of the rights of Soviet Republics. There is no doubt possible about the proposition that we can achieve the future fusion of Socialist nations only by means of their all-around strengthening, an all-around development of culture and their best traditions. Our Party, therefore, shows great solicitude in order to safeguard the further development of all nationalities and a new rise in their economic and cultural status. (Pp. 16–17; italics added.)

On first sight, Gafurov's argument seems to be evenly balanced between the concern for the particular characteristics of Soviet peoples and the distant goal of creating a homogeneous Communist society, which is adumbrated in Lenin's pre-Revolutionary writings on language (see Chapter V) and has never been disavowed by the regime. But upon closer examination the emphasis upon assimilation becomes clear. Moreover, the contrast between the resolution of the Twentieth Party Congress, with its stress on national individuality, is striking. Within hardly more than two years the Party decided to change course again by almost 180 degrees.

Most interesting is Gafurov's listing of obstacles in the way toward complete unity of nations, which he characteristically refers to as "some nationalist prejudices, expressions of national narrowness and national limitations" (p. 17). There is first the question of accepting for responsible positions in the Union Republics alien emissaries of the regime:

In a few places there has appeared the tendency to marshall the cadres of the native nationality against cadres of different nationalities (p. 18).

That approach is exceptionally damaging. Gafurov at first says that leading cadres should be selected without any primary regard to nationality, then contradicts himself by praising in the very next sentence "the fraternal exchange of cadres" of different nationalities. Another hindrance to complete unity are "localist tendencies that are expressed in the failure to fulfil plans of cooperative [i.e., inter-Republican] deliveries, in the attempts of some workers to 'grab' as much as possible for their locality at the expense of the state as a whole." An interesting variation on this is the third obstacle: "Expensive demands of special privileges and higher investments from the All-Union budget in the economy of the Republic" (p. 18). In general, Gafurov deplores the nationalist tendency to pose the interests of a particular Republic against the interests of the Union as a whole. For instance, some Kazakh Party workers acted incorrectly in opposing the settlement of Kazakh lands by Russian and Ukrainian colonists during the so-called virgin lands campaign. Finally, writes Gafurov:

In the field of ideology the nationalist survivals are manifested in the idealization of the historical past, in the uncritical attitude toward various national movements, in forgetting the principle of "Party mindedness" (*partiynost'*) in elucidating questions of culture, literature and arts (p. 18).

As an example he cites the evaluation of the modernist so-called Dzhadidist movement among the Moslems in Central Asia.[90] After the Twentieth Party Congress Central Asian Communists termed the movement progressive arguing that once the Party had corrected its dogmatist attitude toward nationalist leaders abroad (for example, Gandhi) [91] it should do no less with respect to nationalist movements within the confines of the Tsarist Russian Empire. Gafurov takes pains in explaining that such an analogy is "deprived of any historical sense" (p. 19), that anti-Russian nationalists in the Russian Empire cannot claim the same privileges as anti-British nationalists outside. Non-Russian nationalists in the USSR are decried as so-called revisionists (the new term for Titoists; p. 20).

In the concluding part of his article we find the following, seemingly balanced injunction:

The interests of the construction of a Communist society require the strengthening of educational work among the toilers in the spirit of proletarian internationalism, the unshakeable friendship of peoples. We must create an environment (*obstanovka*) of absolute intolerance toward the slightest manifestation of nationalist prejudices. In this connection, we should always keep in mind V. I. Lenin's injunction that it is above all Russians that should combat Great Russian chauvinism, and representatives of a given nationality who ought to struggle against local nationalism (pp. 22–23).

The advice seems eminently fair until one pauses to reflect on how many Russians have come out and criticized Russian nationalism. Despite some qualifying phrases, the tenor of Gafurov's article and especially of its concluding section is such as to indicate that the struggle against Russian nationalism is not to be taken seriously while the struggle against non-Russian nationalism is. Compare, for example, his statement on the role of the Russian language:

Despite the slanderous assertions of our enemies, an immense significance for the peoples of our country attaches to the deep thorough study of the Russian language, the mastering of the very rich achievements of Russian culture, because this facilitates to a significant extent the increased mutual exchange of cultural treasures among the peoples of the USSR.

The Russian language constitutes a mighty medium of communication among the peoples of the USSR. . . . The Russian language is, therefore, justly regarded as the *second native language of all peoples* inhabiting the country of Socialism. But this does not mean at all that one may belittle in any fashion whatsoever the role of the languages and cultures of the fraternal peoples of our Fatherland. The practise of our cadres learning the language of that people among which they live and work, which has justified itself, deserves all possible encouragement (p. 23; italics added).

Gafurov's programmatical article was soon followed by concrete action in the field of education, of which more below; and by a relatively oblique discussion of nationality policy at the extraordinary Twenty-First Party Congress in January, 1959.[92] In some Republics, though not in the Ukraine, important purges took place in 1958–59: some of the purged leaders were openly accused of nationalism.[93] A significant place to combating non-Russian nationalism was also accorded in the important and lengthy Party Central Committee resolution on propaganda, of January 9, 1960.[94] Finally, Gafurov's theses were enshrined most prominently in the new Party program approved by the Twenty-Second Party Congress in October-November, 1961.[95]

In the Ukraine itself the struggle against Ukrainian nationalism was accorded great prominence at several Party Conferences, apparently under prodding from the central Party authorities in Moscow. A month after the Twenty-First All-Union Party Congress, in February, 1959, there took place a conference of selected members of the Kiev Province and City Party Organization, the so-called "activists." The fight against Ukrainian nationalism was not particularly stressed at the Conference.[96] But following a resolution of the All-Union Party Central Committee "On the Position and on the Means of Improving Mass Political Work Among the Toilers of the Stalino [now, Donetsk—Y.B.] Province [in the Ukraine]," [97] a plenary session of the Ukrainian Central Committee was convened in the second half of May, 1959, which put improvement of ideological work as the first item of its agenda. One of the objectives of that work is defined very well in paragraph 4 of its resolution:

. . . Under the conditions of extensive Communist construction, when the rapprochement and mutual help of Socialist nations and nationalities are gathering an *exceptionally* strong (*shyrokoho*) momentum, the work on the internationalist education of toilers, in indoctrinating them with *limitless love for the great Russian people* and all peoples of our Fatherland, should stand in the center of attention of all Party organizations of the Republic.[98]

Similarly the renewed emphasis upon struggle with "survivals of bourgeois nationalism" which was contained in the resolution of the All-Union Party Central Committee on Party propaganda [99] appears to have been responsible for virulent attacks against Ukrainian nationalism at the Twenty-First Congress of the CP (Communist Party) of Ukraine of February, 1960,[100] and especially at the plenary session of the Central Committee of the CP of Ukraine of April, 1960. The latter like that of May, 1959, again discussed improvements in ideological work and again passed a resolution condemning Ukrainian nationalism—a clear sign that central Party authorities were not satisfied with the progress of the assimilationist propaganda campaign.[101] The seriousness of the campaign was stressed by a spokesman of the central apparatus, L. Il'ichev, writing in the September issue of Moscow's *Kommunist*.[102] Not long after the Twenty-Second All-Union Party Congress in Moscow (1961), two important conferences took place in the Ukraine at which the question was taken up again: a huge All-Republican Council on Questions of Ideological Work (February, 1962), which was attended by about 2,000 delegates,[103] and the August plenum of the Central Committee of the CP of Ukraine at which, among other things, were discussed the "Tasks of the Party Organizations of Ukraine to Further Strengthen Ideological Work in the Light of the Resolutions of the Twenty-Second Congress of the CP of the Soviet Union." [104]

The mere listing of the various meetings devoted to "ideological work" evokes the impression that in August, 1958 (publication of Gafurov's article in *Kommunist*), or, at the latest, in March, 1959 (All-Union Party Central Committee resolution on ideological work in the Stalino Province), a decision was made by the leading Party circles in Moscow to reverse the liberal course toward non-Russian peoples and institute a major assimilationist campaign under the slogan of "extensive building of Communism," which was proclaimed from the tribune of the Twenty-First Party Congress in January, 1959. The extent and the intensity of that campaign may be judged from the fact that within a period of less than a year two inter-Republican conferences on the "internationalist" (that is, anti-nationalist) education of peoples were held in the Ukraine: an inter-university conference in Kiev, September 26–29, 1960,[105] and an inter-Republican seminar in Lviv in May, 1961.[106] A Soviet Ukrainian author gives a graphic description of that campaign:

Lecture propaganda has significantly improved in the cities and villages of the Ukrainian SSR. Lectures are read on the topics: "The Friendship of Socialist Nations is the Moving Force of Soviet Society," "Socialist Internationalism is a Mighty Force in the Struggle for Communism," "The Unshakeable Friendship of the Peoples of the USSR Constitutes the Triumph of the Leninist Nationality Policy," "The Flourishing of Soviet Ukraine in the Fraternal Family of the

Peoples of the USSR," and others. In nine months of 1960 there were delivered in the Stalino [Donetsk] oblast (Province) 2,855 lectures on proletarian internationalism, 3,275 on the friendship of peoples of the USSR, and 3,418 on Soviet patriotism. In eight months of 1960 on the friendship of peoples there were given 1,438 lectures in the Stanyslaviv oblast, 1,225 in the Volhynia oblast. In eleven months there were delivered in the Transcarpathian Province 1,323 lectures on the friendship of peoples and 1,250 on Socialist Internationalism. The ideological level of the lectures has risen. Frequently the lectures are supplemented by films, in which the actions of the Ukrainian bourgeois nationalists are exposed ("Ivanna," "The People Accuse," and others).[107]

It seems as if the years 1945–46 have returned with their attacks on Ukrainian "bourgeois nationalism" and the glorification of everything Russian.[108] Is there any difference between the period of reaction after the near-defeat in World War II and that following the challenge from Gomulka, Imre Nagy, Tito, and their sympathizers abroad and at home?

Symbolic for the atmosphere after the Twentieth Party Congress was the cautious rehabilitation of Sosyura's "Love the Ukraine": Three Soviet literary critics writing in Moscow's *Kommunist* rejected as unjustified the characterization of the poem as "nationalist propaganda." Significantly, they did not refer to the primary source of that calumny—Moscow's *Pravda*—but to a statement in a textbook which in turn was based on *Pravda*.[109] But there were in 1956 many other significant developments in the cultural field.

Almost immediately after the Twentieth Party Congress in 1956 the educational and cultural policies of the regime were exposed to an oblique attack. In his article written in July, 1956, Yemel'yanenko said:

Nor can one pass in silence the fact that here and there [*v otdel'nykh mestakh*] the nationality policy in the sphere of education is being violated. There are zealous administrators who attempt to assign children to [public] schools without considering which language is spoken by the parents of the child and thus by the child itself.[110]

From the context it would appear that the "zealous administrators" were attempting to send Ukrainian children to Russian language schools, for in the next paragraph, as in passing, the author mentions that Lenin opposed forced Russification.

Potentially more important have been certain changes in the administration of higher schools. I have not been able to find conclusive evidence that after Melnikov's fall the higher educational institutions in Western Ukraine began to be "de-Russified." But late in 1954 a counterpart Ministry of Higher Education was set up in the Ukraine—the single non-Russian Republic to be given a formal measure of control over its higher education.[111] Precisely what this transfer involved is hard to say.

According to Holubnychy, "Most of the universities and colleges in the Ukraine were transferred back to the jurisdiction of the Ukrainian ministry, and the latter regained the right to establish its own curriculum there." [112] But there is one small indication that the transfer apparently did not remain without effect as far as the language of instruction was concerned. In a letter to the editor of *Molod' Ukrainy,* the Ukrainian Komsomol newspaper of December 8, 1956, a student complained that there were not enough Ukrainian textbooks though "this year [1956–57] the majority of the higher educational institutions in the Ukraine have started teaching in Ukrainian." [113] To make inferences that are really meaningful we should have to know what kind of colleges in the Ukrainian SSR are now teaching in Ukrainian, for a large proportion of the so-called *vuzy* are teachers colleges, and not universities and engineering schools in our sense of the word. But there is no doubt as to the fact that advanced instruction in Russian was hampering the educational progress of many Ukrainian students and that recently central authorities have had to take their plight into consideration.

While the protests against Russian as the language of instruction in elementary, secondary, and higher schools should be traced primarily to the dissatisfaction of ambitious Ukrainians at being deprived of educational opportunities and thus hampered in their socio-economic advancement, there are also clear indications that Ukrainians demand the fulfillment of their cultural needs. A series of complaints has been registered against the Republican book distribution agencies for printing Ukrainian books in too little quantities. In its editorial of September 27, 1956, *Literaturna Hazeta* wrote:

We must remark in passing that in all this there appears an *extremely cautious* approach to Ukrainian publications.[114]

Yemel'yanenko, writing two months earlier, was slightly more explicit:

For example, one cannot regard it as normal that some Party workers bypass such important problems as the distribution of books and journals published in Ukrainian. . . . For can one regard it as normal, for instance, that on the Lviv railroad, which predominantly employs Ukrainians, the newspaper for railroad workers is published in Russian.[115]

The classic example of the silent behind-the-scenes struggle that is carried on within the Party between the proponents of Russian-tinted "internationalism" and the nationally conscious Ukrainian cadres is provided by the publication history of a deluxe four-volume anthology of Ukrainian poems. The anthology, first published in 1957, is remarkable in two ways: First of all, it contains some purged quasi-nationalist poets who were rehabilitated in 1956. The most important of them are

Panteleymon Kulish, a contemporary of Shevchenko's and Oleksander Kandyba-Oles', a first-rate lyricist who emigrated in 1919 (and died in Prague in 1942), both of whom were not included in Volume I of the official *History of Ukrainian Literature* of 1954. Secondly, the anthology covers in a certain way Ukrainian poetry from the eighteenth century to the 1950's in an edition that is technically not outstanding, but nevertheless, rather good. As to the size of publication, that is another story. To obtain the flavor of the debate let us quote from the official summary of Ya. Bash's statement at the Fifth Plenary Session of the Presidium of the Union of Soviet Writers of the Ukraine. The Ukrainian writer said:

One should devote the most serious attention to the problem of the numbers of copies in which Ukrainian books are published. Facts show that despite an increase in the number of new titles, the average number of copies has decreased from year to year. This is to be explained primarily by the faulty practice of the Ukrainian Book Marketing [Agency]. It went so far that initially the agency ordered only 3,000 copies of the *Anthology of Ukrainian Poems,* [the Ukrainian people numbering more than 30 million—Y.B.]. Only after some time, under the pressure of public opinion [*hromads'kosti*], the order was increased to 8,000 copies. But even this is a pitifully small edition. No wonder that very few people succeeded in obtaining the *Anthology* in the bookshops. Now 20,000 additional copies are being printed of that edition.

He continued:

Our publishing houses, too, have started to approach original Ukrainian works in a formal manner. Suffice it to say that the editions of new books by such distinguished masters of the word as A. Holovko or Ivan Le, do not exceed 15,000 copies, while a book "of the usual type" (often of doubtful quality) is published in editions of 100,000, if not half a million. This shows that the book trading agencies and the publishing houses forget about the political aspect of the matter [*sic*], about the great ideologically-educational importance of literature.[116]

Similar complaints have been voiced by readers who pointed out that there were not enough Ukrainian books in rural libraries.[117] It can be safely assumed that both Ya. Bash and his readers know very well where to look for the shortcomings, though in a politic form they are demanding from the regime that it pay more attention to the cultural needs of the Ukrainian people.

But the most interesting indication that in 1956–57 Ukrainian cadres were no longer content to assume the role of the very junior brother as they had been forced to do from 1946 to 1954 is contained in two trends. Occasionally one reads protests against the use of Russian idioms in Ukrainian. There is, for example, a remarkable review of a collection of Ukrainian fairy tales, legends, and anecdotes, in which one of the

compilers had included several quasi-Ukrainian folk tales. The reviewer
cites a ten year old girl who after listening to these tales told her mother:
"Don't read these stories to me any more because if I shall use such
language at school, they'll give me a 'two' [the lowest mark—Y.B.]." He
then pointedly asks:

Can one imagine that in Moscow or Leningrad one would publish, let's say,
a collection of Russian epic songs that consisted of accidental, anti-artistic versions which would mutilate the Russian language, would reduce it to the level
of some dialect, a good for nothing patois. We think it is impossible.[118]

The second trend consists in the effort to establish direct international
contacts, as if to prove that in today's world Ukrainian culture has
greater than provincial significance. At a plenary session of the Union
of Soviet Writers in Moscow, Yury Smolych complained that the enemies
of the Soviet regime abroad were spreading slander about the successes
of Leninist-Stalinist nationality policy and that the regime was not doing enough in refuting them. Specifically he proposed that the journal
Soviet Literature which is published in several world languages, should
present "very complete information not only about Russian literature
but about the literatures of the whole of the Soviet Union." [119] In 1957
Ukrainian historians obtained the permission of the regime to publish a professional journal of their own. In 1958 Ukrainian writers
started the publication of *Vsesvit* (The Universe)—a journal devoted
exclusively to foreign literature, like Moscow's *Inostrannaya Literatura*
(Foreign Literature).[120] It was further announced that at the first international conference on Ukrainian philology to be held in Moscow
within the general framework of the Fourth International Congress of
Slavists in September, 1958, Academician O. Biletsky was to give a paper
on the significance of Ukrainian literature for the development of the
culture of Slavic peoples.[121] From 1946 to 1953, it seems to me, such
a paper would have looked distinctly out of place at a meeting of Soviet
scholars, and one would have expected Biletsky to speak on the bene-
ficial influence of Russian culture. The times appeared to have changed.

In the summer of 1958, as we have already seen, the nationality policy
of the regime changed. Soon the strength of Ukrainian national sentiment was put to a test in one of the most significant developments of
modern Ukrainian cultural and political history. The issue involved
was seemingly obscure: the obligatory or non-obligatory nature of the
second language in primary and secondary schools of the Ukrainian SSR.
But many prominent Ukrainians correctly perceived the political implications of that measure.

On November 12, 1958, the Central Committee of the CP of the
Soviet Union and the USSR Council of Ministers approved "theses" in

which the forthcoming educational reform was outlined. For our purpose the most important was Thesis 19. Though not the shortest one it is so carefully drafted and so pivotal for our discussion that we have reproduced it *in extenso:*

Instruction in the Soviet school is conducted in the native tongue. This is one of the important achievements of the Leninist nationality policy. At the same time, in schools of the Union and autonomous republics the Russian language is studied seriously. This language is a powerful means of international communication, of strengthening friendship among the peoples of the USSR, and of bringing them into contact with the wealth of Russian and world culture.

Nevertheless, we must note that in the area of language study in the schools of the Union and autonomous republics children are considerably overloaded. It is a fact that in the nationality schools [non-Russian schools—Y.B.] children study three languages—their native tongue, Russian, and one of the foreign languages.

The question ought to be considered of giving parents the right to send their children to a school where the language of their choice is used. If a child attends a school where instruction is conducted in the language of one of the Union or autonomous republics, he may, if he wishes, take up the Russian language. And vice versa, if a child attends a Russian school, he may, if he so desires, study the language of one of the Union or autonomous republics. To be sure, this step could only be taken if there is a sufficient number of children to form classes for instruction in a given language.

To grant parents the right to decide what language a child should study as a compulsory subject would be a most democratic procedure. It would eliminate arbitrary decisions in this important matter and would make possible the termination of the practice of overloading children with language study. Permission should be granted not to require a foreign language among the required subjects in schools where appropriate conditions do not exist.[122]

The theses on educational reform were discussed at numerous public meetings and in the press of all the Republics. Not unexpectedly Thesis 19 met with very strong opposition in all three Baltic Republics and in the three Transcaucasian Republics (Azerbaydzhan, Armenia, and Georgia).[123] In the Ukraine, too, popular opposition to the Thesis was rather extensive. It was criticized explicitly by teachers, writers, and even Party officials of intermediate rank. An instructor at the Zaporozhe Teachers College warned that children graduating from a Russian-language school at which Ukrainian was not taught might be unable to gain admission to a university or college at which it was the main language of instruction.[124] The most eloquent defense of the status quo was from the pen of the eminent Ukrainian poets M. Rylsky and M. Bazhan, who published a joint article in Moscow's *Pravda.* In their opinion, the only correct solution of the problem was the compulsory teaching, on a basis of equality, of both the Russian and the Ukrainian languages in all schools of the Ukrainian SSR. "Such a solution would correspond to the principles of Leninist nationality policy. Consequently, such a solution would be really democratic." [125] (This last point is a reply to the final paragraph of the thesis.) Of even greater significance than the impassioned defense by writers is the statement by P. Tronko, a Secretary of the Kiev *obkom* (Provincial Committee) of the Communist party of the Ukraine, in the authoritative monthly journal of the CPU: "Under conditions of our Republic, in our opinion, the study of Russian, Ukrainian and of one foreign language should be required in all schools." [126] (It should be borne in mind that Kiev is the capital of the Ukraine and that this and the publication of Tronko's "opinion" in *Kommunist Ukrayiny* indicate that Tronko had probably been chosen to act as the spokesman for the Ukrainian Party organization.)

A legislative bill based on the theses of November 12 was debated in the two chambers of the USSR Supreme Soviet on December 24, 1958. Though, apparently as a result of its hostile reception in the Republics, the Government *withdrew* Thesis 19 from the bill (the matter was left up to the individual Republics, at least for the time being),[127] the delegates of many of the Republics used the forum of the USSR Supreme Soviet in Moscow to challenge in unmistakable terms the projected policy devised by the country's leaders in the Soviet capital. Both deputies from the Ukraine upheld the status quo. One of them, S. V. Chervonenko, the Secretary in charge of ideological indoctrination of the Central Committee of the CP of Ukraine, bluntly asserted that many years of experience had proved that requiring both Russian and Ukrainian was fully justified. Any change in the existing arrangement would be, in his judgment, a step backwards. If exceptions to the rule had to be made for children of military personnel and other transients, Ukrainian authorities would do so.[128]

In the following three months strong pressure was apparently exerted by the regime, for in the spring of 1959 all Republics—with a few significant exceptions, upon which I have commented elsewhere—included Thesis 19 in the Republican laws on educational reforms, after perfunctory discussions, with little variation in wording. The Ukrainian SSR accepted Thesis 19 in Article 9 of its law.[129]

Today the wider implications of Thesis 19 are clear to every observer of the Soviet Union; it suffices merely to place Thesis 19 in the context of Gafurov's programmatical article. The assimilationists were again to be openly supported by the regime as during the 1930's, 1940's, and early 1950's. The Soviet Ukrainian scholar H. Yemel'yanenko, who in the summer of 1956 complained of administrative restrictions on the use of the Ukrainian language,[130] in the spring of 1959 declared flatly that the "wide spread of the Russian language in all the Soviet Republics [was] a . . . deeply progressive phenomenon, which corresponded to the interests of the construction of Communism." [131] Approximately a year later, I. Kravtsev published an article in the same vein, in which he exclusively dealt with the language problem. In that article he specifically mentions the extensive opposition to the adoption of Thesis 19 in various Republics, including the Ukraine.[132]

A former Soviet Ukrainian journalist who is now living in exile has stressed that by solemnly reiterating the well-established principle that parents have a right to choose which school their children are to attend, the regime has actually extended a veiled invitation to assimilationists and their official patrons to enroll their children in Russian schools.[133] We know from two sources that after the adoption of the law on school reform in April, 1959, the number of Russian-language schools in the Ukraine has indeed increased.[134] Moreover, some materials bear out our suspicion that the democratic choice of parents is not altogether free. An editorial in the professional journal for teachers of Ukrainian clearly states:

This principle of being able to choose the language of instruction, in our opinion, *must under no circumstances be left to take care of itself (na samoplyv)*. The press, the radio, the public must conduct insistent explanatory work among the parents and workers.[135]

From the context it is not clear whether this "explanatory work" is to be in favor of the Ukrainian rather than the Russian language. But judging by Yemel'yanenko's and Kravtsev's commentaries on the recent Soviet nationality policy, it is Russian that is strongly to be preferred.

We have recounted the events of 1958–59 in some detail to document that, unlike Stalin's restoration of Russian hegemony in 1946, the second shift in nationality policy under Khrushchev was not accepted without extensive, vocal and seemingly futile opposition from Ukrainians in various walks of life—from a college teacher up to a Secretary of the CP of Ukraine Central Committee. It is also of utmost significance that though the official policy changed in the middle of 1958, some Ukrainians have continued to publicly resist its implementation to date (spring, 1963). Complaints about the shortage of Ukrainian books, ostensibly because of the faulty practices of the official book distribution agencies, have continued. For instance, the Soviet Ukrainian writer Malyshko complained of this from the tribune of the Twenty-Second Congress of the CP of Ukraine in 1961.[136] In January, 1963, Dyachenko, a Soviet Ukrainian publicist, in a letter to the editor, bitterly attacked an employee in one of such distribution agencies. She had, among other things, refused to order his own pamphlet on national character (in Ukrainian), saying that it was probably nationalistic; he threatened to bring her to court for unjustly accusing him of Ukrainian nationalism.[137] For some years there has been waged on the pages of the USSR and the Soviet Ukrainian press a thinly veiled polemic between non-Russian assimilationists (for example, the Daghestani writer Akhed Agaev,[138] and the Soviet Ukrainian publicist I. Kravtsev[139]) and their opponents (the foremost Ukrainian poet M. Rylsky,[140] the older writer Antonenko-Davydovych,[141] and Dyachenko).[142] One of the wittiest arguments is that by Borys Buryak, who boldly raises the question of national character versus "a-national abstractions." In an imaginary dialogue he has his opponent defend the (officially endorsed) thesis that in the period of extensive building of Communism, which is characterized by such technological feats as the launching of sputniks, national differences are bound to disappear. How do you reconcile this with the fact, asks the author, that while orbiting the earth in 1962 cosmonaut Popovych sang *"Dyvlyus' ya na nebo ta dumku hadayu . . ."* (I look at the sky and think a thought—a popular Ukrainian folk song). Buryak cites Lenin in defense of his conviction that national differences "will persist very, very long even after the realization of the dictatorship of the proletariat on a global scale." To speak of the fusion of nations at this moment is a "nonsensical, wishful thought," says Lenin.[143]

Very noteworthy are also the resolutions of a five-day Republican conference on the culture of the Ukrainian language. The conference took place in Kiev from February 11–15, was sponsored jointly by the Shevchenko University of Kiev and the Potebnya Institute of Linguistics of the Academy of Sciences of the Ukrainian SSR. The assembled linguists, college teachers, writers, and other persons engaged in the field of communications (staff members of publication houses, the press, radio and television) are reported by a Kiev educator to have participated in a rather frank exchange of opinion while discussing the twenty-seven papers read at the conference.

Some of them indignantly pointed out that restrictions on the usage of Ukrainian, which had been made during Stalin's rule (the "cult of the individual") have not yet been lifted. The supporters of "linguistic nihilism" (read: Russification) had then brought about that Ukrainian was excluded from the engineering sciences. Those "anti-Leninists" had also been instrumental in the closing of all Ukrainian-language schools outside the Ukrainian Republic in the 1930's and 1940's. The participants at the conference also "unanimously condemned the absurd theory that a nation has two languages." (This is a sharp criticism of the officially favored tendency to establish Russian as the "second native language" of the non-Russian peoples of the USSR, which is apparent, for example, in Gafurov's and Agayev's previously mentioned articles [144]— Y.B.) The conference found no explicit authority for that trend in the new Party program of 1961. Other far-reaching demands were made. But it might be best to let the Soviet Ukrainian reporter, who apparently attended the conference, speak for himself. In his own words: *Those present ardently and approvingly took up* (vidneslysya do) *the proposition to make representations before the Central Committee of the Communist Party of Ukraine and the Government of Ukraine on behalf of the following:*

1. *In all higher and secondary specialized schools* [that is, colleges and vocational high schools—Y.B.], *training schools and courses for artisans instruction should be conducted in Ukrainian. Textbooks for those schools should be published in Ukrainian.*
   In all pre-school institutions (no matter who supports them financially) in which there are Ukrainian children, the education should be conducted in Ukrainian.
2. *In all* [public] *offices and enterprises, on the railroad and other modes of transportation, in commerce all business should be conducted in Ukrainian.*
3. *The Academy of Sciences, the institutes and publishing houses should publish scholarly works mostly in Ukrainian.*
4. *The cinema studios should produce artistic and scientific films only in the Ukrainian language, and the films produced in other republics should be dubbed into Ukrainian.*

It was also proposed that in Republics of the Soviet Union where there live Ukrainians, general [elementary and secondary] schools with Ukrainian language of instruction should be established (as has been done in the Ukraine for the Russian and other peoples).

All in all, these demands appear perfectly reasonable in the context of the "de-Stalinization" policy of 1956, but in 1963, when they were voiced, they constitute a not inconsiderable challenge to the central government. Not surprisingly, those demands were passed over in silence by the Kiev press; and we have learnt about them only in an indirect way.[145]

In reviewing Soviet policy toward Ukrainian nationalism we have seen that in the 1920's the regime was forced to make certain concessions to Ukrainian feelings. Those concessions were withdrawn during the following decade and many of its beneficiaries liquidated at a time when Russian nationalism became acceptable again. Sometime in the early 1930's Stalin had made the conscious decision to use the Russian national heritage as a cement to hold together the multi-national Soviet Union in the face of German aggression.

During World War II the policy of Russification was suspended and with an eye to flamboyant constitutional trappings Belorussia and the Ukraine were admitted to the United Nations. After the war, however, the emphasis upon all things Russian assumed a particularly strident note, and there are indications that towards the end of his life Stalin was planning a purge not only of Jews but of other bourgeois nationalists, including those in the Ukraine.

After Stalin's death, Beria tried to use the discontent in the non-Russian Republics to bolster his bid to power—he lost his life in the attempt. Khrushchev used it much more adroitly: first courting the non-Russians (in the administrative reorganizations of 1954–56; most clearly at the Twentieth Party Congress), then restoring favor to Russians and their supporters (since 1958). On the surface it would appear as if Khrushchev were repeating Stalin's policy of the 1930's and 1940's.

Khrushchev's position, however, is more difficult, nor is it rendered any easier by his obvious reluctance to resort to mass terror. The Soviet Ukrainian leaders of the late 1950's—whether politicians, or men in cultural life—had been cleared in numerous anti-nationalist purges under Stalin. They are politically loyal Communists, cannot be easily dubbed "bourgeois nationalists" as could the Ukrainian leaders of the 1920's and 1930's. The official policy may have been changed after the revolts in Poland and Hungary, but they have not remained silent, and oppose assimilation—though within certain limits set by the dictatorial regime. The assimilationists cite Lenin on the fusion of nations—very well, their opponents will quote Lenin on the need to hasten slowly, against "nonsensical, wishful dreams." It would seem as if the Ukrainian Communist leaders, so subservient under Stalin, had recovered their spine under Khrushchev. Is it perhaps because the Ukrainian people have advanced in economic and social terms, despite Stalin's terror? Let us turn for evidence to the next chapter, in which we propose to look at the demographic bases of Ukrainian nationalism.

Chapter II

SOME FACTORS UNDERLYING UKRAINIAN NATIONALISM

A student of a political movement must sketch its territorial setting. He should also strive to calculate its strength with the greatest possible precision; the more so, because since 1956 the Soviet government has released a flood of statistics, some of which are very useful. This chapter serves the double purpose of locating the Ukrainian people on the map of the world and of evaluating, in quantitative terms, their demographic and socio-economic progress. I shall give the latest figures on the natural endowments of the Ukraine and her agricultural and industrial production; the number of Ukrainians in the Republic and the Union as a whole; the socio-economic characteristics of all the citizens of the Ukrainian SSR and those of the Ukrainians living in the Republic.

According to the Soviet census of January, 1959, the number of Ukrainians in the USSR is 37.3 million, 32.2 million of whom reside in the Ukrainian SSR. At the present time, the Ukrainian Republic comprises an area of 601,000 square kilometers (less than 3 per cent of the total area of the Soviet Union), with a population of 43.1 million, as of January 1, 1961, which equals one-fifth of the Union total of 216.2 million. Comparing the Ukraine with independent European countries we find that she has a territory somewhat larger than that of France (551,000 sq. kilometers), but with a smaller population (there were 45.8 million Frenchmen as of April 1, 1961).[1]

1. *Natural Endowments, Agriculture and Industry*

In terms of natural endowments, the Ukraine combines fertile agricultural soil with rich mineral deposits; long famous as the granary of Europe, she has also remained "the primary mineral producing area" of the Russian Empire and its Soviet successor ever since the turn of the century.[2] On the basis of her agriculture and mining, food-processing, light and heavy industries were developed. Whether one considers her

36

from the viewpoint of population or economic potential, the Ukraine ranks second among the Soviet Republics, next to the Russian SFSR. (The following paragraphs will document this proposition.) Nor should it be forgotten that on a European scale the Ukraine appears as a highly industrialized country, at least with respect to her output of a few selected, key commodities. Table II-1 shows the per capita output of pig iron, steel, coal, iron ore, and sugar in the Ukrainian SSR, England, France, West Germany, and Italy in 1955.

Table II-1

PER CAPITA PRODUCTION OF SELECTED COMMODITIES IN THE
UKRAINIAN SSR AND SOME WEST EUROPEAN COUNTRIES, 1955
(In Kilogram Per Capita)

	Pig iron	Steel	Coal	Iron ore	Sugar
Ukrainian SSR	413	421	3,131	993	60.3
United Kingdom	247	392	4,388	322	11.8
France	252	290	1,302	1,162	33.8
West Germany	330	427	3,157	300	22.8
Italy	33	111	26	28	20.6

Source: TsSU SRSR—Statystychne upravlinnya Ukrayins'koyi RSR (USSR Central Statistical Administration—Ukrainian SSR Statistical Administration), *Dosyahnennya Radyans'koyi Ukrayiny za sorok rokiv—Statystychny zbirnyk* (Achievements of the Ukrainian SSR in 40 Years—A Statistical Handbook, Kiev, 1957), p. 20.

The figures indicate that in that year the Ukraine had the highest per capita output of pig iron and sugar in Europe, occupied the second place in the smelting of steel (after West Germany) and in the mining of iron ore (next to France), and held a third position in the mining of coal (almost as much as West Germany). According to a more recent, general source in 1962 the Ukraine exceeded in the *per capita* production of pig iron and steel such countries as the United States, England, France, and Western Germany; in coal mined per capita—all those four states; in iron ore per capita—"all main capitalist countries." [3]

Within the economy of the Soviet Union the Ukraine is remarkable both for her agricultural and industrial wealth. The fertility of the Ukrainian black soil has been proverbial since the days of the Tsarist Empire. Now the Republic contains approximately one-sixth of the total cultivated area of the USSR, but a decade ago, prior to Khrushchev's large-scale attempts to till the virgin lands in Kazakhstan and

Western Siberia, her share was one-fifth.[4] Until recently, the two principal Ukrainian crops were wheat and sugar beets, but in the late 1950's
the government introduced corn on a large scale, at the expense of wheat.
Ukrainian herdstocks contain somewhat less than one-third of all the
hogs and less than one-fourth of the big horned cattle in the Soviet
Union.[5] But even a cursory glance at the attached tables shows that
in most instances the output of Ukrainian agriculture is significantly
higher than that in the USSR as a whole or the Russian Republic in
particular, if production is weighted by units of input (see Table II-2,
p. 39). Attention should be drawn to the fact that while in 1960 the
total cultivated area under cereals in the Ukrainian SSR was but one-
eighth (13.0 per cent) of the corresponding total acreage in the USSR,
the Ukrainian cereal crop amounted to one-*fifth* (20.0 per cent) of the
USSR total harvest of cereals. In plain language, Ukrainian soil is, on
balance, more fertile than in the USSR as a whole or in the Russian
SFSR in particular. Because of the density of population in the Ukraine
we find, however, that the per capita output of all cereals combined is
in the Ukraine only slightly above that of the USSR as a whole (624
kilogram compared with 622 kg.) and actually below that in the RSFSR
(654 kg.).[6] In cattle raising and dairy farming the Ukrainian SSR out-
produces the Russian Republic as well as the USSR as a whole on a
per capita basis, but it does not achieve the considerably higher yields
in the three Baltic Republics (see Table II-3). Another table (Table II-4)
shows that the Ukraine occupies a respectable place in the Soviet food-
processing industry.

   The mineral wealth of the Ukraine is even more remarkable than her
agricultural assets. While the deposits of individual minerals are exceeded in size by those in the Russian SFSR, as a rule, they are more
conveniently located, thus reducing the problem of long railroad hauls
which has plagued Russian industry perennially. For instance, Ukrainian
deposits of the classic pair—iron ore and coal—are both substantial and
easily accessible. According to Shimkin, "Nearly half of the measured
reserves [of iron ore in the USSR] lie in the Ukraine and in Crimea,
over 20 per cent each in Central and Northwest Russia, and in the
Urals."[7] Moreover, the quality of the ore that is mined at Krivoy Rog
in the Ukraine is quite high.[8] In the larger deposits at Kerch in the
Crimea, the most plentiful measured in the USSR, the Ukrainian Republic possesses an abundant reserve of lesser quality ore. In 1960, 55
per cent of the total Soviet output of iron ore were mined in the Ukraine.[9]

   Besides iron, the Ukraine also has the Soviet Union's largest deposits
of manganese ore, the second largest being in Georgia. (Manganese is a
metal which is used in the production of steel.) The Georgian ore is better in quality, but harder to mine. The USSR claims to possess about

Table II-2

SELECTED CEREALS IN THE UKRAINIAN SSR, THE RUSSIAN SFSR, AND THE USSR, 1960: AREAS UNDER CULTIVATION AND HARVESTS

	All cereals combined				Wheat				Corn			
	Cultivated area		Harvest		Cultivated area		Harvest		Cultivated area		Harvest	
	Thousand hectares *	Distribution percentage	Thousand metric tons *	Distribution percentage	Thousand hectares	Distribution percentage	Thousand metric tons	Distribution percentage	Thousand hectares	Distribution percentage	Thousand metric tons	Distribution percentage
Ukrainian SSR	16,963	13.9	26,898	20.0	3,952	6.6	6,788	10.6	6,271	55.8	10,639	56.9
Russian SFSR	73,574	60.5	78,865	58.7	35,700	59.1	39,630	61.6	3,494	31.1	5,386	28.8
USSR Total	121,690	100.0	134,369	100.0	60,393	100.0	64,299	100.0	11,239	100.0	18,702	100.0

* A hectare equals 2.471 acres; a metric ton—2,204.6 lbs.

Source: Tsentral'noe statisticheskoe upravlenie pri sovete ministrov SSSR (Central Statistical Administration of the USSR Council of Ministers), *Narodnoe khozaystvo SSSR v 1960 godu—Statisticheskiy ezhegodnik* (USSR National Economy in 1960, A Statistical Yearbook, Moscow, 1961), pp. 394–99, 419–23. The source will henceforth be abbreviated as: *Nar. khoz. SSSR 1960.*

Table II-3

PER CAPITA OUTPUT OF MEAT AND MILK IN
SELECTED SOVIET REPUBLICS, 1960
(In Kilograms *)

	Meat and Fat †	Milk
Ukrainian SSR	48.1	325
Russian SFSR	37.3	286
Lithuanian SSR	75.6	624
Latvian SSR	71.0	686
Estonian SSR	81.9	702
USSR Average	40.2	286

* One kilogram equals 2.2 lbs.
† In slaughter weight.

Sources: Calculated from tables in *Nar. khoz. SSSR, 1960*, pp. 464, 467. Population figures for January 1, 1961, *ibid.*, p. 8.

Table II-4

PROCESSING OF SELECTED FOODS IN THE UKRAINIAN SSR,
THE RUSSIAN SFSR, AND THE USSR, IN 1960

Commodity	Ukr. SSR	Per cent of USSR	Rus. SFSR	Per cent of USSR	USSR	Per cent of USSR
Sugar, granulated *	3,877.1	60.9	1,625.6	25.5	6,363.2	100.0
Meat *	911.4	20.6	2,434.7	55.3	4,406.4	100.0
Animal fats *	189.9	25.8	383.6	52.0	737.2	100.0
Vegetable fats *	449.2	28.4	598.8	37.8	1,585.5	100.0
Canned goods †	1,157.4	23.8	2,118.0	43.6	4,860.6	100.0

* By thousand metric tons.
† By million standard cans.

Source: Nar. khoz. SSSR, 1960, pp. 346, 349, 351, 353, and 355.

one-third of the world's known resources—she has exported significant amounts of manganese to the United States, Poland, Germany, France, and Belgium-Luxemburg. In 1947, for example, the Soviet Union provided 24 per cent of the American supply of manganese; before the war she used to furnish about 40 per cent.[10]

Until quite recently, it was held that Ukrainian deposits of other non-ferrous metals were exceedingly poor, with the possible exception of mercury (small deposits exist near Nikitovka, probably the largest in the Soviet Union).[11] But in the last years geologists found titanium deposits in the Dniepropetrovsk and Zhytomyr provinces as well as new deposits of nickel. Above all, in the near future the Republic is to become self-sufficient in bauxites, the raw material for aluminum.[12]

Most of the Soviet coal and lignite reserves (82 per cent of an estimated total of one trillion metric tons) lie in Western and Eastern Siberia (e.g., some 375 billion tons in the Kuznetsk Basin).[13] Nevertheless, the Ukraine with about 3.5 per cent of the total reserves,[14] provided in the 1950's and early 1960's about one-third of the Soviet coal output.[15] Most of the Ukrainian coal is mined in a single field, the Donets Basin,[16] four-fifths of which lie within the territory of the Ukrainian SSR. There are several reasons why Donets coal is preferred. Historically, the Donets Basin was the first to be exploited on a modern scale; before World War I, in 1913, the Ukraine supplied not one-third, but almost four-fifths of the total demand of the Empire.[17] Secondly, for military reasons the Soviet government might have wanted not to tap the relatively protected Siberian fields to the full extent warranted by their reserves. But there is also a sound economic reason why the Donets Basin has been exploited in preference to the Kuzbas. A great deal of coal is consumed in the metallurgical process. In the Ukraine, the production of one ton of pig iron involved, on the average, 700 ton-kilometers of freight haulage; in Magnitogorsk and Kuznetsk, 4,500 ton-kilometers were needed.[18]

Other mineral deposits in the Ukraine are less significant. Oil drilling is of local importance only; the production of natural gas, however, is considerable.[19] The country also possesses large and varied resources of non-metallic minerals: at the outbreak of World War II virtually all of the Soviet china clay manufacturing was centered in the Ukraine, where ores of a very high quality are found (at Glukhovtsy, Turbovo, Lozoviki, Prosyanaya); superior graphite is mined near Dniepropetrovsk; and, last but not least, the Ukraine is also a significant producer of superphosphates, potash, and salt.[20]

On the basis of these resources, a powerful industry has been erected. As of 1955, 20.2 per cent of the total fixed capital in the industry of the Soviet Union was invested in the Ukraine. Her share equals more or less that invested in the Central Russian industrial complex (18.8 per cent), exceeding by a wide margin the capital equipment in the Urals (13.8 per cent). The size of industrial investment in the other Republics is much smaller (3.4 per cent in the Kazakh SSR, 3.1 per cent in the Azerbaydzhan SSR, and so forth in a rapidly descending proportion).[21]

On January 1, 1960, Soviet statisticians have re-evaluated all capital investment throughout the Union.[22] Some of the resulting figures, which have been reproduced in the table below (Table II-5), provide us with a graphic illustration of the structure of Ukrainian industry compared with industry in the RSFSR and with Soviet industry as a whole (as measured in terms of fixed capital—a valid approach in view of the gen-

Table II-5

RELATIVE STRUCTURE OF INDUSTRY IN THE UKRAINIAN SSR, JANUARY 1, 1960: PER CENT OF THE TOTAL CAPITAL FUNDS INVESTED IN DIFFERENT BRANCHES OF THE INDUSTRY OF THE UKRAINIAN SSR, RUSSIAN SFSR, AND USSR AS A WHOLE

	UkrSSR	RSFSR	USSR
Ferrous Metallurgy	22.5	8.2	9.6
Non-Ferrous Metallurgy	1.0	4.8	4.2
Fuel Industry	23.1	15.6	17.0
of which: Coal	21.5	6.9	8.8
Production of Electric Power and			
Heat Energy	8.3	12.8	11.9
Machine-Building and Metal Working	16.0	21.7	20.3
Chemical	4.7	5.6	4.9
Forestry, Paper, and Wood Processing	2.0	8.1	5.9
Construction Materials	5.0	5.2	5.3
Light Industry	2.1	5.0	4.5
of which: Textile Industry	1.2	3.8	3.2
Food Processing	9.8	9.2	9.1
Other industries	5.5	3.8	7.3
Totals	100.0	100.0	100.0

Source: Tsentral'ne statystychne upravlinnya pry Radi Ministriv URSR (UkrSSR Council of Ministers Central Statistical Administration), *Narodne hospodarstvo Ukrayins'koyi RSR v 1960 rotsi* (National Economy of UkrSSR in 1960, Kiev, 1961), pp. 30–31; Tsentral'noe statisticheskoe upravlenie pri Sovete Ministrov RSFSR (Central Stat. Adm. of the Russian SFSR Council of Ministers), *Narodnoe khozaystvo RSFSR v 1960 g.* (Nat. Economy of RSFSR in 1960, Moscow, 1961), p. 20; *Nar. khoz. SSSR, 1960,* p. 87.

erally capital-intensive modern industry). We see that in the Ukraine there has been a strong emphasis upon the development of coal mining and ferrous metallurgy. Relative investments in Ukrainian chemical, construction, and food processing industries are more or less equal to the Soviet average and to Russian figures. But the Ukraine tends to lag behind in the development of her machine-building and metal processing industry. It should, however, be pointed out that a decade before, on January 1, 1951, only 3.3 per cent of the total industrial capital in the Ukraine had been invested in her machine-building industry, against a corresponding figure of 27.7 per cent for the USSR as a whole.[23] In the 1950's, in other words, the Ukrainian machine-building industry was developed at an accelerated rate to bring it closer to the USSR average. Moreover, the new "perspective plan" for the 1960's and 1970's calls for a continued rapid growth of that Ukrainian industry. Machine-building and metal processing is to assume the first place in the industrial production of the Republic. Automated equipment is to be manufactured in the Ukraine, the country will specialize in the output of heavy trucks and small passenger compact cars.[24] In summary it would appear that until the 1950's certain crucial sectors such as machine-building were neglected, giving the industry of the Ukraine a somewhat lopsided structure reminiscent of typical colonial economies with their emphasis on extractive industries and their relative lack of modern manufacturing facilities. In the last decade (under Khrushchev?) steps have been taken to remedy that structural defect.

The present structure of Ukrainian industry is also reflected in its output figures. Containing approximately one-fifth of the Soviet Union's population, the Ukraine supplied in 1960 51.7 per cent of the total Soviet output of pig iron, 40.1 per cent of steel, and 41.4 per cent of rolled metal.[25] Her share in the production of electrical power, however —a good indicator of technological progress—is more modest: in 1960 it amounted to 53.9 billion kwh out of 292.3 billion, or 18.4 per cent of the Soviet Union total.[26] It is interesting to note that while in absolute terms Ukrainian output in those branches has nearly doubled since the eve of the German invasion (1940), the relative share of the Republic in the total Soviet production has fallen appreciably owing to the development of the eastern industrial regions of the USSR. In 1940, the Ukraine produced, e.g., 64.7 per cent of Soviet pig iron, 48.8 per cent of steel, 49.7 per cent of rolled metal, and 25.7 per cent of electrical power.[27]

The per capita output of Ukrainian chemical and construction material industry approximates that of the Soviet Union, that is, it is close to 20.0 per cent of total USSR output.[28] Minor exceptions are the production of calcinated soda,[29] mineral fertilizers,[30] and ceramic floor tiles.[31] More interesting from the viewpoint of a student of political economy is the output of her machine-building and consumer goods industries. Besides railroad stock, certain coal mining equipment, and agricultural machinery in which Ukrainian enterprises specialize,[32] the Ukrainian machine-building industry is outproduced by factories in the Russian SFSR. As of 1960, for example, only 13.2 per cent of Soviet metal cutting lathes were built in the Ukraine.[33] Similarly, in 1960 only 7,268 automobiles (trucks, buses, and passenger cars) came off Ukrainian assembly lines. They constitute but 1.4 per cent of the total Soviet output. Curiously enough, in 1957 Ukrainian automobile production had reached as many as 22,684 units, or 4.6 per cent of USSR production.[34]

Similarly, several important branches of the consumer goods industry, such as textiles, have concentrated their manufacturing facilities in Russia. Possibly as a result of the earlier, pre-1917 specialization or of deliberate government policy, in 1960 Russia produced as much as 86.8 per cent of Soviet cotton textiles, 79.5 per cent of woolens, 84.5 per cent of linens, and 79.8 per cent silk textiles, the Ukrainian share in the total output reaching but 1.5, 5.6, zero, and 4.9 per cent.[35] For some unexplained reason, however, the relative output of hosiery, knit underwear, and knit outerwear in the Ukrainian SSR is close to the Soviet average per capita (the Ukrainian figures for 1960 are 22.1, 22.6, and 19.5 per cent).[36] Production of leather shoes, on the other hand, lags somewhat behind the Union average with 18.3 per cent of the total.[37] The relative output of the Ukrainian machine-building and consumer goods industry is summarized in the diagram below (Chart II-1).

Part of the explanation for the slowed development of several branches of Ukrainian industry (particularly heavy industry) should be sought in the sharp increase of capital allocations to the eastern areas of the USSR.[38] Official figures, in so far as they are meaningful at all, indicate that in the twenty years since 1940 the development of industry in the Ukrainian Republic has been considerably under the Union average. Total industrial output in the USSR as a whole increased in that period 5.2 times, in the Russian Republic, in which most of the new industrial complexes are located, it grew 4.9 times, in the Ukraine only 3.6 times.[39]

A simple question is now in order: what do all these figures mean? The share of a Republic in the total production of the USSR has been frequently used as an index in Soviet statistics. If we compare the relative productive share of a Republic with her share of the Soviet population, could we draw from this any valid inferences about Soviet policy vis-à-vis the various nationalities? This would be possible only if the other factors of production (above all, natural resources) were distributed homogeneously. That cannot be assumed. But if the distribution of productive factors is known and is properly taken into account, then figures on the relative output of the Soviet Republics can be used as a *rough*

Chart II-1

OUTPUT OF SELECTED COMMODITIES IN THE MACHINE-BUILDING AND
CONSUMER GOODS INDUSTRIES OF THE UKRAINIAN SSR, 1960:
PER CENT OF USSR TOTAL OUTPUT

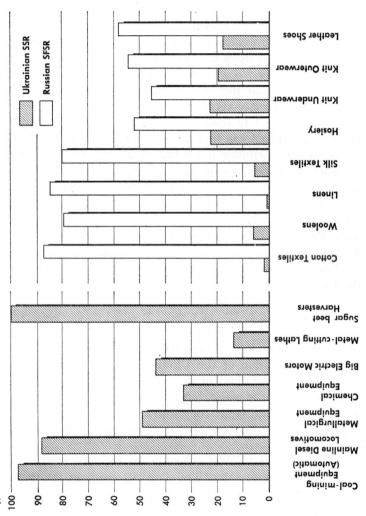

Source: A. Nesterenko, ["The Role of the Ukrainian SSR in the Establishment
of the Material Technological Base of Communism"], *Ekonomika Sovetskoy Ukrainy* (Economy of the Soviet Ukraine), Vol. 1961, No. 6
(November-December), p. 20.

indication of economic policy as it affects the nationalities, or of the economic aspect of nationality policy—depending on the weight we attribute to nationalities in the formulation of economic policy.

Nor can the relative output figures be used as a precise measure of economic self-sufficiency. The whole concept of autarky is meaningless unless it is considered against demand over time, with due allowance being made for likely changes in the demand. Special caution must be used in interpreting industrial data because we do not always know exactly how the listed items have been produced: the Ukraine may build a relatively high proportion of the total Soviet output of a certain kind of machinery using in the process machine tools which are available only in Russia, and vice versa.[40]

To sum up, subject to some qualifications the relative output figures for the Ukrainian SSR can be used as a rough measure of the economic status which that Republic has achieved in the whole Soviet economy and as a tentative indicator of the economic aspect of Soviet nationality policy. Nevertheless, albeit in very rough terms, the relative output figures do indicate the extent of interdependence between the economy of the Ukraine and that of the rest of the Soviet Union. We may, for example, draw the important political conclusion that as the share of the Ukraine in the output of certain key commodities (coal and pig iron) diminishes over time, so does the dependence of the rest of the USSR on the Ukraine.

2. The Demographic Base: Population Totals

The census of January 15, 1959, has provided us with some important data on the population of the Ukrainian SSR. Admittedly, compared to the extensive tabulations of the 1926 census, the published material from the latest count is sparse, but it is considerably more revealing than the mysterious general figures of Stalin's census of 1939. First about the total population of the Republic, then its national and social composition.

According to official Soviet estimates, in 1913 the population of the territory later to become the Ukrainian SSR (without the western provinces) was 27.2 million, that of the future USSR—139.3 million. (In 1897, the population of Eastern Ukraine, the future Ukrainian SSR, had amounted to 21.2 million.) When the census of 1926 was taken, the population of the Eastern Ukraine amounted to 29.0 million, that of the USSR to 147.0 million. The corresponding figures for January, 1939, are 31.0 million for the Ukraine, and 170.5 million for the Soviet Union as a whole. The annexation of West Ukrainian territories in 1939–1945 brought the Ukrainian population figure "in 1940" up to 40.5 million within a total Soviet population of 190.7 million, if we accept official estimates. The census of 1959 showed that the total population of the Ukrainian Republic numbered 41.9 million out of a Soviet total of 208.8 million. (See Table II-6, with notes and sources, p. 48.)

If we compare the rates of growth, we find that between the censuses of 1897 and 1926, the population of the Eastern Ukraine increased by 36.8 per cent as against 41.6 per cent for the USSR as a whole, despite the losses in World War I.[41] Between the two censuses of 1926 and 1939, however, the increase amounted to 15.9 per cent for the Soviet Union, but in Eastern Ukraine it was only 7 per cent.[42] From "1940" to 1959, or within roughly twenty years, the population of the Soviet Union increased by 9.5 per cent, that of the whole Ukrainian SSR including the Crimea by only 3.5 per cent.[43]

Our task would now be to account for the considerably lower rate of population increase in the Ukrainian SSR as compared to the Soviet Union as a whole in the years 1926–39 and "1940" and 1959. For this purpose it may be useful to give the only detailed figures that are available through 1959: the number of urban and rural population. Between 1926 and 1939, the urban population of the Eastern Ukraine increased by 5.8 million or 8 per cent, that of the Soviet Union as a whole by 29.6 million or 12 per cent. The rural population, on the other hand, decreased by 3.9 million (16 per cent) in the Ukraine and 6.2 million (5 per cent) in the USSR.[44] Between "1940" and 1959, however, the urban population of the Ukraine as a whole increased by 5.6 million, or 41.2 per cent, and that of the Soviet Union by 39.6 million (65.5 per cent), whereas the population in the Ukrainian countryside decreased by 4.2 million (15.5 per cent) as against 21.4 million (16.5 per cent) for the Soviet Union as a whole.[45]

Striking are the disproportionately large population losses in the Ukrainian countryside between 1926 and 1939 without a corresponding increase in the number of urban dwellers. The Soviet geographer Lyalikov seeks to explain this by citing the emigration to eastern industrial centers outside the Ukraine.[46] Lorimer points out that as a result of the mechanization of agriculture, large human resources were released for industry, but he also hints at losses incurred during the forcible collectivization.[47] For whatever reason—the famine of 1932–1933, deportations, and emigration—the Ukraine lost between 1926 and 1939 *at least* 2.7 million people, if we choose as a basis for computation the average Soviet figure for population increase (15.9 per cent).[48] Actually, the population losses in the Ukraine must run considerably higher. Elsewhere in his work, Lorimer has calculated that as a result of forcible collectivization and industrialization the Soviet Union as a whole between 1926 and 1939 showed an *excess* (abnormal) number of deaths as high as five mil-

Table II-6*

POPULATION OF THE UKRAINIAN SSR AND THE USSR, 1897–1959

	Millions	
Period and Character of Data	Ukrainian SSR	USSR
1897, Census	21.2 ª	103.8 ª
1913, Soviet estimates	27.2 ª	139.3 ª
1926, Census (December 17)	29.0 ª,ᶜ	147.0 ª
1933, V. Kubiyovych's estimates (January 1)	41.0 ᵇ	—
1939, Census (January 17)	31.0 ª	170.5 ª
1940–1945 ("1940"), Official estimates	40.5 ᵈ	190.7 ᵈ
1959, Census (January 15)	41.9 ᵉ	208.8

ª The figures pertain to the territories of the Ukrainian SSR and the USSR within the boundaries prior to September 17, 1939, i.e., the Western provinces are excluded.

ᵇ Within the boundaries of 1948, i.e., including Western Ukraine, but not the Crimea.

ᶜ The figure is Lorimer's. A more recent Soviet source (*Narodne hospodarstvo Ukrayins'koyi RSR* [National Economy of the Ukrainian SSR, Kiev, 1957], p. 7), for some reason, gives the figure as 29.5 million. I cannot explain the discrepancy, have chosen the lower figure, which is also found in a *contemporary* Soviet source: Arsen Khomenko's *Natsional'ny sklad lyudnosty USSR* (National Composition of the Population of the UkrSSR, Kharkov, 1931), p. 22.

ᵈ Within the boundaries of 1945. The Ukrainian figure probably includes the population of Crimea (incorporated in 1954), though this is not clearly specified in the sources. The preface to *Narodne hospodarstvo Ukr. RSR* (p. 3) states, however, that economic statistics for the Ukraine have been given for the years specified, with data on the Crimean economy counted in, even *before* 1954. Was the same done in the case of population?

* The most up-to-date and accurate Soviet source on the population of the Ukraine in 1913, 1926, 1939, and 1959 was obtained while this book was in print. It is Tsentral'noe statisticheskoe upravlenie pri Sovete Ministrov SSSR (Central Statistical Administration of the USSR Council of Ministers), *Itogi vsesoyznoy perepisi naseleniya 1959 goda : Ukrainskaya SSR* (Results of the All-Union Population Census of 1959, Moscow, 1963), Table 1, p. 1. A comparison of our table with the latter shows that the figures are either identical or wholly compatible (for example, in the 1963 Soviet data the Crimea has been included even in the figures for 1913). The latter source also explains the discrepancy mentioned in Table II-6, Note (c) above: Recent Soviet sources *include* for 1926 the population of the Crimea (annexed in 1954) but *exclude* the population of certain small districts ceded to the Moldavian SSR in 1940. It also affirmatively answers our question posed in Note (d), above.

lion.[49] We see, in other words, that the USSR rate of population growth is itself significantly depressed by the losses of the 1930's and that any calculations based on that rate are, therefore, likely to lead to an *under-estimation* of the losses. A Ukrainian statistician living in the West has estimated the population losses in Eastern Ukraine as 7.5 million between 1926 and 1939. It should be pointed out that this is a *net* figure. The original losses had amounted to some 10 million, but they were covered by some 2.5 million settlers who immigrated to the Ukraine from other Republics. The immigrants were non-Ukrainians, mostly Russians.[50]

The lower rate of population increase since 1940 appears primarily a result of the war. Had there been no war, the population of the Ukrainian SSR in 1959 would have amounted to a figure between 44.5 and 49.6 million, depending on the rate used for projection, instead of the actual figure of 41.9 million.[51] Had the impact of World War II been equally spread throughout the Soviet Union, the population of the Ukrainian SSR would have been 44.3 million: in other words, had the Ukraine kept equal pace with the average Soviet rate of population increase since 1940 (9.5 per cent), her population would have increased by 3.8 million instead of only by 1.4 million. To use Lorimer's terms, between 1940 and 1959 the "redistribution decrement" of the Ukrainian population amounted to 2.4 million. Compared with the earlier period (1926–39) no abnormally high losses have been incurred in the countryside: on the contrary, it appears that between 1940–59, the process of leaving farms went more slowly in the Ukraine than in the Soviet Union as a whole,[52] which may be an indication of shortage of labor in agriculture as a result of war. What factors do then account for the population losses since 1940? Some incomplete information has been released and may serve as a starting point for further research.

According to the statisticians of the Soviet Ukrainian Academy of Sciences, 1.5 million civilians were killed and another three million deported to work in Germany during World War II.[53] Furthermore, when

---

e Within the boundaries of 1959.

Sources: For 1897, see Khomenko, *op. cit.* (in note above), p. 130n, on the Ukraine, and Richard E. Pipes, *Formation of the Soviet Union* (Cambridge, Mass.: Harvard University Press, 1954), p. 290, on the USSR. For 1926 and 1939, see Frank Lorimer, *The Population of the Soviet Union* (Geneva: League of Nations, 1946), p. 162. Figures for "1940" and 1959 in *Nar. khoz. SSSR, 1960,* pp. 8–9. Estimate for 1933, see V. Kubiyovych in *Entsyklopediya ukrayinoznavstva* (Encyclopedia of Things Ukrainian, Munich and New York: Molode Zhyttya, 1949), Vol. I, p. 166.

German troops approached, Soviet authorities evacuated "millions of industrial workers, collective farmers, and officials, together with their families" [54] into the eastern provinces of the Soviet Union, and drafted into military service millions of citizens of the Ukrainian Republic. The number of civilian evacuees and deportees has been estimated by Holubnychy as 4 million, that of army draftees in 1941 as no more than 3.5 million.[55] Finally, when the Polono-Soviet frontier was re-adjusted in 1945, Holubnychy estimates that the Ukraine lost about one million people. Not all of those who had left the Ukraine in one way or another returned. On the basis of figures on the industrial labor force he has calculated that as of the end of 1946, *in addition* to the 1.5 million civilians slaughtered by German occupation forces, some 4.7 million out of a total of 11 million who had left the Ukraine were still missing: they had been killed, had remained in the eastern provinces and had stayed in the West as Displaced Persons.

Another Ukrainian statistician living in exile (Solovey) has drawn attention to some strange revisions of Ukrainian population figures "of 1940" and has suggested other reasons for the low figures after World War II. In 1948 the special volume on the USSR of the Great Soviet Encyclopedia gave for 1939, 41.250 million as the official estimate of the population of the Republic within the boundaries of 1945 (including all Western provinces, but excluding Crimea). According to the census of 1939, Crimea had a population of 1,127,000. Consequently, in 1939 or 1940 the population of the Ukraine within the present boundaries should have been around 42.4 million. But the 1956 statistical handbook (*Narodnoe khozaystvo SSSR*)—the first published after a long silence—unaccountably revised that figure down to 41,027 thousand; after the 1959 census was taken, that figure was further reduced to 40,469 thousand, which we have used in this work. It is possible, of course, that the 1948 figure had been based on an overestimate of the population of Western Ukraine. It may be that the later figure was reduced because of population transfers from Western Ukraine, mainly of Poles, in 1940–41 and after 1944, though such a change ought to have been recorded in the 1948 volume. (See also below.) But it is equally possible, as Solovey suggests, that the earlier figure had been tampered with in order to disguise the full extent of Ukrainian population losses after 1939.[56]

By comparing various official Soviet figures on the number of persons who had been deported from the Ukraine to Germany as civilian laborers and those who had disappeared in German POW camps, with figures on the number of those who had been repatriated to the USSR and those who had arrived in the Ukraine herself, Solovey convincingly demonstrates that roughly 1.9 million or 60 per cent of the Ukrainians who had been repatriated from Germany to the USSR were actually not allowed to return to the Ukraine. There have been several indications that the repatriates were very carefully screened to weed out real and presumed collaborators, but Solovey is the first to indicate the numbers involved.[57] The exile of 1.9 million Ukrainian returnees, in addition to the losses directly caused by the war, may be a contributing reason for the abnormally low population increase in the Ukraine. Other reasons are the punitive deportations, mostly from the Western Ukraine in 1939–41 and after 1944. By way of punitive action, citizens of the Ukrainian SSR have been deported for two main causes: collaboration with the Germans[58] and cooperation with the Ukrainian Nationalist Underground in Western Ukraine.[59] No quantitative data have been released by Soviet authorities to indicate the scope of those actions. Not very convincingly in this particular instance, Solovey estimates that punitive deportations have cost the Ukraine another 1.75 million people.[60]

Population transfers resulting from boundary shifts must also be taken into account. In the postwar years a number of population transfers have taken place, but for lack of pertinent data it is impossible to appraise most of them in quantitative terms. (It is worth noting, in this connection, that a question about the place of birth, which was included in the 1926 census, has been deliberately omitted from the 1939 and 1959 censuses.) The most important one is perhaps the exchange of population between the Ukraine and Poland on the basis of an agreement of October 1, 1944. According to the American demographer Kulischer, by December, 1946, when the transfer was terminated, approximately 1 million Poles and 140,000 Polish Jews were repatriated from the whole USSR. In exchange, about 520,000 Ukrainians from Poland were settled in the Ukrainian SSR.[61] An interesting feature of this transfer is that apparently most of the Ukrainians from Poland (or, to be more precise, from the Ukrainian-inhabited territories that had been ceded to Poland) were not settled in Western Ukraine but farther east in the underpopulated southern steppes of the Ukrainian SSR.[62],* A similar agreement with Czechoslovakia involved the repatriation of about 33,000 Czechs from Volhynia.[63] One can also approximately determine the population increase as a result of territorial annexations since 1944. By incorporating the formerly Czechoslovakian province of Subcarpathia in 1945, the population of the Republic increased by roughly 800,000 people,[64]

---

* A good scholarly Soviet source, obtained while this book was in print—viz., V. I. Naulko, "Sovremenny etnicheskiy sostav naseleniya Ukrainskoy SSR (The Contemporary Ethnic Composition of the Population of the Ukrainian SSR)," *Sovetskaya etnografiya* (Soviet Ethnography, Moscow), Vol. 1963, No. 5 (September-October), pp. 49–50—confirms and makes precise those figures. According to it, 788,000 Poles were repatriated from the Ukrainian SSR alone, and 518,000 Ukrainians, Lithuanians, and Belorussians from Poland settled in the Ukrainian SSR, mainly in the Ivano-Frankivska (Stanyslaviv), Lviv, and Nikolaevsk provinces. The last is in southern Ukraine.

by incorporating the Crimea in February 1954, by less than 1.1 million.[65] But there are virtually no quantitative data on such processes as emigration in connection with Khrushchev's virgin lands campaign and inter-republican assignments of professionals.

The materials on the virgin lands campaign are rather inadequate. We know that Khrushchev's appeal to cultivate the virgin lands was primarily directed to the youth. A reference book for Komsomol propagandists gives the figure of more than 350,000 "young patriots" who had set out to cultivate new lands, besides 120 odd thousand who went to the east to work in industry, between February, 1954 (when the action started), and January, 1957.[66] These are, however, figures pertaining to the Soviet Union as a whole. To obtain figures for the Ukraine, we must consult the press. By March, 1958, 80,000 young people from the Ukraine had actually gone east, revealed a Komsomol leader to a Western correspondent.[67] On the other hand, by using an official estimate of the Republican population in 1954 and the 1958 rate of natural increase Solovey has been able to show rather persuasively that the total number of persons resettled from the Ukraine in the virgin lands campaigns between 1954 and 1959 could run as high as 1.0 million.[68] A small part of that figure covers the emigration for other reasons (professional personnel shifts outside the Ukraine, for example). V. Kubiyovych, a well-known Ukrainian demographer now living in exile, has pointed out in this connection that in all probability the 1959 census data on Ukrainians in Kazakhstan, the destination of the virgin lands drive, to wit, 762,000, has been falsified. According to the census of 1926, there lived as many as 861,000 Ukrainians in Kazakhstan. Kubiyovych estimates their present number as anywhere from 2.5 to 3.0 million, which would be compatible with the high estimates for the recent settlement by Solovey.[69]

The inter-Republican assignments of specialists is very important, though the numbers involved need not be large. That it takes place is admitted by the regime, but no comprehensive summary data has been released.[70] In the opinion of former Soviet citizens there is an unwritten Soviet policy to intermingle the nationalities by assigning the graduates of one Republic to work in another—a policy which has been perfected in the training and stationing of Soviet troops.[71] Holubnychy has estimated that

. . . Apart from [normal] mortality, the Ukraine lost out of 30 higher school [college] graduating classes [1925–55] 112,800 specialists with higher education, including 37,300 engineers. This amounts to 21.4 per cent of all graduated specialists with a higher education and 27.8 per cent of all engineers.[72]

He assumes that most of them had been transferred to work outside the Ukrainian SSR. Actually, the number transferred between 1925 and 1955 might have been even greater owing to the particular nature of the data. The figure of 112,800 is a figure of *net* loss which may include a countervailing influx of specialists· into the Ukraine from other Soviet Republics.[73] We are almost at a complete loss when it comes to estimating the scope of immigration into the Ukrainian SSR. That the place of the of the Crimean Tatars has been partly filled with Russian settlers has already been mentioned; [74] in the following chapter, I shall say a fèw words about the immigration of Russians into Western Ukraine. No official figures, however, are available.[75]

Last, it may be of some interest to mention the migrations *within* the Ukrainian SSR. Already a few weeks after the first Soviet occupation of Galicia, by October 19, 1939, seven thousand unemployed were taken to work in the coal mines of Donbas.[76] After the reoccupation in 1944 such labor recruitment was continued on a large scale.[77] Moreover, Galician peasants, too, were encouraged to settle in the sparsely populated eastern provinces of the Ukraine, especially in the South.[78] In other words, there has been a flow of unqualified labor and impoverished peasants from overpopulated Western Ukraine into the southern and southeastern provinces of the Republic.

3. *The Demographic Base: Nationality*

So much for a discussion of the Republican population as a whole. But how many of them are Ukrainians and how many are Russians, Jews, and Poles, to name only the most numerous minorities? Are the non-Ukrainian minorities increasing, or is it the other way round? Where are they concentrated?

According to the latest census (1959), there were 37.3 million citizens who gave Ukrainian as their nationality—32.2 million of them, or 86.3 per cent lived in the Ukrainian Republic. There they constituted 76.8 per cent of the total population.[79] Several questions may be raised about these figures. Quite apart from the difficult problem of defining nationality (see Note II-1, in the Appendix), it is of interest to know the distribution of Ukrainians outside the Ukrainian SSR, the strength of the non-Ukrainian minorities in that republic, and, above all, the movement and growth of the Ukrainian people in the USSR as a whole and in the Ukraine in particular.

The largest number of Ukrainians outside the Republic in absolute terms live in Russia (3.4 million or 2.9 per cent of the total population). In the Kazakh Republic there are 762,000 Ukrainians (8.2 per cent),[80] in the Moldavian Republic—421,000 (highest relative concentration, with 14.6 per cent), 137,000 (6.6 per cent) live in the Kirghiz Republic, and 133,000 (1.7 per cent) in Belorussia. In virtually all other Union Republics there are Ukrainians in smaller numbers (under 100,000). From this data it would appear that, with the possible exception of areas contiguous to the Ukrainian SSR in which Ukrainians form a majority,[81] the Ukrainians outside the Ukrainian Republic are so scattered that they can be passed over in a political analysis like this. For in all those other areas the Ukrainians will remain a permanent minority.

What is the numerical position of the non-Ukrainian minorities in the Ukraine? According to the 1959 census, Russians account for 7.1 million (or 16.9 per cent) of the Republican population. Jews come a distant next with 840,000 (or 2.0 per cent). The other minorities, down from the 363,000 (0.9 per cent) Poles to the 101,000 Rumanians (0.2 per cent) do not appear to be politically significant any longer.[82] Numbers by themselves may be, of course, grossly misleading: we shall see in our discussion of socio-economic strata that some of the minorities have had a very great influence upon Ukrainian economy, culture, and politics.

What about the movement and growth of the Ukrainian population? According to the census of 1926, there were 31.2 million Ukrainians living in the USSR in that year, 23.2 million of them lived in the Ukrainian SSR, where they formed 80.1 per cent of the total population of 29.0 million.[83] The census of 1939 gave 28.1 [sic] million as the number of Ukrainians in the Soviet Union.[84] (No data was released on the number of Ukrainians in the Ukrainian SSR.) According to Lorimer, the reasons for this decline must be sought in the growing identification of Ukrainians with Russians, particularly of those living outside the Ukraine.[85] That such a process may have taken place appears from the data on intermarriages between various nationalities in the Ukraine. Statistics show that in 1927 about 96.5 per cent of the Ukrainians living in the Ukraine married within their nationality. In the cities, however, only 87.2 per cent of Ukrainian men took Ukrainian brides and 83.4 per cent of Ukrainian girls married Ukrainian men. The others, more likely than not, married Russians: for only 62.0 per cent of the Russian men in the Ukraine found Russian wives and only 70.2 per cent of the Russian women found Russian husbands.[86] By 1937, that is, within the next decade, the number of ethnic intermarriages increased; but only rough aggregate figures have been made available, which do not permit a conclusive interpretation. According to Pisarev, 7.5 per cent of the total number of marriages in the Ukrainian SSR had been concluded between members of different nationalities in 1927; in 1937, that number amounted to 19.0 per cent.[87]

Two things should be pointed out in this connection. In the first place,

these figures comprise marriages contracted between members of all the
nationalities living in the Ukraine. The figure will probably be lower
when only those intermarriages are considered that involve Ukrainians:
in 1927 it was 3.5 per cent compared to the broader figure of 7.5 or 8.2
per cent (see footnote 87). Furthermore, the objection might be raised
that 1937 is an a-typical year, that it represented the climax of Stalin's
Great Purges, in which many families must be presumed to have been
dissolved and in which new "political" marriages were contracted in an
atmosphere of official terror that was directed, among others, against
Ukrainian "bourgeois nationalists." It is most probable that owing to
the industrialization of the country ethnic intermarriages involving
Ukrainians would have increased even without the terror, but it would
seem that a few points must be credited to the drive against Ukrainian
"bourgeois nationalism."

While subjective identification with the Russians may account in part
for the extraordinarily low figure of Ukrainians in the USSR in January, 1939, at least as far as the immediately preceding, suppressed census
of 1937 is concerned, there is some evidence of such identification on the
part of the census takers. One of our respondents was in Kazakhstan
when the 1937 census was taken. He declared himself a Ukrainian only
to be set back by the remark, "Oh, so you are a Ukrainian bourgeois
nationalist?" [88] We should keep in mind that in the minds of some Russians Ukrainians simply did not exist outside of Galicia, and it is likely
that in the atmosphere of the late 1930's those particular Russians may
have tried to substantiate their convictions. The severe famine in the
Ukraine in 1932–33 must also have played a certain part in the over-all
decrease of Ukrainians, probably the major part. On the other hand, it
is worth noting that between 1926 and 1939 the number of Russians in
the Soviet Union increased from 77.8 to 99.0 million (27.3 per cent).[89]
As a result of the annexation of Western Ukrainian territories, however, the total number of Ukrainians in the Soviet Union increased
by 7.5 million until it stood at 35.6 million.[90]

The number of Ukrainians in the *expanded* Ukrainian Republic has
not been given directly, but it can be inferred from another figure in the
Soviet Encyclopedia. According to the "final results of the 1939 census,"
32,828,500 persons in the Ukrainian SSR "spoke Ukrainian," presumably
as their native language.[91] As the "final results of the 1939 census" probably include the Soviet annexations by 1945 (and Crimea) and as the
estimated total population of the Ukrainian SSR in the expanded area
amounted to some 40.5 million (as of "1940"), the linguistic figure provided by the *Encyclopedia,* when discounted by the number of Ukrainians in Transcarpathia (600,000),[92] allows us to calculate the percentage
of Ukrainians in the Ukrainian SSR and Crimea on the eve of the Soviet-

German war. It is 80.0 per cent. Moreover, subtracting from the *Encyclopedia* figure the 7.5 million Ukrainians added by the annexations, we can make a rough estimate of the number of Ukrainians in the Eastern Ukraine at the time when the 1939 census was taken: a figure that has not been disclosed by the Soviet government so far. It is about 25.3 million out of a total population of 31.0 million, or 81.6 per cent. This slight increase over the percentage of 1926 (80.1 per cent) seems implausible in the light of the forced collectivization of the predominantly Ukrainian peasantry, the attacks on Ukrainian "bourgeois nationalism," and the fact that the regime has withheld the census figures on the national composition of the population of the Ukrainian SSR in 1939 though it has released corresponding statistics on other republics.[93] On the other hand, while official terror ought to have diminished the number of self-declared Ukrainians in 1939, the higher birth rate in the rural areas and the Ukrainization (Ukrainian *korenizatsiya*) policy (1926–33) worked in the opposite direction. In any case, World War II and the annexation of the predominantly Russian-inhabited Crimea make the January, 1939, figure on Ukrainians in the Ukrainian SSR—whatever it be—of historical importance only.[94]

A comparison of the increase of Ukrainians with the average population increase in the USSR between 1926 and 1939 shows a rather serious lag, too. Owing to the economic policies of the regime and possibly widespread falsification of responses in the census of 1939, the number of Ukrainians in the Soviet Union within the boundaries of September 17, 1939, actually *diminished* by 9.0 per cent, whereas the total Union population went up by 15.9 per cent.[95] In the period 1940–1959, even with the annexation of Western territories, the Ukrainian group in the Soviet Union increased by no more than 4.8 per cent in almost twenty years [sic], the total population rising by 9.5 per cent during the same time. It could be shown that the beneficiaries on the all-Union scale have been the Russians who increased at a rate faster than the Soviet average,[96] but it would be more to the point to analyze the increase of the Russian minority in the Ukraine.

According to the census of 1926, 2.7 million or 9.2 per cent of the population of the Ukrainian SSR in her prewar boundaries were Russians.[97] Lew Shankowsky has made careful calculations of the number of Russians in West Ukrainian provinces in 1930, when the Rumanian and Czechoslovak, and in 1931, when the Polish censuses were taken. In his judgment, Russians in all those areas numbered no more than 22,400.[98] (See also Table II-7, p. 57.) The Russian population of the Crimea, however, was more substantial, numbering 301,000 or 42.2 per cent of the total, in 1926.[99] We may conclude, therefore, that in 1926, for all practical purposes, the Russians constituted no more than 3.0 million

Table II-7

NATIONAL COMPOSITION OF THE PROVINCES OF THE UKRAINIAN SSR

Province	Years	Total population (thousands)	Percentage of total population					
			Ukrainian	Russian	Belorussian	Jews	Poles	Others
Vinnitsa	1926	2,407.3	87.3	1.7	0.1	7.7	2.7	0.5
	1959	2,142.0	91.8	4.4	0.2	2.3	1.0	0.3
Volhynia *	1931	999.3	74.7	0 6	0.0	10.7	10.6	3.4
	1959	890.0	94.6	4.2	0.5	0.2	0.2	0.3
Dniepropetrovsk	1926	1,823.1	84.4	8.1	0.8	5.1	0.4	1.2
	1959	2,705.0	77.7	17.2	1.3	2.7	0.2	0.9
Donetsk (Stalino)	1926	1,642.2	60.2	26.3	0.7	2.5	0.3	10.0
	1959	4,262.0	55.6	37.6	1.5	1.0	0.2	4.1
Zhytomyr	1926	1,777.2	74.9	2.1	0.1	9.2	8.8	4.9
	1959	1,604.0	84.5	5.4	0.4	2.6	6.4	0.7
Transcarpathian *	1930	725.0	62.1	0.0	0.0	14.1	0.0	23.8
	1959	920.0	74.6	3.2	0.1	1.3	0.0	20.7
Zaporozhe	1926	1,071.2	65.9	17.9	0.2	3.1	0.1	12.8
	1959	1,464.0	68.3	25.9	0.7	1.4	0.1	3.6
Kiev (*City*)	1926	513.6	42.1	24.4	1.1	27.3	2.7	2.4
	1959	1,104.0	60.1	23.0	1.2	13.9	0.8	1.0
Kiev (*Province*)	1926	2,421.2	83.1	5.9	0.2	8.4	1.6	0.8
	1959	2,823.0	80.3	11.9	0.7	5.9	0.6	0.6
Kirovograd	1926	1,421.0	87.5	5.7	0.1	4.0	0.2	2.5
	1959	1,218.0	88.7	8.4	0.8	0.8	0.1	1.2
Crimea *	1926	714.1	10.8	42.2	0.5	7.0	0.6	38.9
	1959	1,201.0	22.3	71.4	1.8	2.2	0.3	2.0
Lugans'k (Voroshilovgrad)	1926	1,339.9	71.9	24.9	0.2	0.9	0.2	1.9
	1959	2,452.0	57.8	38.7	1.1	0.6	0.2	1.6
Lviv *	1931	2,315.0	59.3	0.0	0.0	12.8	26.8	2.1
	1959	2,108.0	86.3	8.6	0.4	1.4	2.8	0.5
Nikolaev	1926	984.9	69.6	12.7	1.5	7.5	0.7	8.0
	1959	1,014.0	81.2	13.7	1.2	2.0	0.3	1.6
Odessa	1926	1,264.2	50.2	16.2	0.3	16.1	1.1	16.1
Odessa and Izmail	1926	1,894.2	45.7	15.1	0.2	11.7	0.8	26.5
Odessa, united	1959	2,027.0	55.5	21.7	0.5	6.0	0.4	15.9
Poltava	1926	2,212.0	95.0	1.3	0.1	3.2	0.1	0.3
	1959	1,632.0	93.4	5.1	0.3	0.8	0.1	0.3
Rovno *	1931	1,033.6	74.7	0.6	0.0	10.7	10.6	3.4
	1959	926.0	93.4	4.2	1.2	0.3	0.5	0.4
Ivano-Frankivska (Stanyslaviv) *	1931	1,400.8	72.7	0.0	0.0	12.3	13.5	1.5
	1959	1,095.0	94.8	3.5	0.1	0.4	1.0	0.2
Sumy	1926	1,842.3	87.6	10.5	0.1	1.4	0.1	0.3
	1959	1,514.0	87.9	11.1	0.3	0.4	0.1	0.2
Ternopil *	1931	1,339.7	59.8	0.0	0.0	12.0	27.3	0.9
	1959	1,086.0	94.9	2.5	0.2	0.1	2.2	0.1
Kharkov	1926	2,314.5	75.1	19.9	0.1	3.8	0.3	0.8
	1959	2,520.0	68.8	26.4	0.5	3.3	0.2	0.8
Kherson	1926	772.4	73.1	17.9	0.4	3.5	1.0	4.1
	1959	824.0	81.1	15.6	0.8	1.3	0.4	0.8
Khmelnitsky (Pereyaslav)	1926	1,773.8	81.8	1.2	0.1	7.9	8.4	0.6
	1959	1,611.0	90.2	3.8	0.2	1.2	4.3	0.3
Cherkassy	1926	1,876.2	93.8	0.8	0.1	4.8	0.3	0.2
	1959	1,503.0	94.0	4.5	0.3	0.9	0.1	0.2
Chernihiv	1926	1,837.5	93.5	3.2	0.2	2.4	0.1	0.6
	1959	1,554.0	94.5	3.9	0.4	0.8	0.1	0.3
Chernivtsi *	1930	854.0	67.2	1.2	0.0	14.0	3.3	14.3
	1959	774.0	66.9	6.6	0.2	5.4	0.8	20.1

* The provinces have been listed in the order of the Ukrainian alphabet. Those incorporated after September 1939, have been marked with an asterisk (*).

Source: Calculated by Lew Shankowsky, of Prolog Research Associates, New York City, and used with his permission. The percentage figures for 1959 have been taken by the compiler from *Narodne hospodarstvo Ukrayins'koyi RSR v 1959 r.: Statystychny shchorichnyk* (National Economy of the Ukrainian SSR in 1959: A Statistical Yearbook, Kiev, 1960), p. 22. Figures for 1926 are from the USSR census, other figures from the Rumanian census of 1930 and the Polish census of 1931 and the Czechoslovak census of 1930, the Polish figures adjusted somewhat to correct apparent falsification with respect to the number of Ukrainians. The administrative units in the 1920's differed from those of 1959; in order to make them compatible, Professor Shankowsky has used detailed, village-by-village results of the earlier censuses and detailed administrative maps.

out of a total of some 38.9 million people in the Ukraine in her *present* boundaries,[100] or about 7.7 per cent of the total population. As we have already seen, however, by 1959 the Russian minority more than doubled to 7.1 million or 16.9 per cent of the total. Even if one allows for the high average rate of increase of the Russian group in the USSR (46.6 per cent in the 33 year period), it appears that the Russian minority in the Ukraine cannot have increased that much by themselves. The inescapable conclusion that within one generation (1926–59) at least 2.7 million Russians have immigrated into the Ukrainian SSR within its present boundaries. That is a number almost equal to the original strength of the Russian minority in 1926.[101, *]

On the other hand, the size of the second largest minority in the Ukraine—the Jews—has been drastically cut, primarily through Nazi extermination policies. In 1926 the Jews in the Eastern Ukraine only numbered 1.6 million (5.4 per cent of the total population); there lived an additional 1.1 million of them in the seven Western provinces and the Crimea.[102] Altogether some 2.7 million Jews were, in 1926, citizens of the Ukraine *within her present boundaries,* constituting about 6.9 per cent of the total population. In 1959 only 840,000 were left (2.0 per cent of the total population). According to a Soviet source previously cited, the Germans slaughtered about 1.5 million civilians in the Ukraine.[103] A majority of those, at least 900,000 according to one Western estimate, must have been Jews.[104] The third largest minority, the Poles, is surprisingly small if one considers the fact that in 1939 the Soviet Union annexed territories with substantial Polish minorities. According to the 1959 census, there are but 363,000 Poles in the Ukraine, or 0.9 per cent of the whole. In 1926, the Poles numbered 476,000 (1.6 per cent) in the Eastern Ukraine alone.[105] The war and evacuation apparently have cut their number down.

The official nationality data for 1959 have been broken down into provinces. With the help of figures from the 1926 census in the USSR, the Rumanian census of 1930, the Czechoslovak census of 1930, and the Polish census of 1931, which figures have been recalculated by Lew Shankowsky to make them comparable to the 1959 census,[106] we can draw important conclusions about the regional distribution of non-Ukrainian minorities (see Table II-7, p. 57).

The highest relative concentration of Poles exists, to our great surprise, not in the Western Ukraine but in two agricultural provinces of the so-called Right Bank Ukraine (that is, Eastern Ukraine right of the Dnieper).[107] In 1959, in the Zhytomyr Province Poles numbered 6.4 per

---

* Naulko, *op. cit.,* p. 47, also points out that between 1926 and 1959 the number of Russians in the Ukraine doubled. He attributes this to an influx into the Ukrainian cities of young Russian males.

cent of the total population, in the Khmelnitsky Province 4.3 per cent, compared with a Republican average of 0.9 per cent. In all Ukrainian provinces, however, the number of Poles has declined. In Western Ukraine, apparently owing to the mutual struggle between the Ukrainian and Polish undergrounds in World War II (see on this Chapter V, below) and the evacuation of Poles under Soviet rule, that decline has reached precipitous proportions. In the Lviv Province, for example, the Polish population decreased from 26.8 per cent of the total in 1931 to 2.8 per cent in 1959; in Ternopil Province from 27.3 to as low as 2.2 per cent.

The highest concentration of Jews is to be found in the capital city Kiev (13.9 per cent of all inhabitants in 1959; as many as 27.3 per cent in 1926), and in the Provinces of Odessa (6.0 per cent), Chernivtsi (5.4 per cent) and Kharkov (3.3 per cent). (Their republican average is 2.0 per cent.) Kiev is the administrative and cultural center, with some industry; Chernivtsi in Bukovina is an agricultural province that had formerly been under Rumanian rule; the other two provinces contain important commercial and industrial cities. In all provinces of the Ukraine, however, the proportion of Jews has dropped, the sharpest decline being registered in the West Ukrainian provinces of Transcarpathia (14.1 per cent in 1931—1.3 per cent in 1959), Ivano-Frankivska, formerly Stanyslaviv (12.3 to 0.4 per cent), to cite only two examples. This decline is possibly the result of both the Nazi extermination policy and the migration of Jews from the overpopulated and economically underdeveloped Western provinces into Poland.

On the other hand, the proportion of Russians in the Ukraine has increased in every province but Kherson (an agricultural oblast in the south) and the city of Kiev itself (in 1926, Russians numbered 24.4 per cent of Kiev's population, in 1959 they numbered slightly fewer—23.0 per cent). The sharpest increases are to be found in the Western areas (in Lviv Province, for example, the percentage of Russians increased from practically zero in 1931 to 8.6 per cent of the total population in 1959). At the present time there are five out of the twenty-five provinces in the Ukrainian SSR in which the share of Russians exceeds one-quarter of the population (the republican average is 16.9 per cent). They are, in descending order: Crimea (71.4 [sic] per cent in 1959 compared with 42.2 per cent in 1926), Lugansk (38.7 per cent, formerly 24.9 per cent), Donets (37.6 per cent, formerly 26.3 per cent), Kharkov (26.4 per cent, formerly 19.9 per cent) and Zaporozhe (25.9 per cent, formerly 17.9 per cent). It is worth noting that with the exception of agricultural Crimea, in which Russian settlers have apparently displaced the exiled Crimean Tatars, all the other provinces listed are distinguished for their industrial potential: Donets (until recently, Stalino) and Lugansk are in the coal rich Donets

Basin, Zaporozhe is a metal forming center, Kharkov a center for machine-building industry. Very interesting also is the sharp influx of Russians into the agricultural Poltava Province (1.3 per cent in 1926, 5.1
per cent in 1959). Poltava Province, together with Kiev Province, has
long been regarded as the cradle of modern Ukrainian culture. Apparently the increase in the number of Russians in Poltava Province, which
is, incidentally, an area with a declining population, is due to the influx
of Russian settlers who have taken the place of Ukrainian peasants
killed in the Big Famine of 1932–33. Another possible reason for the
influx of Russians into Poltava Province may be territorial reorganization. In 1926 there were numerous Russian villages along the border of
today's Kharkov and Poltava Provinces. Had those villages been later
included in the Poltava Province this might have accounted for some
increase of the Russian population of the province.[108]

4. A Socio-Economic Profile of the Population

One of the most significant aspects of Soviet nationality policy has
been the increase in the number of socio-economic opportunities for the
various peoples of the Union. That such an increase must have taken
place can be easily inferred from the obvious economic growth. But it is
not always realized that such a "sociological development" may be uneven. Some nations profit more from economic growth than do other
nations, and the different rate of advancement may become a political
issue. It is true that for the time being the question cannot be squarely
posed in the Soviet Union where all the nations are theoretically equal
or at least rapidly becoming so. But the existence of the problem of
"local cadres" was frankly acknowledged by Khrushchev himself at the
Twentieth Party Congress,[109] and within three years of the Congress the
First Secretary of the Communist Party of Turkmenia, Babayev, was dismissed because of mistakes committed in the placement of Turkmenian
and non-Turkmenian cadres.[110] But what is the problem of local cadres
if not the most pointed aspect of the different rate of socio-economic
development among the various nations of the USSR? Fortunately, recent Soviet statistics shed considerable light on this problem. In the
following paragraphs I propose to approach the question step by step,
discussing first the socio-economic structure of the population of the
Ukrainian SSR with nationality omitted, then injecting the available
data on nationality.

The comparative occupational profile of the Ukrainian SSR (Table
II-8) shows that in the broad economic field of industry relatively fewer
persons are employed in the Ukraine than in the USSR as a whole and
the Russian SFSR in particular (22.9 per cent compared with 25.9 and

Table II-8

A COMPARATIVE OCCUPATIONAL PROFILE OF THE UKRAINIAN SSR; OR, WORKERS AND EMPLOYEES ENGAGED IN THE NATIONAL ECONOMIES OF THE UKRAINIAN SSR, THE RUSSIAN SFSR, AND THE USSR AS A WHOLE, 1960–61,[a] BY NUMBER (IN THOUSANDS) AND BY PERCENTAGE OF TOTAL

	Ukrainian SSR		Russian SFSR		USSR	
	Thou-sands	Per-centage distri-bution	Thou-sands	Per-centage distri-bution	Thou-sands	Per-centage distri-bution
Agriculture and Forestry:						
Collective Farmers[b]	6,396.4	36.353	9,226.5	18.507	21,733.3	25.278
Supervisory and Higher Technical Staff on Collective Farms[c]	132.5	0.753	247.0	0.495	545.0	0.634
Lower Technical Staff on Collective Farms (Tractor Drivers, etc.)[d]	407.3	2.315	875.2	1.756	1,665.2	1.937
Workers and Staff on State Farms[e]	815.0	4.632	3,751.0	7.524	6,324.0	7.356
Staff of Machine Tractor and Repair Stations	87.0	0.494	197.0	0.395	348.0	0.405
Other Agriculture[f]	67.0	0.381	222.0	0.445	458.0	0.533
Forestry	70.0	0.398	211.0	0.423	359.0	0.418
Sub-Total: Agriculture and Forestry	7,975.2	45.326	14,729.7	29.546	31,432.5	36.560
Productive Industry	4,028.0	22.893	15,139.0	30.367	22,291.0	25.927
Services:						
Transportation	1,062.0	6.036	4,004.0	8.032	6,279.0	7.303
Communication	113.0	0.642	471.0	0.945	738.0	0.858
Commerce, Communal Food Supply	854.0	4.854	2,868.0	5.753	4,675.0	5.438
Housing	315.0	1.790	1,277.0	2.561	1,920.0	2.233
Construction	891.0	5.064	3,137.0	6.292	5,136.0	5.974
Health Services	689.0	3.916	2,026.0	4.064	3,461.0	4.026
Education	881.0	5.007	2,782.0	5.580	4,803.0	5.586
Science and Scientific Services	199.0	1.131	1,266.0	2.539	1,763.0	2.051
Banking and Insurance Services	46.0	0.261	162.0	0.325	265.0	0.308
Government and Administration Personnel, Staff of Public Organizations	216.0	1.228	744.0	1.492	1,245.0	1.448
Others	326.0	1.853	1,248.0	2.503	1,967.0	2.288
Sub-Total: Services	5,592.0	31.781	19,985.0	40.087	32,252.0	37.513
Grand Total	17,595.2	100.000	49,853.7	100.000	85,975.5	100.000

[a] Military personnel excluded. The figures are taken at somewhat different dates, which will be specified in the notes below.

[b] Annual average figure for 1960.

[c] As of April 1, 1961.

[d] As of April 1, 1960.

[e] All the data from this point down refer to September 1, 1960.

[f] The term "other agriculture" refers to the difference between the total of "workers and employees" in agriculture and the two specified sub-categories ("workers and staff on state farms" and "staff of machine-tractor and repair stations"), on p. 640 of source. Soviet agricultural statistics are rather complicated owing to Marxist dogma. Only workers and employees of state farms and machine-tractor and repair stations are listed as *"workers and employees* in agriculture." Collective peasants and related persons are listed separately, since they do not completely belong to the working class engaged in the Socialist form of production.

Sources: Based upon absolute figures in tables in *Nar. khoz. SSSR, 1960*. Figures for collective peasants on p. 522; for supervisory and higher technical staff on collective farms—p. 525; lower technical staff—p. 528; all the rest from p. 640.

30.4). Whereas the difference between the Ukrainian figure and the USSR average is small, that between the former and the Russian statistic is quite considerable. The small number of persons employed in Ukrainian industry is counterbalanced by a disproportionately large number engaged in agriculture and forestry (45.3 per cent compared with 36.6 for the USSR and 29.5 for the Russian SFSR). But the growth of the service sector is probably the best indication of the health of a modern industrial economy. In that sector, in terms of employment, the Ukraine is considerably behind the USSR average and the Russian figure (31.8 compared with 37.5 and 40.1 per cent of all employed). Particularly disturbing is the small number of persons engaged in scientific research (1.1 per cent compared with the USSR average of 2.1 and the Russian figure of 2.5). Remembering the ample resources of the Republic we have gained a suspicion that the industrial underdevelopment of the Ukraine, when viewed against Soviet and Russian standards, may be attributed to other than economic reasons.

Even more interesting is the educational profile of the citizens of the Ukrainian SSR as presented in Table II-9 (p. 63). The table combines the data of the 1959 and 1939 censuses—judging from the inclusion of the Baltic Republics, data on the West Ukrainian provinces must have been included, too. It is striking that the relative level of educational achievement in the Ukrainian SSR has fallen in those twenty years. At the outbreak of World War II the number of college educated persons in the Ukraine was one of the highest in the Soviet Union, being exceeded only by that in the small but well-developed Georgian Republic and those in the not yet incorporated Latvian and Estonian Republics. Rather significantly, the relative number of persons with a higher education in the Ukraine was a little larger than that in Russia (6.7, compared with 6.5 college graduates per one thousand population in Russia). Twenty years later, the relative number of college graduates in the Ukraine was below not only those of Georgia, Latvia, and Estonia, but was also exceeded by those of Russia, the Azerbaydzhani SSR, and Armenia. Moreover, the Ukrainian figure had fallen slightly below the all-Union average it had topped in 1939.

The Ukrainian position with respect to the supply of persons with completed or incomplete secondary education seems slightly better (the Ukrainian figure of 1959 is *above* that of Russia but is *below* those of Georgia, Azerbaydzhan, Latvia, Armenia, and Estonia (see Table II-10, p. 64). But it should be kept in mind that the lumping together of persons with completed and incomplete *secondary* education has resulted in a very artificial category embracing semi-educated peasants and workers together with semi-professionals, some of whom may have graduated

Table II-9

NUMBER OF PERSONS IN THE UNION REPUBLICS WITH A
HIGHER EDUCATION, 1939 AND 1959

Republics	Persons with higher education (in thousands)		1959 as per cent of 1939	Number of persons with higher education per 1,000 of population	
	1939	1959		1939	1959
USSR	1,177.1	3,777.5	321	6.2	18
Russian SFSR	709.5	2,265.9	319	6.5	19
Ukrainian SSR	272.0	715.4	263	6.7	17
Belorussian SSR	33.0	95.7	290	3.7	12
Uzbek SSR	19.7	104.9	532	3.1	13
Kazakh SSR	27.4	114.0	415	4.5	12
Georgian SSR	39.7	153.4	386	11.2	38
Azerbaydzhan SSR	21.6	77.2	357	6.7	21
Lithuanian SSR	6.4	35.4	553	2.2	13
Moldavian SSR	7.3	29.5	402	3.0	10
Latvian SSR	13.9	44.4	319	7.4	21
Kirghiz SSR	3.3	27.2	837	2.2	13
Tadzhik SSR	3.0	20.7	694	2.0	10
Armenian SSR	7.6	48.8	648	5.9	28
Turkmenian SSR	4.0	19.8	491	3.2	13
Estonian SSR	8.7	25.2	290	8.3	21

Note: A comparison of this table with the preceding one (Table IV on p. 22 of source) shows that the figures for 1959, at least, include only persons who have *completed* higher education.

Source: Table V in *Nar. khoz. SSSR, 1960*, p. 23.

from vocational high schools and possibly even briefly attended higher educational institutions. In both tables the figures on the percentage increase from 1939 to 1959 show that the Ukrainian rate of educational growth has been one of the lowest, below that of Russia and also below that of the Union as a whole.

Of utmost importance are Soviet data on the various kinds of specialists engaged in the economic and cultural institutions of each republic. The Soviet Government has released detailed figures on the numbers employed in various professional and semi-professional occupations, and aggregate data on the nationality of professional employees in each

Table II-10

NUMBER OF PERSONS IN THE UNION REPUBLICS WITH A COMPLETED
AND AN INCOMPLETE SECONDARY EDUCATION, 1939 AND 1959

Republics	Persons with secondary and incomplete secondary education (in thousands)		1959 as per cent of 1939	Persons with secondary and incomplete secondary education per 1,000 of population	
	1939	1959		1939	1959
USSR	14,689.3	54,929.6	374	77	263
Russian SFSR	8,291.0	30,903.6	373	76	263
Ukrainian SSR	3,625.1	11,972.7	330	90	286
Belorussian SSR	595.2	1,814.0	305	67	225
Uzbek SSR	245.5	1,896.7	772	39	234
Kazakh SSR	364.9	2,215.2	607	60	239
Georgian SSR	401.4	1,270.7	317	113	315
Azerbaydzhan SSR	234.5	967.3	412	73	261
Lithuanian SSR	184.3	476.1	258	64	175
Moldavian SSR	97.3	534.6	549	40	186
Latvian SSR	264.5	722.2	273	140	344
Kirghiz SSR	47.3	470.3	993	32	227
Tadzhik SSR	40.3	425.6	1,060	27	214
Armenian SSR	104.5	508.1	486	81	289
Turkmenian SSR	57.9	388.4	671	46	256
Estonian SSR	135.6	364.1	269	129	304

Source: Nar. khoz. SSSR, 1960, p. 23 (Table VI).

republic. By combining the two sets of figures it is possible to arrive at some tentative conclusions on who, in effect, manages the republics and how the professional personnel of a given nationality are distributed throughout the Union.

In Table II-11, p. 65, we give the numbers of professionals and semi-professionals in the Ukrainian SSR, the Russian Republic, and the Soviet Union as a whole on January 1, 1941, and December 1, 1960. The numbers are presented both in absolute figures and in relation to 10,000 of the total population. An analysis of the figures shows that in 1941 the per capita number of college graduates (professionals) engaged in the Ukraine substantially exceeded the all-Union average (54 compared with 48 per 10,000 citizens) and the number of professionals in Russia (49 in 10,000).[111] But in 1941 there were relatively fewer semi-professionals in

Table II-11

EMPLOYMENT OF HIGHER, AND SECONDARY VOCATIONAL SCHOOL
GRADUATES (PROFESSIONALS AND SEMI-PROFESSIONALS) IN THE
UKRAINIAN SSR, THE RUSSIAN SFSR, AND THE USSR IN
1941 AND 1960 *

Occupations	Time	Ukrainian SSR		Russian SFSR		USSR	
		Thou-sands	Per 10,000 popula-tion ‡	Thou-sands	Per 10,000 popula-tion ‡	Thou-sands	Per 10,000 popula-tion ‡
Engineers	1941	60.9	15	187.7	17	289.9	15
	1960	200.1	46	748.8	62	1,115.5	52
Agronomists, zoologists, veterinar-ians, foresters	1941	14.8	4	40.3	4	69.6	4
	1960	46.6	11	126.2	10	241.8	11
Physicians, exclusive of dentists	1941	33.4	8	82.2	8	141.8	7
	1960	79.9	19	232.7	19	400.6	18
Educators and university graduates (except geologists, lawyers, phy-sicians and economists); librar-ians, employees in cultural fields	1941	73.1	18	165.5	15	300.4	16
	1960	283.4	66	739.7	61	1,378.1	64
Total: Professionals †	1941	217.7	54	527.6	49	909.0	48
	1960	685.9	159	2,083.3	173	3,545.2	164
Technicians	1941	58.5	14	211.6	19	320.1	17
	1960	334.5	78	1,320.9	110	1,931.3	89
Agronomists, zoo-technicians, vet-erinary technicians, foresters	1941	22.4	6	53.5	5	92.8	5
	1960	85.9	20	198.2	16	380.8	18
Medical staff (incl. dentists)	1941	81.5	20	239.2	22	393.2	21
	1960	236.8	55	696.8	58	1,187.3	55
Educators, librarians, employees in cultural services	1941	109.1	27	311.9	29	536.4	28
	1960	185.5	43	635.4	53	1,061.9	49
Total: Semi-Professionals	1941	295.4	73	915.8	84	1,492.2	78
	1960	975.1	226	3,247.6	269	5,238.5	242

* Professional military personnel have been excluded. The exact dates when the censuses were taken are: January 1, 1941, and December 1, 1960.
† The items do not add up to totals because some occupations have apparently not been listed but included in the totals.
‡ To determine the population, official estimates for 1939 (with Western provinces included) and January 1, 1961, have been used (see *Nar. khoz. SSSR, 1960*, p. 8). We do not believe that a more exact calculation of the population figures for January 1, 1941, would have served any purpose because (1) the base figure for 1939 was already an estimate and (2) the population of the Ukrainian SSR underwent considerable changes in the turbulent years 1939–40 (in the newly annexed territories).
Source: Nar. khoz. SSSR, 1960, pp. 654–57.

the Ukraine: only 73 per 10,000 compared with 78 per 10,000 in the USSR and as many as 84 per 10,000 in Russia. In the individual occupational categories the per capita numbers were more or less even, except that the Ukraine led in the number of university trained educators, librarians, and university graduates in related fields (18 per 10,000 compared with the Union average of 16 and the Russian figure of 15).

Within the following twenty years, however, the Ukraine has lost her advantage in the distribution of professionals without gaining a predominance in the semi-professional categories. Especially striking is the small number of graduate engineers (46 in 10,000 compared with the Union average of 52 and the Russian figure of as many as 62) and a similarly small number of technicians. If anything, that is another visible proof of the low priorities which Ukrainian industry has received in Soviet economic planning since the outbreak of World War II. Soviet

Table II-12

BUDGETARY ALLOCATIONS TO THE UKRAINIAN SSR FOR
SOCIAL AND CULTURAL PURPOSES, 1960 *

(Absolute figures [N] in *millions* of rubles; per capita figures also in *rubles*)

Republics	Social and Cultural Purposes		Education		Training of Cadres		Higher Education	
	N	Per cap.	N	Per cap.	N	Per cap.	N	Per cap.
Ukrainian SSR	3,058.1	71	1,396.5	32	390.7	9	182.1	4
Russian SFSR	10,536.9	87	4,695.8	39	1,424.0	12	698.9	6
USSR (I) †	17,387.0	80	8,097.4	37	2,292.2	11	1,110.9	5
USSR (II) ‡	24,936.7	115	10,322.7	48	2,419.8	11	1,167.0	5

* Though the source gives data on budgetary allocations in selected years since 1940, I have chosen not to give data on years 1940 and 1956 for the following reasons: per capita figures for 1940 were likely to be imprecise because of the necessity both to estimate the population in the newly annexed Western Ukrainian territories and also to adjust the 1939 census figures; the per capita figures for 1956 may have suffered from being based on official population estimates *prior* to the census of 1959.
† Sum total of all the Republican budgets.
‡ Sum total of all the Republican budgets plus undistributed All-Union budget.

Sources: Ministerstvo finansov SSSR—Byudzhetnoe upravlenie (USSR Ministry of Finances, Budget Administration), *Gosudarstvenny byudzhet SSSR i byudzhety soyuznykh respublik* (State Budget of the USSR and Budgets of the Union Republics, Moscow, 1962), pp. 28, 29, 47, 48. Population figures for end of 1960 (January 1, 1961) from *Nar. khoz. SSSR, 1960*, p. 8.

budget figures for 1960 also disclose that for some reason *per capita* budgetary allotments for cultural and social purposes in the Ukraine are below the Soviet average for sums distributed among the Republics and below the allocations for the Russian SFSR (see Table II-12, especially the figures on financing of higher education). It should be kept in mind that the Republics have no independent budgets, but that all revenues are collected by central authorities and that a part of those is then distributed among the Republics at a session of the USSR Supreme Soviet in Moscow.[112] It is not implausible to assume that such figures may be interpreted by some Soviet Ukrainians as evidence of discrimination against the Ukraine and in favor of Russia.

To reinforce our impression that either because of her superior endowments or possibly also the policy of the regime the Russian Republic is becoming by far the richest in the Soviet Union we have culled some official data on saving bank deposits in the Soviet Union (the data refer to 1956, but no later figures have been released, to my knowledge). In the USSR as a whole, 184 persons in a thousand had savings accounts with an average balance of 1,732 rubles. In the Ukrainian SSR there were 173 per thousand with average savings of 1,482 rubles. In Russia, more than one-fifth of the population (216 in 1,000) were saving an average of 1,837 rubles each. If calculated on a broader, per capita basis, it would appear that there were 318 rubles saved per Soviet citizen, but that the savings in the Ukrainian SSR amounted to only 256 rubles per inhabitant, whereas in the Russian SFSR they ran as high as 397 rubles per head.[113]

Data on retail turnover per capita in different Republics may also be used as an indicator of relative living standards (see Tables II-13 and II-14). Unless the prices and the assortment of goods in various parts of the Soviet Union were greatly dissimilar—of which we are not aware—it would appear that in 1955 citizens of the Ukraine bought a smaller amount of comparable goods and services than the average Soviet citizen and a *considerably* smaller amount than citizens of Russia. Moreover we see that between 1940 and 1955 retail turnovers increased more slowly in the Ukrainian SSR than in the Russian SFSR and the USSR as a whole. Trained economists may differently interpret the disparities in the retail turnovers in the various Republics but thoughtful Ukrainians in the Soviet Union who have access to official data may try to explain those disparities as indications of economic discrimination. This impression of theirs will be further reinforced if they see in Table II-14 that turnover per head of population in Kiev is less than two-thirds of the comparable figure in Moscow and somewhat below that in Leningrad and that among thirteen Soviet cities with high retail turnovers per

Table II-13

An Indication of Living Standards in the Ukrainian SSR (I):
Retail Turnover in State and Cooperative Shops, Including
Restaurants and Dining Halls, Per Capita, in 1955

	In rubles, actual prices			1955 as per cent of 1940 (comparable prices)		
		Of which:			Of which:	
	Total turnover	Life necessities	Other goods	Total turnover	Life necessities	Other goods
Ukrainian SSR	2,005	1,027	978	187	154	234
Russian SFSR	2,895	1,658	1,237	196	169	247
USSR Average	2,541	1,394	1,147	202	171	254

Source: Tsentral'noe statisticheskoe upravlenie pri Sovete Ministrov SSSR (Central Statistical Administration of the USSR Council of Ministers), *Sovetskaya Torgovlya* (Soviet Trade, Moscow, 1956), p. 32.

Table II-14

An Indication of Living Standards in the Ukrainian SSR (II):
Retail Turnover in State and Cooperative Shops, Including
Restaurants and Dining Halls, in 13 Soviet Cities in 1955,
Per Capita, in Descending Order
(Figures in Thousands of Rubles)

Moscow (RSFSR)	9.2	Rostov-Don (RSFSR)	4.6
Leningrad (RSFSR)	6.2	Perm (Molotov; RSFSR)	4.6
Kiev (UkrSSR)	5.8	Gorky (RSFSR)	4.3
Minsk (Belorussia)	5.5	Chelyabinsk (RSFSR)	4.3
Vilnius (Lithuania)	5.3	Krasnoyarsk (RSFSR)	4.3
Sverdlovsk (RSFSR)	5.1	Tbilisi (Georgian SSR)	4.4
Alma-Ata (Kazakh SSR)	4.9		

Source: As in preceding table (II-13), pp. 194–95.

Table II-15

An Indication of Living Standards in the Ukrainian SSR (III):
Retail Turnover in State and Cooperative Shops, Including
Restaurants and Dining Halls, Per Capita, in 1960

	In rubles, actual prices			1960 as per cent of 1940 (comparable prices)		
		Of which:			Of which:	
	Total turnover	Life necessities	Other goods	Total turnover	Life necessities	Other goods
Ukrainian SSR	312 *	159	153	292	233	381
Russian SFSR	407	232	175	281	232	365
USSR Average	367	200	167	287	234	376

* There is a marked discrepancy in the magnitude of figures in this table and in
Table II-13. The 1960 figures have been divided by 10 to convert them into new
rubles (equal to 10 old ones), though the new currency was introduced only on
January 1, 1961. See preface to *Nar. khoz. SSSR, 1960*, p. 4.

Source: *Nar. khoz. SSSR, 1960*, p. 685.

capita eight are to be found in the Russian Republic. On the other hand,
more recent figures indicate that in the five years from 1955–1960 the
living standards of citizens of the Ukraine have somewhat improved
(compare Table II-15 with Table II-13). Retail turnover sales in the
Ukraine are still below both the USSR and Russian SFSR standards. But
while in 1955 the Ukrainian turnovers were only 69 per cent of the
Russian and 79 per cent of the average Soviet turnovers, in 1960 they
had reached the levels of 77 per cent and 85 per cent respectively. Moreover, for this time the turnovers relative to those in 1940 show a different
picture: the increase in the Ukraine is a little more rapid than both in
the Russian Republic and in the USSR as a whole. Is it a result of
Khrushchev's more liberal policies after the Twentieth Party Congress
in 1956?

Tables II-16 and II-17 show the national composition of the professional cadres in the Ukraine and, secondly, the distribution of professionals of Ukrainian nationality throughout the Soviet Union. No comparable figures on semi-professionals have come to our attention. Little,
however, is lost by this omission; for professionals are likely to hold the
better positions anyway, also the more important ones from a political

Table II-16

NATIONAL COMPOSITION OF PROFESSIONALS WITH HIGHER EDUCATION
WHO WERE ENGAGED IN THE NATIONAL ECONOMY OF THE UKRAINIAN SSR,
DECEMBER 1, 1960, IN DESCENDING MAGNITUDE

Nationality	Number	Percentage Distribution tion	Percentage Strength of Total National Group in Total Population (1959 census)
1. Ukrainians	399,931	58.31	76.8
2. Russians	181,489	26.46	16.9
3. Jews	83,689	12.20	2.0
4. Belorussians	6,272	0.92	0.7
5. Armenians	1,800	0.26	<0.2
6. Moldavians	823	0.12	0.6
7. Tatars	806	0.12	<0.2
8. Georgians	578	0.08	<0.2
9. Chuvashes	228	0.03	<0.2
10. Latvians	209	0.03	<0.2
11. Ossetins	183	0.03	<0.2
12. Mordovians	175	0.03	<0.2
13. Lithuanians	143	0.02	<0.2
14. Komis	123	0.02	<0.2
15. Udmurts	118	0.02	<0.2
16. Estonians	114	0.02	<0.2
17. Azerbaydzhanis	101	0.02	<0.2
Other nationalities *	341	0.05	2.2
Unspecified [Aliens?]	8,738	1.27	—
Total	685,851	100.00	100.00

* Nationalities represented by less than one hundred professionals each have not been included in the table. They are, in descending order, with the number of professionals in parentheses: Maris (61), Yakuts (45), Bashkirs (40), Karelians (32), nationalities from Daghestan (31), Uzbeks (31), Kazakhs (23), Tadzhiks (18), Balkars (14), Buriats (11), Abkhazians (9), Kabardians (7), Turkmenians (6), Kirghiz (4), Kalmyks (3); Chechens, Ingushes, and Karakalpaks (two each).

Source: Tsentral'noe statisticheskoe upravlenie pri Sovete Ministrov SSSR (Central Statistical Administration of the USSR Council of Ministers), *Vysshee obrazovanie v SSSR: Statisticheskiy sbornik* (Higher Education in the USSR: A Statistical Handbook, Moscow, 1961), pp. 70–71. Henceforth abbreviated as *Vys. obraz.* Census figures from *Nar. khoz. SSSR, 1960*, p. 18.

viewpoint. Table II-16 shows that the Ukrainians have either not been able or not been allowed to fill a share of professional positions in the Ukrainian SSR which would correspond to their share of the republican population: they hold but 58.3 per cent of the posts though their share of the total population is 76.8 per cent. On the other hand, Russians, with only 16.9 per cent of the total population, occupy 26.5 per cent of all professional positions. Jews, who constitute 2.0 per cent of the total population, hold some 12.2 per cent of such posts. Other nationalities, notably the Armenians and Belorussians may also be overrepresented, but the numbers involved are relatively small: all but two odd per cent of the professionals working in the Ukraine are either Ukrainians, Russians, or Jews.

The next table (Table II-17) shows that a substantial number of professionals of Ukrainian nationality—117,798, or almost one-quarter of the total—are employed outside the Republic. The largest contingent (85,155, or more than 16 per cent of the total) work in the Russian Republic, where they constitute 4.08 per cent of the total professional force in RSFSR; the second largest contingent work in Kazakhstan (10,984, or 2.1 per cent of the total Ukrainian professional force, or almost 9 per cent of the total of professionals working in the Kazakh SSR).

A comparison of the two tables suggests an important conclusion. Had it been possible to pool all professionals of Ukrainian nationality who are now scattered throughout the USSR in the Ukraine herself they could fill approximately 75 per cent of the vacancies in the Ukrainian economy. This would have been slightly below the number of vacancies strictly proportional to the Ukrainian share in the total Republican population (76.8 per cent). Such a consolidation of professional cadres presupposes, of course, that their individual training is such that they could be fitted into the Republican economy and, above all, a fundamental change in the policy of the regime. Some evidence presented elsewhere also suggests that, depending on the way the statistics were collected, a larger or a smaller number of Ukrainians may have been counted as Russians, for there is some evidence of linguistic assimilation among better educated Ukrainians.[114]

In the long run, of greatest political significance will be data on the availability of research and academic personnel and the training of university students, for the students of today will be the chief engineers and factory directors of tomorrow. To a large extent, their political attitudes will be influenced by their teachers, their fellow-students, and the location of the school; it does not seem implausible to assume that the political attitudes of a Ukrainian student enrolled at Moscow University and studying under Russian professors may differ from those of

Table II-17

DISTRIBUTION OF PROFESSIONALS OF UKRAINIAN NATIONALITY, WITH
HIGHER EDUCATION, IN THE VARIOUS REPUBLICS OF THE USSR,
DECEMBER 1, 1960

Republic	Number	Percentage Distribution	Percentage of Total Professional Group in Given Republic	Percentage of Ukrainians in Total Population of a Given Republic (1959 census)
Russian SFSR	85,155	16.45	4.09	2.9
Ukrainian SSR	399,931	77.25	58.31	76.8
Belorussian SSR	5,441	1.05	4.94	1.7
Uzbek SSR	2,984	0.58	2.74	1.1
Kazakh SSR	10,984	2.12	8.80	8.2
Georgian SSR	579	0.11	0.54	1.3
Azerbaydzhan SSR	615	0.12	0.84	— *
Lithuanian SSR	519	0.10	1.39	0.7
Moldavian SSR	5,702	1.10	17.13	14.6
Latvian SSR	1,135	0.22	2.78	1.4
Kirghiz SSR	2,201	0.43	7.39	6.6
Tadzhik SSR	1,108	0.21	4.74	1.4
Armenian SSR	168	0.03	0.41	— *
Turkmenian SSR	787	0.15	3.50	1.4
Estonian SSR	420	0.08	1.74	1.3
Total: USSR	517,729	100.00	14.60	17.8
USSR minus Ukraine	117,798	22.75		

* Dashes (—) connote that the percentage of Ukrainians in a given Republic is not available, apparently because it is negligible.

Source: Vys. obraz., pp. 70–71. Census figures from *Nar. khoz. SSSR, 1960*, pp. 14ff.

a Ukrainian studying under Ukrainian and Russian professors in Kiev. In recent years Soviet authorities have released useful data on both academic personnel and students. As before I shall first present figures on research, teaching, and higher educational opportunities in the Ukrainian Republic without considering the factor of nationality. The results of this statistical survey will then be interpreted in the light of relevant nationality statistics.

Table II-18 shows the distribution of research and academic personnel in the Ukrainian and Russian Republics in 1940 and 1960, both in absolute numbers and per 10,000 of the total population. Figures for the USSR as a whole have also been given for comparison. In analyzing our occupational profile of the Ukrainian SSR (Table II-8, p. 61) we have already noticed the disproportionately small number of persons who in 1960 were engaged in scientific work in the Ukraine. The figures in Table II-18 only confirm this sad fact. Moreover, they reveal that although in 1940 the relative number of research and academic personnel in the Ukraine had been only little below the Union average, by 1960 the gap had widened. For certain reasons it has not publicly disclosed, the regime has chosen to concentrate most of the highly skilled personnel in the Russian Republic, which now considerably exceeds the Union average both with respect to the total number of personnel and their higher qualifications, as attested by advanced academic degrees.

But what is the nationality of Soviet research and academic personnel? Official figures have been released for the years 1939 (before the annexation of Western territories), 1947, 1950, 1955, 1957, 1958, 1959, and 1960.[115] The 1959 data clearly indicates that the number of research and academic personnel who were officially listed as Ukrainians was disproportionately low compared with the Ukrainian share of the total population of the USSR (9.8 compared with 17.8 per cent). If we make the double assumption that Ukrainian researchers would not leave the Ukrainian Republic and that their specializations met the demand in

Table II-18

RESEARCH AND ACADEMIC PERSONNEL IN THE UKRAINIAN SSR,
THE RUSSIAN SFSR, AND THE USSR, 1940 AND 1960

	1940		1960					
		Per 10,000 of Total Population		Per 10,000 of Total Population	Of whom with the following degrees			
					"Doctor of Sc." *		"Candidate of Sc." *	
Territory	Total	Total	Total		Total	Per 10,000	Total	Per 10,000
Ukrainian SSR	19,304	4.8	46,657	10.8	1,343	0.31	13,622	3.16
Russian SFSR	61,872	5.7	242,872	20.2	7,929	0.66	67,146	5.57
USSR	98,315	5.2	354,158	16.4	10,945	0.51	98,262	4.54

*"Doctor of Science" is the highest academic degree in the USSR, which has no equivalent in the United States. "Candidate of Science" roughly corresponds to our "Ph.D."

Sources: For absolute figures see *Nar. khoz. SSSR, 1960,* p. 786. Relative figures calculated by author on the basis of population figures for 1939 (including the Western provinces) and January 1, 1961, from table on p. 8, *ibid.*

that Republic, we still would have to admit that Ukrainians could have filled only 75.8 per cent of appropriate openings in the Ukraine in 1959, in which Ukrainians constituted 76.8 per cent of the total population.[116] Actually, in 1960, a year later, Ukrainians filled but 48.3 per cent of the research and academic teaching positions in their Republic.[117]

The following table (II-19) shows the growth of the college student body in the Ukrainian Republic from 1940 to 1960 compared with the increases in the Russian SFSR and the USSR as a whole. It should be borne in mind that not all of the students are attending school full-time. In the academic year 1940–41 3.3 per cent of all Soviet students were evening and 28.0 per cent were correspondence students; by 1960–61 their proportion had risen to 10.2 and 41.5 per cent respectively.[118] The table clearly demonstrates that either because of disproportionately heavy wartime losses or because of deliberate government policy, the Ukraine, which on the eve of the German invasion had a higher proportion of college students than either Russia or the USSR as a whole, by 1960–61 was trailing behind the USSR average and the per capita number of students in the Russian Republic. On the other hand, to judge by the figures of Table II-20, which have been culled from the latest statistical annual of the Ukrainian SSR, the proportion of college students among the total population of the Ukraine compares favorably with most countries of the world. It is nudging the relative number of college students in the United States, exceeding by a wide margin the figures for West European countries and Japan.

Table II-19

COLLEGE STUDENTS IN THE UKRAINIAN SSR, THE RUSSIAN SFSR,
AND THE USSR AT THE BEGINNING OF THE ACADEMIC YEARS
1940–41 AND 1960–61

Territory	1940–41		1960–61	
	Total	Per 10,000 of Total Population	Total	Per 10,000 of Total Population
Ukrainian SSR	196,800	49	417,700	97
Russian SFSR	478,100	44	1,496,700	124
USSR	811,700	43	2,396,100	111

Sources: Nar. khoz. SSSR, 1960, pp. 769 and 8, and reference note to Table II-18, p. 73.

Table II-20

<small>College Students in the Ukrainian SSR and in Selected Countries</small>

Country	Year	Totals in Thousands	Per 10,000 of Total Population
Ukrainian SSR	1960–61	418	97
Ukrainian SSR	1961–62	461	106
United States	1960–61	1,913	106
England	1958–59	150	29
France	1958–59	186	41
Italy	1958–59	173	35
West Germany	1959–60	180	34
Japan	1959–60	574	61
India	1957–58	823	21
Pakistan	1958–59	127	14
Iran	1959–60	19	9
Turkey	1959–60	50	19

Source: Tsentral'ne statystychne upravlinnya pry Radi Ministriv URSR (Central Statistical Administration of the Ukrainian SSR Council of Ministers), *Narodne hospodarstvo Ukrayins'koyi RSR v 1961 rotsi: Statystychny shchorichnyk* (National Economy of the Ukrainian SSR in 1961: A Statistical Annual, Kiev, 1962), p. 27.

With respect to nationality DeWitt has clearly shown that at least since 1927 through 1959 the share of Ukrainians among the *full-time* college students in the USSR has always lagged behind the proportion of Ukrainians in the total USSR population. For instance, while in December, 1926, Ukrainians constituted 21.2 per cent of the total Soviet population (within the boundaries of 1926), Ukrainian students made up only 14.6 per cent of the total Soviet student body. From 1929–35 the average share of Ukrainian students amounted to 15.7 per cent, only to fall to 12.7 per cent in 1950, despite the annexation of predominantly Ukrainian territories in the West and Southwest. In 1959, Ukrainians constituted but 13.3 per cent of the total Soviet student body (full-time students).[119],* Assuming that all Ukrainian youths would study only in

* DeWitt's findings on the unequal share of Ukrainians in the total Soviet body is indirectly confirmed with respect to the Ukrainian SSR by the official compilation of relevant 1959 census results made public only in 1963, while this book was already in print. The data gives the educational levels of the different national groups in the Ukrainian SSR in January 1939 (that is, before the incorporation of Western Ukraine) and in January 1959. It differs from DeWitt's data and our data in Table II-16, p. 70, in that they refer to all persons with a higher, completed and incomplete secondary

the Ukraine, we should obtain, for the same year, a maximum hypothetical nationality representation in higher schools of the Ukrainian SSR of 89.5 per cent.[120]

As in the case of professionals, semi-professionals and the special category of research and academic personnel, that assumption cannot be held. But in this particular instance we know from a specialized source that in 1960–61 the total number of students—regular, evening, and correspondence—in higher schools of the Ukrainian Republic was divided as follows: Out of 417,748 students, 260,945 (62.5 per cent) were Ukrainians, and 125,464 (30.0 per cent) were Russians, though the Ukrainians in 1959 constituted 76.8 per cent and the Russians 17.1 per cent of the total population.[121] The same source also shows to what extent Ukrainian students have been scattered through other Republics (see Table II-21, p. 77).

To summarize our argument so far: The figures show that at the time when the 1959 census was taken, that is, after more than forty years of Soviet rule and fourteen years after the conclusion of World War II, the Ukrainians have not yet achieved a proportionate share of Soviet professional and semi-professional employees, research and academic personnel, and students in higher educational institutions. The greatest disparity will be found among the research and academic staff. Nor is the total number of positions in the Ukrainian Republic for such qualified persons, *regardless of nationality,* proportionate to the number of posts in other Republics. These are two interdependent but sufficiently distinct phenomena, which call for a separate analysis.

---

education, which constitutes an irresponsible lumping together of highly educated engineers with semi-literate skilled workers. But it does provide a breakdown according to nationality, which is missing, for example, in our Tables II-9 and II-10, pp. 63, 64.

In January 1939, 103 in 1,000 people in the Ukrainian Republic had an education equivalent or superior to incomplete secondary schooling (first seven grades). But among the Ukrainian group, only 81 per thousand had such an education, compared with 151 among the Russians and as many as 280 among the Ukrainian Jews. Twenty years later, 303 per 1,000 had such an education in the Ukrainian SSR, but only 278 among the Ukrainians compared with 384 among the Russians and 582 among the Jews. See Table 57 in *Itogi vsesoyznoy perepisi naseleniya v 1959 godu: Ukrainskaya SSR,* p. 194.

It is obvious from these figures that the educational level of the Ukrainians in their own Republic in both 1939 and 1959 was below that of the Russian and especially that of the Jewish minority. But the figures also disclose that as far as this minimum general education is concerned the Ukrainians are slowly catching up: Between 1939 and 1959, the number of educated Ukrainians increased 3.4 times compared with a Republican average increase of 2.9 times, an increase among the Russians of 2.5 times, and one among the Jews of 2.1 times. In a footnote to that table Soviet statisticians try to reassure their readers that there are 10.751 million educated Ukrainians in the USSR, of whom 8.957 million live in the Ukrainian SSR and 1.794 million in other Republics—a hint that educated Ukrainians are being "siphoned off" into the other Republics. See, however, our discussion in the main text, below, on the changing socioeconomic profile of the Ukrainians since 1926.

Table II-21

DISTRIBUTION OF STUDENTS OF UKRAINIAN NATIONALITY IN THE USSR
AT THE BEGINNING OF THE ACADEMIC YEAR 1960–61

Republic	Number	Percentage Distribution
Ukrainian SSR	260,945	75.9
Russian SFSR	67,793	19.7
Belorussian SSR	2,255	0.7
Uzbek SSR	2,492	0.7
Kazakh SSR	3,891	1.1
Georgian SSR	419	0.1
Azerbaydzhan SSR	279	0.1
Lithuanian SSR	115	0.0
Moldavian SSR	2,961	0.9
Latvian SSR	541	0.2
Kirghiz SSR	899	0.3
Tadzhik SSR	511	0.1
Armenian SSR	92	0.0
Turkmenian SSR	278	0.1
Estonian SSR	147	0.0
Total	343,618	100.0

Source: Vys. obraz., pp. 128–57.

Analyzing the total number of positions in the Ukrainian SSR we find a significant fact: On the eve of World War II, they were equal to or even above the Union per capita average, with the exception of jobs in research and college teaching. The Ukraine has, of course, suffered terribly as a battle field between German and Soviet forces and has been further devastated by Nazi occupation. But it is also known that after the war the regime has deliberately emphasized the economic development of so-called eastern areas in the Russian and Central Asian Republics, for strategic and, possibly, also for political reasons. This has made Soviet economy less dependent upon the vulnerable Ukraine but has also resulted in a relatively slower economic and social growth in that Republic. Insofar as the decision is motivated by other than economic criteria there is no reason why the Ukraine could not again accelerate her development under more favorable circumstances.

Official data on the nationality of professional and semi-professional employees, professors, and students are rather few. Unlike the census data, they should be treated with very great caution for we do not know how these figures are determined. In discussing the nationality of students, for example, DeWitt suggests that in the middle 1930's the concept of nationality was changed from one of "root nationality" (ethnic descent) to one of self-declared nationality.[122] Since, from the mid-1930's on, the policy of the government has been to integrate its subjects on the basis of Russian culture and language, it may be suspected that in the case of nations closely related to Russians, both external and internalized pressure for assimilation has been very strong.[123] How many persons in the West know, for example, that the controversial Soviet biologist Trofim Lysenko as well as the universally respected nuclear physicist Peter Kapitsa are Ukrainians by descent? Pressures for assimilation are particularly strong among Ukrainians who find themselves outside the borders of their Republic: though there are many Russian-language schools in the Ukraine to serve the Russian minority and some Ukrainians, since the mid-1930's the 3.4 million Ukrainians in Russia have not had a single school with Ukrainian as the main language of instruction.

Voluntary or involuntary assimilation, however, is only one reason why the number of highly qualified Ukrainians has remained disproportionately low. Another cause—perhaps the weightier one—has been the necessity to overcome the low level of socio-economic development which had marked the Ukrainian nation in 1917. In the following pages I should like, therefore, to give a quick survey of historical data to show the socio-economic dynamic of the Ukrainian group from the 1920's through the 1930's. The section is relatively short since in the 1930's the government had withheld detailed systematic data on nationality.

The 1926 census furnishes invaluable data on the socio-economic profile of the Ukrainians, Russians, and Jews living in the Ukraine. There are also relevant bits of evidence from the 1930's and more recent years which may be used to discover certain trends of development. Had the distribution of nationalities been homogeneous, about one-fifth of each would have lived in cities in 1926. Actually, only one Ukrainian out of nine (11.8 per cent) lived in a town, but every second Russian (50.2 per cent) and roughly three out of every four Jews (77.4 per cent) did so. Thus it came about that an absolute majority of the urban population in the Republic was made up of national minorities, Russians and Jews each accounting for about one-quarter of the total urban population (see also Table II-22).

Our impression that in 1926 the Ukrainians were primarily a nation of peasants is confirmed by a breakdown according to occupations—89.3 per cent of the total number of peasants were Ukrainians, but only 4.8 per cent were Russians and 0.5 per cent were Jews.[124] On the other hand, among industrial workers only 50.2 per cent were Ukrainians, as

Table II-22

NATIONAL COMPOSITION OF THE URBAN POPULATION OF THE UKRAINIAN SSR, 1926 AND 1959

(Absolute numbers in thousands)

				Percentages			
	Number		Com-parison	of given nationality		of urban population †	
Nationality	1926 *	1959	1959:1926	1926	1959	1926	1959
Ukrainians	2,536.5	11,782.0	4.6	11.8	36.6	47.4	61.8
Russians	1,343.7	5,726.0	4.3	50.2	80.6	25.1	30.2
Jews	1,218.6	810.0	0.7	77.4	96.4	22.8	4.3
Others ‡	233.1	717.0	3.1	—	—	4.7	3.7
Unknown	6.9	112.0	16.2	—	—	—	—
Total Urban Population, excluding foreigners	5,359.2	19,147.0	3.6	18.5 §	45.7 §	100.0	100.0
Foreigners	14.3	— ‖					
Total Population, UkrSSR, excluding foreigners	28,996.5	41,869.0	1.4	100.0			
Foreigners	23.2	— ‖	—	—			

* Figures for 1926 include the Eastern Ukraine only; they exclude Crimea also.

† The percentages have been calculated after omitting persons of unknown nationality and foreigners.

‡ Others are, in descending order of their numbers in *1926:* Poles (2), Belorussians (1), Germans (9), Tatars (4), Moldavians (5), Greeks (6), Armenians (8), Latvians (12+), Czechoslovaks (12+), and Bulgarians (3). The number in parentheses indicate the ranking in *1959.* In 1959 add Hungarians (7).

§ Per cent of total Republican population.

‖ Unknown.

Sources: On 1926 see O. Pytel', ["National Relations in the Ukraine in the Light of Statistics"], in T. Olesiyevych *et al., Ukrayins'ka lyudnist' SSSR* (The Ukrainian Population of the USSR, Warsaw: Ukrainian Scientific Institute, 1931), Table VII, p. 56, and Table I, p. 44.

On 1959 see *Narodne hospodarstvo Ukrayins'koyi RSR v 1959 rotsi,* p. 14.

against 32.4 per cent Russians and 10.0 per cent Jews.[125] Particularly
important, in view of the following discussion, is the national composition of miners and metal workers. Of the miners less than one-third declared themselves Ukrainians (31.3 per cent), whereas 57.9 per cent were
Russians. On the other hand, the Ukrainians held an absolute majority
among the metal workers (52.9 per cent), who, as a group, had been recruited more recently, the Russian share approximating one-third (32.7
per cent).[126]

Of even greater interest is the composition of the civil service. In 1926
Ukrainians comprised about one-half of all the civil servants in the
Republic (51.7 per cent), Russians—one-quarter (25.0 per cent), and Jews
a goodly part of the rest (16.8 per cent). If one considers, however, only
the top five categories ("managing personnel"; legal, technical, and economic personnel; "workers in arts"), the Ukrainian share drops to 41.9
per cent to the benefit of the Jewish one, which rises to 27.1 per cent,
that of the Russians remaining constant at 24.3 per cent. Among the
managers, the proportion of Ukrainians was at the start of the Ukrainization (korenizatsiya) policy 50.4 per cent (22.1 per cent were Russians,
and 20.0 per cent were Jews). It was the lowest among the economic
personnel (factory directors?) with 33.8 per cent, as against 19.8 per cent
Russians and 40.8 per cent Jews; the highest among the educators (that
is, mostly school teachers) with 68.1 per cent, 15.7 per cent Russians,
and 9.9 per cent Jews.[127]

These data may be supplemented by those on student enrollment. Out
of 27,511 college students in the Ukraine on January 1, 1927 (in 1960,
there were 417,700 of them!), only 48.7 per cent were Ukrainians, while
20.1 per cent were Russians, and 29.7 per cent were Jews. We also notice
that the Ukrainians tended toward the less profitable occupations: As
many as 71.7 per cent of the student body in agricultural institutes were
Ukrainians, 62.9 per cent in teachers colleges, and 55.9 per cent in schools
of fine arts, whereas their proportion among the students of engineering
schools was but 32.9 per cent (32.2 per cent were Russians and 31.9 per
cent Jews).[128]

To sum up the picture so far: While in 1926 the Ukrainians, with
80 per cent of the total population, formed an overwhelming majority
among the citizens of their Republic, it was a majority of the subject
rather than one of rulers; for the two chief minorities—the Russians and
the Jews—were greatly superior to them in socio-economic status. But
has not the Ukrainian position changed over time?

When the twentieth anniversary of Soviet Ukraine was being celebrated in 1937, S. Kosior, the First Secretary of the Communist Party
of Ukraine released a few important data. They bear out our expecta-

tion that during the first two Five Year Plans the rural-urban dispro-
portion of the Ukrainians had been remedied to some extent. Ukrainian
peasants took industrial jobs and settled in cities that had been undis-
puted Russian strongholds before. Whereas in 1923 Ukrainians formed
only 35 per cent of the inhabitants of Kharkov, eleven years later, in
1934, their share amounted to 50 per cent. Significant also is the increase
of the Ukrainian element, during the same period, in two cities of the
steppe industrial region: from 28 to 56 per cent in Zaporozhe, from
16 to 49 per cent in Dniepropetrovsk. Most dramatic, however, was the
influx of Ukrainians into the Donbas: Whereas in 1923 Ukrainians constituted but 21 per cent of the inhabitants of Lugansk (Voroshilovgrad),
ten years later they comprised 60 per cent; in the same period, their
proportion in Donetsk (Stalino) jumped from 7 to 31 per cent.[129] No
data were revealed on the national composition of the capital, Kiev, in
the 1930's. In 1926 Ukrainians had comprised 42.1 per cent of its total
population of 513,700, Russians 24.4 per cent and Jews 27.3 per cent.[130]
From the census of 1959, however, we can infer that the proportion of
Ukrainians probably rose in the 1930's; for in 1959 Ukrainians numbered 60.1 per cent of the city's population, the Russians 23.0 per cent,
and Jews 13.9 per cent.[131] While part of those changes might be explained by persons shifting their national allegiance, it does not appear
likely that it would have been a major part. For the population in the
Ukrainian cities did grow between 1926 and 1939; for example, the
population of the heavily urbanized Yuzivka (Stalino) district increased
by as much as 91 per cent, that of the Lugansk (Voroshilovgrad) district,
also in the Donbas, by 37 per cent.[132]

The reason for the influx of Ukrainian peasants into the cities seems
to have been a combination of "drive" and "pull": on the one hand,
the forcible collectivization of agriculture, and on the other hand opening job opportunities in industry, which in turn influenced the trends in
education. According to Kosior's figures, the national composition of the
workers in the Ukraine changed somewhat in favor of the Ukrainians.
Whereas in 1926 their share among the industrial workers was 50.2 per
cent, in 1935 it approached 60 per cent and went as high as 65 per cent
in the newer branches of the economy: the machine-building and chemical industries. Among the lower officials there were more than 70 per
cent Ukrainians; among the higher their proportion was only 60 per
cent (the corresponding figure for 1926 is apparently that of "managing
personnel"—50.4 per cent).[133]

Kosior's figures on college enrollment are interesting. In 1924, Ukrainians had comprised 30 per cent of the total student body. By 1927, their

share had risen to 48.7 per cent. In 1937, it amounted to 60 per cent.
Kosior added:

In the majority of educational institutions such as teachers and agricultural colleges, medical schools, etc., in which instruction is in Ukrainian, the number
of Ukrainians reaches 70–75 per cent.[134]

Somewhere else Kosior gave figures for other schools: in institutes of
communications, Ukrainians formed only 52.0 per cent of the student
body, in institutes of heavy industry only 40.0 per cent, of local industry 31.0 per cent.[135]

For our purpose it is rather unfortunate that only fragmentary data
has been published after the war which lacks the comprehensiveness and
depth of the figures from the 1920's. A Soviet Ukrainian author, as an
exception to the rule, has released comparable figures on the student
body in the Ukraine in the academic year 1955–56. In the full-time divisions of higher schools in the Republic there were enrolled 212,193
students, of whom 130,530, or 61.5 per cent, were Ukrainians, 61,493, or
29.0 per cent, Russians, and 13,277, or 6.3 per cent, Jews. But when institutions of a "technical profile" (apparently, engineering schools) are considered separately, the Ukrainian share drops to 51.8 per cent, while the
Russian and Jewish increase to 36.4 and 8.2 per cent, respectively.[136]
In short, compared with other nationalities, Ukrainian students in the
middle 1950's took about as much advantage of the higher educational
system of the Ukrainian SSR as they had done twenty years before, with
the significant difference that more Ukrainians are now entering the
better paying technical professions.

After the population census of 1959, the regime revealed in great
detail the various occupations represented in the Ukraine, without, however, giving any breakdowns according to nationality.[137] Such breakdowns were given only for the urban population of the Ukrainian SSR.
Nevertheless, those data yield important insights, especially when juxtaposed to the data from the 1926 census (see Table II-22). We note, for
example, that the population of the Republic has become much more
urbanized (18.5 per cent of all the citizens, or roughly one-fifth lived in
cities in 1926; by 1959 that proportion had risen to 45.7 per cent, or
almost one-half). What about the different nationalities? Almost all the
Jews (96.4 per cent) and four-fifths (80.6 per cent) of the Russians in the
Ukraine lived in cities—a higher proportion than in 1926, which would
probably indicate that even more than in 1926 members of those two
minorities tend to belong to the somewhat higher, urban socio-economic
groups. The share of the Jews in the total urban population has been
drastically diminished—mainly a result of the Nazi atrocities. The share
of the Russians has increased somewhat (from 25.1 to 30.2 per cent). But

the share of Ukrainians in the urban population has grown considerably (from 47.4 per cent—or less than the majority—to 61.8 per cent, about three-fifths). The influx of Ukrainians into the cities of the Republic has been, moreover, faster than the growth of those cities—an encouraging sign that over a period of time Ukrainians have been making more of urban opportunities, and have been able to rise a little on the socio-economic ladder from peasant to skilled worker to professional.*

We conclude this chapter by observing that the Ukraine is one of the most richly endowed Republics of the Soviet Union, which may even out-produce certain West European countries in some key commodities. Since the 1940's, however, her industrial development has been deliberately held back to favor the Asiatic portions of the Soviet Union. She has also suffered tremendous population losses during the forcible collectivization of 1928–33 and World War II.

Partly the result and partly the cause of slowed down development has been a somewhat unfavorable social structure, the heritage of a time when the Ukraine was predominantly agricultural country. That unfavorable social structure is particularly apparent in the case of Ukrainians who for centuries have formed a large but subject majority in their Republic. The present regime does not seem to have put major obstacles in the path of their socio-economic growth, but it has continued the old Tsarist policy of scattering educated Ukrainians into all corners of the Empire, by encouraging those who want to win their laurels in far-off posts of the Imperial service, and by keeping a close watch on those who would rather serve the needs of their home country. One of the most significant conclusions, however, to emerge from our survey of Soviet personnel statistics is that the Ukrainians in the Soviet Union have developed sufficiently strong cadres of all types of professionals as to assume, with some consolidation of forces and some cooperation from non-Ukrainian citizens of the Ukraine, most of the responsible positions in the Republic, and to achieve self-rule. This presupposes, of course, a radical change in political climate. But it cannot be overstressed that from 1917 to 1961 a people of peasants, with a sprinkling of intellectuals, have matured into a sociologically balanced nation.

In the following chapters I shall address myself to concrete problems of Soviet nationality policy. First, a series of questions encountered in the annexation and integration of Western Ukrainian territories.

* In order, however, to fully evaluate this development we must bear in mind that by 1959, when the census was taken, the boundaries of the cities were redefined in such a way as to include within the city limits the predominantly Ukrainian settlements and suburbs. The effect of these boundary changes cannot be precisely assessed in this book. See Naulko, *op. cit.*, p. 47.

Chapter III

INTEGRATION OF WESTERN UKRAINE I:
ADMINISTRATIVE, AGRICULTURAL, AND
RELIGIOUS POLICIES

The so-called Western Ukraine comprises seven provinces, with a total area of 110,600 square kilometers (or more than one-sixth of the area of the Republic) and a population of 7.8 million (according to the 1959 census). The most important are the five provinces that have been acquired from Poland (89,800 sq. kilometers and 6.1 million inhabitants). In terms of socio-economic development, the Western Ukraine appears a predominantly rural area; in 1959, the urban population in all these provinces was still below the average for the Ukrainian SSR.[1]

In integrating the Western Ukraine into the fabric of Soviet society, the regime was faced with a veritable Gordian knot of problems. After the war the Soviet government undoubtedly possessed the power and the necessary determination to cut it in twain—and so it did—but to establish itself in the area permanently it also had to gather the loose ends as neatly as possible so as not to divert to the administration of its new acquisition too many human resources that were badly needed elsewhere, in reconstructing the damaged economy in its old territories. It is with this process of integration that this and the following chapter are concerned.

The most immediate problem in 1944–45 was how to deal with Ukraine's neighbors: Poland, Rumania, Hungary and Czechoslovakia, who claimed these territories as their own. To some extent, its solution was facilitated by the fact that Rumania's and Hungary's war records were not unobjectionable from the Allied point of view. As far as Poland and Czechoslovakia were concerned, the Soviet regime used moral pressure against the background of overwhelming physical force. But the relinquishment of Polish and Czech territorial claims did not, by itself, solve the question of both Polish and Czech minorities in these provinces, especially the former.

But the fundamental problem was that, with the exception of Bessarabia and Volhynia, these provinces had never been a part of the Soviet Union nor of the Russian Empire, for any considerable length of time. Their inhabitants belonged to a different spiritual world, and the foremost institution that bound them to the West was the Greek Catholic, or Uniate, Church. The area had little industry and the peasantry were, on the whole, impoverished—which was a political weakness as well. On the other hand, as we have already seen, the Ukrainian national movement in that area was solidly based on a network of cultural and economic organizations that had been established in the second half of the nineteenth century. How did the Soviet regime proceed to integrate those provinces?

So as not to disrupt the continuity of exposition, I have put a summary of events in the relatively less important Transcarpathia, Northern Bukovina, and Bessarabia in Note III-1, in the Appendix. In the main text I shall deal with formerly Polish Eastern Galicia and Volhynia. After sketching the conditions in the interwar period, I shall discuss in this chapter Soviet administrative, agricultural, and religious policies; the struggle with the Ukrainian underground will be analyzed in the chapter following. Soviet cultural policy will be considered only in passing since it does not differ essentially from that in Eastern Ukraine.

1. *Western Ukraine under Poland and Her Annexation in 1939 and 1944*

As a result of her victory in the armed struggle against the Western Ukrainian (Galician) Republic in 1918–19 and the Soviet-Polish war of 1920–21, Poland acquired Eastern Galicia and parts of Volhynia and Polessye, together with the district of Kholm. Her annexation was sanctioned by two main instruments: the Polish-Soviet Treaty of Riga (March 21, 1921) and the decision of the Conference of Allied Ambassadors of March 15, 1923. Eastern Galicia had formed part of the Hapsburg Empire, the other provinces had been under Russia. The population of the entire region was ethnically mixed, with Ukrainians forming a majority almost everywhere in the countryside, but not in the cities. The relations between the Polish government and its Ukrainian subjects were generally tense and marred by frequent eruptions of violence.[2]

In all fairness, it must be stated that the problem was anything but tractable if both the Polish and the Ukrainian presuppositions were accepted as valid. The Poles considered the region as being historically a part of Poland, though on ethnographic grounds their title would have seemed dubious. But their historical case was reinforced by three other considerations, apart from the maxim of the happy possessor (*beati possedentes*): Poles lived interspersed throughout the whole area; secondly, as a rule they comprised a strong plurality in the towns (a majority with the Jews); and thirdly, in the countryside itself the big landlords were Poles. The Ukrainians, on the other hand, formed a majority of the rural population, small Polish enclaves excepted, but they had all the disadvantages of seeming to be historical upstarts, though their medieval ancestors had been perfectly respectable members of the European community of nations. They demanded at first that the Western powers annul the Polish occupation of Eastern Galicia, and, once that had proved impossible, that the Polish government should grant them autonomy guaranteed by the League of Nations. This the Poles promised to do, but the promise was never kept, apparently because they feared— and not without ground—that the Ukrainians regarded self-government only as a steppingstone to independence. Being the stronger, the Polish government took hold of the land and decided to Polonize it.[3]

The government's policy proceeded along several paths. In the first place, Ukrainian national consciousness was to be destroyed by the Polonization of the school system. In 1919, the Ukrainians managed to introduce Ukrainian as the language of teaching in some 3,000 elementary schools in Eastern Galicia and some 500 schools in Volhynia, Polessye, and Kholm.[4] By 1929–1930, however, the number of Ukrainian schools was reduced to 716 in Galicia and 7 in Volhynia; 1,794 schools in Galicia, and 523 in Volhynia had become so-called bi-lingual (that is, Polish-Ukrainian) schools.[5] This meant in practice that the Ukrainian intelligentsia were called upon to renounce their achievements of the years 1918–19, nay, of the constitutional struggle under Austria as well.

But what made the Polono-Ukrainian struggle so bitter and what lent it a mass character, were other policies which solidified the various grievances of the Ukrainian minority into a firm core of resistance. Because of suspicions concerning their political loyalty, Ukrainians were discriminated against in the distribution of public offices. As a Polish author justly remarks, a good side of this was that many educated young Ukrainians who were unable to obtain jobs in the cities went to work in the countryside, which resulted in an outstanding cultural and socio-economic development of Ukrainian villages, especially in Galicia.[6] But the other side of the coin was that those who would not go back into the countryside were faced with the alternative of either swelling the ranks of the intellectual proletariat or joining the Nationalist underground. In other words, the official policy of keeping the administrative apparatus in Polish hands facilitated the task of recruiting agents for the Organization of Ukrainian Nationalists (OUN).

Moreover, the government embarked on a policy of agricultural reform by dividing up large estates. In Eastern Galicia and Volhynia, big landholdings were also in Polish hands, and this appeared a good opportunity for colonizing the area with Polish settlers. Thus Polish landowners in the eastern provinces were strongly discouraged from selling their land to Ukrainian peasants, though the economic plight of the latter was very grave. According to the American demographer Kulischer, however, the trend of migration in Poland ran in the opposite direction, from east to west, not vice versa. Polish landlords in those provinces thus attracted only an "insignificant" number of colonists from central and western Poland, but the local Polish minority "received a share out of proportion to their number." [7]

It would appear, therefore, that the Polish colonization policy in the so-called eastern provinces was both economically unsound and politically dangerous; it alienated not only the Ukrainian intelligentsia, of whom there were not overly many, but the bulk of the Western Ukrainian population as well: the peasants.[8] No analysis of the socio-economic basis of the Ukrainian national movement in Galicia has yet been made, but in the opinion of qualified observers, towards the outbreak of World War II more than half of the Galician youths supported the extreme nationalists of the OUN.[9] Most of them seem to have been youths from the villages. There were, of course, more Ukrainians living in the countryside than in the cities, but it also seems plausible that many of them joined the OUN because, outside of the essentially unromantic and hence unattractive educational and cooperative movement, their socio-economic advancement was being seriously impeded by the regime.[10]

On September 17, 1939, Stalin ordered Soviet troops to occupy the eastern provinces of Poland. Within a few weeks so-called People's Committees were formed, a general election held to the "People's Assembly" in Lviv, and a delegation despatched to Moscow to petition for the incorporation of the whole territory into the USSR. This request was duly granted by the USSR Supreme Soviet November 1, 1939; two weeks later the Supreme Soviet of the Ukrainian SSR followed suit.[11]

Though initially at least the Soviet title to Western Ukraine was based on the secret additional protocols to the Molotov-Ribbentrop pact of August 23, 1939, and the supplementary frontier treaty of September 28, 1939,[12] this did not prevent Stalin from claiming the right to retain the annexed territories, energetic Polish protests notwithstanding. He was helped in this by the fact that the German-Soviet demarcation boundary of 1939 followed more or less closely the line which Lord Curzon had proposed as a basis for an armistice in the Polish-Soviet War of 1920 and which had been drawn up earlier, in late 1919, to serve as a possible frontier of an autonomous Eastern Galicia under a League of Nations mandate. In any event, the "Curzon Line" took ethnographic conditions into account and was more than a temporary line for cease-fire.[13] The British, who in 1920 had been skeptical of a possible overextension of the Polish state in the east, in 1941 were the first to doubt the validity of Polish arguments, and by March, 1943, Eden had persuaded President Roosevelt to accept in principle Stalin's claims in regard to former eastern Poland. At Yalta (February 1945) that decision was finally confirmed.[14]

The question may now be asked: Why did Stalin insist upon the annexation of Western Ukraine in 1939 and during the war? There are two official explanations which have been advanced in Molotov's radio address of September 17, 1939: In the chaos resulting from the downfall of Poland, the Soviet government had to take special measures to ensure the country's security "from any eventualities and surprises"; secondly, it could not remain indifferent to the plight of the Ukrainians and Belorussians that were inhabiting that territory.[15] Considerations of defense must have played a great, if not predominant, role in the conclusion of the Ribbentrop-Molotov pact; and it was probably considerations of prestige more than anything else that prevented Stalin from yielding to Polish demands after 1941. But as an astute American student of wartime diplomacy has pointed out, political motives should not be ignored either. Stalin's avowed solicitude for the fate of Western Ukrainians, as broadcast to the world in September, 1944, and reiterated in a private conversation with the Polish statesman Mikolajczyk in 1944, need not have been insincere. In the first place, to leave several millions of Ukrainians in Poland after solemnly reuniting them with their Soviet compatriots might have been not only somewhat awkward but would have created bad blood among the Ukrainian Communists, some of whom were looking forward to resuming their jobs in the relatively prosperous Western Ukraine. Secondly, as the Galicians, with and without German support, had developed a nationalism as fierce as that of the Poles, it might have been more politic to control them oneself rather than to entrust their suppression to the weakened Polish ally.[16] Not in vain did Stalin assure the Polish general Anders, during an exchange on the future frontiers of Poland, that they—the USSR and Poland—would together destroy the Western Ukrainians.[17] Finally, in the perspective of Stalin's toast to the Russian people of May, 1945, the linguistic (Marrist) controversy of 1950, Khrushchev's revelations at the Twentieth Party Congress in February, 1956, and the decisions of the Twenty-Second Party Congress of October, 1961, we may surmise that sometime during

World War II the leaders of the regime had become impatient with the resistance of the non-Russian nations of the USSR against the "final solution of the national problem," that is, total assimilation. It is plausible to argue that the Ukraine, being the most important non-Russian Republic, had to be completely integrated in the Soviet Union before the national problem could be attacked in a decisive way. Western Ukraine had, therefore, to be re-annexed for the sake of combating Ukrainian as well as other non-Russian nationalists.[18]

2. *Soviet Administrative and Land Policies with Sidelights on Soviet Cultural Policy*

One of the first measures of the Soviet government upon reoccupying Western Ukraine was to pressure the Poles living in that area to leave for central and western Poland, and the Ukrainians living west of the new Polish-Soviet frontier to settle in the eastern provinces of the Ukrainian SSR. As a result, as we have already seen, the Polish minority in Galicia and Volhynia has been greatly diminished.[19] Moreover, the remaining Poles are apparently being discriminated against in the provision of cultural services. As of January, 1958, there were only three Polish language schools in the whole of the Ukraine, though in 1955–56 there had been 5,617 schools in the formerly Polish western provinces alone. For comparison it ought to be mentioned that in 1958 there were 155 schools in the Ukraine in which Moldavian was the language of instruction and 100 others in which the subjects were taught in Hungarian.[20]

Soviet cultural policy may be best described as an effort to telescope the two decades of Ukrainization and Russian-tinted regimentation into a few years. Great care was taken to impress the Galicians with the status of Ukrainian culture in the east: the first Ukrainian theatre in Lviv, the T. H. Shevchenko Dramatic Theatre, was decreed to be opened early in October, 1939;[21] Ukrainian was introduced as the language of instruction in the University of Lviv, which was renamed Ivan Franko University; artistic ensembles from Eastern Ukraine would tour Galician cities giving concerts of Ukrainian folk songs.[22]

After Stalin's toast to the health of the Russian people and Zhdanov's call to ideological vigilance, however,[23] Russian theatres began to be established in Western Ukraine, too,[24] and letters from schoolteachers appeared in the press calling for an improvement in the study of Russian.[25] That the Russification of the school system met with popular resistance may be gauged from the fact that one count on which Melnikov was indicted in June, 1953, was that he crowded out the Ukrainian language from higher educational institutions in Western Ukraine.[26]

After the liberal policy following Stalin's death (1955–57) was abandoned in favor of accelerated Russification, Western Ukraine, and in particular its capital, Lviv, were again strongly exposed to assimilationist pressures. Judging by reports of recent tourists, Russian rather than Ukrainian or Polish has become the dominant language in the streets of Lviv.[27] Recently several Western Ukrainian writers and journalists (R. Bratun', M. Romanchenko, Ya. Stetsyuk and T. Myhal') complained in a letter to the editor of Kiev's *Literary Gazette* that many factories and other economic and public institutions, as if deliberately, failed to subscribe to Ukrainian language periodicals and newspapers.[28] Nevertheless, at least since 1953 it is difficult and probably pointless to look for any distinction between the cultural policy of the regime in Western and in Eastern Ukraine.

Much more important has been Soviet policy in staffing the Western administrative apparatus. Already in 1940 a decision was made to industrialize the region.[29] The objective seems to have been to relieve the agrarian overpopulation of that area and thus to win the allegiance of its inhabitants. In 1944, when Soviet troops reoccupied those provinces, the German administrative apparatus were routed and local Ukrainians who had held lower positions in it were regarded as disloyal. Hence, East Ukrainian and Russian administrators and Party leaders were channelled into the newly acquired territories, and with them arrived Russian and Eastern Ukrainian industrial workers to assume the better jobs in the newly set up enterprises, particularly in the city of Lviv itself. There is testimony to the effect that an assignment to Western Ukraine in 1944–46 was regarded as highly desirable because, despite all its poverty, in terms of consumer goods the area compared favorably with the rest of the war-ravished Soviet Union.[30] It is a pity that virtually no figures are available on the number and national composition of the new arrivals, so that a researcher is forced to use indirect means of evaluation,[31] for their impact was considerable.

The problem of developing "local cadres" from the ranks of the "intelligentsia of the western provinces" was discussed at more than one Party meeting since 1944; it figures prominently in a reprimand of the Ukrainian Party organization by the All-Union Central Committee in 1946, and it was utilized against Melnikov in 1953. For instance, the following picture emerges from the extraordinary plenum of the Central Committee of the Communist Party of the Ukraine, which met August 15–17, 1946, to discuss the reprimand from the center.[32]

Apparently for lack of trained local personnel, the cadres division of the Central Committee of Ukraine would assign to so-called "leading posts" in the western provinces (mostly First Secretaryships of District Party Committees or Chairmanships of District Soviet Executive Committees) "comrades" from the eastern regions. In the course of time, the new arrival would surround himself with a circle of equally experienced Party workers from wherever he had come from, and it would be difficult for him to find a common language with fledgling Galician Communists. But it was those latter who presumably enjoyed a better rapport with the masses, and whenever anything went wrong, Moscow ordered Kiev to press for the advancement of "local cadres." [33]

The number of these eastern cadres is not given, but it can be inferred to be comparatively large. For instance, the cited editorial in *Radyans'ka Ukrayina* (August 14, 1946) complains that in Lviv "one can count the number of local comrades who have been advanced to leading posts on one's fingers." [34] Lviv is, however, the unofficial capital of Western Ukraine. Professor John A. Armstrong, using an unpublished Soviet dissertation, has found rather interesting figures on the proportion, in 1946, of West Ukrainian officials of local origin under the *nomenklaturas* (personnel jurisdiction) of the provincial (*oblast*), and city and district committees (*gorkom, raikom*). The table, which we have reproduced

Table III-1

PROPORTION OF WEST UKRAINIAN OFFICIALS OF LOCAL ORIGIN, 1946

Oblast	Percentage of Local in Nomenklatura of Obkom	Percentage of Local in Nomenklatura of Gorkoms and Raikoms
Stanislav (now: Ivano-Frankivska)	23	73
Volhynia	14.8	65
Drogobych * (Drohobych)	16.6	59.5
L'vov (Lviv)	11.5	58.3

* In 1959 the *oblast* of Drohobych was abolished and incorporated into the Lviv province.

Source: John A. Armstrong, *The Soviet Bureaucratic Elite* (New York: Praeger, 1959), p. 121; based on M. D. Men'shov, "Bor'ba kommunisticheskoi partii za sozdanie i vospitanie partiinykh i sovetskikh kadrov v zapadnykh oblastiakh Ukrainskoi S.S.R. v chetvertoi piatiletke (1946–50 gg.)" [The Struggle of the Communist Party for Creating and Training Party and Soviet Cadres in the Western Oblasts of the Ukrainian SSR in the Fourth Five-Year Plan (1946–50)], an unpublished dissertation for obtaining the academic degree of candidate of historical sciences in the Institute for Improving the Qualifications of Teachers of Marxism-Leninism, Kiev State University, 1954, p. 43.—Reproduced with the permission of the publisher.

above, shows that among the more responsible personnel (in the *nomen-klatura* of *obkoms*) the proportion of Galician born officials was very low (11.5 per cent in the more important Lviv province, up to 23 per cent in less important ones). Among the lesser officials (those in the *nomenklatura* of *gorkoms* and *raikoms*), local personnel predominated.

Another editorial in *Radyans'ka Ukrayina,* dated July 30, 1952 (almost six years later), in referring to the May plenum of the Central Committee of the CP (Bolshevik) of the Ukraine, complained that the Party leadership in the provinces of Drohobych, Stanyslaviv, Ternopil, Volhynia, and Rovno advanced only a few local people.[35] As a horrible example it was cited that among the chairmen of the Executive Committees of Town and District Soviets in the Drohobych Province (that is, among the town mayors and similar first rank local administrative officials) there were only six native Galicians, and only nine Galicians served as vice-chairmen of those bodies. To evaluate those figures it should be borne in mind that as of January 1, 1956, there were twenty-five rural districts and seventeen townships in that province.[36]

Nor was the situation in the Lviv Province much better. Writing about a month before Melnikov's ouster, Lazurenko, the Secretary of the Provincial Party Committee, cited in *Pravda Ukrainy* as a good example that two Galicians had been elevated to First Secretaryships in two District Party Committees, and that in the second District the chairman of the Soviet Executive Committee was a local man, too. For contrast, he referred to District Party Secretary Petrusenko, probably a new man from Eastern Ukraine. In his district only three out of eleven kolkhoz chairmen were local people. Similar conditions were said to exist in a number of other districts.[37]

In the light of what we know about Soviet personnel policy, it would have been of the utmost importance to determine the nationality of the cadres that have been assigned to Western Ukraine. By relying on an unpublished Soviet dissertation, Professor John A. Armstrong has been able to present more comprehensive statistics, but they still fall short of the aggregate figures we would have wished to obtain. His most important conclusions are as follows.

Judging by the data for one Western Ukrainian province (Drohobych) [38] and some indirect evidence (establishment of Russian-language secondary schools in Lviv), "a considerable proportion of the influx of personnel from the east was Russian." [39] For instance, in the Drohobych oblast in 1947, 25 per cent of the Party officials were Russians and 71 per cent were Ukrainians; two years later, in 1949, 16 per cent of the Party officials were Russians and 84 per cent Ukrainians.[40] It should be borne in mind that the number of Russians among the Party apparatus was disproportionately high; before World War II, Russians formed but a negligible part of the province's total population, by January, 1959, their share in the entire Lviv province, which had incorporated the Drohobych province, amounted to only 8.6 per cent.[41]

On the other hand, by tracing, wherever possible, the backgrounds of the First Provincial Secretaries in the Western Provinces from 1939 to 1956 Professor Armstrong has established that at least thirteen out of the twenty-six First Secretaries in the formerly Polish provinces had held posts in the East Ukrainian apparatus before being transferred to Western Ukraine.[42] It may be, therefore, not implausible to assume that a considerable number of Russians who had been sent to occupy important posts in Western Ukraine were Russians from Eastern Ukraine, who were likely to have a better understanding of Ukrainian aspirations than new arrivals from, let us say, Moscow or Tula.

A fascinating sidelight on the personnel and resettlement policy of the regime is provided by several reports that recently a number of Central Asians have settled in Western Ukraine, for the first time in the history of that area. The Ukrainian refugee, statistician Solovey, has found among the delegates to the Twentieth Party Congress in 1956 a certain Mamsurov Hadzhi-Umar Dzhiorovich representing the Ivano-Frankivska (Stanyslaviv) oblast. Judging by his name, Mamsurov is clearly a non-Ukrainian of Moslem origin.[43] The present writer was also told on reliable authority that in several private letters from the Western Ukraine that were received in the United States the presence of Central Asians in that area was confirmed. Moreover, some racial intermarriages (between Central Asian men and West Ukrainian girls) have also been reported. Unfortunately, it is impossible even to estimate the numbers involved.*

We are in a somewhat better position as far as the number of Russians is concerned. As we have already commented,[44] the proportion of Russians in the western provinces has significantly increased between the two censuses of 1931 and 1959. Altogether, by 1959 their net influx into formerly Polish territories was about 300,000 persons.[45] A correspondent of the *New York Times* has estimated that at the end of 1957 the Russians in Lviv alone comprised 35 per cent of the total population of some 387,000 (about 135,000).[46]

Nor should it be assumed that in recent years the regime has ceased its resettlement policy, which on balance has resulted in a weakening

* In his article the Soviet scholar V. I. Naulko confirms the presence of Asians in Western Ukraine. He writes that, for example, after the resettlement of skilled Polish workers from the Galician oil fields at Boryslav the jobs were taken over by Russian, and by Tatar and Azerbaydzhani specialists. See ["The Contemporary Ethnic Composition of the Population of the Ukrainian SSR"], *Sovetskaya etnografiya* (Soviet Ethnography), Vol. 1963, No. 5 (September-October), p. 50.

of the Ukrainian element in the Ukraine. According to a radio broad-cast from Lviv that was monitored in Washington in December, 1959, there was started a "planned resettlement of families from the Lviv oblast into the collective and state farms of the Crimean oblast. In Janu-ary, 1960, a similar resettlement to collective and state farms in *Dzham-bul, Karaganda, and Kustanay oblasts of the Kazakh SSR [would]* be-gin." [47] With the emigration of Ukrainians from the Western provinces continuing, there is no reason to assume that the parallel immigration of Russians has been suspended. But let us now turn to a brief sketch of Soviet agricultural policy.

That the Soviet government would not allow Western Ukrainian peas-ants to keep their landholdings was a foregone conclusion. The average living standard of the individual landowners was likely to be higher than that of collective peasants, as was demonstrated in the winter of 1946–47 when *kolkhozniks* from the Eastern Ukraine, Belorussia, and Central Russia came to Galicia in search of food.[48] After emerging victorious from a terrible war, Soviet authorities evidently made no attempt to stop this migration of hungry kolkhoz peasants, unlike in 1939–41, when the collectivization of western farmsteads was started. At that time, Western Ukrainians had been encouraged to go east, but the old Polish-Soviet frontier was still kept intact and persons coming from the east were not allowed to cross it without an official permit.[49] An exception, however, was made for the newly acquired Subcarpathian province, which was sealed off in 1945–46, as had been Galicia and Volhynia six years before.[50]

The collectivization of Western Ukraine did not start in full swing until 1947–48, but within three years, by 1951, it was extended to all farms.[51] The techniques that were used are nothing new to students of Soviet affairs; at first the more prosperous landholders were driven out of existence by heavy taxation, then the villagers were harangued in full assembly, and, at the end, individually "persuaded" behind closed doors until they put their signatures to the statutes of the newly formed kolkhoz. Often the most respectable members of the village community were appointed kolkhoz chairmen against their will, and even priests were used by enrollment in the collective farms to give their parishioners a good example.[52] A special facet of the collectivization drive was that it had to be carried out against the resistance of the Ukrainian under-ground. In the words of the *Outline Economic History of the Ukrainian SSR,* "The collectivization in the western provinces of the Ukrainian SSR was carried out in the face of bitter class struggle with the *kulaks,* with Ukrainian bourgeois nationalists." [53] There is little doubt that many dissatisfied peasants joined the Insurgent Army, but it is equally clear that the setting up of kolkhozes made the problem of supply for the underground much more difficult. Conversely, that task was facilitated for Soviet authorities who, before the collectivization, had been compelled to secretly re-induct demobilized airmen to help agents of the Ministry of Procurements and the NKVD (secret police) to "collect" the harvest from a great number of recalcitrant individual peasants.[54]

3. *The Liquidation of the Greek Catholic Church*

The forcible dissolution of the Greek Catholic (Ukrainian Catholic, or Uniate) church of Western Ukraine * in 1946 was no less severe a blow to the Ukrainian national movement than the collectivization of the countryside. As a very brief sketch will show, the Greek Catholic church in Western Ukraine had become a national church par excellence, and to destroy it meant to destroy some of the leaders of the national movement.†

In 1596 a number of Ukrainian Orthodox Bishops pledged allegiance to the Pope in return for his protection from the extreme measures of Counter Reformation. During the preceding six centuries, since the acceptance of Christianity by Prince Volodymyr the Great, Orthodox traditions had become so intermeshed with the Ukrainian national heritage that conversion to the Latin rite of Catholicism would have entailed an undermining of everything that was dear to an overwhelming majority of the Ukrainians. Moreover, as it was the Poles who furnished the shock-troops of the Counter Reformation in the east, to have accepted *Roman* Catholicism would have resulted in rapid Polonization. Hence the pro-Uniate bishops at Brest persuaded the Holy See to make a com-

---

* A controversy might possibly arise about the proper designation of that church. The most correct term, as far as the protocol of the Vatican is concerned, would be "The Byzantine-Slavic Rite of the Roman Catholic church among Ukrainians," as communicated to the author by Professor Roman Smal-Stocki, of Marquette University. But that is much too cumbersome a term to be used in daily life and political literature. Among the faithful in the Ukraine, that part of the Roman Catholic church was known as the "Greek Catholic" or, occasionally, as the "Uniate Church." (See Rev. Dr. Ivan Hrynioch, "The Destruction of the Ukrainian Catholic Church in the Soviet Union," *Prologue* [New York], Vol. IV, No. 1–2 [Spring-Summer 1960], p. 13n.) I shall, therefore, use those two terms. The term "Ukrainian Catholic church" originated in the West at a more recent date—it has now been adopted by Ukrainian Catholics living in exile.

† In the Eastern Ukraine the regime had already destroyed the Ukrainian Autocephalous Orthodox church before the war—see John S. Reshetar, "Ukrainian Nationalism and the Orthodox Church," *The American Slavic and East European Review*, February, 1951, pp. 38–49. See also the brief account by the late Alexander V. Yurchenko, "The Ukrainian Autocephalic Orthodox Church," in Institute for the Study of the USSR, Munich (Nikolai K. Deker & Andrei Lebed, eds.), *Genocide in the USSR: Studies in Group Destruction* (New York: Scarecrow Press, 1958), pp. 172–177. The role of the Autocephalous Church in Eastern Ukraine between the wars was great; but I have found no evidence of any link between the present Russian controlled Orthodox church in Eastern Ukraine and Ukrainian nationalism—hence I have not mentioned this latter church in this work.

promise: The Ukrainian clergy would subordinate themselves to the Roman hierarchy and would accept Catholic dogma, but they would retain the eastern (Greek) rite and some eastern institutions such as the permission to marry. Hence they were called the *Greek* Catholic or Uniate church. From the Ukrainian point of view the acceptance of papal supremacy was a guarantee against Polonization in the name of the Catholic church. From the viewpoint of the Holy See, the non-insistance upon their adopting all of the externals of the Catholic faith was a very skillful first step in the gradual conversion of the European East. As Pope Urban VIII (1623–44) put it: "Per vos, mei Rutheni, Orientem convertendum spero." (It is through you, my Ruthenians, that I hope to convert the East.) [55]

When Austria occupied Galicia at the end of the eighteenth century, she noticed that virtually the only literate Ukrainians in Galicia were Uniate priests, who were increasingly becoming Polonized through contact with Polish burghers and landowners. Whatever might have been the reasons: Whether it was monarchical solicitude for the pious and thus conservative elements of society, or whether it was the calculated policy of enlightened despotism to keep its stronger subjects down by favoring the weaker (the Ukrainians against the Poles)—in any case, Hapsburg authorities supported the Uniate church in Galicia. This had the unexpected result that when the Ukrainian national movement in Galicia started walking on its own feet (in the late 1830's and 1840's) many of its leaders turned out to be either Uniate priests themselves or their descendants.[56]

In the first half of the twentieth century, the Greek Catholic (Uniate) church was fortunate in being headed by a man of extraordinary vision and stature: Metropolitan Count Andrew Sheptytsky (1865–1944). Count Sheptytsky was the scion of a noble Ukrainian family which had given the Greek Catholic Church several bishops in the seventeenth and eighteenth centuries, but had become Polonized and converted to Roman Catholicism in the nineteenth. One of his brothers served in the Austrian and then in the Polish army, where he attained high rank. Another, Clement, became prior of a Uniate monk order. He himself entered the Greek Catholic church against his father's will, became a novice with the Basilian Fathers, and in 1901 was appointed Metropolitan of the Uniate Church in Galicia. He held that post for more than forty years until his death in November, 1944, after the Soviet reoccupation.[57]

Metropolitan Sheptytsky devoted his full life to one overriding aim: He would realize the hope of Urban VIII and convert the East through his Uniate church. For this purpose he aspired to establish a Ukrainian Catholic patriarchate in Kiev. He went incognito to Eastern Ukraine and Belorussia in 1908, established contacts with Ukrainian, Belorussian, and Russian clergy in Kiev and Moscow. He also initiated annual congresses at which church leaders of various Slavic peoples were invited to discuss the problem of how the Churches could be united. During the Russian occupation of Galicia in World War I, he was arrested and deported into Central Russia where he remained until the outbreak of the Revolution.

Upon his return to Galicia in 1917, Metropolitan Sheptytsky began to strengthen the Eastern elements in the Greek Catholic church against what appear to this writer to have been fundamentally alien Latin influences. If his church was to serve as the missionary of the East it had to sink its roots deeper into Eastern traditions, as far as was compatible with Catholic dogma. Metropolitan Sheptytsky was a fine connoisseur of Ukrainian culture and throughout his reforms one can discern an attempt to blend Catholic faith with ancient Ukrainian institutions. For instance, he revived the monastic order of Studites, modeling their rules of life upon those of the monks in ancient Kievan Pecherska Lavra. In 1936, he issued a new prayerbook, making it obligatory upon the priests and the faithful to abandon a few specifically Catholic features of the liturgy in favor of those practiced in Orthodox Ukraine. It was he who encouraged Greek Catholic priests to celebrate Mass in Ukrainian rather than in Old Church Slavic, which was less well understood.[58]

In line with his grand conception and out of his noble character, Metropolitan Sheptytsky was not afraid to defend the interest of Orthodox Ukrainians, even if it went against the grain of some Catholic authorities. Not only did he protest publicly against the forcible collectivization in Eastern Ukraine,[59] but he raised his voice when the Polish government, with the silent consent of the Vatican, started closing down Orthodox churches in Volhynia, Polessye, and the Kholm Province.[60] According to a Soviet source, he allowed his priests to celebrate commemorative masses in honor of Ukrainian national figures who belonged to the Orthodox church, and toward the end of his life, March 10, 1944, he allegedly went so far as to allow seven Orthodox priests to celebrate a commemorative service for the Orthodox poet Taras Shevchenko in a Greek Catholic church in Lviv.[61]

As result of his courageous pan-Ukrainian policy, Metropolitan Sheptytsky won the deep respect not only of the Greek Catholics in Western Ukraine but of the Orthodox as well. When the Soviets occupied Galicia first in 1939 and then again in 1944, they found themselves confronted by a man whose moral authority could easily match that of a monarch in a Western constitutional state. On the eve of World War II, Sheptytsky's "realm" in Western Ukraine numbered some 4.2 million faithful, 10 bishops, 5 dioceses, 2,950 priests, 520 monastic priests, 1,090 nuns, 540 students of theology, 3,040 parishes, 4,440 churches and chapels,

127 monasteries, 1 theological academy and 5 theological seminaries.[62]

Soviet policy toward the Greek Catholic church during the first occupation of Galicia was seemingly one of militant atheism pure and simple. That is, except in retrospect and upon careful analysis, it does not seem to have been specifically directed against the Greek Catholic church, but against the Church as such. Religious instruction was excluded from the curricula of schools, and priests were not allowed to visit the sick in hospitals. Antireligious meetings were held everywhere and antireligious pamphlets were distributed far and wide, whereas the printing of religious literature was forbidden. Even the mimeographs of church authorities were confiscated so that the Metropolitan's pastoral letters had to be written one by one. The theological seminaries at Lviv, Stanyslaviv,* and Peremyshl were closed; heavy taxes were imposed on all monasteries and on the priests themselves, who were officially addressed as "ministers of the cult" and unofficially looked down upon as useless members of the Communist society. Many priests were driven from their parishes, many were jailed and then executed during the retreat from the Germans.

Metropolitan Sheptytsky vehemently protested against the actions of the Soviet government, and when such protests were of no avail, he ordered his priests to resist. It was made obligatory upon them to give religious instruction and "to teach some pious and intelligent individuals how to administer the Sacrament of Baptism to the newly born in case of lack of priests." [63] Priests living near hospitals were ordered to visit them immediately. Furthermore, they were permitted to bring the Holy Communion to the patients in secret.[64] To counteract official propaganda in schools, he issued an appeal to the school children warning them against the "sin against the Faith," and recommending "above all . . . frequent reception of the Sacraments." Sheptytsky's indomitable spirit of resistance is best shown in his convocation of an Archdiocesan Synod in Lviv in May, 1940. The NKVD (secret police) carefully shaded the assembly and later arrested several of its prominent members. Another challenge to the regime was the public announcement of a contest for Greek Catholic missionaries in February, 1940. (Those missionaries were to go to the Eastern Ukraine.) The first two sentences from the announcement are worth quoting:

A contest has been announced for the parishes of Kiev, Odessa, Vynnytsya, Kharkiv, and Poltava. It is requested that all [candidates] be prepared for any sacrifice which may be necessary or at least useful for the cause of the Union of our separated brethren and the baptized or nonbaptized atheists.[65]

---

* Within the last two years the latter town was renamed Ivano-Frankivsk.

On the other hand, when considered with the benefit of time, it appears that already in 1940–41 the regime made preparations for the destruction of the Greek Catholic church through a union with the Russian Orthodox church. Early in 1940, an Orthodox bishop—Nikolay Yaroshevych—was appointed by the Moscow Patriarchate for Western Ukraine and Western Belorussia, though at that time no Orthodox bishop was active in the whole of predominantly Orthodox Eastern Ukraine. In March, 1941, Panteleymon Rudyk, a former Galician Russophile, was consecrated Orthodox bishop of Lviv, though the population in Galicia was predominantly Greek Catholic.[66] Moreover, Soviet authorities conceived the plan of creating an officially sanctioned Uniate Counter-Metropolitan for Lviv and Halych. The post was offered to an outstanding Greek Catholic priest and theologian, author of religious poems and songs, the editor of the ecclesiastical review *Nyva* (The Field) Rev. Gabriel Kostelnyk, D.D. Rev. Kostelnyk rejected the proposition emphatically. Nevertheless, the NKVD would not give up so easily and often invited him to nightly "conversations." There can be no doubt today that it was only the outbreak of the Soviet-German war that prevented the liquidation of the Greek Catholic church already in 1941–1942.[67]

In order to convey the particular atmosphere of the relations between the Communist government and the Greek Catholic church the following account of the nightly "conversations" between Reverend Kostelnyk and a secret police (NKVD) interrogator may not be inappropriate. It comes from a reliable source (Interview #12) who has met Reverend Kostelnyk afterwards and heard the story from him. The account cannot be supported by library research as yet. But it is worth retelling because it provides an interesting sidelight on the degree of refinement which secret police methods are capable of.

Rev. Kostelnyk had three sons, two of whom stood close to the OUN. After he refused the Soviet offer to replace Metropolitan Sheptytsky, the NKVD, in February, 1940, arrested his favorite son Bohdan, who was then seventeen years old. Quite often, the father was "invited" to come to the NKVD building in Lviv where a colonel of the secret police would try to persuade him to change his mind.

What impressed Dr. Kostelnyk most was that, first of all, the colonel spoke beautiful Ukrainian, and secondly, that he must have had a very solid theological education. The secret police man was, in fact, so accomplished a theologian that the two of them would engage in extremely involved theological disputes, and more than once the colonel would get the better of the argument, though the Reverend had always prided himself on being very erudite (he held a double doctorate in theology and philosophy). He would come home exhausted; his intellectual wrestling matches with the NKVD theologian wore him out, interspersed as they were with standard tricks of interrogation procedure. (He was, for example, forced to sit in a brightly lit room, and whenever he had to concentrate on his thoughts especially hard, his conversation partner would, as if playingly, train the beam of a powerful spotlight on his face.) Above all, Rev. Kostelnyk was racked by fears as to what had been done to his son.

One night, he heard groans and screams from an adjoining room, a heavy fall, then piercing screams again. The colonel obviously seemed annoyed, but he dismissed the whole matter with the remark, "That beastly X.—he used a Russian name—he always beats his prisoners until they are half dead." Then he affably continued with the theological dispute as if nothing had happened. Rev. Kostelnyk tried to concentrate on the intricate problem suggested by his partner, but he could not take his mind off the screaming victim next door.

Suddenly, the door to the next room opened, and he saw a bleeding prisoner stagger out, prodded on by the blank bayonets of the prison guards. As if by a prearranged signal, the lamps in his room went out, except for the spotlight. The colonel turned its powerful beam so that it caught the group and, as if on a stage, he let it follow them until they disappeared through a second door opening into the corridor. The prisoner was Rev. Kostelnyk's son. Almost gently the colonel asked, "Have you no pity for your son, Reverend Father? One word of yours will release him. If not—we know that you have two other sons, and we know who is to blame for their upbringing."

In June, 1941, Kostelnyk remained in Lviv, but his son vanished together with the retreating Soviet armies. His fate is unknown.[68]

Soviet policy during the first months of the second occupation in the fall of 1944 was in remarkable contrast to the blunt atheistic drive of 1939–41. To quote the *Catholic White Book:*

Soldiers and officers attended the religious services; hostile propaganda was imperceptible; perverse literature was prohibited. Even crucifixes were allowed in civil hospitals. But all religious propaganda was persistently prevented from the outset; no more religious books or papers treating on religious subjects were allowed to circulate. In fact all religious publications and diocesan printing offices stopped operating. Religious instruction was permitted in the churches; however, schools were obliged to remain secularized, and abstain from any religious manifestations. Churches were reopened so that religious holidays could be celebrated. On Easter Day, to add to the joy of the population, even the price of liquor was lowered. Seminaries were allowed to exist. Not only priests and students of Theology were exempted from military service and obligatory work, but even the seminarians and ecclesiastical singers, and in some places, the Presidents of Confraternities. The churches paid very moderate taxes. Convents that the German Command had returned to religious communities were allowed to remain as religious property. It seemed that after the concessions made to Christianity by the USSR in 1941–43, and the following years, the Catholic Church could now breathe freely under the Bolshevik regime.[69]

But this picture changed after November, 1944. On the first day of that month old Metropolitan Sheptytsky died. His office was immediately taken over by his "co-adjutor" whom he had designated as his successor several years before: the Right Reverend Joseph Slipy, the Rector of the Greek Catholic Theological Seminary in Lviv. A most elaborate funeral was held for the deceased head of the Uniate church. Among the Ukrainians there circulated rumors that the funeral had been paid for by the State and that it was attended by high Soviet dignitaries, including Khrushchev, who is said to have laid down a wreath on behalf of Stalin. I have not been able to obtain a confirmation of these not very plausible rumors, but their very existence is characteristic of the more liberal Soviet policy at that time. Nevertheless, already in November there were signs of an impending storm: It appears that the Soviets had only waited for the death of the immensely popular Metropolitan before embarking on an all-out persecution of the Greek Catholic church. (Metropolitan Sheptytsky, incidentally, seems to have died from natural causes—at least, no serious allegations of foul play have been made.)

The first sign of a change may be sensed in the cool reception of a Greek Catholic delegation in Moscow. In order to achieve a modus vivendi with the regime the new Metropolitan Slipy had 100,000 rubles collected by the Church and offered them to the Soviet Government for the care of its war wounded. Contrary to their expectations, the Church delegates who brought that sum to Moscow were not received by Stalin himself, but by a few of his lower functionaries. They were told that the Government's attitude toward the Greek Catholic church depended on one thing: the help she would render in the struggle against Ukrainian Nationalist Insurgents. Metropolitan Slipy had several times reminded his faithful of the obligations imposed by the Fifth Commandment and the Golden Rule, but these exhortations of his were not considered sufficient. A Ukrainian exile writer asserts, apparently referring to this delegation, that Soviet authorities also suggested to them to unite with the Russian Orthodox church. Later the two most influential members of the Uniate hierarchy—Metropolitan Slipy and Bishop Gregory Khomyshyn—were said to have been summoned to Kiev and thence to Moscow, where the same proposition was made to them. They declined, as had already done the brother of the late Metropolitan Sheptytsky,

Rev. Clement Sheptytsky, who had been a member of the first delegation to Moscow, together with Rev. Kostelnyk and two other priests.[70]

The Soviet policy quickly gathered momentum. According to the official *Catholic White Book,* already in the fall and winter of 1944 priests
were forced to attend "re-education" conferences, at which the Papacy
and the Catholic church were attacked in general terms.[71] Toward the
end of 1944, there also appeared in the press violent denunciations of
the Catholic church which was accused of not having taken a sufficiently
firm stand against Hitler,[72] and the late Metropolitan Sheptytsky was
now openly called "an agent and spy of Austrian and German militarism
for decades" and attacked for having allowed his residence to become
"a refuge for the *otamans* [chieftains] of various Fascist bands, their staff
headquarters." [73]

A few months later the storm broke loose. On April 6, 1945, wide
publicity was given to an article by a certain Volodymyr Rozovych—
reputedly, a pseudonym of the Western Ukrainian Communist writer
Yaroslav Halan—entitled "With Cross and Knife." [74] The burden of his
argument was that the Greek Catholic church, together with the Vatican,
supported the Nationalist underground movement and could, therefore,
no longer be tolerated. Five days later, the Archbishop's palace in Lviv
was thoroughly searched by the NKVD. Metropolitan Slipy was arrested,
and so were his bishops throughout the area. They were tried behind
closed doors not in Lviv, but in Kiev, and sentenced to exile for alleged
collaboration with the Germans. The efforts of the clergy to elect a Vicar
Capitular (the previous Vicar General had been arrested together with
the Metropolitan) proved of no avail; he was arrested soon afterwards.[75]

After the destruction of the top hierarchy arrived the turn for the
lower: the deans were forbidden to issue any orders, then a decree was
issued outlawing all religious ceremonies except those specifically sanctioned by the government. "Only those priests were allowed to celebrate
who were 'registered' by competent state officials. In every parish, a committee of twenty persons was appointed and charged with the administration of the Church's property." [76] Those committees were being encouraged to opt for a conversion to the Orthodox faith—if that was
accomplished, the Greek Catholic priest was dismissed and an Orthodox
minister appointed in his place.[77]

In April, 1945, there was also published an undated appeal by Alexis,
the Patriarch of Moscow and of all Russia, "To the Pastors and Faithful
of the Greek Catholic Church in Western Ukraine." It invited them to
"break, tear the bonds which [tied them] to the Vatican," and to "hasten
[to] return to [their] Mother's embrace, to the Russian Orthodox
Church." [78] On May 28, 1945, the Establishment of an "Initiative Group
for the Union of the Greek Catholic Church with the Russian Orthodox

Church" was made public. It was headed by Rev. Gabriel Kostelnyk, representing the diocese of Lviv, and included Rev. Dr. Michael Melnyk and Rev. Anthony Pelvetsky as members for the dioceses of Drohobych and Stanyslaviv. On the very same day, the group issued an appeal to the Uniate clergy and petitioned the Ukrainian Soviet Government to legalize its existence.

Their petition, while sprinkled with obsequious references to the "incomparable Stalin" and the "admirable Soviet Army," and containing a bow in the direction of the Ukrainian Party chief Khrushchev, nevertheless strives to present rationally persuasive arguments for the dissolution of the Greek Catholic church (of which more will be said at the end of this chapter), and not slight the difficulties inherent in its rapid dissolution. Two short paragraphs are worth quoting because they bear testimony either to the civil courage of the undersigned, or to their ignorance of Soviet conditions. For instance, the connection of Galicia with the West is acknowledged in the following words:

As it is common knowledge, we shall not make a secret of the fact that our people in Galicia since the fourteenth century have been in touch with the progress of vital conditions and movements in Western Europe, that they have been imbued with the ideas which have grown in West European soil.[79]

A plea for tactful caution in bringing about the union is couched in the following terms:

The psychology of religion is of a very delicate nature—one can, therefore, hardly assume that the transformation of our Uniate Church into the Orthodox could be achieved on the spot. One needs time for that in order to preserve the personal honor of priests [*sic*], in order to persuade and re-educate the clergy, to calm and to prepare the faithful, etc. . . .

On the whole, [the Initiative Group] wants to proceed in such a way that there be as little strife and friction as possible (for victims in such an action will only discredit it) and that no stubborn resistance be provoked.[80]

On June 18, 1945, arrived the reply from a certain Khotchenko, the appropriate official of the Soviet Ukrainian Council of People's Commissars. In terse bureaucratic language he advised the group that it had been sanctioned "as the only administrative organ of the church which [had] the right to fully direct the existing Greek Catholic parishes in the western provinces of the Ukraine." [81] In the same letter the group was ordered to report to the authorities the names of all deans, parish priests, and abbots who refused to submit to the jurisdiction of the group. Thus after the arrest of the canonical hierarchy of the Church, a group of self-appointed or officially selected priests was decreed to be the supreme authority in the Church and ordered to act as an informer on those who refused to recognize it as such. The protest of over three hundred priests addressed to Molotov was ignored.[82]

All through the rest of 1945 and the first two months of 1946, Kostelnyk travelled with an entourage of secret police from one decanate to another in an attempt to persuade the priests to break with the Vatican. The character of his companions was such as to indicate that not only verbal arguments were used.[83] Official sources admit that notwithstanding all efforts at persuasion and intimidation, little progress was made:

The influence of Roman education and discipline was very strong. Rome knew how to break minds, how to intimidate human conscience and to stultify men's ability to conceive independent critical thoughts. . . . It was especially hard for the old to join our action, which is wholly understandable if their age is considered; likewise for the young, unmarried priests who had just left the walls of divinity schools. Among the young priests, besides the influence of Roman education, the emotional element would prevail as against healthy, sober reasoning, and this emotional element would present the whole action in a false light. They did not see and could not comprehend that our present action of reunification with the Orthodox Church of our ancestors was only the beginning of a great action of Christian revival all over the world.[84]

On February 24 and 25, 1946, Rev. Pelvetsky and Rev. Dr. Melnyk were consecrated Orthodox bishops at St. Vladimir's in Kiev. Rev. Kostelnyk could not become a bishop because he was married, but already in April, 1945, the Orthodox priest and theologian Makary, a native of the Kholm province, had been appointed bishop of the most important Galician dioceses of Lviv and Ternopil.[85] On March 8–10, a synod of the Greek Catholic church was staged at St. George's in Lviv, which formally completed the *fait presque accompli*. The result was a foregone conclusion, but the strength of the pro-Orthodox forces was anything but impressive and merits a few lines of comment.

According to the report Bishop Pelvetsky delivered at the synod on behalf of the Initiative Group, in March, 1946, the Group had a membership of 986 priests, 281 stubborn clergymen having refused to join it.[86] But according to a list which Bishop Makary published shortly afterwards, the number of priests who had joined the Orthodox Church was 1,111 out of a total of 2,303.[87] Moreover, Catholic circles point out that some of the names in that list are those of priests already deceased or executed.[88]

The synod was attended by 216 priests, all pro-Orthodox, and 19 representatives of the laity. An unstated number of more prominent priests from the opposite camp had been invited to attend but they did not come.[89] Furthermore, despite the strong probability that the proceedings were controlled by the NKVD, the official record mentions one instance of disagreement: Rev. Lesyuk proposed that the resolutions of the synod should be considered as a declaration of intention rather than as binding decisions and that the synod should constitute only a preparatory stage in the action for reunification. The record says that his motion was over-ruled by a show of hands.[90] Nor does the record anywhere state explicitly that the resolutions were actually signed by all the delegates present; [91] underground reports claim that half of them did not sign them.[92]

The liquidation of the Greek Catholic church outside Galicia—in the Transcarpathian province, in the Ukrainian settled areas in Poland and Slovakia—was undertaken a little later and completed by 1951. The methods were rather similar, with the difference that the youthful bishop of Transcarpathia, the Right Reverend Romzha, was severely wounded in a road accident in October, 1947, and died soon afterwards in a hospital. From a detailed account by an "absolutely trustworthy" person, published in the *White Book,* it appears that the "accident" was engineered and that, moreover, when Bishop Romzha showed signs of recovery he was speeded on to death by a suspicious new arrival on the staff of the hospital where he was lying.[93]

The subsequent fate of the Greek Orthodox church is not difficult to imagine. Under administrative pressure its priests joined the Russian Orthodox church; those who remained recalcitrant, however, were removed from their posts and in many instances deported to Siberian labor camps. Yet it should not be fancied that the Greek Catholic church could simply be decreed out of existence. For some reason best known to the Soviet police, in September, 1952, the editors of *Radyans'ka Ukrayina* were told to reprint on the pages of their newspaper an entire pamphlet by the octogenarian poet Karmans'ky entitled "The Vatican—The Inspirer of Frenzied Obscurantism [*mryakobissya*] and World Reaction." In that pamphlet the Vatican and the Uniate church in Galicia were attacked for collaborating with Hitler and fostering the Ukrainian nationalist movement.[94] Generally speaking, printing space in the central Ukrainian newspaper is too valuable to waste on dead issues. Informed Ukrainian exiles close to Rome also told the author about the existence of an underground Church in Western Ukraine; this was confirmed in a transmission of Radio Vatican.[95]

Moreover, the conversion to Orthodoxy seems to have been rather superficial; in the course of the *détente* after Stalin's death many priests are reported by well-informed sources to have celebrated typically Catholic holidays, apparently without any interference from the authorities.[96] Soviet sources have confirmed this unofficial information. In February, 1957, for example, an antireligious West Ukrainian publicist complained that "his opponents in cassock" and "modernized laymen" were conducting Catholic propaganda and asking Ukrainians "to support the action for the reopening of the treacherous Uniate church." [97] More than two years later, in the summer of 1959, another Communist writer voiced similar complaints:

We must not forget that not all former Uniate priests broke with the Union. Some of them continue their work among the believers, conducting "soul saving" preachings on openly pro-Uniate and anti-Soviet themes, attempting to give lessons of religion to school children, and fabricating all sorts of "miracles" which were allegedly performed by the Late Metropolitan, Andrew Sheptytsky, and so on. . . .[98]

It may be nevertheless interesting to enquire why the Soviets succeeded in enlisting the support of some Greek Catholic priests and in the acceptance of their coup by many others. Analyzing the apostasy from the official Catholic viewpoint, Rev. G. Mojoli has listed six reasons why about half of the Catholic clergy have yielded. They are:

(1) The confusion of minds caused by the imprisonment of the whole Episcopate; (2) The complete disruption of all Catholic organization; (3) The draconian methods of the Soviet police; (4) The powerful support of the Orthodox Church in the campaign of intimidation; (5) The anxiety of the clergy (for the most part married) concerning the fate of their families, who would be destitute if they refused to yield; (6) The tales told to deceive the more ingenuous priests, especially in the country districts.[99]

None the less, this list does not exhaust the motives of the apostates. In the opinion of this author, it fails to explain why the Soviets gained for their purposes so intelligent a person as Rev. Dr. Kostelnyk who, after all, had enjoyed the full confidence of the late Metropolitan Sheptytsky and who had always been regarded as a firm Ukrainian patriot, if not an altogether orthodox Catholic.[100] For all we know, his resistance may have simply been broken down by threats of repression against his family. It has also been asserted by a person who had known him well that his determination to resist might have been impaired by a human frailty of his: great self-assurance and ambition. But it is also possible that the causes for the limited but nevertheless tangible success which Soviet authorities achieved in the reunification action may have lain somewhat deeper. At the risk of idly playing the devil's advocate, the following considerations might be borne in mind.

The establishment of the Uniate church was a compromise solution, which had stood the Ukrainian people in very good stead during the emergence of a Ukrainian national movement in Galicia in the nineteenth century. But like any other compromise it contained within itself strong inner tensions which sooner or later were bound to come to the fore. The most important controversy in the Church centered around the problem of how closely it should be integrated with the Roman

Catholic "Mother Church." Sheptytsky looked toward the East, and he did everything in his power to adapt the institutions of the Greek Catholic Church to those of the Orthodox, arguing that this would make a reunification with the latter that much easier. But not all of his subordinates followed his lead. His great adversary was the Bishop of Stanyslaviv, Khomyshyn; another was the Rector of the Lviv Seminary and later his successor, Rev. Slipy. They were known as ardent "Latinists." They argued among other things for the introduction of celibacy, though, from the national point of view, the advantages of having a married clergy had been clearly proven by history in the nineteenth century. Dr. Kostelnyk, on the other hand, was a prominent member of the "Eastern" wing of the Church. In 1930, on the intervention of higher Church authorities, he was dismissed from his post at the Uniate Theological Seminary of Lviv, where he had taught philosophy, following charges that he was unsure in his faith; and it has been alleged, by a Soviet source, that unless his personal friend, Metropolitan Sheptytsky, had stood up in his defense, he would have been defrocked.[101]

Be that as it may, he is known as the foremost representative of the questioning, somewhat malcontent group in Greek Catholic circles, and as such he was rather popular, especially among the youth—both ordained priests and laymen. A few priests may have joined the movement for similar rational reasons: one delegate to the synod—Rev. Joseph Kyshakevych, of the Lviv diocese—and one representative of the laity—Mr. Pavlo Burbak—have been identified by a well-informed source as belonging to the pro-Orthodox wing in the Uniate church, which goes back at least to the second half of the nineteenth century and had been connected with the Galician Russophile movement.[102]

A second, related motive, which is always stressed in the publications of the pro-Union group, may have been the fact that the Vatican did not always regard the Uniate church as possessing equal rights with the Roman Catholic. Kostelnyk's leading idea in the speeches that have been published—which may have been his sincere conviction—was that the Uniate church had no future because Rome had changed the policy of Urban VIII and forsaken the Uniates in a critical moment in history. As proof he adduced the fact that according to the concordat which had been concluded between the Polish government and the Vatican in 1925, the jurisdiction of the Greek Catholic church under Sheptytsky was restricted to the boundaries of Galicia. Outside of that province a sort of neo-Uniate church (or Church Department, rather) was set up under the jurisdiction of Roman Catholic bishops, and staffed with clergy who were not Ukrainians. If anything, this looked like an attempt to convert the Ukrainian population outside Galicia to the Roman rite of Catholicism, which implied Polonization.[103]

Subsequent developments in the Greek Catholic church in the free world would seem to imply that the Latinist wing has won the upper hand; or that with the approval, if not on the orders of, Rome Sheptytsky's Eastern policy has been reversed. Celibacy of the priests has become obligatory, and the unofficial, but commonly used designation "Greek Catholic church" has been quietly withdrawn in favor of "Ukrainian Catholic church." That in the event of a breakdown of Soviet power the Latinization of the Uniate church would have immense consequences for the development of Ukrainian nationalism, need not be emphasized. Moreover, some relatively recent pronouncements of the Vatican may indicate that the Catholic church would not necessarily support Ukrainian national aims, even if they may serve an extension of Catholicism in the East. The pastoral letter of Pius XII, of July 7, 1952, entitled "To All Peoples of Russia" received much adverse comment in the Ukrainian exile press because it clearly shows the possibility, if not actually the probability that the Vatican would directly appeal to Orthodox Moscow over and against the wishes of a Greek Catholic Lviv.[104]

This would serve to indicate that Kostelnyk's arguments against ties with the Holy See, and, more specifically, his thesis that the Vatican itself had abandoned the Greek Catholic church as a church of the past, have not been completely unfounded. At least this author has become convinced that, barring the emergence of another Metropolitan Sheptytsky, the Greek Catholic church will become so closely integrated with the Roman Catholic church as to forego its historical role of being a national Church of the Western Ukraine with well-founded ambitions to create a Ukrainian Catholic patriarchate in Kiev. This is not to deny that all the leaders of the Greek Catholic church, including its late Metropolitan Sheptytsky, were devout and sincere Catholics who primarily wanted to advance the interests of the universal Catholic church. Nevertheless, in insisting that in her externals, the Church should adapt herself to Ukrainian conditions, they showed a statesman-like insight and at least an indirect, secondary concern for the cultural and political advancement of their fellow-countrymen of Orthodox faith.

Last should be mentioned another hypothesis. Rev. Kostelnyk is assumed to have helped to bring about the reunification because he believed that only an outward submission to the Patriarch of Moscow would save the Church from utter destruction and preserve it until the time when the Ukraine would become free with the help of the West. This hypothesis is partly strengthened by reports that Dr. Kostelnyk maintained his previous connections with the Nationalist underground.[105] When it was suggested to him that he should leave with the Germans in 1944 he is said to have replied that he was an old man, that his wife was very ill, and that they would rather stay behind. But so popular was he among certain sections of the Nationalist youth that he did not lose their confidence even when he helped to engineer the conversion to Russian Orthodoxy. After the operation was completed he is reported to have taken to drink, and being in his cups he would exclaim in company that he had sold himself to the devil.[106] In 1948 he was assassinated with explosive bullets in a street in Lviv; the murderer escaped. Soviet sources blame the act on the Ukrainian underground,[107] but in their conversations with the author several exiles have expressed their conviction that he was killed by the NKVD, who never trusted him completely.[108] A historian may later be able to unearth the relevant facts—this author must restrict himself to retelling a few versions of what happened to the foremost Soviet instrument in the liquidation of the Greek Catholic church in Western Ukraine.

What conclusions can be drawn from our account of Soviet policies in Western Ukraine?

The Soviet Union took full advantage of her international good will in 1944-45 to brush aside the territorial claims of Ukraine's neighbors; furthermore, she resettled a great part of the Polish minority westward and is apparently bent upon denationalizing those Poles who have remained. She has "Ukrainianized" and "de-Ukrainianized" the western provinces within a matter of a few years, and she had been in a hurry to collectivize their peasants by 1951. That the cultural and economic institutions once connected with the Ukrainian national movement (the "Shevchenko Scientific Society," "Prosvita," the union of co-operatives) have either been destroyed or absorbed in Soviet bodies, is to be understood. But the two most important facets of Soviet policy are: the industrialization of the area and the liquidation of the Greek Catholic church.

The industrialization of those provinces, Galicia in particular, has been accompanied by an influx of Russian workers and administrative personnel, which in turn aggravated the problem of finding loyal "local cadres" and must have exerted a stimulus toward further Russification of the educational system, particularly of universities and of cultural life in general (theaters, for example). To what extent Soviet policy has been effective in this particular sector is a rather complex problem, and I shall consider it on an all-Ukrainian scale in Chapters VIII and X, below. Here we may note only two things: As the Ukrainian national movement in Galicia had partly rested on the socio-economic grievances of the overpopulated countryside, industrialization struck at one of the movement's roots. But in the very process of industrialization, new grievances were created which had to be officially recognized in June, 1953.

The liquidation of the Uniate church, almost a political necessity for such a regime if one considers (1) her close links to the Ukrainian national movement, (2) her allegiance to the Holy See, and (3) her relatively small membership (some four million out of Ukraine's thirty odd million of believers), does not seem to have been a great success; for many ex-Uniate priests have become Orthodox only by name. Nevertheless, it would also seem that the regime's success is greater than is often assumed in the West. Under the leadership of Metropolitan Count Sheptytsky the Greek Catholic church had grown into a Ukrainian National Church par excellence. After his death, however, it became apparent that his successors had not quite worked out a Ukrainian counterpart of Gallicanism; nor, to be fair, were they given an opportunity to do so either by the Roman Catholic Poles nor the ostensibly pro-Orthodox Soviet Russians. The Soviet government utilized the inner tensions within the Uniate church so as to evoke the impression that the Church dissolved herself by her own free will; they did not completely succeed in doing so, but they did not fail altogether. To achieve a status in Ukrainian affairs comparable to that which it had enjoyed in the 1920's and 1930's the Ukrainian Catholic church would need another Metropolitan Sheptytsky.

Chapter IV

INTEGRATION OF WESTERN UKRAINE II: ARMED RESISTANCE—THE UKRAINIAN INSURGENT ARMY (UPA) AND THE UNDERGROUND

The armed resistance in Western Ukraine and the Soviet measures to combat it have been singled out in a separate chapter not only for reasons of space. While Soviet policies offer much to complain about and while they often create acute dissatisfaction, there exists a certain border line which most people do not dare to overstep for fear of suffering even greater hardships. But when not one, not ten, but hundreds and thousands are ready to sacrifice not only their daily bread but their very lives for a seemingly abstract idea, we sense that we are in a different realm.

From the Soviet point of view, Ukrainian armed resistance after World War II constituted a problem by itself. True, there had been Ukrainian nationalist guerrillas in the early years of the regime (1920–24), and the Turkic peoples of Central Asia produced the Basmachi movement which lasted through the 1920's. True, Ukrainian resistance after 1945 was mainly limited to the formerly Polish territories: Soviet West Ukraine and certain districts west of the Curzon Line, which were left to the Poles in 1944–45. Some things could be explained by the comparative lack of Soviet indoctrination and the particular background of the area, by abnormal war circumstances, by collaboration with the Germans and later with the Allies. But Soviet authorities knew very well that this did not exhaust the list of possible explanations; for the Ukrainian Insurgent Army (UPA) and the Ukrainian Nationalist [1] underground (OUN) did include bona fide Soviet citizens, products of their own educational system, and it was hardly plausible to designate thousands of men and women as treacherous agents of imperialism, even if this was done for public consumption. The ordinary Soviet citizen must have wondered who those men were to challenge the victors of Stalingrad and Berlin. Why did they take up arms and what for?

1. *General Survey*

Soviet Russian, Polish, and Czechoslovak sources partly confirm the accounts of Ukrainian exile writers in regard to the area in which Ukrainian guerrillas were active.[2] It comprises the western provinces of the Soviet Ukraine, where they fought in considerable numbers at least until the beginning of 1950, and in isolated groups as late as February, 1956; the territories immediately west of the Polish Soviet frontier, the so-called Trans-Curzon Land (1944–48); and mountainous Slovakia, where they appeared temporarily on armed raids and during the Great March to the Austrian-German frontier. Ukrainian exiles also assert that actions of the underground did take place in eastern Ukraine, at least until the middle of 1949; but they appear to have been much less numerous than those in her western provinces.[3]

By far the most detailed and penetrating Communist analysis of the Ukrainian Insurgent Army (*Ukrayins'ka Povstans'ka Armiya,* UPA) is that by a Polish general officer, published in a Polish military review. Brigadier General Blum describes why and how from the end of World War II until March, 1948, some six thousand armed Ukrainians operating near the new Soviet frontier presented "a grave danger to the young People's [that is, Communist—Y.B.] Government" in Poland.[4] He characterizes their activity as follows:

In Poland the UPA detachments . . . resisted the resettlement of Ukrainians into the territory of the Soviet Union, by setting up ambushes for units of the Polish Army which were protecting the moving operations; by destroying the outposts of MO [Citizens' Militia]; by setting fire to the deserted villages; blowing up railroad stations and bridges; by ruining forests, and similar methods.

The UPA bands disorganized the normal course of life in districts which constituted their area of activity. Thus, for example, in 1945 public administration in the province of Rzeszow was completely set at a standstill: cantonal offices were working in only two communities, in some villages authorities were formed four times only to be liquidated each time by the UPA platoons. Only 10–12 per cent of the tax in kind were collected in that province. The bands destroyed and liquidated the majority of the Citizens' Militia outposts.[5]

Using archival material, Blum presents invaluable information on the organizational structure and military effectiveness of the Ukrainian Insurgent Army in that area. The entire land was administered by a Ukrainian underground executive board, with a leader ("*krayovy provid-*

nyk") and deputy leader presiding. They were assisted by an officer ("referent") for military affairs, who commanded the military-like units of UPA, an officer in charge of political organization, an indoctrination officer, the officer of the Security Service, the officer for economic affairs, and the editor of the regional organ of the Organization of Ukrainian Nationalists (OUN). One of the most interesting persons in the group was the economic officer whose job it was to supervise, among other things, the collection of taxes for purposes of the UPA from the Ukrainian population of the area.[6]

As a military formation, the UPA in the Trans-Curzon Zone was divided into 17 platoons. Each platoon was well armed, containing two heavy machine guns and eight to ten light machine guns in addition to automatic small weapons, such as burp guns. Several platoons shared small caliber artillery and mortars. Officers of the Insurgent Army systematically replaced their arms with the latest types available, thus achieving "great fire power." [7] After the end of hostilities in Germany, in June, 1945, three Polish infantry divisions were thrown into the struggle with Ukrainian guerrillas without obtaining any visible success.[8] April 17, 1947, the Polish government decided on a large scale action (code name "Wisła," or "Vistula") to wipe out the UPA in Poland and simultaneously to resettle the remaining Ukrainian peasants from the southeastern frontier zone into the northwestern provinces of Poland. The operation called for the deployment of some five infantry divisions, assisted by one regiment of engineers, a motorized regiment, and a squadron of ten planes. A Deputy Chief of the Polish General Staff, Brigadier General Mossor, was named as chief commanding officer. In that action, which lasted until July 31, 1947, the Ukrainians suffered 1,509 casualties in killed and captured. But it was not until March, 1948, that the Poles could finally claim to have defeated the Ukrainian insurgents, though Polish forces were vastly superior.[9]

Interesting sidelights on that struggle are given by Blum in another publication. On the basis of the data of the Polish General Staff and the Corps of Internal Security he lists the total casualties in the civil war against the anti-Communist underground (both Polish and Ukrainian), in the period from June, 1945, to April, 1948. They are—on the government side:

1,300 soldiers of the regular Polish Army killed;

3,000 soldiers of Internal Security troops killed;

4,500 members of the Polish Workers' [Communist—Y.B.] Party and activists of the Democratic Bloc [fellow-travellers] killed;

3,000 regular Army soldiers and members of Internal Security troops wounded;

    1,200 civilians wounded;
  10,000 farms burnt down;
   8,000 hectares of forests either burnt or cut down;
      40 bridges dynamited,
      20 railroad stations and 6 oil wells ruined.

On the side of the anti-Communist underground (the "bands") the casualties were about 7,500 killed and 2,000 wounded.[10]

It is impossible to tell from these summary figures exactly how many casualties were incurred in the struggle against the *Ukrainian* underground. But from two significant details it would appear that those casualties probably made up the majority of the total losses. For one thing, the struggle against the Ukrainian Insurgent Army lasted longer. The Provincial Security Committees that had been set up by the government to combat the underground were dissolved in western and central provinces on November 12, 1947, whereas in the southeastern provinces they had still their hands full until the middle of 1948. It was the Polish anti-Communist underground that was active in the western and central sections of Poland; the southeastern was the scene of operations against the UPA.[11] Furthermore, Blum gives an interesting distribution of underground members who surrendered during the amnesty period from January until April 21, 1947. Out of the total of 41,427 who gave up the struggle only 145 (0.3 per cent) were members of the UPA.[12]

What was the secret of the long Ukrainian resistance? Gen. Blum cites the topography of the area (wooded and mountainous); treacherous fighting methods, which, for example, cost the life of Gen. K. Swierczewski, Polish Deputy Minister of Defense and hero of the Spanish Civil War, who was killed in an ambush in March, 1947; and excellent intelligence on the part of the Ukrainians.[13] Another high Polish officer, writing in the same journal, Colonel of the General Staff Gerhard, stresses that Polish intelligence was relatively poor because Polish agents failed to obtain the cooperation of the Ukrainian peasants in that area.[14] On the other hand, Gerhard stresses the effectiveness of Ukrainian counter-intelligence, especially when compared to that of Polish anti-Communist guerrillas of the Freedom and Independence (WIN) group. Writes Gerhard:

Thanks to our intelligence agents we had exact information on them [the Polish WIN guerrillas]. [But] that form of intelligence did not give any results as far as the Ukrainian Fascist bands were concerned. . . .[15]

The Banderovists [16] constituted a wholly distinct (special) group in the underground. They were the best organized and their conspiratorial system surpassed that created by the WIN group. For that reason the struggle with UPA was particularly hard.[17]

But as Gerhard and Blum are forced to admit one of the most decisive factors was that the Insurgent Army enjoyed the support of the Ukrainian population. Blum is quite frank on this:

The most conscious section of the Ukrainian population [that is, those who listened to the appeals of Soviet authorities—Y.B.] were resettled to areas of the Soviet Union; *the remaining [peasants] for the most part succumbed to the terror of the UPA bands.* Many reasons were responsible for such a state of affairs. It is a fact that the support an important part of the Ukrainian population furnished the Ukrainian bands *of their own free will,* and in many cases under duress, made the struggle with the bands more difficult.[18]

The Polish government succeeded in defeating the Ukrainian insurgents only when it physically removed their source of support, by resettling Ukrainian peasants from its southeastern border region into formerly German lands in the west and northwest of Poland.

Soviet sources are much more reticent on their government's struggle with the Ukrainian underground, so much so that a well-informed Polish author has had to tactfully indicate to his readers that he was unable to draw a complete picture because of the lack of cooperation on the part of Soviet archival authorities.[19] It need not follow from Blum's and Gerhard's accounts that the UPA was equally strong in Soviet occupied Western Ukraine; from interviews with former members of the underground this writer has gained the impression that the UPA-OUN were indeed not so prominent east of the Polish-Soviet frontier. On the other hand, it is plausible to assume that the superior organization of the Trans-Curzon West Galician insurgents was not solely due to more favorable circumstances, but also reflected the organizational principles of the entire movement; that the East (Soviet) Galician detachments of the insurgents, which were under the command of the top leaders in the movement, would also try their utmost to create and maintain a viable organization adapted to the Soviet milieu. In other words, *mutatis mutandis,* we may infer from the two Polish articles some of the dimensions of the problem which Soviet authors would like to hide; for example, the considerable popular support without which any guerrilla movement is soon doomed to failure. Conceding less important points, Soviet writers admit that the struggle of the Ukrainian underground in the USSR took the form of terroristic acts such as assassinations of prominent personalities of the regime,[20] the burning of collective farm buildings and resistance to collectivization in general.[21] Ukrainian insurgents are also said to have engaged in gathering information for "imperialist intelligence" [22] and in "ideological diversions." [23]

Ukrainian sources add several new features to this composite picture which they obviously paint in somewhat warmer colors. They freely admit that when the Soviet and the Communist Polish governments, after agreeing on the Curzon Line as the new frontier, began to liquidate the remaining national minorities by means of large scale resettlement, Ukrainian insurgents fought a losing battle to retain the Ukrainian hold on the western outskirts of their ethnographic territory. Long before they started combating collectivization in Galicia and Volhynia they would help Ukrainian peasants from behind the Curzon Line to burn their deserted homesteads so as to prevent Polish settlers from taking the area over.[24] Generally speaking, in the period of interregnum that followed the breakdown of effective German rule in Western Ukraine in 1943–44, Ukrainian insurgents would protect their countrymen against hostile actions on the part of both Soviet partisans and the Polish minority.[25]

The Soviet complaint against "ideological diversions" Ukrainian exiles have plausibly interpreted as an official admission of the existence of a secret Ukrainian propaganda apparatus. Primitive printing presses, especially those using letters cut from wood, might have been fairly easily hidden in the forests, especially if they had been set up during the German occupation. The Ukrainian underground claims to have distributed quite a number of periodical news sheets, propaganda leaflets, and brochures, some of which found their way to the West.[26] This allegation appears the more plausible if coupled with another that during the winter months, when footprints were particularly difficult to hide, the guerrillas literally had to go underground in artfully prepared earth fortresses. Willy-nilly, they had to hibernate, and to pass their time away they would engage in ideological and political discussions. If there were intelligent people among them they would try to put their ideas down in writing and to spread them among the population; where there is a will a way can often be found.[27] Moreover, Ukrainian Nationalists had always attached much importance to ideology and propaganda.[28]

From the viewpoint of insurgents the most attractive way of spreading Ukrainian Nationalist ideas was to set out on extended propaganda raids across the borders. Thus, according to underground sources, carefully selected and instructed units of the Insurgent Army made two successful raids into Slovakia in the summers of 1945 and 1946. Similar raids were made into eastern Ukrainian provinces bordering on Volhynia, into Belorussia, Poland (East Prussia in the winter of 1947–48), and Rumania (summer of 1949).[29]

But the most important feature of the insurgents' political activity was to establish psychological rapport with the Soviet-educated Ukrainians from the east. Official sources remain largely silent on this side of their activity, but information from the underground is so plausible that it merits attention. Units of the Insurgent Army are said to have been issued instructions to spare regular soldiers and officers, in contrast to members of the MVD (security police). These instructions were not always followed,[30] but on the whole the relations between the regular Soviet Army and the UPA were less hostile than might have been supposed. Instances are reported of Soviet units "forgetting" some of their arms near villages known as strongholds of the insurgents and of not attacking them in critical moments when they were expected to do so by their—universally detested—"colleagues" from MVD detachments.[31] Whenever the UPA captured a regular soldier of the Red Army they would ask him the usual questions, then give him a good Nationalist propaganda talk and release him, his pockets full of foodstuffs and—propaganda leaflets.[32] It is remarkable that it was not only Ukrainian front line soldiers who at times showed their sympathy toward the Nationalist underground, but Russians as well.

When, in the fall and winter of 1946–47, tens of thousands of peasants came to Galicia from the eastern Ukraine in search of food, the underground handed out leaflets urging the local population to help their fellow countrymen. They did so, distributing bread together with nationalist propaganda.[33] The influx of hungry peasants from the socialistic east did not, as a Soviet writer later candidly pointed out, make collective farms more attractive to the "backward" small peasant proprietors.[34] When by 1951 the collectivization was carried out it made the supply of the underground very difficult indeed, as we have already remarked in a previous chapter.[35]

The Soviet government also decided to break the alliance between the countryside and the Insurgents by sending into the western provinces a large number of Ukrainian school teachers from East Ukraine. Before leaving to assume their new assignments, they had been carefully briefed on the fallacies of "bourgeois nationalist" ideology, and it was hoped that they would instill the proper doubts in the minds of their pupils who would trust them more than they would Russian school teachers. The Insurgents did their best to turn the tables on their enemy, allegedly not without success; in 1949 a great many of these teachers were recalled to the eastern provinces.[36]

Soviet sources remain silent about the number of their opponents. A dependable Ukrainian estimate puts the maximum strength of the resistance movement as such at about 20,000 men on the eve of the Soviet occupation of Galicia (in the fall of 1944). This number includes—it should be noted for later reference—both the members of the open military-like formations of the UPA and secret members of the Nationalist underground (OUN).[37] It represents the peak strength of the movement —as the Soviet authorities established themselves firmly in Western Ukraine, it diminished quite rapidly. Nevertheless, the magnitude of the resistance can be gauged from two facts: A movement of that size must have had the passive and active support of a considerable number of peasants who supplied it with food and intelligence.[38] Secondly, in May, 1947, Poland was forced to conclude an agreement with Czechoslovakia and the USSR to coordinate their actions against the UPA.[39]

Who were those men to challenge the Soviet Union and Poland to an armed struggle? Soviet authors try to ward off this question with standard imprecations against "bourgeois nationalist bandits." [40] On the basis of underground publications, however, and testimonies by participants who escaped to the West, a rough picture can be pieced together which would indicate the roots of the movement.

2. *The Roots of the Ukrainian Insurgent Army*

From the early history of the resistance movement [41] and the biographical data of its leaders that have been posthumously released by underground sources, it appears that from the fall of 1943, its top leadership rested in the hands of the Bandera faction of the Organization of Ukrainian Nationalists (OUN). It appears equally certain that a very considerable proportion of the guerrillas, possibly more than half of them, were members of that organization.[42] In view of the OUN's great contribution to the resistance movement, especially after 1943, it might be worth while to stop for a moment to sketch the history of that organization. (This is not to deny that other groups outside the OUN contributed to the genesis of the Insurgent Army during World War II; but as we are primarily concerned with the postwar years it seems fit to pass over those complex events which are treated elsewhere.) [43]

The Organization of Ukrainian Nationalists evolved by 1929 from the Ukrainian Military Organization (UVO), which in turn had been founded in Galicia in 1920. This is not the place to trace that development in detail,[44] but it is necessary to lay bare some of the roots of that organization in order to understand the emergence of the UPA in the 1940's.

As we have already seen, it was not until 1923 that Polish rule in Galicia was finally recognized by Allied statesmen. So long as the fate of the province had not yet been finally decided, a group of Ukrainian officers, who had participated in the struggle for independence in the Eastern Ukraine as well as in Galicia, resolved to form a quasi-military underground organization. Its aim was to prove both to the outside world and to the Ukrainian Galician community that the Poles were unable to establish effective government in that region. From the material presented by Martynets', himself a prominent member of that organization, it would appear that its members were beset by a sense of guilt for letting themselves be defeated by their enemies. This guilt was to be expiated by acts of personal bravery, by force rather than by peaceful, diplomatic appeals. Said Captain Vasyl Kuchabsky, one of the early ideologists of UVO:

I start from the presupposition: *For a healthy development of the nation, i.e., for ensuring the free development of individuals of whom the nation consists, it is absolutely necessary that there be a national state.*

The Wilsonian theory [of national self-determination] has left unsolved the problem of the ability for establishing a state [*derzhavnoho zhyttya*—note the implicit doubt as far as his fellow countrymen were concerned—Y.B.]. We clarify this problem by regarding self-determination not as an established fact, but as an organically connected process of social development. Thus we return to the ancient truth that *the question of life is a question of force, and force alone.*[45]

Unfortunately, as we have already seen,[46] the policy of the Polish government in the interwar period was scarcely designed to pull away the rug from under extreme Ukrainian nationalists of the brand of Kuchabsky. The Ukrainians in Poland were not regarded as full-fledged Polish citizens, but alternatively as material for future Polonization or *personae non gratae*. To be fair, Polish doubts about the loyalty of some of their Ukrainian minority were also not unfounded; neither the terroristic acts on the part of the UVO, nor its foreign connections could be expected to contribute much to the Polish fund of good will that had been very meager to start with.[47] Nor was the international situation propitious for a *détente* in the tense relations between Warsaw and the Ukrainians: there was that rumbling in revisionist Germany and the West, and the nationalist fervor generated by the Ukrainization policy in the Soviet East. Nor was the scene at home inherently stable: Pilsudski's military *coup d'état* of 1926 revealed tensions within the democratic foundations of the new Polish state.

In this atmosphere the Organization of Ukrainian Nationalists was founded at the Congress in Vienna, in 1929. Its program starts out with a laboriously extensive quasi-Hegelian chapter on Weltanschauung. But however dull and incomprehensible it might have been to the rank and file, it contained a few striking and memorable expressions such as

[The principles on which the new organization rested were:] active idealism, moral autonomy [sic], and individual action (para. 15) . . . pan-Ukrainianhood, non-partisanship, and monocracy (para. 16).[48]

Each member was required to memorize the "Ten Commandments of a Ukrainian Nationalist" (adopted a few months later, in June 1929):

1. You will win a Ukrainian State, or you will perish in the struggle for Her.
2. You will not allow anybody to sully the glory and honour of Your Nation.

5. Avenge the death of the Great Heroes.

7. Do not hesitate to carry out the most dangerous act, if required to do so for the good of the Cause.[49]

These paragraphs have been quoted at length to give an idea of the attraction they must have exercised upon a people that was dissatisfied with its social condition (for example, the exclusion from government jobs) [50] and that was constantly reminded of its political failures by the distinctly nationalist policy of its conquerors.

No complete account has been published so far about the Organization in Poland before 1939. It was certainly popular with the Galician youth, especially from the countryside. Moreover, a Western observer may be struck by the fact that most of its leaders appeared to be college students. But he will find this surprising only if he does not bear in mind that in East European countries universities have in the late nineteenth and the twentieth centuries furnished political revolutionaries. As far as political sophistication was concerned, most of the rank and file tried to make up for the lack of it by unquestioning belief in and an unshakeable devotion to, the Cause, no matter what it might bring: jail, torture, or even execution. While some problems of the OUN in Poland would bear further investigation (for example, the link between the grievances of the Ukrainian countryside and the rural descent of most of the OUN leaders, including Bandera—but not Shukhevych), one thing is certain: basing itself on the cells of the UVO, between 1929 and 1939, the OUN developed a good organizational network, centered in Galicia, but extending also to the other Polish held provinces, with possible feelers into the Soviet Ukraine. The underground OUN, which, incidentally, had inherited some of the foreign connections of UVO and gained a few others, was strong enough to weather the first Soviet occupation (1939–41) without substantial damage,[51] and under the Germans (1941–44) it is said to have infiltrated all of the lower German administrative apparatus in Galicia.[52]

The emergence of the OUN at the head of the Ukrainian resistance movement by the fall of 1943 might appear as the culmination of a logical process of development from a closed totalitarian party to the leaders of a national revolution. In reality, this process illustrates the role of historical contingencies rather than human foresight. An analysis of it is indicated for an understanding of the resistance movement after 1942.[53]

Armed struggle was first undertaken in Volhynia in early 1943, not so much because the province was relatively well suited for this kind of activity (it is rather wooded), but because by the end of 1942, living conditions had become so insupportable that to take up arms seemed the only way of self-defense. In the first place, Rovno in Volhynia was the seat of the notoriously cruel *Reichskommissar* Erich Koch who ordered savage repressions whenever one village did not fulfill its quota of grain deliveries. Secondly, Volhynia being full of forests, Soviet partisans would appear from time to time, blow up a bridge, derail a train, assassinate a German official, and then disappear in the woods leaving the local population to meet the Nazis' wrath. The situation was further complicated by the existence of Polish settlements in Volhynia. The relation between the Poles and the Ukrainian majority was rather tense. According to dependable Ukrainian sources, Soviet partisans would use these Polish settlements as bases for their operations against the Germans, for which Ukrainians often had to foot the bill.[54] The cooperation between Poles and Soviet partisans has been confirmed by later Communist accounts.[55]

By the fall of 1942, the Volhynian Ukrainians had become so exasperated with Soviet provocations and the German misrule of terror that the regional leadership of the OUN advised the establishment of armed groups for self-defense lest in despair the Ukrainian population should join Bolshevik partisans. They did so contrary to an instruction from the top leaders of the OUN from the summer of 1942 against large scale armed struggle.[56] In October, 1942, the supreme leadership had to give in to the pressure of their subordinates, and towards the end of 1942, the first *Nationalist* formations of the Ukrainian Insurgent Army (UPA) were formed in Volhynian forests. They were joined by former Soviet prisoners of war; by local youths who refused to go to Germany as common laborers; and by a battalion of the Ukrainian police that went underground when German authorities ordered it into action against their fellow countrymen.

By the spring of 1943, Volhynia had become a witches' cauldron of guerrilla struggle and German repression. It was Soviet operatives and German flying squads that kept it boiling, but it was the substance of the Ukrainian and Polish nations that was destroyed in the process. This is not the place to ascertain who fired the first shot—the Ukrainians or the Poles—but it is a well attested fact that in the spring of that year the two nationalities started to slaughter each other on a grand scale. German authorities fed fuel to the flames when after the defection of Ukrainian security police they recruited Poles for the job of pacifying the Ukrainian countryside.[57] The emergence and the growth of the Ukrainian Insurgent Army in Volhynia must, therefore, be explained primarily as an effort to protect the local peasants against the provocations of Soviet partisans, the hostility of Polish settlers, and brutal repressions on the part of the Germans.

The immediate cause for the organization of Ukrainian military-like formations in Galicia was similar. Undoubtedly the position of Ukrainian Nationalists in Galicia was much stronger than that in Volhynia, for it was Galicia that had been the foremost base of the OUN in the interwar years. Moreover, German policy in Galicia, which had been annexed to Frank's Polish *General Gouvernement,*[58] differed greatly from that practised in Koch's *Reichskommissariat Ukraine.* While the Gestapo arrested and executed a number of Galician OUN members after the political demonstration of June 30, 1941,[59] it was a far cry from breaking the backbone of that organization. On the contrary, two prominent OUN leaders escaped: Mykola Lebed' ("Ruban")—an outstanding organizer and the chief of the OUN security service, and the foremost military expert of the OUN, Roman Shukhevych. The wave of arrests over, German authorities in Galicia pursued a relatively mild policy. They contented themselves with occupying the top echelons of the administration, leaving Ukrainians in charge of the lower posts.[60] This resulted in the OUN assuming control over a large proportion of the socio-economic life in Galicia. The OUN leadership wished Galicia to remain their chief base of supply—in terms of manpower, arms and foodstuffs—and they did not want to provoke the Germans into repressive measures.[61] But one circumstance sufficed to upset Ukrainian plans: in the spring of 1943, Stalin ordered the partisan leader Kovpak to make an extended raid into Western Ukraine. In the late summer of 1943, his units reached Galicia;[62] and the Ukrainian leaders decided on the spot to organize armed popular resistance to protect the civilian population against Kovpak because they did not trust the effectiveness of German forces. This entailed, however, a partial "deconspiration" of the underground network, and brought forth German reprisals.

The burden of these paragraphs has been to show how much the development of the Ukrainian resistance movement in 1942–1943 hinged on events that did not necessarily correspond to OUN's conception of a "national revolution." These events were responsible for changing the character of the resistance movement and ultimately of the OUN itself.

Before 1942, the movement was in large part identical with the OUN, a tightly knit organization of young conspirators who looked to the Nazi and—less explicitly—to the Communist Party as their models. In 1942–1943, as we have already seen, the resistance movement expanded to include not only OUN members, but also ordinary peasant youths who refused to go to work in Germany or who wanted to defend their native villages. The top leadership remained in the hands of the OUN, but at the intermediate levels served men who did not necessarily share the attitudes of the pre-war OUN. There were many former officers of the Red Army—Soviet educated Ukrainians—who helped out as badly needed military instructors,[63] and there were also several prominent old *émigrés* from the Eastern Ukraine who leaned toward cooperation with the democratic center of the Ukrainian National Republic, the Ukrainian government-in-exile.[64] A Soviet Ukrainian served in a highly responsible post in the propaganda section of the movement.[65] Finally, the insurgents found themselves in great need of doctors and pharmacists to take care of their wounded. There were not many Ukrainians available who possessed the necessary qualifications. Nationalist leaders found a solution: They would save Jewish doctors and pharmacists from Nazi concentration camps on condition that they would serve in UPA underground hospitals. Many of them are said to have performed their extraordinary tasks with exemplary courage and ingenuity.[66]

All this, plus German occupation policy, made nonsense of the Fascist-like ideology of the interwar OUN. Moreover, there was a change of attitude among the OUN members themselves. During the German occupation OUN leaders from the Western Ukraine had come to know intimately the political attitudes of Soviet educated Eastern Ukrainians. This contact served to convince them that several important tenets of the OUN creed, above all, its totalitarian *Fuehrer-Prinzip* and the ill-considered stress upon Ukrainianhood by descent as contrasted to Ukrainian patriotism by conviction, were unacceptable to the bulk of the Ukrainian people.[67]

The changes in the composition of the resistance movement as a whole and the changes in the attitudes of its OUN core in particular were registered in the silent decision to absolve OUN members from memorizing the Decalogue of 1929 and in an equally unstated resolution to find a broader organizational basis for resistance.[68] This latter resolution was implemented when in July, 1944, the Ukrainian Supreme Council of Liberation (*Ukrayins'ka Holovna Vyzvol'na Rada* [UHVR]) was established. The Council was designed to incorporate representatives from all Ukrainian groups committed to the independence of their country and to serve as a political guiding body for the UPA, which had outgrown the stage of being only the military arm of the OUN. The OUN was to subordinate itself to the UHVR as did the UPA command. To emphasize the unity of the Ukrainian resistance movement, Roman Shukhevych was elected Secretary-General of the UHVR under the pseudonym "Roman Lozovsky." Under the pseudonym "Taras Chuprynka" he had assumed chief command over the UPA a year earlier; he was also the head of the Leadership (*Provid*) of the OUN, where he was also known under the name "Tur." It need hardly be stressed that the initiative for creating the UHVR lay with the OUN, which thus tried to win a broader popular basis.[69]

The relationship between the OUN and the newly created UHVR might have formed a most fascinating chapter in the history of the Ukrainian resistance movement, but it cannot be written as yet because complete data on the personal composition of the two organizations have not yet been released for reasons of security. That their leadership interlocked, is clear, but not to what extent. The point that emerges from a personal interview is that the apparatus of the OUN did not merge completely with that of the Insurgent Army which was immediately subordinate to the UHVR and its Secretary-General Shukhevych. There would be a military commander of a UPA district, who in most cases would also be a member of the OUN, and there would be a political district "leader" who would invariably be a member of the Organization, and sometimes the two would work at cross-purposes. Moreover, the OUN district leader had small conspirated military forces of his own, which during military operations were formally subordinated to the UPA district commander.[70] Who used to resolve emerging conflicts: The OUN hierarchy as such, which had a well-developed local network, or the UHVR which, though superior in status, was deficient in local roots, with the exception of the military-like chain of command of the UPA? More likely than not, the stronger man on the spot won out, and his standing in the OUN must have been an important element in his strength.[71]

On the basis of the slim, available evidence the following hypothesis may be advanced: Owing to lack of time and the pressure of the enemy the relationship between the UHVR and the OUN was not completely resolved. The UHVR was created primarily to provide political leadership for the numerous Ukrainian Insurgent Army, which had been recruited from deconspirated OUN members, defectors from the Red Army, and local peasant youths. The OUN furnished many of its cadres to the UPA and the UHVR, but generally speaking it remained somewhat aloof in the underground.[72]

To press this hypothesis a little further, it may be said that there were two tendencies represented in the OUN itself. There were the "military men" (*viys'kovyky*): People who felt more at ease in rationally deploying relatively large groups of trained fighters, who would insist upon maintaining rigorous professional standards, as expressed in military ranks and an orderly chain of command. It was they who insisted that the movement be organized like an army, and it was not merely for creating a favorable impression that the name Ukrainian Insurgent

Army had been chosen.[73] On the other side stood the "conspirators," those who believed that a totalitarian state could be damaged only by a totalitarian organization striking from below; those who gloried in the slogan "each man for himself." They would look upon the whole de-conspirated UPA with suspicion, believing that the UPA soldiers had chosen the fastest route to death, though one decorated with laurels.[74] It would seem to this writer that the parallel existence of the UPA and OUN should be partly explained by the presence of these two tendencies within the OUN. So also can the very emergence of the UPA be explained.

The question may now be raised whether in the conditions of Soviet reality the OUN would not have been better off if it had refused to come into the open within the UPA, all the great temptations notwithstanding. The answer is that at the time when the OUN decided to link itself with the UPA (late 1942–early 1943), the complete re-establishment of Soviet authority could hardly have been foreseen. According to a well-informed source,[75] in the beginning of 1943 responsible Ukrainian Nationalist circles envisaged a repetition of the events of 1918: Germany and Soviet Russia would mutually exhaust themselves in the struggle; German forces would have to retreat, while Soviet troops would be too decimated to pursue them. At the same time, the Western Allies would land on the southern shore of the Ukraine to bring order to a weary country. In that situation, went their reasoning, it was imperative to build up a large professionally trained military force which would be ready to assume effective authority not only over Galicia and Volhynia, but over parts of Eastern Ukraine as well. Once the Germans had started to retreat through Western Ukraine, Ukrainian Insurgents would disarm them and then set up an independent rump state and await a union with the Anglo-American invasion corps to liberate the rest of the country. Special UPA units, designated to take root farther east in the Chernihov province (northeast Ukraine) were already being trained, when the German defense of the Dnieper line broke down unexpectedly in October, 1943, and with it the leading conception of UPA strategists.

In the beginning of 1944, particularly after the "New Stalingrad" at Korsun-Shevchenkivsky, where in a two weeks' battle ten German divisions and one brigade were surrounded and destroyed,[76] it became abundantly clear that Red troops would reoccupy Soviet territory at least as far as the boundaries of September, 1939. But Ukrainian leaders—together with resistance leaders of other nations—did not abandon hope that the Western Allies, especially England, would be more forceful in reasserting their influence in Eastern Europe and that the Soviets, weakened as they were, would not be able to ignore Western demands. Great hopes were placed particularly in Winston Churchill, who was known

as a staunch anti-Communist and the moving spirit behind Allied intervention in the Russian Empire after World War I. In that situation, too,
it appeared imperative that the UPA be built up so as to become a
force on the spot, a factor which would have to be taken into account
in the hostilities that would foreseeably break out as a result of Anglo-
Soviet rivalries in the Middle East and Eastern Europe. In short, so great
was England's historical prestige and so disgraceful had been Soviet defeats in 1941–42 that Ukrainian Nationalist leaders refused to consider a
possible shift in power between Berlin and Moscow, London and Washington.

So much for Ukrainian thinking at a higher level. But even if the
OUN leaders had assessed the situation correctly, it remains doubtful
whether they would have been able to restrict armed resistance. They
had failed to do so in the fall of 1942; and after a year and a half of
fairly successful fighting, in military-like formations, in military uniforms, and under semi-professional officers who were being rapidly
trained by former officers of the Red Army and the Ukrainian National
Republic of 1917–20, the UPA caught the fancy of the local population,
and efforts to curtail its activity had little chance of success. In this connection we have invaluable testimony by an intelligent German who in
his capacity as high official of the German political police in Galicia
could observe the developments at fairly close range. In his memoirs he
describes the situation in the last weeks of 1944 as follows:

That part of the population who regarded themselves as particularly exposed
to Soviet repressions, left the province, going west. Town residents started flow-
ing off into the countryside. He who stayed behind did not entertain any illu-
sions about the future; everyone was conscious of the harsh lot which he would
have to suffer for years to come. But in this attitude there was also a will to
fight, a will to last through the hard times and an admirable, unshakeable faith
in the indestructibility of the biological force of the Ukrainian people, regardless of mass-deportations and the all-embracing brutal regime of terror. *The
will to resist, which could no longer be forced into the mold of the OUN or
UPA ideologies, literally imbued the whole of the population. Organized resistance became a movement of the whole people.*[77]

At every step one could sense a feverish activity: The forests became
filled with volunteers joining the insurgents; new supply depots were
being set up where arms, ammunition, military equipment, and foodstuffs were to be stored; and an underground administrative apparatus
was organized. He continues with the following important comment:

It is true that in UPA circles there existed different views in regard to the future. Some discussed the possibility of a universal popular uprising which would
have had the aim of attracting the population of other territories occupied by

the Red Army for united common action; others favored limited military operations having the object of sapping, weakening the forces of the enemy; still
others envisaged only the possibility of protecting the population, that is the
biological substance of the nation, against enemy terror by means of defensive
actions. A careful German observer noticed that the forms and methods of revolutionary struggle had not yet been agreed upon in details. But everybody noticed the firm decision to link the active spirit of resistance with the vital will
of the people: to fight and to win.[78]

So much for the situation in Galicia. But what about the Eastern
Ukraine? A similar feverish activity on the part of Eastern Ukrainians
could not be reported because it did not exist. One of the reasons why
the Insurgent Army established itself in Western Ukraine, but not in
the eastern provinces was that it could base itself on the well-established
OUN network that had been developed in the formerly Polish territories
in the 1920's and 1930's. But was it not also a question of different attitudes on the part of the citizens of the different areas? The problem is
so important that we shall return to it in the concluding chapter of this
study.

3. Soviet Policy against Ukrainian Armed Resistance, 1944–56

Soviet authorities were fully informed about the activities of the UPA.
They thought of combating it by issuing a long appeal "To the Members of the So-Called UPA and UNRA," dated February 12, 1944, that is,
before Soviet troops entered the main area of resistance. In the proclamation the leaders of the UPA were depicted as heinous collaborators
with the Germans—a half truth, on the black side—and the misguided
rank and file were offered amnesty upon their surrender.[79]

The same theme was elaborated at great length in a relatively important section of Khrushchev's major policy speech of March 1, 1944.[80] In
that part, Khrushchev cited several instances of Ukrainian-German collaboration and then tried to explain away some anti-German actions
on the part of the UPA as German inspired and innocuous. After the
plenary meeting of the Central Committee of the Communist Party
(Bolshevik) of Ukraine, November 22–24, which discussed the resolution
of the Central Committee of the All-Union Party on "Deficiencies in
Political Work among the Population of the Western Provinces of the
Ukrainian SSR," of September 27, 1944, a second appeal was issued "To
the Population of the Western Provinces of the Ukraine." [81] A more
careful analysis of the first appeal and of Khrushchev's speech are indicated because they show rather clearly the extent of Soviet concern over
the Ukrainian underground in 1944.

To inculcate the alleged facts of Ukrainian German collaboration, UPA leaders are always referred to as "Ukraino-German nationalists." Moreover, it is also important how sparing those two sources are in the use of the term "Ukrainian Insurgent Army." With the qualification "so-called UPA" it is found in the first appeal; but never does it occur in Khrushchev's speech in which the insurgents are always identified by the apparently less popular terms "Nationalists," "Banderovists," *Melnykovtsi* [82]—terms which are designed to stress the exclusive nature of the movement and its connections with those partly discredited political organizations. This would seem to indicate that the term "Ukrainian Insurgent Army" had caught the imagination of the people. Furthermore, in prominent places the authors of the two documents emphasize that the struggle of the UPA is senseless because the aspirations of the Ukrainian people have already been achieved under Soviet rule; for example, the third paragraph from the end of the first appeal reads:

As a member of the Great Soviet Union the Ukrainian people has achieved its statehood, liberty, and independence [sic]. Only the Soviet government, the Bolshevik Party and the great Stalin have enabled the Ukrainian people to unite all its lands in a single Soviet Ukrainian State.

Khrushchev, too, tries to depict Ukrainian Nationalists as a "gang of hireable careerists," "Quislings," who "on their knees had begged Hitler to give them at least the appearance of Ukrainian statehood"—the desired implication being that the Soviet government had unquestionably given all that. If anything, this would mean that Nationalist propaganda for Ukrainian independence had a certain measure of success, and probably not only in Western Ukraine, since the speech was delivered to a Kiev audience.

In another section of his speech Khrushchev emphasizes the alleged loyalty of the Ukrainian people toward the Soviet regime. To show the reasoning behind these sentences it is worth while to reproduce some paragraphs in full:

Attacking our Soviet Union, Hitler counted upon creating dissension among our peoples. Through their agents—the Ukraino-German nationalists—German Fascists began to circulate fairy tales that they were coming to liberate the Ukraine, the Ukrainian people.

In the mind of every honest Ukrainian patriot there unwittingly arose the question—from whom are the Germans going to liberate the Ukraine, from whom are they going to liberate free Ukraine, the free Ukrainian people which lives and works in the fraternal family of Soviet peoples? . . .

Having put out the slogan of the liberation of the Ukraine, the Germans counted upon finding dunces among the Ukrainian people who would swallow that hook. But apart from a small band (*kuchki*) of German agents, those hirelings, the Ukraino-German nationalists, nobody went in for the Germans. . . .[83]

In the war, the affection that all peoples of the USSR feel towards our Soviet State, our Soviet Union, has appeared with even greater clarity. The Ukrainian people fighting for the Soviet Union is thus fighting for Soviet Ukraine. Victory in the struggle of the great [sic] Ukrainian people [84] against the occupants for the liberation of its Fatherland, for its national independence and freedom is conceivable only if it remains a member of the Soviet Union. The reason for this is that one can beat the enemy and clear our holy soil from the German conquerors only with the great force that is at the disposal of the Soviet Union, which united all our peoples. . . .

In the Great Fatherland War there has been fully demonstrated the full expedience for each Soviet Republic and its people to be a member of the great Soviet Union.[85]

Twelve years later, in his "de-Stalinization" speech Khrushchev admitted that towards the end of the war Stalin had been so pleased at the loyalty of the Ukrainian people that he considered its wholesale deportation on the model of other "affectionate" peoples of the USSR—the Crimean Tatars, the Chechens, and the Ingushes.[86] Thus, taken at their face value, Khrushchev's references to the unity of Soviet peoples appear as a single brazen lie. But to those who could read between the lines they were an unmistakeably clear expose of the aspirations of the Ukrainian people and the weaknesses of Soviet policy in fulfilling them, coupled with a set of instructions on how to counteract the influence of UPA by means of propaganda.

In line with Khrushchev's directives, the second appeal of December, 1944, is alleged by a generally reliable source to have engaged in ideological polemics with the UPA. It contained the following characteristic sentence:

How can there be an independent Ukraine, when the Ukraine is already free, enjoys the Soviet [form of] government, under which the Ukrainians are the masters of their fate? [87]

On January 6, 1945, a meeting of West Ukrainian school teachers was held in Lviv, which was attended by Khrushchev and Manuilsky. At this meeting Manuilsky delivered an address on "Ukrainian German Nationalists in the Service of Fascist Germany," which does not contribute any new ideas but elaborates the main theme of Khrushchev's previous speech.[88]

Soviet policy in the newly occupied territories, however, resulted at first in a strengthening rather than a diminution of insurgent activity. Upon the arrival of Red troops all the male population, starting with fourteen-fifteen year old youths, were drafted into the Soviet army.[89] Word got around that to enter the Army at this stage was to court death. From two interviews it appears that the new draftees were sent to the front badly trained and very poorly equipped, as if they were to serve merely as cannon fodder.[90] While we should be on guard against elements of ethnocentricity in evaluating general Soviet policies, it is not implausible, as Ukrainian nationalists assert, that one of the purposes of the draft policy in reoccupied Ukraine was to kill a maximum number of Ukrainians with the least amount of suspicion—after all, Stalin's feeling toward them was somewhat less than cordial.[91] Be that as it may, the local population countered this action by hiding in the woods, and many of these asked admission to the UPA.

The unconditional surrender of Germany in May, 1945, served as the occasion for the third appeal to the UPA, dated May 18. This time a final deadline for the amnesty was set—July 20, 1945. This appeal was apparently quite successful. In the first place, most of those who were merely hiding from the Red Army now came out of the woods and surrendered. To the UPA this might have been a blessing in disguise, for it simply could not absorb such a number of people. But with them went a number of old UPA fighters and OUN members who had become disillusioned at the prospect of fighting the conquerors of Germany.[92]

Nevertheless, Shukhevych would not give up. He thought that the halcyon bliss which prevailed among the Allies in May, 1945, would not last long: Anglo-Soviet rivalry would sooner or later erupt in armed hostilities. In his opinion, it was important for Ukrainian Nationalists to be ready for such a contingency, even if they had to wait some fifteen years for it to occur.[93] Starting in 1945, he gradually broke up the UPA into smaller and smaller units that could more easily go underground.[94] Many UPA officers were simply ordered to leave the armed formations and join the underground network of the OUN—much to their chagrin. Some UPA units in the Carpathian mountains which would not obey the reorganization order, had to be disarmed by force. After fighting for years in groups of twenty to one hundred men, the soldiers were afraid to disappear in the underground nameless and unsung, where they would be alone with two or three fellow-conspirators in a large village and would have to shift for themselves. The small-scale open war that was conducted by relatively large UPA units in the Ukrainian inhabited districts west of the Curzon Line and the propaganda raids into neighboring Slovakia and Rumania were greeted as a welcome psychological relief from the strict conspiratorial regime that Soviet authorities had imposed upon the UPA in Western Ukraine.[95] When the Poles, with Soviet help, liquidated Ukrainian settlements in Poland, the Galician underground apparently proved unable to absorb all of its "unemployed" colleagues from the west; those who had managed to keep their identities secret from the regime were urged to go to the eastern Ukraine in the guise of settlers,[96] others were ordered to make their way to the American occupation zones in Germany and Austria, which incidentally served as a tangible demonstration of the existence of the Ukrainian underground movement.

While the position of the UPA and the OUN underground became increasingly difficult after May, 1945, Soviet authorities in West Ukraine could take but little comfort in this fact as they increasingly realized how strong the popular basis of that movement was. The "final deadline" of July 20, 1945, was extended indefinitely in the fourth appeal to the residents of Western Ukrainian provinces signed by Khrushchev (November 5, 1945),[97] and in the subsequent order (of November 15, 1945) by the Ukrainian SSR People's Commissar of Interior Affairs, the Gen. Lieut. of NKVD troops Ryasny. The reason for the extension was given that "some people could not make their escape from the bands." [98] The fifth appeal was issued February (or March) 26, 1946, after the elections to the Supreme Soviet. As cited by the underground author Orlenko, the appeal stressed that "the election results had proved that the toilers of the western provinces followed the lead of the Party of Lenin and Stalin and to a man supported the Soviet government, whereas the traitors and hirelings of the Ukrainian people—the Ukrainian-German nationalists had suffered a complete defeat; that they had never enjoyed the support of the population." [99] Ukrainian sources maintain that, on the contrary, the Galicians largely boycotted the elections—not an implausible allegation of the appeal is read in the light of the exaggerated claims of Khrushchev's speech of March, 1944.

The sixth appeal to surrender is said to have been broadcast over Radio Lviv on Ukrainian Christmas Eve, January 6, 1947.[100] But in the fall of that year Soviet authorities in the Galician countryside still felt as if they were in hostile territory. Says Pirogov, who had been detailed to "collect grain" in the village of Ispass, near Kolomyya:

At night I took every precaution for our safety for we were jittery—more than we had ever been in enemy territory during the war. I put a second man on guard. The bloodhound detailed to us by the MVD was chained in the yard. Some of the men slept fully dressed. The rest kept their guns by their bedside. I was ashamed to look my sergeants in the eyes as I made all these arrangements. We were, after all, within the borders of our own country, in the Soviet Union, in territory only recently liberated from the "oppression of the Polish squires." Still, I was responsible for their safety and must follow all instructions.[101]

Finally, as late as December 30, 1949, we have a well-authenticated report, the Order No. 312 by the Ukrainian Minister of the Interior

Koval'chuk, proclaiming an amnesty to those members of "nationalist bands" who would give themselves up.[102] The order is interesting in one other respect besides its date: It admits that among the "bandits" there were youthful escapees from factory and artisan schools. A later Soviet source adds to this that among them were youths who had been called up to go to work in the Donbas coal mines.[103]

Soviet evidence on the existence of a Nationalist underground after 1949 is quite sparse. On May 19, 1954, Kiev radio announced the execution of "one of the chiefs of the so-called Organization of Ukrainian Nationalists," V. O. Okhrymovych, for espionage on behalf of the United States.[104] He had been "recently" parachuted into the Ukraine from an American plane. As if to stress the importance of the announcement, it was printed in Kiev's *Pravda Ukrainy* on the same day and reprinted in the central newspaper of the Red Army *Krasnaya Zvezda* (Red Star, Moscow) the day following. Okhrymovych had been indeed a leading figure in the OUN and a prominent member of the UHVR. After 1945 he had been in the West on a special mission.[105] His stature in the Nationalist movement and the boast in the official communique that he had revealed the identities of "his accomplices in espionage activities in the Ukraine" may lead one to suspect that alleged espionage was not the main purpose of his mission. As an anonymous correspondent of the *Manchester Guardian* put it:

[This] must be taken to mean that some underground organizations do exist, for espionage in this context is merely a label affixed in order to discredit the nationalists.[106]

Another cryptic piece of evidence is an appeal published in a Volhynian provincial newspaper around February 10, 1956, calling upon "armed anti-Soviet partisan bands" to surrender.[107] Has there been a Ukrainian underground as of February, 1956? That evidence would indicate that there has been one indeed unless it be assumed that the partisan bands near Rovno (Ukraine) were not composed of Ukrainians. But how widely is it spread? Even to make an intelligent guess it would be necessary to briefly review Soviet policies in combating it.

A few Soviet policies have already been shown, such as the issuance of highly publicized appeals, with promises of pardons, and ideological polemics. Other policies, such as blockading off whole strips of territory, torturing suspects during interrogations (sometimes public)—these and similar measures can easily be imagined. So can the brutal terror inflicted upon the population by roving bands of former Soviet partisans, whose purpose was to provoke the UPA to rush to the defense of the innocent people and thus to reveal their own location.[108] Collectivization of individual peasant households as a means of combating insurgent activity has already been mentioned.[109] I would like to draw attention to other methods that are less well known and have often proved more effective.

The foremost objective of the Soviet authorities was to isolate the underground from the support of the local population, and a favorite method of theirs consisted of provoking the insurgents into unpopular actions. One of the most ingenious moves was to enlist almost openly dozens and dozens of villagers for spying on the activities of the Nationalists although the Soviet network of secret agents functioned as usual. The OUN security service very quickly established the identity of the new agents, but they were baffled as to who should be considered an active one and who was only a dud. Before the motive of the Soviet authorities became clear, some rash Nationalists executed many of such agents who later turned out to be innocent people—which did not improve relations between the underground and the village of which the victims had been members. Sometime later the security service issued a secret appeal to those whom they thought to be harmless but impressed agents to declare themselves as such; the result of this was that those who had been recruited as a kind of gun fodder for Soviet intelligence found themselves in the very difficult role of double agents.[110]

How cruel mistakes were sometimes committed by immature OUN personnel may be illustrated by the following true story. The UPA command had issued orders that the peasants west of the Curzon Line were to resist Soviet-Polish efforts to dislodge them from ethnographic Ukrainian territory. One day a Soviet Ukrainian major harangued the assembled villagers to leave for the fertile steppes of southern Ukraine. The peasants stood around him nodding their heads in a fashion of theirs, as if to indicate that they had heard what he was saying. This was noticed by an underground agent who reported it to the district officer of the security service. The latter ordered one of the peasants seized and hanged without much of a court-martial. It turned out that the victim was the brother of a prominent UPA supporter and, secondly, that the higher UPA command had forbidden any actions whatsoever in that particular village because it served them as an important meeting place. When questioned by his superiors why he had the peasant hanged, the security officer replied: "He was nodding his head—that means that he agreed with what the Bolshevik was saying, did he not?" [111]

Another Communist approach was revealed in recruiting the so-called "extermination battalions" (*istrebitel'nye batal'yony*), who were to cooperate with the MVD in fighting the underground. As a rule, those battalions were recruited from local people who knew virtually everybody in a given village. There would be volunteers from Party and Komsomol members, but the bulk of those units would be made up of demobilized Red Army soldiers, sometimes defectors from the underground, and, above all, men who had been simply impressed into that service. Whenever an action was undertaken, MVD soldiers and members of the extermination battalions would alternate in the advancing line. The insurgents had little choice but to shoot people whom they knew to be innocent—and with every such casualty they would alienate his relatives and friends in the village upon which they were dependent for support.[112]

A third method of provocation was the employment by the regime of phony UPA soldiers on a large scale; locally unknown MVD operators would don shabby uniforms and Ukrainian national insignia and mercilessly plunder the population in the name of an independent Ukraine. Whenever a villager in spite of everything showed sympathy with the Ukrainian cause, the proper police authorities would be notified.[113]

But the most widespread technique was probably systematic deportation of families who were suspected of having connections with the underground or of being otherwise potentially disloyal to the regime. According to a top secret instruction by Profatilov, First Party Secretary of the Volhynia Province, which had been issued sometime before March, 1945, the procedure appears to have been as follows.[114] In the area in which Nationalists were operating, a very careful census of the population was taken (by March 5, 1945, in the Volhynia oblast). The census takers were to pay special attention as to whether the families were complete, particularly, as to whether all the males were present. Any absence of a family member had to be justified by show of documents or the testimony of a reliable witness, otherwise a full investigation of the case was ordered. Whenever the suspicion arose that a member of a given family was among the insurgents, the family was given an ultimatum, and, if the suspected member did not show up in the allotted time, his family was deported.[115]

Such a drastic action must have had an effect in restraining the actions of the underground. A non-Ukrainian who, in official capacity, witnessed the execution of such deportation orders on Galician villagers was astounded. Once a whole village were deported to Siberia, but not a single whimper or sob was heard. Never before in his life had he encountered such fortitude, "except in novels." [116] Another observer confirms this but adds that the second and the following waves of deportations were not borne so bravely.[117]

Another weak point of the underground involved the necessity of providing medical care for its wounded. Sometimes, Soviet operatives would spread dangerous contagious diseases, for example, typhoid fever, in villages reported to be UPA supply bases, then flood the black market with poisoned vaccine.[118] There are reports that the commander of the

UPA General Chuprynka-Shukhevych himself suffered from serious rheumatism—apparently contracted while staying in damp earth fortresses during the winter—and had to seek medical help. According to underground sources, he was killed in a skirmish with the MVD in his secret lodgings in a village near Lviv, March 5, 1950. It would appear that he was recovering from his illness when spotted by an agent of the secret police.[119]

In the light of these policies it appears safe to conclude that if there is any underground in the Ukraine today (which is possible) it is greatly restricted in its activities. In the last paragraphs of this chapter we shall raise the question of what might have been the effect of the decade of brave struggle in Western Ukraine. Before attempting to answer it we must ask ourselves again, in greater detail: What did the UPA fight for, what did it want to establish?

4. The Aims and the Results of Armed Resistance (Preliminary Conclusions)

Part of the answer may be found in the writings of "P. Poltava," the head of the political education section of the UPA, and for a time its Vice Commander in Chief. In the underground brochure "The Conception of an Independent Ukraine and the Basic Tendency of Political Development in the Present World," he attempts to disprove the Soviet notion that the Ukrainian national movement is a reactionary one, that it is, so to speak, "out of step with the march of history" and thus doomed to failure.[120] The article is remarkable for its endeavor to defend the nationalist position within the context of thinking that would be familiar to a Marxist. Incidentally, it also provides a conception of the desired social structure of independent Ukraine: In the future Ukraine there must not be any "exploitation of man by man." This is to be ensured by state and cooperative ownership of industry, banking, and commerce, state ownership of soil with the right to collective or individual use, according to the wishes of the population.[121] (Note the desire to meet the socio-economic attitudes of Eastern Ukrainians.) [122]

At a meeting of the OUN leadership in August, 1949, some ideological tenets of the Ukrainian underground that had been approved by the Third Extraordinary Grand Congress of 1943 were revised. The changes are said to have been endorsed by a Conference of OUN in June, 1950. The Conference abandoned the quasisocialist insistence upon state ownership of land which formally prevails in the Soviet Union and came out "for a complete destruction of the kolkhoz serfdom in the Ukraine; against the return of big landlords and capitalists; for a free transfer of land to the *property* of the peasants on the basis of family homesteads [one man 'labor farms']." Furthermore, it added to the old program the point that the Ukrainian underground was "for the freedom of political and public [*hromads'kykh* means communal, etc.] organizations." [123] On the whole, it is remarkable how in the struggle against the pseudo-democratic Soviet regime, the ideology of the OUN has evolved in the direction of liberal democracy, probably under the pressure of Soviet educated Eastern Ukrainians fighting in its ranks.[124] So much for ideology. More to the point is the question what were the immediate objectives of armed resistance against such a world power as the Soviet Union; for it is this question rather than problems of ideology that the UPA fighters must have discussed among themselves.

Poltava tries to give the answer in another pamphlet written in 1949.[125] According to him, the Ukrainian "national Revolution" had won an important bridgehead in the shape of Western Ukraine, where (1) the national consciousness of the population was particularly high and where the people were especially eager to proceed with the establishment of an independent state; (2) where the population was used to revolutionary struggle, and (3) where an elaborate Nationalist organization had been built up over decades.[126] Wrote he, "Under no circumstances have we the right to retreat from this bridgehead." [127] Finally, by way of encouragement he quoted from a few letters to demonstrate the "resonance" of the struggle among Soviet citizens, not only Ukrainians.

When the Korean War broke out, Poltava expressed the unmistakeable hope that it would spread to Europe and thus to the Ukraine. Apart from that, he gives in the later article the clearest exposition of what drove the OUN leaders to continue their struggle against hopeless odds: the firm conviction that Ukrainian statehood can be won only in struggle; and, secondly, a hardly concealed desire for martyrdom—the first commandment of the Nationalist Decalogue. In this connection it is worth remembering that the Greek word "martyr" means a witness—a witness to the vitality of a faith, or of the national idea perhaps. Writes Poltava:

Since in the USSR there are no opportunities for legal peaceful struggle, the Ukrainian nation can fight for its rights, the cause of freedom and justice only by means of armed struggle, by means of insurgent and underground war.[128]

Even more revealing, because more outspoken, are the words of a certain girl "Tetyana," formerly a student at a teachers college in the western outskirts of the Ukraine—the Kholm District—and in 1947–48 a member of the underground and secretary to the UPA officer "Khrin." During the conversation in the earth fortress, one of the soldiers had put the question: "How long shall we keep on fighting?" Khrin gave him the stock answer, "Until our country will be liberated from the last oppressor, etc., etc." Thereupon Tetyana took the word and said:

Friends, more than once have I turned that question over in my mind. There is only one answer to it—that which has been given by our commander. But I have learnt for myself that it is better not to torture oneself with that question. One must organize one's life in such a way that in the fervor of work and struggle time will pass away like a train speeding across the steppe. Behind us will remain the work we have given to the people, [our] success in struggle, the model of our idealism, and, if need be,—of heroic courage. In work man finds oblivion. Thus we shall not have the time to ponder such affairs. This is a sign of weakness, of people who are exhausted or those who are living in servitude. We have got arms, we have a sacred idea and a clear aim before us. We must, therefore, go on without indulging in moods of depression and sadness, without regard to casualties and sacrifices, onward to victory.[129]

Without any doubt there were people who had been caught up in the underground for other than idealistic reasons: as men, they had been defending their homesteads against Soviet partisans, German police, or hostile Polish settlers; as youths, they had been looking for excitement. When Soviet troops reoccupied the area those persons found themselves with arms on their hands, which in many cases meant the alternative between being deported (or perhaps even shot) with their hands bound, and dying a free man in battle—and they chose the latter. But the influence of idealists, those Nationalist martyrs, should not be minimized. They may have become disillusioned about the immediate prospects of their struggle, as Poltava and the girl Tetyana, but it appears that gnawing doubts only served to spur them on to further action.

The problem that arises in this connection is: What influence had armed resistance upon (1) Soviet nationality policy and (2) upon Ukrainian nationalism. This question can only be answered at the end of our study, but the reply can nevertheless be prepared by a survey of possible media of information about their resistance.

To start with official Soviet media, there is no doubt that the struggle of the Nationalists in Western Ukraine was publicized in a number of speeches,[130] lectures,[131] leaflets,[132] appeals, and newspaper articles.[133] It was also presented in at least one theater play,[134] films,[135] and numerous books of fiction.[136] Recent Soviet literature on the Ukrainian underground has been carefully examined in a bibliographical article by Professor Shankowsky.[137] Some of the items cited by Professor Shankowsky were read by the present author.[138] Curiously enough, works of Soviet fiction reveal more about the true nature of the Ukrainian underground than publicistic pamphlets and memoirs by Soviet partisans. Thus the Soviet Ukrainian dramatist Vasyl' Mynko draws a rather persuasive and not unattractive picture of a nationalist infiltrator (handsome; can

speak fluently on Soviet literature and music, i.e., is *kul'tyrny* [cultured]
in the Soviet sense of the word, has a winning approach with women).
Ihor Shevchuk's orders from his organization are to collect military
intelligence for Western powers, but he pretends to be a Ukrainian
patriot. In recruiting a new assistant he says: "My ideal is to see a free
and flourishing Ukraine. This is the reason why a struggle is necessary
in order to stop the humiliation of the Ukrainians and destroy all that
is called communism." [139] Rather eloquent words these from the mouth
of a despicable hireling, a German-Ukrainian nationalist! Another Soviet
writer in attempting to glorify the work of the secret police has in effect
written a good testimonial to the effectiveness of some Ukrainian underground operatives. The hero of his spy thriller, Drobot, chief of a provincial health department in Western Ukraine, member of the Communist Party, former Red Partisan and recipient of a Soviet order in the
end turns out to be none other but an agent of Ukrainian Nationalists
planted into the Soviet administrative apparatus. That such a method
of struggle is not fictitious has been confirmed by a Soviet Ukrainian
scholar in 1959.[140]

One of the great difficulties of analyzing Soviet materials is to determine the precise distribution of these media: Have they been restricted
to Western Ukraine, or have they been freely available in the eastern
provinces, too? This can be stated with assurance only in regard to
articles published in the Kiev press, but it is plausible to assume that
the films made in Moscow and Kiev and the books that were published
in Kiev were given an all-Ukrainian circulation. As a general hypothesis
it may be stated that Soviet accounts of the struggle with the Ukrainian
underground are more voluminous in Western Ukrainian publications
less accessible in Eastern Ukraine and in the West, but that the general
outlines of it were officially communicated to all Ukrainians. For instance, in 1957 and 1959 the regime staged show trials of former underground members who were accused of having committed atrocities during the period of armed resistance. The very fact that the regime has reopened the issue some ten years after the events seems to indicate that
it does not consider it to be dead. In this context it is worth noting that
the trials were referred to in the Kiev press.[141]

Among the unofficial media of communication must be reckoned the
underground press, personal connections, and reports of persons who
came into contact with the underground more or less accidentally.

There is little doubt that the UPA was well known in Western
Ukraine. But did people know about it in the East, except as they learnt
about it in official sources? The underground press must have been effective enough to have elicited a complaint from a correspondent in Kiev's
Radyans'ka Ukrayina against "ideological diversions." [142] But except

in the case where the UPA succeeded in furnishing leaflets to persons going to the Eastern Ukraine (soldiers, settlers) the distribution of underground material in those provinces must have been very restricted for lack of an organizational network as well developed as that in Galicia.

Personal connections have constituted, perhaps, a more effective channel of communications. While the bulk of UPA membership were recruited from Western Ukrainians, there was also a considerable number of Eastern Ukrainians serving in the UPA in various capacities. Most of them would have a family or friends in the East, and however much attention they might devote to conspiratorial secrecy, it is not implausible to assume that news of their activity would seep through. But fear of Soviet repressions would keep that news confined to the smallest circle possible.

This cannot be assumed of the thousands of peasants and workers who were exchanged between Eastern and Western Ukraine. Whereas the disguised OUN members among them might have been reluctant to talk, the Galician peasants who were settled in the southern steppes and the boys and girls drafted into the Donbas mines were likely to be more outspoken.[143] Likewise the Eastern Ukrainian and Russian workers who came to the Western Ukraine in 1946–47 have presumably written to their relatives in the East about the UPA, albeit in guarded language, for armed resistance in the Soviet Union is sensational news and ought to provide a welcome relief from accounts of drab everyday life of ordinary Soviet citizens.

Of greater importance, from the qualitative point of view, were numerous representatives of Eastern Ukrainian and Russian intelligentsia who were temporarily stationed in Western Ukraine in one official capacity or another. To some of them the ground might have been made too hot to stay by the OUN and UPA, but others would remain and spread the news about the resistance movement in carefully written letters to the relatives and friends in the East. Last but not least, Soviet officials who had to travel were made painfully aware of the existence of the underground when the heavily guarded trains would slow down when going through Volhynia and Galicia in 1945–46.[144]

Instead of a period this chapter really ends with a question mark. We have seen that the cadres of the Ukrainian Insurgent Army were largely inherited from the Organization of Ukrainian Nationalists, whose roots go back to the 1920's. The OUN had developed as a response to the attempted Polonization of Galicia. The conspirated members fought for an independent and united Ukraine, but before 1943 their concept of freedom was tainted with strong totalitarian overtones. In that year a series of historical circumstances in Volhynia and Galicia forced the OUN to expand its ranks so as to defend the local population. While this did some damage to the tightly knit conspiratorial organization, it broadened the popular base of an elitist West Ukrainian party by the inclusion of a great many unindoctrinated village youths and a considerable number of Soviet-educated Eastern Ukrainians. A political movement grew into a small army—thus the Ukrainian Insurgent Army (UPA) was born.

Almost against their will, a group of OUN leaders, who wisely sought to strengthen their position by creating a non-partisan Supreme Council of Liberation (UHVR), thus found themselves in 1944 with a considerable military force. Their assumptions as to the strength of Germany and England proved incorrect, and after May, 1945, they were faced with the victorious Soviet armies at their peak strength. Against all odds, in the hope that an armed conflict between the Allies was not far behind, and with the conviction that the West Ukrainian "bridgehead of the National Revolution" must be held under any circumstances, they challenged the Soviet Union and Poland to a duel and stood ground at least until 1950—for five years after the conclusion of the war. This they could do only with the support of the local people, which Soviet authorities tried to cut off by various methods, starting with ideological persuasion and ending with mass deportations and widespread executions. By 1956, at the latest, the Soviet government liquidated the bridgehead physically: armed resistance does no longer exist on any considerable scale. The question is: Have they also liquidated the *psychological* bridgehead? We are not so much concerned with the attitudes of Western Ukrainians, but with the resonance of their struggle in Eastern Ukraine. Has it all been in vain? We have seen that it has been well publicized by official and non-official sources throughout the Ukraine, but what reactions has it produced in the minds of non-participating Eastern Ukrainians? This is the question we shall have to answer at the end of the study.

Chapter V

SOVIET LINGUISTIC POLICY: EXTENT OF THE UKRAINIAN LANGUAGE IN THE UKRAINIAN SOVIET SOCIALIST REPUBLIC

That the struggle for language rights has formed a significant chapter in the history of nationalism is well known.[1] But how significant has it been? Is not language in many cases *the* distinguishing characteristic of nationality, particularly when, as in the case of Ukraine and Russia, historical development has been at times closely interwoven but the two nations have continued to differ in language? What does this imply?

It appears that the problem can be attacked by singling out two basic functions of language which are interrelated, and yet separable for the purpose of sharpening our discussion: language may be said to serve as a means of everyday intercourse and as a bearer of culture. In the words of the authors of the Royal Institute report on nationalism:

The adoption of uniform languages over considerable areas must obviously have exercised a potent influence both in binding the inhabitants of any single area to one another and in differentiating them from the rest of the world. The full importance of this influence lies in the fact that culture follows language, and that the literature written in that language will form one of the proudest parts of the national heritage.[2]

Professor Jacob Ornstein, a professional linguist, has put the issue even more sharply. In his article "Soviet Language Theory and Practice" he wrote:

. . . History shows that when a people is deprived of all else, language remains as a symbol of solidarity—the ultima Thule of ethnic aspirations.[3]

Nevertheless, it would seem that when it comes to the question of why a certain group of men preserve their national identity and why others

141

do not, the role of national culture based on language should not be overestimated. Deutsch has aptly pointed out that the German minority, living in Rumania before World War II, who were socio-economically and culturally less advanced had preserved their sense of national identity, while the prosperous Milwaukee Germans did not, despite the existence of modern facilities of communication, which enabled them to maintain contact with their country of descent. He observes:

The effects even of radio and airplanes look quite different from a quantitative point of view: both adults and children still spend most of their hours living and working, and not in ships, trains, or airplanes, nor in minority school classrooms, nor in listening to broadcasts or reading books in the old language of their parents. *With whom they live, with whom they work,* and with whom as a result of those experiences they will continue to communicate in daily life will be decisive.[4]

In other words, Professor Deutsch, a political scientist, unlike Professor Ornstein appears inclined to see the use of a particular language as a *dependent* variable, changing with, rather than itself determining the direction of, deep socio-economic processes. The cited example is certainly an extreme case contrasting the New with the Old World, but then it shows the more clearly that unless a language is used in daily life, it is liable to die out however magnificent a culture it might bear.

   With these considerations in mind it is proposed to analyze Soviet linguistic policy in two stages. In this chapter I shall discuss it with reference to Ukrainian as a means of everyday intercourse. After a glance at Soviet theoretical pronouncements, I shall try to ascertain how many people in the Ukraine speak the Ukrainian language regularly, and then ask whether the regime has favored its persistence and further extension. The officially induced changes *within* the Ukrainian language itself shall only be touched upon; in other words, I shall concentrate upon the "extra-linguistic" policies of the regime, leaving it up to professional philologists to explore the "intra-linguistic" aspects.[5] In the following chapter Soviet manipulation of Ukrainian cultural symbols will be analyzed, by considering in some detail how the regime has interpreted the life and work of Ukraine's greatest poet, Taras Shevchenko. In a way the following chapter is closely related to the subsequent one on Soviet historiography—for both deal with official interpretation and distortion of symbols of Ukrainian nationhood; viewed from another angle, however, it forms a logical unity with the present linguistic one, since it analyzes Soviet policy toward language as a bearer of culture.

1. *A Glimpse of Soviet Linguistic Theory*

Late in 1913, Lenin wrote very much in the spirit of the *Communist Manifesto:*

Marxism is incompatible with nationalism, even the most "just," "pure," re fined and civilized nationalism. Marxism puts forward in the place of any kind of nationalism an internationalism which is the fusion of all nations in a higher unity, which is growing before our eyes with every mile of railroad, with every international trust, with every workers' association.[6]

He approved of population transfers and intermarriages between members of various nationalities and expressed his hope that as a result of this intermixture the Russian language would spread throughout the Empire. But while in the mind of any politician less astute than Lenin, the acceptance of the internationalist thesis would have led to the unqualified support of Tsarist Russification efforts, Lenin and his followers perceived correctly that such a policy only delayed the widespread voluntary assimilation on the part of the non-Russian intelligentsia. Similarly as the slogan of "the right to self-determination up to the point of secession" had been adopted in order to exorcise the resentment of the non-Russian peoples towards the Russians and thus keep them within the Empire, concessions in the matter of native languages were designed to point out the beauty and usefulness of the Russian language, for as Lenin put it graphically: "We do not want to drive [them] into Paradise with a stick." [7]

Stalin has left us several interesting pronouncements on the future of national languages under "socialism." He fully shared Lenin's internationalist ideal, but as a practicing statesman he had to express it in a more guarded fashion. For instance, in his speech on "The Political Tasks of the University of the Peoples of the East," of May 25, 1925, at the height of the policy of *korenizatsiya,* he attacked Communist "internationalists" for belittling the importance of national languages. Said he:

Some people (Kautsky, for example) talk of the creation of a single universal language and the dying away of all other languages in the period of socialism. I have little faith in this theory of a single, all-embracing language. Experience, in any case, speaks against rather than for such a theory.[8]

At the Sixteenth Party Congress in 1930, Stalin shifted his emphasis somewhat. Replying to a question from the floor, he stated in reference to Kautsky's doctrine:

I still object to this theory. . . . I object to it because the theory of the fusion of all the nations of, say, the USSR into one common *Great Russian* nation with one common *Great Russian* tongue is a national-jingoist, anti-Leninist

theory, which is in contradiction to the basic principle of Leninism that national distinctions cannot disappear in the near future, and that they are bound
to remain for a long time, even after the victory of the proletarian revolution
all over the world. As for the development of national cultures and national
tongues taken in a more distant perspective, I have always maintained, and
continue to maintain, the Leninist view that in the period of the victory of
socialism *all over the world,* when socialism has been consolidated and become
a matter of everyday life, the national languages must inevitably fuse into one
common language, which, of course, will be neither Great Russian nor German,
but something new.[9]

Not so long ago, Stalin attracted attention by his participation in the
Marr controversy in Soviet linguistics. For almost two months a public
discussion was held in *Pravda,* starting May 9, 1950, until July 4 when
Stalin spoke his final word.[10] What prompted the all-powerful dictator
to intervene in a dispute among philologists?

As summarized by an eminent Soviet-educated linguist, who is now
teaching in the United States, the doctrine of the late Academician Marr
(he had died in 1934, long before the controversy broke loose) appears
to have been as follows:

There are no national languages; there are only class languages. Each class has
a language of its own. The old school of philology had established linguistic
families: the Romance, Germanic, Slavic, and Indo-European families of language. That school compared the languages within those families. It considered that each linguistic family had developed from a single original language
(*Ursprache*) which had once been the same for all nations. There are no linguistic families and never have there been any original languages, says Marr.
All languages are interrelated on the basis of class similarities and differenti-
ated according to class differences—every word of every language can, therefore, be compared to every word of any other language. The number of languages has been steadily diminishing, and before long mankind will speak a
single language.[11]

Stalin said in effect that Marr's thesis of class languages was nonsense.
Language, being "the product of a whole number of epochs, in the
course of which it takes shape, is enriched, develops, and is polished," [12]
cannot be regarded as a mere superstructure on the economic base—otherwise we should arrive at the absurd conclusion that the superstructure
is more stable than its basis. What this proposition may entail for Marxist epistemology is not my task to discuss—we shall be concerned only
with its practical application in the realm of policy.

In one of his pronouncements on the Marr controversy Stalin hastened
to point out that as a result of ethnic intermixture no new language
would emerge, but that one of the old languages would come out on top:
It would retain its grammatical system and its basic word stock.[13] Where-

upon one Soviet citizen—a certain Kholopov—asked Stalin how this could be reconciled with his previous statement at the Sixteenth Party Congress. Stalin explained that that was quite easy in terms of Marxist dialectics; before the world-wide victory of socialism, national languages would struggle among themselves for supremacy; whereas after the establishment of socialism on a world-scale, national languages would gradually merge into "zonal languages," and "zonal languages" would then coalesce into a general international language.[14] The implication was very strong that Russian was to become at least one of the "zonal languages."

Marr's theory, as Yury Sherekh-Shevelov has justly observed, was a relic from the period of romantic proletarian internationalism. The surprising thing is not that it was buried with such a great fanfare, the mighty dictator himself delivering the funeral oration, but that it was buried so late. For one of the embarrassing features of the highly original doctrine was that by putting all languages on an equal "class" basis, it challenged the autonomous and pre-eminent position of the Russian language and culture which they had acquired during centuries of imperial rule. Even if they had wanted to, neither Marr nor his pupils have been able to stop the recurrence of linguistic Russification in the name of progress toward a universal proletarian language,* and the amount of energy that has been spent on refuting his doctrine can, to my mind, be explained only in terms of a pedantic disposition that is unusual even among Marxists.[15]

Khrushchev himself has not engaged in any lengthy discussion of the position of the various languages in the Soviet Union. But in the summer of 1958, or little more than two years after Khrushchev's anti-Stalin speech at the Twentieth Party Congress, Stalin's linguistic pronouncements were revived in Gafurov's crucial article on Soviet nationality policy. As we have seen in the introductory chapter of this book (Chapter I), Gafurov's piece signified the recession in Khrushchev's liberal attitude toward the non-Russian peoples, which had reached its high

---

* Already in 1945, V. V. Vinogradov, a leading Russian philologist and genuine opponent of Marr praised "the *national* originality and creative strength" of the Russian language. He wrote:

> The Russian language has carried the sacred light of the thousand-year-old Russian culture through all trials and disasters, through all abysses, and hostile camps. (*Velikiy russkiy yazyk* [The Great Russian Language], Moscow, 1945, pp. 168–69.)

In the same book he candidly admitted that the enforced primacy of Russian "is creating suitable conditions which, in the future, will shorten the path to one single language for all mankind" (p. 113).

For a more thorough analysis of the linguistic problems involved see the valuable article by Jindrich Kucera, "Soviet Nationality Policy: The Linguistic Controversy," *Problems of Communism*, Vol. III, No. 2 (March-April, 1954), pp. 24–29, from which the quotations by Vinogradov have been taken (pp. 25, 29).

point shortly after the Twentieth Party Congress. It is noteworthy that during the progress toward the "inevitable disappearance of national differences and the fusion of nations" under Communism "the emergence of a single language for all the nations" was postulated. The development of such a language was also clearly implied in the section on nationality interrelations in the ambitious new Program of the Communist Party of the Soviet Union, as approved by the Twenty-Second Congress in October, 1961.[16] In his second major speech to the same Congress Khrushchev endorsed that section in the following important words:

The draft Program charts *a course towards the further economic and cultural flowering of Soviet republics and a drawing together of nations still more closely and comprehensively during the full-scale building of communism.*

. . .

The Party will continue to make sure that the languages of the peoples of the U.S.S.R. develop freely and will prevent any restriction, privilege and compulsion in the use of a particular language. Every citizen of the U.S.S.R. enjoys and will continue to enjoy full freedom to choose the language of instruction for his children. Nothing impedes the development of national languages in our country. But their development must tend not to reinforce barriers between peoples but to draw nations closer together.

One cannot help noticing the growing eagerness of non-Russian peoples to master the Russian language, which has become virtually *a second native tongue for the peoples of the U.S.S.R.,* a means of intercourse among them, *a vehicle for bringing each nation and nationality into contact with the cultural achievements of all the peoples of the U.S.S.R., and with world culture. (Applause.) This voluntary study of Russian is a process of positive significance for the development of cooperation among the nations. (Applause.)* [17]

But Khrushchev is likely to be remembered less for his programmatical pronouncements on the linguistic question than for his role in changing the position of the Ukrainian language in the educational system, of which more will be said in a later section.

To sum up: Lenin and Stalin have always approved of linguistic Russification as a preliminary step to the establishment of an ill-defined international language of socialism. By 1950 when Marr's internationalist "class" theory was formally repudiated, Stalin's emphasis had shifted perceptibly from the eschatological goal of world communism to the strategic objective of building and maintaining a powerful Soviet state the "most outstanding nation" of which was the Russian. For our topic the significance of his pronouncements in the Marr controversy is that in the summer of 1950 Stalin put the official seal of approval to a proposition that had been practically enforced ever since the late 1930's: to wit, the predominance of the Russian language as the national language of the Soviet Union. In his speech to the Twenty-Second Party Congress and especially in contemporary policies Khrushchev has shown that he was continuing Lenin's and Stalin's policy of linguistic assimilation, without Lenin's political subtlety and without Stalin's doctrinal obfuscations.

2. *Direct Evidence on the Extent of Ukrainian*

Before analyzing Soviet linguistic policy we must know how many people in the Ukraine actually speak, write, or read Ukrainian in their daily lives. The 1926, 1939, and 1959 censuses included questions about native language, native language being defined in such a way as to roughly suit our purpose.[18] Complete data from the 1926 census are available. The findings of the 1939 census with respect to native language have been withheld, with the exception of a single aggregate figure. The 1959 census figures that have been released so far (end of 1962) are more detailed than those of 1939 but still considerably less revealing than those of 1926.* Outmoded as they may seem, I shall nevertheless use the results of the 1926 census. I shall not do so because I think that one could infer from them the situation after the war, but in order to indicate the nature of the problems involved. Then I shall try to bring those results up to date by adding fresh information that is available.

For 1926 breakdowns are available according to nationality, sex, age, and residence (urban and rural, in different regions).[19] What is their significance for our study? Discrepancies between the numbers of members in the different national groups and the numbers of persons who declare the language of the group to be their native language can be used to point out the direction in which and the rate at which, linguistic assimilation proceeds. Off hand, it would appear to be a transfer to Russian. This impression is confirmed by the following figures. Out of 23.2 million self-declared Ukrainians in the Ukraine in 1926, 21.9 million (or about 94.2 per cent) gave Ukrainian as their native language, whereas 1.3 million, or 5.7 per cent, preferred Russian. Of the 2.7 million declared Russians, however, 2.6 million spoke Russian (98.0 per cent), and only 37,117 (or 1.4 per cent) used Ukrainian as their main instrument of communication ("native language"). A clearer picture of linguistic Russification emerges if we break up the aggregate figures according to the place of residence. Of the 2.5 million Ukrainians living in cities, only 1.9 million (ca. 74.5 per cent) spoke Ukrainian, whereas 0.6 million (24.9

---

* Additional data has been released later in 1963 when this book was in print. It will be briefly considered in footnotes.

per cent) declared Russian to be their native language. But in the countryside, 20.0 million out of 20.7 million Ukrainians (96.5 per cent) gave Ukrainian as their native language, and only 3.2 per cent were linguistically Russified. Among the Russian minority in the Ukrainian countryside we find, on the contrary, that only 2 per cent (24,000 out of 1.3 million) have adopted Ukrainian.[20] We see thus that it was the Ukrainians rather than the Russians who were liable to linguistic assimilation, especially in the cities.[21]

The data of the 1959 census confirm that the general direction of linguistic assimilation is that of more and more persons adopting Russian. Out of a total Republican population of 41.9 million, 38.1 million or ca. 91 per cent gave as their native language the language of the nationality to which they declared they belonged. The linguistically assimilated group amounted to some 3.7 million or 9 per cent. Of that latter group, 3.2 million declared Russian to be their native language and only 490,000 had adopted Ukrainian. If we take up the different nationalities individually we find that about 2.1 million Ukrainians out of a total of 32.2 million, i.e., 6.4 per cent, declared Russian to be their native language, compared to only 131,000, or 1.8 per cent, of 7.1 million self-declared Russians who had adopted Ukrainian. It is also interesting to note that self-declared Jews are strongly assimilated to the Russians, the Poles to the Ukrainians [22] (see also Table V-1).

A comparison of the linguistic data of the 1926 and 1959 censuses is rather hazardous, partly because of a possible change in the definition of "native language," mainly because the 1926 data do *not* cover the Western provinces, and it is extremely difficult to incorporate Polish, Czech and Rumanian figures on languages.[23] Being aware that this pitfall may impair the value of the following comparison, we may nevertheless give its essential results. When the last Soviet census was taken in January, 1959, a somewhat higher percentage of self-declared Ukrainians gave Russian as their "native language" than in December, 1926: 6.4 compared with 5.7 per cent. On the one hand, the proportion of self-declared Ukrainians who in 1959 continued to speak, write, and read Ukrainian is still rather high—93.5 per cent of the total national group. (This may be, incidentally, cited as quantitative proof of the high correlation between national feeling and the use of national language.) On the other hand, the inroads of Russification policies may actually be greater than revealed by the small percentage increase (0.7 per cent) in the number of persons who use Russian. We must not forget that the first population census of 1926 was followed by six to seven years of Ukrainization policy in the East and by the incorporation of more strongly nationalistic West Ukrainian areas during World War II. As

Table V-1

Native Languages of Citizens of the Ukrainian SSR,
Selected Nationalities, Census of January 15, 1959 *

		Out of whom regard as their native language				
	Total	The language of their nationality		Ukrainian		Russian
		Thousands of persons and percentage				
			%		%	%
Total population	41,869	38,136	91.0	490	1.2	3,213	7.7
Out of whom:						
Ukrainians	32,158	30,072	93.5	—	—	2,075	6.4
Russians	7,091	6,959	98.1	131	1.8	—	—
Jews	840	142	16.9	23	2.7	672	80.0
Poles	363	68	18.7	249	68.6	45	12.4
Belorussians	291	107	36.8	27	9.3	157	54.0
Moldavians	242	201	83.1	16	6.6	24	9.9

* A comparative table incorporating the data for 1926 has not been drawn up because of the extreme difficulty in incorporating the figures on Western provinces in 1926. For a brief critical discussion of the linguistic data of the Polish census of 1931, see Volodymyr Kubijovyč (Kubiyovych), *Western Ukraine within Poland, 1920–1939: Ethnic Relationships* (Chicago, Ill.: Ukrainian Research & Information Institute, Inc., 1963), pp. 14ff.

Source: *Narodne hospodarstvo Ukrayins'koyi RSR v 1959 r.* (National Economy of the Ukrainian SSR in 1959, Kiev, 1960), p. 15.

far as the Russians living in the Ukraine are concerned, only a few more of them adopted the Ukrainian language in 1959 than in 1926 (1.8 compared with 1.4 per cent). The proportion is so small as to be almost negligible. The linguistic Russification of the Republic appears to continue, albeit at a relatively slow rate.

Unfortunately no figures have been released that would have permitted us to gauge the different impact of Russification in the cities and the villages of the Ukrainian SSR. For the *USSR as a whole* we know, however, that 88 per cent of self-declared Ukrainians gave Ukrainian as their native language in 1959: 94 per cent of those living in the villages, but only 77 per cent of those living in urban areas.[24] As in the 1920's, cities seem to have remained the strongholds of Russification. Rather significantly, however, in Soviet urban areas *as a whole* the Ukrainian language seems to be gaining as the primary means of communication among Ukrainians (in 1926, only 74.5 per cent of Ukrainians in the cities of the Ukraine habitually spoke Ukrainian).*

A revealing breakdown of the earlier 1926 figures has been made by the Soviet Ukrainian statistician Khomenko who has grouped self-declared Ukrainians with Ukrainian as native language in different categories according to residence, age, and sex, with a special tabulation of four of the then largest cities (Kiev, Kharkov, Dniepropetrovsk, and Odessa).[25] Among the *rural* population, he found significant differences only in the northern wooded region close to the Belorussian frontier (*Polessye*), where only some 84.7 per cent of the declared Ukrainians spoke Ukrainian, compared with the national rural average of ca. 96.5 per cent; likewise in the southern mining region (some 89.8 per cent). More important were regional differences among the *urban* population. In the Polessye, Right Bank (including the present capital Kiev), and Left Bank regions (that is, in areas to the right and the left of the Dnieper), the percentage of self-declared Ukrainians speaking Ukrainian approximated the national urban average of 75.3 per cent for men and 73.7 per cent for women. But in the Donbas, linguistic Russification had progressed rather far: only 54.3 per cent of the men and 53.8 per cent of the women who had given their nationality as Ukrainian actually spoke that language. The explanation for that divergence is to be found in the fact that the mining pits of the Donbas have traditionally attracted many alien workers and personnel who made their language prevail.

Even more interesting is the tabulation for the capitals Kharkov and

* The newly released data from the 1959 census fills in this gap. In the Ukrainian SSR, as distinct from the Soviet Union as a whole, 98.6 per cent of the self-declared Ukrainians living in the countryside listed Ukrainian as their native language, compared with 84.7 per cent of self-declared Ukrainians in the cities. This bears out our observation above that, compared with 1926, self-declared Ukrainians living in the cities and towns of the Soviet Union as a whole are slowly adopting Ukrainian as their primary means of communication. The process appears more strongly pronounced if we consider only the cities in the Ukrainian Republic. See Tsentral'noe statisticheskoe upravlenie pri Sovete Ministrov SSSR (Central Statistical Administration of the USSR Council of Ministers), *Itogi vsesoyznoy perepisi naseleniya 1959 goda: Ukrainskaya SSR* (Results of the All-Union Population Census of 1959—Ukrainian SSR, Moscow, 1963), Table 53, pp. 170–73. A word of caution, however, is in order. If we want to fully evaluate this development we must bear in mind that by 1959, when the census was taken, the city limits had been redefined in such a way as to include within the cities the predominantly Ukrainian neighboring settlements and suburbs. The effect of these boundary changes cannot be precisely assessed without undertaking painstaking city-by-city studies. Cf. V. I. Naulko, "Sovremenny etnicheskiy sostav naseleniya Ukrainskoy SSR (Contemporary Ethnic Composition of the Population of the Ukrainian SSR)," *Sovetskaya etnografiya* (Soviet Ethnography, Moscow), Vol. 1963, No. 5 (September-October), p. 47.

Kiev,[26] commercial Odessa and industrial Dniepropetrovsk. In the four cities combined, only 62.5 per cent of the Ukrainian men and 58.8 per cent of Ukrainian women gave Ukrainian as their native language. Moreover, we notice a sharp divergence in the male group aged 20–24 (70.7 per cent) and 25–29 (65.4 per cent). It seems that this might be explained by the influx into those cities of Ukrainian males from the linguistically less Russified countryside, who were seeking work. Of greatest importance would have been to follow their speaking habits through the two next censuses (1939 and 1959) so as to ascertain whether that particular age group had maintained its Ukrainian language or succumbed to Russification. Unfortunately, no comparable figures have been released later. Another striking thing in the 1926 data is that Ukrainian women living in those four cities were more strongly Russified than Ukrainian men. For all age groups, the difference amounts to only some 3.5 percentage points, but for the ages 20–24 and 25–29 it is very considerable. In the first group, only 58.8 per cent Ukrainian women spoke Ukrainian, compared with 70.7 per cent men, in the latter 56.5 per cent women, compared with 65.4 per cent men. The inference from these figures might be twofold: Either fewer Ukrainian women immigrated to those cities than men, or if this is not the case, female immigrants lost their Ukrainian language faster, probably upon marrying foreigners.[27,*]

On the extent of the Ukrainian language on the eve of the war, there is only one figure: According to "the final results of the 1939 census" (that is, results that had been adjusted to include the annexed territories, probably through 1954), 32,828,500 persons in the Ukrainian SSR spoke Ukrainian. As we do not know the exact number of Ukrainians it refers to, this figure cannot be used for measuring linguistic Russification without complicated calculations which are likely to impair the accuracy of the results.[28]

All these figures raise the interesting problem: Who were those people who in 1926 declared themselves to be Ukrainians but did not give Ukrainian as their native language? Some light on this is shed by the responses to the Harvard Nationality Questionnaire.[29]

Under the Harvard Project on the Soviet Social System, 511 Ukrainians who had left the Ukraine during or after World War II filled out a questionnaire on the nationality problem in the USSR. Fifty-two of the respondents turned out to be Western Ukrainians who had not had long experience of Soviet rule; they were, therefore, eliminated from the sample. An error of 1 has crept into some tabulations, which has reduced

* See, however, Note V-2, in the Appendix: "New Data from the 1959 Population Census on Ukrainian as a Means of Primary Communication in the Cities and in the Countryside and in Different Provinces of the Ukrainian SSR."

our sample to 458 Eastern Ukrainians without materially affecting the results, provided only large numbers are considered. It should be emphasized at the outset that this sample is not a representative cross-section of the population. In the first place, it also includes those Ukrainians who lived most of the time outside the Ukraine in other Soviet Republics (32 cases, or 6.8 per cent of the total sample). It may be assumed that many of them, perhaps all, would have been excluded from the census results which refer to the Ukrainian SSR only. In the second place, as many as 60.5 per cent of the respondents (277 in number) either lived in the cities most of the time or moved from the countryside into the cities, which gives the sample a strong urban bias (according to the census of 1939, apparently adjusted to include the western provinces, only 34 per cent of *all* citizens of the Ukrainian SSR lived in the cities—see *Narodnoe khozaystvo SSSR v 1960 godu* [National Economy of the USSR in 1960 (Moscow, 1961)], p. 10; the percentage of Ukrainians living in the cities of the Republic was 36.6 in *1959*—see Table II-22, above). Moreover, it would have been very important to learn precisely through which channels the respondents had been approached, for the contacts of a respondent with a Ukrainian "separatist" or a Russophile *émigré* organization are indicative of his political views and probably also of his linguistic habits. While these remarks would indicate that the questionnaire data (see Table V-2) should be approached with caution, the fact remains that they are the best unofficial material available on the extent of Ukrainian spoken by Soviet Ukrainians around 1941.

The striking thing about this data is that though all of the respondents were Ukrainians by definition of the Harvard team and only three came from families without a Ukrainian parent, not more than 91.9 per cent gave Ukrainian as their native language, and only 76.4 per cent spoke it at home. The latter figure might have been increased by up to 6.8 per cent if we consider that had those 32 respondents not been exposed to a particularly heavy Russification outside the Ukraine, they might have continued to speak Ukrainian. Another striking thing is that the number of bilingual persons virtually always exceeds by a substantial margin the number of those who speak only Russian—a feature which makes comparisons with Khomenko's 1926 data particularly difficult. The concept of "language spoken at home" may also be closer to the Soviet 1926 definition of "native language" than that of "native language" as used in the Harvard questionnaire. Moreover, the general sample is too urban to be representative of the Ukraine as a whole.

The relatively low number of rural inhabitants who spoke Ukrainian as compared with the 1926 figure may be interpreted as a result of 11 respondents' living most of their time outside the Republic; the figure of urban dwellers is particularly hard to interpret because of the large

Table V-2

HARVARD REFUGEE QUESTIONNAIRE DATA ON THE EXTENT
OF UKRAINIAN SPOKEN BY UKRAINIANS *

Total sample N	Breakdown	Ukrainian		Russian		Ukrainian and Russian	
		N	%	N	%	N	%
458	RESPONDENTS:						
	Native language	421	91.9	9	2.0	19	4.1
	Language spoken at home	350	76.4	32	7.0	64	14.0
	Desired language for children	357	77.9	27	5.9	46	10.0
32	persons lived most of the time outside the Ukraine, which gives a discount factor for Russification of 6.8 per cent maximum.						
169	RURAL DWELLERS:						
	Native language	161	95.3	3	1.8	1	0.6
	Language spoken at home	149	88.2	4	2.4	12	7.1
	Desired language for children	149	88.2	4	2.4	3	1.8
11	villagers lived most of the time outside the Ukraine, which gives a discount factor for Russification of 6.5 per cent maximum.						
157	URBAN DWELLERS:						
	Native language	137	87.3	11	7.0	5	3.2
	Language spoken at home	101	64.3	19	12.1	34	21.8
	Desired language for children	107	68.1	14	8.9	28	17.8
9	urban dwellers lived most of the time outside the Ukraine, maximum discount—6.2%						
120	PERSONS MOVED FROM VILLAGE TO CITY:						
	Native language	111	92.5	4	3.3	3	2.5
	Language spoken at home	94	78.3	8	6.7	14	11.7
	Desired language for children	92	76.6	8	6.7	15	12.5
	Maximum discount factor—9.2 per cent (11 cases).						
11	PERSONS MOVED FROM CITY TO VILLAGE—NOT ANALYZED (NUMBER TOO SMALL)						

Table V-2 (Continued)

HARVARD REFUGEE QUESTIONNAIRE DATA ON THE EXTENT
OF UKRAINIAN SPOKEN BY UKRAINIANS *

Total sample N	Breakdown	Ukrainian		Russian		Ukrainian and Russian	
		N	%	N	%	N	%
120	COLLECTIVE FARMERS:						
	Native language	113	94.2	3	2.5	1	0.8
	Language spoken at home	107	89.2	3	2.5	7	5.8
	Desired language for children	105	87.5	1	0.8	5	4.2

Maximum discount for Russification outside the Ukraine—6.5 per cent.

Total sample N	Breakdown	N	%	N	%	N	%
89	SEMI-SKILLED WORKERS:						
	Native language	81	91.0	2	2.2	4	4.5
	Language spoken at home	65	73.0	7	7.9	17	19.1
	Desired language for children	69	77.5	5	5.6	11	12.4

Maximum discount factor—2.4 per cent.

Total sample N	Breakdown	N	%	N	%	N	%
398	BORN INTO FAMILIES IN WHICH BOTH PARENTS WERE UKRAINIANS:						
	Native language	383	96.2	3	0.8	6	1.5
	Language spoken at home	332	83.4	18	4.5	43	10.8
	Desired language for children	329	82.7	19	4.8	33	8.3
57	BORN INTO FAMILIES IN WHICH ONLY ONE PARENT WAS UKRAINIAN:						
	Native language	34	59.7	5	8.8	13	22.8
	Language spoken at home	15	26.3	12	21.1	20	35.1
	Desired language for children	25	43.8	8	14.0	12	21.1

* The absolute numbers and the percentages may not add up to the totals, mainly because not all of the respondents have answered all questions.

Source: Harvard Project on the Soviet Social System, Nationality Questionnaire.

number of bilingual persons: Had it been possible to count all the latter toward the Ukrainian column, it might be taken to indicate a slight de-Russification of the Ukrainian cities since 1926. On the other hand, the figures bear out the continuing Russifying influence of the cities (compare the rows on persons who had moved from villages into cities, and on the semi-skilled workers most of whom presumably fall into the same category).

The tables would have provided a graphic picture of linguistic Russification of the respondents, were it possible to interpret "native language" as the language spoken by their parents and the "language spoken at home" as that used in their own households. Unfortunately, both concepts appear somewhat ambiguous. For example, in the light of what we know about Ukrainian cities it is implausible to assume that as many as 87.3 per cent of the parents of our urban respondents actually spoke Ukrainian; furthermore, a number of our respondents were too young to have had households of their own—in their cases the word "home" obviously refers to the household they were born into. Assuming these respondents to be more or less a representative sample, we are left with the impression that, as of the outbreak of the Soviet-German war, a relatively high proportion of Ukrainians—up to one-third in the cities— were not exclusively speaking Ukrainian at home, but either exclusively Russian (up to one-eighth), or both Ukrainian and Russian. Nevertheless, nine-tenths of them and more (except in the cities) claimed Ukrainian as their native language. What does this mean?

In my opinion, this signifies that the adoption of Russian for everyday use does not, except in the course of several generations, entail complete alienation from the nationality of one's ancestors. Those who speak Russian may still refer to Ukrainian as their native language though it is likely that in some cases their parents, too, did not exclusively speak Ukrainian at home. Even some of those who do not claim Ukrainian as a native language regard themselves as Ukrainians (8.2 per cent of our total sample). On the other hand, we notice from the last two sets of figures (on persons born into families in which both parents were Ukrainians and on persons born into families in which only one parent was Ukrainian) that the nationality of parents exerts a very strong influence not only on the language spoken at home (Ukrainian in 83.4 per cent of purely Ukrainian households compared with only 26.3 per cent of the mixed households) but also on the declaration of the "native language" (Ukrainian in 96.2 per cent compared with 59.7 per cent of the households). The nationality of the parents is in fact the strongest factor of all, as can be easily noticed from a quick comparison of the differences between the various categories (rural or urban residence, the occupation of collective farmers versus that of semi-skilled workers). We may thus provisionally conclude that the most prone to linguistic Russification are those Ukrainians who are descended from ethnically mixed parentage. Residence and occupation as such do not seem to be quite so influential.

But the interpretation is not so simple. To some extent, the strongly pronounced bilingualism of the persons from mixed households (35.1 per cent, or more than one third, of them spoke both languages at home) may obviate clear cut Russification. We also notice a curious phenomenon: for some reason, which I cannot explain, a significantly larger number of such persons desire their children to speak Ukrainian than speak Ukrainian themselves (43.8 compared with 26.3 per cent). Finally, it can be argued that Ukrainians who marry Russians or others may have been originally predisposed toward assimilation because of some other considerations. Mixed parentage may thus be only the immediate but not the weightiest reason why some Ukrainians prefer to speak Russian at home. The relationship between linguistic Russification and declared nationality, and what it involves in terms of political action, appears a complex problem indeed—it is proposed to examine it in connection with other material bearing upon attitudes, in the last chapter. Meanwhile let us keep this warning in mind when relating the more impressionistic evidence on the 1930's, 1940's, and 1950's.

For the period after 1945 we have data for a number of cities by American tourists who visited the Ukraine in the middle and late 1950's. I have also obtained a statement from a former Soviet citizen who received part of his education in Kiev in the early 1950's. Unsystematic though it may be, their testimony clearly shows that in the larger Ukrainian cities—Kiev, Kharkov, and particularly in cosmopolitan Odessa, a port city—Ukrainian usually can only be heard on the markets where collective peasants are selling their foodstuffs, and occasionally at theaters, in scientific institutions,[30] and at public meetings. No clear testimony is available on Lviv, but an anonymous letter writer complained in November, 1957, that it has been made most impolitic for Ukrainians in that city to speak in Soviet offices anything but Russian.[31] An American political scientist, who visited the Soviet Union in 1957, vividly summed up his impressions in a letter to this writer:

. . . I did hear some Ukrainian spoken in Kyiv [Kiev] (and even a little bit in Kharkiv). For example, I saw a large group of school pupils who were being herded about Kyiv by their teachers; they were looking at all of the public buildings and monuments and spoke exclusively in Ukrainian. I also heard Ukrainian spoken in the little Shevchenko (house) museum, in which the poet had lived for a while (at "Shevchenko Pereulok [Place]"); it was in the office of the museum and was being spoken behind closed doors. The woman guard in this little museum was reading a Russian newspaper. Two female guards in the museum of Ukrainian art were speaking in Russian when I visited it on a Sunday afternoon. Of course, one did hear both Russian and Ukrainian on the loudspeakers in the parks and squares. While in the park overlooking the Dnipro [Dnieper] I heard two women conversing in a controversial tone and heard one of them say "*ty katsapka* [you are a Russian, with a pejorative connotation—Y.B.]."

When I visited the Institute of History of the Ukrainian SSR Academy of Sciences I was warmly received by the director as well as by others; they spoke with me in Ukrainian at all times. While in the Cathedral of St. Sophia [in Kiev] with two Intourist guides and another American, we encountered a Ukrainian from Galicia. The American who was with me asked about the bishop's throne which is behind the altar. I kept quiet wanting to see if the Intourist guides knew their business; when they didn't seem to be able to explain this seat, the Galician (who had overheard us) explained in Ukrainian what its purpose was. I then began speaking with him in Ukrainian and we had a brief conversation. I told him I was from New York, and he commented that there were many Ukrainians there. We shook hands warmly, but I didn't want to keep him too long in the presence of Intourist people and others.

I did encounter various manifestations of Russian great power chauvinism: in Kiev in the Intourist Hotel the Intourist personnel in the office were showing me announcements of what was playing in the opera and theater and when we came to the listings of the Franko Theater one of them said, "That's not interesting; it's the Ukrainian theater." They didn't know that I spoke Ukrainian (as they were later to discover). In the course of my travels I met a Moscow *yuriskonsul't* [legal counsel to an administrative bureau, a factory, or similar enterprise] who in the course of our talk actually ventured to assert that he did not consider Ukrainian to be a separate language but a "variant of Russian." These were chance occurrences. Also a middle aged Intourist woman employee who was from Leningrad expressed her dislike for Ukrainian signs and for the language until she found out that I spoke it and then endeavored to make some remarks calculated to attempt to correct the earlier statements of a disparaging nature. *Thus many Russians, it would appear, would not even tolerate Ukrainian if they had their way; of course, the language receives little more than bare toleration from the regime in the larger cities* [italics added].

Yet Russians in Ukraine must listen to all operas in Ukrainian—even [the Russian operas] *Prince Igor, Boris Godunov* and *Ivan Susanin* as well as *Ruslan and Lyudmila*. While in Kiev I attended an excellent performance of Leoncavallo's *I Pagliacci* and of Mascagni's *Cavalleria Rusticana* in Ukrainian. The Franko Theater in Kyiv performs plays exclusively in Ukrainian and many of these are written by Ukrainian Soviet writers although there are also Russian plays presented there in Ukrainian translation. . . .

Though most persons spoke Russian on the streets and in public places in Kyiv it was interesting to observe these same people actually lining up in front of news stands to purchase the Ukrainian language evening newspaper, *Vechirniy Kyiv* [Kiev in the Evening]; they would also be reading it while sitting on the benches in the parks and on the Shevchenko Boulevard. In Kharkiv I could not obtain a copy of the Ukrainian-language oblast newspaper, *Sotsialistychna Kharkivshchyna* [Socialist Kharkov Region], but I did see it under glass in a park.

As concerns signs: In Kyiv the trolley busses have signs in Russian while the trolleys have signs in Ukrainian for the most part [sic]. One also sees large neon signs in Ukrainian.

I was rather impressed and even surprised to see so much technical, scientific and medical literature available in the bookstores in the Ukrainian language. [—Printed with permission.]

What are some of the motives why Ukrainians speak Russian in the Ukraine? A person who attended a Ukrainian ten-year school in Kiev in the late 1930's told the author how great the pressure was to speak Russian. We know that at that time Soviet policy encouraged the use of Russian language, but even so, from the testimony of our respondent it would appear that, in some cases at least, the official pressure had been internalized: he would date a Ukrainian girl, a native of Kiev, and he felt very strongly that unless he wanted to appear a country-bumpkin (he himself had been born in a village) he had to express his sentiments in a Russian language that was not only correct, but exquisite. Ukrainian was simply not modern enough.[32] Another respondent who had been born in the countryside, too, and who went to college in Odessa at about the same time, pointed out to this writer that the student community was socially divided into a Ukrainian circle and a Russian circle. This division coincided more or less with the students' origin. Peasant children would join the Ukrainian circle to speak Ukrainian and sing Ukrainian folk songs. On the other hand, children of towns-people and would-be urbanites had a group of their own, in which the use of the Ukrainian language was frowned upon and Ukrainian culture in general was regarded as somewhat rustic. Another distinguishing characteristic of the urbanite Russian circle was their infatuation with modern Western dances: tangos, fox trots, and the like.[33]

Nor was the price of speaking Ukrainian always so low as making a social misstep. As another respondent put it:

At the time when Postyshev [one of Khrushchev's predecessors in the Ukraine, Second Party Secretary from 1933–37—Y.B.] wore a Ukrainian embroidered shirt in public, a friend of mine who was teaching in a Ukrainian school sent his son to a Russian school which was farther off, lest they should brand him as a Ukrainian nationalist.[34]

We may conclude from this that if an educated Ukrainian who lived in one of the large cities and was fluent in both Ukrainian and Russian chose to speak his native language, this was regarded not only as a sign of *mauvais ton,* but as Ukrainian nationalism, an act of political insubordination. This was at least the case on the eve of World War II. As far as the countryside and smaller towns are concerned, Ukrainian seems to predominate.[35]

The nature of the cited evidence is such as to preclude more probing analysis: we do not know in any significant detail how many people actually speak Ukrainian compared with those who did so in 1926 or who those people are.* The over-all impression is that the decade of Ukrainization notwithstanding, the large cities have remained linguistically almost as Russified as they used to be before the Revolution of 1917. Apparently, the Ukrainian immigrants from the countryside upon entering the cities have gradually acquired the habit of speaking Russian at work and at home, although this process encountered some resistance, as shown in the account of the Odessa student. In summary, according to the census of 1959, 6.4 per cent of the Ukrainians in the Republic, a slightly higher percentage than in 1926 (5.7 per cent), have adopted Russian as their primary means of communication. If only Ukrainian city-dwellers are considered, the percentage is likely to be higher.† Linguistic Russification, which is not necessarily synonymous with holding pro-Russian political attitudes, seems to have been brought about for a variety of reasons: some persons married Russians; some were economic status seekers; others were status seekers in the political sense: by adopting Russian language and culture they achieved a feeling of belonging to the ruling nation of the Soviet Empire. Still others felt that they were politically suspect and had to demonstrate their loyalty by dropping the language of their ancestors.

At the same time it should be pointed out that for certain purposes the Ukrainian language has been maintained even in the large cities. Haggling over the price of eggs and cabbages in the peasant market is in Ukrainian, as it used to be even in Tsarist times. On the other hand, though before the Revolution there were also some dramas and operas performed in Ukrainian, at the present time there are undoubtedly more of such (see Table V-3).[36] Now, however, virtually all residents of the Ukrainian Republic who have attended its elementary and secondary schools can speak, read, and write Ukrainian more or less well, as one would expect them to know a second state language, even if not all of them use it as a primary vehicle of communication.[37] American tourists noticed, for example, Russians reading a Ukrainian local evening paper in Kiev, and the facade of shop signs to a large extent is

---

* See, however, Note V-2, in the Appendix.

† According to a newly released census information in 1959, 15.3 per cent of Ukrainian city-dwellers in the Republic (1,802,510 out of a total of 11,781,750) gave Russian as their native language. See Tsentral'noe statisticheskoe upravlenie pri Sovete Ministrov SSR, *Itogi vsesoyznoy perepisi naseleniya 1959 Ukrainskaya goda: SSR* (Moscow, 1963), p. 170.

Table V-3

LANGUAGE OF THEATERS IN THE UKRAINIAN SSR

Year	Total	Ukrainian	Year	Total	Ukrainian
1914 [a]	47	— *	1946 [a]	103	—
1928 [a]	74	—	1951 [a]	81	—
1933 [a]	90	—	1953 [d]	79	56
1937 [b]	85	53	1956 [a]	79	—
1938 [a]	89	—	1958 [e]	80	—
1939 [c]	101	75	1960 [e]	68	—
1941 [a]	140	—			

* A dash (—) indicates that no information is available.

Sources: [a] *Kul'turnoe stroitel'stvo SSSR* (Cultural Progress of the USSR, Moscow, 1956), pp. 294–95. The 1914 data refer to 1956 boundaries, those for 1928 through 1939, to pre-September, 1939, frontiers. Figures give the number of theaters at the beginning of the year.

[b] *Pravda*, 24 December 1937, p. 2.

[c] *Kul'turnoe stroitel'stvo SSSR* (Moscow, *1940*), pp. 184–86, as of January 1, 1939. The total of 75 Ukrainian theaters includes 31 theaters on collective and state farms.

[d] *Kul'turnoe stroitel'stvo SSSR* (Moscow, *1956*), p. 298.

[e] *Narodnoe khozaystvo SSSR v 1960 g.* (USSR National Economy in 1960, Moscow, 1961), p. 804.

still kept Ukrainian. One American visitor, who was particularly bold, went into private apartments in Kiev to find out whether Ukrainian was spoken at least within the privacy of one's own walls. He was consistently disappointed until he dropped in on a group of persons who *did* speak Ukrainian. It turned out to be a meeting of the Communist Party.

3. *Indirect Evidence: Soviet Linguistic Policy*

The problem of ascertaining the effectualness of the Ukrainian language as a vehicle of everyday communication can also be attacked by analyzing Soviet linguistic policy. Some figures on the use of Ukrainian in schools and publications are available through the 1950's. We also know a few things about the language of certain government establishments; and in the realm of "intra-linguistic" policy, about the direction followed in the development of Ukrainian vocabulary, especially in the technical fields.

In Table V-4, I have tried to compile all the available evidence on the language of instruction in elementary and secondary schools of the Ukrainian SSR from 1914–62. A glance at the figures will show that during the struggle for independence (1917–20) the Ukrainian intelligentsia succeeded in "Ukrainizing" quite a number of schools and similar educational institutions, some 63.0 per cent by 1921, but not uniformly throughout the country. For instance, about 90 per cent of the schools in the agricultural Podolia, Poltava, and Kiev provinces taught in Ukrainian, compared with only 20 per cent in the industrial Kharkov and Don provinces. When the Soviet Ukrainization policy started in 1923, their proportion rose within a few years to about 80 per cent and, except for a temporary drop in 1930 (to 69.5 per cent), stayed at that level throughout the anti-nationalist periods of the 1930's, 1940's, and 1950's. On the other hand, the share of Russian schools, after a fairly rapid decline from 100 per cent before World War I to 6.7 per cent in the heyday of the Ukrainization policy in 1928–29, started climbing back in the 1930's, until it reached 9.8 per cent on the eve of World War II in 1938–39 and full 13.7 per cent in 1955–56, after the incorporation of predominantly Russian inhabited Crimea. In the school year 1959–60, after the school reform, judging by the rather imprecise figures that have been released, the number of Russian schools may have increased to more than 16 per cent of the total (see p. 173). It is significant to note that the number of schools with Russian as the language of instruction has increased not so much at the expense of Ukrainian as of smaller minority schools (Polish, Yiddish, and others).

What do these data imply for the development of Ukrainian national consciousness, for the growth of a strong, well-balanced Ukrainian nation? Before we try to answer this fundamental question, let us attack another not unimportant problem: To what extent do those data reflect the policy of the regime? The only information on who formally decides on the language of instruction in elementary and secondary schools has been unearthed by Holub. He found an official statement to the effect that when the Western Ukraine was incorporated in the Soviet Union in 1939 and the problem became acute in that area, the People's Commissariat of Education of the Ukrainian Republic ordered that "the problem of the language of instruction in every school [should] be solved by the local city or county board of education according to the composition of students and the wishes of their parents." [38] That a similar practice has been followed in the Eastern Ukraine, too, may be inferred from the following complaint in an instruction of the People's Commissariat, of September 20, 1940: "The registration for the first grade of the Ukrainian schools in Kharkov, Kiev, and Nikolaev has not been satis-

Table V-4

LANGUAGE OF INSTRUCTION IN SOVIET UKRAINIAN SCHOOLS (ELEMENTARY AND SECONDARY)

	Schools							Students			
	Total number	Language of instruction						Total number	Language of instruction		
Year		Ukrain.	%	Russian	%	Other	%		Ukrain.	%	Russian	%
1914–15 [a]	20,197	[none	0.0	20,197	100.0	none	0.0]	1,728,313	[none	0.0	1,728,313	100.0]
1921	21,968		(63.0) °	—*				2,023,680 [b]			—	
Podolia, Poltava & Kiev provinces			(ca. 90)									
Kharkov & Don provs.			(ca. 20)									
Kiev City			(ca. 25)									
Kiev Prov.			(ca. 95)									
Dniepropetrovsk City			(ca. 20)									
Dnpr. Prov.			(ca. 80)									
1922	20,579 [b]		0.35 [d] [sic]					1,724,380 [b]			—	
Donets prov.												
Kiev & Poltava provs.												
1923–24	16,004 [e] rural		95 [u]					1,575,538 [e]			—	
urban			69.7									
1925	15,555 [b] rural		33.7 [f]					1,795,190 [b]			—	
urban			81.9 [f]									
			43.8									
1926 [z]	—	elementary	79.4		6.5		9.4	—			—	
elem. bi-lingual			+4.7									
seven-year schools			53.6		13.3		25.5					
same, bi-lingual			+17.6									
1927–28 [a]	20,463 [a]	—						2,448,044 [a]			—	
1928 [g]	19,620	16,172	82.4	1,314	6.7	2,134	10.9	—			—	
1929–30 [h]	20,764 [h]	—		1,287 [i]	6.2	(incl. Jewish: 469)	2.4				285,000 [i]	

Year												
1930 [j]	20,764	69.5	14,430	1,504	7.2	4,830	23.2	—	2,400,000	83.2 [r]	—	
1932–33 [h]	21,971	—	—	1,004 [i]	4.6	291	1.4	—	—	—	211,000 [i]	
				(incl. Jewish:)								
1932–33 [a]	22,632	—	—	—	—	—	—	4,555,615	—	—	—	
1934–35 [k]	21,941	78.9	17,327	1,394	6.4	3,220	14.7	4,685,000	—	—	—	
				(Incl. Jewish: 432)			(2.0)					
1935–36	—	—	—	—	—	—	—	—	—	83.0 [s]	12.7 [s]	
1936–37 [zz]	21,947	80.8	17,736	—	—	—	—	5,564,000	—	82.8	—	14.0
1937–38	23,539 [a]	—	—	480	2.2	—	—	5,501,570 [a]	—	82.8 [t]	—	
1938–39 [l]	21,882	84.8	18,557	2,149	9.8	480	2.2	5,250,882	4,107,676 +329,614	78.2 / 6.3	737,219	14.2
	Bilingual +696	0.7										
GRADES I–IV			3,238,785						2,549,110 +188,394	78.7 / 5.8	460,669	13.6
GRADES V–VII			1,695,089						1,317,793 +117,070	77.7 / 6.9	229,766	14.7
GRADES VIII–X			317,008						240,773 +24,150	76.0 / 7.6	46,784	
(1939–40) [m]	24,677	85.8	—	2,509	8.7	1,572	5.5	—	—	—	—	
(1940–41) [m]	24,940	86.0	—	2,571	8.9	1,524	5.2	6,762,700	—	—	—	
					(Jewish: 231)		(0.8)					
1940–41 [aa]	29,597	—	—	—	—	—	—	6,491,500	—	—	—	
1945–46 [aa]	27,407	—	—	—	—	—	—	4,939,200	—	—	—	
1946–47 [n]	28,703	80.0	22,957	—	—	—	—	—	—	—	—	
	(7,430 in Western provinces only) 6,931 in Western provinces only											
1950–51 [aa]	29,900 [30,063]	93.3	6,931	249	3.4	250	3.4	6,698,700	—	—	—	
1955–56 [p]	24,977	85.1	—	4,008	13.7	251	0.9	5,283,623 [5,524,754]	3,814,869	72.2	1,369,145	25.9
	29,361 Bilingual +125	0.4										
1955–56	Crimean oblast: 1,013 [q]	1.5	—	—	—	—	—	145,800	—	—	—	
1958 [y]	30,077	84.7	25,464	4,355	14.5	258	0.9	—	—	—	—	
1961–62 [v]	40,564	82.1	33,309	6,292	15.5	361	0.9	7,300,000	—	—	—	
	Bilingual +602	1.5										

* A dash (—) indicates that no information is available.

Sources: [a] *Kul'turne stroitel'stvo SSSR* (Moscow, 1956), p. 88. Some care should be exercised in interpreting these figures. They comprise all non-specialized elementary and secondary schools, including special schools for the deaf, mentally retarded, etc., at the start of the school year. The figures through 1937–38 refer to the territory of the Ukrainian SSR before September 17, 1939, i.e., are exclusive of western provinces and the Crimea. Moreover, as appears from *Narodne hospodarstvo Ukrayins'koyï RSR* (Kiev, 1957), pp. 429 & 433, the figures for 1940–41 and 1945–46 are exclusive of schools and pupils in the Transcarpathian province. It is well known that under the Tsarist government (in 1914–15) there were only Russian schools in Eastern Ukraine. Bracketed figures for that year added by compiler.
[aa] Adjusted figures from *Nar. hosp. URSR* (1957), *ibid.*: figures for the Crimea have been deducted.

Table V-4 (Continued)

b S. Siropolko, *Narodna osvita na sovyets'kiy Ukrayini* (Public Education in Soviet Ukraine, Warsaw: Ukrainian Scientific Institute [Works, Vol. 23], 1934), p. 23. Work is exclusively based on Soviet materials.

c *Ibid.*, p. 201. Figures may not be strictly comparable: they refer to "schools and other institutions of social education"—hence the parentheses.

d Basil Dmytryshyn, *Moscow and the Ukraine, 1917–53* (New York: Bookman Associates, 1956), p. 73.

e *Ibid.*

f V. Zatonsky, *Natsional'na problema na Ukrayini* (National Problem in the Ukraine, Kharkov, 1927), pp. 24, 43.

g Siropolko, *op. cit.*, p. 25: data as of December 1, 1928.

h V. P. Zatonsky, *Pro tchytelin ta shkolu* (About Teachers and School, Kharkov, 1935), p. 25.

i *Ibid.*, p. 77. Data are intended to demonstrate the excesses of the Ukrainization policy, and may be distorted in that direction.

j Dmytryshyn, *op. cit.*, p. 128.

k *Ibid.*, p. 154.

l *Kul'turnoe stroitel'stvo SSSR* (Moscow, *1940*), p. 73. Figures below the Ukrainian data show bilingual instruction: Ukrainian and another language, most probably Russian.

m Decision No. 54 of the Collegium of the People's Commissariat of Education of UkrSSR, July 4, 1940, "Concerning the Confirmation of the School Network of the UkrSSR for the Year 1940–1941," in *Zbirnyk nakaziv i rosporyadzhen' narodnoho kommissariatu osvity UkrSSR* (Collection of Orders and Instructions of the People's Com-at of Educ. of the UkrSSR), Vol. 1940, No. 18, pp. 14–15. These are planned figures—hence parentheses. The figures for 1940–41 are given directly, some figures for 1939–40 can be calculated from them.

n H. I. Ponarovs'ka, "Teaching Russian in Elementary Schools with Ukrainian as the Language of Instruction," *Radyans'ka Shkola* (Soviet School, Kiev), Vol. 1947, No. 1 (January–February), p. 32.

o P. M. Dudnyk (Vice-Minister of Education, UkrSSR), "Raise onto a Higher Level the Work of Schools in the Western Provinces of the Ukrainian SSR," *Ibid.*, Vol. 1947, No. 2 (March–April), pp. 1ff.

p I. Ye. Kravtsev, *Marksysts'ko-lenins'ki prymtsypy proletars'koho internatsionalizmu* (Marxist-Leninist Principles of Proletarian Internationalism; Kiev, 1956), p. 51. Kravtsev's figures do not add up to the totals he gives—I have bracketed them and computed the totals anew. All percentages refer to these newly computed totals for which alone information on language of instruction has been given (see also *Kult. stroitel'stvo* [Moscow, 1956], pp. 186–87). Robert S. Sullivant in his *Soviet Politics and the Ukraine, 1917–1957* (New York: Columbia University Press, 1962), p. 295 has also used Kravtsev's figures but computed his percentages on the basis of the larger totals.

q *Narodne hospodarstvo URSR* (Kiev, 1957), pp. 429 and 433.

r John S. Reshetar, "The Nationality Problem in the Soviet Union" (Russian Research Center MS, 1954), p. 39.

s Harold R. Weinstein, "Language and Education in the Soviet Ukraine," *Slavonic and East European Review*, Vol. XX (1941), p. 142.

t Vsevolod Holubnychy, "The Language of Instruction: An Aspect of the Problem of Nationalities in the Soviet Union," *Horizon* (New York: Ukrainian Students' Review), Vol. II, No. 1–2 (Fall-Spring, 1956–57), p. 31.

u Sullivant, *op. cit.*, p. 108.

v *Ukrayins'ka Radyans'ka Entsyklopedia* (Ukrainian Soviet Encyclopedia, Kiev, 1962), Vol. IX, p. 514.

y Speech by I. Bilodid (Minister of Education, Ukrainian SSR), in *Pravda Ukrainy*, February 1, 1958, p. 2.

z Volodymyr Zatons'ky, *Natsional'na problema na Ukrayini: Dopovid' na plenumi TsK LKSMU, cherven' 1926 r.* (National Problem in the Ukraine: Address to the Plenum of the Komsomol of Ukraine Central Committee, June, 1926, Kharkov, 1926), p. 4.

aa Total figure of all schools from *Kult. stroitel'stvo SSSR* (Moscow, *1940*), p. 41; total number of *Ukrainian* schools from *Pravda*, December 24, 1937, p. 2—confirmed by Dmytryshyn, *op. cit.*, p. 154; total of all pupils from Dmytryshyn, *ibid.*; percentage of Ukrainian pupils from *Pravda, loc. cit.*

factory. *The boards of education in those cities* have not carried out the necessary work of explanation among the parents concerning the admission of pupils to the first grades of Ukrainian schools; and in some instances they have permitted first grades to open in Ukrainian schools with Russian as the language of instruction." [39] But while the particular decision may have been made by local education officials, the extent of their autonomy must not be overestimated. From an earlier instruction of the Commissariat's Collegium (No. 54) we can infer that the languages of instruction in the school network as a whole must be approved by the People's Commissariat (or, to use modern terminology, Ministry).[40] In general, it seems that in a would-be monolithic state like the Soviet Union significant changes cannot be introduced by local action alone. In other words, allowing for minor variations, the figures on the language of instruction in schools provide an accurate reflection of the regime's policy.

But how can those variations be accounted for? While the endeavor to have Russian taught from the first grade of Ukrainian-language schools may have been officially inspired, this need not be so. A respondent cited instances of Ukrainians in Kiev sending their children to Russian schools to prepare them better for assuming responsible positions in Russia, or simply to facilitate their admission to Moscow colleges.[41] It is quite possible that such a group of practical Ukrainians were responsible for the incidents reported in the official complaint. On the other hand, comparatively recently there has been a different complaint in the Soviet Ukrainian press against zealous officials who "have tried to assign children to [Russian] schools without considering which language was spoken by the child's parents and thus by the child itself." [42]

Another problem is: Can figures on the language at schools give us a reliable picture of the prevalence of Ukrainian as a means of everyday communication? A student of Hungarian nationality policy before World War I remarked pointedly:

Where the nationalities live in their close settlements far away from Magyar culture, all school Magyarization is impossible because the school with its four hours of instruction is quite impotent against the twenty hours of real life.[43]

Cannot the same verdict *mutatis mutandis* be applied to Ukrainians attending Russian schools in the Ukrainian villages? This may be so, but a continuous exposure over seven to ten years to a body of knowledge as varied as that provided by the curriculum of Soviet elementary and secondary schools should not be underestimated as a strong influence on the communication habits of a particular individual.[44] Four hours of elementary instruction may not prevail against the twenty hours of real life, but some five or six coupled with a few hours' allowance for home-work may do so, if they include a sufficiently large slice of real life.

This brings us to the central problem of the language of instruction. To many, education in the native language may seem primarily a guar-antee of preserving the cultural heritage of a people. This is a familiar nationalist stand. But there is also another aspect. If instruction is pro-vided in a language the mastery of which presents considerable diffi-culty for a certain group of students (let's say, Russian to Ukrainians from the villages) but not for others, this will result in favoring one group over the other in their quest for socio-economic advancement. This function of the language of instruction has been recognized in an editorial of *Radyans'ka Ukrayina,* of June 28, 1953. It refers to higher education, but it can be applied to secondary schools as well. Writes the central Ukrainian paper:

It is quite natural that the introduction of Russian made study difficult for thousands of students and had a negative impact on their progress. It is neces-sary to end once and for all the under-privileged position of the Ukrainian language in the higher educational institutions and to organize the instruction in the native language all over the country.[45]

We have seen that more than four-fifths of all elementary and secondary schools in the Ukraine carry out their program of instruction in Ukrain-ian. What we would like to know now is: How good are the educational opportunities they offer compared with those provided by schools with Russian as the language of instruction?

From the 1930's until the early 1960's, when the 1958–59 school reform became effective in the Ukraine, there were four-year elementary schools, so-called "incomplete secondary schools" with seven grades, and ten-year elementary-secondary schools. The reform changed that structure some-what by the addition of an extra, eleventh year for those who want to go on to universities.[46] The following discussion will be largely in terms of the school system before 1960, but for accuracy's sake we shall speak of ten-or-eleven-year schools, whenever appropriate.

As admission to Soviet institutions of higher learning presupposes, as a rule, graduation from a complete secondary school (ten or eleven years), it would have been extremely important to determine how many of such schools have Ukrainian as the language of instruction. Statistics on this are not available, but certain inferences can be drawn from a comparison of the number of such Ukrainian-language schools with the number of pupils attending them. We know, for example, that in 1930 only 69.5 per cent of the schools were Ukrainized, but that they were attended by 83.2 per cent of the school children. In 1938–39, however, 84.8 per cent of the schools taught in Ukrainian, but they accounted for only

78.2 per cent of the student body. By 1955–56 this gap widened further. In that year the proportion of Ukrainian schools remained virtually unchanged (85.1 per cent), but the number of students taught in Ukrainian had further declined to 72.2 per cent of the total student body. As Professor Sullivant aptly pointed out, in that year Ukrainian schools had an average enrollment of 153 pupils each, Russian schools—342 pupils each.[47] What does this mean? In our opinion, the explanation must be sought in the greater Russification of *city* schools which show a higher student enrollment per school than rural schools that presumably teach in Ukrainian. While the difference in enrollment can be easily documented,[48] the relatively greater Russification of city schools is a hypothesis for which there is suggestive proof only (see Table V-5, p. 168). We find that in all three cities—Kharkov and Odessa in Eastern Ukraine, and Lviv in Western Ukraine—Russian language schools predominate. (Unfortunately, we have no recent data on the national composition of the residents in those cities, so that we cannot say by how much, compared with the population.) There are more Russian than Ukrainian schools even in Lviv though there were hardly any Russians in that city at all before World War II. What is even more significant: in all cities, most of the larger and presumably better ten-year schools are Russian.[49]

But even if this had not been the case, it would not have made too great a difference. In schools with Ukrainian as the language of instruction, teaching of Russian starts with the second term of the second grade (see Table V-6). In grades IV to VI almost as many hours are devoted to Russian language and literature as to Ukrainian; and in the last four grades the number of lessons devoted to Russian exceed those devoted to Ukrainian even in the Ukrainian-language schools of the Republic. This is a great change from the years of Ukrainization, when Russian was not taught in Ukrainian schools until the third grade, and when in the higher grades for which information is available (V–VII) the hours devoted to Ukrainian and Ukrainian literature outnumbered those assigned to Russian at least two to one.[50] We see that the higher the grade, the less attention is devoted to Ukrainian language and literature.

Nevertheless, there is subtle discrimination in favor of Russian-language schools, which may cause Ukrainian parents to send their children to them rather than to Ukrainian schools, merely to help them "make the grade." So far as could be ascertained, at least one-half of the 132 higher schools of the Republic in 1956–57 taught in Russian (see Table V-7). This does not tell us anything, however, about the kind of schools that were doing so (technical institutes? medical schools?). Prior to the fall of 1955, all secondary school graduates applying for admission to any Soviet college had to pass a rigorous examination in Russian language and literature, both written and oral.[51] Since the academic year

Table V-5

NUMBER AND TYPES OF ELEMENTARY SECONDARY SCHOOLS
IN THREE UKRAINIAN CITIES

	Elementary (Grades I–IV)		Incomplete Secondary (I–VII)		Secondary (I–X)		Total	
	N	%	N	%	N	%	N	%
KHARKOV, 1957:[a]								
Ukrainian language								
of instruction	4	50.0	6	40.0	28	31.8	38	34.2
Russian language	4	50.0	9	60.0	60	68.2	73	65.8
Total	8	100.0	15	100.0	88	100.0	111	100.0
ODESSA, 1957:[b]								
Ukrainian language	2	66.7	7	36.8	9	15.8	18	22.8
Russian language	1	33.3	12	63.2	48	84.2	61	77.2
Total	3	100.0	19	100.0	57	100.0	79	100.0
Plus schools for which no information on languages is given							10	
							89	
LVIV, 1955:[c]								
Ukrainian language	1	16.6	14	66.7	14	37.8	29	45.3
Russian language	4	66.7	7	33.3	20	54.1	31	48.4
Polish language	1	16.6	0	0	3	8.1	4	6.3
Total	6	100.0	21	100.0	37	100.0	64	100.0

Sources: [a] *Khar'kov: Spravochnaya kniga* (Kharkov: A Citizen's Guide Book, Kharkov, 1957), pp. 216–20.

   [b] *Odessa: Spravochnik* (Odessa: A Handbook; Odessa, 1957), pp. 155ff.

   [c] *L'viv: Dovidnyk* (Lviv: A Handbook, 1955), pp. 207–8.

Table V-6

WEEKLY HOURS DEVOTED TO UKRAINIAN AND RUSSIAN IN ELEMENTARY AND SECONDARY SCHOOLS OF THE UKRAINIAN SSR, 1959–60 *

	Grades	I	II	III	IV	V	VI	VII	VIII	IX	X
Schools with Ukrainian as language of instruction	Ukrainian language & literature	12	11/8 †	8	6	6/5	5	4	4	3	3
	Russian language & literature	0	0/3	4	5/4	4/5	4/5	4/5	4	4	4
Schools with Russian as language of instruction	Ukrainian language & literature	0	0/3	4	5/4	4/5	4/5	4	4	3	3
	Russian language & literature	12	11/8	8	6	6/5	5	4/5	4	4	4
	Total Hours	24	24	25	27	33/32	33	34	36/35	37	37

The rest of the programs for both types of schools are identical.

* Based on so-called variant No. 1 for schools which start implementing the educational reforms of 1958–59 somewhat faster.

† Numerator gives the no. of weekly hours in the first term, denominator—no. of hours in the second term.

Source: "School Plans for Schools of the Ukrainian SSR for the 1959–60 Academic Year," *Radyans'ka osvita* (Soviet Education, Kiev), June 6, 1959, p. 4.

Table

LANGUAGE OF INSTRUCTION IN HIGHER

	Total	Ukrainian		Ukr.-Russ.		Russian		Others	
Year	N	N	%	N	%	N	%	N	%
1914–15 [a]	19	—†		—		19	100.0	—	
1914–15 [b]	27	—		—		19	70.4	8	29.6
1920 [c]	38	—		—		—		—	
1921 [d]	42	—		—		—		—	
1923–24 [e]	—	—	19.5	—		—		—	
1925 [f]	35	6	17.1	21	60.0	8	22.9	0	
1925–26 [g]	35	10	28.6	16	45.7	9	25.7	0	
1927 [f]	37	9	24.3	25	67.5	3	8.1	0	
1927–28 [b]	39	—		—		—		—	
1928 [f]	38	11	29.0	24	63.2	1	2.6	2	5.3
1929 [f]	42	14	33.4	19	45.2	2	4.8	3	7.1
				4 *	9.5				
1932–33 [a]	203	—		—		—		—	
1933–34 [b]	173	—		—		—		—	
1938–39 [a]	129	—		—		—		—	
1939 [i]	142	—		—		—		—	
1940–41 [b]	173	—		—		—		—	
1945–46 [b]	154	—		—		—		—	
1950–51 [b]	160	—		—		—		—	
1956–57 [j]	132 [j]	—	ca. 50 [k]	—		—		—	
1960–61 [l]	135	—		—		—		—	
Out of Total N 35 in 1925–26 [g] there are:									
Industrial Technical Inst's.	4	—		1		3		—	
Agricultural Colleges	7	2		5		—		—	
Socio-Economic Institutes	3	—		1		2		—	
Teachers Colleges	12	5		7		—		—	
Medical Schools	5	1		—		4		—	
Advanced Schools of Fine Arts	4	2		2		—		—	
Out of Total N 42 in 1929 [h] there are:									
Agricultural Colleges	9	3		6		—		—	
Industrial Technical Schools	5	1		1;2 *		1		—	
Transportation Institutes	1	—		1		—		—	
Socio-Economic Institutes	4	2		2		—		—	
Medical Schools	5	1		2;1 *		1		—	
Teachers Colleges (including 3 tri-lingual)	13	6		4		—		3	
Advanced Schools of Fine Arts	5	1		3;1 *		—		—	

V-7

SCHOOLS IN THE UKRAINIAN SSR

	STUDENTS TAUGHT IN							
Total	Ukrainian		Ukr.-Russ.		Russian		Others	
N	N	%	N	%	N	%	N	%
26,700	—		—		26,700	100.0	—	
35,204	—		—		26,700	75.8	8,504	24.2
27,205	3,512	12.9	16,054	59.0	7,639	28.1	0	0
28,207	3,983	14.1	20,712	73.4	3,512	12.5	0	0
29,141	—				—			
33,406	6,218	18.6	22,675	67.9	1,822	5.5	2,691	8.1
40,890	11,197	27.4	18,727	45.8	3,442	8.4	4,338	10.6
			3,186 *	7.8				
—	—		—		—		—	
97,533	—		—		—		—	
124,400	—		—		—		—	
123,135	—		—		—		—	
196,775	—		—		—		—	
136,999	—		—		—		—	
201,544	—		—		—		—	
344,000 [j]	—		—		—		—	
417,000	—		—		—		—	

* Numbers of bi-lingual Russo-Ukrainian higher schoools in which Russian predominated.

† A dash (—) indicates that no information is available.

Sources: [a] *Kul'turnoe stroitel'stvo SSSR* (Moscow, 1940), p. 106: figures do not include the western provinces.

[b] *Kul'turnoe stroitel'stvo SSSR* (1956), pp. 208–09. The 1914–15 figures include western provinces and Crimea (refers to 1956 boundaries). Two universities—in Lviv and in Chernivtsi (North Bukovina)—then offered certain courses in Ukrainian. The coverage of the statistics for 1927 through 1956 is identical with those for elementary and secondary schools (see Table V-4, note "a").

[c] Siropolko, *op. cit.*, p. 85.

[d] *Ibid.*, p. 87.

[e] Zatonsky, *Natsional'na problema na Ukrayini* (1927 ed.), pp. 24, 43.

[f] Siropolko, *op. cit.*, p. 92. Figure for 1928 is confirmed by *Kult. stroitel'stvo* (1940), *loc. cit.* Figure for 1929 (33.4%) of completely Ukrainized institutes or colleges shows, however, a discrepancy from figure for 1929–30 given by *Entsyklopediya Ukrayinoznavstva*, Vol. I, p. 939. The latter gives for the academic year 1929–30 Siropolko's figures for 1928.

[g] Siropolko, *op. cit.*, p. 206. Figure for completely Ukrainized institutes (28.6%) confirmed by source of note e: 28.5%.

[h] Siropolko, p. 204: as of November 1, 1929.

[i] As of January 1, 1939: E. N. Medynsky, *Prosveshchenie v SSSR* (Education in USSR. Moscow, 1955), p. 30.

[j] *Nar. hosp. Ukr. RSR* (1957), p. 510.

[k] Student's letter to *Molod' Ukrayiny* (Kiev), Dec. 8, 1956: "This year the majority of higher educational institutions in the Ukraine have changed to Ukrainian as a language of instruction." This statement should be taken with a grain of salt, but there are no official data to contradict it.

[l] *Nar. khoz. SSSR, 1960*, p. 769.

1957–58 the examination rules for the graduates of non-Russian schools have apparently been relaxed.[52] Nevertheless, even now it appears that graduates of Ukrainian schools are at a comparative disadvantage if they apply to a college even in the Ukrainian SSR, unless they want to study such disciplines as Ukrainian linguistics, journalism, and the like. Even before the reform of 1958–59, which is likely to have diminished the study of Ukrainian even further, Ukrainian was neglected as a subject in the Russian-language schools of the Ukrainian Republic. In those schools Ukrainian was not included as a required subject on yearly promotional examinations in secondary schools, despite the protests of Ukrainian educators.[53] In Ukrainian-language schools both Ukrainian and Russian figured on the required yearly examinations, with the result that pupils attending Ukrainian-language schools had one more subject to study quite seriously. Assuming that the abilities of the different pupil groups are about equal, it would follow that students of Russian-language schools in the Ukraine could obtain better grades with less effort than their fellow students at Ukrainian-language schools. Better grades at the secondary school mean, however, a better chance to be admitted to college.

After the school reform of 1958–59, the system of general elementary and secondary schools in the Ukraine has been gradually broken up into a compulsory division embracing the first eight grades and an optional division which includes the last three years. The emphasis appears to have been to force every child to complete the first eight years and then look out for employment opportunities. Only the ablest of them would be allowed to finish the last three grades with minimum interruption from various sorts of part-time labor.[54] More relevant in our context is that, as we have already seen,[55] despite considerable opposition from parents, educators, writers, and Party officials, it has been left up to the parents to decide if they wanted their children to learn Russian (if enrolled in a Ukrainian-language school) or to study Ukrainian (if enrolled in a Russian-language school). The parents were also to decide what type of school to send their children to: one with Russian or one with Ukrainian as the language of instruction. With the regime dedicated to hastening the assimilation of Soviet peoples on the basis of Russian language and culture, it is hardly surprising that the voluntary decisions of parents seem to have been a little one-sided. (After all, the term "voluntary" must be read in the Soviet context: the people are to "choose" only what is "good for them.")[56] Shortly after the reform was announced, the number of Russian-language schools in the Republic increased—apparently at the expense of Ukrainian-language schools. We know this on the authority of S. Chervonenko, then Communist Party of Ukraine Central Committee Secretary in charge of ideological indoctrination, but unfortunately he has not given any figures.[57] Rather imprecise statistics were supplied by Republican Minister of Education, Bilodid. According to him, in the school year 1959–60 there were 36,432 elementary and secondary schools in the Ukraine, out of which "approximately 6,000" taught in Russian.[58] His colleague, Minister of Culture Babiychuk gave the number of Ukrainian-language schools as "more than 30,000." [59] Volume IX of the Ukrainian Soviet Encyclopedia, which was published in 1962, finally disclosed the precise number of Russian-language schools in the Ukraine in the academic year 1961–62: 6,292 compared with 33,309 Ukrainian-language schools out of a total of 40,564 including part-time schools.[60] These figures reveal that the proportion of Russian schools in the Ukraine has increased at the expense of Ukrainian schools. (In February 1958 there were 25,464 Ukrainian and 4,355 Russian schools in the Republic—see Table V-4.) In July 1962, the implementation of the educational reform was reviewed at a session of the Supreme Soviet of the Ukrainian SSR—but no information at all was released on the number of Ukrainian-language schools.[61]

In reviewing Soviet policy toward elementary and secondary schools in the Ukraine we see that there appears to be a hardly concealed discrimination against Ukrainian-language schools as such and against Ukrainian language and literature as subjects in all schools. To judge from figures on student enrollment and a single eye-witness account, Russian-language schools are larger and presumably better equipped. Ukrainian language and literature are not taken quite seriously in the last three years because they are not required in entrance examinations to most higher schools, even in the Ukraine. While it is true that the regime does not lay insurmountably high obstacles in the way of those who prefer their education in Ukrainian, those pupils who want to enter higher schools to study other than Ukrainian disciplines are subtly channeled into entering Russian-language schools. If language of instruction at school is linked with national consciousness it follows that, quite apart from the contents of instruction, the policy of the government has been to induce Ukrainians to de-nationalize themselves in looking for better educational opportunities. This is especially true of higher educational institutions.

To ascertain how many institutions of higher learning now teach in Ukrainian and how many in Russian is singularly difficult (see Table V-7), and this writer has not been able to come to any definite conclusions. As of the outbreak of World War II, no official instruction existed as to the criteria according to which one or the other language was to be adopted.[62] It varied from one university to another. More likely than not, Russian professors would teach in Russian, with a few notable exceptions, but one could never be certain as to which policy would be followed by Ukrainian professors and for what reasons. Some of them refused to lecture in Ukrainian because they felt the results were not worth the extra trouble of introducing a new terminology; some did so because they wanted to conform; others for fear of being branded bourgeois nationalists.[63]

Another direct approach would have been to examine the language of university publications. So far as one can judge from the extensive holdings of Harvard College Library (Widener), a great many scientific articles that have been written at the universities of Kiev, Lviv, and Odessa after the war—probably the majority—are in Russian. But in order to yield any conclusive results, the whole body of scholarly writing at the universities would have to be examined, journal by journal, for even if the title page has been in Ukrainian, spot-checks have revealed that some of the articles contained in the journals were written in Russian.[64] Such an examination is impossible since not all of the journals have found their way abroad.

Another way of finding out the language of instruction in higher schools would have been to analyze their announcements in the daily press before the start of the academic year. It is customary for Soviet universities to publicize their rules of admission, and if we see that a particular college in the Ukrainian SSR requires an entrance examination only in Russian, we can be reasonably certain that in that particular school the instruction is in Russian. But the difficulty with this particular method is that not all of the colleges advertise in the press, and there is no way of telling whether the sample thus obtained is representative of the whole.

All these are painful gaps in our knowledge, for the problem of the language of instruction in higher schools appears to be quite serious. This has not only been acknowledged in the Soviet Ukrainian press (see the editorial in *Radyans'ka Ukrayina,* cited above), but has also been confirmed by a former Soviet student at an engineering school in Kharkov. His essays were graded not only on the basis of contents, but also on style and grammar. As they had to be written in Russian, graduates of Ukrainian-language schools found themselves at a considerable disadvantage compared with their fellow students who had come from Russian-language schools.[65] Does this all mean that we cannot make any generalizations about the language of higher instruction in the Ukraine? Perhaps we can, but let us consider other aspects of Soviet linguistic policy first.

More revealing than school figures are statistics on books, journals, and newspapers that have been published in Ukrainian. From Table V-8 we see that before World War I, the proportion of books that came out in the vernacular in Eastern Ukraine was almost negligible (3.2 per

Table V-8

LANGUAGE OF BOOKS PUBLISHED IN THE UKRAINIAN SSR

	Titles					No. of copies (in 1,000)		
	Total	Ukrainian		Russian		Total	Ukrainian	
Year	N	N	%	N	%	N	N	%
1913 [a]	5,283	170	3.2			9,986	431	4.3
1917 [b]	1,373	747	54.4	452	32.9	— *	—	—
1918 [b]	1,526	1,084	64.4	386	25.3	—	—	—
1919 [b]	1,414	665	47.0	726	51.3	—	—	—
1920 [b]	860	457	53.1	369	42.8	—	—	—
1921 [b]	667	214	32.0	448	67.3	—	—	—
1922 [b]	1,312	385	29.3	927	70.7	—	—	—
1923/24 [b]	2,757	855	31.0	1,848	67.1	—	—	—
1924/25 [b]	4,508	1,813	40.2	2,535	56.2	—	—	—
1925/26 [b]	4,726	2,162	45.8	2,365	50.1	—	—	—
1926/27 [b]	5,028	2,445	48.6	2,427	48.3	—	—	—
1927/28 [b]	5,413	2,920	53.9	2,232	41.2	—	—	—
1928 [a]	5,703	3,225	56.5	—	—	36,665	24,238	66.1
1929 [b]	6,480	—	—	—	—	—	—	—
1930 [b]	8,079	—	—	—	—	—	—	—
1931 [b]	8,086	6,218	76.9	2,104	26.0	—	—	—
1932	—	—	—	—	—	—	—	—
1933 [a]	5,187	3,629	70.0	—	—	83,693	66,712	79.7
1938 [a]	4,147	2,159	52.1	—	—	76,908	64,377	83.7
1939 [c]	4,369	1,865	42.7	—	—	51,209	41,188	80.4
1940 [d]	4,836	2,012	41.6	—	—	51,370	41,327	80.4
1946 [d]	2,151	1,311	60.9	—	—	43,841	37,714	86.0
1950 [d]	4,136	1,856	44.9	—	—	77,649	62,155	80.0
1953 [e]	3,251	1,924	59.2	—	—	85,674	71,512	83.5
1954 [d]	4,021	2,267	56.4	—	—	92,261	73,341	79.5
1955 [d]	4,821	2,378	49.3	—	—	86,268	63,006	73.0
1956 [e]	5,982	2,671	44.7	—	—	97,577	68,306	70.0
1957 [e]	5,808	3,054	52.6	—	—	100,647	75,977	75.5
1958 [e]	6,618	3,975	60.1	—	—	116,222	88,395	76.1
1959 [f]	6,817	4,048	59.4	—	—	99,426	75,272	75.9
1960 [f]	7,889	3,844	48.7	—	—	113,109	79,060	69.9

* A dash (—) indicates that no information is available.

Sources: [a] *Kul't. stroitel'stvo* (1940), p. 205.
  [b] Siropolko, *op. cit.*, p. 184.
  [c] *Kul't. stroitel'stvo* (1940), p. 260.
  [d] *Kul't. stroitel'stvo SSSR*, 1956, pp. 318–19.
  [e] *Nar. khoz. SSSR, 1958*, pp. 872–73.
  [f] *Nar. khoz. SSSR, 1960*, pp. 810–11.

cent). During the few years of the Ukrainian national revolution (1917–20) their share rose to more than one-half of the total, only to fall again to less than one-third during the subsequent reaction (1921–23–24). In the decade of *korenizatsiya* (1924–25—1933) Ukrainian book production increased quite rapidly to reach an unprecedented peak of 6,218 titles or 76.9 per cent of the total of 8,086 titles published in the Republic in 1931. During the Great Purges which strongly affected the Ukrainian intelligentsia, the production of books in Ukrainian fell both in relative and absolute terms to 1,865 titles (42.7 per cent) in 1939. After the war, the number of Ukrainian books amounted on the average to one-half of the total number of titles published in the Republic.

Several things should be noted about these figures. Unlike the data on schools, where minor local variations are possible, statistics on the publication of books directly reflect the policy of the central government in Moscow. As of 1955, all plans for publication had to be approved by a section of the USSR Ministry of Culture, the so-called *Glavizdat*. Another division of that ministry (*Glavknigotorg*) was in charge of distributing the books throughout the Soviet Union.[66] In both cases—publication and distribution—the appropriate organs of the Union Republics acted merely as agents of the central ministry and should be assumed to have wielded only very little influence on its decisions. This state of affairs may have been responsible for the relatively low book production in the Ukraine, if compared with the early 1930's, and above all, for the small share of Ukrainian books. Whereas the book production in the Soviet Union as a whole shows a steady rise from 26 thousand titles in 1913 to some 76 thousand in 1960, with a temporary dip in the post war years (see Table V-9), book production in the Ukraine had been relatively high before World War I, reached its peak in the early 1930's, and then fell off to a level which again exceeded that of 1913 only as late as 1956.

The second feature which should be noted is that since 1913 the relative number of copies of Ukrainian books has always, by a substantial margin, run higher than the relative number of titles. Apparently it is the more "popular" books that have been published in that language: political tracts, selected literary classics, modern Soviet novels; while the more esoteric (for example, scientific) literature seems to have continued to be published in Russian.[67] Occasionally, there have been complaints in the Soviet Ukrainian press about inadequate editions of particular books. For instance, an editorial in the professional journal of teachers of Ukrainian language and literature blamed the shortage of methodological handbooks on "the wrong and shortsighted practice of the Ukrainian *knigotorg* [book distribution agency] which approaches the problem from a commercial point of view [sic]." It appears that the

Table V-9

RUSSIAN BOOKS PUBLISHED IN USSR

Year	Titles			Copies		
	Total No.	Russian	%	Total No.	Russian	%
1913 [a]	26,174	23,805	91	86,739	80,218	92
1928 [a]	34,767	25,169	72	270,482	221,399	82
1938 [b]	39,992	30,321	76	692,678	545,731	79
1940 [a]	45,830	34,404	75	462,203	345,738	75
1950 [a]	43,060	30,482	71	820,529	640,391	78
1954 [a]	50,109	34,881	70	996,962	785,895	79
1955 [a]	54,732	39,375	72	1,015,028	827,058	81
1958 [c]	63,641	45,312	71	1,103,186	886,322	80
1960 [d]	76,064	55,337	73	1,239,647	1,016,356	82

Sources: [a] *Kul'turnoe stroitel'stvo SSSR* (Moscow, 1956), p. 320.
[b] *Kul'turnoe stroitel'stvo SSSR* (Moscow, 1940), pp. 205, 206.
[c] *Nar. khoz. SSSR, 1958*, pp. 871–73.
[d] *Nar. khoz. SSSR, 1960*, pp. 809–11.

Pedagogical Research Institute of the Ukrainian SSR had prepared a collection entitled *Literatura v shkoli*, i.e. "[Ukrainian] Literature at School." But the Ukrainian *knigotorg* ordered only 350 copies to be printed in 1956 to satisfy the demands of almost 25,000 Ukrainian-language schools.[68] Finally, it is obvious that the cited publication figures cannot be made the basis for any conclusions as to the proportion of Ukrainian and Russian books that are actually read by the citizens of the Ukrainian Republic, because many Russian books are imported from other Republics.

Statistics on periodicals (see Table V-10) confirm our inferences from the analysis of book production. As the journals are mostly published by the same houses that are publishing books, their production appears to be subject to the same controls as that of books. The difference between the relative number of Ukrainian titles and number of copies is even more pronounced, showing that the more esoteric journals are published in Russian. Unfortunately, no breakdown according to subject matter is available for journals published in the Ukraine, only for the entire USSR. From the latter it appears that it is the literary magazines which have the highest circulation (175 titles—110 million copies in 1955), followed by 381 political and socio-economic journals with a combined circulation of 139 million copies.[69]

Table V-10

Language of Newspapers and Periodicals Published in the Ukrainian SSR

	NEWSPAPERS						PERIODICALS					
	Total No. of Titles	Ukr.	%	Copies per issue (in thousands)	Same in Ukr.	%	Total No. of Titles	Ukr.	%	Copies (in thousands)	Same in Ukr.	%
1917	168 a	106 b	63.1(?)	*	—	—	—	—	—	—	—	—
1917 c	* (923) b	(172)	(18.6 ?)	—	—	—	* (923)	same	—	—	—	—
1918	—	218 b	—	—	—	—	—	—	—	—	—	—
1918 c	* (573)	* (252)	44.0	—	—	—	* (573)	same	—	—	—	—
1919 c	* (465)	* (243)	52.3	—	—	—	* (465)	same	—	—	—	—
1920 c	* (290)	* (139)	47.9	—	—	—	* (290)	same	—	—	—	—
1921 c	* (369)	* (181)	49.1	—	—	—	* (369)	same	—	—	—	—
1922 c	* (455)	* (168)	36.9	—	—	—	* (455)	same	—	—	—	—
1924 d	—	—	—	—	90 d	—	—	—	—	—	—	—
1925 b	74	39	52.7	—	—	—	—	—	—	—	—	—
1926	—	—	—	—	—	—	—	—	—	—	—	—
1927 d	—	—	—	—	500	—	—	—	—	—	—	—
1928 b	137	82	59.8	—	—	—	180	124	68.9	—	—	—
1928 e	234	117	50.0	1,675	975	58.2	—	—	—	—	—	—
1929 b	251	232	92.4	—	—	—	—	—	—	—	—	—
1933	2,037 e	1,721	84.4	5,894	4,936	83.7	272 f	204	75.0	17,708	16,688	94.3
1935 q	—	—	90.0	—	—	—	—	—	75.0	—	—	—
1936 a	1,830	1,402	76.6	—	—	—	—	—	—	—	—	—
1938	1,570 e	922	58.7	5,800	3,806	65.6	254 f	138	54.3	12,183	10,558	86.6
1939 g	1,655	970	58.6	6,899	4,560	66.1	202	103	51.0	13,189	12,996	98.5
1950	1,192 m	972	81.6	4,627	3,253	70.3	160 h	72	45.0	9,249	8,216	88.8

Year											
1953 [n]	—	—	—	—	—	—	168	82	48.8	18,986	15,628	82.3
1954 [h]	—	—	—	—	—	—	209	101	48.3	21,759	17,834	81.9
1955	1,061 [i]	—	5,593	—	—	—	245 [h]	115	46.9	22,983	19,154	83.3
1956	1,273 [k]	76.9	6,217	69.0	4,290	979	303 [l]	133	43.9	24,800	20,195	81.4
1957	2,964 [m]	80.6	7,495	70.7	5,298	2,392	379 [n]	169	44.6	28,991	24,117	83.2
1958	3,329 [m]	81.6	8,209	71.8	5,895	2,715	488 [n]	214	43.9	31,746	26,197	82.5
1959	3,518 [o]	82.3	9,380	72.1	6,774	2,896	502 [p]	236	47.0	34,767	28,713	82.6
1960	3,280 [o]	82.0	10,408	72.5	7,547	2,692	369 [p]	192	52.0	44,809	37,775	84.3

Note: Starting with 1957 newspaper statistics have included kolkhoz papers published more than once.

* A dash (—) indicates that no information is available.

Sources: [a] "Figures and Facts," *Pravda*, December 24, 1937, p. 2.

[b] Siropolko, *op. cit.*, pp. 190ff. Note that for the years 1928 and 1929 the totals of newspapers (137 and 251) have not been given explicitly. I have added up the number of Ukrainian and Russian newspapers.

[c] Jurij Lawrynenko, *Ukrainian Communism* . . . , p. 356. Periodicals and newspapers have not been listed separately, hence asterisks and parentheses. Publications in languages other than Russian and Ukrainian have been ignored.

[d] V. Rudnyev, *Ukrayins'ki burzhuazni natsionalisty—ahentura mizhnarodnoyi reaktsiyi* (Kiev, 1955), p. 87.

[e] *Kul'turnoe stroitel'stvo SSSR* (Moscow, 1940), p. 220.

[f] *Ibid.*, p. 214

[g] *Ibid.*, p. 260.

[h] *Kult. str. SSSR* (Moscow, 1956), p. 323.

[i] *Ibid.*, p. 326.

[k] USSR Ministry of Culture—Glavizdat, *Pechat' SSSR za sorok let, 1917–1957* (Moscow, 1957), p. 131.

[l] *Ibid.*, pp. 112–14. Ukrainian figure gives number of periodicals published in the USSR as such, but it is identical with that published in the Ukraine.

[m] *Nar. khoz. SSSR, 1958*, p. 876.

[n] *Ibid.*, pp. 874–75.

[o] *Nar. khoz. SSSR, 1960*, p. 814.

[p] *Ibid.*, pp. 812–13.

[q] Sullivant, *op. cit.*, p. 215.

Figures on the number of newspapers are even less satisfactory and should be taken with much caution since it is not known what they cover: for example, how many small factory and kolkhoz newspapers are included in their number (see Table V-10). As a matter of general principle it would appear that at the Republican and oblast level there is one newspaper in Ukrainian and one in Russian.[70] It is also interesting to note that since 1950, unlike the practice with books and journals, the relative number of Ukrainian newspaper titles has exceeded the relative number of copies per issue in Ukrainian by a considerable amount. This can only mean that though after World War II the number of Ukrainian papers is quite high they are likely to be papers with a smaller circulation than the relatively few Russian papers published in the Republic.

Another serious difficulty is that we cannot use the publication figures exclusively in order to determine what is actually read in the Ukraine, for many Russian books, journals, and periodicals are in addition imported from Russia. The only quantitative evidence we have been able to obtain is from an address delivered by a leader of the Communist Party (Bolshevik) of Ukraine, Volodymyr Zatons'ky, at a meeting of Ukrainian Komsomol leaders in June, 1926. He pointed out that in 1924 a total of 90,000 newspaper copies were published in the Ukrainian Republic in Ukrainian, compared with 445,000 copies in Russian. Two years later, as a result of the policy of *korenizatsiya*, on March 1, 1926, the number of Ukrainian newspaper copies reached 612,000, that of papers published in Russian diminished to 420,000. But actually in 1924 885,000 Russian-language newspapers were read in the Ukraine compared with 90,000 Ukrainian; and in 1926, as many as 1,000,000 Russian-language papers were perused, compared with 612,000 Ukrainian. The explanation of this is that in 1924 440,000 Russian-language papers were imported, in 1926 as many as 580,000.[71] Later evidence could not be found, but there are no grounds to assume that the situation would be radically different in the period after World War II.

Our discussion of the extent to which the Ukrainian language is used in schools and publications raises the cardinal question: How good is it as a means of everyday intercourse? Does its vocabulary cover all walks of modern life or is it rather a literary language of the past? Or to use the apt term of a German philologist: To what extent can we say that Ukrainian is a "sociologically" complete language?[72] Furthermore: Has the Soviet government improved Ukrainian as a vehicle of communication? While it is true that an exhaustive answer to those questions could be given only by a professional linguist with an intimate knowledge of cultural life in the Soviet Ukraine, a political scientist may be able to establish enough pertinent facts to indicate in general terms the direction of the development.

4. *Soviet Policy and the Quality of Ukrainian*

During the 1920's, the problem of the quality of Ukrainian as a medium of communication was squarely faced by a group of Ukrainian linguists. We read, for example, in the editorial of the first issue of the *Bulletin of the Institute for a Ukrainian Scientific Language* the following paragraphs, which are indicative of the spirit at the time of *korenizatsiya:*

The October Revolution, which has transferred power into the hands of the toiling masses, has given the Ukrainian people an opportunity, unique in its history, to create its political life, to build the public order on a socialist basis.

But awakened in the fire of revolution to struggle, and to a new, magnificent and creative life, the Ukrainian popular masses have found themselves without such an important spiritual weapon as a developed cultural language.[73]

The authors of the editorial point out that there is needed a developed native language not only for "household use," [74]

but for the whole multi-faceted life of the state; for science, for the press, for offices; for political organizations; for school education; for military affairs; for industry and commerce.

The editorial concludes on the ardent note:

We conciously enter upon the path of rendering scientific assistance to broad strata of the Ukrainian public in linguistic matters; and on the tenth anniversary of the October Revolution we, too, lay our brick to the magnificent construction of the Republic—the Bulletin of the Institute of Ukrainian Scientific Language of the Ukrainian Academy of Sciences—with the inscription: "To protect them I shall set the Word." [75]

We already know that the premise of those linguists about the building of a Ukrainian state was not correct, as far as Stalin was concerned, and in the 1930's Stalin's viewpoint was made to prevail. Efforts to create a scientific terminology based on the vernacular, were declared to be manifestations of Ukrainian bourgeois nationalism.[76] The point that emerges from a quick survey of the literature is that central authorities were especially critical of the so-called de-Russification of the Ukrainian proletariat.[77] As the country was just embarking upon a program of centrally directed industrialization, the stand of the regime becomes understandable, though it is more than likely that not only questions of technological efficiency were involved. Furthermore, an argument could be made that in some cases the introduction of an easier terminology based on Ukrainian would have allowed more workers to master their craft more quickly. This might have furthered rather than decreased technological efficiency.

What is the situation today? Without any doubt the rapid development of the Ukrainian language toward sociological completeness was
cut short in military affairs, science, and technology. From refugee testimony it appears incontrovertibly that Russian is the exclusive language
in the Soviet armed forces: Not only has the Ukrainian language been
"demilitarized" by cutting it off from access to the Army, but it has also
been put on defense, so to speak. There is universal conscription in the
USSR. For the duration of the basic military training the recruits are
usually moved into another Republic. For rural youths who do not continue their education beyond the fourth or eighth grade and thus do not
come into close contact with Russian, the army serves as a powerful
alternative instrument of Russification.[78] Most scientific papers that are
published in the Ukraine today appear to be in Russian. To judge from
remarks of tourists, the language in the factories appears to be Russian,
too.

Nevertheless, the vitality of Ukrainian should not be underestimated.
The fact is that Ukrainian is a state language, though not the first one.
Proceedings of the Republican Supreme Soviet and of the much more
important congresses of the Communist Party of Ukraine are available
in Ukrainian, and it is well known that at the meetings of the Communist Party practically everything on earth is being discussed. Unfortunately, the documents do not show what language is used by the speakers, but it is possible that even Khrushchev speaks in Ukrainian when
he is in the Ukraine. To consider a lower level: The Republican Ministry of Agriculture is known to issue its instructions in Ukrainian, and it
is very possible that the same holds true for the Ministry of Education,
both of which employ a considerable number of officials.[79] A number
of doctors are trained in the vernacular, too: This writer has seen medical textbooks in Ukrainian. Intensive research would have been able to
map out further areas of political and socio-economic life in which
Ukrainian has continued to be used, but from the cited evidence it
appears already that, restricted though it may be, since 1917 the Ukrainian language has definitely advanced on the road toward sociological
completeness.

While this particular problem straddles the borderline of extra-linguistic and intra-linguistic policy, changes in Ukrainian orthography,
grammar, and general word stock clearly belong to the realm of linguistics. Here I shall simply refer interested readers to the works by Roman
Smal-Stocki, the article series by Sherekh, and a very good survey article
by Weinreich that also touches upon the Ukrainian problem.[80] The general principle from which the individual policies are derived is simple
enough: The Ukrainian language is to be made as similar to Russian
as possible.[81]

5. Conclusions

What general conclusions can be drawn from this survey of Soviet language policy in the Ukraine? The foremost is that it has been an integral part of its general policy toward the nationalities. As seen from the viewpoint of the Bolshevik leaders, the problem before the outbreak of World War I was a rather delicate one. As Marxist internationalists and Russians either by descent (Lenin) or by adoption (Stalin) they did not conceal that ultimately they favored linguistic Russification. But as astute politicians they realized that the brusque rejection of the linguistic demands of the national minorities, as practised by the Tsarist government, was the worst possible way to achieve that ultimate goal. The considerable support which the nationalist movement enjoyed in the Ukraine after the Revolution convinced them that they had to be very careful so as not to alienate large strata of the population; for the Ukrainians might demand linguistic equality, but what they really meant was equality of educational opportunities. Hence, relatively great freedom was given to the use and development of Ukrainian in the Republic until the early 1930's.

The purpose of the so-called Ukrainianization policy was essentially threefold. In the first place, it constituted an attempt on the part of the regime to penetrate with its apparatus every nook and cranny of society, and this could only be achieved if language barriers were removed that had been clogging up the channels of communication. In the second place, the regime appears to have been honestly concerned with giving the non-Russian peoples an opportunity to climb up a little on the socio-economic ladder of advancement. Thus the Soviet government would be able to tap a larger pool of better qualified manpower than used to be the case under the linguistically inflexible policy of the Tsars. Moreover, it was assumed that the newly emerging non-Russian intelligentsia would be loyal to the regime and could under circumstances be used as a counterweight to holdovers from the Tsarist regime: officials and military personnel whose devotion to the Communist goals evoked considerable doubt.[82]

But rapid industrialization in the 1930's, coupled with threats of German aggression, and a growing spirit of independence in the national Republics, led to a revision of the internationalist or pointedly a-Russian attitude of the top Soviet leaders. Henceforth, certain carefully selected parts of the Russian national heritage were incorporated into the body of Communist dogmas. More likely than not, the Russian heritage was regarded as a means rather than an end—as unifying cement for the forces of world revolution—but whatever its object, this meant an increased emphasis upon the use of Russian in the national Republics, which is clearly seen in the decree of March 13, 1938, making Russian an obligatory subject in all Soviet schools.

In the post war years, the glorification of everything Russian attained considerable lengths, but for reasons which are still as valid today as they were in the 1920's, the regime has not dared to crowd out Ukrainian from all sectors of public life. It understands that to do so would be to impede the socio-economic progress of a large part of the Ukrainian people, especially from the countryside. This is true even now, although since 1958 (the Twenty-First and Twenty-Second Party Congresses—January, 1959 and October, 1961) much emphasis has again been laid on the "voluntary" study of Russian, in preparation for "the fusion of nations in the period of Communism." The achievements of the 1920's were grounded on genuine socio-political aspirations of the Ukrainian people. The reactions of the 1930's and the 1940's were not able to destroy those achievements completely; there are no reasons to assume that the reaction of the late 1950's will have a greater success.

In interpreting Soviet language policy this author has found it quite useful to employ a recent formula invented by a Soviet historian of Kazakhstan. Speaking of the "Rooting of the Soviet Apparatus in Kazakhstan in the First Decade of the Existence of the Republic (1920–30)," A. P. Kuchkin has coined the expression of "functional *korenizatsiya.*" It meant that only those offices which were close to native life were actually filled with natives.[83] Applying this formula *mutatis mutandis* to Soviet linguistic policy in the Ukraine we find that wherever feasible, wherever little opposition would be provoked by its use—that is, in the traditionally Russified cities, in industry, and higher education—the Russian language would be used in the interests of preserving the *unity of power.* But whenever certain officials would come into close contact with a population habitually speaking Ukrainian, whether in the capacity of Party officials, agronomists, rural teachers, or doctors, they would be encouraged to speak Ukrainian in the interest of maintaining the *pervasiveness of Communist power and of fully utilizing the available human resources of the native population.* How successful this policy has been—whether linguistic Russification has become synonymous with pro-Russian political views—can only be determined by examining the attitudes of the Soviet Ukrainians (see Chapter X).

Chapter VI

SOVIET INTERPRETATION
OF TARAS SHEVCHENKO

This chapter deals with Soviet policy toward the Ukrainian language as a bearer of culture. I have selected the greatest Ukrainian poet, Taras Shevchenko (1814–61), to point out how the regime has interpreted this part of the nation's cultural—and political—heritage.

1. *Literature and the Regime*

The question may be raised: Why should a study on nationalism and nationality policy enter the province of literary historians? One answer would be that, some exceptions notwithstanding, it is idle to speak of disinterested literary history in the Soviet Union: Soviet interpretation of writing must follow the current literary criticism of the regime, which is but a part of its general policy and hence the legitimate concern of political scientists. Moreover, literature being the most articulate expression of man's thoughts, his doubts, and aspirations, literary policy ought to provide us with a relatively clear account of the general policy of the regime.[1]

Apart from illustrative purposes, an analysis of the official exegesis of literature is important in itself. National movements have always depended on symbols, and what symbol could be more powerful than the poet's word infused with the glory of the past and inspired with the hope for a future that would be more glorious still? It is known that in the case of some East European nations, such as the Serbians and the Czechs, the Slovaks and Bulgarians, whose states had been conquered by their neighbors, a literary revival in the nineteenth century preceded the formulation of political demands. The development in the Ukraine was quite similar. But is it historically valid to adduce the experience of the nineteenth century as proof of the importance of literature in the twentieth? There is some evidence to indicate that, first of all, the politically sensitive Soviet regime has always devoted much attention to literature; that literary works are widely read, and, finally, that classics form a large proportion of them.

With few exceptions, all Soviet secondary school graduates applying to institutions of higher learning must pass entrance examinations in Russian and in Russian literature.[2] Furthermore, all of them must be acquainted with the major Party decisions concerning literature, besides a number of literary works by thirty-odd authors.[3] As late as 1955, Zhdanov's well-known Leningrad speech of 1946 was still a "must" in the curriculum.[4] In that speech, sprinkled with references to Lenin, Zhdanov said:

We demand that our comrades—those who direct literature as well as those who write it—be guided by that without which the Soviet system cannot live—to wit, by politics.[5]

In an earlier speech of his, in 1934, he quoted Stalin's dictum about writers being the engineers of human souls.[6]

For performing their constructive task well, Soviet writers and literary critics are rewarded very handsomely indeed. According to a Western student of the problem, in the mid-1950's a Soviet author would receive for a novel of 320 pages from 30,000 to 80,000 rubles, depending upon its artistic quality and ideological value. That sum exceeded the average annual income of a Soviet worker by five to thirteen times. Scientific and political works are paid for similarly. In addition, Soviet writers are entitled to a good apartment in the city and a country villa, both at low rent; they are also given the opportunity to travel widely in the country and to take their vacations at luxurious rest homes in the south.[7]

The same student points out that as a matter of government policy books are priced relatively low compared with foodstuffs and clothing. If it is kept in mind that so-called light literature is not permitted and that other opportunities for entertainment, such as television, are relatively limited, it would appear that the average Soviet citizen reads quite a number of books, belles-lettres and other. Kalnins writes, "In 1956, a kilogram of butter cost 28 (old) rubles; but one could buy a 425 pp. dictionary for 9 rubles, a politico-historical work of 500 odd pages for 8 rubles, and a novel of 800 pages for 18 rubles."[8] The hypothesis that Soviet citizens read a great deal also seems to be borne out by Soviet library statistics. In 1956 public libraries of the USSR Ministry of Culture lent out a total of approximately 782 million books, the estimated total population of the country then being 200.2 million. Forty-five per cent of the books were belles-lettres, 19 per cent children's books and only 9 per cent socio-political tracts.[9] Another author complained that when left to themselves, Russian kolkhozniks would read "one-sidedly, mainly belles-lettres." [10] Additional evidence for this hypothesis may be found in the fact that literary periodicals have the highest circulation [11] and that discussion of literature, both native and Russian, occupies an important place in the curriculum of Soviet secondary schools.[12]

But what about the classics? Before the reform, pre-Revolutionary literature was analyzed systematically in Grades VIII and IX, though it already comprised about one-half of the reading assignments in Grades V through VII.[13] No significant changes were made after the reform: Programs in Russian literature call for an intensive analysis of pre-Revolutionary writings in Grades IX and X, the last year, Grade XI, being reserved exclusively for the interpretation of Soviet literature.[14] To judge from the manner of presentation in Ukrainian readers, great care is devoted to the study of literary classics because, wrote the Russian nineteenth century critic Chernyshevsky:

> The study of every discipline should help to educate the pupils. History of literature contains more of such an educational element than many other disciplines.[15]

Furthermore, while the literary quality of a number of Soviet works cannot be denied, it would appear at least to the present writer that, as a rule, nineteenth century authors are more human and more interesting.[16]

2. Shevchenko's Life: General Evaluation of His Work

Of all Ukrainian poets, the greatest and at the same time the most popular is Taras Shevchenko. His collection of poems *Kobzar* (The Bard) has been published many times in editions totaling millions of copies; his life and his works are discussed in Grades V through VIII of Ukrainian schools; and, as of 1957, he was the only non-Russian poet besides Shakespeare and Goethe, of whom a knowledge was required of all students entering Soviet institutions of higher learning.[17] This is not the place to thoroughly and critically discuss his work, nor would this writer be competent to do so; inevitably distorting Shevchenko's contribution to literature, I shall try to give an objective picture of those aspects of his life and work that are politically most relevant and then account for the various interpretations made of it by the regime.

Admittedly, a comprehensive analysis of Soviet literary policy would have had to consider more than one major Ukrainian writer, including both classic and modern. I have, nevertheless, decided to focus this chapter on one, Shevchenko. Not only is Taras Shevchenko the most outstanding Ukrainian poet, but, with the possible exception of the West Ukrainian poet Ivan Franko (1856–1916), he alone has reached the stature of a spiritual national leader, a national prophet par excellence whose words have become flesh and blood of the living cultural—*and political*—heritage of the Ukrainian people. Furthermore, in this and the following chapter it is not my primary concern to record every change of Soviet policy toward the sum total of Ukrainian cultural and political symbols. Rather would I analyze how potent and fertile those symbols are likely to prove in the thinking of Ukrainians living in the USSR today. This calls for an often minute analysis of changes and logical inconsistencies in the official interpretation, which could be detected by interested Soviet Ukrainians who might then draw conclusions not always acceptable to the regime. (It is with the feeding roots of nationalism that I am concerned.) Such detailed analysis, in turn, entails concentration on a few cases, of which that of Shevchenko is one of the most meaningful.

Taras Shevchenko was born a serf in a village near Kiev, in 1814. From his early childhood he showed a great desire to paint. Recognizing the boy's talent and deciding that he was not good for anything else, his master apprenticed him to a Russian painter in St. Petersburg. One night Shevchenko accidentally met a fellow countryman of his—Ivan Soshenko —who was a student at the St. Petersburg Academy of Fine Arts. The gifted young serf evoked his interest. Soshenko helped him with his painting, introduced him to the Ukrainian poet Hrebinka, who in turn told his friends about the exciting discovery he had made. Hrebinka's friends included Bryulov, a fashionable painter and professor at the Academy, and the Russian poet laureate Zhukovsky, a tutor of the Crown Prince who was later to rule as Alexander II. Bryulov, too, was deeply touched by Shevchenko's desire to become a famous painter. He remonstrated with his master to release him, but the latter named what was then a very high price (2,500 rubles). Yet Bryulov would not give up; he painted a portrait of Zhukovsky which was sold at a lottery at the Imperial Court, and with the proceeds he literally bought Shevchenko free in 1838. Shevchenko was enrolled at the Academy of Fine Arts where he became a favorite student of Bryulov's. He made good progress and after seven years was graduated with the diploma of an "independent artist."

But even before he had been bought free, Shevchenko began to write poetry in Ukrainian. In 1840 he published his early poems in a small collection entitled *Kobzar*—it was immediately hailed as a work of talent. The two major themes of his poetry that grew increasingly prominent in the following years are: his protest against social oppression (serfdom, in particular) and his hatred of the political subjugation of his country by the Russian Tsars.

After graduating from the Academy he went to Kiev where he obtained a position as an artist with the Archeographic Commission. His job enabled him to travel widely to sketch Ukrainian historical monuments. In Kiev he also joined the secret political society of the Saints Cyril and Methodius, whose hundred members set themselves the goal of working for the abolition of serfdom and of absolute rule, and for transforming the Slavic states of Eastern Europe into free Republics, united in a common Federation (1846–1847). Their methods were less radical than their aims: they were to be achieved by propaganda and popular education, not by terroristic activities. Nevertheless, when the existence of the Society was discovered by the Russian police in the spring of 1847, its leading members were tried and sentenced to various terms of exile. Shevchenko's verdict was the most severe of all because in one of his poems ("The Dream," written in 1845) he had caricatured the Tsar and the Tsarina. He was to be drafted as a private into disciplinary barracks of the Russian Army and sent to eastern Russia, forbidden to paint or to write poetry, an express prohibition which Nicholas I added to the sentence in his own handwriting.

After the death of the Tsar in 1855, a number of political prisoners were amnestied, but Alexander II struck out Shevchenko's name from the list of those to be pardoned. Only two years later influential friends in St. Petersburg, most notably the freethinking Vice-President of the Academy Count Fedor P. Tolstoy and his wife Anastasia, succeeded in having the poet's sentence revoked. In 1858, he returned to the capital. He was cordially received both in Ukrainian and in radical Russian circles. He met his old Ukrainian friends of the Cyril and Methodius Society: the writer Kulish and the historian Kostomarov; became acquainted with the gifted Ukrainian lady writer Marko Vovchok, whose short stories on peasant life were greatly admired by Turgenev;[18] was introduced to Turgenev himself; briefly saw Leo Tolstoy; became quite friendly with the minor Russian poets Kurochkin and the brothers Zhemchuzhnikov; met the Russian poet Nekrasov, and the Russian revolutionary critics Chernyshevsky and Dobrolyubov. At one public reading he stole the thunder from Dostoyevsky and the Russian poets Maykov and Benediktov: the audience is said to have gone wild with applause when Shevchenko appeared on the stage, however cordial their reception of Maykov and Benediktov may have been.[19]

But Shevchenko had returned to St. Petersburg a sick man. Throughout his exile he managed to paint and to write verse surreptitiously, and after liberation he wrote some of his large masterpieces. He also authored some twenty novelettes in Russian, under the pseudonym "Kobzar Darmohray," of which only nine have been preserved. But he was depressed by the official prohibition to live in the Ukraine and his inability to find a wife who, like himself, was a "child of the people" and at the same time would prove a match for a man who was exuberantly praised as a poet and highly respected as an artist (in 1860, the Petersburg Academy of Fine Arts conferred upon him the honorary title of Academician). Shevchenko died in March 1861, mourned by all Ukrainians as well as by a number of prominent Russians.

Although it may seem overenthusiastic, the best general appraisal of Shevchenko's work has been given by the foremost Ukrainian literary historian of the 1910's and 1920's, Academician Serhiy Yefremov. He said:

> For the Ukraine the significance of Shevchenko's genius transcends the limits that are set even to great poets in their native countries: he was for her the sun who "leads the day after him"—the day of the rebirth [of a people] as a great civilized [kul'turnym] nation. His poetry became the best expression of national self-consciousness in the Ukraine, similarly as one would regard his personal life as the symbol of the fate of the whole Ukrainian people.
>
> . . . Shevchenko's work has introduced Ukrainian literature into the circle of world literature, has set it on a new path, by providing it with fresh themes and new poetical forms.[20]

In the comparatively liberal period of the NEP, a number of Soviet Ukrainian scholars under the direction of Yefremov set about exploring the rich heritage of Shevchenko's work in a disinterested way. But at the same time, several "proletarian" critics who stood close to the Party raised the demand for a "class study of Shevchenko." V. Koryak, in a series of newspaper articles that were later published in a book—Borot'ba za Shevchenka (Struggle for Shevchenko; 1925)—attempted to reinterpret the poet as "the prophet of the proletariat," "the prophet of the social revolution," "the poet of the peasants," and "the poet of the hoboes," thus overstressing the social aspects of Shevchenko's poetry.[21] The more influential critic A. Richyts'ky wrote in 1923 that Shevchenko could only be understood as a pre-proletarian poet. Referring to the famous lines in a poem written in 1857,

> When shall we have our Washington
> With new and righteous laws?
> We surely will, someday!

Richyts'ky wrote that Shevchenko's was

> [Quite obviously a] bourgeois democratic concept of the nation's problems. . . . Shevchenko poses the problem of a united national front and the revolutionary struggle of the bourgeoisie for a national state. . . . Shevchenko's image of Washington expresses his program of a revolutionary war for the independence of the Ukraine and for a republic.[22]

In the 1930's, Richyts'ky was executed as a Ukrainian nationalist. From 1933 until 1935, when he, too, was arrested for Ukrainian nationalism, the leading Party authority on Shevchenko was a certain Ye. S. Shablovsky. He pointed out that

In his works Shevchenko educated the masses in the spirit of recognizing the right of the Ukraine to be an independent state, and in denying the political privileges of any nation;

the apparently desired implication being that precisely this had been achieved in the Ukrainian Soviet Republic.[23] He admitted the "narrowness, the limitation" of Shevchenko's nationalism, but tended to exonerate him by showing that under the "given concrete historical circumstances it was nevertheless a great instrument that molded the consciousness of the peasants into revolutionary action." [24] In 1934, the "Division of Culture and Propaganda of Leninism of the Central Committee of the Communist Party of Ukraine" classed Shevchenko in their theses as a "bourgeois democrat and ideologist of petty bourgeois peasantry, with nationalist and religious remnants." [25]

There came the late 1930's when parts of Russian history would be reevaluated in the spirit of Soviet Russian patriotism; at the same time the 125th anniversary of the poet's birth was approaching in 1939. The regime decided to celebrate it with considerable pomp. Shevchenko was rehabilitated in some fashion: as comrade in arms of the radical Russian critics of the late nineteenth century Chernyshevsky and Dobrolyubov. The *Pravda* editorial of March 6, 1939, called him "a great son of the Ukrainian people, the founder of Ukrainian literature, a popular poet revolutionary, an ardent fighter for the happiness of the toilers." It was acknowledged that

Shevchenko had disclosed to the world the power and beauty of the Ukrainian language. He has carried Ukrainian literature onto a height worthy of a people with a rich historical past, a people that had never reconciled itself with [its] loss of freedom, and serfdom.

But in the fourth paragraph the main point of the new interpretation was laid down in the sentences:

In the poetry of Shevchenko were *reflected* the ideals of Russian revolutionary democracy of the 1860's. [He died in 1861.—Y.B.] In vain have Ukrainian bourgeois nationalists endeavored to tear Shevchenko apart from his Russian friends, from Chernyshevsky and Dobrolyubov. For the freedom of his people Shevchenko fought side by side with the best sons of the Russian people. He would bow before the Decembrists, regarded Herzen with deep reverence.[26]

The full implication of this obligatory link to Russian radicalism—an attempt to fit Shevchenko's genius to the Soviet "elder brother" theory

—was not yet perceived in Kiev, where the newspaper *Komunist* wrote in 1939:

He had a boundless love for his native land, for his own Ukraine . . . he dearly loved his people with their heroic past and with their great and glorious future. The best traits of the nation found embodiment in the person of Taras Shevchenko: love of freedom, hatred of servitude, flaming love for the fatherland, and a wish to make life beautiful, . . . the people happy, the land flowering . . . This manly call of the poet revolutionary went out to all nations enslaved by the nobles and oppressed by the autocratic rule of the Tsarist henchmen . . . The prominent leaders of Russian revolutionary democracy, Chernyshevsky and Dobrolyubov, *paid attention* to his voice. Filled with hatred of the oppressors and love for the oppressed, the inspired poetry of Shevchenko was near and dear to all subjected nations of autocratic Russia.[27]

During the war, the foremost Ukrainian literary scholar, the late Academician O. I. Bilets'ky, was still left free to declare:

There is no analogy between Shevchenko and foreign poets. . . . Shevchenko and Franko are the two summits of modern Ukrainian literature, which, since their time, has followed the course of European development.[28]

But after Zhdanov's speech (1946) the newly published *Outline History of Ukrainian Literature* was severely taken to task for

. . . not showing the great and fruitful influence of Russian culture and literature on the development of Ukrainian culture and literature; for keeping silent about their connection; for exaggerating the influence of West European literatures.[29]

An editorial in *Radyans'ka Ukrayina* in 1949 not only presents a new interpretation of Shevchenko's work, it clearly illustrates the humiliating length to which Soviet Russian patriots were prepared to go during the anti-Western and anti-nationalist campaign. As quoted by Odarchenko:

Great and burning was the love of Taras Shevchenko for the genius of the *Russian people*. From the life-giving sources of Russian culture, he avidly absorbed all the best creations of the genius of the Russian nation. Taras Hryhorovych *learned* from Herzen, Dobrolyubov, and Chernyshevsky . . . Leaning on the brotherly aid of his *Russian* friends . . . Shevchenko rose to heights of world culture. Shevchenko *hated all those who bowed before the moribund idealistic art of the West.* Shevchenko demonstrated passionately that nowhere else in the world were there such creations of genius, as those contributed to the treasury of the world's culture by the Russian people.[30]

Not much changed in the first year after Stalin's death. The authoritative theses of the Central Committee of the Communist party of the Soviet Union on the tercentenary of Ukraine's "reunification" with Russia stressed Shevchenko's connection with Russian democrats, adding the new touch that Shevchenko had always fought Ukrainian bourgeois nationalists and liberals—quite an interesting revision of the theses of Richyts'ky (1923) and Shablovsky (1933).[31]

The 100th anniversary of Shevchenko's death was in 1961. It was celebrated rather modestly when compared to the big fanfare attending the tercentenary of the Treaty of Pereyaslav seven years before. In Moscow, an All-Union Shevchenko Memorial Committee sponsored a festive session in the *Bolshoy* Theater on March 10, 1961, which was attended by most of the Party Presidium members with the significant exception of Khrushchev who seems to have left Moscow to make a political speech.[32] In Kiev, among other celebrations, there took place a festive plenary meeting of the Ukrainian SSR Academy of Sciences on March 6, at which the late Academician O. I. Bilets'ky, the dean of Ukrainian literary historians read a paper on "Shevchenko's Work and Its Significance for the World." On March 9, at a session sponsored by the Academy's Institute of History V. H. Sarbey addressed himself to the topic "Shevchenko as the Protagonist of the Fraternal Friendship of Peoples." [33]

Judging from the anniversary editorial in *Radyans'ka Ukrayina* [34] the interpretation of Shevchenko's work had remained essentially that prescribed by the 1954 Party Theses: Shevchenko was depicted as the protagonist of the friendship between the Russian and the Ukrainian people and a bitter enemy of Ukrainian nationalism. But the tone of the editorial and especially that of Professor Kyrylyuk's accompanying article "Immortality" [35] appear less stridently pro-Russian than the writings on Shevchenko in 1954, quite apart from the pseudo-scholarship under Stalin. If besides the inevitable formulas on Shevchenko's friendship with Russian radicals the Soviet Ukrainians in 1961 were able to detect a slight change in the Shevchenko image that was presented in popular media, they have to thank for this the much more outspoken discussion in Soviet Ukrainian scholarly circles. I shall take over only a few highlights from the careful bibliographical article by Professor Odarchenko, who is now living in the West.

The first timid criticism of the falsification of Shevchenko was heard in 1955, at the fourth annual scholarly conference devoted to Shevchenko. Novikov criticized two books published during Stalin's reign as being full of empty declarations and fabrications; one of the authors had suppressed evidence that did not fit into his predetermined thesis of Shevchenko's materialism.[36] But after the Twentieth Party Congress in February, 1956, criticism has grown sharper. The veteran Shevchenko-scholar Ayzenshtok dismissed the legend of Shevchenko's friendship with Russian revolutionary democrats as "subjectivist rubbish," which, "in some instances, is bordering on phantasy." [37] Some Ukrainian scholars, especially those writing for a wider audience, have continued to write all kinds of prescribed interpretations, and it may be assumed that the change of the Party's nationality policy in 1958 did clearly indicate that that was indeed the safe thing to do.[38] But it is of considerable significance that—Party policy or no Party policy—in their more esoteric publications they subtly or openly undermined the official image of Shevchenko, which, occasionally, they themselves had helped to propagate. The clearest example of this is the late Academician Bilets'ky's report to the ninth scholarly conference on Shevchenko, which took place in 1960. He bitterly remarked, in a quasi-aside, that the Pushkin House of the USSR Academy of Sciences had so far done more for the study of Pushkin's work than the Shevchenko Institute of the Ukrainian SSR Academy had done for the study of Shevchenko. The complete ten-volume edition of Shevchenko's works, begun in 1949, had not yet been completed; moreover, that so-called academic edition "[could] not be regarded as a definitive one [sic]." [39] Too many bad biographies of Shevchenko were being published. But the full acid of Bilets'ky's ridicule was reserved for the misinterpretation of Shevchenko's philosophical and political views:

As a rule, the recipe for compiling books on Shevchenko's Weltanschauung is quite simple: Shevchenko is a revolutionary democrat. Once he is a revolutionary democrat, he is the friend of Russian revolutionary democrats, and he is, therefore, a materialist, atheist, utopian socialist, and so on. It is easy to find quotations to fit the scheme, so easy in fact, as they are being found by our enemies in order to prove that Shevchenko was an idealist and a mystic. The text is here like "a thill, it points wherever you turn it." [40]

No wonder that after Ayzenshtok's and Bilets'ky's savage criticism the official interpreters moderated the tone of their controversial assumptions in 1961.

So much for a general appraisal of Shevchenko's work by Soviet critics. To sum up its essence as of 1954, before the less than outspoken qualifications that were added later: The social theme in his poems is overemphasized at the expense of the national, and together with the former much stress is put upon his links with Russian radicals. What I would like to do now is to explore the unity theme a little more closely in the light of Western and Soviet scholarship.

3. Shevchenko and the Russians: His Political Views

It is true that having lived for many years in St. Petersburg Shevchenko had many acquaintances and friends among the cream of Russian and Ukrainian intelligentsia. For the regime the task would, therefore, appear rather simple: From the wide circle of his acquaintances it has merely to select for emphasis those who are acceptable radicals, and to dismiss the others with perfunctory and often hostile remarks. Nevertheless, it seems that the particular method with which Soviet critics have tried to achieve the task—to wit, the neo-scholastic quoting of Stalin, Lenin, Herzen, Belinsky, Chernyshevsky, and Dobrolyubov to sanction every major thought in Shevchenko's work—is self-defeating. Chernyshevsky wrote in his review of the Ukrainian literary journal *Osnova* (Basis) that as with the appearance of Mickiewicz Polish literature has ceased to be in need of condescending reviews by French and German critics, so with Shevchenko Ukrainian literature no longer needs anybody's condescension.[41]

From a detailed analysis of Shevchenko's attitudes toward his Russian and Ukrainian contemporaries (see Note VI-3, in the Appendix) the conclusion may be drawn that at least until the middle 1950's Soviet interpretation was very tendentious; the influence of prominent Russians on Shevchenko has been exaggerated, sometimes grotesquely (as in the case of the hostile Russian critic Belinsky), while the Ukrainians' role in the poet's life has been unduly minimized. Furthermore, it would appear that this distortion can be detected by interested Ukrainians in the USSR, even those who have no access to the full, politically unexpurgated editions published in the West. Reasonably complete editions of Shevchenko's works that have been printed in the Ukraine contain materials inconsistent with the official line.

This brings us to the second and third important problems of interpretation: Shevchenko's attitude toward Ukrainian language and literature, and, beyond that, his political views. The curriculum in Ukrainian secondary schools includes the discussion of Shevchenko's autobiographical novel *The Artist,* which was written in 1856, in Russian.[42] Whatever the other merits of the work, the teachers are reminded to stress the political implications of the greatest Ukrainian poet's writing of *The Artist,* his diary, and his novelettes in Russian. They are advised that

It is well to begin the characterization of the novelettes by telling the history of these works. The pupils should know that for a long time Ukrainian bourgeois nationalists kept silent about everything the poet had written in Russian. Throughout his life the poet gladly used the language of the fraternal Russian people. He wrote in that language the poems "Banquet" and "The Blind Woman," the intimate *Diary,* dramas and novelettes. This shows the love which the Ukrainian national poet had for Russian culture.[43]

That Shevchenko's Russian prose is artistically inferior to his Ukrainian poetry, that, with the exception of *The Artist,* none of his novelettes has come to us in final polished form—this is not to be brought up in Soviet schools. But why indeed did Shevchenko write in Russian?

In his letter of January 25, 1843, which was omitted from the 1949 Soviet edition of his works, he confided to a Ukrainian friend of his that he had written a poem in Russian to show his Russian critics that he could be a poet in that language, too.[44] In an earlier letter to another Ukrainian friend (Yakiv Kukharenko) he complained that he was everything but pleased with his Russian poem "The Blind Woman." [45] (That letter, too, has been excluded from the Soviet collection apparently because it contains an uncomplimentary reference to the Russian language.) But the clearest expression of Shevchenko's views on the merits of writing in Ukrainian or Russian is contained in the preface to the planned 1847 edition of his *Kobzar*.[46]

The preface is in part a strongly worded polemic against the "horde of foreign journalists" who do not write original works themselves and produce only unreadable translations but who, at the same time, try to prevent Ukrainian authors from writing in their native language as do the other Slavic peoples: the Poles, Russians, Czechs, Serbs, Bulgarians, and Montenegrans. Apparently in reply to Belinsky's argument of 1841 that a Ukrainian *language* does not exist, that there is only a provincial dialect,[47] Shevchenko writes

. . . Do not pay any attention to the Muscovites. Let them write in their own language, and us—in our own. They are a people and have a language (*slovo*), and we are a people with a language of our own; let others judge which language is the better one.

Shevchenko concludes his preface with an appeal to his fellow writers to go to work and create a Ukrainian literature.

This preface—a literary manifesto, in effect—is much too important a document to be ignored by Soviet critics. They have met the challenge in a certain way: withheld the full text from publication and re-interpreted whatever they had not been allowed to quote. Thus the secondary school pupils are to be told that in that preface Shevchenko called upon his Ukrainian fellow poets to create works for the benefit of their people (which is correct), by referring primarily to the writings of progressive Russian authors (which is a Soviet interpolation).[48] In the "academic" history of literature we learn for the first time that in the preface Shevchenko sharply condemned "liberal Ukrainian squires" for looking down upon the Ukrainian language.[49] To sum up: An interested reader who has access to the full *Western* editions of Shevchenko will readily perceive that before 1847, in any case, the poet did not show great desire to become a Russian author. Soviet editors and critics, nevertheless, have tried to maintain a consistent image of Shevchenko as a Russophile by unceremoniously cutting his words and transforming Russian critics into —liberal Ukrainian squires.

Nor is there any evidence that Shevchenko changed his attitude toward the Ukrainian language during his exile, though it is in those years that almost all of his Russian works were written. For instance, in his biography Zaytsev refers to a letter that the poet wrote to his Ukrainian friend Kukharenko either in 1859 or 1860.[50] Apparently suffering from a mood of Russophobia, Shevchenko bitterly scolded his old friend for forgetting the Ukrainian language; he seems to have used a single Russian word in a previous letter addressed to the poet. Moreover, despite his friendship with many prominent Russians, Shevchenko remained as sensitive as ever to any insults directed at his people. When in 1858 the Russian Ivan S. Aksakov started publishing a new literary journal he invited Shevchenko to take part in it. Shevchenko, however, promptly refused on the ground that while enumerating all Slavic peoples in his editorial statement, Aksakov had omitted the Ukrainians. He remarked full of sarcasm,

"I am much obliged to him; for are we not very close relatives? When our father's house was burning, his [father] warmed his hands.[51]

But the question still remains why Shevchenko wrote in Russian.

Zaytsev has advanced the hypothesis that after the arrest of the members of the Cyril and Methodius Society in 1847, official repression of anything Ukrainian became so stifling that the only way to have something published was to write in Russian. He shows that most of the novelettes, with the exception of the autobiographical *Artist,* show a moralizing, publicistic tendency, and that one of the points in those novelettes which Shevchenko wanted to impress upon his Russian and Ukrainian readers alike, was respect for Ukrainian language and Ukrainian national heritage. For instance, in *The Musician* the character of Maria Yakymivna, an educated woman who prefers to speak Ukrainian, has been drawn with a great deal of sympathy. In seven out of nine novelettes, Shevchenko's positive heroes are men and women who have not forsaken their Ukrainian heritage.[52]

Zaytsev's hypothesis does not, however, explain why Shevchenko wrote *The Artist* or his diary in Russian. It would appear that the poet was broadminded enough to write in another language if he could thus approach his audience better; in his time there were few educated Ukrainians and even fewer who would regularly speak Ukrainian. A novelette whose action was set in the artistic circles of St. Petersburg would have been incomprehensible even to most of his fellow countrymen had it been written in Ukrainian, and would have been very hard for his Russian friends to follow—hence the choice of Russian as the medium of expression. Why Shevchenko kept his diary in Russian, I cannot explain; but the evidence shows that it was *not* because he had changed his views on Ukrainian language or culture. One of the warmest passages in the diary is devoted to a casual meeting with a fellow country-man of his, a certain Andriy Oberemenko. (This passage has *not*, of course, been included in the school reader.) [53]

What were Shevchenko's political views? It is not necessary to delve into the poet's life very deeply in order to recognize that his antagonism toward any kind of reforms has been vastly overdrawn.[54] Shortly before his death he became very interested in the Sunday school movement and himself wrote a first reader for children. The printing of the reader was to be financed with the proceeds from the sale of the 1860 edition of *Kobzar*. The costs of the *Kobzar* were in turn borne by a Ukrainian ex-serf who had become a rich factory owner—Symyrenko. The poet had visited Symyrenko on his trip to the Ukraine. He was much impressed with Symyrenko's management of his sugar factory; his workers were well paid and well housed; there was a beautiful church, an adequately equipped infirmary, a library, and a school with 150 children who were taught by qualified teachers, most of whom had university degrees. Need-less to say, Shevchenko was very grateful for Symyrenko's offer of a con-siderable sum for the printing of his works. In their desire, however, to remake Shevchenko into a precursor of communist revolutionaries, re-cent Soviet authors have overlooked these episodes in his life.[55]

What were Shevchenko's explicit views on the political status of his country? Being primarily a poet, he held certain definite convictions about the past and entertained a vision of future goals, but he did not offer a detailed prescription of the means by which those goals were to be achieved. It is relatively easy to show what the poet rejected: the political and social oppression of his country by Russian Tsars, among whom Peter I, Catherine II, and Nicholas I were singled out for special condemnation. He viewed political and social oppression as an insep-arable whole; recent Soviet critics are right when they stress this unity, but unlike their executed predecessors in the 1920's and 1930's they mini-mize the *political, national* element in Shevchenko's works.

In particular instances it becomes very clear that postwar Soviet in-terpretation is not based on a disinterested reading of Shevchenko's poetry, for example, when it is alleged that Shevchenko was in favor of the "reunification" with Russia in 1654. While respecting Khmelnytsky as a "rebel of genius," [56] Shevchenko never forgave him for concluding the Treaty of Pereyaslav, which in his opinion had led to the current oppression. This idea is most forcefully expressed in the "mystery poem" *Velyky L'okh* (Great Dungeon), of 1845,[57] and in a short bitter piece written in 1859 on the occasion of visiting Pereyaslav, "If you, tipsy

Bohdan, would look at Pereyaslav now. . . ." The poet thinks that Khmelnytsky would have become thoroughly drunk, if not worse, had he been able to foresee the results of the treaty. The poem is very important because it contains Shevchenko's mature appraisal of Bohdan Khmelnytsky in a pithy form:

> Amen to you, great man!
> Great and famous! but not very much so . . .
> If you had not been born
> Or had drunk yourself [to death] in your cradle . . .
> I should not have dragged you, most glorious man,
> Through the mud. Amen.[58]

It need not be stressed here that these poems, although reprinted in some Soviet editions, are not included in the secondary school curricula. Moreover, in the "academic" history an unsuccessful attempt has been made to revise Shevchenko's attitude toward Khmelnytsky and the Union of Pereyaslav.[59]

The clearest indication of Shevchenko's positive views is contained in his famous "Message to My Dead, Living and Yet Unborn Fellow Countrymen, in the Ukraine and Abroad," that was written in 1845. That poem is essentially directed against Ukrainians who forget their national descent and go to serve either Russia or Poland, or, even worse, pride themselves on their famous Ukrainian ancestors, but oppress their very countrymen as ignorant serfs.[60] The poem is analyzed in detail in Grade VIII, and excerpts from it are also read in Grade VII.[61] As was to be expected, Soviet commentators stress Shevchenko's critique of the social order (the oppression of serfs) at the expense of his protest against the political (assimilation to the dominant nationalities, ignorance of the history of one's own people). But the attentive Soviet reader may form his own conclusions when he comes to the lines that are reprinted even in the anthologies for Grades VII and VIII:

> Only in the house of one's own is there justice-truth (*pravda*),
> Strength and freedom.
> There is not another Ukraine in the world,
> There is no second Dnieper . . .

These lines, however, are glossed over in recent Soviet commentaries. More honest was Shablovsky, when in 1933 he cited them as an example of the poet's "nationalist limitations." [62]

In the same year, 1845, Shevchenko wrote his "Will." In the first two stanzas, the poet appeals to his countrymen to bury him on a mound in the Ukrainian steppe from which he could see the Dnieper. The last stanza of the poem contains his famous political testament:

> Grant me burial, then uprising
> Shatter every gyve;
> Drench with evil blood of foeman
> Freedom, that it thrive.
> And my name in your great kindred,
> Kindred free and new,
> Ye shall cherish, lest it perish,—
> Speak me fair and true.[63]

The only legitimate inference that can be drawn from these lines and from "The Message," when considered in the light of Shevchenko's biography, is that the poet called upon the Ukrainians to work and, if necessary, to fight for the social and political liberation of their country. But it also becomes clear that he was vague as to the precise forms in which this freedom was to be realized. Taking advantage of this, Soviet critics have tried to interpret Shevchenko as a prophet of the Soviet order. In discussing the last stanza of his most popular poem, "My Will," the teacher is supposed to point out to his pupils that his legacy has been realized in the Soviet Union.[64] Only after considering the attitudes of Soviet Ukrainians in my Chapter X will it be possible to say how convincing that argument may sound in their ears.

The last problem which ought to be considered, if only in the form of a brief postscript, is Shevchenko's connection with world literature. One might have expected that with the beginning of postwar isolation research on that particular aspect of Shevchenko's work would become politically dangerous, the more so since the method of isolating the Soviet Union from the West consisted in emphasizing everything Russian. In a book that was published by the Ukrainian Academy of Sciences in 1939, the influence of Western poets upon Shevchenko was still discussed in a fairly objective way.[65] During the war, his poetry was recognized for what it was: a significant contribution to world literature.[66] But after Zhdanov's speech (1946) the line changed: Russian influences—real and imagined—have been cited to the exclusion of any others, and Shevchenko has been depicted as a "people's poet," sometimes in the sense of being somewhat provincial, favorite with the lower classes, etc., which does not do justice to his full genius. There were some indications that during the "decompression" after Stalin's death and the Twentieth Party Congress, which entailed an expansion of cultural contacts with the world, Ukrainian scholars would be allowed to investigate more fully Shevchenko's position in world literature.[67] But with the restoration of Russian language and culture to the place they had held under Stalin and Zhdanov, that is from the summer of 1958 on, any hope for a full analysis of that facet of Shevchenko's work has had to be abandoned.

4. Conclusions

In our analysis of the Soviet interpretation of Shevchenko we have seen that the regime has tried to enlist Ukraine's most popular poet to reinforce its ideological policy, sometimes with scant regard for historical truth. Similar tendencies could be detected in the Soviet presentation of other Ukrainian classics, but we think that the example of Shevchenko will suffice. In essence, the Soviet image of him consists of certain officially prescribed themes: the unity of thought and action with nineteenth century Russian radicals, which tends to be depicted as a relationship between pupil and master; the hatred of everything anti-Russian, which means the "decadent West" and "Ukrainian bourgeois nationalism" in particular. Those themes had been laid down in the Zhdanov inspired decree against "distortions" in Ukrainian literary criticsm (1946) and the Central Committee Theses on the Re-Unification with Russia (1954); and it need not be emphasized that with the exception of some works that appeared before Zhdanov's speech, post war literary criticism in Soviet Ukraine has served the aim of general Soviet policy. The following is important: How can the discrepancy between the official interpretation and the correct, historically ascertainable sense of Shevchenko's works be detected by readers in Soviet Ukraine? What effect would such a discovery have upon them?

We submit that the problem is in part a mechanical one, and in part one of motivation. Shevchenko's most important work, his Ukrainian poems collected in *Kobzar*, is not voluminous, so that it is not easy to justify any cuts on the ground of space limitations. Selections of his poems were printed, but there were also reasonably full editions, with important prefaces to the original editions omitted. Without a very painstaking analysis of their distribution (how many copies were printed? in what year?),[68] it is not possible to state with absolute assurance whether the access to some poems presents special difficulties. My impression is that a Soviet Ukrainian reader who wants to look up a particular poem by Shevchenko can do so relatively easily, because reasonably full editions of the *Kobzar* were published in the Soviet Union not only in the 1920's but also in 1939 and 1949. On the other hand, there might also be a strong temptation for certain readers to rely on shortened versions in school anthologies. In those anthologies the cuts are, as a rule, not clearly indicated. Moreover, because Shevchenko had written comparatively little and that little had captured the imagination of all strata of the Ukrainian people, his work might not be a typical example of the effectiveness of Soviet textual censorship. In the case of more esoteric classics (Ivan Franko, Lesya Ukrainka) who have left more and longer

works, it is always possible for the regime to suppress certain objectionable pieces on the grounds that a selection had to be made, that a complete edition of their works would have been too expensive, and the like.

Even more serious than the problem of the availability of texts is
that of motivation. Why should Soviet Ukrainians want to approach the
official interpretation critically? In quest of truth? Undoubtedly there
are such men and women in whom the pure curiosity to learn the truth
has survived in spite and perhaps because of, Soviet distortion of facts.
But we need not be cynics to recognize that the majority of mankind
are not philosophers in the classic sense of the word, that general con-
tentment is a poor stimulus for critical and politically dangerous inquiries. Only after examining whatever evidence there is on the attitudes in the Soviet Ukraine, can we make any inferences as to the possible effect of the discovery that the Soviet interpretation of Shevchenko
does not always do justice to the poet. Such an analysis will also reveal to
us to what extent Shevchenko's innermost hope has been fulfilled. Inspired by the Eleventh Psalm he wrote in 1859:

> . . . I shall exalt
> Those petty, dumb slaves!
> To protect them, I shall set
> The Word.

Chapter VII

SOVIET INTERPRETATION OF UKRAINIAN
HISTORY: SOME PROBLEMS

This chapter will concentrate primarily on the interpretation of one key problem of modern Ukrainian history, the Treaty of Pereyaslav (1654), or the so-called reunification of Ukraine with Russia, the 300th anniversary of which was celebrated with such fanfare in 1954. As in my approach to Soviet literary criticism I shall be guided by certain principles. I am not primarily interested in whether Soviet historical writings express the "truth," that is, whether non-Soviet historians using the same materials, or Soviet historians working under different circumstances, might have arrived at conclusions other than those reached by Soviet historians now, allowing for legitimate differences of opinion. What I should like to do is not only to prove that deliberate misinterpretation of history exists, but also to ask why history has been misinterpreted, to enquire whether this falsification can be detected by Soviet Ukrainians, and—so far as this can be ascertained—what effect such a discovery might have upon their thinking. In other words, I am directly concerned with the presumable *impact* of historical knowledge, and only indirectly with the problem of *arriving at* that knowledge—which is the business of a professional historian. Cyril E. Black in his introductory essay to a valuable collection of historiographical articles has drawn attention to the contribution an analysis of the Soviet interpretation of history can make to political science. In his terse words: "The relationship between historical writing and the Communist Party line offers some valuable insights into the working of the Soviet system." [1] My task is to consider the relationship between historiography and the party line in regard to the Ukraine. From this I hope not only to obtain a clearer picture of the nature of Soviet policy, but also to draw some inferences as to its results.

To refute Soviet arguments I have relied to a great extent upon the large, scholarly history of the Ukraine by Michael Hrushevsky.[2] I am well aware that in the interpretation of certain events Hrushevsky differs from such Russian historians as Klyuchevsky. Sometimes it is hinted by Western authors that Hrushevsky might be a Ukrainian nationalist first and a historian second,[3] but the fact remains that Hrushevsky is too careful and too productive a scholar to be dismissed without due attention to his work.[4] I have divided the chapter into three parts: a survey of Soviet Ukrainian historiography after 1945, the case study of the interpretation of Pereyaslav, and conclusions.

1. *Soviet Interpretation of Ukrainian History Since 1945*

The general problem of interpreting Ukrainian history was the subject of a protracted discussion on the pages of the Kiev and Moscow press from the summer of 1946 until the end of 1947.[5] Under attack were all semi-popular histories of the Ukraine published by the Institute of the History and Archeology of the Ukraine of the Ukrainian SSR Academy of Sciences in 1941–44.[6] The evidence strongly suggests that the "discussion" was inspired by central authorities in Moscow and that in passing its ideological decrees the Central Committee of the Communist Party of Ukraine was merely re-phrasing instructions from above.[7] In 1947 the Central Committee of the Communist Party of Ukraine took the Historical Institute of the Academy under its immediate supervision,[8] and at the end of that year Soviet Ukrainian historians began to write a new semi-popular *History of the Ukraine* in two volumes.[9] The first volume covering the events before 1917, did not appear until 1953. The second volume on the Soviet period was published in 1958.[10]

Six to eleven years is a decidedly long time for a semi-popular work, even if the two volumes are quite bulky.[11] This shows beyond doubt how much care the regime devotes to the proper interpretation of a subject that is politically as important as the history of a constituent people of the USSR. The most authoritative statement in the historiographical discussion of 1946–47 was printed in the theoretical Party organ *Bol'shevik*. On the tercentenary of the Treaty of Pereyaslav (1954) the Central Committee published appropriate historical theses, which in effect provide a binding guide line for the interpretation of the whole of Ukrainian history, and not only of that particular event. Those theses are still binding today (late 1962).

The 1947 article "On the History of the Ukrainian People" was written by K. Lytvyn, then Secretary of the Central Committee of the Communist Party of Ukraine in charge of ideological matters.[12] The keynote of his article is sounded in the second and third paragraphs where the author states that:

[In the Soviet Union], for the first time in its history the Ukrainian people has been given limitless opportunities for the development of its economy, culture and science.

. . . .

[It] has become convinced that . . . outside that family [of Soviet peoples] it is threatened with enslavement, destruction of its culture.[13]

In the first part of his article Lytvyn denounces various heresies committed by Ukrainian historians during the war, two of them being their failure to adopt a Marxist periodization of history and their acceptance of Hrushevsky's thesis of the essential unity of the Ukrainian people, as contrasted with the Marxist emphasis upon a sharp division between the exploited and exploiting classes.[14] But the quintessence of his criticism is contained in four directives at the end of the article:

1. Ukrainian historians must delimit historical periods in accordance with Marxist socio-economic principles.
2. They must depict the unity of the historical processes of the Ukrainian and Russian peoples, and disprove Hrushevsky and his followers who asserted the contrary.
3. They must present the Kievan Rus, the medieval East Slavic Empire whose capital was Kiev, as "the cradle of three peoples: the Great Russian, the Ukrainian, and the Belorussian."
4. They must devote attention to the historical struggle of Slavic peoples for unity, which heretofore had been ignored by "bourgeois historians." [15]

The entire history of the Ukrainian nation up to 1917 is thus to be interpreted as a prelude for its joining the USSR, and later the Eastern European Soviet Empire of postwar creation.[16]

A comparison of the 1954 Central Committee Theses with Lytvyn's article is rather instructive.[17] Being addressed to a broader audience, they do not mention the problem of Marxist periodization. But even the "class character" of history is not stressed; the Ukrainian and the Russian people are essentially depicted as single units and not aggregates of warring classes. Even the pan-Slavic theme has been virtually sacrificed [18] to the overriding purpose of the Theses: to present the entire Ukrainian history as a teleological process, the *telos* being not so much the creation of the USSR (as in Lytvyn's article) but the so-called reunification with the Russian people.[19]

The four main points of the Theses are:

1. "The Russian, Ukrainian and Belorussian peoples trace their origin to a single root—the ancient Russian people who founded the early Russian state—Kiev Rus" (from Thesis I).

2. Throughout its history, the Ukrainian—and, for that matter, the Belorussian people, too—desired reunification with the Russian people (Theses I–VI).[20]
3. The reunification was a progressive act (Thesis VI).
4. Throughout its entire history, the Russian people had been the senior brother in the family of East Slavic peoples. Its main virtue consisted in giving rise to a strong working class, which in turn produced its vanguard, the Communist Party (*passim*).

As late as 1954, Stalin's toast to the Russian people was thus reaffirmed on highest authority by virtually identifying the Communist Party before 1917 with the (Great) Russian working class—a proposition that is substantially correct—and the Russian working class with the Russian people. This was a political requirement. In its light, Ukrainian history had to be reinterpreted as a continuous process toward reunification with the Russian people in 1654 and again in 1917–20.

A politically motivated interpretation, however, entailed a great disadvantage to the regime, which became painfully obvious during Stalin's time. Evidence had to be selected to fit a predetermined pattern; and unless this was done very carefully, the works turned out to be all too schematic, too "black and white," and therefore less convincing. Thus, referring to Volume I of the large semi-popular history of the Ukraine, the well-known writer, former partisan leader and Stalin prize winner, P. Vershyhora, could not help exclaiming in print: "A history without history." [21] Anastas Mikoyan in his important speech to the Twentieth Party Congress went further in criticizing the output of historians under Stalin. He ridiculed the work of an unnamed Moscow historian who had blamed certain weaknesses of the Ukrainian Communist Party (Bolshevik) organization in 1918–20 on the activities of two of their Party leaders, Antonov-Ovseyenko and Kosior. More importantly Mikoyan issued a challenge to Ukrainian historians:

I believe that Ukrainian historians will be found who will write a rather better history of the emergence and development of the Ukraine socialist state than the Moscow historians who undertook the job but who would perhaps been better advised not to. (*Laughter in the hall*.) [22]

Implicit in Mikoyan's criticism of "such historical nonsense" appears to be the admission that under Stalin some historical subjects had become so sensitive that Soviet Ukrainian historians left it up to their Russian colleagues to deal with them.

The Ukrainians were not slow to take up Mikoyan's challenge. In the summer of 1956 a very important conference of Soviet Ukrainian historians took place. K. H. Huslysty asserted that it was no longer possible to ignore the contributions of gentry and bourgeois historians of the Ukraine. He further criticized those of his colleagues that had written about the friendly relations of Russian Tsars toward the Ukraine. I. A. Boyko, from the Institute of History of the Ukrainian SSR Academy of Sciences proposed to study the work of Michael Drahomanov—the well-known Ukrainian liberal thinker of the latter half of the nineteenth century.[23] F. Ye. Los, of the same institute, termed the emergence of the Ukrainian bourgeois national movement in the nineteenth century progressive, criticized his colleagues who had depicted it otherwise. Ye. H. Fedorenko, a representative from Kiev University, criticized Vol. I of the textbook of Ukrainian history, published in 1954 (Vol. I of the semi-popular history perhaps?) as misleading. Specialists had not been consulted when it was written [sic]. Two historians demanded the establishment of a Ukrainian historical journal (D. V. Pohrebyns'ky and Doniy). They were successful: starting with 1957 the *Ukrayins'ky istorychny zhurnal* (Ukrainian Historical Journal) appeared. A. D. Voyna demanded better access to non-Soviet historical studies, especially those on the post-Revolutionary history of the Ukraine.[24]

Rather significantly, the conference was not publicized in the Soviet Ukrainian press and we learned about this in a rather indirect way. But after the summer of 1956 three important articles were published in which some of the findings of the conference were made public. I. Boyko complained that "a thorough research work on Ukrainian-Russian relations in the period of the liberation war of the Ukrainian people, 1648–54 [did] not exist"—a shattering commentary on the flood of publications that appeared in connection with the Pereyaslav Tercentenary in 1954.[25] Similarly, M. M. Lysenko, the director of the historical methodology section of the Scientific Research Institute of Pedagogy of the Ukrainian SSR, suggested that the progressive significance of the reunification with Russia may have been overstressed at the expense of "objective facts." [26] (More will be said on this in Section 2 below.) As far as the period of 1918–20 is concerned, we have the very important admission of historian N. Suprunenko:

A serious lacuna is that in recent historical works nobody has posed the question about [Russian] great power chauvinism in the Ukraine and the great damage, which it inflicted upon the cause of fighting Ukrainian bourgeois nationalism, the cause of constructing a sovereign Ukrainian Soviet State.[27]

With the change in nationality policy in 1958, the guide lines for Ukrainian historians have presumably been changed too, but I have not been able to find any direct evidence in the form of a programmatical article comparable to that of Boyko's or Suprunenko's. That the atmosphere has changed can be clearly inferred from the extremely interesting review in *Pravda* of the *Outline History of the Communist Party of Ukraine,* which was published in 1961. Hardly had the history appeared than Academician Mints called for a new, second edition, revised in the light of the Twenty-Second Party Congress' resolutions. It appears that the authors of the history had admitted some weaknesses of the Bolsheviks vis-à-vis Ukrainian bourgeois nationalists in 1917–20, had insufficiently stressed "how alien nationalism was to the Ukrainian people." [28] Have Mikoyan's and Suprunenko's protests of 1956 been in vain? Must Soviet Ukrainian historians return to Stalinist-like falsifications?

Before analyzing in detail a prime example of such "historical nonsense"—if we may extend Mikoyan's term to cover the interpretation of the Treaty of Pereyaslav—I should like to touch upon two problems closely related to Soviet Ukrainian historiography: the teaching of a separate course in Ukrainian history in Soviet schools and extended polemics with Ukrainian historians living in exile.

In a system in which the state controls all school curricula, it is crucially important to find out how history is being taught. The contents of Ukrainian history presented to school children may be inferred from our summary of the 1946–47 historiographic discussion and of the 1954 Party Theses. But it is also of considerable significance for the outlook of the child whether Ukrainian history is presented in a separate course or intermixed with the discussion of the so-called history of the USSR (i.e., mostly Russian history), as was the case under Stalin. In 1956 Lysenko suggested that Ukrainian history be taught at the schools of the Republic instead of the history of the USSR. Insofar as the program of instruction for 1956–57 did not envisage such a change, he proposed that in teaching the history of the USSR the teachers should pay "special attention" to local sources. [29]

Other Ukrainian historians took up the idea. In the fall of 1958, in discussing the impending educational reforms Lysenko and his co-author I. M. Skrypkin, advocated as a "logical supplement to the general course of the history of the USSR a separate course in the history of the Ukrainian SSR." That course was to be taught in the second semester of Grade VII and in both semesters of Grade VIII (the two last grades of compulsory universal education). [30] Ten months later, another writer pointed out that, despite some improvements, children were still not receiving an adequate knowledge of Ukrainian history. *"The material from Ukrainian history had to be considerably increased."* But how was this to be accomplished? Though "frequently the thoughts were expressed" that a separate course of Ukrainian history ought to be set up, V. O. Puns'ky felt that the "history of the Ukrainian people was so closely interwoven with the history of the Russian people that in a school, in which only the bases of historical science were studied, repetition of teaching material would have become unavoidable when the history of the Ukraine would be taught as a separate course." Moreover, such a combined presentation would be better for "the elucidation of the centuries-old friendship between the Russian and Ukrainian peoples, for educating the pupils in the spirit of unshakeable friendship of all Soviet peoples [sic]." Nevertheless, he advocated separate textbooks for pupils in the Ukrainian SSR and not only in the field of history.[31] In the same issue of the journal I. F. Chernikov shot back that there should be a separate course in Ukrainian history in addition to the course in the history of the USSR and that the argument that such a course would lead to a repetition of material "could not stand up to any criticism. Avoidance of repetition did not present any practical difficulties whatsoever." [32]

Finally, in 1961 the issue was resolved by administrative fiat.[33] In Grade IV highlights of the history of the USSR were to be taught. In Grade V ancient history was considered, in Grade VI history of the Middle Ages. In Grades VII–VIII introductory history of the USSR and modern history of foreign countries was to be taught; in Grades IX–XI (that is, beyond the level of compulsory universal education) a systematic course on history of the USSR and current events in the USSR and abroad was placed in the curriculum.[34] What had happened to the proposed course in Ukrainian history? Starting with the school year 1961–62 material from the history of the Ukraine was to be systematically integrated into the course on Soviet history, either in the form of supplementary remarks or separate lectures or series of lectures. Writing that such an approach "would ensure the understanding by the pupils of Grade VII of questions relating to the common descent of the Russian, Ukrainian and Belorussian peoples from the common root of the ancient-Rus nationality, the centuries old friendship of the Ukrainian and Russian peoples . . . ," Lysenko admitted that he had been overruled on political grounds.[35] Nevertheless, the Ukrainian historians gained a limited concession in that they were allowed at first to publish school readers on Ukrainian history,[36] and then a school textbook.[37] It need not be stressed that the publication of the thin (182 pp.) text took an inordinately long time; the manuscript was discussed at a historians' conference in 1959,[38] but it was not until 1962 that it was finally published. Obviously it was not only historians that had to be consulted.

The second problem—the polemic with non-Soviet authors—can be dealt with more briefly. Since its inception in July, 1957, an important function of the *Ukrayins'ky istorychny zhurnal* appears to have been to engage in detailed and acrimonious disputes with Western authors who in one way or another had touched upon Ukrainian history. In the Vol-

umes 1957–59 (total of fifteen issues), for example, I have counted no less
than eight such review articles.[39] There was also a sharp and detailed
attack on Ukrainian historians living in the West who attended the International Historical Congress in Stockholm. They were "very active." [40]
It would have been tedious to enter into the merits of those attacks. But
it should be borne in mind that after 1957 college professors, secondary
school teachers of history, and other interested Ukrainians who read the
journal can obtain a fairly complete, though distorted picture of Western
publications relating to the Ukraine. Many of the reviews are detailed
enough to permit those Ukrainians to reconstruct the Western argument,
a great contrast to the deliberate isolation under Stalin.

Let us now turn to our case study: the historical facts behind the
political celebration of 1954.

2. The Treaty of Pereyaslav (1654) and the "Reunification" of the Ukraine with Russia

The celebration of the tercentenary of the Treaty of Pereyaslav in
1954 was undoubtedly a major propaganda campaign. It produced a
flood of semi-popular literature which need not be analyzed in detail
because it follows the Party Theses.[41] What I would like to do in this
section is to consider two problems in historiography. The first, and the
narrower one, is whether the Treaty of Pereyaslav may legitimately be
interpreted as a treaty of unification with Russia. The second, broader
question is how the union with Russia has been evaluated by Soviet
historians; why they have done so; and what have been the presumable
results.

Recent Soviet historiography has attempted to interpret the Treaty of
Pereyaslav as the climactic fulfillment of the age-long desire of the
Ukrainian people to be reunified with their Russian brethren. We read
in Thesis VI:

The Pereyaslav Rada's [Council's] move culminated the people's struggle to
reunify the Ukraine with Russia; it was the realization of the Ukrainian people's
age-long hope and desire and marked a turning point in their history.

This is not the place to review Ukrainian history from the Middle Ages
to the seventeenth century in order to establish how closely Soviet claims
correspond to reality.[42] I should like to concentrate on the Treaty itself.
If the Party statement means anything beyond a sweeping generalization
it must be proved that (1) the Agreement which grew out of the decision
of the Council of Pereyaslav was intended by its signatories as a treaty
of incorporation; [43] and that (2) in 1654 the Ukrainian people as a whole
desired to be united with the Russian people and vice versa. Let us

briefly recount the incidents that led to the conclusion of the agreement and summarize its contents. From there we shall proceed to examine some of the interpretations.

Almost since the beginning of his uprising against Poland in May, 1648, Hetman Khmelnytsky sought to establish contact with Tsar Alexey Mikhaylovich of Russia. In his first letter to the Tsar, of June 8, 1648, Khmelnytsky hinted at what great benefits would accrue to Orthodox Christians in general and Ukrainians in particular if Alexey Mikhaylovich were elected King of Poland. He also suggested that if the Tsar was willing to attack Poland he would aid him with all his troops. But Moscow remained cool to the repeated advances of the rebellious Cossack leader, mindful of her eternal peace treaty with Poland that had been concluded in 1635.[44] In search of allies, Khmelnytsky turned to the Crimean Khan. The latter, however, proved susceptible to presents and as the Polish treasury was ample, the Crimean Tatars would desert Ukrainian troops at crucial moments, forcing Khmelnytsky to conclude with Poland a series of increasingly unfavorable peace treaties. In 1651, Khmelnytsky concluded a treaty of alliance with the Sultan, accepting for this purpose the status of a Turkish vassal. But he would not give up his hope of obtaining aid from the Muscovite Tsar. For reasons of her own, Russia broke off diplomatic relations with Poland in the summer of 1653, and on October 1 of that year the *Zemsky sobor* (Assembly of Estates) in Moscow decided that the Tsar "should graciously accept Hetman Bohdan Khmelnytsky and the whole Zaporozhian Host with its towns and lands under His Majesty's high hand for the sake of the Orthodox Christian faith and Holy Divine Churches." [45]

Envoys of the Tsar were despatched to the Ukraine to accept from Khmelnytsky a solemn oath of allegiance. Sworn in also were his troops and the Ukrainian towns. The main ceremony was performed at Pereyaslav—hence the resulting agreement has been called the Treaty of Pereyaslav. In view of later controversy, one detail of the procedure should be noted. All accounts agree that immediately before the oath was to be administered, Khmelnytsky demanded from the Muscovite envoys that they should swear for the Tsar that he, too, would keep his faith. This they refused to do, saying that the Tsar need not make an oath to keep faith with his own "subjects." Thereupon Khmelnytsky and his Ukrainian retinue withdrew. After some time, Khmelnytsky returned and swore the oath of allegiance to the Tsar; his retinue and rank and file Cossacks followed suit and within a short time the oath was also administered to the citizens of several Ukrainian cities. There is some difference of opinion as to what changed Khmelnytsky's mind to swear the oath without a symbolical *quid pro quo:* some Ukrainian contemporaries alleged that the envoys reconsidered and swore in the name of the Tsar. The most plausible interpretation is that they did not swear a formal oath but gave strong assurances that the Tsar always kept his "word," which was interpreted by Khmelnytsky as the equivalent of an oath.[46]

After the ceremony at Pereyaslav (January 8, 1654) Khmelnytsky despatched his envoys to Moscow, and in March, 1654, an agreement between him and Tsar Alexey was drafted and agreed upon by the *Zemsky sobor*. The so-called Treaty of Pereyaslav consists of two documents: the "Articles of Bohdan Khmelnytsky," and a Gracious Writ of Tsar Alexey Mikhailovych, both of March 27, 1654.[47] The most important of the eleven articles are the first and fifth. Article I provided that the taxes collected in the Ukraine should go to the Muscovite treasury. Article V regulated the external relations of the Cossack Host. Ambassadors in "good affairs" were to be received and freely dismissed and the Tsar was merely to be notified of the results of the conversations. Ambassadors hostile to the Tsar, however, were not to be dismissed without Moscow's approval. Furthermore, Khmelnytsky was not to negotiate with the Sultan and the Polish king without permission from the Tsar. In the "Gracious Writ" the Tsar confirmed the previous "rights and privileges of the Cossacks." The most significant of them was the right of self-government. The Cossacks were to elect their Hetman by themselves. The Tsar, however, was to be notified of their choice and the new Hetman was to swear an oath of allegiance. Secondly, the Cossacks were to be judged in their own courts, according to ancient Cossack law.[48]

The Treaty of Pereyaslav has been interpreted in various ways. At one extreme have been scholars who have seen it as a treaty of complete incorporation (D. Odinets, and V. Myakotin in his later works); at the other extreme it has been regarded as a military alliance between two independent states (V. Lypyns'ky).[49] In order to arrive at the presumed intention of the signatories two methods may be followed: one, a close reading of the terms of the agreement in the light of contemporary diplomatic usage; the second, an interpretation of the treaty in the light of the actions of the parties before and after its conclusion, that is, an attempt to ascertain how the parties interpreted the treaty for themselves. If the narrower textual interpretation conforms with the parties' subsequent actions, then it may be assumed with a great degree of certainty that the intention of the parties has been established correctly.[50]

Whereas the agreement of Pereyaslav is now being depicted as the act of the "reunification of the Ukraine with Russia," it is very significant to note that none of the original documents employs this term.[51] The two formulas that are constantly used in the most important documents (the "Articles of Bohdan Khmelnytsky" and the "Tsar's Gracious Writ" of March, 1654) are: to take Khmelnytsky "under His Majesty's high hand" [52] and, when viewed from Khmelnytsky's side, to swear "an oath of eternal subjection." [53] This may seem a worthless quibble, for does not the term "subject," as used by Khmelnytsky, clearly express his desire to make the Ukraine part and parcel of the Muscovite state? If so, why should we not speak of a *unification* of the Ukraine with Russia, dropping the prefix *re-* because of legitimate doubts as to whether the Ukrainian and Russian peoples had ever been closely united in the Middle Ages? Actually, there is more to textual analysis than appears at first sight.

In his careful analysis of the Treaty of Pereyaslav and the subsequent documents defining the legal status of the Ukraine within the Russian Empire, the eminent Russian jurist Baron Nolde has found what he called a "duality of juridical nature." As he put it, "They had the . . . peculiarly mixed nature of grants by 'grace' and of treaties at the same time." [54] He noted, for example, that until the time of Peter II the Russian Foreign Office regarded the agreement of Pereyaslav as a treaty binding upon Russia, though it was full of expressions like "in accordance with the *grant* of our imperial majesty, the *subject* of our imperial majesty, Bohdan Khmelnyts'ky." [55] Nolde's observation does not support the view that the agreement of Pereyaslav entailed the unconditional surrender of rights on the part of Khmelnytsky. Nolde interprets it, therefore, as an act of incorporation providing for the Ukraine a certain autonomy, the precise limits of which were to be agreed upon between each successive Hetman or Tsar. [56]

More recently, Ukrainian scholarship has confirmed Nolde's doubts about the admissibility of regarding the Treaty as a unilateral grant on the part of the Tsars. Furthermore, it has also proved that Nolde's assumption of a dual juridical nature of the agreement of Pereyaslav was unwarranted: The treaty did have a single intent. The clue to the solution lies in the contemporary usage of the term "subject" as followed by the Muscovite Foreign Office. In his thorough article Prokopovych has established that this particular concept as used in the Treaty of Pereyaslav does *not* connote a subject ("citizen," "national") in the modern sense of the term. [57] Before Catherine the Great, the Russian people were —with a few exceptions—referred to as "the people of all ranks of the Muscovite state," not "subjects," and in addressing the Tsar they always called themselves "servants" (*kholopy*). [58] It was only in 1786 that the term "subject" was introduced into Russian public law to designate the population of the Empire. [59] Conversely, Prokopovych found after a careful investigation that:

The tsar's subjects were *vassals* in various degrees of dependency; sometimes, and this must be emphasized, this dependency was purely nominal. There were lands which accepted "subjection" to the tsar on certain conditions, i.e., the tsar's defense protection was only formally recognized by them. In such a case, the tsar's supremacy was a *protectorate*.[60]

From an analysis of the crucial terms used in the Treaty of Pereyaslav we have concluded that the agreement should not be regarded as one of unconditional incorporation but rather as a treaty of protection, Khmelnytsky accepting the *suzerainty* but not the *sovereignty* of the Russian Tsar. What positive proof is there of our thesis that a strong element of defensive alliance was involved? We have to consider some historical facts preceding the conclusion of the treaty and the most important of the subsequent events.

Recent Soviet historiography seems to be very inclined toward facile generalizations. We read, for instance, in the Academic history of the Ukrainian SSR that the important decision of the Russian *Zemsky sobor* to accept Bohdan Khmelnytsky "under the sovereign's high hand" was ". . . the expression of the will and desire of the entire Russian people to aid their fraternal Ukrainian people in its struggle against the Poland of the squires." [61]

A Soviet Ukrainian publicist tries to explain the union by postulating that ". . . History of mankind does not know of another example of such sincere, selfless and ardent friendship as the friendship and brotherly unification of two great Slavic peoples—the Russian and Ukrainian." [62]

The documents, however, suggest that a good deal of *Realpolitik* was involved, too. The union was decided upon under the impression that if in 1653 the Tsar would not help Khmelnytsky, the latter would seek a closer union with the Turkish Sultan or the Khan of Crimea and might conceivably make war on the Tsar, which would have been rather dangerous.[63] While the Ukraine was greatly weakened in the long struggle with Poland, Khmelnytsky could, nevertheless, marshall more than 300 thousand battle-hardened troops—a force not to be overlooked.[64]

In reviewing Soviet historiography on this subject, Krupnytskyj has drawn attention to its tendency to ignore the years 1654–57, that is, from the conclusion of the Treaty of Pereyaslav until Khmelnytsky's death.[65] If we look at the facts, the reason becomes obvious: No matter how the Russian court wanted to interpret the Treaty Khmelnytsky was not willing to become more than a nominal vassal of the Tsar. This appeared clearly in his international relations.

In 1654–55 Ukrainian and Russian troops joined to attack Poland which was ideal from Khmelnytsky's point of view. But in Muscovy there was strong opposition against the war with Poland: a powerful faction of *boyars* looked upon southward expansion as a secondary matter, for, in their opinion, the foremost task of Russia was to occupy the Baltic states. By the spring of 1656 this faction won out, and Russia concluded an armistice with Poland: the Poles offering Tsar Alexey the Polish crown, subject, however, to the approval of the *sejm* (Parliament). The Muscovite government took the position that the Ukrainians being vassals of the Tsar their envoys need not be invited to the armistice negotiations at Vilna. Khmelnytsky appeared outwardly calm, for he did not want to break with Alexey, but privately he and his officers raged at this insult to a faithful ally. When in the summer of 1656 Russia declared war on Sweden, he repaid Alexey by remaining neutral. Moerover, in September, 1656, Khmelnytsky concluded a military alliance with Rakoczy of Transylvania, which in December of that year was joined by Sweden. The object of the alliance was to conquer Poland. Under its terms, Khmelnytsky sent a Cossack detachment of 15,000 men under one of his colonels to invade his old enemy's country together with Transylvanian and Swedish troops, while his protector Tsar Alexey had concluded an armistice with the Poles and was at war with Sweden.[66]

The joint Transylvanian-Ukrainian-Swedish campaign miscarried, but it aroused the anger of the Tsar. Two Muscovite envoys were sent to Khmelnytsky, who had been stricken mortally ill, to remonstrate with him over the alleged breach of the Pereyaslav Agreement. Their conversation was rather angry, Buturlin [67] complaining that the Tsar had not received Ukrainian taxes as promised, apart from small sums from the city of Kiev itself, and that Khmelnytsky had shown himself disloyal in concluding an alliance with Karl Gustav of Sweden. Khmelnytsky retorted that the taxes had turned out not to be so high as he had hoped; that it had been the Tsar who had shown himself "merciless" in making an armistice with the Poles against the wishes of the Ukrainian Cossacks; and that his relations with Sweden preceded the Treaty of Pereyaslav and that the Tsar could not object to his dealing with an old friend. He later apologized for his anger: he did not want to give the impression that he would break the oath given to the Tsar while already on his death bed.[68] But the very incident shows that as of 1657 Khmelnytsky did not regard the Treaty of Pereyaslav as one of unconditional subjection and that, most probably, in 1654 it had never entered his mind that it could be interpreted as such.[69]

It is very important to ascertain precisely how Soviet historiography treats those last three years of Khmelnytsky's rule. Pankratova's textbook for Grade VIII ignores the Ukrainian treaty with Sweden, but this might be explained by lack of space.[70] But so does the college textbook of 1947: it only hints that the Treaty included "internal contradictions." [71] The new history of the Ukrainian republic deals with the years 1654–57 rather cursorily, but it admits in passing—as facts of minor importance, so to speak—that Russia declared war on Sweden, whereas Khmelnytsky gave military aid to Rakoczy and the Swedes against Poland.[72] On the next page a statement by Khmelnytsky is quoted to the effect that he was "a loyal subject of the Tsar and would never be separated from the Tsar's high hand," so as to refute the claims of Ukrainian "bourgeois nationalists" who allegedly have interpreted Khmelnytsky's treaty with Sweden as an indication of his desire to break with Russia.[73] But that is not the point: not a complete break with Moscow was at issue in June 1657, but significant differences of opinion as to the status of the Ukraine under the Muscovite protectorate, Khmelnytsky reserving himself a freedom of action whose extent struck the Russians as a sign of disloyalty.

Unfortunately for the regime, which may have preferred to leave these three years in semi-darkness, conscientious Soviet biographers of Khmelnytsky could not help taking their position on the events in 1654–57. Thus, by a simple juxtaposition of the general histories with two biographies of Khmelnytsky—the scholarly one by Kryp"yakevych and the popular by Osipov, any Soviet reader may discover by himself that though the Treaty of 1654 allegedly expressed the desire of the entire Ukrainian people to be reunified with Russia, all was not harmony between the two peoples after its conclusion.[74] In the first edition of his book (1939), Osipov was able to characterize Khmelnytsky's diplomacy in 1657 as follows:

He showed himself a loyal subject of the Muscovite Tsar, but, above all, an ardent patriot of his country. The duties which the Muscovite subjecthood imposed upon him, he put in second place after the interests of the Ukraine.[75]

Very characteristically, this passage was omitted when Osipov's biography was republished in 1948.

So much for an analysis of the diplomatic history of 1654–57. But the Party Theses postulate that the Treaty was an act of reunification of two brotherly peoples, long prepared by cultural and economic ties. This is an extremely complicated subject, and all I can do is to cite the opinion of the most competent historians.

It is true that Khmelnytsky proved either unable or unwilling to depart from the semi-feudal conception of political order which he had inherited from the Poles. When he tried to subordinate the Ukrainian peasants, whom several years before he had led against the Polish magnates, to Ukrainian Cossack officers or even to Polish landlords (who returned to the Ukraine as a result of the more stringent of his peace treaties) the peasants simply fled behind the Muscovite border.[76] Soviet accounts stress that Russian officials treated these refugees very well; but in reviewing the three volumes of documents published by the USSR Academy of Sciences, the late Professor Yakovliv has found instances of friction.[77] Khmelnytsky and his officers, who were mostly descended from the gentry, did not understand the needs of the cities and tried to tax them mercilessly, with the result that Ukrainian burghers appealed to the Tsar to safeguard their liberties.[78] To interpret these moves as an expression of the desire to be united with the Russian people seems to be rather far-fetched; but at the same time it is clear that the rapprochement with Russia corresponded to certain socio-economic interests of the Ukrainian people. In this connection the verdict of Hrushevsky is very remarkable. Referring to the emigration of Ukrainian peasants to the Left Bank Ukraine, often behind Muscovite borders, he wrote: "The cause of the independence of the Ukraine was killed at the price of her territorial expansion," for "the matter of the union of the Ukraine with Moscow and of later compromises with Poland and Muscovy was to a certain extent already prejudged by that emigration movement." [79]

Other economic and cultural relations existed, too. According to Yakovliv, who has examined the voluminous Soviet document collection of 1953, the Ukraine sent to Russia saltpeter and gunpowder in return for grain and foodstuffs; Ukrainian artisans were invited to come to Moscow, and so were Ukrainian monks and clergymen. But in the light of these relations the theme of indebtedness which appears in the 1654–1954 Party Theses (the Russians inspired the Ukrainians toward their uprising against Poland—see the end of Thesis III) is highly implausible: If the Ukraine in the seventeenth century exported to Muscovy skilled artisans and learned monks, it was not a country to look for inspiration to the north.[80]

Furthermore, the diplomatic documents of that period furnish conclusive evidence against the Party Theses that the Ukrainians and Russians of the seventeenth century considered themselves brotherly peoples. The bond that united them was not ethnical, but common danger from Poland and common Orthodox faith. To conclude my analysis of the evidence on the actual character of the Treaty of Pereyaslav, I should like to quote from Yakovliv's findings:

The authors of the introductory article [to *Vossoedinenie I*] conclude their presentation of the idea of common origin and affinity of the Russian and Ukrainian people by saying: "The community of origin of the two brotherly peoples and of the language roots have caused, over the entire period of history, *the closest proximity of culture and the recognition of the oneness of the Russian and Ukrainian people.* . . ."

In their declaration of "oneness of the Russian and Ukrainian peoples" the authors of the introductory article ignore completely the historical documents collected and published under their own editorship. These documents corroborate neither the "oneness" of these people[s], nor the close affiliation of the Ukrainian and Muscovite-Russian language. Some Ukrainian documents call the Ukrainian people a "Russian people" (*rosiys'ky narod*). In B. Khmel'-

nyts'ky's writ of March 17, 1654 (No. 236, Vol. iii) to the tsar, reference is made to "All the Christian Russian clerics and the lay people of all ranks" (and the Ukraine is called a "Russian state," *ibid.*) while the Russian people are called "Muscovite people" or "Muscovites." Muscovite documents, on the other hand, call the Ukrainian people "Cherkassy" or "Zaporozhian Cherkassy" (Vol. i, Nos. 164, 193; Vol. ii, Nos. 140, 142, 152, 192, and many others). At that time in Muscovy the Ukrainian language was called the "Byelorussian language." Ukrainian documents of the seventeenth century had to be translated into the Muscovite language and negotiation with Ukrainian envoys were conducted with the aid of interpreters.[81]

The broader problem of how the regime has interpreted the union of the Ukraine with Russia is rather instructive of the possibilities and limitations of officially controlled historiography, nay, of official propaganda as such. Fortunately, the problem has been considered in scholarly literature in connection with the "lesser evil" doctrine of Soviet historiography, and I can, therefore, limit myself to a few supplementary remarks.[82]

In the 1920's and early 1930's the Soviet regime wanted to emphasize its break with the Russian Tsarist tradition. Ukrainian historians, both Marxist and non-Marxist, were given free hand to examine the facts of Imperial Russian policy toward the Ukraine, which in many respects was one of colonial exploitation.[83] It was at that time that Khmelnytsky to whom the Tsarist government had erected a monument in Kiev would be regarded very critically for concluding the Treaty of Pereyaslav. Hrushevsky judged him severely for his failure to understand the desires of the Ukrainian popular masses and the tasks of modern government.[84] M. Yavorsky, the head of the Marxist school of Ukrainian historians, arrived at the same conclusions but formulated them in even more striking terms.[85] But the most explicit condemnation of Khmelnytsky was contained in the 59th volume of the first edition of the *Large Soviet Encyclopedia,* published in 1935, in which a certain historian with the initials V.K. characterized the result of 1654 as follows:

. . . The well-known Pereyaslav Treaty . . . meant the union of Ukrainian feudal lords with [their] Russian [counterparts]. In essence, it juridically formalized the beginning of the *colonial domination of Russia over the Ukraine.* Basing himself on the Ukrainian feudal class, which had grown significantly by that time, Khmelnytsky aspired to become *an autocrat in the Ukraine.* Wishing to ensure the political rule of his descendants he had his son George appointed hetman during his lifetime.[86]

In short, as of 1935, the Treaty of Pereyaslav was officially regarded as the selfish act of a socially reactionary Cossack officer who did not want so much to "reunify" his country to Russia as to become an Ukrainian autocrat with the help of Russian "feudal lords."

With the revision of the official attitude toward Russian history, the orthodox Marxist position of Yavorsky and the contributor to the Soviet Encyclopedia became politically objectionable. It is interesting to note that Yavorsky was officially condemned for Ukrainian nationalism already in 1929–30 and exiled to the Far North soon thereafter: the Russian historian N. Pokrovsky and his school who were also very critical of the colonial policy of the Tsars were tolerated until 1936—an indication that Russians were allowed a greater freedom of expression than the non-Russian peoples.[87] In any case around 1930 Yavorsky's textbooks on Ukrainian history—the only ones admitted in Soviet Ukrainian schools— were withdrawn. In 1937 the authors of the projected textbook on the history of the Soviet Union were reminded on highest authority to pay more attention to concrete historical circumstances. In 1654, the Ukraine was faced with the alternative "either to be swallowed by the Poland of the squires and Sultan's Turkey, or to accept the domination of Russia. . . . The second alternative was nevertheless the lesser evil." [88]

As was to be expected, after Stalin's toast of May 24, 1945, it became somewhat embarrassing to characterize the union with Russia as the "lesser evil." Two and a half years later one N. Yakovlev published in the *Bol'shevik* a very important programmatical article "On the Teaching of the History of the Fatherland," in which he tried to take the sting out of the "lesser evil" formula without repudiating it completely. His reasoning went like this: According to Marx, every nation is divided into the exploiters and the exploited, and so are the Russian and the non-Russian peoples. Being the representatives of the exploiting minority, the Tsars oppressed not only the non-Russian peoples but the bulk of the Russian people as well. On the other hand, each non-Russian people had its own class of exploiters which the Russian Tsars supported. The lower classes of the non-Russian peoples gradually realized how much they had in common with their exploited brethren among the Russian people, and finally, under the leadership of the Russian proletariat and its vanguard, the Communist Party, they destroyed Tsarism and established the multinational Soviet Union based on the friendship of peoples. The implication of the article is rather obvious: As the union with Russia led toward the establishment of the USSR it should be regarded as a progressive act rather than a lesser evil. The proof lies in the division of each people into two hostile classes and the assertion that the majority felt a bond of common interest with the Russian people, if not with the Russian government.[89]

In the light of Yakovlev's article it becomes clear why the regime opposed so violently any interpretation of Ukrainian history which stressed the social unity of the Ukrainian people. The second remarkable thing about his article is that despite being published in the most authoritative party organ next to *Pravda* its message went unheeded by the majority of Soviet historians until Professor Nechkina picked up his argument in her well-known letter to *Voprosy istorii,* the journal of the Soviet historical profession, in 1951.[90] That her letter provoked a lively discussion on the pages of *Voprosy istorii* and that the discussion had to be called off on demands from the Party is well known.[91] What we are interested in is to ascertain why the Party reprimanded both Nechkina and the editorial board of the journal for initiating the discussion.

At first sight, in her letter Nechkina clung to the Party line to the extent that she virtually repeated Yakovlev's arguments of 1947. The only new thought she added was that one ought to investigate whether at the time of incorporation into Russia the people in question was independent or whether it was already included in another state. Only in the first instance could one interpret the union with Russia as the lesser evil because it involved a certain loss of freedom. But the transfer of authority over a people from a neighboring empire to Russia was progressive, because by definition Russia was more progressive than her neighboring states. Furthermore, Nechkina advanced the following ingenious formulation:

All phenomena of the life of a people after its incorporation in Russia can be . . . divided into two groups: the first refers directly to the colonial regime, to the colonial policy of Tsarism, to suppression, it *expresses* that oppression; the second group is related to the struggle *against* it and to the general communication of one people with another.[92]

The implication of this division for the work of Soviet historians was simple: They were to stress the latter group of facts (i.e., the cooperation with the Russian people, increasingly interpreted as the influence of the latter upon all non-Russian peoples) and they were to minimize the former (colonial oppression) which was to be charged exclusively to Tsarism.[93] Like Marx–Hegel, and Lenin–Marx, the Party speaking through Nechkina now put the "lesser evil" formula on its head. Why did Nechkina who, more probably than not, did not write her programmatic letter without political authorization, incur Party criticism a year and a half later? As put by her colleague Pankratova on the pages of *Kommunist* in 1953, the discussion of the formula was a political mistake because it "returned historians to the [already] decided question of the progressive nature of the peoples' being incorporated in Russia." [94]

The Party spokesman on the progressive significance of the union with Russia was, characteristically, not a Russian (that would have been impolitic) but the leader of the Communist Party of Azerbaydzhan, Bagirov. Bagirov, however, was also a supporter of Beria's, which brought him before an execution squad in the spring of 1956. Taking advantage of this opportunity the Party repudiated his thesis of the unqualified benefits of Russian help and allowed M. M. Lysenko, the scholar in charge of historical methodology at the Scientific Research Institute of Pedagogy of the Ukrainian SSR to reinterpret the formula of "lesser evil" so as to bring it closer to its original meaning of 1937. Lysenko complained that while on the whole the reunification of the Ukraine with Russia in 1654 was progressive:

The majority of the writers, however, . . . [did] not show the objective facts of the feudalistic serf policy of Russian Tsarist oppression in relation to broad masses of the Ukraine. One also keeps silent about the internal policy of the Hetmanate administration of Bohdan Khmelnytsky, which was directed against the interests of ordinary peasants and which reflected the interests of Cossack officers—the class of Ukrainian feudal lords.[95]

Furthermore, while reassuring his readers that the union with Russia was a good thing, Lysenko cites the Russian historian Fadeev to prove that the foreign policy of Catherine II was aggressive.[96] He chides Ukrainian historians for overstressing the progressive features of Ukrainian-Russian cooperation against Napoleonic invasion. After all, Nicholas I had justly been called the "gendarme of Europe" and—in his own words—"Ignoring this aspect of the consequences of the war of 1812 leads to a mistaken glorification of Tsarism." [97] The pro-Russian interpretation of the "lesser evil" formula, as initiated by Yakovlev and Nechkina, could not receive a more cruel blow than in the criticism of a Ukrainian official writing in the journal of Ukrainian teachers. The interesting thing is that more likely than not it was the Party which inspired Nechkina's letter and which speaking through Lysenko restored the "lesser evil" formula to some of its original meaning. Had the Party realized that by 1956 the extreme adulation of everything Russian adopted as a means of cementing the Soviet Empire had reached a point of diminishing returns?

3. Conclusions

We have seen that the regime devotes considerable time and effort to the presentation of Ukrainian history. Respect for the historical heritage of the Ukrainian people is the ostensible reason, but much more important is probably the fact that in the absence of official history the Ukrainians might interpret their history by themselves. Interviewing refugees from Soviet Central Asia Richard Pipes found that not having been taught their history they had exaggerated notions of the past glory of their peoples.[98] Nor does the regime commit the mistake of Russian nationalists before World War I who denied the existence of a Ukrainian nation. Embittered about his people being deprived of its name and

national face, Hrushevsky set about writing a magnificent monument
to its history which would inspire his fellow-countrymen. To judge by
the frequent attacks against him in latest Soviet Ukrainian historiography, the regime has been unable to raze it completely: Some of
Hrushevsky's theses have been incorporated in Soviet historiography.
Lest a second Hrushevsky should emerge, the regime has decided not
to deprive the Ukrainians of their national face outrightly but to reinterpret the Ukrainian heritage to serve its needs. Unlike extreme nationalists of Fascist tendencies, the Communists never reject the national
heritage of their subject peoples in toto, but often—in effect. In doing
so, they are helped by the fact that as opposed to Fascism, Communist
ideology is a-national in principle, though sometimes it takes on strong
nationalistic coloring, as after World War II, before 1954. Whether a
"proletarian internationalist" ideology is the cause rather than the effect
of a relatively flexible policy of constant reinterpretation I find it impossible to decide; the important thing in our context is that the regime
interprets Ukrainian history selectively rather than rejects it altogether.

In our analysis of one crucial problem in the history of the Ukrainian
people—its union with Russia in the seventeenth century—we have seen
that for political reasons recent Soviet historians have depicted a unity
of the Russian and Ukrainian peoples which did not actually exist. The
question that should be raised now is: Can the average Soviet Ukrainian
detect this discrepancy between fact and official interpretation?

It would seem that in history the mechanical obstacles on the road to
truth are extraordinarily high, much higher certainly than in the interpretation of well-known literary classics. Primary documents are not
easily available; if they are printed, the editions are doctored to suit the
regime's political aims. In any case, their interpretation requires much
painstaking research which must not be expected from anybody but the
professional historian, whose activity can be easily controlled. The more
remote the period, the fewer documents are available, the more difficult
is it to reconstruct the true character of the past, and the greater becomes
the latitude for honest difference of opinion.

As far as the average intelligent Ukrainian is concerned, he must rely
on secondary sources. They are, of course, slanted in that the opposite
viewpoint is not presented fairly. For instance, it has been observed that
Soviet Ukrainian historians since the late 1930's have not been allowed
to quote Hrushevsky—he was merely to be mentioned as a *bête noire*—
whereas their Russian colleagues have not suffered from similar restrictions and sometimes quoted him approvingly.[99] To arrive at the historical truth is not facilitated by the regime's withholding of certain information it wants suppressed (that is, on the Ukrainian-Russian relations
between 1654–57). I should nevertheless argue that given a certain

amount of curiosity, it is relatively easy to detect Soviet falsification of history. The most interesting problem would have been to ascertain what Soviet Ukrainians think once they detect that something is wrong with the official interpretation, but I have not been able to find this out directly. Let us see why falsification is not hard to detect.

In the first place, as we have seen in our discussion of the "absolute or lesser evil" formula, the Party line has changed rather drastically from the 1920's to the 1950's. An individual with access to Soviet literature of the 1920's and 1930's can by a simple juxtaposition of it with later works see for himself that "something is wrong." Some determined individuals treasure such "interesting" early books.[100] But with a reasonable degree of assurance it can be said that they are in the minority and that they must be extremely cautious in lending out their treasures. The majority of the population can be intimidated not to inquire too closely into the different interpretations of the 1920's if they have the books in their homes, and as for the libraries, the Soviets are not the first nor the last who are versed in burning printed heresy, or, at best, transferring it to locked collections. Hence, a comparison with earlier writing cannot serve for the average Soviet Ukrainian as a means of detecting historical misrepresentation.

Nevertheless, I am quite optimistic that the average intelligent person can detect presumable falsification. In issuing their programmatic statements, the ideological functionaries of the Party are very often placed in the uncomfortable position of men who know that they are lying and yet want to be believed. I maintain that this generates uncertainty in their ranks and that this uncertainty is communicated to every Soviet citizen who is intelligent enough to read between the lines. Let us take the "lesser evil" formula again. For fear of being accused of sundry deviations, Soviet historians have adhered to it faithfully throughout the late 1930's and 1940's. But any schematic presentation of history, especially if a certain formula is repeated almost verbatim in one textbook after another, must arouse the suspicion of intelligent readers that the facts have been tailored to fit the thesis. Obviously, their suspicion must become acute when the scheme is suddenly changed. But I should like to ignore this obvious effect for the sake of another which, in my opinion, seems to be more general.

It appears to me that Soviet historians are *always* faced with the problem of how many qualifying facts to introduce so as to make their argument convincing and yet stay within the bounds of the Party formula. If they paint everything in black and white they will be ideologically correct, but they will not convince anybody who is somebody. But if they introduce some grays, they might sound more convincing but they are likely to be accused of spreading doubt that the white is really white and the black actually black. To my mind this is precisely what happened to Nechkina when as a result of her professional training she committed the political blunder of making the revision of the "lesser evil" formula palatable to rational minds—by introducing the criterion of previous independence. I deem it improbable that her letter was published without prior consent of the Party. But when the Party functionaries saw to their dismay that her rational argument provoked a fairly rational discussion they quickly declared the matter *res adjudicata* and rebuked Nechkina for the oversight which they had committed themselves. As Pankratova acknowledged later, the very fact that the issue was once opened to discussion or, in more general terms, the very fact that grays were introduced, shed doubt upon the white progressiveness of the union with Russia.

On the orders of the Party speaking through Bagirov, Soviet Ukrainian historians subordinated every single fact to the black and white scheme of the unification with Russia. But to employ a Ukrainian idiom, such a schematic exposition is "sewn with white thread," i.e., all too obvious.[101] All of a sudden, the Party line was changed in 1955 when in an editorial in *Voprosy istorii* the second volume of the History of the Ukrainian SSR, then being prepared for publication, was criticized for not including enough gray tones to make the exposition convincing. To quote two excerpts from the editorial:

The authors of the second volume of the History of the Ukrainian SSR have so shortened the material from the history of the Ukraine herself that the concrete peculiar development of the Ukrainian people has virtually disappeared.

The drafts of the second volume of the History of the Ukrainian SSR have been discussed for years. The endless revisions of that volume have not always improved its quality. Often they have been made to give this work a more "streamlined" shape, to take out controversial and sharp questions and thus to obviate possible criticism. But criticism deserves precisely such an approach in preparing the given work, for it damages scholarship [sic].[102]

We have already seen that a year later, in 1956, Lysenko called upon Ukrainian historians to add some grays in their exposition of the Khmelnytsky period, as well as that of Catherine II and of Nicholas I. To give more scope for the presentation of the "concrete peculiar development of the Ukrainian people" the regime in late 1957 allowed Ukrainian historians to publish a professional journal of their own: the bi-monthly *Ukrayins'ky istorychny zhurnal*.

All this, it seems, proves our point that it is not so easy to paint in black and white and yet appear convincing. Not only does the regime find it hard to remain consistent in attributing the two colors, but it has to be very careful as to how many grays it will allow its historians to add: A total absence of grays provokes skepticism as to the whole scheme, but if one adds a certain amount of them they will overshadow both the whites and the blacks. As of late, the pendulum has swung toward a greater emphasis upon convincingness; but how long will it stay in that position? There are signs that it is again swinging toward the other extreme—see *Pravda's* criticism of the *Outline History of the Communist Party of Ukraine* in 1962. To sum up, it does not take much intelligence to discover that something is wrong with Soviet historiography, but the regime can make it very difficult, if not altogether impossible, to discover precisely what.

Chapter VIII

THE COMMUNIST PARTY OF UKRAINE AND THE COMMUNIST PARTY OF THE SOVIET UNION, WITH EMPHASIS ON THE YEARS AFTER STALIN'S DEATH

The primary aim of this chapter is to elucidate the inter-relationship between the Communist Party of Ukraine and the All-Union Party. In broader terms, it is a study of the nature of ties between the rulers of an Empire and the political elite of one of its subdivisions. It is also an analysis of power, for as Carl J. Friedrich puts it:

Power . . . [is] a human relationship in which the leader and the led are banded together for the accomplishment of some common objective, partly by consent, partly by constraint.[1]

During Stalin's life the relative character of Soviet power became obscured through deliberate cultivation of the myth of an omnipotent dictator who held the substance of power in his own hands; his death revealed that he had been dependent upon a number of associates. While the struggle among his successors is no direct concern of mine, I shall touch upon it insofar as it bears immediately upon the events in the Ukraine. It is now widely accepted that in his rise to power Khrushchev has been helped by his friends in the CP of Ukraine.[2]

In this chapter I shall stress the events after Stalin's death for two reasons. First, it is only after the dictator's passing away that the struggle for power had broken out into the open, and it is in the light of the events after March, 1953, that we can interpret some of the moves made in the preceding eight years since 1945. A would-be monolithic regime keeps the secrets of the ruling clique to itself, until it cannot help revealing them. Furthermore, the general policies of the regime have already been discussed in the introduction to this work. In this chapter I shall give figures on the strength and composition of the CP of Ukraine; analyze the most important event in its recent history—Melnikov's dis-

missal in June, 1953; briefly relate the continuing mystery of Kirichenko's abrupt fall in January, 1960; examine the careers of some
prominent graduates of the Ukrainian Party organization in the All-
Union apparatus; and scrutinize the link between nationality policy and
the re-organization of industrial administration.

1. *The Strength and Composition of the Communist Party of Ukraine (CPU)*

In 1958, on the fortieth anniversary of the CP of Ukraine, the central
Party journal *Partiynaya Zhizn'* (Party Life) dedicated the better part
of an issue to articles on the Ukrainian Communist organization. Of
utmost importance is an editorial summary of Ukrainian Party statistics:
It is a rare event that such detailed political information has been published in the Soviet Union, even after the avalanche of economic figures
that was set off in 1956.[3] Analyzing those and related data we come to
the following three conclusions: the membership of the CP of Ukraine
is still disproportionately low if compared with the Union average (although in recent years the difference has been diminishing); like everywhere else in that bastion of socialism, its members have been recruited
primarily from the better classes; and the share of Ukrainians in the
CPU as a whole and its leading organs is still below that of Ukrainians
in the total population of the Republic, though much larger than in the
1920's.

There are two ways of ascertaining the membership of the CP of
a given Republic. At every Republican Congress the exact figures are
given in the so-called political report of the Central Committee. Many
of these Congresses immediately precede the All-Union Congresses, and
that makes it very easy to obtain the Republican membership at the
time of the All-Union Congress. The other method is to calculate the
Republican membership on the basis of its representation at the Moscow
Congress; for every voting delegate stands for a certain number of full
Party members. The second method looks very inaccurate, but as Fainsod
has pointed out it may actually yield better results for some purposes,
because the figures announced at the Republican Party Congresses usually do *not* include the Party members in the armed forces and the
security police stationed in that particular region.[4] According to the first
method, we find that as of September 1, 1952, shortly before the first
All-Union Party Congress held after the war, the Communist Party (Bolshevik) of Ukraine * had 676,190 full members, or—assuming that the
population of the Ukrainian SSR was then about 38.1 million—more

---

* Prior to the Nineteenth Congress of the All-Union Communist Party (October,
1952) the official name was Communist Party (Bolshevik) of Ukraine, or CP(B)U. For
simplicity's sake I have omitted "Bolshevik" from now on.

than 17 (17.7) Party members per 1,000 people.[5] According to the second method, the membership of the Communist Party of Ukraine would be 765,000, or 20 (20.1) Party members per 1,000 population.[6] At the same time, the All-Union Party included 6,013,259 full members, or more than 30 (30.4) Party members per 1,000 population, assuming that in 1952 the total population of the Soviet Union was around 198,080,000 people.[7] For October, 1961, we obtain for the CPU the (full) membership figures of 1,432,806 or 1,566,000, depending on which method we choose. This would give us about 33 or 36 (32.8 or 35.9) Party members per 1,000 population in the Ukraine, compared with the Union average of 40.6.[8]

Why is the CPU membership so low? I cannot explain it. It is true that the Ukraine is somewhat less industrialized than Russia, which has furnished Party representations high above the Union average,[9] but the difference in urbanization does not seem to be so great as we should have expected had there been a high correlation between Party membership, residence, and occupation. Is it perhaps also a question of historical roots? This is too big a topic to discuss in this work. But against the background of Khrushchev's struggle for power it is worth noting that the membership of the Communist Party of Ukraine has increased disproportionately fast. Between the Nineteenth and the Twenty-Second CPSU Congresses (1952–61), the number of full members of the All-Union Party (CPSU) grew by 2,859,257, or 47.6 per cent, whereas that of the Ukrainian Party members jumped by 756,616, or as many as 111.9 per cent. High leaders of the CP of Ukraine helped Khrushchev into the saddle; did Khrushchev, in turn, help to expand the CPU?

In terms of length of membership, the Ukrainian Party organization appears fairly new, which may be, in part, attributed to the high turnover during and immediately after World War II. The 1958 article indicates that one third of the total membership of the CPU in 1958 joined the Party during the war (about 365,000) and that more than 463,000 (ca. 42 per cent) became members after 1945.[10] The extent of the turnover may be judged by the fact that on the eve of the German invasion the CPU numbered 559,235 members.[11] If all these figures are added together we obtain the total of 1,387,235 members for 1958 instead of 1,095,250 (the figure given for 1958), which gives us a deficit of some 292,000. How many of these latter Communists have died of natural causes, how many perished during the war, and how many have fallen victim to purges?[12] The number of Party members who left the Party for one reason or another between 1941 and 1958 may actually be still higher for the statistics give no more than the Party seniority of the *1958* members ("one third of the Ukrainian Party organization"). Former Party members would thus *not* be counted, and there is no way of telling how many citizens were actually recruited by the Party in those 17 years and how many of them left the Party. That considerable turn-over in the CPU had two significant effects: similarly to the Party or-ganizations in other parts of the Union, the CPU membership has be-come further outbalanced in favor of higher social groups; and owing to special circumstances the number of Ukrainians in the Party has risen sharply in absolute terms.[13]

There are several indications that at least the younger members of the CPU belong to the middle and upper classes. At the Sixteenth CPU Congress in January, 1949, Khrushchev decried the fact that among the candidate members that had been admitted to the Party in the Dniepro-petrovsk oblast in 1948, only 17.2 per cent were workers and 9.6 per cent collective farmers. The rest—as many as 73.2 per cent—were em-ployees and students.[14] The 1958 summary admits the preponderance of members from the more educated social classes: It indicates that in that year members with higher and secondary education (completed or incomplete) numbered 773,342 men and women. Above all, it is pointed out that between 1940 and 1958 the number of "Communist specialists with higher and secondary education" (Party members who are profes-sionals and semi-professionals) increased fourfold, while the total mem-bership increased less than twofold. To counteract this tendency more workers and peasants have been admitted to the Party in recent years: in 1957, for example, they constituted 65 per cent of the new recruits to the CPU.[15] The same source also gives a very interesting breakdown of the various occupations represented in the CP of Ukraine, which are summarized in Table VIII-1, p. 230. From the context it appears that the very large category of "others" includes other white collar workers, as well as military and police personnel.[16]

A sharp image of the social composition of the CPU emerges as soon as we juxtapose in the same table the occupational distribution of CPU members with the total number of persons engaged in a given occupa-tion. Striking is the quantitative proof of the widely held thesis that the higher a person advances in the Soviet Union, the more likely he is to be a member of the Communist Party. In the Ukraine, for example, every fifth doctor, every fourth technician and every third engineer be-longs to the Party, compared with every *thirty-fourth* worker and every *forty-fifth* collective farmer. In connection with the social composition of the Party it should also be mentioned that women constitute a rela-tively small if increasing percentage of the total membership. In 1939, they made up only 13.2 per cent of the total, by 1958 their proportion had gone up to 17.5 per cent. In January, 1959, however, in the total population of the Soviet Union, women outnumbered men by 55 to 45.[17]

Of particular importance is the national composition of the CPU on

Table VIII-1

OCCUPATIONAL COMPOSITION OF THE COMMUNIST PARTY OF UKRAINE (CPU)
COMPARED WITH THAT OF THE TOTAL POPULATION OF THE UKRAINE, 1958

| | CP of Ukraine | | Total population (comparable data) | |
| | N | Per cent | N | Ratio columns |
Occupations	(1)	(2)	(3)	(3):(1)
Workers	225,000	20.5	7,763,000 *	34
Collective farmers	155,000	14.2	6,903,400	45
Engineers and architects	48,639	4.4	139,400	3
Technicians	54,117	4.9	203,200	4
Agronomists, veterinarians, zoo-technicians and other farm specialists	38,929	3.6	102,500	3
Physicians	13,533	1.2	68,800	5
Educators	59,213	5.4	— †	
Others	500,819	45.7	—	
Total	1,095,250	100.0	—	—

* From the general statistical annuals that have been consulted it is impossible to extract the number of workers directly because in transport, construction, communications, and commerce the number of workers has been lumped with that of employees. I have derived the above figure in the following way: taken the official figure for all workers *and* employees in the Ukrainian SSR (*Narodnoe khozaystvo SSSR v 1958 g.*, p. 661) and *discounted* it by the average percentage of engineering, technical personnel, and salaried employees (i.e., by "employees") in industrial jobs. This gives a rough figure for workers alone in all branches of the economy, assuming of course that the number of supervisory personnel in each branch is similar to that in industry (see *ibid.*, p. 131).

† In the statistical annuals teachers have unfortunately been lumped together with other "cultural workers," such as librarians and museum staff.

Sources: On the CPU, see "KPU v tsifrakh," *Partiynaya Zhizn'*, 1958, No. 12 (June), p. 58. See also H. McClosky & J. E. Turner, *The Soviet Dictatorship* (New York, etc.: McGraw-Hill, 1960), p. 263. See *Narodnoe khozaystvo v 1958 g.*, pp. 131 and 661 (on workers), 677–679 (all others, except collective farmers); *Nar. khoz.*, *1960*, p. 522 (on collective farmers).

which only very sparse data have been released. In May, 1940, Ukrainians reportedly constituted 63.1 per cent of the total membership, Russians 19.1 per cent, Jews 13.4 per cent, and others 4.4 per cent. But in the Central Committee of the CPU, the highest *functioning* representative organ of the Party, there were only 40.0 per cent Ukrainians.[18] From 1940 to 1956 only the nationality of the *delegates* to Party Congresses has been publicly announced, but as Dmytryshyn points out those data are rather misleading.[19] The only intermediate figure is one gleaned by Professor Armstrong from an unpublished Soviet dissertation: According to that as of January 1, 1951, Ukrainians comprised 71.4 per cent of so-called "directing cadres" of the CPU.[20] After the Twentieth Party Congress a published Soviet source gave the number of Ukrainians among "directing workers" of the CPU as 68.8 per cent. Russians constituted then 28.5 per cent and other nationalities 2.7 of those directing cadres. (The figures refer to January 1, 1956.) [21] So long as we do not know exactly who those "directing cadres" or "workers" are, those aggregate figures are not too meaningful, but they give us nevertheless a very rough indication of the political status of Ukrainians. The author continued to say that in the "apparatus of the CC CPU [CPU Central Committee]" there worked 75.1 per cent Ukrainians, 24 per cent Russians, and 0.9 per cent other nationalities.[22]

Finally, in 1958 the regime for the first time since 1940 published full figures on the national composition of the CPU. Those figures are particularly striking when juxtaposed to the data from the January, 1959, census (see Table VIII-2).

Table VIII-2

NATIONAL COMPOSITION OF THE COMMUNIST PARTY
OF UKRAINE (CPU) IN 1958

	Percentage of Party members	Percentage of total population, UkrSSR, January 15, 1959
Ukrainians	60.3	76.8
Russians	28.2	16.9
Others	11.5	6.3

Source: "KPU v tsifrakh," *Partiynaya Zhizn'*, 1958, No. 12 (June), p. 59. Population data from *Narodnoe khozaystvo SSSR v 1960 godu*, p. 18.

In a more recent Soviet article we find another important figure: In 1960 as many as 73.2 of the newly accepted candidate members in the Ukraine were Ukrainians.[23] At the same time it was disclosed that Ukrainians in the *All-Union* Party numbered, as of July 1, 1961, 1,412,-200 full and candidate members out of a total of 9,626,700, or 14.7 per cent.[24] (The reader will recall that in 1959 Ukrainians constituted 17.8 of the population of the Soviet Union.)

What do all those data mean? First of all, though the Communist Party of Ukraine has come a long way from being an ethnically alien party on Ukrainian soil (at the end of 1920 only 19.0 per cent of the Communist Party of Ukraine were Ukrainians),[25] the Party, after forty years of Soviet rule, still does not fully represent the Ukrainian element in the Republic, but favors the Russian and other minorities. It is possible that Ukrainians, many of whom have rural backgrounds, have continued to suffer from not being attracted by the urban oriented Party that provided easy access to Russian and Jewish laborers and intellectuals. On the other hand, there is also some evidence that Ukrainians as such were distrusted by Stalin and might, therefore, have been deliberately discriminated against in Party recruitment.[26] It is also remarkable that the percentage of Ukrainians in the CPU has declined as compared to that of May 1940 by almost three per cent. To what extent this is due to the high losses during the war and to what degree it should be traced to a deliberate policy of personnel intermixture is difficult to tell; an unpublished Soviet dissertation shows that "on April 20, 1944, 2,965 persons were sent from the 'eastern oblasts of the USSR' to take [Party and state] posts in the Ukraine." By 1946, 800 had been sent to one small province alone (Vinnitsa).[27] It should also be noted that in the five years from January, 1951, to January, 1956, the number of Ukrainians among the "directing cadres" dropped off by a few percentage points: quite possibly the result of Stalin's comprehensive attack on Ukrainian "nationalism" in 1951. As if to obviate any such charges of political discrimination, the regime announced in 1962 that two years before it had accepted—on probation—73.2 per cent of the new Party members in the Ukraine from among Ukrainians. But this is still a disproportionately low number, for Ukrainians comprise almost 77 per cent of the total population. In the All-Union Party there were also disproportionately few Ukrainians as late as July, 1961.

If the figures on so-called leading cadres are viewed in longer perspective they appear more favorable to the Ukrainians. Insofar as they are meaningful at all, they show that the Ukrainian majority in the Republic have not yet achieved a share of leading Party positions commensurate with their share in the population at large. At the same time, a great advance has been made compared with 1940 and certainly with the

1920's and 1930's. Holubnychy found that in the spring of 1924 the proportion of Ukrainians in the Central Committee of the CPU—which probably corresponds roughly to the "leading Party workers" as defined by Kravtsev—amounted to only 16.0 per cent. By November, 1925, it rose to 25.0 per cent, and by the summer of 1930, as a result of the Ukrainization policy, to 43.0 per cent, only to fall to 40.0 per cent after the Great Purges in 1940.[28] In 1956, it amounted to 68.8 per cent.[29] Another important sidelight on recent personnel policy is shed by Professor Armstrong, who traced the careers of many high officials. He writes:

It seems . . . that most of the Russians in the higher levels of the Ukrainian apparatus elite are natives of the Ukraine or that they went there at an early stage of their careers.[30]

What is the reason for this abrupt rise of the Ukrainian cadres, despite the strongly pro-Russian policy after the war? Basically, it would seem that as the Ukrainian people advanced toward higher socio-economic status it became increasingly more difficult to keep their abler and more ambitious representatives down, the more so since those who were promoted were loyal to the regime. But by itself this hypothesis is probably not sufficient to explain the silent "Ukrainization" of the CPU apparatus after 1945. The more welcome is, therefore, the thesis of a student of the CPU who found that the majority of the members of the CPU Central Committee and almost 75 per cent of the *obkom* Secretaries in the Ukraine have achieved their high positions during World War II, as organizers of the anti-German Communist underground. By force of circumstances, it was people intimately acquainted with local conditions, that is, mostly Ukrainians, who were assigned to such tasks and thus it happened that most of the new leading cadres in the CPU after the War turned out to be Ukrainians.[31] This is important to keep in mind when we come to discuss the changes after Stalin's death: The Ukrainian cadres of the CPU were not created after March, 1953, they had been forged already in World War II.

2. *Exit Melnikov, Enter Kirichenko; or, a Brief Essay in "Kremlinology"*

The curt dismissal of Melnikov for committing distortions of the "Lenin-Stalin nationality policy" in the Ukraine in June, 1953, was almost unprecedented in the history of the Communist Party of Ukraine. A parallel has been suggested in the dissolution of the Soviet Ukrainian government under Rakovsky in the fall of 1919—but the Moldavian Rakovsky never headed the Communist Party of the Ukraine.[32] The action of the Ukrainian Central Committee in unseating its First Secretary for Russification of higher educational institutions in Western Ukraine appears the more dramatic if we consider that towards the end of February of the same year the same body convened to discuss short-comings of the Kiev Party organization in combatting Ukrainian nation-alism.[33] What happened within three months after Stalin's death? It is believed that only a close analysis of the careers of the top Communist leaders in the Ukraine can furnish clues to the events of June, 1953.

Since January, 1938, that is, since the Great Purges, the First Secretary of the CPU had been Khrushchev.[34] Before his Ukrainian assignment Khrushchev had been First Secretary of the extremely important Moscow Province and Moscow City Committees (1935–38). Khrushchev com-pleted the purge of the CPU and apparently as a reward was admitted to full membership in the Politburo in 1939. During the war Khru-shchev's closest assistant was Demyan S. Korotchenko, apparently a Ukrainian, who by late 1944 was listed as Second Secretary of the CPU, while Khrushchev since 1943 held the double position of First Secretary of the CPU and Chairman of the Ukrainian Council of People's Com-missars.[35]

After the war, Khrushchev must have run into difficulties: We have already noticed that a minor famine broke out in the fall of 1946. Kaganovich, Stalin's perennial troubleshooter, was sent to the Ukraine and in early March, 1947, he replaced Khrushchev as First Secretary of the CPU.[36] Kaganovich left again for Moscow on December 26 of the same year (1947), and Khrushchev was reinstalled as First Secretary of CPU.[37]

This whole episode might have been passed over in this context but for two significant details: A few weeks after Kaganovich's arrival Khru-shchev was also relieved of his First Secretaryship in the Kiev oblast and city Party organizations, and when he resumed his old post in December, 1947, his assistant was no longer Korotchenko, but a new man, Leonid G. Melnikov. In December, 1947, Korotchenko was made Chairman of the Ukrainian Council of Ministers and since that time he has stayed in the less powerful administrative branch of the Party (the State adminis-tration), occupying inferior positions in the late 1950's and early 1960's.[38]

On March 25 and 26, 1947, *Pravda Ukrainy* reported with several days' delay that Khrushchev had been relieved of the two Kiev posts, allegedly on his own request. According to one line of thought, these two moves added to the loss of the First Secretaryship and to repeated previous criticisms of the Ukrainian Party organization in the All-Union Central Committee (while it was headed by Khrushchev),[39] created a strong im-pression that Khrushchev's position in the Ukraine was being attacked and that but for the intervention of a powerful figure in the Kremlin—possibly Stalin himself—Khrushchev might have gone the way of his physically purged predecessors Postyshev and Kosior.[40] That hypothesis is elaborated very plausibly by Lazar Pistrak, a Western biographer of Khrushchev. Pistrak points out, for example, that in June, 1946, Khrushchev, who usually restricted himself to rather insignificant articles, wrote a weighty piece on "some problems of intra-Party work" in which he critically discussed the personnel policy of the Ukrainian Party organization, thus anticipating the All-Union Central Committee resolution by six weeks.[41] Further credibility is lent to Pistrak's hypothesis that in 1947 Khrushchev narrowly escaped the quiet post-war purge by Khrushchev's revelations after Kaganovich joined the "anti-Party" group in June, 1957. In a speech to writers Khrushchev accused Kaganovich of wrongly persecuting the eminent poet Rylsky for being a Ukrainian "bourgeois nationalist," added the pregnant phrase that Kaganovich's actions might have "led to serious consequences not only for literature." [42] It is rather significant that the official and highly authoritative *Outline History of the Communist Party of Ukraine* does not even mention Rylsky by name, but stresses the broader political threat of Kaganovich's rule.[43] On the other hand, given the utilitarian character of Soviet historiography, the possibility must not be excluded that Kaganovich's temporary replacement of Khrushchev was an act of assistance rather than a play for power: Khrushchev had been Kaganovich's protégé in Moscow, there is not definite *contemporary* evidence of a struggle between the two men. Kaganovich might have done Khrushchev a favor by taking over the leadership of the Ukraine when she was suffering from the drought of 1946–47.[44]

But there is some circumstantial evidence to indicate that though Khrushchev returned to his previous post in the Ukraine in December, 1947, his position in that Republic was being undermined by one of his rivals for Stalin's succession. Leonid G. Melnikov, the new Second Secretary of the Communist Party of Ukraine, is said to be a Russian from the Moscow Province. Shortly before World War II he joined the important Stalino (now Donetsk) Province Party Committee in the Donbas (Ukraine) rising from chief of the coal division, to a Secretary in 1939, to First Secretary in 1944.[45] On Kaganovich's departure in December 1947 his election to the Second Secretaryship of the CPU Central Committee was announced; he had become a junior Secretary of the CPU Central Committee already in July, 1947.[46] The thing that is important to keep in mind is that Melnikov was appointed to the Secretariat of the Ukrainian Central Committee while it was formally headed by Kaganovich, not Khrushchev. Of even greater importance is the admittedly tenuous evidence of connections between Melnikov and Stalin's ambitious lieutenant Georgiy Malenkov.[47]

Khrushchev remained First Secretary of the Ukraine until the middle of December, 1949, when he was called to the Soviet capital to resume his old post as head of the Moscow Party organization and was also designated a Secretary of the All-Union Central Committee.[48] This transfer is worth noting for two reasons. In the light of the duel between Khrushchev and Malenkov after Stalin's death, it appears as the second but last stepping stone to supreme power. At the end of 1949 Khrushchev was either allied with Malenkov against the Zhdanovites,[49] whom he purged from the Moscow Party organization after his arrival; or Stalin had chosen Khrushchev, who was Malenkov's senior both in years (born in 1894 as against Malenkov's 1902) and political status (member of the Politburo since 1939 as against 1946), as a possible counterweight to the ambitions of his first lieutenant. Secondly, the changes in the Ukrainian Party organization are notable, too.

In the Ukraine, Khrushchev was succeeded by Melnikov. But the same plenum that elected Melnikov First Secretary of the Party appointed Alexei I. Kirichenko, a relatively obscure provincial Secretary from Odessa, Second Secretary. In view of his brilliant if relatively short career after Melnikov's dismissal it is worth while to give a few pertinent data from his official biography. Kirichenko was born in 1908 into the family of a railroad construction worker in the village of Chornobayevka (Kherson Province), in southern Ukraine. To judge by the ending of his name he should be a Ukrainian, but he might easily come from a Russified family since the Kherson Province is an ethnically mixed territory and since before World War I Ukrainian workers tended to be assimilated to the Russians. In 1928, he graduated from a school for tractor mechanics and occupied several posts in the repair shops of various state farms. Kirichenko did not join the Party until 1930 and continued to work in agricultural engineering. Like Khrushchev, who made his career as Party Secretary at the Stalin Industrial Academy in Moscow (1930), Kirichenko advanced as head of a "study unit" at the Akhtyrka Farm Mechanization "Tekhnikum" (vocational school) and member of the Party Committee at the Azov Black Sea Institute for Socialist Farm Engineers. His star rose when apparently Khrushchev himself, who was greatly interested in agriculture, in March, 1938, assigned him to work in the Central Committee of the CPU first as an instructor, then as responsible organizer, sector, and department head. In February, 1941, Kirichenko was made Central Committee Secretary in charge of industry. During the war he served as a high political commissar ("Member of the War Council") on various military fronts, similarly to Khrushchev. In January, 1944, he was elected Central Committee Secretary in charge of cadres. Not long afterwards he must have fallen into temporary disfavor, for in July, 1945, he relinquished his Central Committee Secretaryship to become First Secretary of the none too important Odessa oblast and city committees, a post he held until December, 1949.[50]

Melnikov's tenure as First Secretary and Kirichenko's superior was not a very calm one. In the spring of 1950, a plenum of the CPU Central Committee was called to consider organizational problems in the newly created Western Ukrainian *kolkhozy*.[51] In July, 1951, the storm over Sosyura's poem broke loose. In May of the next year, a plenum of the CPU Central Committee met again to discuss two problems: the lagging state of agriculture and "The [Present] State of and Measures [Taken] to Improve the Preparation, Selection, Training, and Assignment of Leading Party Cadres." [52] The content of the discussion was not disclosed but, in the light of Soviet political protocol, the particular phrasing of the second item on the agenda suggests implied criticism. Incidentally, it was Kirichenko who reported on it; he was responsible for personnel matters; and the criticism may have been directed as much against him as against his superior. The release of T. Z. Serdyuk from Central Committee Secretaryship to head the Lviv Party organization points to the Western Ukraine as the trouble spot. To justify the confidence of the Kremlin Melnikov emphasized in his report to the Seventeenth Congress of the CPU, September 24, 1952, that more than 22,000 Party members or candidates had been purged since the last Congress in January, 1949, and that "Party influence in the rural areas of the Republic's western provinces had been strengthened considerably." Then he launched into a vehement tirade against "bourgeois nationalism" and "homeless cosmopolitanism," that is, nationally conscious Ukrainians and Jews.[53] Nevertheless, on June 12, 1953, Melnikov was summarily dismissed for "shortcomings in political work and in the guidance of economic and cultural work" and for "distortions of the Leninist-Stalinist nationality policy" in the Western Ukraine. This latter he had committed by advancing cadres from the eastern provinces of the Ukraine and by Russification of higher schools.[54]

A widely accepted hypothesis is that Melnikov was unseated by Beria.[55] In turn, the most plausible explanation of Beria's downfall—which the present writer shares with two analysts [56]—is that the veteran chief of the secret police, who had been universally feared and loathed, tried to overcome the stigma of his past by a series of popular policy moves and, above all, by a frantic effort to create for himself a territorial mass-base in the non-Russian Republics by taking advantage of the legitimate grievances of their citizens. These bold moves alarmed the other leaders of the Party Presidium, the more so because Beria appeared to have strong influences in the East European satellites, East Germany especially.[57] In the long run, Beria might have created a very strong position for himself by gaining control not only of the Soviet border Republics, but of the satellites as well. But the unexpected popular uprising in Berlin and other cities in June, 1953, gave Beria's rivals an excellent argument against the ambitious secret police officer. Moreover, it probably brought them the support of the Soviet Army who had a large stake in the possession of East Germany. On June 28, alert Soviet citizens learnt that something must have happened to Beria the night before; his arrest was formally announced July 10.[58] A more detailed account of Beria's moves in the preceding months shows a haste that may have been born out of despair.

At the Nineteenth Party Congress in October, 1952, Beria had devoted a major part of his speech to the achievements of Soviet nationality policy, in the course of which he made a few laudatory references to the state of Ukrainian economy.[59] The ominous doctors' plot charges of January 13, 1953, were directly aimed at Jews, but indirectly at Beria, too.[60] Beria may have been responsible for issuing the limited amnesty of March 27, 1953,[61] but the manner in which the doctors' plot was repudiated left no doubt that it was Beria who was behind that move. Probably it was also he who inspired the *Pravda* editorials "Soviet Socialist Law Is Inviolable" (April 6, 1953) and "Soviet Ideology of Friendship of Peoples" (on the next day).[62] Within a week Beria started placing his men in charge of the secret police in all the Republics: His protégé Meshik was appointed Ukrainian Minister of Internal Affairs early in April.[63] At about that time, Beria must also have made a trip to Western Ukraine. According to later accusations, he went to that troublesome region to establish contacts with Ukrainian "bourgeois nationalists" who wanted to set up an independent capitalist Ukraine. As Armstrong points out, this particular charge is ludicrous.[64] It is plausible that Beria helped to install in Lviv as chief of the local secret police a man of his own choice, a certain Menshtein. On April 14, 1953, Beria moved to repossess his old bailiwick in Georgia, in which an allegedly nationalist conspiracy (the so-called Mingrelian nationalist organization) had been discovered in November, 1951, and March, 1952, which led to the purge of many of Beria's political friends. He promptly reinstalled them in April, 1953.[65] Already at the end of that month Beria's influence in the two Republics must have been rather strong. Armstrong observes that at the May Day celebrations in Kiev and Tiflis "Beria's picture was more prominently displayed than any other living leader's." [66] Early in May Beria appears to have engineered a few personnel changes in the Uzbek Republic: for example, on May 7 N. A. Mukhitdinov, who from 1956 to 1961 rose very high as Khrushchev's apparent protégé, was demoted from Republican Prime Minister to First Deputy Prime Minister.[67]

In June Beria was ready for his major coup in the Ukraine. On June 12 Melnikov was ousted from the leadership of the Ukrainian Party organization under rather humiliating circumstances. A brief extract from the resolution of the Ukrainian Central Committee is in order to characterize the new mood in Party policy:

The bureau of the Central Committee and the secretary of the same Committee of the Ukrainian Communist Party, Comrade Melnikov, committed in their practical work distortions of the Leninist-Stalinist national policy of our Party; these distortions took the form of the shameful practice of promoting to leading Party and Soviet posts in the Western regions of the Ukraine mostly people from the other regions of the Ukrainian S.S.R. and of introducing teaching in Russian at the Western Ukrainian universities.[68]

Melnikov was succeeded by Alexei Kirichenko. On June 17 the Central Committee of the Lithuanian Communist Party and on June 27 the Central Committee of the Latvian CP similarly criticized the Republican leaders for not promoting local cadres. The latter session was held on the very day when Beria was probably arrested and perhaps even killed in Moscow. Among the reasons that were later given for Beria's arrest were:

By various cunning methods Beria sought to undermine the friendship of the peoples of the USSR—the foundation of foundations of the multi-national socialist state . . . , to sow friction among the peoples of the USSR and to activate bourgeois nationalist elements in the Union republics.[69]

An editorial in *Pravda Ukrainy* entitled "The Indestructible Force of the Friendship of Peoples of the USSR," of July 14 was a little more explicit. It says, echoing *Pravda* of July 10:

Under the false pretense of fighting distortions of the Party's nationality policy that bourgeois degenerate attempted to sow enmity between the peoples of the USSR, to activize in the Union Republics, *including the Ukraine,* bourgeois nationalist elements.[70]

The Georgian Beria appears thus as the champion of the nationalities at the Nineteenth Party Congress, a champion of the Georgians in April, and of Ukrainians, Lithuanians, and Latvians in June, 1953, and *Pravda Ukrainy* admits in so many words that it was he who dislodged Melnikov.

But this explanation is not altogether satisfactory. Apart from the difficult problem whether or not Beria had any supporters in the Presidium of March, 1953, and if so, who they were (Bagirov? possibly Malenkov at one time, or Khrushchev?) there is the puzzling fact that Beria who seems to have concentrated his effort in the Ukraine was unable to staff the Ukrainian Party organization with men of his choosing. It will be noted that though the Ukrainian Central Committee resolution of June 12, 1953, condemned the entire Bureau of the Central Committee along with Melnikov, a member of the Bureau, Kirichenko, was chosen to succeed Melnikov. Later, Kirichenko turned out to be Khrushchev's protégé. In other words, in the Ukraine Beria seems to have advanced the interest of Khrushchev rather than his own. In this connection, note should be taken of a very ingenious and plausible suggestion by Robert Conquest, a British scholar, that the sudden political rehabilitation of the old Ukrainian Bolshevik Petrovsky on April 28, 1953, who during the Great Purges had been demoted from the Presidency of the Ukrainian Republic to a minor job in Moscow, was Beria's work.[71] Beria may have hoped to organize a pliable Ukrainian leadership under the figurehead of Petrovsky, but failed in the attempt. Be that as it may, in removing Melnikov from the Ukraine, Beria seems to have walked into a carefully laid trap.

We may add that Melnikov was succeeded by Kirichenko and that in August, 1953, Nikolay V. Podgorny, whose career had been almost exclusively in state administration, was suddenly appointed Second Secretary of the CPU and eventual successor to Kirichenko.[72] The official spelling of his name—Podgorny, instead of the Ukrainian version Pidhirny—at first suggested the idea that the new First Secretary of the Ukraine (a post Podgorny has held since December, 1957) was a Russian. A Ukrainian exiled publicist interpreted Podgorny's appointment as "linked with the necessity of finding a new form of balance between the Ukrainian and Russian wings in the CP of Ukraine." [73] But in 1960, when attending the Fifteenth session of the United Nations General Assembly in New York together with Khrushchev, Podgorny addressed the delegates in Ukrainian. In more recent years, Kiev's *Radyans'ka Ukrayina* has used a Ukrainized form of his name.[74] Apparently, Podgorny, like Kirichenko, is of Ukrainian descent. Thus in the summer of 1953, for the first time in the history of the Communist Party of Ukraine, two Ukrainians were entrusted with the important posts of First and Second Secretaries of the Party. Once established, this precedent has been followed until to date (end of 1962).[75]

When the book was going to press, Soviet newspapers revealed that on July 2, 1963, Podgorny was relieved from his position of First Secretary of the Ukrainian Party Central Committee in connection with his election as a Secretary of the All-Union Party Central Committee—probably an advancement in rank. Podgorny's successor in the Ukraine, the new First Secretary of the CP of Ukraine, became P. Yu. Shelest, formerly a Secretary of the Central Committee of the Ukrainian Party Organization and the Chief of its Bureau for the Direction of Industry and Structure—a bureau set up late in 1962. Judging by his name, Shelest, too, appears to be of Ukrainian origin. M. O. Sobol' was elected as Second Secretary of the Ukrainian Party.[76]

How relevant is this excursion into "Kremlinology" to the topic of

Ukrainian nationalism? It would have been of utmost importance if one could demonstrate that in June, 1953, the dissatisfaction of Ukrainians in general and of Western Ukrainians in particular had reached such a critical stage that the dismissal of Melnikov became necessary—no matter who was actually responsible for it. If such evidence exists I have not been able to find it. In other words, I have not been able to establish that nationally conscious cadres of the CPU actively participated in the power struggle in Moscow on their own initiative. But this is not to deny the proposition that real grievances against Stalin's nationality policy in the Ukraine did exist and that Beria and the regime acknowledged their existence in June, 1953. While Melnikov's removal may not have been necessary, it was certainly politic: even after Beria's fall, a Russian was not made First Secretary of the Ukraine. Furthermore, while there is no evidence to show that the cadres of the CPU forced this or that policy upon Moscow there is ample proof of the fact that Khrushchev found their service useful in his rise of power. The crucial problems which arise in this connection are: Who are Khrushchev's new men from the Ukraine? What effect has their political advancement had upon Soviet policy toward Ukrainian nationalism, if any?

3. *The Advance of Ukrainian Party Cadres after June, 1953*

A comparison of the membership lists of the Communist Party of the Soviet Union Central Committees elected at the Nineteenth, Twentieth and Twenty-Second Party Congresses [77] shows the most prominent members of the Ukrainian Party organization who have been advanced under Khrushchev's Secretaryship. The *crème de la crème* of those have been selected for brief sketches. I have refrained from tracing the careers of members of the Soviet Ukrainian Government: The Party is the more important branch of Soviet political institutions; moreover, it has the advantage of being the stabler one as compared with the ministries that were constantly being reorganized after Stalin's death. But I have not withstood the temptation of briefly indicating the careers of some military figures who had been connected with Khrushchev before Stalin's death and who have been advanced after his assumption of power.

One of the first of Khrushchev's former subordinates in the CPU to obtain an important post in the All-Union Party organization was Mzhavanadze, who in September, 1953, replaced Beria's appointee Mirtskhulava as First Secretary of the Georgian Party, a post he has held to date (end of 1962). Mzhavanadze, apparently a Georgian, has been identified as an old *politruk* (political indoctrination officer in the armed forces) who after World War II was engaged in the Ukraine.[78] Mzhavanadze was first elected candidate member of the All-Union Presidium in

June, 1957, after the defeat of Malenkov's "Anti-Party Group," has remained in that position through the last Congress in October, 1961. Another Communist Party of Ukraine officer to head a Republican Party organization is Serdyuk, from February, 1954, till May, 1960, the head of the relatively small CP of Moldavia.[79] Of greater importance is the career of Leonid I. Brezhnev, formerly of the Dniepropetrovsk *obkom* in the Ukraine,[80] who at one time was in charge of one of the most important projects of Khrushchev's: the development of the virgin lands in Kazakhstan. Since February, 1954, as soon as the project had been decided upon, Brezhnev served as Second, then First Secretary of the Kazakh Party organization.[81] Upon his promotion to alternate membership in the Presidium and the Secretariat of the All-Union Party (CPSU) Central Committee at the Twentieth Party Congress (February, 1956), Brezhnev yielded his post in Kazakhstan to another graduate of the Ukrainian Party apparatus: Ivan D. Yakovlev.[82] Brezhnev's career after the Twentieth Party Congress is not without interest. After the ouster of the Anti-Party Group in 1957, Brezhnev was appointed full member of the Presidium. In May, 1960, he replaced Voroshilov as Chairman of the Presidium of the USSR Supreme Soviet, two months later relinquished the post of Secretary of the Central Committee he had held since February, 1956, thus giving rise to speculations that he might have been demoted upward, for reasons unknown.[83] When the book was already in press, it was reported that Brezhnev had been re-elected a Secretary of the All-Union Party Central Committee.[84]

A few former CPU members achieved high positions in the Party apparatus of the Russian Republic (RSFSR). By February, 1956, Stakhursky, formerly of the Vinnitsa Province in the Ukraine, had been entrusted with the leadership of the strategically important Khabarovsk Territory in the Soviet Far East; and Struev, who had held posts in the Donbas, had taken over the industrial Molotov (now: Perm) province in the Urals.[85] Both Secretaryships entitled their holders to full membership on the Communist Party of the Soviet Union Central Committee. But neither Stakhursky nor Struev lasted long in those prominent posts; at the Twenty-Second Congress in October, 1961, Stakhursky was not re-elected to the Central Committee, and Struev was demoted to alternate membership. The most successful of this particular group has been A. P. Kirilenko. Formerly a Secretary of the Zaporozhe, Nikolaev, and Dniepropetrovsk *obkoms* in the Ukraine—all of them industrial areas. In 1955 Kirilenko was appointed First Secretary of the important Sverdlovsk *obkom* in the Urals, which in 1956 comprised 119,784 Party members. Since 1956 Kirilenko has been a member of the Central Committee's Bureau for the RSFSR, and since July, 1957, a candidate member of the Presidium.[86] Somewhat surprisingly, at the Twenty-Second

Party Congress Kirilenko was re-elected to the Bureau on Russian Republican Affairs, but not to the Presidium. Within half a year, however, in late April, 1962, Kirilenko was elected full member of the Presidium.[87]

A little less prominent but more stable has been the career of Dmitriy S. Polyansky, who had been born into the family of a poor peasant in the Donets Basin in 1917. After attending the Kharkov Agricultural Institute Polyansky joined the Party in 1939 and was detailed to Komsomol work in Kharkov. From 1945 until 1949 he served in responsible positions on the staff of the All-Union Party Central Committee, in its personnel division. From 1949 he occupied a series of regional posts: In the Crimea (1949–December, 1955; First Provincial Secretary from December, 1953); First Secretary of the Chkalov *obkom* (1955–February, 1957) and the Krasnodarsk Territorial Committee (February, 1957–March, 1958), both in the Russian Republic. Since the end of March, 1958, Polyansky has been the Premier of the Russian Republic, and apparently as such he was elected to the Party Presidium: a candidate member in June, 1958, a full member in May, 1960.[88]

Several other members of the Ukrainian Party apparatus have advanced to responsible positions within the central Party organization in Moscow. A. M. Rumyantsev, formerly First Secretary of the Kharkov Province Committee, in 1956 was editor-in-chief of the most authoritative Party journal *Kommunist* (Moscow); since 1958 he has edited the *Problems of Peace and Socialism,* the journal of the Communist international movement.[89] Of even greater importance than the career of the ideologist Rumyantsev,[90] is the transfer to the central apparatus of V. M. Churaev and V. N. Titov. At the session of the CPU Central Committee in August, 1946, Victor M. Churaev was identified as First Secretary of the Kharkov *obkom*.[91] Later he is said to have served as deputy director of a major staff agency in the Ukrainian Party. In February, 1956, he was appointed Head of the Central Committee Department of Party Organs for the RSFSR, or in plain English, Party personnel director for the Russian Republic.[92] Churaev attracted attention when he was appointed chairman of the mandate commission at the extraordinary Twenty-First Congress in January, 1959, and delivered its report. He was identified as a former Director of the Central Committee Department of Party Agencies in the Union Republics until March, 1961. At the Twenty-Second Party Congress in October, 1961, Churaev was elected a member of the Central Committee Bureau for the RSFSR.[93] At that Congress, the credentials report was given by V. N. Titov, who until March, 1961, had served as First Secretary of the Kharkov *obkom*. He has been identified as the Director of the Central Committee Department of Party Agencies in the Union Republics at the time of the Congress.[94] Both Churaev and Titov have thus been engaged in personnel work at the highest level.

To supplement the picture on the military side, we note that after Beria's fall, General of the Army Moskalenko took over the extremely important Moscow Military District from Colonel-General Artemyev. Moskalenko is known as a close associate of Khrushchev's, under whom he worked in the Moscow Party Committee from 1949–51.[95] In the summer of 1953 he apparently helped Khrushchev to disarm Beria's followers in Moscow; in March, 1955, he was awarded by promotion to the highest military rank, Marshal of the Soviet Union; since February, 1956, he has been elected full member of the Central Committee of the All-Union Party. Moskalenko became very prominent again when in October, 1960, he succeeded General Nedelin as Commander in Chief of Soviet Rocket Troops (the officer in charge of Soviet long-range missiles). Nedelin had been killed in a plane accident.[96] Early in November 1962 Moskalenko yielded the rocket command to Marshal Biryuzov, assuming another important position—that of chief inspector general of the Soviet armed forces.[97]

Apart from Moskalenko, it is worth while to mention some other general officers who were promoted to Marshals of the Soviet Union in March, 1955. Following rather close upon Malenkov's resignation from Premiership (early February, 1955) and upon Bulganin's succession, those promotions, albeit they went to competent officers, may well have been politically motivated. Besides Moskalenko five other officers were advanced: Bagramian, Biryuzov, Grechko, Chuykov, and Yeremenko.[98] Of the five, Bagramian alone cooperated during World War II with Bulganin, all the others were commanders on the southern front for which Khrushchev held political responsibility.[99] Next to Moskalenko the marshal closest to Khrushchev appears to be A. A. Grechko. (Judging by their names both appear to be Ukrainians.) Grechko had been elected full member of the Central Committee CP of Ukraine in 1949 and 1952, a post he held as Commander of the Kiev Military District. After the June 17, 1953, uprisings in Eastern Germany he was given command of Soviet forces in that advanced strategic area. Since November, 1957, Grechko has served first as Commander in Chief of Ground Forces (fourth ranking position in the Ministry of Defense), then First Deputy Minister for General Affairs (second ranking post in the Ministry), since July, 1960. Grechko has been identified as a personal supporter of Khrushchev; [100] he was elected a candidate member of the All-Union Party Central Committee at the Twentieth Party Congress (1956), promoted five years later to full membership.[101]

But the two most distinguished careers made by Ukrainian Party graduates are those of Kirichenko and Semichastny. (At the beginning of

1960 Kirichenko's star had fallen, but Semichastny's is still on the ascendancy at the time of writing, the end of 1962.)

In the reorganization of the top leadership immediately after Stalin's death, on March 6, 1953, L. G. Melnikov was demoted from full to alternate membership on the Presidium. In May, 1953, a few weeks *before* Melnikov's fall in the Ukraine, Kirichenko took the latter's place on the Presidium.[102] Two years later, at the July plenary session of the Central Committee, Kirichenko was promoted to full membership on the Presidium in an evident move to strengthen Khrushchev's position in the Presidium after Malenkov's resignation from Premiership.[103] In December, 1957, Kirichenko achieved the top ranks of Soviet leadership: a full Presidium member, he was, in addition, made Secretary of the Central Committee. (At this juncture, however, he had to yield the First Secretaryship of the CP of Ukraine to Podgorny.)

At the Twenty-First Party Congress in January, 1959, Kirichenko, at the peak of his power, delivered a report on Party personnel,[104] which indicates that by that time he had been entrusted with the very important but also very dangerous task of supervising Party cadres throughout the Soviet Union. That is a position which has been traditionally exercised by the second-ranking secretary; in other words, in the beginning of 1959 Kirichenko appeared very much Khrushchev's first deputy. But a year later he was suddenly demoted to the First Secretaryship of the comparatively insignificant Rostov Province, a post from which he was also ousted six months hence to disappear from Soviet politics altogether.[105]

No reason for Kirichenko's abrupt dismissal has been given. But it is not unlikely, as Conquest assumes, that in fulfilling the duties of his sensitive position Kirichenko had laid himself bare to charges that he, being a non-Russian, unduly favored the local cadres in the Republics. For instance, Babayev's dismissal from the First Secretaryship of the Turkmenian CP in December, 1958, amidst criticisms that he had violated the precepts of Leninist nationality policy in giving preference to Turkmenians, occurred while Kirichenko was in charge of Party cadres.[106] But given the long and close association between Kirichenko and Khrushchev, it would be safe to assume that Kirichenko was merely carrying out his superior's policy. If so, early in 1960 Khrushchev must have sacrificed him as a scapegoat for the reverses in nationality policy, as he sacrificed Belyaev, when the latter failed to produce sufficient grain in the virgin lands, a favorite scheme of Khrushchev's.[107]

Vladimir Ye. Semichastny, who has been successful so far, is a veteran Komsomol leader from the Ukraine. After serving as First Secretary of the Ukrainian Komsomol from 1947-50, he became a junior and then the First Secretary of the All-Union Komsomol.[108] In that latter capacity he gained notoriety in the West when during the fortieth anniversary meeting of the Komsomol in late 1958 he denounced the late Nobel Prize winner Boris Pasternak in the vilest language possible.[109] From April till August, 1959, Semichastny served as a Director of the Central Committee Department of Party Agencies for the Union Republics.[110] From August, 1959, until November, 1961, Semichastny occupied the post of Second Secretary of the Azerbaydzhani Central Committee, after the dismissal of First Secretary Mustafaev. On November 13, 1961, Semichastny was appointed head of the Committee on State Security, that is, the Soviet secret police.[111] Judging by his name, Semichastny may be a Ukrainian.[112]

What is the significance of the advancement of former members of the Ukrainian Party organization to leading posts in the Russian and All-Union Party apparatuses? On first sight, the nationality of the new appointees seems to have very little relevance to their being appointed. Insofar as names can be taken as reliable evidence of a person's nationality—which is questionable—we notice that some of the appointees from the Ukraine (for example, Brezhnev) are probably Russians. Moreover, a broader study would have revealed that it was not only members of the Ukrainian Party organization that were advanced by Khrushchev, but his protégés in the Moscow apparatus as well (most notably the woman Furtseva).[113] Thirdly, Khrushchev's new appointees with Ukrainian names cannot plausibly be regarded as Ukrainian nationalists in disguise, that is, men who are committed in the long run to the establishment of an autonomous or independent Ukrainian state. The biography of Kirichenko reveals that he was an *aparatchik* who had made his career at a time when bona fide Ukrainian nationalists and Ukrainian "National Communists" were being executed right and left. The most certain conclusion that can be drawn from their advancement after Stalin's death is that they confirm Friedrich's thesis of political power. No established dictator is powerful enough to dispense with the help from a clique of trusted lieutenants, far less a would-be dictator like Khrushchev was in 1953–57. Power is indeed a bond that in a certain fashion unites the leader and the led: Kirichenko and Podgorny needed Khrushchev to rise to the Presidium, but for a number of reasons, which we shall try to explain in a moment, Khrushchev also needed both Kirichenko and Podgorny.

While the role of nationality in advancement within the Party should not be exaggerated, can we discount it altogether? It is true that we do not possess any hard and fast evidence as to what criteria are used in the selection of top Soviet cadres. We know that so-called family circles are formed between Party and administrative officials working in one area.[114] Assuming that a higher Party functionary has some freedom in the choice of his associates, would he, other things being equal, give preference to a fellow-national? High ranking Party members have not defected to the West to tell their experiences, and not much can be expected from interviewing the present officeholders in the Soviet Union, should they ever consent to answer questions on their working methods.[115] But for the purpose of establishing hypotheses, logical inferences from official actions and statements may suffice.

What has struck this observer most about the composition of the All-Union Presidium is that since the fall of the so-called "Anti-Party Group" in June, 1957, it has always included two or more Ukrainians: the First Secretary of the CPU and another prominent member of the Republican Party organization. Thus in June, 1957, the Presidium contained Kirichenko, as a full member, and Khrushchev's old assistant D. S. Korotchenko as an alternate. (Korotchenko, by the way, had been a full member of Stalin's enlarged Presidium of 1952; he was dismissed from the Presidium altogether in March, 1953, reappeared as an alternate member in 1957.) In June, 1958, Podgorny, First Secretary of the CPU, was also admitted to the Presidium as a candidate member; after Kirichenko's fall he took the latter's place among the full members in May, 1960. Podgorny was re-elected to that post at the Twenty-Second Party Congress in 1961. At that Congress, Korotchenko was dropped from the roster of alternate members, but a substitute was quickly found in V. V. Shcherbitsky, then Premier of the Ukrainian SSR, formerly a junior Secretary of the Ukrainian Central Committee. It seems as if in the last five years a decision has been made to allot to the Ukrainian Party organization at least two seats on the Presidium, one of them being a full membership. Similar allotments can be found in the case of other important Republics. On closer examination we find that the First Secretary of the Communist Party of Ukraine has always been a member of the Presidium at least since 1952 (Melnikov from October 1952 to May or June, 1953; Kirichenko from May, 1953, to January or May, 1960; Podgorny from June, 1958, to date). Another fact which is even more important is that since 1953 the top posts in the Ukraine have been held by Ukrainians. What does this add up to?

In the light of an important passage from Khrushchev's political report to the Twentieth Party Congress it can be plausibly suggested that nationality did indeed play a role in Kirichenko's advancement, as it figured in the almost simultaneous, precedent-making promotion of the Uzbek Mukhitdinov.* They may have been young and competent

---

* Nuritdin A. Mukhitdinov, born in 1917, was appointed First Secretary of the Uzbek CP in December, 1955; became an alternate member of the Presidium at the Twentieth Party Congress, and a full member upon his election to the Secretariat of the Central Committee CPSU in December, 1957. See *Pravda*, December 22, 1957. For reasons unknown, Mukhitdinov was *not* re-elected either to the Presidium or the Secretariat at the Twenty-Second Party Congress. But another Uzbek, Sh. R. Rashidov, was elected a candidate member of the Presidium. See *Pravda*, November 1, 1961, p. 1.

men,[116] intensely loyal to Khrushchev personally; the regions they were heading may have been economically very important; but to my mind it does not explain everything.[117] A large part of the explanation for the precedent-making admission of a Ukrainian and an Uzbek into the Secretariat and Presidium of the CPSU should be sought precisely in their being a Ukrainian and a Uzbek. Why? Speaking on the organization of Soviet economy at the Twentieth Party Congress, Khrushchev said:

The rapid development of the economy and culture of the Union republics places on the order of the day certain questions of improving the guidance of the economy and of cultural development.

Before, when there were few specialists locally, when the cadres were weak in a number of republics and when there were not so many industrial enterprises either, the management of nearly all enterprises was exercised through Union ministries. Now the situation has changed: *Along with industry, people have developed in all the Union republics; national cadres have been forged, and the general cultural level of all the peoples of the USSR has risen sharply.* Under these new conditions, the old methods of managing the economy require *substantial revision.* While leaving the Union ministries in charge of general direction . . . it is necessary at the same time to enlarge considerably the powers of the republic ministries.*

The notion that the problem of native "cadres" is not limited to economic administrators is almost explicit in Khrushchev's statement. Would it be, therefore, implausible to suggest that Kirichenko and Mukhitdinov, and later Podgorny and Rashidov, have been advanced not only on strength of their loyalty and competence but also because they were also representing the non-Russian Communist cadres in a Party dominated by Russians? The rapid promotion of Mukhitdinov may also have been dictated by considerations of foreign policy: Mu-

---

* *Pravda,* February 15, 1956; and Gruliow (ed.), *Cur. Soviet Policies II,* p. 52. The discussion appears under the heading of "Some Questions of Our Nationality Policy." Italics added. Copyright 1957, the Joint Committee on Slavic Studies. Reprinted by permission. In this context attention should be drawn to a statement by Merle Fainsod, which had been made three years earlier. He wrote: "One of the most serious points of tension in . . . Soviet [nationality] policy involves the position of the Soviet-trained native intelligentsia. Once these persons have been educated for administrative and other responsibilities, *they aspire to real as well as formal authority,* and they become increasingly restive under the rigid control exerted by the plenipotentiaries whom Moscow despatches to supervise their activities. When they express their restiveness, they are charged with bourgeois nationalist deviations, removed from office, and drastically punished. This phenomenon of *incipient internal Titoism* has been little noted, yet it would appear to be of considerable significance, and it constitutes an interesting counterpart to the difficulties encountered by Western imperial powers in dealing with the native intelligentsia in their colonies." (*How Russia Is Ruled* [1953 ed.], pp. 495–96. Italics added. Reprinted by permission of Harvard University Press.)

khitdinov is an Asian and since 1955 the Soviet Union has increased its appeals to the Middle East.

In order to gain a deeper understanding of the relationship between the Party elite in Moscow and its subordinates in the Ukraine let us briefly reconsider the dismissal of Melnikov in the light of Khrushchev's later statement. It is basically the pressure of native cadres for further advancement that made Melnikov's removal politic, even if, more likely than not, he merely served as a scapegoat for the policy of Moscow. Apart from the official indictment, there is other evidence that the problem was particularly acute in Western Ukraine. In the first place, it has been calculated on the basis of the representation at the Seventeenth CPU Congress in 1952 that the Party coverage of West Ukraine was comparatively thin. In 1952, seven provinces of the Western Ukraine (Lviv, Drohobych, Ternopil, Stanyslaviv, Volhynia, Rovno, and Trans-carpathia) * contained about 100,000 Party members, or as much as the Kiev Province alone.[118] The conflicts between native and "imported" cadres have already been noted in an earlier chapter.[119] We have also seen that in May, 1952, Serdyuk of the CPU Central Committee was despatched from Kiev to take over the Lviv Province Committee. Shortly after Melnikov's fall K. Z. Lytvyn, who in 1949 had been CPU Central Committee Secretary in charge of ideology and who in 1953 fulfilled the same function as Second Secretary of the Lviv Province Committee, was withdrawn from that post to become Ukrainian SSR Minister of Culture. His function was taken over by a native communist, B. K. Dudykevych who has been identified by Ukrainian exiles as a former member of the CP of Western Ukraine, the Ukrainian Section of the Polish CP in the interwar period.[120] While the Western Ukraine presented the greatest difficulties, it is not implausible to argue that the problems were not restricted to her. We have already seen at the beginning of this chapter that in the nine year period between the Nineteenth and the Twenty-Second Party Congresses the membership of the CPU grew disproportionately fast.[121] Would most of the new members come from Western Ukraine? This is possible, but not very likely. It looks as if under Stalin Party recruitment (or, in other words, admission to the Soviet political elite) had been neglected in the Ukraine as such, and that efforts were made to rectify that situation under Khrushchev.

4. *Changes in the Administration of Ukrainian Industry*

The advance of Ukrainian cadres in the Party apparatus found its parallel in important changes within the administration. In 1957 the

* In 1959 the province of Drohobych was incorporated into that of Lviv, around 1963 the province of Stanyslaviv was renamed Ivano-Frankivska.

Soviet Union embarked upon her most ambitious scheme of administrative reorganization since the early 1930's. It seemed as if in industrial management the autonomist national cadres had won the struggle against stultifying and politically frustrating centralization.

Until the summer of 1957, all industrial enterprises in the Soviet Union had been divided into four categories: plants of All-Union, Union-Republican, Republican, and local importance. All-Union enterprises were directly subordinated to an All-Union Ministry in Moscow, and Republican and local enterprises were under Republican Ministries (each Republic had a Ministry of Local Industry). The situation was not always standardized as far as the Union-Republican enterprises were concerned. According to Fainsod, those factories were, in most cases, responsible both to the Ministry in Moscow and its counterpart Ministry in the capital of the Republic, the central Ministry exercising general guidance and the Republican counterpart Ministry carrying "a substantial part of the burden of operative control." [122] But in some cases Union-Republican enterprises were themselves subdivided into two categories: those directly responsible to Moscow and those responsible both to Moscow and the Republican capital.[123]

While Soviet administrative structure thus shows a confusing variety of form, its content since the 1930's has shown notorious centralization. It has been achieved by three principal means: central planning of output coupled with central distribution of all important producers' and consumers' goods (so-called "funded" and "quota" commodities); [124] central financing; and a single apparatus for gathering statistics. The last item is self-explanatory, but the extent of centralization in planning and financing merits some further comment.

From the elaborate division of Soviet enterprises into four classes it might have been supposed that while the next higher administrative organ controlled the working of its subordinate organs in *general* terms, the latter had substantial freedom in allocating productive tasks and resources among the enterprises under its immediate jurisdiction. But this was certainly not the case before 1957, nor has it been realized to a substantial degree at the time of the writing (end of 1962). So far as I could learn from the general materials released after Stalin's death the principle that has prevailed in Soviet administration was a kind of "double vertical control" along the line of administrative responsibility. This meant in practice that the enterprise was immediately controlled by a certain administrative organ, but that organ lacked the authority to allocate resources without a detailed authorization from the organ above. The result of this peculiar arrangement was that two organs did virtually the same work of detailed operational control, which in most cases involved a decision from Moscow. Let me illustrate. In the beginning of 1956, *Pravda* reported the following:

Union-republican Councils of Ministers [that is, the Council of Ministers of the Soviet republics] approve the plans for production and distribution of all types of industrial output drafted by the enterprises of republic ministries and producers' cooperatives. They also allocate capital work among the various ministries and agencies on the republican level, fix the number of personnel and the amounts to be paid as wages and approve plan indices for public health, education, culture, public welfare, and communal economy.

The [recent] government decision to authorize the Union republican Council of Ministers to use the additional funds that have been allocated or derived from local and republican budget [revenues] for financing above-[the-]plan housing, communal economy, social and cultural measures is of great importance. In the first half of 1955 alone such additional [revenue] was used for above plan financing of enterprises, housing construction and other measures in amounts totaling 525 million rubles for the Russian Republic, 506 million for the Ukraine, 20 million for Belorussia, 19 million for Georgia.[125]

In other words, before 1956 the Republican governments could not freely dispose of the profits derived from enterprises under their *exclusive* jurisdiction. The principle of "double vertical control" becomes even clearer when the rights of local administrative organs are examined. Said Deputy M. M. Lazurenko from the Lviv electoral district in a debate during the May, 1957, session of the USSR Supreme Soviet:

At the present time the province executive committees cannot even redistribute capital investment among enterprises of one and the same system without the approval of the corresponding republic ministry. Province executive committees do not even have the right to allocate completely their own funds received as deductions from the profits of industries of district, city, or province subordination.[126]

Implied in both examples is the Soviet system of tax collection. Unlike the United States, where each governmental unit determines its necessary revenue and then collects the taxes through its own channels,[127] all taxes in the Soviet Union are raised by the central government which then allocates a certain percentage from the total revenue for the disposition of the Republican governments and their subdivisions. As Harry Schwartz puts it:

The Supreme Soviet of the USSR determines the budgetary revenues and expenditures of the constituent Republics and also the relationships between the budget of each republic and the total budget of all local governmental units in that republic.[128]

Faced with economic inefficiencies and political disadvantages (the sheer weight of the bureaucratic apparatus in Moscow, the restiveness of local cadres) the regime decided to shift some operational controls from Moscow to the Republican capitals. Published figures show that in 1953, 64 per cent of the gross industrial output of the Ukrainian SSR were produced in enterprises under All-Union jurisdiction, and only 36 per cent in Republican, provincial, and district enterprises. In the next year (1954) only one third (33 per cent) was produced by enterprises under central jurisdiction, in 1956 less than one quarter (24 per cent).[129] In reviewing these developments during a session of the USSR Supreme Soviet the Ukrainian Prime Minister N. T. Kalchenko stated that about 10,000 enterprises were transferred from Union to Republican jurisdiction, that the value of the industrial output of the Union Republican and Republican enterprises had risen from 43 billion rubles in 1953 to 145 billion rubles by 1957 and the Republican budget increased during the same period from 18 to 43.7 billion rubles.[130]

Precisely what this meant in terms of the change in powers of the Ukrainian Council of Ministers is extremely difficult to ascertain. We know, for example, that in 1954 counterpart ministries for ferrous metallurgy and coal mining were set up in Kiev, but we do not know which particular enterprises were put under their immediate control, quite apart from what that control really involved.[131] Furthermore, in the summer of 1957 the elaborate transfer from All-Union to Union-Republican Ministries was scrapped in favor of a more complex structure of territorial economic councils, so that within this context there would be little point in investigating the developments of 1954–56 in detail.

At the CPSU Central Committee plenum of February, 1957, it was "discovered" that so-called interdepartmental barriers entailed a lot of waste. Khrushchev, therefore, proposed to abolish all industrial ministries and set up territorial economic councils instead. Before long, after a nation-wide discussion, in which 40,820,000 are said to have participated at 514,000 meetings, Khrushchev's proposals were embodied, with some modifications, in the Law of May 10, 1957, "On Further Improving the Organization of the Management of Industry and Construction." [132] The main provisions of that law are as follows:

The whole reorganization was to be carried out within less than two months: by July 1, 1957. The country was to be divided into economic regions. Their number was to be established by the Republican Supreme Soviets, but from the deputies' speeches it became apparent that the Russian Federation would be divided into 68 such regions, the Ukrainian SSR into eleven.[133] (See Note VIII-1, in the Appendix, for a list of economic regions in 1957.) Article 5 of the law read:

The economic council of an economic administrative region [was] to be directly subordinate in all its activities to the Council of Ministers of the Union Republic. The USSR Council of Ministers [was] to exercise direction of the economic councils through the Council of Ministers of the Union Republics.

What was the competence of those administrative councils? Their decisions could be vetoed by the Republican Councils of Ministers and by the USSR Council of Ministers, with the *formal* difference that the Republican Council could revoke them (absolute veto) while the USSR Council had the right only to suspend them (suspensive veto)—see Article 8. The positive competence of the economic councils the law left undefined. But in his speech before the Supreme Soviet Khrushchev said:

The economic councils must be given the right to engage in financial planning and redistribution of profits and of working capital among the various industries of the region, and also to set up necessary financial reserves.[134]

Articles 9 and 11 listed the Ministries that were to be dissolved and whose enterprises were to be completely subordinated to the economic councils. They were the All-Union Ministries of

> Automobile Industry
> Machine Building
> Instruments and Automation
> Machine Tools
> Construction Machinery and Road Machine Building
> Construction for the Oil Industry
> Tractor and Farm Machine Building
> Transport Machine Building
> Heavy Machine Building
> Electrical Equipment Industry;

and the Union-Republican Ministries of

> Paper and Wood Processing Industry
> Urban and Rural Construction
> Light Industry
> Lumber
> Oil
> Meat and Dairy Products Industry
> Food Products Industry
> Building Materials Industry
> Fishing Industry
> Construction
> Construction for the Metallurgical and Chemical Industries
> Construction for the Coal Industry
> Coal
> Non-Ferrous Metallurgy
> Ferrous Metallurgy

A small but strategically important group of All-Union Ministries were to be retained, viz.:

The Ministries of:
  Aviation Industry
  Defense Industry
  Radio Industry
  Shipbuilding Industry
  Power Plants (formerly: Power Plants and
    Power Plant Construction Ministries).

As far as chemical industry was concerned, some of the enterprises were to be placed under the direct jurisdiction of economic councils, in accordance with a list approved by the USSR Council of Ministers. The same article (13) admonished the remaining All-Union Ministries to restrict themselves to planning and maintaining high technical standards, but letting the economic councils carry out their decisions. The article did not mention two Ministries which Khrushchev seems to have wanted to disband, too: the Ministry of Transport Construction and that of Medium Machine Building,[135] the latter reportedly a cover name for the defense industry. Article 18 described the enlarged functions of the *Gosplan* (State Planning Commission) which was envisaged as an economic superministry; and Article 20 stipulated that all chairmen of the Republican Councils of Ministers should be included in the new Council of Ministers of the Soviet Union.

So much for a summary exposition of the law. What are its political implications? A western observer is sorely tempted to describe those measures as a decentralization of the administrative apparatus of the Soviet industry. Khrushchev and his associates, however, were well aware of the danger that some regional councils might develop tendencies toward autarky, or *mestnichestvo* (localism). "Such fears are not unfounded, and they must not be forgotten," said Khrushchev in his speech before the Supreme Soviet. But he reassured his audience that "integrated national economic planning, centralized finances, and nationwide statistics" would prevent such a state of affairs,[136] and—we may add—so would the Party so long as it remains the powerful centralized instrument it is now.

What appears to have been the true significance of the reform? There may be convincing economic reasons why it was undertaken.[137] An examination of all the relevant evidence would have gone far beyond the scope of our enquiry; the hypothesis, that we shall offer now may, therefore, be somewhat one-sided but, we hope, not unfounded. As we see the matter, one of the chief reasons for the reform was political.[138] The Ukrainian exile economist is right when he points out that it was hardly solicitude for the people as such that prompted Khrushchev to "bring management nearer to production." [139] In what we consider his most important speech to date, the secret speech "On the Cult of Personality" at the Twentieth Party Congress, Khrushchev showed no signs of regret for the millions of ordinary Soviet citizens who perished during the drive for collectivization and during the Great Purge. But he was concerned with the Party workers, the cadres. Having spent much of his time outside Moscow he had grasped one important phenomenon to which Stalin and perhaps even Malenkov had shown themselves blind: the Kirichenkos, the Mukhitdinovs, the Brezhnevs, and Kirilenkos were forging ahead. He accepted their help in his rise for power and in return gave them responsible positions in Moscow. Furthermore, in order to demonstrate his good will to those loyal Party workers who could not be accommodated in the capital, he gave them opportunity to exercise greater administrative responsibility on the spot.[140]

This appears clearly from several pronouncements of Khrushchev, for example, in his speech to the Supreme Soviet in May, 1957, and from the preamble to the reorganization law, which reads:

. . . To expand even more the powers of Union republics in the sphere of economic construction and to transfer the center of gravity of operational guidance and construction projects to the localities, to economic administrative regions.

On the other hand, there is clear evidence that non-Russian cadres welcomed the expansion of their administrative powers and deplored the old Stalinist methods of management. In the discussions on the 1957 industrial reform Mukhitdinov, then First Secretary of the Uzbek Party, pressed for only one economic council in Uzbekistan when it looked as if Moscow would reserve for itself the right to directly intervene in the affairs of the economic region, without formally going through the Republican government. (That had been Khrushchev's original proposal.) When the economic regions were formally subordinated to Tashkent, Mukhitdinov changed his mind and accepted four economic councils in Uzbekistan.[141] In the Ukraine, prior to the reform, we notice a complaint in *Radyans'ka Ukrayina,* the organ of the Central Committee of the Ukrainian Party, of August 12, 1955, that the Zhytomyr Province exported most of its linen fiber outside the Ukrainian SSR only to import them back as expensive linen cloth. It was officially suggested that a large textile factory be built in Zhytomyr (Northwest Ukraine) to process the local crops. Baranovsky, the chairman of the Ukrainian Planning Commission, promised in 1955 to build such a factory.[142]

How has the industrial reorganization of 1957 worked out in practice? What have been its effects on the Republican cadres?

A Ukrainian economist living in exile predicted in June, 1957, that "in spite of its centralist foundations the reform [would] evidently strengthen the decentralizing tendencies." [143] Alec Nove points out that within two months after the adoption of the reform strong complaints were voiced about the extent of those tendencies. He cites the chairman of the Belorussian national economic council: [144]

There are instances when officials bother only about enterprises subordinate to them and do not think of the difficulties their irregularities cause for enterprises in other regions. It is necessary to speak about this frankly, so that these defects do not grow worse. . . . *We have met clear instances of tendencies toward [autarky].* [A. Nove's italics.] The Dzerzhinski factory of the Dnepropetrovsk region supplies rolled wire to the Rezhitsa nail-making works. In July, the Dzerzhinski factory underfulfilled its plan by 15 per cent, but sent to Rezhitsa only 300 instead of 1,020 tons of rolled wire. When this outrageous fact was investigated, the managers of the Dzerzhinski factory declared that they had orders from the Dnepropetrovsk sovnarkhoz [economic council—Y.B.] to give priority to enterprises in their own region and to supply them in full.[145]

It will be recognized that the Dzerzhinski factory is located in neighboring Ukraine.

To combat the tendency toward "localism" the central government in January, 1958 (that is, six months after the reform), issued a decree making the heads of economic councils liable to criminal persecution if it could be shown that they had obstructed inter-regional delivery plans.[146] This put the chairmen in a difficult quandary of priorities. They were criticized if they did not deliver the goods to another, more remote region, but they would also be castigated if enterprises in their own region or the neighboring one failed to meet the output plans set by the Gosplan. If those latter enterprises were also dependent on goods produced in his region he was likely to favor them on the ancient principle that the shirt is next to the body. Nove is quite right in stressing that to counteract their self-interest by legal means (such as the punitive decree of January, 1958) the regime must be very explicit which priorities it is going to enforce.[147] Occasionally an economic council chairman will get caught. For instance, at the Twenty-Second *Ukrainian* Party Congress in September, 1961, Podgorny announced that a severe Party penalty had been imposed on Lviv council chairman Ivonin and his deputy dismissed. Ivonin, while not fulfilling his supply plans, retained for his enterprises more resources than had been allotted to him by the planning agencies. Furthermore, he sent on his own initiative, without proper authorization, important products of his region to other regions—apparently in a form of illegal barter trade, necessary to keep his enterprises functioning as he wanted them to function.[148]

The central government, however, has not limited itself to legal pro-

hibitions, but has strengthened central controls by administrative measures. In the fall of 1959, for example, the Supreme Soviet of the USSR
passed a law in which it reaffirmed the basic centralized character of
the USSR budget.[149] A corresponding law was passed by the Ukrainian
SSR Supreme Soviet in the summer of 1960.[150] In the debate in the Supreme Soviet in Moscow it was made clear that Republican governments were allowed "to increase the general amounts of revenue and
expenditure established for [their] Republic[s] in the USSR state budget
without changing the amounts paid into the Union-Republican budget
from All-Union state income." [151] In simpler language, the Republics
were allowed to dispose only of budgetary surpluses not foreseen by
central authorities. Even then, unutilized capital investment allocations
made by the central government to enterprises and organizations of *economic councils*—by far the most important enterprises supervised by Republican governments—were exempted from that provision. As the economic councils had been forbidden to reallocate those funds themselves,[152] the central authorities in effect continued to control the development of industry throughout the USSR over the head of Republican governments. A vivid degree of the centralization involved was
provided in *Pravda* on July 20, 1959. The First Secretaries of the Kherson and Nikolaev Provinces and the Chairman of the Kherson Economic
Council in southern Ukraine thought they had found a way of achieving certain economies by changing the investments allocated by the State
Planning Commission (apparently the USSR Gosplan, not the Republican Commission). But the planning officials turned them down, so the
trio appealed to none other but Khrushchev and the All-Union Party
Central Committee. Khrushchev personally approved and praised the
initiative of the local administrators. But how many instances must there
be of the local people not being able to "catch the dictator's ear"? In
any case, the exchange of telegrams in *Pravda* appears centralization
writ large.

In the following year (1960) superior, All-Republican economic councils were set up in Republics having several economic regions, including the Ukraine. Interviewed about the functions of the new administrative body Ukrainian Prime Minister Kalchenko was not able to give
a satisfactory answer. He merely remarked that it would coordinate the
activities of the old economic councils and would relieve the Republican Gosplan of its duty to "solve operative problems." [153] Almost simultaneously, however, the number of economic councils in the Ukraine
was expanded from the original eleven to fourteen, by the creation of
the new councils of Poltava, Cherkassy, and the Crimea.[154]

That administrative reshuffle did not apparently achieve its purpose,
so in the middle of 1961 new coordinating bodies were set up; the eco-

nomic regions were grouped in "major economic reasons," complete with "councils for coordination and planning." [155] There were three such major economic regions in the Ukraine. Very important is the announced purpose of setting up those intermediate coordinating bodies, after the establishment of Republican coordinating councils a year before, viz. "carrying out the rational territorial division of labor and implementing the *struggle against all kinds of localist tendencies.*" [156] Simultaneously the territorial departments of the central planning agencies in Moscow were being strengthened. Hardly were those councils established and given a chance to function, when in November, 1962, Khrushchev embarked upon a most ambitious reorganization indeed: the division of the entire Party organization into an industrial and an agricultural production branch. It is too early to assess the effects of that policy (see Note VIII-2, in the Appendix, on the resulting structural changes, however). We may note in this connection that the fourteen economic councils were reduced to seven; the intermediate councils may have been scrapped.[157]

There can be no doubt that by 1961 the pendulum of Soviet policy has again swung toward a thinly disguised centralization, even though the Moscow Gosplan itself has not been given absolute authority over the direction of the economy, as it had under Stalin.[158] Nevertheless, it would be a mistake to ignore the effects of the more liberal policy upon both the rights and the prevailing attitudes of the Republican cadres. From 1957 to 1961 some tangible achievements were made. Alec Nove summarized them as follows in 1961:

The tendency to extend the rights of republics has been noticeable at least since 1955. . . . The *sovnarkhoz* reform in 1957 speeded up the process. The fact that the republican Gosplan plays an essential role in drafting its own republican plan, that the republic government is the immediate superior of the *sovnarkhozy,* and that the allocation of materials within the republic is most often the responsibility of the republican authority, all strengthens the position of the men in charge at that level. They also control, through their power over "their" *oblasti,* the operations of local industry, and have a wide range of powers over retail trade, including that of fixing retail prices for a range of commodities which amounted to 45 per cent of total turnover.

The republican governments and Gosplans remain subordinate to the all-union authorities in all important economic questions. Output plans, many basic material allocations, the pattern of investments and so on are still primarily a central responsibility. *However, the influence of the republics in the process of taking central decisions, as well as their rights in detailed application of policy, have certainly increased.* The premiers of each of the republics are, since 1957, *ex-officio* members of the all-union government.[159]

Of even greater significance may be some less tangible consequences of the reforms of 1955–61. Foremost among these should be counted the greater willingness of the administrators of Ukrainian industry to criticize both Republican and central authorities for not helping them to produce what the people in the Ukraine want. For instance, at the Twentieth Congress of the Communist Party of Ukraine in 1959 First Deputy Prime Minister I. Senin—who appears, incidentally, to be a Russian by nationality—announced with obvious relief that in the current seven year plan the Ukraine would "finally" obtain facilities for finishing all raw materials grown by Ukrainian agriculture. The plan provided for the construction of Europe's largest linen textile mills in Zhytomyr and Rovno. (One of those mills had been promised as early as 1955, by Ukrainian planner Baranovsky.) [160] Also for the first time in Soviet rule passenger automobiles would be built in the Ukraine: the small compact "Zaporozhets." [161] Just a few days later the start of its production was announced with great pride in the press. It was significantly emphasized that the initiative had come from the local economic council in Zaporozhe.[162] Within a few years, by the way, the "Zaporozhets" compacts had become very popular throughout the Soviet Union. Only 8,500 such cars were produced in the first six months of 1962, but annual production was scheduled to reach 150,000 in 1965. The "Zaporozhets" story will present an interesting test case of how far local administrators will be allowed to go in the face of displeasure in the center. In March, 1962, Khrushchev grumbled in a public speech that the production of cars should not have been authorized in the first place, that "the country could, of course, get along without these cars at the present time." He admitted, incidentally, that the authorization was the result of energetic lobbying in the capital:

You remember the Kommunar harvester combines. They were being made in Zaporozhe. They were highly valued by farm workers. *Suddenly Ukrainian comrades started to insist* that another product be made by the plant instead of combines. The request was unfortunately granted.[163]

If Senin's criticism of central authorities in January, 1959, was only implicit, a few days later, at the Twenty-First All-Union Party Congress in Moscow Hayovy, the First Secretary of the Dniepropetrovsk oblast was quite outspoken in requesting more investment funds for the industry in his province. He went so far as to challenge the central Gosplan; he cited figures to show that it was not economically sound to allot so many funds to the Karaganda and Bernaul plants in the Asiatic part of the USSR because their production costs were higher than those of the Dniepropetrovsk mills.[164] I have not been able to find whether Hayovy got his way, but in one of his most important recent speeches

(November 19, 1962), Khrushchev virtually admitted that lobbying by Republican leaders has become widespread and, occasionally, successful. He referred to a dispute in the Gosplan in Moscow as to whether any further hydroelectric stations should have been built on the Dnieper in the Ukraine. Upon his personal intervention the Ukrainians obtained their stations, despite much opposition in the Gosplan.[165] It does not seem implausible to assume that Khrushchev merely played the supreme arbiter between the rival Ukrainian and Siberian hydro-electric lobbies.

Many similar examples could be cited of outspoken criticisms of the centralized administrative procedures of the Gosplan in Moscow and its counterpart in Kiev, of budgetary restrictions, and, above all, of inadequate output plans. Let us cite only the most prominent voices. At the Twenty-First Congress of the CP of Ukraine early in February the chairmen of the Stalino (now Donetsk) and Kiev economic councils criticized both the Republican and central planning agencies—the latter in a more guarded fashion—for excessively detailed controls "shackling the initiative of the economic and Party organizations on the spot." [166] It appeared, for example, that for the year 1960 the Gosplan, against the advice of the economic council, had obligated a certain factory in Kiev to produce 200 types of machine tools most of which could have been more easily and profitably built elsewhere.[167] At an All-Union conference in Moscow half a year later Senin took public issue with the budget law that had been passed less than a year before (October, 1959). He complained among other things that the Republics had not been granted the right "to redistribute capital investments to any appreciable extent among the branches of industry. This makes it difficult to use the funds allocated to capital work effectively." He suggested:

It is advisable to leave at the disposal of the Union republics a reserve of up to 3% of capital investments in the form of a reserve ensured by material and technical resources. Moreover, Union republics should be allowed to redistribute up to 5% of capital investments among branches of industry without lowering assignments for putting production capacity into operation, reporting this later to the USSR State Planning Committee.[168]

Finally, there was a very significant exchange of opinions between Khrushchev and Podgorny at the January, 1961, CPSU Central Committee Plenum on agriculture. The Ukrainian Party organization was being accused of shortcomings in agricultural production, but Podgorny used the occasion to make counter-demands on central authorities. To preserve the tenor of the exchange I quote the longish passage in full:

Podgorny [delivering his report]: Special commissions have been established under the Central Committee of the Ukraine Communist Party and the province Party committees to check on the progress of the measures for integrated mechanization of work in animal husbandry.

However, the amount of machinery on the collective and state farms of the Ukraine is disproportionately low for the tasks of fulfilling the seven-year plan. Much manual labor is still employed, particularly in harvesting corn, beets, and other crops. Nevertheless, the need for tractors and other machines is far from fully met year after year. For example, the number of tractors allocated [by the central authorities, obviously—Y.B.] is only half what is needed, and is barely enough to make up for the number scrapped. Few trucks, tractor-drawn carts, silage- and corn-harvesting machines and many other farm machines are supplied, as well as tires and spare parts.

N. S. Khrushchev [interrupting]: Comrade Podgorny, think about the initiative of Odessa Province tractor drivers in employing tractors at higher speeds. This is a progressive trend, for it makes it possible to double the work performed by the tractor pool without enlarging the latter. Have you read about this?

N. V. Podgorny: I have read about it. They are working on this in our Odessa and Kherson Provinces.

N. S. Khrushchev: Tell about it; you say you ought to be given more tractors, but you don't tell about what is being done with the ones that exist.

N. V. Podgorny: I said in my speech that we are working on increasing the speeds, *but we ought to be given what should be given us*.[169]

N. S. Khrushchev: In this case you're pronouncing the word "give" louder. [*Stir in the hall.*]

N. V. Podgorny: Nikita Sergeyevich, I consider that in speaking of the shortage of machinery I am merely confirming what you said about the abnormal situation that has arisen in respect to the production of a number of agricultural machines, and that increasing the output of machinery in short supply is a task that is being placed on the agenda.

N. S. Khrushchev: Look, comrades, he is trying to make me a partner. [*Laughter in the hall.*][170]

Podgorny repeated his demands for more agricultural machinery from the tribune of the Twenty-Second All-Union Party Congress, and was greeted with applause.[171]

From both Senin's and Podgorny's criticisms it would appear that while the central government has succeeded in restricting the power of the economic councils as well as the Republican authorities it can no longer count on their willing acquiescence; the war between the extreme centralists and the moderate autonomists has not yet been won. But in any event, the present situation is a far cry from the Stalinist years when local Party leaders had to be abjectly grateful in public for whatever came their way and dared not openly criticize the Moscow government on pain of death.

5. *Conclusions*

The current attempts by Ukrainian Party leaders and administrators to win greater freedom for themselves in executing the general Party policy can be best understood as the result of a complicated process of socio-economic development of the Ukraine (see Chapter II, above), coupled with their own personal advancement under Khrushchev. Beria, in trying to grasp supreme power in Moscow with the help of leaders in Soviet borderlands and satellites, merely dramatized what was no longer a secret among the rivals for Stalin's succession. As if taking his clue from the late chief of the Soviet secret police, Khrushchev utilized the support of the "-enkos" (Moskalenko, Kirichenko, Kirilenko) and their equivalents from other non-Russian Republics in establishing himself in the Kremlin. Obviously, Khrushchev did also enjoy substantial backing among Russian Party leaders (for example, Frol Kozlov in Leningrad). But this does not change the fact that at least until 1960 Khrushchev's most trusted lieutenants were his former subordinates in the Ukraine, some of whom were Ukrainians by nationality. The most dramatic indication of a change in Party policy toward the non-Russian nationalities were the administrative reforms since 1955, especially the reorganization of 1957, which were undertaken as much for political as for economic reasons.

Almost inevitably, a reaction set in—visible most clearly in the re-emphasis upon assimilation since 1958 (Chapter I, above) and Kirichenko's fall in early 1960. The writers, poets, and educators (the "cultural cadres") have stubbornly tried to preserve the particular features of Ukrainian culture. The administrators, supported by high Party leaders (for example, Senin and Podgorny) have boldly criticized the efforts to re-establish a system of petty tutelage over Ukrainian industrial production. This is not to say that the emerging Republican cadres must be assumed to be politically disloyal, though the centralists in the Party may be expected to do their best to interpret their demands in such a light.

In recent years the centralists appear to have won a series of battles: the abolition of non-Russian languages as compulsory subjects in the schools of the non-Russian Republics; national assimilation being incorporated as a plank in the new Party Program of 1961; the disappearance of Kirichenko and Mukhitdinov; and the emasculation of regional economic councils. Basically the Soviet Union remains a centralized regime, drawing heavily on the Russian national heritage. But during the struggle with Beria and Malenkov in 1953–57 Khrushchev explicitly recognized the increasing pressure from the non-Russian borderlands. Will he be able to satisfy both the centralists in Moscow and the local rulers in Tashkent and Kiev without permanently alienating either the first or the second group and without resorting to the corrective of mass terror, which might be too costly a luxury in the present international situation?

We must leave the answer to that question to Khrushchev and his future historians. In the last two chapters we shall deal with the international position of the Ukrainian SSR and, by way of conclusion, with the attitudes of Ukrainians in the USSR.

Chapter IX

THE UKRAINIAN SOVIET SOCIALIST
REPUBLIC IN INTERNATIONAL AFFAIRS

Several years ago the *New York Times* printed a brief notice about a vote taken in the General Assembly of the United Nations. The delegate of the USSR said *da,* which is the Russian equivalent for "yea." "Oui," voted the representative of Belorussia in French. The delegate of the Ukrainian SSR, however, said "yes" in English.

This episode is perhaps characteristic of the role which the two Soviet Republics play in world politics. Nevertheless, we might profitably speculate on why the USSR has decided for a multiple international representation different in form, though not in content. In a study of Ukrainian nationalism, one cannot but examine the foreign relations of the Ukrainian Republic, however limited they may be at the present time, for the very fact that the Ukraine now appears on the world stage is likely to be important in the future. In this chapter, I propose to sketch how Ukrainian participation in international affairs was decided upon, examine the possible reasons for this, and finally consider the potential impact of the representation upon the long-range development of Ukrainian national feeling. Legal aspects will be mentioned only in passing.

1. *Activity of the Ukrainian SSR in International Affairs*

The invitation of the Ukraine to the San Francisco Conference on International Organization, which was tendered by the Executive Committee of the Conference on April 30, 1945, following a unanimous decision of forty-seven nations,[1] may have surprised many a student of international affairs. For had not the Ukrainian SSR in 1923, upon "joining" the Soviet Union, relinquished her right to foreign representation and thus left the community of formal and actual sovereign states?[2] The evidence that has been made public does not permit us to draw a complete picture of the negotiations which preceded the event, but it suffices for a brief sketch.

Late in 1943 the Soviet government requested that the "Ukraine, Bielo-Livonian [Belorussian?—Y.B.], Moldavian, Lithuanian, Latvian, Estonian, and Karelo-Finnish Republics" be represented on the United Nations War Crimes Commission, "contending that these entities were no less sovereign than the British Dominions and that their war sufferings gave them a moral right to representation." This request was rejected by the other Allies—Great Britain and the United States.[3] Two months later, February 1, 1944, after listening to a report by Molotov, the Supreme Soviet of the USSR passed a law enabling the Soviet Republics to enter into direct relations with foreign powers.[4]

It was during the Conference at Dumbarton Oaks that Soviet Ambassador Gromyko suddenly raised the question of admitting all of the sixteen Republics to membership in the United Nations (August 28, 1944).[5] Great Britain and the United States showed "an attitude of reserve toward this proposal and anticipation of great difficulty from it," [6] and on August 31 President Roosevelt remonstrated to Stalin in a telegram. Stalin replied on September 7. What appears to be a part of his telegram has been quoted by Sherwood. It throws some light on the possible motives behind Gromyko's suggestion:

You, of course, know that the Ukraine and Belorussia, which are constituent parts of the Soviet Union, are greater in population and political importance than certain other countries which we all agree should belong to the number of initiators of the establishment of International Organization. Therefore, I hope to have an opportunity to explain to you the political importance of this question which has been brought up by the Soviet delegation at Dumbarton Oaks.[7]

But, on the whole, the question seems to have been of minor importance so far as the Soviet Union was concerned; after August 28 it was brought up at Dumbarton Oaks only twice.[8] On January 11, 1945, while reviewing the documents of the Conference Gromyko urged Leo Pasvolsky of the United States Department of State to give further thought to the admission of all sixteen Republics.[9] But sometime in January Soviet leaders abandoned their insistence on the admission of all the constituent Republics.

It was at the fourth plenary meeting of the Yalta Conference, February 7, 1945, that Molotov formally requested the inclusion of at least two, or perhaps three, but not all sixteen Soviet Republics in the membership of the United Nations. The three named were the Ukrainian, Belorussian, and Lithuanian Republics.[10] The proceedings of the Yalta Conference that have been published by the Department of State do not reveal why the United States finally acquiesced in the admission of the two republics.[11] One may surmise, however, that it was Churchill's support of Molotov's proposal that more than anything else helped to change the American attitude.[12] With the backing of the Big Three, the Ukrainian SSR (as well as Belorussia) had no difficulty in being admitted to the United Nations.[13] Since attending the San Francisco Conference, the Ukrainian SSR has actively participated in a number of United Nations organs and agencies,* with the conspicuous exception of the International Bank for Reconstruction and Development (IBRD) and the International Monetary Fund (IMF). In November, 1947, she was even elected to the Security Council, albeit on the twelfth ballot, after the rival candidate, India, had withdrawn.[14] Among the major actions of the Soviet Ukrainian delegation to the UN have been its appeals to the Security Council on behalf of the nationalist government of Indonesia [15] and of the Greek Communist guerrillas,[16] and Manuilsky's orations in the General Assembly on disarmament.[17] A scanning of the accounts in the Soviet Ukrainian press (mainly *Radyans'ka Ukrayina,* Kiev) from 1946 to 1962 leaves the impression that the activity of the Ukrainian delegation to the United Nations does not differ in any significant way from that of the delegation of the USSR,[18] with the possible exception of Podgorny's address to the General Assembly on October 4, 1960 (of which more below).

Outside of the United Nations, the Ukrainian SSR has been represented at a few postwar diplomatic conferences and has been a party to a number of bilateral and multilateral conventions.† She has, for example, participated in the making of peace treaties with Italy and the

---

* Including the Atomic Energy and Conventional Armaments Control Commissions of the UN General Assembly (1948-49); The Economic and Social Council (1946) and the following of its commissions: Economic Commission for Europe (1946), Human Rights (1948-), Statistical (1948-), Population (1948-); the ILO (1954-), UNESCO (1954-); furthermore, the Universal Postal Union (1947-), the World Meteorological Union (1950-), the World Health Organization (1946-). In 1957 the Ukrainian SSR became a charter member of the International Atomic Energy Agency. United Nations *Yearbook,* 1946-47 through 1960. See also, below in the main text, for the Security Council and UNRRA.

† In chronological order, as follows: (a) A bilateral treaty with the Soviet sponsored Polish Provisional Government, of September 9, 1944. The agreement provided for the evacuation of Ukrainians from the territory of Poland and of Polish citizens from the territory of the Ukrainian SSR. See L. Kh. Palamarchuk, ed., *Ukrayins'ka RSR v mizhnarodnykh vidnosynakh* (Ukrainian SSR in International Relations, Kiev, 1959), pp. 193ff. This source (a publication of the Ukrainian SSR Academy of Sciences, Division of Political Science and Law) cites all agreements that the Ukrainian SSR concluded or acceded to, from 1945 to 1957. (b) The series of peace treaties signed in Paris, February 10, 1947, with Italy, Rumania, Hungary, Bulgaria, and Finland. See *ibid.,* pp. 58ff.; or UN *Treaty Series,* Nos. I:747 (Vol. 49, pp. 3ff.), I:645 (42:3), I:644 (41:135), I:643 (41:21), I:746 (48:203). (c) The Danube Convention of August 18, 1948. See text in *Ukrayins'ka RSR . . . ,* pp. 267ff.; or UN *Treaty Series,* I:518 (33:181).

former allies of the Axis powers (Bulgaria, Hungary, Rumania, and Finland), and she has been guaranteed a seat at the eventual peace conference with Germany.[19] She has also signed the Danube Convention of 1948. On the other hand, she is not a party to the 1955 peace treaty with Austria, nor has she been invited to participate in a number of conventions that affect her interests directly and vitally (the treaties that were to legalize the incorporation of the formerly Polish and Czech provinces into the Ukrainian SSR and settle related matters).* The incorporation of Bessarabia and Northern Bukovina, on the other hand, was legalized in the peace treaty with Rumania, and Hungary renounced her claims to the Subcarpathian Ukraine in the sister treaty,[20] both of which agreements were signed by the Ukrainian SSR.

The membership of the Ukrainian Republic in the United Nations Relief and Rehabilitation Administration (UNRRA) deserves separate mention, for it was as a recipient of UNRRA aid that the Republic had the most extensive relations with Western representatives since the early 1920's. (After the East-West split those relations were ended in August, 1947.) Together with the Belorussian Republic, the Ukrainian SSR was admitted to membership in the UNRRA Council at its third session in August, 1945,[21] and on December 18, 1945, Mr. Herbert L. Lehman, Director General of UNRRA, and Mr. Anatoliy M. Baranovsky, Member of the UNRRA Council for the Ukrainian SSR, signed an agreement stipulating the amount of aid and the conditions on which the Ukrainian SSR was to receive it.[22] One of the conditions was that UNRRA inspectors would be free to travel all over the country and make contacts with Ukrainian citizens through their own interpreters, if necessary, in order to supervise the proper distribution of UNRRA supplies.[23] According to two independent sources, that agreement was kept to the letter.[24] At first, it is true, members of the UNRRA staff in Kiev were not allowed

---

* The most important is the Polono-Soviet Treaty, signed in Moscow, July 16, 1945, in which Poland ceded her eastern provinces to the Ukrainian and Belorussian SSRs. The text of the treaty is in the UN *Treaty Series*, No. I:61 (Vol. 10, pp. 193ff.); its ratification was announced in *Vneshnaya politika Sovetskogo Soyuza, 1946 g.* (USSR Foreign Policy, Moscow, 1952), p. 85. The precise course of the frontier was not settled until May 22, 1951, when the USSR and Poland signed a new treaty in Warsaw. In that treaty Poland ceded to the USSR a strip of territory near the river Bug, through which a Soviet railway line passed, in exchange for a strip of Ukrainian territory west of Drohobych. Populations were exchanged. The Ukrainian government, however, was not a party to this agreement (see the *New York Times*, May 23, 1951, and Holubnychy, *Ukrayina v Ob"yednanykh Natsiyakh* (Ukraine in the UN, Munich, 1953), p. 71. Nor was the Ukrainian SSR made a party to the three treaties on the regime of the Polono-Soviet frontier, all of which were directed against the Ukrainian Insurgent Army. The first was a secret accord of May, 1947, between the USSR, Poland, and Czechoslovakia (see the *New York Times*, May 13, 1947, p. 3). The texts of the two Polono-Soviet agreements of July 8, 1948, are under Nos. 575–76 in UN *Treaty Series*, Vol. 37, pp. 25ff. See also Holubnychy, *op. cit.*, p. 70.

to make social contacts with the population, but later the regime let
them see anyone they wished, provided they were accompanied by a
"guardian angel" from the NKVD (secret police).[25] As far as their official
tasks were concerned, the UNRRA mission in Kiev found the Ukrainian
government most cooperative in the efficient and proper distribution of
UNRRA shipments, which totaled about 188 million dollars.[26] But there
was one fly in the ointment: The UNRRA mission experienced difficulty
in publicizing its work through the Soviet press.[27] In 1947 UNRRA
funds ran out, and the mission had to leave the country in August, 1947.
Before long Kiev was barred to foreigners—the hopeful start of direct
contacts between the Soviet Ukraine and the West was thus brought to
an abrupt halt—and was reopened only in 1953.

In view of the Ukrainian membership in the United Nations and of
the political and economic importance of the country, and perhaps also
as a result of the encouraging experience of the UNRRA mission, the
establishment of diplomatic relations with the Ukraine has been considered twice in Anglo-American official circles. In August, 1947, the British
chargé d'affaires in Moscow "requested the Soviet government to trans-
mit to the Government of the Ukraine a proposal that [the United
Kingdom] and the Ukraine should exchange diplomatic representatives." [28] Neither this note nor a personal visit of the chargé d'affaires
to the Ukrainian Ministry of Foreign Affairs proved of any avail [29]—the
Soviet government refused to allow the Ukraine direct diplomatic representation.

In 1952 Senator H. Alexander Smith, of New Jersey, and Representative Lawrence H. Smith, of Wisconsin, raised the question of the United
States offering to establish diplomatic relations with both the Ukrainian
and Belorussian Soviet Republics.[30] This time it was the State Department that opposed such a move.[31] While hearings on Representative
Smith's resolution in favor of establishing such relations were held in
July, 1953, it was never reported out of the Committee on Foreign Affairs. In all justice, it must be admitted that the purpose of the move
was unmistakably to embarrass the Soviet government by giving moral
support to Ukrainian and Belorussian aspirations for independence and
by exposing the "sovereignty" of those two Republics for what it was
worth.[32] Most probably such an offer would have been rejected by the
government of the USSR, if not by those of the Soviet Ukraine and
Belorussia themselves.

Limited though the activities of the Ukrainian Ministry of Foreign
Affairs may be (the Soviet Ukraine has, of course, no diplomats accredited abroad, and it was not until 1958 that the Ukrainian delegation
to the United Nations established permanent mission headquarters in

New York), the Ministry does exist. John Fischer tells us that, when the UNRRA mission arrived in Kiev in 1946, "the welcoming delegation included an assistant minister from the fledgling Ukrainian Foreign Ministry, resplendent in a tight-waisted gray uniform with silver shoulder boards and a gray lamb hat. He greeted us, somewhat euphemistically, as the 'first foreign ambassadors to the Ukraine.' " [33]

MacDuffie mentions one other very rare facet of the Ministry's work. Leaving the country in 1946, he requested that the exit visa be issued by the Ukrainian Foreign Ministry, not by Moscow. After a long delay his request was granted. The visa he received bore the number 100,001, though he was positive that he had been the first person to have made such a request.[34] Besides the few formalities it performs when the Ukraine becomes a party to a convention, the purpose of the Foreign Ministry of the Ukrainian SSR seems to be primarily to provide personnel for the Ukrainian delegation to the UN and its agencies and, secondly, to greet foreign dignitaries arriving in Kiev.[35]

Mr. Fischer's impression of 1946 should be supplemented by that of a more recent visitor, Professor Aspaturian, who travelled in the Soviet Union in July, 1958. He writes that "the principal function of the Republican Ministry is ceremonial, ornamental, and symbolic." It has no geographic area desks but possesses such functional divisions as "Political Affairs" (UN representation?), a Protocol and Consular Department, a Press Department, and possibly an Economic and/or Legal Department.[36]

On the semi-official level of cultural exchanges, however, as well as in international economic relations, the role of the Ukrainian SSR is fairly extensive. Borys Lewytzkyj has recently assembled valuable data, especially on the "rather intensive cultural relations between the Ukraine and the People's Democracies." He regards those as a " 'sublimated' form of the political aspirations of the Ukrainian intelligentsia, Party, and administrative bureaucracies to play a role in the field of international relations." In that field the central government has granted the Union Republics a "certain initiative and freedom of movement." [37]

2. *Reasons for Admitting the Ukrainian SSR to the UN*

The question why a particular state has made a certain move under a peculiar set of circumstances can seldom be answered without recourse to hypotheses. Several assumptions have been made to explain why Stalin granted a modicum of international representation to the Ukrainian and Belorussian Republics—which acquired amendment to the Soviet constitution. In February, 1944, unidentified British diplomats who were queried by James Reston of the *New York Times* viewed the amendment as (a) a device to increase Soviet voting strength in international bodies, especially vis-à-vis the British Empire; (b) a means of making the annexation of the Baltic countries more palatable; and (c) a convincing way of inviting other East European nations to join the multinational Soviet Union. Other factors regarded as important were (d) the strength of the idea of self-determination, especially in Georgia and the Ukraine, and (e) increased efficiency (on issues of lesser importance, the British diplomats thought, the Soviet government might prefer the constituent republics to negotiate directly with foreign powers, in order to alleviate the burden upon the People's Commissariat of Foreign Affairs in Moscow and thus increase the efficiency of Soviet foreign policy making). In the opinion of these diplomats, Stalin was neither so weak nor such a legalist as to amend the constitution solely for the purpose of obtaining extra votes.[38]

Later interpretations of Stalin's policy have added but little to that perspicacious earlier judgment—they have been only attempts to assign the proper weight to each of the factors listed. Three basic hypotheses have been advanced since 1944. The first hypothesis, which is implicit in the accounts of American policymakers—most clearly perhaps in the memoirs of Cordell Hull [39]—assumes that the Ukraine and Belorussia were admitted to the United Nations in order to obtain two additional votes for the Soviet Union. The second hypothesis, which has been advanced by Aspaturian, is that Stalin anticipated concrete diplomatic benefits to accrue to the Soviet Union not only from multiple representation in the United Nations but also at various postwar conferences. In particular, Aspaturian stresses the utility of the multiple arrangement in making the absorption of Western Ukraine, Western Belorussia, and, above all, the Baltic Republics look better in Western (chiefly, American) eyes. The third hypothesis, which has been held independently by authors as diverse as a Ukrainian exile scholar (Holubnychy) and an American editor and publicist (John Fischer), is that, although Stalin gained two extra votes by having the two Republics admitted to the United Nations, it does not follow that his main motive had been to obtain these votes. A "far weightier," [40] perhaps the exclusive,[41] reason was the necessity or, at least, the expediency of placating anti-Soviet Ukrainian feelings in 1944–45.

The argument in favor of the first assumption (that the USSR desired to gain additional votes in the UN) would run as follows: Since the Munich Conference of 1938 at the latest, the Soviet Union had grown deeply suspicious of the motives of the Western Allies and their instrument, the League of Nations. The delay in establishing the second front reinforced that old feeling. It is against this background of Russian suspicion—the argument continues—that Gromyko's unexpected proposal at Dumbarton Oaks must be viewed. To quote W. H. Mc-Neill:

The U.S. wished that all nations which had signed the United Nations Declaration of January, 1942, should become members, together with eight other nations which were not at war with the Axis. Six of these were Latin American republics; and to the Russians this proposal must have seemed like a device for packing the Assembly with American puppets. The principle upon which the Russians wished to base the new international organization—a continuation of the wartime Grand Alliance—would have excluded states which had taken no part in the war. Consequently, they opposed the admission of nonbelligerents. When the Americans showed signs of insisting, Andrei Gromyko, the head of the Russian delegation, announced that each of the sixteen republics, too, should have separate representation in the Assembly.[42]

In other words, the timing of Gromyko's proposal strongly suggests that, at least on August 28, 1944, when that issue was raised, the Soviets were concerned with counterbalancing American influence in the Assembly. When President Roosevelt emphatically opposed the Soviet "absurdity"[43] and when the British, too, showed an attitude of "reserve," the Soviet Union scaled down its demands to three, or at least two, additional votes. Another point to buttress this contention is made by Aspaturian: In 1945–46 the Soviet position in Eastern Europe was not yet wholly assured, and Stalin was, therefore, greatly interested in any additional support in the United Nations.[44]

Yet, however plausible at first sight, this first assumption is open to several criticisms. The request for the admission of all sixteen Soviet Republics to the United Nations in August, 1944, was preceded by the constitutional amendment of February, 1944. The question of creating an international organization to succeed the League of Nations had admittedly been debated since late 1943. But in February, 1944, was the United Nations as much in the minds of Soviet planners as in those of Americans? Were there not other, more compelling reasons why Stalin had the Constitution amended? The hypothesis that Stalin wanted additional votes in the Assembly seems to imply that he, like President Roosevelt and Secretary Hull, viewed the United Nations as a promising instrument for creating a new world order. But the evidence indicates the opposite: Stalin did regard the United Nations as a not unimportant "meeting ground for great opponents,"[45] but he was far from overestimating the organization's effectiveness in changing the tone and mode of international relations. Hence, runs the counterargument, the number of Soviet representatives in the United Nations was a matter not to be ignored, but hardly the only reason for demanding the admission of two constituent Republics. In support of this, we may refer to Stalin's speech of November 6, 1944, which illustrates his traditional,

Realpolitik approach toward international organization. In that address Stalin said that the United Nations should primarily be an organization that would be able to prevent aggressive nations (read "Germany") from attacking peace-loving nations (read "the USSR") and asserted that such an organization would be effective only if the Big Powers remained in agreement among themselves.[46]

Furthermore, it may be argued that the Soviet Union did not really expend much effort in obtaining the admission of all sixteen Republics, that Gromyko's proposal at Dumbarton Oaks was not meant to be taken seriously, that it was a trial balloon rather than a working proposition. It may be pointed out that the whole issue was raised at that Conference only three times, and quite briefly at that. While in his telegram of September 7, 1944, Stalin referred to the "political importance" of the whole question, he explicitly mentioned only two Soviet Republics, the Ukraine and Belorussia. Did he do so because he realized from the beginning that he had not the slightest chance of obtaining sixteen additional votes? But why single out those two Republics and not, for example, Georgia or Armenia? It is true that as late as January, 1945, Gromyko referred to the "extreme importance" of admitting all sixteen Republics to the UN, but the occasion for the statement was a review of Dumbarton Oaks documents prior to Gromyko's departure for Moscow for new instructions.[47] Finally, at Yalta when, as an afterthought, Roosevelt requested Stalin's support for two extra votes for the United States should circumstances warrant his asking for them, Stalin agreed, apparently with no further ado. Had Stalin really cared about a larger number of votes in the Assembly for himself, the argument goes, he would have opposed American parity right then and there.[48]

Summing up the pros and cons, we find that the first hypothesis, while explaining one reason for Stalin's insistence upon the admission of two Soviet Republics to the United Nations—his desire to obtain additional votes—exaggerates its importance.

Aspaturian's argument—the second hypothesis—is more persuasive because, like that of the British diplomats, it takes more factors into account. On the issue of UN representation he feels that more significant than the increased numerical strength was the "psychological comfort, procedural advantage, and legal precedent for future action" that the admission of the Ukraine and Belorussia afforded the USSR.[49] He also seems to imply that in late 1944 and early 1945 Stalin foresaw the advantage of having more votes at peace conferences. Aspaturian makes the point that "were it not for the separate admission of Belorussia and the Ukraine, the British Commonwealth would have numerically dominated the Commissions [for the individual Axis satellite states], although the Soviet Union bore the brunt of the war in Eastern Europe." [50] In this connection it should also be stressed that separate Ukrainian representation on the International Danube Commission was quite advantageous to the Soviet Union: The Ukraine signed the new Danube Convention as the bona fide riparian state she had become in 1940, and thus further strengthened the pro-Soviet majority on the Commission.[51]

But above all, Aspaturian sees in the Soviet constitutional amendment of February 1, 1944, an instrument for facilitating territorial expansion. The timing of the amendment seems to indicate this strongly. On December 31, 1943, a pro-Communist National Committee of Poland had been set up, five days before the Soviet troops crossed the Polish boundary of September 1, 1939. One of the members of that Committee was the Polish communist writer Wanda Wasilewska, then married to the Ukrainian dramatist Alexander Korniychuk. On February 7, that is less than a week after the adoption of the amendment, Korniychuk was abruptly relieved of his post as Deputy Foreign Commissar of the USSR, appointed Foreign Commissar of the Ukrainian SSR, and ordered to start negotiations with the Polish National Committee, including his wife. As was to be expected, the Polish Committee agreed to the incorporation of Eastern Galicia into the Ukrainian SSR.[52] The amendment also seems to have been designed to help persuade President Roosevelt to accept the incorporation of the Baltic Republics, and to counter the expected opposition from American citizens of Baltic descent, by demonstrating that those Republics might also have "independent" international representation. This is why at Yalta Molotov and Stalin suggested the admission of Lithuania to the UN,[53] and this is why the Soviet Union tried hard to have separate Baltic representatives appointed to the satellite peace conferences of 1946–47. Rebuffed by the Western powers on both these counts, Soviet Russia resorted to the expedient of attaching the foreign ministers of the Baltic Republics to the Soviet delegation at the peace conferences.[54]

Aspaturian's argument has the merit of the multi-causal approach; it comes to grips with a real concern of Stalin's in 1944 (how to make the incorporation of additional territory more palatable to Western, chiefly American, statesmen), and it does explain why Stalin pressed the issue of international representation not for all Soviet Republics but only for two located in the western part of the USSR. If one could demonstrate that the cultural and political relations of the Eastern European satellites with the Ukraine and Belorussia are more extensive than those with the USSR as a whole, credence would be lent to a most provocative corollary assumption: International representation has been given precisely to those Republics in order to offer to the satellites an inducement to enter the USSR in the distant future. But while the second basic hypothesis plausibly explains the diplomatic benefits derived from the constitutional amendment, it may slight the advantages which would accrue to the regime in its domestic policy. Here we must turn to the third hypothesis; namely, that Stalin's moves in 1944 and 1945 were prompted by his difficulties in the Ukraine.

What positive evidence is there to indicate that there is a link between Ukrainian nationalism in 1944 and 1945 and the admission of the Ukrainian SSR to the UN? Molotov's speech in the USSR Supreme Soviet of February 1, 1944, and a remark which Stalin made in a conversation with President Roosevelt at Yalta and which the latter passed on to his Secretary of State, Stettinius, are referred to in the attempt to establish such a link.

In explaining the constitutional amendment of 1944, Molotov adduced the following reasons for granting the Soviet Republics greater powers in the realms of defense and foreign relations: (a) the political, economic, and cultural development of the Republics—their growth resulting from Leninist-Stalinist nationality policy; (b) the greater power of the Soviet Union as a whole; (c) the large extent of Soviet diplomatic relations during the war, raising questions which would touch upon "quite a few specific economic and cultural needs of the Union Republics and which could not be dealt with to the full extent by the All-Union representations abroad"; [55] (d) the interest of the Soviet Union as a whole in "extending international relations and strengthening the co-operation of the USSR with other countries"; and, finally, (e) the contribution of this action, made possible by the successful Leninist-Stalinist national policy, toward the moral victory of progressive mankind over Fascism.

Upon analysis, the motif of the speech appears to be the strength of the Soviet Union as a result of applying the "Leninist-Stalinist national policy." It is with nationality policy that Molotov starts elucidating the reasons for the changes. At another crucial spot—the end of the main body of the speech—he quotes from Stalin's address at the twenty-sixth anniversary of the Bolshevik Revolution (November 6, 1943):

All the peoples of the Soviet Union have unanimously risen to the defense of their native land, justly considering the present Patriotic War the common cause of all toilers, regardless of nationality and creed. Now even the Nazi politicians themselves [have come to] realize *how hopelessly foolish their speculations upon creating dissension and conflicts between the peoples of the Soviet Union have proved. The friendship of the peoples of our country* has survived all the hardships and trials of war, it has been tempered in the common struggle of all Soviet peoples against the Fascist invaders.[56]

From the evidence available today we know that Stalin's and Molotov's protestations of the friendship of the peoples expressed an ideal rather than the current state of affairs. The Chechen-Ingush and the Crimean Tatars had proved so disloyal that in the same year 1944 their Autonomous Republics were dissolved and the inhabitants deported to the East.[57] If we can trust Khrushchev's account, Stalin would have dealt equally with the Ukrainians had he known where and how to deport a people of forty million.[58] Five days after Molotov's speech in Moscow, February 5, 1944, those assembled at "a meeting of the intelligentsia" in Kiev, including the Chairman of the Presidium of the Ukrainian Supreme Soviet, M. Hrechukha, issued an appeal to the Ukrainian underground to surrender.[59] There followed an official appeal "To the Members of the So-Called 'Ukrainian Insurgent Army,'" of February 12, 1944, which was signed, among others, by Khrushchev himself.[60] Finally, addressing the session of the Ukrainian Supreme Soviet which amended the Constitution of the Republic in line with Molotov's proposal (March 1, 1944), Khrushchev launched into a long diatribe against "Ukrainian-German nationalists." [61] It may thus be argued that a basic reason for the constitutional changes of February 1, 1944, was precisely an attempt on the part of the regime to conceal the cracks in the "friendship of the Soviet peoples" because this façade was useful in its foreign policy as well as in its dealings with the non-Russian peoples within the Soviet Union.

This hypothesis has been indirectly confirmed by a Soviet author and is wholly consistent with Stalin's remark at Yalta. In his article on the "International Representation of the Ukrainian SSR" E. L. Kurishkov interpreted Khrushchev's standard explanation of the constitutional amendment as follows:

The adoption of the historic law by the USSR Supreme Soviet had great significance in unmasking the anti-popular, treacherous character of bourgeois nationalism and cosmopolitanism, and especially Ukrainian bourgeois nationalism. Ukrainian bourgeois nationalists have endeavored to weaken the power of the Soviet state . . . to kindle separatist and national-deviationist tendencies and movements. They have made efforts to weaken the political, economic, and cultural bonds between the Soviet Republics, to tear asunder the close union of socialist nations.

The changes in the USSR connected with the enlargement of the rights of the Soviet Republics were a mortal blow to the Ukrainian nationalist band. . . .[62]

This may be an interpretation from the perspective of 1954, when the article was written, but it does not appear implausible in the light of other evidence on Ukrainian nationalism in 1944–45. It should also be borne in mind that Soviet scholars may have access to materials not available in the West.

The final piece of evidence in support of the "nationality trouble" hypothesis is a somewhat cryptic reference by President Roosevelt to a remark made by Stalin at Yalta. In Stettinius' account of a conversation with the President on the day when Molotov first raised the issue of two or three additional votes (February 7, 1945) we read:

In reviewing the entire matter of additional seats for the Soviet Union the President told me that evening at Yalta that Stalin felt his position in the Ukraine was difficult and insecure. A vote for the Ukraine was essential, the Marshal had declared, for Soviet unity. . . . The President had been indignant at the Soviet request at Dumbarton Oaks for votes for each of the sixteen republics. He had told me it would be just as logical for us to ask for forty-eight votes. However, he told me that from the standpoint of geography and population he did not believe there was anything preposterous about the Russian proposal for two extra votes for the Ukraine and White Russia.[63]

As the Stettinius papers have not been released for publication in the United States Department of State collection of Malta and Yalta documents, it is hard to put this remark of President Roosevelt's into its proper context. It seems that he had a private talk with Stalin; possibly that was the conversation Stalin had in mind when, in his telegram of September 7, 1944, he expressed his desire to have an opportunity to explain to President Roosevelt the political importance of the question. Stalin may have exaggerated his difficulties in order to make it more palatable for Roosevelt to change his mind, but his statement was by no means unfounded if read against the background of difficulties in the Western Ukraine.[64]

Proponents of the "nationality trouble" hypothesis face several difficulties. First of all, the admission of the Ukraine to the United Nations was coupled with that of Belorussia. It is harder to prove the existence of a strong nationalist movement in Belorussia than it is in the Ukraine or the Baltic states. A possible answer would be that Stalin preferred not to single out the Ukrainians for that favor, since his feelings toward them were somewhat less than cordial. Secondly, it has been argued very plausibly that, whenever negotiations reached a difficult stage and the other side was about to block any further concessions, Stalin invoked domestic difficulties with the Ukrainians. He had used that technique in his talk to German Ambassador Count von Schulenburg sometime in 1940; now he used it as an argument against President Roosevelt in the talk reported by Secretary Stettinius.[65] As summed up by Asaturian: "While Stalin's problems with the Ukrainians were real enough, he was putting them to use in the service of Soviet diplomacy. In negotiations, a statesman finds it useful to have a source of internal pressure allegedly beyond his control to use as a bargaining lever." [66] The third difficulty with the argument that it was primarily Ukrainian nationalism which induced Stalin to grant the Ukrainian and

Belorussian SSR representation in the United Nations is that all the Soviet documents previously cited in this chapter refer to friction in the newly incorporated *Western* Ukraine, not the larger and more important central and eastern areas of the country. But a careful study of the political developments under German occupation has revealed that Eastern Ukrainians were susceptible to the brand of nationalism imported by their fellow countrymen from the West.[67]

Thus, while suggestive evidence in support of the "nationality trouble" hypothesis is relatively easy to obtain, conclusive proof requires a more careful and elaborate analysis than can be undertaken here. Such an analysis in depth, however, is made impossible by the lack of local Central and Eastern Ukrainian data for the crucial wartime year 1944. A study of the interrelation of the Ukrainian national feeling and Stalin's decision to create a modicum of international representation for the Ukraine would envisage a series of difficult questions. Was there in 1944 a gathering threat of Ukrainian action (for instance, the formation, when circumstances permitted, of a nationalist government supported by the Western Allies and inevitably hostile to the USSR) which the Soviet government sought to avert by its concessions of February 1, 1944? Possibly, efforts of the Organization of Ukrainian Nationalists (OUN) to broaden their popular base in late 1943 might have led to the formation of such a government, or so its proponents hoped.[68] How were the measures of the Soviet government publicized in its appeals to the Ukrainians of various regions? There is no data on this.

Finally, a corollary to the "nationality trouble" hypothesis should not be excluded as a *minor* reason for the admission of the Ukrainian SSR to the United Nations—to wit, the advantage of having Soviet *Ukrainian* spokesmen officially protest the actions of Ukrainian exiles and American and Canadian citizens of Ukrainian descent. That activity of the Soviet Ukrainian representation to the United Nations became considerable in 1960, as we shall see later.

To conclude so far, after surveying the history of the admission of the Ukrainian SSR to the United Nations and briefly describing her diplomatic activities in the UN and other areas, an attempt was made to determine the reasons for her admission, starting with the interpretation of the constitutional amendment of 1944 by British diplomats. All the factors cited in that interpretation help to explain Stalin's policy in 1944, but in the writer's judgment factors (b) and (c), to wit, the disguise of territorial expansion into Eastern Europe and the standing invitation to East Europeans to join the USSR were the foremost reasons, to be followed by the internal factors (d) and (e), namely, the strength of the idea of nationalism in the Soviet Union and the greater efficiency and coherence resulting from giving the constituent Republics a small outlet onto the international scene. Paradoxical as it may sound, I should put the role of the two Republics in the United Nations as the last consideration; until after Stalin's death the USSR did not pay much attention to the United Nations except as a meeting ground for the big powers. In summary, the truth appears to lie somewhere between the second and the third of the hypotheses as characterized above. Stalin's difficulties in the Ukraine were "real enough" in 1944–45, but so were the benefits which he hoped to derive from the admission of the Soviet Republics to international councils in the United Nations and elsewhere.

3. Possible Effect of the Admission to the UN upon Ukrainian Nationalism

If we accept the hypothesis that the admission of the Ukrainian SSR onto the world stage—if not as a star, at least as a supernumerary—has been connected with the rise of Ukrainian patriotic feelings during World War II, it becomes very important to inquire what impact the international activity of the Republic might have had upon the thinking of the Ukrainian people. Has it passed unnoticed? Has it led them to believe that they were living in a "free, sovereign state" within the Soviet Union?

In approaching this question it is necessary to make a few basic assumptions, not all of which can be adequately documented. (1) In states that are largely self-contained only a small proportion of citizens are directly engaged in foreign affairs. When it comes to discussing international affairs, the overwhelming majority show a deplorable lack of the "pungent sense of reality." [69] (2) In totalitarian states, this effect is further reinforced by a deliberate policy of isolation on the part of the regime. The authors of the report of the Harvard Refugee Interview Project found:

. . . Ignorance and distorted views of the outside world are deeper and more widespread—even among the intelligentsia—than heretofore had been realized by most students of the USSR. It is almost impossible to exaggerate the ignorance of the outside world prevalent among Soviet citizens.[70]

After Stalin's death, of course, more Soviet citizens have traveled abroad, but they have been carefully screened and often channeled into the countries of the socialist or neutralist camps. (3) The participation of the Ukrainian SSR in world affairs is comparatively recent. On the one hand, this must have added an attraction of novelty for every international step reported at home; at the same time it is unlikely that the news would have produced such a deep response, as in countries where foreign affairs had been conducted for generations and where an "attentive public" had been developed. (4) Furthermore, most of the international activity of the Republic has been confined to the United Nations. International organizations, however—with the exception of those that serve only as a means of international *administration* (such as the World Postal Union) and thus have little popular appeal—serve as the framework for intricate multilateral diplomacy. If "old-fashioned" *bilateral* diplomacy has not been easy to comprehend by ordinary mortals, multilateral relations are still more complex. (5) Finally, to judge from several interviews with former Soviet citizens, the essential subordination of the Soviet Ukrainian government to Moscow in domestic affairs is so obvious, as not to encourage any hope that it would be any less in foreign affairs, where additional considerations of world prestige are involved. So much by way of a preliminary warning that the impact of the representation in the United Nations upon the more thoughtful sections of the Ukrainian public should not be overestimated.

If we accept the proposition that in the Ukraine only a relatively small proportion of citizens are engaged in foreign relations of any kind, an analysis of secondary sources of information is indicated. Foreign press is, of course, not available to any significant number of educated Ukrainians.[71] Radio receivers are comparatively scarce, too. According to the official statistics for 1960, only 1 person in 18 owns a radio set in the Ukraine.[72] The corresponding proportions for 1945, 1950, and 1956 were approximately 1:2,700, 1:112 and 1:31.[73] How many of those sets are equipped for receiving foreign broadcasts this writer does not know. But we need not follow this argument of exclusion any further to realize that the overwhelming majority of Ukrainians are dependent upon official media to obtain information on the outside world.

Though the Ukrainian representation in the UN has not reached out for the stars, its very presence in that body raises a few interesting questions in the minds of students of international law and organization. As the UN "is based on the principle of the sovereign equality of all its Members" (Art. 2 of its Charter), does this mean that the Ukraine is a state in the legal sense of the word?[74] What have been the historical precedents for the admission of that country? Can any parallels be drawn between the legal status of India in the League of Nations, and of the Ukraine in the UN?[75] What is the significance in international law of the Ukraine being a signatory to a number of European peace treaties and the Danube Convention? No Soviet author has dared even to raise those questions, apparently because they were all taboo.[76] Apart from the two articles cited and Foreign Minister Palamarchuk's collection of treaties, this writer knows of only three serious efforts in this field: a scholarly survey of the Ukrainian role in ILO,[77] Professor Lisovskiy's schematic but competent pamphlet on the international status of the

Ukraine since the seventeenth century,[78] and L. O. Leshchenko's well-documented study of the participation of the Ukrainian SSR in the International Danube Conference of 1948.[79] In none of those works have those sensitive problems been broached. There is also the question of how well-publicized those scholarly writings have been among the general public.

Needless to stress, the image that the Ukrainian public receives of the activity of its representatives abroad is thus highly selective.[80] Most international events have been covered by the All-Union news agency TASS that presents identical reports to all Soviet papers, without any regard to developments which might specifically interest the Ukrainians. Occasionally, however, an important speech by a Soviet Ukrainian representative will be commented upon by a special correspondent of *Radyans'ka Ukrayina* or *Pravda Ukrainy*.[81] Moreover, a careful reading of a dozen or so speeches by Ukrainian delegates to the UN have convinced this writer that they contain very little of what might affect Ukrainian patriots. Three speeches are an exception. In one the Ukrainian delegate was bold enough to use Beria's statement at the Nineteenth Party Congress to favorably compare the "fraternal aid" of Russia to the Ukraine, with the American contribution toward the development of French economy under the Marshall Plan. His speech on the floor of the General Assembly was summarized in detail in the Soviet Ukrainian press—an obvious appeal to Ukrainian pride at having overtaken one of the leading European nations in the production of several key commodities.[82] The second instance has been a vitriolic speech by Kyzya of the Ukrainian SSR, in which he assailed both Ukrainian "bourgeois nationalists" abroad and the Government of the United States. In his opinion, the United States had infringed upon the sovereignty of the Ukrainian SSR by allowing Secretary of Labor Mitchell to make a speech at the freedom rally that had been organized by the Ukrainian Congress Committee of America in New York, December 30, 1956.[83]

But perhaps the most significant international action of the Ukrainian SSR to date (most significant, certainly, in the context of this study) has been First Secretary Podgorny's speech on the floor of the UN General Assembly October 4, 1960. In 1960 a whole series of newly independent African states were admitted as members of the UN, and in their honor many heads of state and heads of governments attended the Fifteenth Session of the General Assembly, such as Khrushchev, Nehru, Nasser, Nkrumah, and others. It is of some significance that among the numerous prime ministers of East European satellites Khrushchev chose to include Podgorny and Mazurov, First Secretary of the Party of Belorussia, as if to indicate that, so far as the Soviet Union was concerned, there was little difference in the international status of Poland, for example, and the Ukraine and Belorussia. On September 18 Khrushchev delivered a lengthy address on disarmament, some critical weaknesses of the United Nations structure (that is, weaknesses in Soviet eyes), and colonialism.[84] In reply, Prime Minister Diefenbaker of Canada reminded Khrushchev that the USSR's Eastern European satellites might still be suffering from a colonial yoke, and that the "freedom-loving" Ukrainian people, too, had been deprived of the "right of free election." [85]

Mr. Diefenbaker's reference to the plight of the Ukraine was made only in passing, but that sufficed to provoke Podgorny to a lengthy rebuttal on the floor of the Assembly—delivered, incidentally, in Ukrainian [86]—and to inspire a campaign of "popular" protests in the Ukraine herself.[87] In Podgorny's speech Ukrainian exiles were awarded a few choice epithets ("Hitlerite scum . . . dozen-odd brawlers who are now picketing the delegations attending the Session"), but in the protests in the Ukraine they were attacked at length.

This episode is important in our context not only because it shows the high sensitivity of Soviet leaders toward any statement by a prominent Western personality in which the real state of affairs in the Ukraine is mentioned and not only because it demonstrates their growing annoyance with the actions of Ukrainian exiles and their sympathizers, but because it dramatically proves the use toward which the United Nations forum can be put in protesting the actions of Ukrainian nationalists abroad. Let us recall here that Soviet actions toward the exiles are not limited to verbal attacks. As was brought out at Stashynsky's trial in Karlsruhe, West Germany, he had, on orders from the KGB (Soviet secret police), assassinated two prominent Ukrainian Nationalist leaders in Germany: Lev Rebet (1957) and Stepan Bandera (1959).[88]

Nevertheless, we should be on our guard against attributing too much importance to the activities in the United Nations; there is evidence to indicate that in the 1950's at least neither the Soviet government [89] nor Soviet citizens [90] have paid much attention to that body, and thus to the Ukrainian representation in it. As far as direct relations with foreign countries are concerned, the censorship of the regime has been tight indeed; the British offer of August, 1947, had been announced in the Soviet Ukrainian press as late as April 7, 1950, in the form of a translation from the Russian *Novoe Vremya* (New Times).[91]

But on the other hand, it cannot be stated with absolute assurance that the Ukrainian people do not attach any significance whatsoever to their international representation. It would appear that the official policy of news selection itself tends to exaggerate the role of Soviet and incidentally also of Ukrainian delegates because, as a rule, it is only their speeches that are extensively summarized in the Soviet Ukrainian press.[92] In order to fill out some gaps in the All-Union news coverage, in March,

1945, a group of Kievan journalists together with some officials of the new Ukrainian Ministry of Foreign Affairs, established a monthly under the title *Suchasne i maybutnye* (The Present and the Future) which was in everything but the name a Soviet Ukrainian journal of international affairs.[93] A poem and a novelette by two Soviet Ukrainian authors, in which the presence of the Ukraine in the United Nations is touched upon,[94] might be considered rather dubious evidence of popular interest in the subject, but we know from Fischer's account that in 1946 certain circles in Kiev were much pleased with their Republic entering into foreign relations.[95] It is not without significance that fairly recently, in August, 1957, Kiev was chosen as the site for the Fourth Congress of the pro-Communist World Federation of Democratic Youth, which took place immediately after the Moscow Youth Festival. Delegates from all over the world came to the ancient city; part of the proceedings was in Ukrainian.[96] This was done as if to emphasize that Kiev was the capital of a Soviet Republic and the second city of the Soviet Union rather than merely a provincial town in Soviet Russia. It is not likely that such a choice had been made without the desire on the part of certain sections of the Soviet Ukrainian leadership for establishing direct links with the outside world, a desire that was more than whetted by the admission of the Ukraine to the United Nations.[97]

To sum up the whole argument: The international representation of the Ukrainian SSR, complete with anthem, national flag, and Foreign Minister undoubtedly belongs to the category of Soviet constitutional trappings. They have been granted partly to reap certain diplomatic advantages and partly in response to heightened Ukrainian patriotism during and after World War II. Now, they are not taken very seriously by the majority of the Ukrainians but they seem to be welcomed by sections of the Soviet Ukrainian bureaucracy to whom they imply a certain raise in prestige. In the long run, their importance in the development of Ukrainian nationalism would depend mainly upon whether the regime will succeed in destroying the demographic, sociological, and cultural bases of that movement. Should the regime prove successful in permanently emasculating Ukrainian nationalism, no constitutional provisions will be able to reinvigorate it. Should it fail in doing so, such colorful trappings as an international representation will provide food for thought and, under favorable circumstances, may also provide a spark for action.

Chapter X

UKRAINIAN NATIONALISM
AFTER THE WAR: CONCLUSIONS

At the end of our study of postwar Soviet nationality policy in the Ukraine we are faced with a number of questions. We have seen that in Western Ukraine the regime attempted to destroy the Greek Catholic church. For at least five years after the fall of Berlin it waged a small war against the Western Ukrainian underground. Has this had any repercussions on the attitudes of the Ukrainian people as a whole? The regime has Russified schools, distorted Ukrainian literature and history. On the other hand, recently it has allowed Ukrainians to rise in the Party, to assume greater administrative responsibilities, and to clamor for greater freedom of cultural expression. During the war it even endowed them with a few paraphernalia commonly found in relations between sovereign states. What impact have all these measures exercised upon the thinking of Soviet Ukrainians?

While many of our questions must remain unanswered, for short of radical changes in the Soviet Union the Ukrainian people will not risk their lives for the sake of enlightening Western scholars, it is believed that a survey of Ukrainian attitudes on the basis of interview data will yield some valuable insights which would supplement our inferences from the analysis of Soviet nationality policy. These particular data are admittedly incomplete, but as a Chinese proverb says, "It is better to light at least one candle than to blame the darkness." [1]

Here and there, throughout the study, I have already used interview findings to document or to illustrate single points. Now it is proposed to combine the data from my own interviews with similar material from the Harvard Project on the Soviet Social System in order to obtain a coherent picture of Ukrainian nationalism after the war. The chapter will be organized as follows: First, I shall give a survey of how Ukrainians view themselves and how they are perceived by others. What are their attitudes toward Ukrainian independence and toward the regime? The main part of the chapter will then be devoted to an analysis of the cohesiveness of the Ukrainian people under the Soviet regime. The particular problems to be taken up are: attitudes toward the Russians, the differences between Western and Eastern Ukrainian nationalism, the role of symbols, and the relations between the elite and the common people. In conclusion I shall touch upon the nexus between economic progress and nationalism, and consider the role which contingencies have played in recent manifestations of Ukrainian nationalism.

Our most remarkable finding is that Soviet Ukrainians today identify themselves as Ukrainians. This is a great change from 1917 when many Ukrainians declared themselves to be Russians, Little Russians, or, simply, "local people." This appears not only in interviews from Ukrainian postwar defectors and former camp inmates who incline toward the nationalist point of view, but also from observations of American tourists, and statements by Russians and Ukrainians who take the Russophile position. One of the latter declared that the difference between the Ukraine and Russia was "obvious," that the Ukrainians formed an entirely separate nationality, that you could not compare the character and industriousness of a Ukrainian peasant with that of a Russian.[2] An American traveller also stressed the difference between the exterior of the Ukrainian and Russian countryside; he went even so far as to assert that there was a distinct difference in the outward appearance of the crowds in the streets of Kiev and Moscow.[3] Edward Crankshaw, a well-known British student of Soviet politics, strongly perceives that difference, too. The last chapter in one of his books on the Soviet Union is entitled "Sunshine in Kiev," and he ends it on the following note:

. . . It occurred to me that history is not finished yet and that the Soviet Union may be standing on the threshold of an era of counter-colonization. After all they have suffered at the hands of Romanovs and Bolsheviks, the Ukrainians with their superior energy, their toughness and dourness, their innate practicality, may very well find themselves dominating increasingly a Soviet Union where these qualities are urgently in demand, bringing order and self-respect into a land which for all its rare qualities of the imagination suffers from the lack of both these qualities. The Ukraine has already exported a Khrushchev and a Kirichenko, to say nothing of a host of Party managers loyal to Khrushchev. The day may come when it will export trees and flowers and neat and sturdy cottages to the dusty wastes of the Great Russian villages—and, with these, a stiffening of fibre to resist the emotional excesses of the tyrant of the hour.[4]

We must now ask ourselves the question: What political implication have these differences as perceived by Soviet Ukrainians?

About 90 per cent of the 459 Eastern Ukrainian respondents to the Harvard Nationality Questionnaire stated that they had registered in the Soviet Union as Ukrainians (412 cases), 2 per cent (7) had given another nationality to the Soviet officials, and the rest (40) did not answer that question on the Harvard Questionnaire.[5] The respondents were also asked to indicate various reasons why they had registered as Ukrainians. About one-half of the sample (235) answered, "Because I was born in the Ukraine and lived there all or most of my life"; but about a third (149) gave what Gilliam terms answers of "aggressive identification": they had registered as Ukrainians "because [they] considered [themselves] Ukrainians and liked Ukrainian culture." [6] Because of a possible sample bias,[7] the numbers are less important than the social groups with which the sentiment is associated. Gilliam found that the most aggressively conscious were younger Ukrainian workers of rural background.[8] The younger non-manuals (salaried employees, professionals and the like) and collective peasants were less aggressive; only one out of three checked the latter answer. This is an interesting comment on Deutsch's thesis that nationalism is associated with social mobility—but more of the latter when we shall discuss the problem of the elite. A good *indirect* indication of nationalism is also the image which a people has of itself. Georgian pride and nationalism has been commented upon by many travellers to the Soviet Union. How do the Ukrainians portray themselves?

The general Harvard interview which was given to 76 Ukrainians included the question: "Are there traits distinguishing the following nationalities: Great Russians, Ukrainians. . . ." In surveying the answers, Gilliam found out that even the more nationalistic Ukrainians described their differences from other nationalities, particularly from the Russians, as follows:

The most used adjectives were "good, good-natured, good-hearted, mild." Next in frequency were adjectives describing themselves as "cleaner"; the next most frequent are about six other categories: "more refined, shy, hospitable, individualistic, anti-Communist." Interesting for their absence were all such characterizations as "strong, brave, forceful, proud, determined."

On the other hand, the Russians were most often identified as "imperialistic, [they] have desire to enslave, to conquer, to force their will on others." Almost as often they were called "noisy, vulgar, coarse, cursing," "harbingers and supporters of communism," "insolent, cruel, brutal." Miss Gilliam concludes from this: "Ukrainians in this particular interview apparently consider themselves, when they are nationalistic, as *oppressed* and as having *minority status,* with the force and the initiative on the side of the Russians." [9]

Persons who have met Eastern Ukrainians after the war confirm this finding as a rule, the exception being a school teacher of Ukrainian literature and language. In conversation with a foreigner, he made no attempt to hide his anger at the low status which the regime had assigned to Ukrainian studies at school and to Ukrainian culture in general.[10] One source called the attitude of Ukrainian college students in Kiev toward their nationality "ambivalent": they were bilingual and did not know much Ukrainian history and politics.[11] Returnees from Soviet labor camps observed that while Eastern Ukrainians identified themselves as Ukrainians, they were "little conscious of their nationality,"[12] did not draw a sharp distinction between themselves and the Russians,[13] "did not know what [an independent] Ukraine would bring them."[14] A student of Soviet politics said: "The Russians were more conscious, the Ukrainians softer, but the Georgians were very conscious [of their nationality]."[15] Apparently the three centuries of Tsarist rule and the persecutions of the 1930's have borne fruit: Many Eastern Ukrainians have internalized the oppression in depicting themselves as the innocent and powerless victims of cruel political subjection. One observer, a former inmate of a forced labor camp, noted: "They have not been able to recover completely from the famine [of 1932–33]."[16]

During the Harvard interviews, 28 per cent of the 76 respondents used the question on distinguishing nationality traits to offer spontaneous comments that the Ukraine should be independent; 17 additional per cent were anti-Russian, but did not mention national independence; "33% (25 cases) did not volunteer any discussion of nationalism or separatism or declared that such issues were not current"; but only 3 respondents (4%) opposed the idea of a separate Ukraine and "two others gave generally negative responses to the idea."[17] In summary, the Eastern Ukrainians appear after the war as a somewhat passive and inarticulate group, the very opposite of people ardently aspiring toward political freedom and independence. At the same time, however, this impression does not jibe with the qualities of "toughness and dourness, . . . innate practicality, . . . self respect" which Crankshaw found to admire in them. We should also note that after Stalin's death many Ukrainians have protested in the Soviet press against attempts to destroy the Ukrainian cultural heritage (see Chapter I, above). While it would be perilous to say how widespread those other more aggressive qualities are, they should be mentioned in some detail to obtain a more balanced picture.

Many Ukrainians are known to have made a career of the army which calls for other than soft qualities. A former Soviet army doctor, a Jew by nationality, "estimated that 40–50% of the officer and sergeant cadres were either Ukrainians or Belorussians. The Ukrainians work well with the Russians in the army, but at the same time they are stern and probably make life hardest on the enlisted men. The number of major ranking officers in the Soviet Army who are Ukrainians shows that the Army career has no advancement limitation for the Ukrainians." [18] Moreover, from several independent sources (among them, three returnees from labor camps), this writer has been assured that there are underground circles in the Eastern Ukraine, too, though unlike those in the Western Ukraine they have not engaged in armed opposition to the regime. There would be illegal student circles in which a respected professor would discuss in somewhat cautious language the aims of Ukrainian nationalism; [19] Ukrainians in responsible government positions would maintain a communications network to warn their fellow countrymen of impending arrests; sometimes those arrests could be obviated by self-imposed exile outside of the Ukraine.[20] In the most recent years, according to a defector from the Soviet Union, the constant attacks on Ukrainian "bourgeois nationalism" have, by way of reaction, awakened a feeling of national pride among some younger people. Another competent source, which must not be identified, spoke of circles among Ukrainian college students, in which questions relating to the status of the Ukraine in the Soviet Union were discussed with much frankness. The source expressed the opinion that the West tended to underestimate the strength of Ukrainian patriotism.

To sum up, it appears that the initial portrait of the Ukrainians as a stolid and neither articulate nor aggressive people semi-paralyzed by oppression, may have been overdrawn. In the questionnaire which was focused upon nationality, a large number of younger workers pointedly identified themselves as Ukrainians; a number of the "tougher" of their fellow countrymen have become officers in the Soviet Army, where they would, however, closely cooperate with the Russians; but some of the most resourceful and the toughest men have used their high positions in the state apparatus to engage in action, which, without being vocally nationalistic, has contributed to preserve the substance of the Ukrainian nation. To probe the attitudes of the Eastern Ukrainians more deeply it is proposed to analyze their position towards certain features of the regime.

Remarkable is the pride which Ukrainians show at the economic development of their country. One respondent, a postwar defector who inclined toward the nationalist viewpoint, emphatically rejected my observation that the Ukraine might not be economically self-sufficient to a degree of making separation from Russia an economically feasible proposition; a wartime refugee of mixed parentage (her mother was a Russian) asserted the same, adding that in order to form an intelligent opinion about the economic potential of the country, one ought to take a look at the huge combines (*kombinaty,* or factory complexes) in southern Ukraine.[21] Soviet Ukrainian intellectuals as well as peasants would argue in the labor camps that Ukrainian agriculture should be kept at a high level of productivity, for as soon as the regime falls, the Ukraine should be ready to supply Europe with grain, competing in this with the United States and Canada.[22] Both East and West Ukrainians would say: Give us ten years' time and the Ukraine shall be one of the leading states in Europe from an economic viewpoint. Incidentally, they also advocated keeping the deported Crimean Tatars where they are presently staying, for the Ukraine needed the Crimean ports and a free hand in transforming the Crimea to surpass Switzerland as a center for tourist trade [sic].[23]

The attitudes toward Soviet agriculture would imply that the Ukrainians are not willing to credit the regime with much achievement in this field. At least, from the conversations in the labor camps it follows that they feel that the regime is either not doing enough or that it is actually hampering economic development. One respondent noted that the *Eastern* Ukrainian intelligentsia were sympathetic toward retaining the collective farms or transforming them into more efficient state farms, but they felt that they could not prevail against the wishes of the peasants who wanted to return to a system of privately owned family plots. The *Western* Ukrainian intelligentsia, however, took the liquidation of the kolkhoz system for granted.[24] Nor were the people quite satisfied with the way in which Soviet Ukrainian industry was managed. In discussions held in another camp it was pointed out that "nothing would work under compulsion." The people were to be given freedom to decide on whether they preferred a collective or private enterprise system. It was said that the ideal system would be one combining privately and collectively managed enterprises that would compete with each other for best results.[25] In short, while the collective farms were rejected by the majority as one of the worst features of the regime, Ukrainian intelligentsia were toying with the idea of establishing a middle ground between free enterprise and collective economy.

The feature of the regime which Ukrainians and other Soviet citizens like best is its educational system. In his report to the Sixteenth Congress of the CP of Ukraine Khrushchev cited Himmler's memorandum of May 14, 1943, "On the Position of the Youth in the Ukraine," which makes the point very well. The chief of the Gestapo wrote:

The youth are disturbed by the lack of perspectives for the future. Under the Soviet regime the youth have always been inculcated that if they would make the effort, they could be admitted to higher schools. Among many youths who have now [that is, under the German occupation—Y.B.] been deprived of this possibility, sympathies toward Bolshevism are spreading.[26]

That has been confirmed by the Harvard data and by my own postwar respondents.[27] One of the latter even cited as example two young girls from Galicia. One of the two had formerly been associated with the Ukrainian Insurgent Army and the other was the daughter of a Greek Catholic priest. They said they did not want to defect even if given an opportunity; the regime had set up schools and scholarships; in their opinion, the West would not give them so much.[28] On the other hand, it should be kept in mind that since the school reforms of 1958–59, admission to higher schools and thus to the ranks of the Soviet elite has been made considerably more difficult for any but the ablest secondary school graduates. Within several years young people in the Ukraine and in other Soviet Republics are bound to lose some of their enthusiasm for the Soviet educational system as it becomes increasingly selective.[29]

Important for tapping national sentiment is the perception of the differential impact of certain Soviet policies upon the Ukraine. For a number of reasons I myself have not been able to obtain a sufficiently large number of answers and have to fall back on the evaluation of the Harvard Nationality Questionnaire. Miss Gilliam found that 65 per cent of the respondents answered that there were relatively more arrests from among the Ukrainian intelligentsia, while 31 per cent said that they were suffered equally by all nationalities.[30] Fifty per cent of the sample asserted that the Ukraine was economically more exploited than other regions of the Soviet Union.[31] While it is hard to judge how representative those figures are, we have already inferred from certain official statements that the issue of economic exploitation was rather widespread in the Ukraine after Stalin's death.[32] Furthermore, there exists seemingly conflicting evidence that Ukrainians are being discriminated against in their socio-economic advancement.

On the basis of general questionnaires, in which nationality was not stressed, Irving Rosow found that except for low educated Ukrainians of rural background the educational and life (career) chances of Ukrainians and Russians of similar social background did not differ in any significant degree; and that the Ukrainians who attained high paying positions tended to be more satisfied than comparable Russians, apparently because they had expected some discrimination based upon nationality.[33] The inference from this would be that the regime does not discriminate against ambitious Ukrainians, somewhat to their own surprise. On the basis of another sample, however, viz. that of the Nationality Questionnaire, Miss Gilliam concluded that such a discrimination must exist, for 71 per cent of the well educated Ukrainians *who hid their nationality* said that nationality was important to their career.[34] She also found that the higher the occupational group, the higher was the proportion of those who claimed that nationality was significant in their career advancement.[35] She sums up her observation in the following words:

... It appears that the greater the success attained, the more frequent the complaint that nationality had been a barrier to advancement. This might mean either that the higher the Ukrainian attempts to advance in his academic or professional career, the more obstacles he [thinks he] would encounter by reason of his nationality (many said that Ukrainians were held back because they were under suspicion by the regime) or that the greater a person's ambition the greater the likelihood of feeling himself opposed for irrelevant reasons. A third explanation may be that the ambitious are *correct* in their assessment—that the greater the *ambition,* the higher the ascent, and the more sanctions based on nationality have been encountered.[36]

In putting the question to some of my respondents I have found that a Russophile Ukrainian who did not mind speaking Russian in the Soviet Union found that his Ukrainian nationality did not put any obstacles to his career; whereas another, also a postwar defector, voiced his suspicion that it was his known preference for speaking Ukrainian that wrecked his professional education in that country.[37] Admittedly, most of the respondents were referring back to the Stalinist period. But some *recent* visitors from the Soviet Union (Soviet citizens), after some hedging, admitted in a private conversation that nationality does indeed play a role in making a good career in the ostensibly "internationalist" Soviet system. How can these various findings be reconciled, if at all?

From the statistics presented in Chapter II it appears beyond doubt that the share of the Ukrainians among the well paid scholars and scientists in the Soviet Union is far below the share of Ukrainians in the total population of the state.[38] Somewhat higher is the Ukrainian proportion among full-time college students, but it is still relatively low.[39] The share of Russian scientific personnel and college students, however, exceeds the proportion of Russians among the total population.[40]

How does this data compare with that of the Harvard questionnaires? In the first place, on the basis of these statistics alone it is not possible to establish discrimination between Ukrainians and Russians of *similar social backgrounds,,* because only few data on the social backgrounds have been released since 1926. In that year, only 10.5 per cent of the Ukrainian population of the USSR lived in cities, but 21.3 per cent of the Russians did so.[41] In the Ukrainian SSR, 11.8 per cent of the Ukrainians lived in urban areas in 1926, compared with 50.2 per cent of the Russians. Comparable recent figures for the Soviet Union as a whole have not yet been released (end of 1962),* but in the Ukrainian Republic, according to the census of 1959, 36.6 per cent of the Ukrainians re-

---

* According to the statistical handbook obtained while this book was in print, in 1959, 39.2 per cent of the Ukrainians in the USSR lived in cities compared with 57.7 per cent of the Russians. See *Itogi vsesoyznoy perepisi naseleniya 1959 goda: SSSR* ... (Moscow, 1962), pp. 184 and 190.

sided in cities compared with as many as 80.6 per cent of the Russians.[42] We also know that in all of the non-Russian Republics with the possible exception of the Kazakh SSR, most of the Russians live in cities. If we accept the hypothesis that the urban population is sociologically more mobile than the rural, this may account partly for the fact that the educational and life chances of a Ukrainian *as such* are lower than those of the Russians: for even in the Ukraine a strong majority of Ukrainians still live in the countryside. This need not contradict the findings of Rosow who has controlled both chances by social backgrounds. But over a longer span of time which is, however, short enough to be perceived by the more thoughtful Ukrainians, it will also appear that the regime influences the social structure of the various peoples in the Soviet Union by deciding where to build new industry. This may be implied in the vague answer that it is exploiting the Ukraine more than other areas. Moreover, with the postwar emphasis upon developing the industries in the East (Southern Siberia, Soviet Central Asia), such answers are bound to grow more frequent. Dniepropetrovsk Secretary Hayovy's complaint to the Twenty-First All-Union Congress in 1959 that the current Seven Year Plan allots an undue proportion of investment funds to eastern factories has already been noted.[43]

If we return now to the findings of Miss Gilliam and those of my own and view them against the background of the anti-Ukrainian policy of the late 1940's and early 1950's and the explicit admission by the regime that the Russification of higher schools in the Ukraine hindered thousands of students in their educational advancement,[44] we see that discrimination against *a certain kind* of Ukrainian does exist. It does not appear absolute, on the order of Negroes and mulattoes in South Africa who are discriminated against no matter what they do. Hence Rosow is correct if he concludes that Russians and Ukrainians *by origin,* of similar social background, are treated as equals. The point is that for all we know of his sample these may be Ukrainians who have adopted Russian speech, hidden their Ukrainian nationality, and otherwise assimilated themselves to the Russians.[45] Some of those assimilated Ukrainians may have appeared as Russians in our statistics of scientific personnel and students—for those figures have presumably been derived on the basis of personal declarations by the respondents.

To sum up so far: in our survey of attitudes toward the regime we have seen that—at least before 1958—Ukrainians endorsed the school system of the regime, and prided themselves on the economic achievements of their Republic. Nevertheless, they felt that they could do a better job of economic development if left free to reorganize the economy. All the peasants favored the return to individual plots, though some of the Eastern intellectuals feared that this might entail the loss of some of

the advantages of bigness. In the *general* Harvard questionnaires a pronounced discrimination against Ukrainians by origin in schools and careers was not detected, but under some probing in the narrowly focused
nationality questionnaires it was found that the higher a Ukrainian advanced the more he would complain of his nationality being a negative
factor in his career. We have adduced recent Soviet statistics showing
a disproportionately low number of Ukrainians enrolled at colleges and
working as academic and scientific personnel; and have ended with the
hypothesis that anti-Ukrainian discrimination in the Soviet Union is
conditional upon a citizen's preference for his native culture. It is now
proposed to examine the general problem of the cohesiveness of the
Ukrainian people.

One of the most common ways to cement the cohesion of a group is
to set it up against another group, the so-called "out-group" in the so-
ciologists' parlance. In order to accomplish this, the bad qualities of the
"out-group" are stressed and, justly or not, it is blamed for all kinds
of ills suffered by the "in-group." To what extent are Russians regarded
by the Ukrainians as an "out-group" and blamed for the ills of the Soviet regime? In more technical language, how strong is the deflected
hostility of the Ukrainians?

There is evidence that Western Ukrainians look upon the Russians
almost as the "devils incarnate" for having destroyed their traditional
way of life during the postwar collectivization.[46] Eastern Ukrainians,
however, do not share their extreme rejection of everything Russian,
which is probably to be explained by their centuries' long cohabitation.
In the oral Harvard interviews 17 per cent of the respondents (Eastern
Ukrainians) offered anti-Russian censures. But in the questionnaire
which was focused on the nationality problem 29 per cent said that the
Russians were the group most responsible for the rise of Bolsheviks to
power, 22 per cent checking the suggested answer "Jews," 65 per cent
"Members of the Party" (which, of course, is a redundant reply); 9
per cent blamed the workers and 7 per cent the intelligentsia. But
when given the following choice:

Check one: In general, in comparison with the Russians, the Ukrainians offered
——————————— (more, less, same) support to the Bolshevik regime;

57 per cent answered that the Ukrainians offered less support. In other
words, about one third of the Harvard sample did *not* blame the Russians for the actions of the regime.[47] Nevertheless, the lack of strong
hostility against the Russians apparently does not lead the Ukrainians
to adopt certain symbols which are held dear by the former. From the
general Harvard questionnaire that had been administered to about

2,700 persons, about 17 per cent more Ukrainians than Russians were willing to have an atomic bomb dropped on Moscow.[48]

Qualitative data from my own interviews confirm this picture of a relative lack of hostility between Eastern Ukrainians and Russians. True, the notion that the collectivization of the Ukrainian countryside was carried out with the help of the Russians seems to be widely held. To my counterargument that it was a general policy of the regime and not specifically directed against Ukrainians, the rejoinder was: "The *tysyachnyky* (workers' thousands) were sent from Russia to the Ukraine, not vice versa." * This may explain the observation of an American student of Soviet affairs that while the attitudes of the Ukrainian city population were ambivalent, there was anti-Russian sentiment in the villages.[49] The Ukrainian intelligentsia, however, felt a certain resentment at Russians being given the better posts. One source stated that when Postyshev arrived to take over the Ukrainian Party organization in 1933, he brought with him 10–15 thousand "responsible Party workers" from Russia.[50] Another suggested that the Ukrainians should be loyal to the regime to obviate its need of filling the governmental apparatus with Russians.[51]

Furthermore, there are signs that the Russians as a whole and the Russian community in the Ukraine in particular are divided on their attitudes towards the Ukrainians. This has been noticed by the Eastern

* Interview #31. In the early 1930's, industrial workers were sent into the countryside to carry out the planned collectivization, assisted by police and, occasionally, troop detachments. Respondent's point is that Ukrainian workers were not trusted to perform such a task in Russia, but that the regime relied on Russian proletariat. This is confirmed by a Russophile source from the city, who said that it was Russians who set up kolkhozes in the Ukraine (Interview #54). On the other hand, a Soviet source states that 8,421 of such workers were recruited in the Ukraine. Of these 1,986 were sent to other Republics: 505 persons went to Kazakhstan and 1,300 to Northern Caucasus, which is certainly not Russia in the strict sense of the word but an ethnically mixed territory (Russians, Ukrainians, and mountaineer peoples)—"KPU v tsifrakh (CP of the Ukraine in Figures)," *Partiynaya zhizn'*, Vol. 1958, No. 12 (June), p. 57. A considerable number of those proletarians may have been Russians from the Ukraine (a large section of the workers in the Ukraine was either Russian or Russified), but many of them—contrary to public impression—must have been Ukrainians. It is significant, however, that the official statistics confirm the notion that virtually no Ukrainians were sent to collectivize the peasants in Russia proper.

Even more revealing are the interviews quoted by John S. Reshetar, Jr., "The Nationality Problem in the Soviet Union," in Gilliam, *et al.*, *op. cit.*, p. 12. "'The crops in 1932 were very good in Ukraine, but the Communist Soviet government took by force all the crops from the Ukrainian peasants. There was no famine in Russia proper at that time. Our peasants went by train to Russian territory to buy some grain' (Harvard interview protocol #1719). Or: 'In March and April [1933] one could already see swollen faces. . . . People lived on potatoes. In May when the potatoes were gone, people began to go to the Russian villages to exchange their clothing for food. Interestingly enough, beyond Kharkov where the Russian territory begins there was no hunger. The government did not take away the grain from the Russian peasants' (Interview protocol #1582)."

Ukrainians and hence their reluctance to paint Ukrainian-Russian relations in solid black. On the one hand, there is an authentic Soviet
anecdote which depicts the thinking of some older Russians of the Imperial school. One elderly Russian lady says to a Ukrainian professor
in a Kiev park: "How come, Professor, that you are not ashamed to
raise your daughter in such a language [Ukrainian]! And fancy what a
name you have thought up for her: *Lesya!*"—"But that is really quite
simple, Madam. Lesya means Lenin, Stalin, *i ya* [and I]." [52] On the other
hand, an Eastern Ukrainian in a labor camp defended Russians against
sweeping charges of intolerance by pointing toward the first edition of
Osipov's book—the best popular biography of Khmelnytsky that has
been published so far, written by a Russian. [53]

In all its complexity the problem of the relationship toward the Russian minority was raised during World War II when young Eastern
Ukrainians requested the permission of a Western Ukrainian Nationalist organizer to enroll their Russian friend in the OUN underground
cell they had recently joined themselves. The Galician who had always
been taught that the "Muscovites" were the arch-enemies of the Ukraine
was rather surprised, but yielded. Other organizers had similar experiences, and as a result the Nationalist underground in German occupied
Ukraine enrolled a number of Ukrainian Russians who proved as loyal
as Ukrainians. [54] That relationship has been perhaps best summed up
by two respondents. According to one, the Eastern Ukrainians were not
so anti-Russian as to take revenge on the Russians for the actions of
the regime. [55] Another put it as follows:

[The Ukrainians and Russians] do not show hostility against each other. But
usually the Ukrainians would give to understand that they were not in their
own country, that they [the Ukrainians] wanted to become masters [in their
own house]. [56]

There are also signs that relations with the next largest minority, the
Jews, will tend to be even less hostile. [57]

The problem of Ukrainian-Russian relations merges with that of the
fundamental cohesiveness of the Ukrainian people. Is there a tendency
for it to melt away under the double impact of industrialization and
Soviet terror, to intermarry with non-Ukrainians and to lose its national
face?

In this respect, there appears to be a great difference between the
tightly knit religious and national communities in Soviet Central Asia,
where marriages with outsiders are very rare, [58] and the somewhat looser
and more receptive Ukrainian people. The 1937 census figure on ethnic
intermarriages in the Ukraine (19 per cent), as we have already seen in
Chapter II, seems quite large but is liable to misinterpretation because

it includes marriages not involving Ukrainians and refers to a year of the Great Purge.[59] While there is certainly more social intercourse between Ukrainians and Russians than, for example, between Russians and Tadzhiks, the available evidence does not support the view that the Ukraine is a seething melting pot of nationalities. One item in the Harvard nationality questionnaire asked the respondents to give the nationality of his three closest friends from early school, high school, first and last jobs, and the army. As analyzed by Miss Gilliam the responses were:

With regards to personal friends of the respondents, approximately 80% of the respondents indicated that in each of the life situations enumerated, their best friend was a Ukrainian. An exception was the army situation where only 65% indicated that their best friend was Ukrainian. This might be due to the non-availability of associates of one's own nationality in nationally mixed units. The second and third friend mentioned are also somewhat less likely to have been Ukrainians, especially in the higher schools; but the proportion is still about 60%. In almost every instance, the next nationality mentioned in each context is Russian, but the proportion here is still about 10% to 20%, a very poor second to Ukrainian self-popularity. It is apparent, then, that the Ukrainians of this sample indicate that they confined their friendships largely to their own nationality; however, this pattern was breached more frequently in higher schools and in the army.[60]

The problem is, of course, whether the sample chosen has been a representative one, but it would seem that the differences between the magnitudes involved (60–80 per cent cf. with 10–20 per cent) are so large that short of a *fundamental* bias of the sample—which does not exist—a correction of a few percentage points would not have altered the conclusions. Those conclusions are the more interesting because, as we have seen in Chapter V, the sample is biased toward the more mobile elements of society: those who lived in the cities most of the time, or those who moved from villages into cities.[61] We shall pursue the subject of cohesiveness further by analyzing the relations between Eastern and Western Ukrainians and between the elite and the common people.

Ideally, this study should have included a consideration of Ukrainian nationalism in different regions of the country: the predominantly rural Right Bank Ukraine, with Kiev; Kharkov; the southern steppes, with Crimea and Odessa; the industrial South, with special attention to the Donbas; Volhynia; Galicia; the Transcarpathian region; and Northern Bukovina. There was not sufficient material available for such a task. But the data permit a few more general conclusions on the effect of the annexation of Western Ukraine upon the Western Ukrainians themselves and upon the cohesiveness of the Ukrainian people as a whole. In allowing Western Ukrainian youth to attend schools, and in giving

Western Ukrainians access to lower positions in the governmental apparatus, the regime has removed one of the basic grievances that was responsible for the particular virulence of Galician nationalism.[62] At the same time the Soviets have created even greater resentment by dissolving the Greek Catholic church, collectivizing the countryside, and discriminating against the very same Western Ukrainians once they aspired toward top positions (as it appeared during the Melnikov controversy). The methods by which the underground resistance was finally crushed must also have left a solid fund of hatred behind them.[63]

There is no direct evidence on how Eastern Ukrainians reacted to the plight of their brethren in Galicia, except by former camp inmates who had occasion to observe both Eastern and Western Ukrainians. All of them remarked that the Galician Ukrainians from the Insurgent Army were the more energetic ones in camp activities and that they were more outspoken and ardent in advocating national independence. One source called them "the driving elements," another saw in them the "ferment, the banner carriers" of the struggle for independence.[64] How were the relations between the two groups? According to one respondent, the Eastern Ukrainians in his camp had not heard about the Insurgent Army in the West, but they considered that any bona fide Ukrainian movement was a good thing.[65] One former Eastern Ukrainian film actor, however, who had heard about the UPA was enthusiastic: their heroism reminded him of Gogol's famous hero Taras Bulba.[66] But I have obtained the distinct impression that a difference was felt between the Ukrainians from the East and the West and that it took some time until they drew together. What separated them?

As most of the Western Ukrainians are Greek Catholics and virtually all Eastern Ukrainians Orthodox (a minority are members of Protestant Churches), it might have been supposed that it was a difference in faith which created a barrier between them. But this does not appear to have been the case. From interviews with defectors and former camp inmates one can infer that the Russian Orthodox church in its present form has ceased to have a considerable influence in the lives of the younger Eastern Ukrainians.[67] What separated the Eastern from the Western Ukrainians in the camps was not religious difference—on the contrary, for Easter many Dnieper Ukrainians joined Galicians in a Uniate divine service.[68] The difference stemmed rather from the policy of the camp administration and from a certain lack of consensus upon the political future of their country and the means by which those goals could best be achieved.

It has been noted that Western Ukrainians accused of collaboration with the UPA belonged to the category of prisoners who were treated the worst in all labor camps. Hence some Eastern Ukrainians who might have been imprisoned on ridiculous, petty charges were initially afraid to join the Galicians, lest they should damage their chances of obtaining an amnesty.[69] Other Eastern Ukrainians had allegedly lost all hope that political independence was possible for the Ukraine, and looked upon the "Westerners" as persons addicted to phantasies.[70] Another observer, however, obtained an impression which is not quite so pessimistic.[71] The Western Ukrainians he met rejected the regime *in toto,* while Eastern Ukrainians pointed out that despite all its evils it gave out scholarships and had introduced Ukrainian in public schools. But the Western Ukrainians ignored the first and took the latter for granted. The younger among them would hold regular "seminars" in which they tried to convert the rest to fight for an independent Ukraine. The older men, and especially the Eastern Ukrainians, remained skeptical as to the possibility of achieving independence in the near future. They would point out to the young firebrands that they were not united among themselves (a painful allusion to the Bandera-Melnyk-UHVR controversy in the OUN), and that foreign powers (the United States in particular) would use the Ukrainian government-in-exile * for their own purpose which need not be that of the Ukrainian people. Sometimes their arguments would not stay at the verbal level. But in one respect Eastern and Western Ukrainians would cooperate closely: In awakening and deepening among the labor camp inmates an interest in Ukrainian culture. Ukrainian operas would be performed with joint forces, an Eastern Ukrainian specialized in writing sentimentally patriotic poems and Western Ukrainians would recite poems by Franko. Every performance of the so-called circles of "artistic activity," which the camp authorities encouraged in order to maintain the workers' morale, turned out to be a "national demonstration" jointly organized by Eastern and Western Ukrainians, so that before long the Russians in that camp began to refer half jokingly to "the overabundance of *khokhols*" (*khokhlatskoe zasil'e*).[72]

The comparative facility with which Galicians and Eastern Ukrainians found common language on cultural ground may well mean, as Miss Gilliam has pointed out, that in the Eastern Ukraine the regime has succeeded to some degree in emasculating Ukrainian nationalism by

---

* Ukrainians living abroad are split among several political groupings. The most promising of those, because it enjoys the support of the overwhelming majority of the wartime and postwar refugees from Eastern Ukraine, is the Ukrainian National Council (*Ukrayins'ka Natsionalna Rada*) in Munich, West Germany. It carries on the work of the last democratic Ukrainian government in the Ukraine, that of the Ukrainian National Republic (*Ukrayins'ka Narodna Respublika*), which had gone into exile in 1920. It is of great significance, however, that the President-in-exile of the UNR, Dr. Stepan Wytwytsky, is a West Ukrainian by birth and had once served as a diplomatic representative of the West Ukrainian government.

instilling "cultural pride devoid of aspirations of national independence." [73] But something else might be involved, too. On a limited scale
underground organizations apparently exist also in Eastern Ukraine,
but they do not challenge the regime to an armed clash, in which they
know they would be the losers. The basic political difference between
Eastern and Western Ukrainians seems to consist in how they evaluate
the possibility of fighting the regime. Placed in a unique situation at
the end of the war, the leadership of the Western Ukrainian Nationalists concluded that armed struggle was the only possible means of political action. If challenged by the argument that in the long run such
a struggle was extremely costly they would either point to the laurels
of a heroic death or to the possibility of being saved by foreign intervention in World War III. It would seem that even nationalistic Eastern Ukrainians do not share this essentially pessimistic assumption.
Hence it would appear that the undoubtedly heroic struggle of the UPA
in Galicia and Volhynia has not and could not have produced the resonance in the East which Galician leaders apparently hoped they would
obtain. The "National Revolution" stopped in the West because Eastern Ukrainians have had their bitter experience with armed guerrilla
warfare in the 1920's, the collectivization of the 1930's, and the terror
of the German occupation in the early 1940's.

While it would be, therefore, premature to say that even with some
population exchange between Galicia and the Eastern Ukraine the differences in the outlook of the Ukrainians in these two main regions have
been resolved, it would seem that nationalism in the Eastern part has
been strengthened somewhat. The uncompromising if perhaps not altogether promising stand of the "Westerners" has forced many Eastern
Ukrainians to take their stand on the desirability of creating an independent Ukrainian state. In the labor camps, at least, the discussion has
not resulted in any firm agreement on political action, but it strengthened the mutual desire to cooperate on the cultural plane.

Of even greater importance for the cohesiveness and resilience of the
Ukrainian people is the relationship between the Ukrainian-born elite
and the people at large. We have seen in Chapter II that since the 1920's
the regime has produced a great many Ukrainian administrators, engineers, and other professionals. The question is now whether they are
nationally conscious and whether, should an opportunity for independent action arise, they would throw in their lot with the Ukrainian people rather than with the central authorities in Moscow.

From the interview data we have seen that virtually all Soviet-educated Ukrainians identify themselves as such, so that a certain minimal
degree of national consciousness must be presumed. But we have also
seen that such an identification is not a reliable indicator of the re-

spondents' political views: Some of them would cooperate with Ukrainian nationalist, others with "anti-separatist" Russian émigré organizations. Deutsch warns us correctly:

Only if nationality is valued; if it is seen as the winning card in the social game for prestige, wealth, or whatever else may be the things culturally valued at that time and place; or if it fulfils a need in the personality structure which individuals have developed in that particular culture—or if it is at least valued for lack of any more promising opportunities—only then does it seem probable that consciousness of nationality will strengthen its development.[74]

In discussing linguistic assimilation, he further suggests six qualitative "balances of factors": (1) similarity of communication habits: linguistic and cultural; (2) facilities for learning and teaching [the new language]; (3) frequency of contacts; (4) material rewards and penalties; (5) values and desires; (6) symbols and barriers.[75] In analyzing the Harvard nationality questionnaires, however, it has been found out that it was the attitude toward the language policy of the regime which was most closely correlated with the strength and ready availability, the "saliency" of Ukrainian nationalism as measured by the number of spontaneous nationalist write-ins in the questionnaire.[76]

Viewed in the light of Deutsch's and Gilliam's analysis, the outlook for Ukrainian nationalism would appear rather bleak. Admittedly there were many protests against the Russification of schools in the wake of the reform of 1958–59.[77] But from our postwar interviews it also appears that the struggle for economic betterment occupies most of the attention of Soviet citizens, Ukrainians and non-Ukrainians alike. We also know that since about 1938, and especially since May, 1945, until 1955, and again since 1958, the regime has openly and continuously stressed that Russian nationality or a reasonable facsimile thereof was "the winning card in the social game for prestige and wealth." The present generation of Soviet Ukrainian elite have also grown up in the knowledge that Ukrainian nationalism made one liable to arrest and liquidation—witness the purges of the 1930's. Linguistic and cultural communication habits between Ukrainians and Russians are similar, unlike those between Russians and the Turkic peoples of Central Asia. Facilities for learning and teaching Russian have existed for centuries in the large Eastern Ukrainian cities the majority of whose inhabitants are likely to be Russians; and where those facilities were lacking, the regime has provided amply for them by directing Russian officials and workers into Western Ukraine, and building Russian theaters in Lviv and Mukachevo, ostensibly to satisfy their cultural needs. Higher schools, even in Western Ukraine, were Russified. While this has proved a hardship for ambitious Ukrainians, it is not an insuperable barrier except

for those Ukrainians who cannot or will not learn to speak Russian in
their daily lives. Some discrimination in the assignment of jobs does
apparently exist, but, as Rosow found, it is not absolute. Moreover,
there is indication that some of the mobile Eastern Ukrainians, that
is, those who were born in the cities or moved into them from the countryside, have absorbed a few cultural values tacitly sanctioned by the
regime. They have come to look down upon the Ukrainian language
as a peasant dialect, while Russian has been esteemed as the language
of the drawing room.[78] We know very little about the political attitudes
of the Soviet Ukrainian elite, but if the choice of language is a reliable
indicator of the strength of nationalist sentiment it would seem that
with help from the regime many of the better situated Ukrainians are
rapidly denationalizing themselves.

What can Ukrainian nationalism oppose to the blandishments of rising to the top of the political and socio-economic ladder? What can it
set against assimilating oneself to a culture which ranks high in world
prestige? This calls for an analysis of Ukrainian national symbols and
the channels that are available for their transmission.

The material presented in the historical introduction (Chapter I) and
the analysis of Soviet Ukrainian historiography (Chapter VII) as well as
the chapter on Shevchenko (VI) should refute any possible notions that
the Ukrainian national movement arose sometime during World War I.
While it is true that it was not until 1848 in Austrian Galicia and 1863
in the Russian Ukraine that it achieved considerable political significance, it originated as a cultural and political movement at the end of
the eighteenth century; while the history of the Ukrainian people, as
distinct from a modern Ukrainian nation, begins in the Middle Ages.
But a Ukrainian patriot surveying the history of his country in order
to find powerful symbols that would inspire his fellow countrymen to
struggle for independence, faces several difficulties. In the first place, for
a number of reasons, one of the most important of which is their country's exposed geographical position on the eastern border of Europe,
since the Middle Ages the Ukrainian people have failed to maintain
political independence for longer periods of time. Related to this is
the fact, that with the exception of the four centuries of Lithuanian-
Polish rule (fourteenth through seventeenth centuries) the mainstream
of Ukrainian history cannot be neatly separated from that of the Russian people, though we need not believe the official thesis that ever since
the Tatar invasion in the thirteenth century the Ukrainian people have
aspired to be re-united with their northeastern brethren. Ukrainian literature has achieved a high pinnacle in the nineteenth century, but
there is also the disturbing fact (from the nationalist point of view)
that the greatest Ukrainian poet kept his diary and wrote some of his

inferior works in Russian. Thus, even if it were possible to present the Ukrainian national heritage correctly, this might have only led the people to discuss the advantages and disadvantages of the traditional cooperation with the Russians but would not have offered them a clear-cut historical argument for national independence. An exception may be made for Western Ukrainians who have never been under extended Russian influence until 1945, and who, like the Poles, take pride in representing the European West. But all their differences with Eastern Ukrainians notwithstanding, it is not likely that they would want to separate themselves from the main body of the people. The question should now be raised: Is it possible to present Ukrainian national heritage correctly under the regime? If official textbooks distort it without mercy, do alternative channels exist from which the truth could be learned?

The data of the Harvard nationality questionnaire indicate that the two primary institutions which stimulated or kept Ukrainian national feelings alive by transmission of proper symbols, were the home and the Autocephalous Orthodox church.[79] In our analysis we have also seen that the Western Ukrainian Greek Catholic church was a national church *par excellence*. Of these three institutions the two churches have been dissolved,[80] and there is a plausible hypothesis that the influence of the home may also be waning. It is said that parents are afraid to make hostile statements against the regime in the presence of their younger children lest they repeat them in public, but as the children grow up to an age when they could receive such information critically, they imbibe the official presentation of certain symbols.[81] It would appear that for the majority of the people, and particularly for those who want their children to "get ahead" under the regime, the official version of Ukrainian political and cultural history may prove the most acceptable one; for as one of my respondents put it: "Under Soviet conditions people do not see more than is plainly visible through the window, nor do they care to see more." [82] It is true that all these propositions refer to the Stalinist period. Under Khrushchev more freedom for inquiry and expression is available, but how much more is a rather moot point.

Viewed in this light, the official representation of Ukrainian symbols appears a very insidiously pernicious one indeed. The regime has tried to enlist Ukrainian historical figures for its ends, by depicting them as the collaborators and disciples of Russians. In the opinion of some respondents this deliberate attempt to present Ukrainian national heritage as second best, a provincial component of the Russian culture, as a matter of embroidered shirts, folk dances, and ethnographic opera, is much more dangerous to Ukrainian nationalism than the outright suppression by Tsarist governments.[83] It merely encourages more ambitious

Ukrainians to break away from their village past to embrace the modern world of the largely Russified cities. This appears to have been the main current in the development of Ukrainian leading strata since the late 1930's through Stalin's death.

But this is not the whole story. It seems to me, first, that for certain purposes of its own the regime has had to develop cadres who really know the Ukrainian national heritage *ex officio* and may have become committed to it beyond the point required by the regime; secondly, I would deem it not improbable that under changed political circumstances the denationalized Ukrainian administrative elite would be forced to throw in their lot with the Ukrainian people.

Following the ideological decrees of 1946–48 those cadres that had been engaged in cultivating the Ukrainian national heritage were compelled to sing the praise of the elder brother. Since 1953–54 they have been allowed a somewhat greater freedom of expression. They have used it to demand that Ukrainian culture be accorded an appropriate status. While maintaining their political loyalty to the regime, they have begun to lay the foundations for a dam against the tide of Russian influence, especially in the cities. In my judgment, that tide has flowed from the danger that the Ukrainian arts and sciences in the form tolerated by the Stalinist regime were no longer able to satisfy the cultural needs of the urban educated minority. There is a remarkable passage in the speech by Ya. Starynkevych at a Ukrainian writers session, in which, reviewing the Ukrainian prose output in 1957, he deplores the tendency to link the national to the village, to peasant life. "But we have a national intelligentsia and working class. What they have accomplished is worthy of being depicted in great works of belles-lettres." [84] Why have the Soviet leaders found it expedient to let Ukrainian writers, literary historians, history, and language teachers speak up again after silencing them in 1946?

The possibility of a dangerous political provocation should not be excluded: the bold voices of the 1920's were physically destroyed in the 1930's, and there are some among the Ukrainian exiles abroad who fear that a similar if not quite so brutal fate (viz., the suppression of writings) may now be in store for the outspoken writers of the post-Stalinist thaw. But it may also be that the regime has been relatively permissive because intellectuals who are well acquainted with the Ukrainian national heritage can be made useful to the regime. There is, for example, evidence that the majority of the Ukrainian people who live in villages not only speak Ukrainian but also like to read Ukrainian books. The education in the countryside is not as good as in the cities, but it is education nevertheless and to obtain from today's Ukrainian peasant the most labor at the lowest cost it is necessary to pay at least minimal attention to his cultural needs. Nor are the peasants the only ones who object to the suppression of Ukrainian culture. To judge by Miss Gilliam's findings, their sons, too, who move into the cities to become workers aggressively identify themselves as Ukrainians out of respect for their native culture; even if some of them may, paradoxically, adopt the Russian language. Moreover, there is some evidence that, having received fairly good schooling, they are critical of some propaganda claims. Two independent sources depicted the reaction of Ukrainians to the Pereyaslav "reunification" celebrations in 1954: in one camp, the Ukrainians remained silent and merely spat whenever the word Pereyaslav was mentioned, in another the remark was made that though Russia needed the Ukraine, the Ukraine did not need Russia now.[85] In order to maintain psychological access to the majority of the Ukrainian people, the regime has not only allowed for the teaching of all subjects in Ukrainian in the overwhelming majority of primary and secondary schools but has also tolerated the growth of a small Ukrainian elite who are committed to the study and development of Ukrainian culture.

The Soviet regime has also constantly professed to be impartial towards the various peoples it has ruled, though since the 1930's it has accorded increasing privileges to the Russians and though after May 1945 it has all but ceased to even pay lip service to the notion of the "equality of peoples." But there is no logical reason why a Communist power should irrevocably commit itself to support a single people, be it even the "most outstanding nation" of the country. As Barrington Moore has pointed out, as the regime gains the allegiance of a particular national group it loses its totalitarian flexibility.[86] After Stalin's death and particularly after the Twentieth Party Congress the Soviet leaders have reverted somewhat to "Leninist proletarian internationalism," and the Ukrainian elite—both cultural and administrative—have profited from this move. Has the subsequent reaction (1958 to date) undone all the achievements of that period? It is too early to form a definite judgment on that.

Moreover, the aim of Soviet Communism appears to be not so much to reject the patriotic attitudes of its peoples altogether but to absorb and to transform them into the higher unity of Soviet patriotism. To reinterpret six to ten centuries of a nation's history is not so simple. To sound more convincing, at least the distorters must know exactly what they are distorting, and it is quite possible that in reading the forbidden works of Hrushevsky and Yefremov they will learn much that is not welcome to the regime and that might serve as a good argument for Ukrainian nationalism. Though the Party maintains rigid controls on the admission to ideologically sensitive work,[87] it is plausible to assume that many of the Ukrainian cultural cadres are attracted to their professions by something more than the prospect of earning a living. Throughout this process of reinterpretation, the national cadres from the Republic must be left some freedom of expression, which, as a welcome and not to be neglected by-product, also serves to create good will in the formerly colonial peoples of Asia and Africa.

Finally, there is a very interesting phenomenon which has appeared in full strength only in the years after Stalin's death (since 1954). Already in the immediate postwar period, Soviet spokesmen inveighed against the "Fascist collaborators" among the Ukrainian exiles (displaced persons).[88] In more recent years, those derogatory references have become rather extended polemics against Ukrainians living abroad, especially those in the United States and Canada who have enlisted prominent speakers (for example, Canadian Prime Minister John Diefenbaker and Governor Averell Harriman) to appear at their celebrations of the 40th anniversary of Ukrainian independence in 1958. Three high representatives of the Soviet Ukrainian cultural elite—the poets Maksym Rylsky and Volodymyr Sosyura and the theater director Hnat Yura—published a long polemical article in *Radyans'ka Ukrayina,* of February 22, 1958, entitled "Memorial Services." Three days later the article was reprinted in Moscow's *Pravda.*[89] More recently, as we have already seen, First Party Secretary Podgorny chose the forum of the Fifteenth UN General Assembly (1960) to rebut at length Prime Minister Diefenbaker's brief reference to the subjugated status of the Ukraine and to savagely attack Ukrainian exiles. Podgorny's speech was carried in full in the central Ukrainian press.[90] It may be asked, if the cause of the Ukrainian nationalists abroad is dead, why not let it rest in peace? It would seem on the contrary that the regime does not feel that its Ukrainian subjects in the USSR are immune to such appeals. In any case, this is another use to which the Soviet Ukrainian elite can be put: to refute the arguments of the Ukrainians abroad.

In short, whether to establish psychological rapport with the Ukrainian masses, whether to balance out the various peoples in the interests of political flexibility, to transform the Ukrainian heritage prior to its absorption in "all-Soviet" patriotism, or to fight "bourgeois nationalists" abroad, the regime cannot neglect the men who know Ukrainian symbols even if these men may, in the long run, further Ukrainian nationalism. But why have the Ukrainian writers been given greater leeway only after Stalin's death? The answer is that Khrushchev seems to be a more farsighted man than Stalin. But what has he seen that Stalin ignored?

Actually, the greater tolerance of the views of Ukrainian intellectuals is only a facet of Khrushchev's policy to give greater administrative responsibilities to local cadres, mostly Party members. The policy, which is associated with the general trend of increasing efficiency in Soviet industry, raises a fundamental problem which we can only touch upon here: the interrelationship between industrialization and nationalism.

Industrialization is sometimes alleged to lead inevitably to centralization, to increased frequency of contacts between different peoples and thus to a reduction of national differences. If we consider the growth of the bureaucratic apparatus under Stalin and the linguistic Russification of the Ukrainian administrative elite this would indeed appear to be so. Upon closer analysis, however, some flaws appear in this picture. From historical evidence we know that the period of intense industrial development is also a period of great national tension in which each national group tries to reap the benefits of the development.[91] While the economic development of the Ukraine does no longer proceed at so rapid a pace as in the 1920's and 1930's, the Ukrainian economy certainly does not stand still, and in the process of development friction between the Ukrainians and Russians does ensue, some of which we have documented in Chapter VIII, above.

We have found that the regime has openly acknowledged discrimination in the placement of "cadres" in Western Ukraine. But is the problem limited to the special case of Western Ukraine? From the sharp increase in the total membership of the Communist Party of Ukraine after Stalin's death, from the unprecedented election of two Ukrainians —Kirichenko and Podgorny—to the top positions of the CPU that until June, 1953, had traditionally been held by non-Ukrainians, we have inferred that there seems to be a silent struggle for promotion being waged in the Party of the Ukraine. But as we have seen from the material in this chapter the jockeying for power in the CPU is but an important aspect of similar competition in all walks of Soviet Ukrainian life. The most telling indication of this are the opinions reported by my respondents that it was imperative for Ukrainians to fill all positions in the Soviet administrative apparatus in the Ukraine to obviate their falling into the hands of Russians. They would be loyal to the régime and even pass for Russians if it would give them positions of responsibility. In summary, economic development and widespread education has prepared the native "cadres" for assuming administrative positions and they have challenged the old ruling class, mostly composed of Russians, to move aside and to let them, too, grasp the rewards offered by the regime. This pressure from the native cadres has been acknowledged by none other than Khrushchev at the Twentieth Party Congress; at the Twenty-First Congress Kirichenko made some poignant remarks about *young* Party workers who demanded their place in the sun.[92]

At the same time, utmost centralization as practised under Stalin seems to have reached its point of diminishing returns both in terms of economic efficiency and flexible political control. In order to document this hypothesis it would have been necessary to study the reorganization of industrial management in great detail, and for comparative purposes one also ought to have analyzed the history of the administrative structure of some big American corporation (General Electric or General Motors). But while there may be not enough data to enable use to erect a thesis, the available ones may do for a somewhat speculative discussion.

It appears that the ministerial apparatus centered in Moscow duplicated the controls exercised by the foremost centralized organization in the Soviet Union: the Party. Moreover, the Party functionaries in Moscow whose primary interest was political became so enmeshed with their Party colleagues in the central economic departments that they failed to heed such matters as the resentment of the Party leadership in the Union Republics. Khrushchev, however, who had made his career in one of those Republics, has tried to win the allegiance of non-Russian Republican Party leaders by appointing two of them (Kirichenko and Mukhitdinov) to highest posts in the All-Union Communist Party and by giving those whom he could not take with him into the central apparatus greater responsibilities on the spot. Thus he has also created a political counterweight to the departmentalized bureaucratic apparatus in Moscow, without sacrificing any power at the center, for the new men are all members of one of the most centralized organizations of the world: the Party. Admittedly, during the current reaction, by the time of the Twenty-Second All-Union Party Congress in the fall of 1961, both men lost their high posts in the Secretariat. But others still occupy important positions (for example, the full Presidium member Kirilenko).

Has the appointment of Kirichenko, Kirilenko, and his like to responsible positions strengthened Ukrainian nationalism? It may have actually weakened it, at least in the short run. The authors of the Royal Institute report on nationalism point out that historically one of the greatest weaknesses of multi-national empires has been that they staffed their political administration with aliens "who both socially and politically kept the upper positions strictly to themselves."[93] We have already seen that even during the heyday of Soviet Russian nationalism, the Ukrainians refused to regard the entire Russian people as their inveterate enemies. The appointment of Ukrainians to positions of high authority makes it even more difficult to crystallize nationalism in opposition to an ethnic out-group. Moreover, the new Ukrainians in Moscow are in a politically vulnerable position. As soon as they start to build up their bona fide Communist power base in the Ukraine, their centralist opponents are likely to accuse them of Ukrainian "bourgeois nationalism." It is therefore probable that to prove themselves loyal to the regime, Kirilenko, Podgorny and others will help restrict Ukrainian cultural freedom as much, if not more than native Russians. Nor is it clear at all how much the Ukrainian careerists are committed to the national heritage as shared by the majority of the Ukrainian people. From Soviet belles-lettres and the observation of foreigners, it appears that the higher Party functionaries and the cream of the intellectual elite form a society contained in itself, which has closer ties with the center than with the population among whom they work.[94] So long as the regime maintains its power, they are prone to serve not their subjects, but their masters.

On the other hand, we may speculate that in the *long* run the rise of "native cadres" to responsible positions in Moscow and within the Republic itself will strengthen a form of Ukrainian Titoism. For to say that there is a gulf between them and the population from whom they are descended is to draw attention to only one side of the coin. Our survey of Khrushchev's appointments has shown that it is always useful to have a body of trusted lieutenants whom one can place in key positions should need arise. Granted that a strong competition for important Party posts does exist, it would seem unwise for any highly placed Ukrainian in Moscow to lose touch with his Party organization "at home," for one never knows when the top man in the Kremlin might die and who his successor would turn out to be. While firmly keeping one's finger in the Kremlin pie seems to be one's primary concern, a kind of "grass roots support" on the territorial Party level is not to be neglected even in the Soviet Union. Hence we would suppose that the Ukrainian Party leaders in Moscow and Kiev, while berating Ukrainian "bourgeois nationalists," will *very cautiously* try to build up their own political machines which will primarily consist of their old and trusted associates in the Ukraine. They also probably enjoy having Ukrainian representatives in the United Nations even more than their rivals in Moscow, though the representation also serves to increase the prestige of the Soviet Union as such. In the eyes of the majority of the Ukrainian people, Soviet Ukrainian statehood in international law appears to be a sham, but for the Ukrainian Party elite even the small quantum of prestige it yields may be a useful asset in the battle for political advancement.

In the more distant future, which may see the downfall of the regime, the fact that many top administrative positions in the Republic are already held by Ukrainians may prove of very great advantage indeed. In their conversations with one respondent, Eastern Ukrainians pointed out the relative weakness of the Soviet Ukrainian Party elite. In their opinion, they were too weak to be able to impose their will upon the Ukrainian people should the superior force of the regime be withdrawn. They regarded themselves as a "serving elite," rather than a "ruling elite." [95] This appears to be somewhat idealized thinking. More sound appears the judgment of a source who stated: "If under those conditions they will not throw in their lot with the Ukrainian people, the people will slaughter all of them." [96] We may infer that they will not have another alternative then. In the chaos of destruction local government will be the first to emerge and only local men will be allowed to take over the affairs of the community. The Ukrainians in Moscow will have to yield to Muscovites and any Ukrainian administrators sent to Soviet Central Asia may find that they will be fortunate if they escape with their lives. In the Ukraine, most of the local administrators are now Ukrainians, and they may be presumed to look out for the interests of their communities first, Kiev second, and Moscow only in the last place.

Our speculation on what the Ukrainian political elite would do under different circumstances raises the question as to what role is played in Ukrainian nationalism by contingency. It has been noticed by the Harvard team that a focusing of the respondents' minds upon the problem of nationality produced different answers from those obtained in describing their general life situation in the Soviet Union. From this and the observations of my own sources who encountered Soviet Ukrainians after the war, one may conclude that although Ukrainian nationalism is not dead, it tends to be dormant, not salient, except in the newly annexed regions in the West. What are the reasons for this? Besides the highly absorbing struggle for material rewards in which Ukrainian nationality presents a certain barrier, it has been noticed that Soviet Ukrainians tend to be so preoccupied with abolishing the ills of the regime that little thought is given to what precisely should be put in its place.[97] But as soon as the regime starts breaking apart, as in 1941–42, the resentments are being aired in larger groups, rational and irrational alternatives are discussed, and various clandestine organizations start mushrooming, some of them with distinctly nationalist hues.[98] Enlightening is the experience of a young Ukrainian woman who witnessed the breakdown of the regime in a large industrial city in southern Ukraine, Dniepropetrovsk.[99] Her story is worth quoting in detail as an example.

The source was born in a village in the Province of Poltava and obtained her education the hard way by working in factories and studying at night, until she qualified as a civil engineer. She was a loyal Soviet citizen though she did not like many things: the humiliating comedy of elections ("they made me act like a clown"), the drabness of Soviet cultural life, the senseless terror (it was the time of the Great Purges), and the tendency on the part of newly arrived officials from Russia to call Ukrainians Fascists and to take away their jobs.

As soon as the Germans occupied Dniepropetrovsk she went to the newly organized municipal administration to offer her services in its reconstruction. She noticed a Russian sign on the door and for some reason she cannot explain even today she started talking in Ukrainian, thought most of the time she would speak Russian. The official told her in Russian that there was no work for her, but if she wanted she could help clean up the rubble in the streets. He was a Russian. The source had hoped for a more responsible job, to which she thought her professional education entitled her, and in her resentment she asked the man why he was speaking Russian. "That is none of your business," was his curt reply. It angered her even more, and she left the city hall deeply offended.

She joined her Ukrainian friends outside and told them what had happened. They had had similar experiences, and they started arguing that it was not right for Russians to take over the administration of a Ukrainian city, to refuse decent work to Ukrainians, and, adding insult to injury, to do so in Russian. Rumors cropped up that Hitler favored an independent Ukrainian state and that representatives of the Ukrainian government had already arrived in Dniepropetrovsk by airplane. Friends joined friends, and before she fully became aware of what was happening, she found herself in the midst of a semi-public meeting of prominent Ukrainian citizens. One *litterateur* moved, as a counterpart to the German National Socialist Workers Party (the NSDAP, or Nazi Party), to organize forthwith the Dniepropetrovsk Section of the Ukrainian National Socialist Party. Similar meetings took place everywhere, and before any Galician came to the city the Ukrainian population of Dniepropetrovsk became organized. Within a week or two, the entire city began to speak Ukrainian, though under the Soviet regime that language had been heard only in the outskirts.

The source herself soon joined a Ukrainian Nationalist cell, but she has remained convinced even at the time of the interview that Soviet Ukrainians appreciate the economic and cultural gains made since 1917 and that they would willingly cooperate with the regime on one condition: it must cease to be intolerant of all things Ukrainian.

I have cited her account in detail to show that Ukrainians act differently under the full force of oppression and at the moment when the lid is taken off.

What are the most important conclusions of this study?

Despite terror, population exchange, and ethnic intermarriage; despite the differences between East and West Ukraine and the gulf between the political elite and the common people, the Ukrainians show a rather strong cohesiveness. A degree of national consciousness shared by the people as a whole, however latent, has forced the regime to manipulate Ukrainian national symbols instead of suppressing them altogether. This, for all the distortions, may keep Ukrainian national sentiment alive, even in the absence of alternative channels of communication.

The people do not consider open resistance possible, but wittingly or unwittingly prepare themselves for a struggle by occupying strategic positions in the administrative apparatus. The regime has found it politic to support their endeavor within certain limits because it hopes thus to drive a wedge between the elite and its lesser subjects. In some minds, especially those of Western Ukrainians, the goal of political independence is an axiom; but it may be safely assumed that for the majority of the Ukrainians it is a thesis to be proved. While Ukrainian nationalists will have to show the advantage of separate political existence, their opponents will also be called upon to demonstrate that centralized government from Moscow is the best solution. Insofar as the experience of German occupation can serve as a guide, it would seem that the protagonists of local government by local people will have an advantage over those who uphold central authority. Local people means in any but the Nazi context not only Ukrainians, but Ukrainian Russians, and Ukrainian Jews as well.

To conclude: Should the regime stay in power for a long time, Soviet Ukrainians may find a modus vivendi that would exclude humiliating subservience to the Russians, as practiced during the last decade of Stalin's rule. Should it erode by degrees, in the emerging Kiev the ties to Moscow will be subjected to an extensive scrutiny. A sudden destruction of the center, however, will strain them to the breaking point; for the time when the Ukraine could be regarded as a mere province of the Russian Empire has passed for good. The main task for Soviet Ukrainians and Western statesmen alike is to prepare themselves for all three possibilities, for in statesmanship as in life, "The readiness is all." *

* *Hamlet,* Act V, Scene 2.

NOTES

Notes to Chapter I: Soviet Policy toward the Ukraine after World War II: An Historical Survey

1. See Note I-1, "The Terms 'Nation' and 'Nationalism,'" in the Appendix.
2. See the discussion in John S. Reshetar, Jr., *The Ukrainian Revolution, 1917–20* (Princeton: Princeton University Press, 1952); Richard Pipes, *The Formation of the Soviet Union* (Cambridge, Mass.: Harvard University Press, 1954); and Jurij Borys, *The Russian Communist Party and the Sovietization of Ukraine* (Stockholm, 1960).
3. In my Ph.D. dissertation *Ukrainian Nationalism and Soviet Nationality Policy after World War II* (Department of Politics, Princeton University, 1958), pp. 4–24, I have sketched the development of Ukrainian nationalism since the eighteenth century.
4. See his letter of December 18, 1914 (Old Style) to Dr. O. Nazaruk, a political leader in Galicia and presumably a liaison man for the S.V.U. (Union for the Liberation of the Ukraine), which had been established in Austria, in Symon Petlyura, *Statti, lysty i dokumenty* (Articles, letters, and documents, New York: Ukrainian Academy of Arts & Sciences in the U.S., 1956), pp. 188–90.
5. For two conflicting judgments, see E. Heifetz, *The Slaughter of Jews in the Ukraine in 1919* (New York, 1921) and Arnold D. Margolin, *Ukraina i politika Antanty* (Ukraine and the Policy of the Entente, Berlin, 1921). Mr. Heifetz toured the Ukraine under the auspices of the Red Cross, working for the All-Ukrainian Committee for the Victims of Pogroms; he blames the Ukrainian government for the excesses. The late Dr. Margolin, however, tends to exonerate it. Dr. Margolin had been defense counsel in the famous Beiliss ritual murder case (1911–13) and a member of the Ukrainian government.
6. This refers to the struggle in 1918–20. To be fair, it should be pointed out that in December, 1917, the English and the French offered the Ukrainian Central Rada financial subsidies to continue the war against the Central Powers. The English government seemed to have secretly authorized a sum of £10 million; French agents actually turned over to the Ukrainians an estimated 50 million rubles. See George F. Kennan, *Russia Leaves the War* (Princeton, N.J.: Princeton University Press, 1956), pp. 169, 184.

    In February, 1918, the Central Rada concluded a separate peace with the Central Powers. This might explain why in 1919 the Western Allies would not support the successor government of the Rada.
7. See on this V. Kutschabsky, *Die Westukraine im Kampfe mit Polen und dem Bolschewismus* (Berlin, 1934).
8. Pipes, *op. cit.*, pp. 57ff. See also the verdict of a contemporary Jewish historian, M. O. Rafes, cited in John A. Armstrong, *Ukrainian Nationalism, 1939–45* (New York: Columbia University Press, 1955), p. 13n. The second

revised ed. of the work, entitled *Ukrainian Nationalism* (*ibid.*, 1963), was received too late to be fully considered. Unless specifically indicated, all references are to the first, 1955 edition.

9. See Oliver H. Radkey, *The Election to the Russian Constituent Assembly of 1917* (Cambridge, Mass.: Harvard University Press, 1950), *passim*, esp. pp. 19, 29ff., 79. The Russian Social Revolutionaries (SR's), whose socio-economic program corresponded very closely to that of the Ukrainian Social Revolutionaries, nevertheless obtained fewer votes than the latter.

10. E. H. Carr, *The Bolshevik Revolution, 1917–23*, Vol. I (New York: Macmillan, 1951), p. 300. Pipes, *op. cit.*, pp. 137ff.

11. The Jewish one in particular—see note 5 above.

12. See the appraisals by Reshetar, *op. cit.*, pp. 316–31; Pipes, *op. cit.*, pp. 149–50 and 283–86; and, from a somewhat different viewpoint, in Borys, *op. cit.*, pp. 336–44.

13. Peter Kleist, *Zwischen Hitler und Stalin, 1939–45* (Bonn: Athenaeum, 1950), p. 185. The author was an official connected with the German Foreign Ministry.

14. See Stalin's report to the Congress in *Voprosy Leninizma* (11th ed.; Moscow, 1940), pp. 571ff., and Jane Degras (ed.), *Soviet Documents on Foreign Policy*, (1933–41) Vol. III (London, New York, etc.: Oxford University Press, 1953), pp. 319ff.; the latter issued under the auspices of the Royal Institute for International Affairs (R.I.I.A.). See also Stephen D. Kertesz, *Diplomacy in a Whirlpool: Hungary between Nazi Germany and Soviet Russia* (Notre Dame, Ind.: Notre Dame University Press, 1953), and for an eyewitness report, Michael Winch, *Republic for a Day* (London: Robert Hale Ltd., 1939), *passim*.

15. See e.g., his article written in December 1919, ["Elections to the Constituent Assembly and the Dictatorship of the Proletariat"], in *Sobranie sochineniy* (Collected Works, 2nd. ed.; Moscow, 1923), Vol. XIV, pp. 439–59.

Note that in this and many following references in the book some titles of articles (never books) have been put into square brackets ([ ]). This is to alert the reader that the title has been *translated* from the original Russian or Ukrainian. Both the specialist and the layman will be able to correctly identify the source from the information provided (translated title, journal or book, volume, and pages) and the layman will be spared the transliteration of article titles, some of which are very long.

16. See Stalin's declaration in *Pravda*, December 7, 1917, p. 3 ("Sovet narodnykh kommissarov ob Ukraine"), and Jurij Lawrynenko, *Ukrainian Communism and Soviet Russian Policy toward the Ukraine: An Annotated Bibliography, 1917–53* (New York: Research Program on the USSR, 1953), pp. 76ff.

17. The *Communist International*, No. 7 (December 1924/January 1925), p. 96, as cited by Walter Kolarz, *Russia and Her Colonies* (New York: Praeger, 1952), p. 129.

18. Merle Fainsod, *How Russia Is Ruled* (2nd rev. ed., Cambridge, Mass.: Harvard University Press, 1963), p. 361. The two sections on "Soviet Nationality Policy" (pp. 360–4) and "The Establishment of the USSR and the Constitution of 1924" (pp. 364–70) are a model of condensed, but incisive analysis.

19. See V. A. Slipchenko, ["The CP(B)U (Communist Party [Bolshevik] of Ukraine)—The Organizer of the Destruction of the Kurkul-Nationalist Counter-Revolution in 1921–23"], in Ministerstvo Vyshchoyi Osvity URSR (Ukrainian SSR Ministry of Higher Education), *Naukovi pratsi kafedr suspil'nykh nauk vuziv m. Kieva* (Scholarly Papers of the Social Science Departments of Kiev Higher Schools), Vol. II (Kiev, 1959), pp. 73–90; also A. D. Zalyevs'ky, ["The Destruction of the Kurkul-Nationalist Bands in the Ukraine, 1921–22"], *Ukrayins'ky istorychny zhurnal* (Ukr. Historical Journal), Vol. 1959, No. 4 (August-September), pp. 90–98.

Note that in this and most of the following references to Soviet journal articles throughout the book the volume number has been omitted. Soviet usage attaches little importance to the consecutive numbering of volumes: the numbers are printed in an inconspicuous place and sometimes missing altogether. The uniform Soviet practice is to number anew the pages in each issue and designate the volume by the *year* of publication. This usage may seem incomplete to an American scholar. Actually, it permits unambiguous identification just as easily.

20. For a more extensive discussion of that period see Chapter III in Robert S. Sullivant, *Soviet Politics and the Ukraine, 1917–1957* (New York: Columbia University Press, 1962), esp. pp. 84–96; for a provocatively different account of the reasons for Ukrainization (*korenizatsiya* in the Ukraine) see Roman Smal-Stocki, *The Nationality Problem in the Soviet Union and Russian Communist Imperialism* (Milwaukee: Bruce, 1952), pp. 97–98.

21. On Stalin's letter against the Ukrainian Communist writer Khvylovy, see Fainsod, *op. cit.* (1963 ed.), pp. 369–70. The letter is reproduced in full in George S. N. Luckyj, *Literary Politics in the Soviet Ukraine, 1917–34* (New York: Columbia University Press, 1956), pp. 66–68. See *ibid.*, pp. 66ff. for an analysis of the position of Shumsky, Ukrainian People's Commissar of Education until 1926. A good recent article on that period from the Soviet point of view is F. Yu. Sherstyuk, ["The Exposal and Destruction by the Communist Party of Ukraine of the Nationalist Deviation in 1926–28"], *Ukrayins'ky istorychny zhurnal*, Vol. 1958, No. 3 (May-June), pp. 73–82. Besides Luckyj and Sullivant, *loc. cit.*, see the special study by Iwan Majstrenko, *Borot'bism: A Chapter in the History of Ukrainian Communism* (New York: Research Program on the USSR, 1954), and the annotated documents in Lawrynenko, *op. cit.* The most extensive analytical treatment of the 1920's in the Soviet Ukraine is that by Michael M. Luther: *The Birth of Soviet Ukraine* (unpublished doctoral dissertation, The Department of History, Columbia University, 1963). It is now being prepared for publication.

22. The most complete source of the 1930's is Hryhory Kostiuk, *Stalinist Rule in the Ukraine: A Study of the Decade of Mass Terror, 1929–39* (Munich: Institute for the Study of the USSR, 1960). On a special aspect of that period see also the documents in Ukrainian Association of Victims of Russian Communist Terror, *The Black Deeds of the Kremlin: A White Book* (2 vols.; Toronto, Canada, 1953–56).

23. This expression has been used by Dmytryshyn to denote Soviet nationality policy since 1934—see his *Moscow and the Ukraine, 1918–1953* (New York: Bookman Associates, 1956), pp. 151ff.

24. On German policy in the occupied territories, see the comprehensive monograph by Alexander Dallin, *German Rule in Russia, 1941–45* (London: Macmillan, 1957). On p. 166 Professor Dallin writes: "Germany had entered the Ukraine in the summer of 1941 full of hopes. Handled cleverly, a large part of the Ukrainian population might well have made common cause with the new authorities. The people, by and large, thirsted for relief: their demands were modest. A unique opportunity presented itself. Germany bungled it, and aroused against itself those it had claimed to free." Reprinted with permission of The Macmillan & Company Ltd., St. Martin's Press.

25. *Pravda*, May 25, 1945, p. 1. In the following sentences Stalin said that the Russian people had not done so but had placed complete trust in the Communist leadership. For necessary qualifications, see George Fischer, *Soviet Opposition to Stalin* (Cambridge, Mass.: Harvard University Press, 1952).

26. Armstrong, *op. cit.* (1955 ed.), pp. 287–88. Italics added. Cited by permission of Columbia University Press.

27. Leo Gruliow, ed., *Current Soviet Policies II: The Documentary Record of the 20th Communist Party Congress and Its Aftermath* (New York: Praeger, 1957), p. 182; henceforth cited as *Cur. Soviet Policies II*. Involved were the North Caucasian peoples, such as the Karachai and Kalmyks (end of 1943), the Chechen-Ingush (March, 1944) and Balkars (April, 1944); also the Crimean Tatars. For an earlier admission of disloyalty, see "The Law on the Liquidation of the Chechen Ingush Autonomous SSR and the Transformation of the Crimean ASSR into the Crimean oblast [of the Russian SFSR]," partly cited in Fainsod, *op. cit.* (1st ed., 1953), p. 494. The subject has been treated extensively in R. Conquest, *The Soviet Deportation of Nationalities* (New York: St. Martin's, 1960).

28. See the passage from his speech at the Army Parade in Moscow, November 7, 1941, in his *O velikoy Otechestvennoy voyne Sovetskogo Soyuza* (Great Fatherland War of the USSR, 5th ed.; Moscow, 1952), p. 40.

29. Dmytryshyn, *op. cit.*, pp. 172ff.

30. Before 1944, there existed Lithuanian, Latvian, and Estonian; Georgian, Azerbaidzhani, and Armenian; Kazakh and "some other" national military units. See Molotov's report to the Supreme Soviet and the editorial commentary in *Bol'shevik* (Moscow), Vol. 1944, No. 2 (January), pp. 1ff. Technically speaking, the "All-Union" People's Commissariat of Defense was transformed into a "Union-Republican" Commissariat, dividing the jurisdiction between the Ministry in Moscow and supplementary Ministries in the republics.

31. For a more detailed analysis, see Chapter IX, below.

32. Peter Pirogov, *Why I Escaped* (New York: Duell, Sloan & Pearce, 1950), p. 232. Reprinted by permission of the publisher. See *ibid.*, pp. 215ff., for a perceptive account of how Soviet soldiers came in contact with the western way of life in occupied Germany. Equally revealing of another aspect of the encounter are the short poems "View from the Glorietta [in Vienna]," "St. Stephen's Cathedral," and "Mozart's Cloak," by Ukrainian poet T. Masenko. They were published in the literary magazine *Vitchyzna* (Fatherland [Kiev]), Vol. I, No. 6 (June, 1946), pp. 6off., and later criticized for undue admiration of the West.

33. The resolution is referred to at length in the editorial ["Strengthen the Ideological and Political Work in the Western Provinces"], *Rad. Ukrayina,*

October 29, 1944, p. 1. The original text of the resolution was not available.

34. For a more detailed discussion, see Chapters III and IV, below.

35. See V. Gorshkov, G. Vaulin, L. Rushkovskaya, P. Bol'shakov, "A Harmful Novel," *Bol'shevik*, Vol. 1944, No. 2 (January), pp. 56–64.

36. *Ibid.*, No. 17/18 (September, 1944), p. 4.

37. *Pravda*, May 25, 1945, p. 1. See also Sullivant, *op. cit.*, p. 248.

38. See *Radyans'ka Ukrayina*, May 24, 1946; 1947; 1949; 1950; 1952; and 1953.

39. *Pravda*, February 10, 1946. Reprinted in the highly authoritative *Pytannya partiynoho budivnytstva: Zbirnyk materialiv i dokumentiv na dopomohu partiynomu pratsivnykovi* (Problems in Party "Construction": Collection of materials and documents to help the Party worker, Kiev, 1948), pp. 3–14.

40. "Concerning the Journals *Zvezda* [Star] and *Leningrad*," in *Bol'shevik*, Vol. 1946, No. 17/18 (September), pp. 4–19. Zhdanov's speech elaborated a simultaneous resolution of the Central Committee of the Party, an extract of which was published under the same title. See *Pytannya partiynoho budivnytstva*, pp. 393–96.

41. Cf. the joint decision of the USSR Council of Ministers and the Party Central Committee, "Concerning Measures for the Liquidation of Violations of the Statutes of the Agricultural *Artel'* in the Collective Farms," of September 19, 1946, in *Bol'shevik, ibid.*, pp. 66–70. In the same issue, pp. 70–72, there was reprinted a joint decision "Concerning Measures of Safeguarding the Common Lands of the Kolkhoz from Pilferage," of May 27, 1939.

42. For a list of those resolutions see Note I-2, in the Appendix.

43. "Correct the Mistakes [Committed] in the Elucidation of Some Questions of Ukrainian History," *Kul'tura i zhizn'*, Vol. 1946, No. 3, reprinted in *Rad. Ukrayina*, July 24, 1946.

44. Lazar Sanov, ["The Contemporary Hero and the Feeling of Something New"], *Vitchyzna*, Vol. I, No. 7/8 (July-August, 1946), pp. 260–61.

45. *Pravda*, August 23, 1946. For a more detailed discussion, see Chapters III and VIII below.

46. Pirogov, *op. cit.*, pp. 234ff.

47. See Vsevolod Holubnychy, "Outline History of the Communist Party of the Ukraine," *Ukrainian Review*, Vol. VI (Munich: Institute for the Study of the USSR, 1958), p. 114. Henceforth cited as Holubnychy, "Outline History."

48. See his speech in *Zasedanie Verkhovnogo Soveta USSR (Tret'ya, yubileynaya sessiya): Stenograficheskiy otchet* (Kiev, 1948), pp. 20–25.

49. See Chapter IV, below.

50. See Solomon M. Schwarz, *The Jews in the Soviet Union* (Syracuse, N.Y.: Syracuse University Press, 1951), p. 209.

51. *Pravda*, February 11, 1949, p. 3. See also Note I-3, in the Appendix, on "The Jewish Question in the Ukraine."

52. *Pravda*, May 14, 1950, p. 2. The title of the book was *Iz istorii obshchestvennoy i filosoficheskoy mysli v Azerbaydzhane XIX v.*

53. Cf. "Contrary to the Truth of Life," *Sovetskoye iskusstvo*, April 10, 1951, p. 3; complete translation in *Current Digest of the Soviet Press* [henceforth abbreviated as *CDSP*], Vol. III, No. 15, pp. 11ff.

54. See a biographical sketch entitled "An Inspired Bard of the Socialist Fatherland," in *Rad. Ukrayina* (January 11, 1948).

55. *Ibid.,* April 3, 1948.

56. It was printed, e.g., in the Ukrainian SSR, *Kalendar Dovidnyk na 1945 rik* (Calendar-Almanac for 1945, Kiev, 1945), p. 35.

57. Interview #33.

58. E.g., it is significant that the poem is not mentioned in the anniversary article, cited in footnote 54.

59. *Pravda,* July 2, 1951, p. 2. Condensed translation in *CDSP,* Vol. III, No. 24, pp. 13ff. Most of the following quotations are taken verbatim from the *Current Digest of the Soviet Press,* published at Columbia University by the Joint Committee on Slavic Studies, appointed by the American Council of Learned Societies and the Social Science Research Council. Copyright 1951, the Joint Committee on Slavic Studies. Reprinted by permission.

60. Ukraine, Ministerstvo kul'tury URSR, *Kul'turne budivnytstvo v Ukrayins'kiy RSR* (Cultural Construction in the Ukrainian SSR, Kiev, 1961), Vol. II, pp. 457ff., briefly refers to a Central Committee Communist Party of Ukraine resolution "On the Situation of and Measures for Further Improvement of Ideological Work of the Ukrainian Party Organization," of 1951. That resolution was apparently passed at the Central Committee's plenum of November 20–24, 1951, which discussed that question as the first item on its agenda. See the chronology by P. I. Denysenko *et al.,* ["Materials for the History of the CPU"], *Ukr. istorychny zhurnal,* Vol. 1958, No. 3 (May-June), pp. 130ff.

61. See *Rad. Ukrayina,* September 25, 1952. Local bourgeois nationalism was also denounced at the Party Congresses in Georgia (*Pravda,* September 20), Estonia (*Ibid.,* September 21), Buryat-Mongolia (September 22), Turkmenistan (September 24), Armenia (September 27), Kirghizia (September 27), Uzbekistan (September 28), Lithuania (September 29), and Kazakhstan (September 30). See the convenient summary in *Suchasna Ukrayina* (Today's Ukraine [Munich]), No. 47 (October 19, 1952), p. 4.

62. See Peter Meyer's article "Stalin Follows in Hitler's Footsteps," in Elliott E. Cohen (ed.), *The New Red Anti-Semitism: A Symposium* (Boston: Beacon Press, 1953), pp. 1–18.

63. *Pravda,* January 13, 1953.

64. See, e.g., the article by A. Fadeev, ["On Literary Criticism"], in *Bol'shevik,* Vol. 1947, No. 13 (July 15), pp. 20–35, in which he discusses the correct attitude toward Russian classics (especially, pp. 22ff.). See also A. Pankratova, *Velikiy russkiy narod* (The Great Russian People, 1st ed.; Moscow, 1948), *passim.*

65. *Rad. Ukrayina,* September 16, 1945.

66. Already in 1946 there appeared in *Bol'shevik* a remarkable article rationalizing Soviet nationality policy. See Note I-4, in the Appendix.

67. See Boris Pasternak, *Doktor Zhivago* [in Russian] (Ann Arbor: University of Michigan Press, 1959), p. 530. (The translation of that passage is by the New York *Times,* November 21, 1957, p. 15. Copyright 1957 by The New York Times Company. Reprinted by permission.) For a different English translation see *Doctor Zhivago* (New York: Pantheon, 1958), p. 732.

68. *Pravda Ukrainy,* June 13, 1953, p. 2.

69. See Chapter VIII, below, for a more detailed analysis of developments within the Party.

70. See the statement of the Party Central Committee, the USSR Council of Ministers, and the Presidium of the USSR Supreme Soviet, calling for a country-wide celebration in *Pravda* and *Izvestiya*, December 9, 1953, p. 1 and *CDSP*, Vol. V, No. 49, p. 10; their Theses on the 300th Anniversary of the Reunification of the Ukraine and Russia, *ibid.*, January 12, 1954, and *CDSP*, Vol. V, No. 51, pp. 3ff. The tercentenary celebrations have been well analyzed by John S. Reshetar, Jr., in his article "The Significance of the Soviet Tercentenary of the Pereyaslav Treaty," *Annals of the Ukrainian Academy of Arts and Sciences in the U.S.*, Vol. IV, No. 3 (Winter-Spring, 1955), pp. 981–94. For an analysis of the historical event, see the chapter on historiography (VII), below.

71. Official reasons for the transfer were given as "the integral character of the economy, the territorial proximity and the close economic ties between Crimea Province and the Ukrainian Republic." See the Decree of the Presidium of the USSR Supreme Soviet in *Pravda, Izvestiya*, February 27, 1954, and *CDSP*, Vol. VI, No. 9, pp. 23ff. Voroshilov cited the transfer as "evidence of the further strengthening of the unity and indissoluble friendship between the Russian and the Ukrainian people of the great, mighty fraternal family of the peoples of the USSR." (*Ibid.*, p. 24.) See also Note I-5, in the Appendix.

72. Reshetar, *loc. cit.*, pp. 982ff.

73. *Ibid.*, p. 986. Cited by permission of the Ukrainian Academy of Arts and Sciences in the U.S., Inc.

74. See the report "Response to Party's Call to Develop Virgin Lands," *Pravda* and *Izvestiya*, February 23, 1954; or *CDSP*, Vol. VI, No. 9, p. 7.

75. See Max Frankel's despatch from Kiev on an interview of the American electoral observers delegation with Nikolay Kirichenko, First Secretary of the Ukrainian Komsomol, the *New York Times*, March 11, 1958, p. 11. The word "barren" had been obviously garbled to "*Bahrein* lands in Asia." For a discussion of the figure, see Chapter II, below.

76. See the reports on celebrations in the Ukraine in *Pravda*, August 26, 1956, p. 4, and feature article on p. 2 of *Izvestiya*, same date.

77. *Spravochnik komsomol'skogo propagandista i agitatora* (Reference book for komsomol propagandists and agitators, Moscow, 1957), p. 429. Other cultural anniversaries which were celebrated that year by the World's Peace Council include the 250th anniversary of the birth of Benjamin Franklin and the 200th anniversary of Mozart's birth.

78. *Pravda Ukrainy* (Kiev), September 5, 1956, p. 4.

79. See Chapter VIII, below.

80. N. Kal'chenko at a session of the USSR Supreme Soviet, *Izvestiya*, February 7, 1957, p. 4; or *CDSP*, Vol. X, No. 7, p. 9.

81. Statystychne upravlinnya Ukrayins'koyi RSR (UkrSSR Statistical Administration), *Narodne hospodarstvo Ukrayins'koyi RSR: Statystychny zbirnyk* (National Economy of Ukrainian SSR: A Statistical Handbook, Kiev, 1957), pp. 21, 488. Henceforth abbreviated as *Nar. hosp. URSR (1957)*.

82. *Cur. Soviet Policies II*, p. 182.

83. *Pravda*, February 15, 1956; or *Cur. Soviet Policies II*, p. 52. That excerpt from his speech is quoted in extenso and analyzed in Chapter VIII, below.

84. V. I. Lenin, ["On the Question of Nationalities or 'Autonomization'"], note dated December 30–31, 1922, *Kommunist*, Vol. 1956, No. 9 (June), pp. 22–26; or *Kommunist Ukrainy* (Communist of Ukraine, Kiev, Rus. ed.), Vol. 1956, No. 7 (July), pp. 19–23.

85. Translation also in *Cur. Soviet Policies II,* p. 193.
86. See the editorial ["On the Ideological Firmness (*ideynost'*) of a Communist"], *Kommunist,* Vol. 1956, No. 9 (June), pp. 12–13. This comes out very
well in O. Prosyanyk's review article ["V. I. Lenin on the Unity of Action
and the Fraternal Friendship of the Ukrainian and Russian Peoples"],
Komunist Ukrayiny (Ukr. ed.), Vol. 1957, No. 10, pp. 14–24, esp. on p.
24, where the author discusses Lenin's important "Project of a Resolution
of the Central Committee of the Russian Communist Party (Bolshevik)
(RKP(b)) Central Committee on Soviet Power in the Ukraine," of November 21, 1919, and Lenin's note on "autonomization." The former may
be consulted in Lenin's *Sochineniya* (Works, 1950 ed.), Vol. 30, pp. 142–
44; it has been translated in Borys, *op. cit.,* pp. 349–50.
87. See the editorial ["Under the Sign of Leninist Unity"], *Komunist Ukrayiny* (Ukr. ed.), Vol. 1957, No. 7 (July), pp. 1–6.
88. *K.U.* (Ukr. ed.), Vol. 1957, No. 7 (July), pp. 26–36.
89. "Uspekhy natsional'noy politiki KPSS i nekotorye voprosy internatsional'-
nogo vospitaniya (Successes of the CPSU Nationality Policy and Some
Problems of Internationalist Education)," *Kommunist,* Vol. 1958, No. 11
(August), pp. 10–24.
90. See Pipes, *op. cit.,* pp. 14 and *passim.*
91. Until the middle 1950's Gandhi was denounced by Soviet writers as an
agent of British imperialism. Then the Soviet attitude was suddenly and
drastically changed, and Gandhi was respected as a progressive national
leader. See on this Alvin Z. Rubinstein. *The Foreign Policy of the Soviet
Union* (New York: Random House, 1960), pp. 378–79, 385–86.
92. Khrushchev did not dwell on the problem to any extent, nor was it discussed in the Congress's resolutions. But a fairly clear statement of the
Party's policy is contained in N. Mukhitdinov's speech at the Congress.
See *Pravda,* January 31, 1959, pp. 7–8; or *Current Soviet Policies III* (New
York: Columbia University Press, 1960), pp. 104–08.
93. In December, 1958, the First Secretary of the Central Committee of the
Communist Party of Turkmenia was dismissed with several other responsible officials for his opposition to the employment of non-Turkmen cadres
in his Republic. See *Turkmenskaya Iskra* (Spark of Turkmenia), December 16, 1958 and January 20, 1959; or *CDSP,* Vol. IX, No. 9, pp. 31–32.
Also, *Pravda,* February 5, 1959, p. 3, or *Cur. Sov. Policies III,* p. 166. In
July, 1959, the First Secretary of the Azerbaydzhani Party Mustafaev was
ousted for a number of reasons, apparently including the assertion of
Azerbaydzhani cultural interests against the center—see *Bakinskiy Rabo-
chiy* (Worker of Baku), July 11, 1959, pp. 1–2 (*CDSP,* Vol. XI, No. 37,
pp. 19–22). A similar purge took place in the summer of 1959 in Latvia,
involving ultimately the First Party Secretary of Latvia—see, e.g., *Sovetskaya Latviya,* November 18, 1961, pp. 1–3 (*CDSP,* Vol. XIII, No. 46, p.
45). The purges in Azerbaydzhan and Latvia have been discussed in more
detail in the present writer's article "The Soviet Education Laws of 1958–
59 and Soviet Nationality Policy," *Soviet Studies,* Vol. XIV (October 1962),
pp. 146–48. Professor Herbert Ritvo in his extensive commentary on the
new Program of the CPSU states: "Preference for 'national cadres' was
among the most serious of the charges presented in the 1959 purges of the
Party leaderships in Azerbaidzhan, Kirghizia, Tadzhikistan and Latvia," in
The New Soviet Society (New York: New Leader, 1962), p. 200, note 282.

94. "The Tasks of Party Propaganda in Present Day Conditions," *Pravda,* January 10, 1960, pp. 1–2; or *CDSP,* Vol. XII, No. 2, pp. 17–23. See esp. paragraph 4 (p. 20 in *CDSP*).

95. Part 2, Section IV: "The Tasks of the Party in the Field of National Relations." Several editions, the best is that edited by Ritvo, *op. cit.,* pp. 188–91.

96. *Rad. Ukrayina* and *Pravda Ukrainy,* February 14, 1959. I. V. Shul'ha and V. I. Yurchuk in their article ["Party Organizations of the Ukraine in the Struggle for the Realization of the Decisions of the Twenty-First Congress of the Communist Party of the Soviet Union (CPSU)"], *Ukrayins'ky istorychny zhurnal,* Vol. 1961, No. 5 (September-October), pp. 11–20, refer to a Central Committee of the Communist Party of Ukraine plenary session in February, 1959. A reference to that session could not be obtained from the daily press.

97. The resolution of the Central Committee CPSU was first mentioned in a *Pravda* editorial "Raise Political Agitation to the Level of Seven Year Plan Tasks," March 10, 1959, as having been passed "recently." Its text was not published. See *CDSP,* Vol. XI, No. 21, p. 20.

98. ["The Tasks of the Party Organizations of the Ukraine in Relation to the Strengthening of Non-Political Work among the Toilers"], *Rad. Ukrayina,* May 22, 1959, pp. 1–2.

99. See Note 94, above.

100. See the excerpts from the proceedings of the Congress (A. D. Skaba's, M. Podgorny's addresses, etc.) translated in *Digest of the Soviet Ukrainian Press* (henceforth–DSUP), Vol. IV, No. 4 (April, 1960), pp. 8–10; or *Rad. Ukrayina,* Feb. 19 and 21, 1960.

101. See the announcement of the plenum in *Pravda Ukrainy,* April 27, 1960; the resolution ["On the State of Ideological Work in the Ukraine and Measures for its Improvement"], *ibid.,* April 30, 1960, p. 1, par. 5.

102. ["Towards a New Higher Level of Ideological Work"], *Kommunist,* Vol. 1960, No. 14 (September), pp. 22–40. Since the Twenty-Second Congress of the Communist Party of the Soviet Union Il'ichev has been a Secretary of the CPSU Central Committee.

103. See *Rad. Ukrayina,* Feb. 20, 1962, pp. 1ff.

104. See *ibid.,* August 11, 1962, p. 1 or *DSUP,* Vol. VI, No. 9 (September, 1962), p. 19; also Editorial, ["For a Close Link between Ideological and Organizational Work"], *Komunist Ukrayiny* (Ukr. ed.), Vol. 1962, No. 8 (August), pp. 7–14.

105. Best account in *Ukr. istorychny zhurnal,* Vol. 1961, No. 1 (January-February), pp. 154ff. Very briefly mentioned in *Pravda Ukrainy,* Sept. 30, 1960, p. 2.

106. Best account in *Ukr. istorychny zhurnal,* Vol. 1961, No. 5 (September-October), pp. 165–66. Also *Rad. Ukrayina,* May 28, 1961, p. 1.

107. A. I. Novikov, ["The Education of Toilers in the Spirit of the Friendship of Peoples and Socialist Internationalism at the Current Phase (of Socialist Growth)"], *Ukr. istorychny zhurnal,* Vol. 1961, No. 5 (September-October), p. 24.

108. See above, pp. 12ff.

109. A. Metchenko, A. Dement'ev, G. Lomidze, ["For a Thorough Elucidation of the History of Soviet Literature"], *Kommunist,* Vol. 1956, No. 12 (August), p. 91. *Pravda* was attacked indirectly through criticism of the *Out-*

line of the History of Soviet Ukrainian Literature that had copied *Pravda's* verdict on the poem. It is, however, noteworthy, that the poem was never restored to the place it had held in 1944: neither in 1956 nor later.

110. *Pravda Ukrainy,* July 28, 1956, p. 3.

111. See the decree of the Presidium of the USSR Supreme Soviet, of December 29, 1954: "No. 3: On Transforming the All-Union Ministry of Higher Education into the USSR Union-Republican Ministry of Higher Education," *Vedomosti Verkhovnogo Soveta SSSR,* Vol. 1955, No. 1 (p. 3).

112. V. Holubnychy, "The Language of Instruction: An Aspect of the Problem of Nationalities in the Soviet Union," *Horizon* (Ukrainian Students Review [New York]), Vol. II, No. 1/2 (Fall 1956/Spring 1957), p. 36, *et passim*. Before 1946, most of the higher schools in the Ukraine had been under Republican jurisdiction. As of the summer of 1954, however, only 62,000 college students in the UkrSSR out of a total of 275,000 were studying at higher schools under the jurisdiction of the Republic—213,000 attended All-Union schools. See Panas Fedenko, *Ukrayina pislya smerty Stalina* (Ukraine after Stalin's Death, Munich: Institute for the Study of the USSR, 1956), p. 56 (mimeographed).

113. M. Cholobit'ko, as cited by the monthly newssheet *Vil'ny Ukrayins'ky Robitnyk* (Free Ukrainian Worker, Paris), December, 1956.

114. Cited in M. Dobryans'ky, "Sabotaging the Ukrainian Book," *Hovoryt' Radio Vyzvolennya* (Radio Liberation Speaking, Munich), Vol. II (1957), pp. 66ff. [Italics added.]

115. *Loc. cit.* (Note 110, above).

116. "The Participants of the Plenum Have the Word," *Literaturna Hazeta* (Literary Gazette [Kiev]), Vol. 1958, No. 18 (March 4), p. 3.

117. See, e.g., the notice "Following Unpublished Letters [to the Editor]," *ibid.,* Vol. 1958, No. 8 (January 28), p. 3, in which the official in charge promises to supply rural libraries in the Stalino oblast with Ukrainian books; and the letter "Increase the Editions," in which a certain M. Halushko complains that his village library in the Kirovograd oblast does not contain enough Soviet Ukrainian belles-lettres, because they are printed in very small editions (*ibid.,* Vol. 1958, No. 19 [March 7], p. 4).

118. L. Horovy, "Rejoinder to Folklorists [H. Sukhobrus and V. Yuzvenko (comps.), *Ukrayins'ki narodni kazky, lehendy, anekdoty* (Kiev, 1957)]," *ibid.,* Vol. 1958, No. 16 (February 25), p. 3.

119. See *ibid.,* Vol. 1958, No. 15 (February 21), p. 3.

120. *Ibid.,* and No. 18, *loc. cit. Vsesvit* is a monthly; its edition in October, 1962 was 19,000. See bibliographical article by Bohdan Kravatsiv, ["Journals and Newspapers in the Ukrainian SRR"], *Svoboda, Al'manakh na rik 1963* (Almanac for 1963, Jersey City, N.J., 1963), p. 82.

121. *Ibid.,* Vol. 1958, No. 12 (February 11), p. 4. Other papers that were announced were: M. K. Hudziy, on the Ancient Literature of Kievan Rus; T. Rylsky on problems of translating from one Slavic language into another; Bulakhovsky on the role of the ancient Bulgarian language. All three are top-flight scholars.

122. "On the Strengthening of the Relationship of the School with Life and on Further Development of the System of Public Education in the Country," *Pravda,* November 14, 1958; translation from George S. Counts, *Khrushchev and the Central Committee Speak on Education* (University of Pittsburgh Press, 1959), pp. 45–46. Reprinted with permission of the University of Pittsburgh Press.

123. See Y. Bilinsky, *loc. cit.*, pp. 140–42.
124. S. Bysykalo in *Rad. Ukrayina,* November 25, 1958, p. 3.
125. *Pravda,* December 22, 1958, p. 3.
126. See his article ["Life Demands This"], *Komunist Ukrayiny,* Vol. 1958, No. 12 (December), p. 23.
127. Bilinsky, *loc. cit.* (n. 93), p. 140.
128. *Zasedaniya Verkhovnogo Soveta SSSR, 5 sozyva, II sessiya (22–25 dekabrya 1958 g.) Stenograficheskiy otchet* (Sessions of the USSR Supreme Soviet, 5th convocation, 2nd session [22–25 December 1958]. Stenographic report, Moscow, 1959), p. 356. See also p. 297 for the statement by the other Ukrainian deputy (Hrechukha).
129. *Rad. Ukrayina,* April 19, 1959, p. 2.
130. See above, p. 26.
131. In his article "Along the Path of the Leninist Friendship of Peoples," *Rad. Ukrayina,* March 27, 1959, pp. 3–4.
132. "V. I. Lenin on the Russian and the National Languages of Our Country," *Rad. Ukrayina,* April 13, 1960, pp. 3–4. See also *DSUP,* Vol. IV, No. 5 (May 1960), pp. 6–10, for a condensed translation. Related materials, *ibid.,* pp. 1–6.
133. Iv. M-ko [Majstrenko], "How to Understand the Law of the UkrSSR Supreme Soviet," *Vpered* (Munich), Vol. 1959, No. 7 (July), p. 4.
134. S. Chervonenko, ["Close Connection with Life is the Condition for Successful Ideological Work"], *Komunist Ukrayiny* (Ukr. ed.), Vol. 1959, No. 7 (July), p. 38. Also Yu. Shiraev, "Paths of Further Rapprochement of the Nations in the USSR," *Pravda Ukrainy,* July 25, 1959, pp. 2–3. See also Chapter V, below.
135. See *Ukrayins'ka mova v shkoli,* Vol. 1959, No. 4 (April), p. 5.
136. Said Malyshko: "Only, I think, the editions of our [i.e., Ukrainian—Y.B.] books ought to be increased. Poetry appears in editions of 8,000, prose in those of 15,000. This is a drop in the sea for a population of forty million." *Rad. Ukrayina,* October 1, 1961, p. 6. See also the complaints by Maria Pryhara and Natalia Zabila, Ukrainian children's writers, that between 1958 and 1959 editions of Ukrainian children's books have been drastically cut from 150,000–200,000 to 18,000–40,000 [sic] copies, ostensibly because of "clumsy workers in book distribution." (*Literaturna Hazeta,* December 5, 1958, p. 5; or *DSUP,* Vol. III, No. 1 (January, 1959), pp. 22–24. Similar complaints by O. Mykylenko, *Rad. Ukrayina,* Oct. 8, 1959, p. 3.
137. "Reply to Vira Bondar," by O. Dyachenko, *Literaturna Ukrayina* (Literary Ukraine), January 18, 1963, p. 3.
138. "In a Free, New Family: Notes on the Mutual Enrichment of National Cultures," *Izvestiya,* December 5, 1961, p. 4.
139. See, e.g., his article "Overcoming the Nationalist Survivals Is an Important Task of the Internationalist Education of Toilers," in *Robitnycha Hazeta* (Workers' Gazette [Kiev]), December 17, 1958, pp. 3–4. Also his pamphlet *Razvitie natsional'nykh otnosheniy v SSSR* (Development of National Relations in the USSR, Kiev, 1962).
140. See his ["In a Free, New Family"], *Kommunist Ukrainy* (Rus. ed.), Vol. 1962, No. 12 (December), pp. 45–47. Rylsky's entire article is in effect a polemic against the assimilationist thesis of Agaev's, though he does not mention his name.
141. ["Tons and grams"], *Dnipro,* Vol. 1961, No. 11 (November), pp. 135–45. In that article Antonenko-Davydovych urges great respect for the Ukrain-

ian language that is frequently mutilated in official media. As motto he has chosen Mayakovsky's verse "For about a gram of product, you spend about a year for a single word's sake, [work through] thousands of tons of verbal ore."

142. Dyachenko's article, which was later printed as a pamphlet and was boy-cotted by an employee of the Kharkov book distribution agency, entitled ["Reflections on Human Characters (Depiction in Belles-Lettres of National Character and of Its Evolution)"], *Vitchyzna*, Vol. 1962, No. 11 (November), pp. 139–52, attempts to show that Communism can be reached only through the development of the national, not through the denial of it.

143. "Character and Abstractions," *Literaturna Ukrayina,* January 29, 1963, pp. 2ff.

144. See above, pp. 21 and 33, note 138.

145. See the report by an educator from Kiev "Dolya ridnoyi movy" (The Fate of [Our] Native Language), *Nasha kul'tura* (Our Culture), Vol. 1963, No. 3 (March, 1963), pp. 5–6. *Nasha kul'tura* is a monthly supplement to the weekly *Nashe slovo* (Our Word, a Ukrainian-language paper published in Warsaw for Ukrainians in Poland). This and related material has been conveniently summarized in English in S. Dovhal, "A Fight for the Language," *Problems of the Peoples of the USSR* (Munich), No. 18 (June, 1963), p. 47. Our quotation in the text is a translation from the original, which has been located with Mr. Dovhal's kind assistance.

The two Soviet accounts used by the author—V. Koptilov, ["For a High Culture of the Ukrainian Language"], in *Literaturna Ukrayina* (Kiev), February 26, 1963, and the chronicle entitled ["A Conference on Problems of the Culture of Language"], in *Ukrayins'ka mova i literatura v shkoli* (Ukranian Language and Literature at School, Kiev [the professional journal of teachers of the Ukr. language and literature]), Vol. 1963, No. 2 (April), pp. 91–93—confirm that such a conference took place, give a few details, but do *not* substantiate the report in *Nasha kul'tura*. The Polish paper has the reputation of being more outspoken in such matters than the heavily censored Soviet-Ukrainian publications.

Notes to Chapter II: Some Factors Underlying Ukrainian Nationalism

1. See Tsentral'noe Statisticheskoe Upravlenie pri Sovete Ministrov SSSR (Central Statistical Administration of the USSR Council of Ministers), *Narodnoe khozaystvo SSSR v 1960 godu: Statisticheskiy ezhegodnik* (National Economy of the USSR in 1960: Statistical Yearbook, Moscow, 1961), pp. 14, 18, 858, 860. Henceforth, the source will be abbreviated *Nar. khoz. SSSR, 1960*. (A square kilometer is 0.3861 sq. mile [approximately one-third].)

2. Demitri B. Shimkin, *Minerals—A Key to Soviet Power* (Cambridge, Mass.: Harvard University Press, 1953), p. 310.

3. See D. Korotchenko, ["In the Fraternal Family of Soviet Peoples—Toward Communism"], *Kommunist Ukrainy* (Rus. ed.), Vol. 1962, No. 12 (December), p. 31.

4. In 1953 the total area under cultivation in the Ukrainian SSR comprised 30,970,000 hectares, that in the whole of the USSR—157,172,000 hectares.

(A hectare is equal to 2.471 acres.) In 1960, the corresponding figures were 33,547,000 hectares out of 202,985,000. See *Nar. khoz. SSSR, 1960,* pp. 392–93.

5. See *ibid.,* pp. 454 and 452. (18.2 out of 58.7 million hogs, 17.6 out of 75.8 million big horned cattle, as of January 1, 1961.)

6. Output figure for 1960 from Table II-2, estimated population (January 1, 1961) from *Nar. khoz. SSSR, 1960,* p. 8. (A kilogram equals 2.2 lbs.)

7. Shimkin, *op. cit.,* p. 47.

8. See *ibid.* for a technical description.

9. A. Nesterenko, "Rol' Ukrainskoy SSR v sozdanii material'no-tekhnicheskoy bazy kommunizma (Role of the Ukrainian SSR in the Establishment of a Material-Technological Base for Communism)," *Ekonomika Sovetskoy Ukrainy* (Economy of Soviet Ukraine), Vol. 1961, No. 6 (November-December), p. 20.

10. Shimkin, *op. cit.,* pp. 6off.

11. *Ibid.,* pp. 162ff.

12. P. V. Kryven', ed., *Ukrayins'ka RSR: ekonomichno-heohrafichna kharakterystyka* (The Ukrainian SSR: An Economical and Geographical Characterization, Kiev, 1961), p. 16. Source is a college textbook.

13. Shimkin, *op. cit.,* p. 191.

14. Calculated by author by taking the total Donbas reserves (*ibid.,* p. 189) and subtracting 22 per cent of the total to account for reserves outside the Ukrainian SSR, and by adding 0.5 billion tons of Western Ukrainian reserves. A more recent Soviet source estimates the Western Ukrainian reserves at 1.2 to 2.0 billion tons, but admits that they are hard to mine. See O. T. Dibrova, *Heohrafiya Ukrayins'koyi RSR* (Geography of the Ukrainian SSR, Kiev, 1961), p. 27. Source is a secondary school textbook.

15. In 1950, 29.9 per cent of the total Soviet output or 78.0 out of 261.1 million tons; 32.2 per cent in 1956, or 137.7 out of 429.2 million tons; 33.5 per cent in 1960 or 172.1 out of 513.2 million tons. See Tsentral'noe Statisticheskoe Upravlenie pri Sovete Ministrov SSSR, *Narodnoe khozaystvo SSSR v 1956 godu* (National Economy of USSR in 1956, Moscow, 1957), p. 74 and *Nar. khoz. SSSR, 1960,* p. 258. Former source henceforth abbreviated *Nar. khoz. SSSR, 1956.*

16. In 1960, out of a total of 172.1 million metric tons, the Donbas produced 156.2 million, the coal mines in Volhynia and Lviv oblasts (Western Ukraine) yielded but 3.0 million. See Tsentral'ne statystychne upravlinnya pry Radi Ministriv URSR (Central Statistical Administration of the Ukr-SSR Council of Ministers), *Narodne hospodarstvo Ukrayins'koyi RSR v 1960 rotsi* (National Economy of Ukrainian SSR in 1960, Kiev, 1961), p. 55. Henceforth cited as *Nar. hosp. URSR, 1960.*

17. See *Nar. khoz. SSSR, 1960,* p. 258. (78.2 per cent of the total, or 22.8: 29.2 million tons.)

18. Harry Schwartz, *Russia's Soviet Economy* (1st ed.; New York: Prentice Hall, 1950), p. 207.

19. See *Nar. khoz. SSSR, 1960,* pp. 264 (oil) and 267 (natural gas).

20. Shimkin, *op. cit.,* pp. 222ff., especially pp. 231ff.

21. See Tsentral'noe Statisticheskoe Upravlenie pri Sovete Ministrov SSSR (Central Statistical Administration of the USSR Council of Ministers), *Promyshlennost' SSSR: Statisticheskiy sbornik* (USSR Industry: A Statistical Compilation, Moscow, 1957), p. 18. As of 1957, the Ukrainian share of

industrial capital had remained constant at 20.2 per cent of the USSR total, while the Russian share increased to 64.5 per cent. The Russian figure, however, has not been broken down further. See same author, *Narodnoe khozaystvo SSR v 1958 godu* (National Economy of USSR in 1958), p. 134. The general statistical yearbook for 1960 (*Nar. khoz. SSSR, 1960*) does not give any corresponding figures at all.

22. See *Nar. khoz. SSSR, 1960*, p. 84, for a summary description of the operation.

23. V. Burlin, M. Darahan, Ye. Dolhopolov, "Pereotsinka osnovnykh fondiv URSR ta yiyi znachennya" (Re-evaluation of the Basic [Capital] Funds of the UkrSSR and Its Meaning), *Ekonomika Radyans'koyi Ukrayiny* (Economy of Soviet Ukraine), Vol. 1960, No. 6 (November-December), p. 8, and *Nar. khoz. SSSR, 1958*, p. 133.

24. Nesterenko, *loc. cit.,* p. 20.

25. Calculated from table in *Nar. khoz. SSSR, 1960*, pp. 244–45.

26. *Ibid.,* p. 272.

27. Ts.S.U. SRSR—Statystychne Upravlinnya Ukrayins'koyi RSR (Central Statistical Adm'ion of the USSR Council of Ministers—Statistical Administration of the Ukr. SSR), *Narodne hospodarstvo Ukrayins'koyi RSR: Statystychny zbirnyk* (National Economy of the Ukrainian SSR: A Statistical Compilation, Kiev, 1957), p. 34. Henceforth cited as *Nar. hosp. URSR (1957)*.

28. The author has consulted tables on the output, in 1960, of chemical fertilizer, cement, and bricks. In 1959 (when the census was taken) the population of the Ukrainian SSR was 41.9 million or 20.0 per cent of the total USSR population of 208.8 million. (*Nar. khoz. SSSR, 1960*, pp. 8, 280, 308, and 314.)

29. In 1955, the Ukraine produced about one-half of the Union supply (*Promyshlennost' SSSR*, p. 195).

30. In 1960 27.8 per cent of mineral fertilizers produced in USSR (*Nar. khoz. SSSR, 1960*, p. 280).

31. In 1955 4.8 out of 5.6 million sq. meters (*Promyshlennost' SSSR*, p. 298). The present writer has also consulted 1960 figures on the output of cement (*Nar. khoz. SSSR, 1960*, p. 308) and construction bricks (*ibid.,* p. 314). With respect to the two latter commodities, Ukrainian output is more or less equal to the USSR per capita average.

32. For instance, 97.4 per cent of all Soviet coal mining "combines," 100 per cent of beet harvesters and 88 per cent of main line locomotives. See Nesterenko, *loc. cit.,* p. 20; also Chart II-1.

33. *Nar. khoz. SSSR, 1960*, p. 288.

34. *Nar. hosp. URSR, 1960*, p. 62; *Nar. khoz. SSSR, 1960*, p. 291.

35. Calculated from tables *ibid.* pp. 325–28. Bohdan Vynar proves that in the seventeenth and eighteenth centuries there were solid beginnings of a textile home industry in the Ukraine. Its development was, however, cut short by the policy of the Tsars who favored Russian merchant capitalists. See his *Rozvytok ukrayins'koyi lehkoyi promyslovosty* (Development of Ukrainian Light Industry; Denver, Colo.: Zarevo, 1955), pp. 7ff.

36. Calculated from figures in *Nar. khoz. SSSR, 1960*, pp. 335–36.

37. *Ibid.,* p. 339.

38. This can be easily inferred from the output figures *ibid.,* p. 228. In the 20 years from 1940–60, the output of electric power in the USSR as a whole

increased sixfold from 48.3 to 292.3 billion kwh, but in the eastern regions it increased almost eleven times from 10.7 to 117.5 billion kwh. All the industries for which figures have been given (power generation; production of pig iron, steel, and rolled metals; output of iron ore, oil, and natural gas) are rather capital intensive. On pp. 598–99 the same source gives direct figures on capital investments of various republics, but these figures are less useful since the eastern regions of the Russian SFSR have not been singled out.

39. *Ibid.,* p. 227. Economists may object to the use of these figures since (1) they are based on *three* sets of prices (the constant prices of 1926–27, wholesale prices as of January 1, 1952, and as of July 1, 1955—see *ibid.,* p. 876 for the method of computation) and (2) since Soviet prices may be arbitrary between various products as well as over time. But these are the best figures that have been made available.

40. Vorob'ev remarks in ["Development of National Relations in the Period of Constructing Communism"], *Kommunist Ukrainy* (Rus. ed.), Vol. 1962, No. 1 (January), pp. 35–36, that the Ukraine exports special machine tools receives other kinds of machine tools *(stanki)* from Gorky in the Russian Republic. A. Kochubey, Deputy Director of the UkrSSR State Planning Board, in "Life-giving Associations," *Rad. Ukrayina,* March 20, 1962, pp. 3–4, or *Digest of the Soviet Ukr. Press,* Vol. VI, No. 5 (May, 1962), pp. 8–9 describes the trading activity of the Ukrainian SSR as follows:

> Our Republic is a great supplier of locomotives, tractors, electrotechnical equipment, special tools, metallurgical and mine equipment, freight cars, agricultural machinery, pumps and compressors, and engineering equipment for light, food and printing industries. The Ukrainian SSR covers a wide range of exports of mass produced goods, as well as foundry products, and forged and stamped goods.
>
> In turn, huge amounts of a variety of products made by the hands of the brotherly nations of the USSR, come to Ukraine. The largest percentage of freight comes to us from the R[ussian] SFSR. Our Republic maintains particularly strong economic ties with the Northwestern, Ural, Volga, North Caucasian, and other regions. The Central region of the Russian Federation plays an especially important role. From this region Ukraine gets machine and engineering equipment, tools, precision instruments, trucks, locomotives, truck tires, wool, cotton, linen and other textiles, etc. The West Siberian region gives us lumber and allied material; and the Far East—fish, fish products and minerals.
>
> Our ties are flowering from year to year with Kazakhstan, Georgia, Belorussia, and Moldavia. Transcaucasia, for example, ships us petroleum and oil products, pipe, locomotives, as well as citrus fruit and tea. The Baltic republics give us railroad passenger cars and radio equipment.

41. My calculation, by slide rule, from the data in Table II-6.

42. Frank Lorimer, *The Population of the Soviet Union* (Geneva: League of Nations, 1946), p. 162.

43. Figure for USSR from *Nar. khoz. SSSR, 1958,* p. 7; that for the Ukrainian SSR, my calculation from data in Table II-6.

44. Lorimer, *op. cit.,* pp. 154, 158.

45. Calculated by author on the basis of figures in *Nar. khoz. SSSR, 1960,* p.

10. It should be noted that the Soviet figures for 1939 are, in effect, later figures embodying the boundary changes through 1945, at least; probably also the incorporation of Crimea in 1954.

46. Nikolay Lyalikov, *Sovetskaya Ukraina: ocherk ekonomicheskoy geografii* (Soviet Ukraine: An Outline of Economic Geography, Moscow, 1954), pp. 94ff. The net immigration into the eastern regions of the RSFSR (from all over the country) was over 3 million people in that period; into the Central Asian Republics—1.4–1.7 million (see Lorimer, *op. cit.,* pp. 164, 169).

47. Lorimer, *op. cit.,* p. 161.

48. *Ibid.,* p. 163.

49. *Ibid.,* p. 136. Lorimer's method has been criticized by another demographer, Basilius Martschenko, a former employee of Soviet census authorities. See his "Soviet Population Trends, 1926–39" (New York: Research Program on the USSR, 1953, pp. 28–32. (Mimeographed.)

50. Dmytro Solovey, *Lyudnist' Ukrayiny za sorok rokiv vlady TsK KPSS u svitli perepysiv* (The Population of the Ukraine for the Last Forty Years under the Rule of the Communist Party of the Soviet Union, Detroit, Mich.: Vil'na hromada, 1961), p. 12.

51. For projection the rates 0.55 per cent (annual population increase in Ukrainian SSR, 1926–39) and 1.25 per cent (average USSR increase, 1926–39) have been used. Cf. Vsevolod Holubnychy, "Statistics of the Population of the Ukraine, 1940–56," *Vpered* (Forward [Munich]), No. 71 (October, 1956), pp. 2–3. Holubnychy is an American-trained economist and author of numerous articles on Ukrainian affairs. He has chosen the intermediate rate of 1.00 per cent as the most realistic, it would have given, for 1959, a Ukrainian SSR population of 48.6 million. (The author has extrapolated Holubnychy's figures through the census of 1959.) In all these changes the results from several boundary changes (1945, 1954) have already been taken into account.

  Throughout this paragraph as base population figures for 1940 have been chosen the latest official estimates—40.5 million for the Ukrainian SSR and 190.7 million for the USSR (see Table II-6)—in order to achieve greater consistency. In his article Holubnychy has used another population figure for the Ukraine in 1940—viz., 41.0 million. It is taken from Tsentral'noe Statisticheskoe Upravlenie SSSR (USSR Central Statistical Administration), *Narodnoe khozaystvo SSSR: Statisticheskiy sbornik* (USSR National Economy, A statistical handbook; Moscow, 1956), p. 18. As usual in Soviet statistics, the earlier figure was changed without any explanation (see also the brief discussion in the present book, p. 50). In our projections we have used the time span of 18 years (from the end of 1940 till the beginning of 1959).

52. See the figures on p. 47, above.

53. Akademiya nauk Ukr. SSR, Instytut ekonomiki (UkrSSR Academy of Sciences, Institute of Economics), *Ocherki razvitiya narodnogo khozaystva Ukrainskoy SSR* (Outline of the Development of the National Economy of the Ukrainian SSR, Moscow, 1954), p. 443, as cited by Holubnychy, *loc. cit.*

54. *Ibid.,* p. 442.

55. Holubnychy's estimate was on the basis of Warren Eason's finding that before the war men at the age of 16–59 comprised 26.5 per cent of the total population. The total of 11 million (see below, in main text) has

been thus derived as follows: 1.5 million civilians killed by Germans, *plus* 3 million deported to Germany, *plus* 3.5 million army draftees, *plus* 4 million evacuated to the eastern provinces of the USSR, is 12 million, from which we *subtract* one million people ceded to Poland in 1945.

56. Solovey, *op. cit.,* pp. 14–15. See also the analysis by V. S. Holubnychy, "Unpublished Data of the USSR Population Censuses," *Vestnik instituta po izucheniyu SSR* (Bulletin of Institute for the Study of the USSR [Munich]), Vol. 1960, No. 2 (April-June), pp. 66–72, esp. p. 72.

57. *Ibid.,* pp. 15–24. Among other sources Solovey cites Solomon Schwarz, a very careful student of the Soviet Union. If that figure still seems implausibly high, the reader should bear in mind Khrushchev's well-known statement that after World War II Stalin would have exiled all forty million Ukrainians, except that he did not know where to banish them to.

58. On re-occupation all suspects would be tried; some were deported to the East. Interview #75. On the wholesale deportation of Crimean Tatars see Note I-5, in the Appendix.

59. Such deportations have been officially acknowledged in the Order No. 312, of December 30, 1949, by the Ukrainian SSR Minister of State Security Koval'chuk. The order promised that the families of those insurgents who would surrender to the authorities would be returned from deportation. See Chapter IV, below, and Note IV-1, in the Appendix, for exact citation and discussion of its authenticity.

60. Solovey, *op. cit.,* pp. 32–53. Summary figure, *ibid.,* p. 76.

61. Eugene M. Kulischer, *Europe on the Move: War and Population Changes, 1917–1947* (New York: Columbia University Press, 1948), p. 292. Kulischer has used Polish official statistics.

62. *Ibid.,* p. 301. See also the reports in *Radyans'ka Ukrayina,* November 28, and December 3, 1944; August 17, 1945.

63. Kulischer, *op. cit.,* pp. 287–88.

64. As of 1936, no later data available. See Akademiya nauk URSR, Instytut Ekonomiky (UkrSSR Academy of Science, Institute of Economics), *Narysy ekonomichnoyi heohrafiyi URSR* (Outline of the Economic Geography of the UkrSSR, Kiev, 1952), Vol. II, p. 556.

65. Official estimates as of April, 1956 (*Nar. hosp. URSR, 1957,* p. 7).

66. *Spravochnik komsomol'skogo propagandista i agitatora* (Reference Book for Komsomol Propagandists and Agitators, Moscow, 1957), pp. 108, 109.

67. Max Frankel in the *New York Times,* March 11, 1958, p. 11. In 1959 Soviet Ukrainian historian V. M. Taranenko wrote on ["The Participation of the Toilers of the Ukraine in the Cultivation of Virgin and Fallow Lands (1954–1956"], *Ukr. istorychny zhurnal,* Vol. 1959, No. 6 (November-December), pp. 46–55, but he studiously avoided giving any global figures.

68. Solovey, *op. cit.,* pp. 68–73. Figure on p. 73.

69. V. Kubiyovych, "The National Composition of the Population of the UkrSSR and the Number of Ukrainians in the Light of the Population Census of Jan. 15, 1959," *Ukrayins'ka literaturna hazeta* (Ukrainian Literary Gazette [Munich]), Vol. VI, No. 3 (March, 1960), p. 2.

70. See, e.g., a news item in *Vitchyzna* (Fatherland [Kiev]), Vol. 1946, No. 10/11 (October-November), p. 215: In 1946, medical institutes in the UkrSSR graduated 2,436 young specialists, 700 of whom went to work in the "fraternal Republics."

71. Interview #75, with a former Soviet officer.

72. See his "Engineers in the Ukraine," *Visti Ukrayins'kykh Inzheneriv* (Ukrainian Engineering News [New York]), Vol. VIII, No. 3-4 (May-August 1957), p. 57. See also Table II-17, which confirms the magnitudes estimated by Holubnychy.

73. Holubnychy, *ibid.*

74. See Note I-5, in the Appendix.

75. There is an excellent statistical study which analyzes the migratory processes in and out of the Ukraine from 1897 to 1926 only, to wit, A. Hirshfeld, *Migratsiyni protsesy na Ukrayini* (Migratory Processes in the Ukraine, Kharkov, 1930). No remotely comparable data have been released on the postwar years, so the present author has reluctantly decided not to embody Hirshfeld's conclusions in the present study. See, however, the text below for some rough estimates of Russian immigration into the Ukraine.

76. B. M. Babiy, *Vozz"yednannya Zakhidnoyi Ukrayiny z Ukrayins'koyu RSR* (Reunification of Western Ukraine with the Ukrainian SSR, Kiev, 1954), p. 69.

77. Interview #75.

78. Lyalikov, *op. cit.*, p. 95, confirmed by interview #59: eastern Ukrainian kolkhozes would publish letters in the local Galician press calling upon the peasants to come east.

79. *Nar. khoz. SSSR, 1960*, pp. 14 and 18.

80. *Ibid.*, pp. 17ff. See, however, Kubiyovych's criticism above, to the effect that the number of Ukrainians in Kazakhstan and Russia may have been arbitrarily reduced.

81. See *ibid.* (Kubiyovych) for a concise discussion of where Ukrainians live in the USSR. In his earlier article in *Entsyklopediya ukrayinoznavstva* (Encyclopedia of Ukrainian Studies, Munich: Molode Zhyttya, 1949), Vol. I, p. 164, Professor Kubiyovych gave detailed estimates on the distribution of Ukrainians in the Soviet Union as of 1930. He found, for example, that 3.4 million Ukrainians were living in a compact mass in contiguous areas of the Russian Republic (that is, areas incorporated into the Russian SFSR that were contiguous to the Ukraine). In those areas the Ukrainians constituted about two-thirds of the total population (or, 66.0 per cent). In order of magnitude, those areas were: the Kursk and Voronezh provinces (incidentally, the area in which Khrushchev had been born) contained 1.4 million Ukrainians (64.2 per cent of total population); the western part of the North Caucasus region (known as the Kuban region) with 1.3 million Ukrainians (63.8 per cent of the total); the Don region, with about 600,000 Ukrainians (76.8 per cent). Given appropriate conditions those contiguous areas may be claimed by the Ukraine as Ukrainian ethnic territories.

82. *Nar. khoz. SSSR, 1960*, p. 18. See also the recent analysis by V. Kubiyovych, ["The National Composition of the Population of Soviet Ukraine in the Light of the Soviet Censuses of 12/17/1926 and 1/15/1959"], *Zapysky NTSh* (Shevchenko Scientific Society Notes [Paris]), Vol. CLXIX (1962), pp. 1-16 (in reprint).

83. Lorimer, *op. cit.*, pp. 51, 63; also Olesiyevych, *et al.*, *Ukrayins'ka lyudnist' SSSR* (Warsaw: Ukrainian Scientific Institute, 1931), p. 44.

84. Lorimer, *op. cit.*, p. 138.

85. *Ibid.*, p. 161.

86. A. Khomenko, *Natsional'ny sklad lyudnosty URSR* (National Composition of the Population of UkrSSR, Kharkov, 1931), p. 110. The exact figures for *intra*-ethnic marriages in the Republic are 96.9 per cent for men and 96.0 per cent for women.

87. I. Pisarev, "Naselenie strany sotsializma (K itogam perepisi 1939 g.) (Population of the Country of Socialism: The Results of the 1939 Census)," *Planovoe Khozaystvo* (Planned Economy [Moscow]), Vol. 17, No. 5 (May, 1940), p. 19. Khomenko, however, gives 8.2 per cent as the corresponding figure for 1927 (*op. cit.*, p. 109).

88. Interview #79.

89. Lorimer, *op. cit.*, p. 138.

90. See the article on Ukrainians in the *Bol'shaya Sovetskaya Entsyklopediya* Vol. 44 (2nd ed., Moscow, 1956), p. 172B. The figure is the so-called "final result of the 1939 census," which, judging by other figures published in the same year, probably includes all the Western provinces and possibly Crimea, too. The term "final result" is not explained in the Encyclopedia. The former figure of 7.5 million is the sum of a Soviet and a Western estimate. Babiy, *op. cit.*, p. 56, estimated the number of *Ukrainians* that were added to the Ukrainian SSR upon incorporation of the formerly Polish territories in September 1939 at "close to seven million." The remaining half a million may be accounted for by the 500,000–600,000 Ukrainians that as of 1930 were estimated by C. A. Macartney to live in Bessarabia and Northern Bukovina, the two Rumanian provinces that were annexed by the Soviet Union in June 1940—see his *National States and National Minorities* (London: Oxford University Press, 1934), p. 524. The two figures (7.5 and 35.6 million) do not, however, include the population of the Transcarpathian Province, which was incorporated in 1945.

91. See *B. Sov. Entsyklopedia, loc. cit.*, p. 169A. It will be seen in Chapter V below that not all persons who declare themselves Ukrainians give Ukrainian as their native language and, furthermore, that only relatively few non-Ukrainians do so. The linguistic figure should, therefore, be taken only as a rough approximation.

92. Estimate by C. A. Macartney, *National States and National Minorities* (London: Oxford University Press, 1934), p. 518. Macartney estimated the number as 587,000. The total population of that province in 1930 was 725,000 (see Table II-7, below). By 1941 it would have increased to up to 800,000. Thus, in order to arrive at the total number of people in the Ukrainian SSR and Crimea before the annexation of the Transcarpathian province, we should have to discount 40.5 million by 0.8 million, which would give us 39.7 million. The linguistic figure of 32.8 million discounted by 0.6 million Transcarpathian Ukrainians gives us the figure of 32.2 million. 32.2 million constitute 80.0 per cent of 39.7 million. (See the figure in the main text, below.)

93. E.g., on the Uzbek and the Tadzhik SSR, which were not so much hit by collectivization as the Ukrainian and Kazakh SSRs. See the articles on those two former Republics in *Bol'shaya Sov. Ents.*, 2nd ed., passim.

94. See the analysis by Holubnychy, *loc. cit.* (in note 56, above).

95. Lorimer, *op. cit.*, p. 138.

96. See on this Lew Shankowsky, "The Effects of the Soviet Nationality Policy in the Light of the 1959 Census and Other Statistical Data," *Prologue* (New York), Vol. V, No. 1–2 (Spring-Summer 1961), pp. 27–87, esp. Table

14, pp. 77–78. Shankowsky gives the figure of 4.6 per cent for Ukrainians (p. 77). The discrepancy is probably due to more rounding of figures by this writer.

97. Khomenko, *op. cit.*, pp. 22–23.

98. Results privately communicated to the author (see Table II-7). There were 6,000 Russians living in the Volhynian Province (0.6 per cent of the total population), 6,200 in Rovno Province (0.6 per cent), and 10,200 (1.2 per cent) in Chernivtsi Province (Bukovina).

99. Tsentral'noe Statisticheskoe Upravlenie SSSR—Otdel Perepisi (USSR Central Statistical Administration—Census Division), *Vsesoyznaya perepis' naseleniya 1926 g.* (All-Union Population Census of 1926), Vol. V (Moscow, 1929?), p. 5. Henceforth, cited as *Vsesoyznaya perepis' . . . 1926 g.*

100. Population figures for the seven Western Provinces and Crimea added up from Table II-7. The actual figure would be somewhat higher because we have not adjusted the Eastern Ukrainian data for 1930–31, the date of the Western censuses.

101. See also the calculation by Solovey, *op. cit.*, p. 76. I have taken over his argument but corrected some figures. The original figures for 1926 will be found in Lorimer, *op. cit.*, p. 51; for 1959—in *Nar. khoz. SSSR, 1960*, p. 14. Without any additional immigration the Russian minority would have increased to only 4.4 million.

102. Calculated from the percentage figures in Table II-7. For lack of data no adjustments have been made to account for the population increases between 1926 and 1931.

103. See above, p. 49.

104. By Solomon M. Schwarz. See Note I-3, on the Jewish problem, in the Appendix.

105. Khomenko, *op. cit.*, pp. 22–23.

106. In 1926 Eastern Ukraine was divided into 41 districts (*okrugs*); in 1959 the whole of Ukraine contained only 25 provinces.

107. That part of the Ukraine had been under Polish rule until the Polish Partitions in the last quarter of the eighteenth century.

108. I owe this suggestion to Mr. Holubnychy.

109. See Chapter I, above, p. 20.

110. For a veiled reference, see Karayev's report to the 15th Extraordinary Congress of the Turkmenian Party. *Turkmenskaya Iskra*, Jan. 20, 1959, pp. 1–4 or *CDSP*, Vol. XI, No. 9, pp. 31–32. Clearer in *Pravda*, February 5, 1959, p. 3, or *Cur. Soviet Policies III*, p. 166.

111. There is a discrepancy in the figures given for 1939 in Table II-9 and those for January 1, 1941 in Table II-11. Possibly the discrepancy is due to the difference in time; probably Table II-11 does not include all persons with higher education. Retired people have certainly been excluded from it.

112. For a more extended discussion see Chapter VIII, below.

113. Calculated from tables in *Nar. khoz. SSSR, 1956*, pp. 281–82. Data on savings refer to the end of 1956, estimated population figures as of April 1956 (*ibid.*, p. 18). To avoid additional errors no adjustments have been made for the 8 months in 1956.

114. See Chapter V, below, Sec. 2, *passim*.

115. They have been conveniently assembled in Nicholas DeWitt, *Education and Professional Employment in the USSR* (Washington, D.C.: National Science Foundation, 1961), p. 769.

116. Calculated on the basis of figures in *Nar. khoz. SSSR, 1960*, pp. 785–86. The appropriate positions in the UkrSSR numbered 39,902 in 1959, and there were 30,252 of Ukrainian personnel.

117. They held 22,523 out of a total of 46,657 positions. See Tsentral'noe statisticheskoe upravlenie pri Sovete Ministrov SSSR (Central Statistical Administration of the USSR Council of Ministers), *Vysshee obrazovanie v SSSR: Statisticheskiy sbornik* (Higher Education in the USSR—A Statistical Compilation, Moscow, 1961), p. 215. Henceforth source will be abbreviated *Vys. obraz.*

118. *Nar. khoz. SSSR, 1960*, p. 766.

119. DeWitt, *op. cit.*, Table IV-A-7, p. 656.

120. That is, representation of the titular nationality in the schools of their Republic. Calculated by slide rule from the data in *Nar. khoz. SSSR, 1960*, pp. 769 and 780. I have assumed that 50 per cent of the students in the Ukraine are regular full-time students. It is only for the latter category that nationality data are supplied in the general statistical handbooks.

121. *Vys. obraz.*, p. 130. Population figures from the 1959 census.

122. DeWitt, *op. cit.*, p. 354.

123. This is a most difficult problem. I discuss it throughout the book, but particularly in the chapters on linguistic policy and national consciousness (Chapters V and X).

124. O. Pytel', "Natsional'ni vidnosyny na Ukrayini v svitli statystyky" (Relations between the Nationalities in the Ukraine in the Light of Statistics), in Olesiyevych *et al., op. cit.*, pp. 43–84: Table XIV, p. 70. (For full citation of source see source note to Table II-22.)

125. Cf. *ibid.*, Table XV, p. 76. I have obtained the figures by subtracting the number of agricultural workers.

126. *Ibid.*

127. *Ibid.*, Table XVI, p. 78.

128. *Ibid.*, Table XVII, p. 80.

129. S. Nykolyshyn, *Kul'turna polityka bol'shevykiv i ukrayins'ky kul'turny protses* (Cultural Policy of the Bolsheviks and the Ukrainian Cultural Process; n.p., 1947), p. 88, citing Kosior's figures.

130. *Vsesoyuznaya perepis' . . . 1926 g.*, Vol. XII (Moscow, 1929), p. 27.

131. See this work (Bilinsky), Table II-7, p. 57, above.

132. Lorimer, *op. cit.*, p. 164. It should be noted that in the 1930's the districts were named Stalino and Voroshilovgrad. For clarity's sake the present (1962) names have been used.

133. S. Kosior, "Torzhestvo leninsko-stalinskoy natsional'noy politiki" (Triumph of Leninist-Stalinist Nationality Policy), *Pravda*, December 24, 1937. The lower officials mentioned are chairmen of (district?) executive committees and city soviets (mayors); the others are said to have been employed by "higher organs" of the Republic.

134. *Ibid.* It should be noted that he did not give the figure for 1927—I have interpolated it myself (see p. 80, above).

135. Nykolyshyn, *op. cit.*, pp. 90ff. Primary source was not available.

136. I. Ye. Kravtsev, *Marksysts'ko-lenins'ki pryntsypy proletars'koho interna-*

tsionalizmu (Marxist-Leninist Principles of Proletarian Internationalism, Kiev, 1956), p. 51.

137. See on this Table II-8, above; also the more detailed breakdowns in *Narodne hosp. Ukrayins'koyi RSR v 1960 rotsi,* pp. 9–17.

Notes to Chapter III: Integration of Western Ukraine I

1. Tsentral'ne statystychne upravlinnya pry Radi Ministriv URSR (Central Statistical Administration of the UkrSSR Council of Ministers), *Narodne hospodarstvo Ukrayins'koyi RSR v 1959 r.: Statystychny shchorichnyk* (National Economy of the UkrSSR in 1959: A Statistical Yearbook, Kiev, 1960), p. 16. Henceforth abbreviated as *Nar. hosp. URSR, 1959.* Area figures from same author, *Narodne hospodarstvo Ukrayins'koyi RSR* (1957), p. 11.

2. For a thoughtful and objective appraisal, see the chapter "The Minorities: the Ukrainians," in Raymond Leslie Buell's *Poland: Key to Europe* (New York & London: Knopf, 1939), pp. 253–87. I have used other sources which have led me to the same conclusions.

3. A Polish author writing on the Ukrainian minority deplored that his government, being one of "a national and centralized state (d'Etat national et centralisateur)," did not give sufficient local autonomy to the Ukrainians. Federalist ideals in Poland did not find "any serious response (écho) either in Parliament or in public opinion." Jerzy Stempowski in *Pologne, 1919–1939* (Neuchatel, Switzerland: Editions de la Baconnière, 1946–), Vol. I, p. 413.

4. See E. Ammende (ed.), *Die Nationalitaeten in den Staaten Europas* (Vienna: Braumueller, 1931), p. 63; and *Entsyklopediya ukrayinoznavstva* (Encyclopedia of Ukrainian Studies, Munich & New York: Molode Zhyttya, 1949), Vol. I, p. 945. Dr. Ammende was Secretary General of the Congress of European Ethnic Groups, or Minorities (Europaeischer Nationalitaetenkongress); his book is a collection of competent reports submitted by the national sections of that body.

5. M. Felinski, *The Ukrainians in Poland* (London: author, 1931), pp. 130ff.; his figures are disputed by the contributors to Ammende (ed.), *op. cit.,* p. 63. Ukrainians have always complained that in the bi-lingual schools only very few subjects, usually physical education and arithmetic, were actually taught in their language.

6. Stempowski, *loc. cit.,* p. 417. In his words: "Public administration employed only a minimal number of Ukrainians." The primary vehicle for the process of social growth was the extensive cooperative movement.

7. Eugene M. Kulischer, *Europe on the Move: War and Population Changes, 1917–47* (New York: Columbia University Press, 1948), pp. 128ff. See also Michael Winch, *Republic for a Day* (London: Robert Hale Ltd., 1939), p. 218. Winch's book is mainly devoted to the Transcarpathian province, but contains interesting sidelights on Galicia as well.

8. Another thorn in their flesh was the frontier scheme. It meant that in a frontier district about 20 miles wide, and often extended to 50 miles, only Poles were allowed to settle (Winch, *ibid.*). These settlers lived under a quasi-military regime, more often than not they would be drawn from the most fervently patriotic sections. (See M. Herasymenko & B. Dudykevych,

Borot'ba trudyashchykh Zakhidnoyi Ukrayiny za vozz"yednannya z ra-dyans'koyu Ukrayinoyu, 1921–39 rr. (Struggle of the Toilers of Western Ukraine for the Re-Unification with Soviet Ukraine, 1921–39, Kiev, 1955), p. 57. The tendency of the book is obvious, but the authors take trouble to cite Polish sources and spot checks have proven them to be accurate quotations. Professor Roman Smal Stocki in a communication to the present author has written: "The experience with the Polish settlers in the 20–50 mile frontier zone [was] very disappointing for the Polish government. The younger generation intermarried with local Beloruthenians and Ukrainians and became Ukranized or Beloruthenized. Thus it did not help that originally the settlers were 'drawn from the most fervently patriotic Polish sections.'" Cited with permission.

9. Interviews #5 and 12.
10. Some Galician peasants longed to supplement their incomes by taking jobs on the publicly owned railroads, as did the Poles. But the government did not give them such jobs. Unscrupulous organizers from the Organization of Ukrainian Nationalists (OUN) took advantage of this and promised them "pears growing on willow trees" if they would only join the movement. A great many did, and fought for the Ukraine and—a postmaster-ship in village X. Interview #12.
11. See V. M. Babiy, *Vozz"yednannya Zakhidnoyi Ukrayiny z Ukrayins'koyu RSR* (Re-unification of Western Ukraine with the UkrSSR, Kiev, 1954), *passim;* also, *Vozz"yednannya ukrayins'koho narodu v yedyniy ukrayins'kiy radyans'kiy derzhavi, 1939–1949: Zbirnyk dokumentiv i materiyaliv* (Re-unification of the Ukrainian people in a single Ukrainian state, 1939–49: Collection of documents and materials, Kiev, 1949), *passim.*
12. Cf. Jane Degras (ed.), *Soviet Documents on Foreign Policy* [under the auspices of Royal Institute of International Affairs] (London: Oxford University Press, 1953), Vol. III, pp. 359ff., 377ff.
13. See Harold W. Temperley (ed.), *A History of the Peace Conference* (London: Frowde, Hodher & Stoughton, 1920–1924), Vol. VI, pp. 275, 318–22. A useful recent work is S. Konovalov (ed.), *Russo-Polish Relations: A Historical Survey* (Princeton, N.J.: Princeton University Press, 1945)—pro-Russian viewpoint, but liberal quotations from primary sources.
14. [Royal Institute of International Affairs.] William Hardy McNeill, *Survey of International Affairs, 1939–1946: America, Britain and Russia—Their Cooperation and Conflict, 1941–1946* (London: Oxford University Press, 1953), pp. 167, 320.
15. Excerpts from the speech are translated in Degras (ed.), *op. cit.,* pp. 374ff.
16. R.I.I.A. [McNeill], *op. cit.,* p. 407 and note.
17. Cf. the following exchange: "Anders: 'Many Ukrainians were and have remained Germanophiles. We and later you had, therefore, many troubles.' —Stalin: 'Yes, but those were your Ukrainians, not ours. We shall destroy them jointly.'" Władysław Anders, *Bez ostatniego rozdziału. Wspomnienia z lat 1939–1946* (The Last Chapter Is Missing: Memoirs from 1939–46, 2nd ed., Newtown, Wales, 1950), p. 123, as cited in D. Solovey, *Lyudnist' Ukrayiny za sorok rokiv vlady TsK KPSS u svitli perepysiv* (The Population of the Ukraine for the Last Forty Years under the Rule of the Communist Party of the Soviet Union [in the Light of Census Figures], Detroit: Vil'na Ukrayina [Ukrainian Free Society of America], 1961), p. 40.
18. Wrote Professor Roman Smal Stocki to the author: "It is important also

to understand that for Stalin and Moscow, Ukraine is the most important part of the whole nationality problem; the transfer of this international problem by 'unification' of the Ukrainian territories into an interior Soviet Union problem means for Stalin a 'final solution' of the whole nationality problem of the whole Soviet Union." Cited with permission.

19. See Chapter II, above (p. 57), on the figures involved.

20. From the speech of the Ukrainian SSR Minister of Education, *Pravda Ukrainy*, February 1, 1958, p. 2; the total figure is from *Nar. hosp. URSR, 1957*, pp. 429–30.

21. Babiy, *op. cit.*, p. 75.

22. Myroslav Prokop, *Ukrayina i ukrayins'ka polityka Moskvy* (The Ukraine and Moscow's Ukrainian Policy, Munich: Suchasna Ukrayina [Contemporary Ukraine], 1956), pp. 103ff., 125ff. See also Hryhory Kytasty, former Soviet Ukrainian composer and member of the State Bandurist Choir, for a most vivid and illuminating reminiscence entitled, "Bourgeois Galicia, Shevchenko's triumph over Stalin and—'It's the Ukraine after all,'" *Ukrayins'ky Prometey* (Detroit), March 4, 1954, as quoted by Prokop, pp. 126–27.

23. See on this Chapter I, above (p. 12).

24. Russian theaters in Lviv and in Mukachevo (Transcarpathian province) were built in the fall of 1946. See Danylo Lobay, *Neperemozhna Ukrayina* (Invincible Ukraine, Winnipeg: Ukrainian Canadian Committee, 1950), pp. 190ff.

25. See the article by F. Buhayko, Ed.D., "Master the Language of the Great Russian People," in *Radyans'ka Ukrayina* [spec. edition for western provinces], June 18, 1947; also, "A Letter from Lviv," *Rad. Ukrayina*, April 6, 1950.

26. See Chapter I, above (p. 18).

27. See on this the editorial "Lviv 'na russkom yazyke'" (Lviv in Russian), *Svoboda* (Liberty [Jersey City, N.J.]), October 11, 1962, p. 2.

28. *Ibid.*, citing *Literaturna Ukrayina* (Literary Ukraine [Kiev]), October 2, 1962.

29. Babiy, *op. cit.*, p. 130, refers to a joint decision of the UkrSSR Council of People's Commissars and the Central Committee of the Communist Party (Bolshevik) of Ukraine of 16 February 1940, approving the plan of industrialization. Some aspects of the industrialization have been described by H. I. Koval'chak in his article ["The Industrialization of the Western Provinces of the Ukrainian SSR"], *Ukrayins'ky istorychny zhurnal*, Vol. 1959, No. 6 (November-December), pp. 3–12. Koval'chak gives some figures on nationality, but they do not permit us to calculate the number of Russian immigrants. See, however, below (note 31).

30. Peter Pirogov, *Why I Escaped* (New York: Sloan and Pearce, 1950), p. 197: "It was, indeed, a paradise by comparison."

31. In its editorial of April 26, 1946, *Rad. Ukrayina* wrote:

> "To support [the emerging workers class in Galicia] in the fulfilment of Stalinist directives comes the great Russian people and all fraternal peoples of our Fatherland. Already *hundreds of qualified workers* from the factories in *Moscow, Leningrad, Sverdlovsk*, and other cities are helping the young workers of Lviv enterprises and new constructions to master new professions, are letting them share their long experience. From No-

vosibirsk, Sverdlovsk, Moscow, from Izhevsk and Tula there are arriving transports with machine tools and other equipment. . . ." (Italics added).

13,000 school teachers from the "eastern provinces" (of the Ukraine?) were sent to Western Ukraine between 1939–56; see V. Yu. Nikolayenko, "Fulfilling the Leninist Principles of Public Education," in *Radyans'ka Shkola* (Soviet School [Kiev]), Vol. 1957, No. 4, p. 11. Apparently this number does not include Russian teachers dispatched to that region (cf. Pirogov, *op. cit.,* p. 243). For purposes of comparison it should be noted that in 1955–1956 the total number of school teachers in the Western provinces was 63,331 (*Nar. hosp. URSR, 1957,* p. 436).

In the fall of 1946, among the students in the colleges of Lviv, there were said to have been 80 per cent Ukrainians, half of them local people, and among the Faculty there were "many Galicians" (Lobay, *op. cit.,* p. 184, citing an interview with a Soviet Ukrainian official).

In 1947, 70 per cent of the workers engaged in industry and construction were Ukrainians; the rest presumably Russians or remaining Poles. In 1949 68.3 per cent of the employees of the Lviv railroad administration were Ukrainians. See Koval'chak, *loc. cit.,* pp. 6–7.

In 1947, 54 per cent of all "leading workers" of the province, city and district sections of "people's education," i.e., of all school principals and inspectors, were persons of local (i.e., Galician) origin; see P. T. Dudnyk, "Raise Onto a Higher Level the Work of Schools in the Western Provinces of the UkrSSR," *Rad. Shkola,* Vol. 1947, No. 2, pp. 1ff.

See below for an attempt to establish the aggregate number of Russian immigrants.

32. See the editorial in *Rad. Ukrayina* of 14 August, 1946: "Painstakingly Educate and Boldly Place Local Cadres," partially cited in Lobay, *op. cit.,* pp. 159–160; *Pravda's* report on 23 August 1946, p. 2; Vsevolod Holubnychy, "Outline History of the Communist Party of the Ukraine," *The Ukrainian Review,* Vol. 6 (1958), p. 113. (The journal was published by the Institute for the Study of the USSR, Munich.)

33. As an example to be abhorred, Khrushchev cited at the 1946 plenum the words of a certain Morenko, apparently an Eastern Ukrainian, who was secretary of a district committee in Volhynia: "Once you advance local people to leading work, they demand from you much attention and cause you much work and trouble [*vozni*]. Those, however, who are sent to us from the eastern provinces have got experience and you can make much greater demands on them." *Pravda, loc. cit.*

34. The reason for this may have been the secretary of the Lviv city Party committee, a certain Khlomov, who, judging from his name, hailed from farther east. See the complaint "Incorrect Attitude of the Lviv *gorkom* of the CP(B)U as to Selecting and Educating Cadres," *Rad. Ukrayina,* February 16, 1947.

35. "An Important Task of Party Organizations in the Western Provinces," *ibid.,* July 30, 1952. The plenum met May 27–29, 1952, discussed also the situation in agriculture. See Holubnychy, *op. cit.* (note 32), pp. 117–118.

36. *Nar. hosp. URSR, 1957,* p. 9.

37. *Pravda Ukrainy,* May 12, 1953.

38. See note to Table III-1, above.

39. John A. Armstrong, *The Soviet Bureaucratic Elite* (New York: Praeger, 1959), p. 111.

40. See Table 14, *ibid.*, p. 110, based on M. D. Men'shov, *op. cit.* (Table III-1, above), p. 62.

41. See Table II-7, above.

42. See Table 15 in Armstrong, *op. cit.*, p. 112. I have deducted the figures for the other West Ukrainian provinces that had been under the rule of Czechoslovakia and Rumania before 1945. On pp. 111–112 Professor Armstrong cites a Soviet statement to the effect that the eastern Ukrainian provinces sent to West Ukraine a "significant quantity of Party, Soviet, economic and other Communist workers." It is, however, difficult to obtain a precise picture from such sweeping qualitative terms.

43. Solovey, *op. cit.*, p. 51.

44. See Chapter II, above (pp. 56–58).

45. To be exact 301,900. Calculated by author on the basis of percentage figures in Table II-7, above.

46. Solovey, *loc. cit.*

47. *Ibid.*, p. 52. The date and time of the broadcast were December 3, 1959, 7 P.M., European time. The quotation is from the broadcast, italics added.

48. Pirogov, *op. cit.*, pp. 234ff.

49. Interview #64. I have not been able to find out who issued those permits. Probably it was the NKVD (secret police) upon requests from the Party, State administration, educational institutions.

50. Pirogov, *op. cit.*, p. 243.

51. Interview #74; and Akademiya nauk UkrRSR, Instytut ekonomiki (Academy of Sciences of the UkrSSR, Institute of Economics), *Ocherki razvitiya narodnogo khozaystva UkrSSR* (Outline of the Development of the National Economy of the UkrSSR, Moscow, 1954), p. 524. By January 1, 1948, 9.6 per cent of the farms had been collectivized; as of July 1, 1951, their proportion was 95.2 per cent (49 per cent as of January 1, 1949). A more recent Soviet source gives interesting data on collectivization; as of June 1941, there were about 1.3 million peasant households in Galicia and Volhynia. The regime had succeeded in collectivizing only 13 per cent of the households (172,518). After the war, by the end of 1945, only 2,400 [sic] households could be reorganized as collective farms because of hostile opposition and lack of Soviet personnel. See M. K. Ivasyuta, ["Socialist Reconstruction of Agriculture in the Western Provinces of the Ukrainian SSR"], *Ukr. istorychny zhurnal*, Vol. 1959, No. 4 (July-August), pp. 7–8. See also similar article by I. P. Bohodyst, ["Socialist Reconstruction of the West Ukrainian Countryside"], *ibid.*, Vol. 1957, No. 2 (September-October), pp. 69–82.

52. Interviews #64, 69, 74.

53. Akademiya nauk UkrRSR, Instytut ekonomiki, *loc. cit.*

54. Pirogov, *op. cit.*, p. 245. One of the operations in which Pirogov took part is described by him in vivid detail on pp. 197ff., esp. p. 203.

55. Quoted by His Excellency Msgr. J. Buchko in *First Victims of Communism: White Book on the Religious Persecution in the Ukraine* (Rome, 1953), p. 86. (Henceforth abbreviated as *First Victims . . .*). This is the official Ukrainian Catholic White Book.

      For a concise but objective account of the Union, see the article by N. Polons'ka-Vasylenko and M. Chubaty in *Entsyklopediya ukrayinoznav-*

stva, Vol. I, pp. 607ff. Ivan Wlasowsky describes it in greater detail from the Orthodox viewpoint in his *Outline History of the Ukrainian Orthodox Church* (New York & Bound Brook, N.J.: Ukrainian Orthodox Church of U.S.A., 1956), Vol. I, pp. 239ff., *et passim.*

56. E.g., the initiator of the Ukrainian Galician literary movement was the young poet Rev. Markian Shashkevych.

57. Sources for sketch: Manuscript A; Polons'ka-Vasylenko and Chubaty, *loc. cit.,* p. 616.

58. Interview #12. One of these features was the kneeling during the reception of the Sacrament, which is not customary in Eastern Ukraine. One tolerant Greek Catholic priest looked the other way when the older of his parishioners insisted upon kneeling, with the result that he had to bend down several times while administering it.

59. *First Victims . . . ,* p. 16.

60. Walter Dushnyck, *Martyrdom in the Ukraine: Russia Denies Religious Freedom* (New York: The America Press, n.d.), p. 13; also, *Diyannya soboru hreko-katolyts'koyi tserkvy 8–10 bereznya 1946 r. u L'vovi* (Proceedings of the Synod of the Greek-Catholic Church in Lviv, March 8–10, 1946, Lviv, 1946), p. 44. (Henceforth abbreviated as *Diyannya soboru. . . .*) According to the latter source, a publication of the re-unification synod, Poland obtained her freedom of action upon paying to the Holy See the sum of 2 million *zloty.* The churches involved were so-called "pre-Uniate" churches; their congregations had been forcibly converted to Orthodoxy by the Tsarist government in the 1830's and 1870's.

61. *Diyannya soboru . . . , ibid.*

62. Editor's Note to Rev. Dr. Ivan Hrynioch, "The Destruction of the Ukrainian Catholic Church in the Soviet Union," *Prologue* (New York), Vol. IV, No. 1–2 (Spring-Summer 1960), p. 5.

63. *First Victims . . . ,* p. 26, quoting an instruction of Sheptytsky's.

64. *Ibid.,* p. 27.

65. Cited *ibid.,* p. 28. Cited by permission.

66. Prokop, *op. cit.,* pp. 120ff.

67. *First Victims . . . ,* p. 29.

68. This account is confirmed in essence by Rev. Dr. Hrynioch, *loc. cit.,* pp. 20–21. Father Hrynioch, a priest of the Ukrainian Catholic church, gives an interesting critical evaluation of Dr. Kostelnyk's character *(ibid.).*

69. *First Victims . . . ,* pp. 31–32. Cited by permission.

70. Yevhen Prirva, "The Fifth Anniversary of the Liquidation of the Ukrainian Greek Catholic Church," *Suchasna Ukrayina,* March 18, 1951, pp. 6ff.

71. *First Victims . . . ,* p. 33.

72. Alexander Korniychuk, ["What Is the Vatican So Excited About"], *Suchasne i maybutnye* (Present and Future [Kiev]), Vol. II, No. 1 (January, 1946), pp. 4ff.

73. Yu. Skrypnychenko, ["Reactionary Wiles of the Vatican against Slavic Peoples"], *Ibid.,* Vol. I, No. 10 (December, 1945), p. 24.

74. In 1949 Halan was assassinated by members of the Ukrainian underground.

75. *First Victims . . . ,* p. 36. Metropolitan Slipy was held captive for almost 18 years until he was released in February, 1963, on the intervention of Pope John XXIII. See *Svoboda* (Jersey City), the "Ukrainian Weekly"

Section, February 16, 1963, p. 1; *Time* Magazine, Vol. LXXXI, No. 8 (Feb. 22, 1963), p. 70.

76. *First Victims* . . . , p. 38.

77. Manuscript A.

78. Dushnyck, *op. cit.,* pp. 33–34.

79. *Diyannya soboru* . . . , pp. 17ff.

80. *Ibid.*

81. *Ibid.,* pp. 19ff.

82. Its text is printed in *First Victims* . . . , pp. 39–40n.

83. Prirva, *loc. cit.,* referring to underground sources.

84. *Diyannya soboru* . . . , p. 26.

85. *Ibid.,* p. 27.

86. *Ibid.,* p. 61. The latter number is very possibly a printing mistake, and should have been *1, 281.* See below Makary's figure, also the number of priests in 1945.

87. *First Victims* . . . , pp. 109, 44.

88. *Ibid.,* p. 44n.

89. *Diyannya soboru* . . . , pp. 32, 53.

90. *Ibid.,* pp. 41ff.

91. "This appeal [to Patriarch Alexis, concerning the unity in prayer and in administration], as a historical document, *was to be signed,* according to a decision of the synod, by all the delegates to the synod." *Ibid.,* p. 44. [italics added].

92. Prirva, *loc. cit.* Father Hrynioch, who has exhaustively analyzed the proceedings of the synod from the viewpoints of both Catholic and Orthodox canonic law (*loc. cit.,* pp. 33–46), has come to the conclusion that it had been illegally convened and that its decisions, according to the law of both Churches, were, therefore, null and void.

93. *First Victims* . . . , pp. 58n.

94. *Rad. Ukrayina,* September 9, 10, 11 and 13, 1952.

95. The *New York Times,* July 18, 1954, p. 5: Vatican radio reports over 1,000 priests maintain underground organization.

96. Interview #4.

97. I. Melnychuk, "Retort to a Fanatic," *Literaturna Hazeta* (Literary Gazette [Kiev]), February 5, 1957, p. 4, as cited by Hrynioch, *loc. cit.,* p. 19n.

98. D. Pokhylevych, "Uniates and Their Reactionary Role," *Komunist Ukrayiny* (Kiev), Vol. 1959, No. 7 (July), pp. 77–82, as cited by Hrynioch, *loc. cit.,* p. 30n.

99. *First Victims* . . . , p. 110. Msgr. G. Mojoli is Minutant of the Oriental Congregation of the Catholic Church. Cited by permission.

100. Interviews #4, 5, 12, 37. He has been described by one source as "somewhat of a revolutionary, a malcontent."

101. *Diyannya soboru* . . . , p. 44, and Interview #4.

102. Interview #4. They are listed in *Diyannya soboru* . . . , pp. 54–58.

103. See Kostelnyk's speech on the reasons for re-unification, *ibid.,* pp. 63–74.

104. For a rather moderate criticism see Ye. Vrets'ona, "Render to God What Is God's and to Caesar What Is Caesar's," *Suchasna Ukrayina,* Nos. 22–23 (October 19, November 2, 1952). Rev. Dr. Hrynioch in his address "The Encyclical 'Orientales Ecclesias' Is a Document of Great Significance," *ibid.,* No. 5 (56) (March 8, 1953), p. 2, tries to minimize the importance of the Papal letter, by arguing that it had been superseded by the encyclical of

December 15, 1952, which is more sympathetic towards the Ukrainian viewpoint. (An encyclical carries greater authority than a mere apostolic letter.) After reading both documents there remains one person who is not convinced. Text of letter in Osservatore Romano, July 24, 1952; that of the encyclical, *ibid.,* December 31, 1952; transl. in *First Victims* . . . , pp. 74ff. *Suchasna Ukrayina* was the weekly of a more moderate group of Ukrainian nationalists who had formerly belonged to the OUN.

105. Interviews #37 and 62.
106. Interview #12.
107. See, e.g., *Rad. Ukrayina,* September 23, 1949.
108. Interviews #5, 12, 48 and 62. See also Hrynioch, "The Destruction . . . ," *loc. cit.,* p. 32 (n. 14).

Notes to Chapter IV: Integration of Western Ukraine II

1. Following the example set by John A. Armstrong, I shall capitalize the word whenever I am referring to members of the Organization of Ukrainian Nationalists (OUN).

2. For a critical discussion of sources see the important note in the Appendix (IV-1).

3. See on this the somewhat more detailed discussion below, p. 116. It is worth stressing that during the German occupation a Nationalist underground did exist in the eastern provinces of the Ukraine. See also John A. Armstrong, *Ukrainian Nationalism, 1939–1945* (New York: Columbia University Press, 1955), *passim,* supplemented by Lew Shankowsky, *Pokhidni hrupy OUN* (OUN Raiding Groups, Munich: Ukrayins'ky Samostiynyk, 1958), *passim.* It is not implausible to assume that a few remnants of the Eastern Ukrainian underground organization held out into the postwar years, but all evidence points to the proposition that after 1945 the underground was concentrated in the Western Ukraine. The 2nd edition of Professor Armstrong's book, called *Ukrainian Nationalism* (New York: Columbia, 1963) was published shortly before this work went to press. As the revisions are not very substantial apart from an added chapter, I have not thought it necessary to revise all my references. Unless specifically indicated they are to the first (1955) ed. of Armstrong's work.

4. Brig.-Gen. Ignacy Blum, "Udział wojska polskiego w walce o utrwalenie władzy ludowej: Walki z bandami UPA" (The Share of the Polish Army in the Struggle for the Stabilization of People's Government: Actions against the UPA Bands), *Wojskowy przegląd historyczny* (Review of Military History [Warsaw]), Vol. IV, No. 1 (January-March 1959), pp. 13 (quotation), 9 (figure) and 15 (duration). Gen. Blum's article was later included as Chapter III of his book *Z dziejów Wojska Polskiego w latach 1945–48* (From the Actions of the Polish Army in 1945–1948, Warsaw: Ministry of Defense Publishers, 1960). Unless specifically indicated, all the following references to Blum will be to his article.

5. *Ibid.,* p. 12.
6. *Ibid.,* p. 8.
7. *Ibid.*
8. *Ibid.,* p. 15.
9. *Ibid.,* pp. 17ff.

10. See "Udział Wojska Polskiego w obronie narodowych i społecznych inte-resów ludu polskiego oraz w umacnianiu władzy ludowej w latach 1945–48 (The Share of the Polish Army in the Defense of the Democratic and Social Interests of the Polish People as well as in the Consolidation of the People's Government in the Years 1945–48)," in Polska Akademia Nauk, Wydział Nauk Społecznykh (Polish Academy of Sciences, Division of So-cial Sciences), *Sesja naukowa poświęcona wojnie wyzwoleńczej narodu pol-skiego 1939–45: Materiały* (Scientific session devoted to the liberation war of the Polish people, 1939–45; Materials; Warsaw: Ministry of People's De-fence Publishers, 1959), p. 260. Blum's paper was delivered on October 5, 1958.

11. *Ibid.*

12. *Ibid.*, p. 243n.

13. Blum, *loc. cit.* (journal), pp. 29, 17, 11.

14. Col. of Gen. Staff Jan Gerhard, "Dalsze szczegóły walk z bandami UPA i WIN na południowo wschodnim obszarze Polski" (Further Details on Ac-tions against the Bands of UPA and WIN in the Southeastern Area of Poland), *loc. cit.*, Vol. IV, No. 4 (October-December 1959), p. 320.

15. *Ibid.*, p. 324.

16. The late Stepan Bandera, a prominent OUN leader, was assassinated by a Soviet agent in Munich in 1959.

17. *Ibid.*, p. 327.

18. Blum, *loc. cit.*, p. 16; see also p. 29.

19. *Ibid.*, p. 6.

20. Besides that of Swierczewski, the most publicized assassination was that of the Western Ukrainian Communist, anti-religious writer Yaroslav Halan on October 24, 1949; see Babiy, *Vozz"yednannya Zakhidnoyi Ukrayiny z Ukrayins'koy SSR* [Kiev, 1954], p. 158. Halan's bust is now exhibited in the Leningrad Museum of Atheism (Harry Schwartz, of the New York *Times*, per Shankowsky).

Ukrainian underground sources also claim that the Soviet Marshal Va-tutin died from wounds he had received in an ambush by Ukrainian in-surgents, near Hoshcha, on the road Korets'—Rovno, in Volhynia, on March 20, 1944. Soviet sources have not confirmed this. See Lew Shankow-sky, "Ukrayins'ka povstancha armiya (Ukrainian Insurgent Army)," in My-ron Levyts'ky, ed., *Istoriya Ukrayins'koho Viys'ka* (History of the Ukrain-ian Armed Forces, 2nd rev. ed.; Winnipeg: Ivan Tyktor, 1953), p. 718. Source will henceforth be abbreviated as: Shankowsky, "UPA." Vatutin's assassination by Ukrainian guerrillas, however, has been confirmed by Yu-goslav Communist Party leader Milovan Djilas who visited Kiev in early 1945. See his *Conversations with Stalin* (New York: Harcourt & Brace, 1962), p. 120.

21. See on this Bohodyst, ["Raising the Political Consciousness of the Toilers in the Struggle for the Strengthening of Soviet Authority in the Western Provinces of the UkrSSR (1944–1950"], *Ukr. istorychny zhurnal*, Vol. 1959, No. 6 (November-December), pp. 56–66, esp. p. 66. See also Chapter III, above.

22. Babiy, *loc. cit.*

23. Ryaboklyach, "Indestructibility of Friendship," *Rad. Ukrayina,* August 12, 1951.

24. Shankowsky, "UPA," p. 775; Interviews #12, 62, 77.

25. See below.

26. Shankowsky has counted 21 titles of various periodical publications, 60 pamphlets and 81 leaflets that have appeared under Soviet rule, 1944–1950. ("UPA," pp. 796–97, n. 187.) On the practice of cutting type from wood, see *ibid.*, p. 748, n. 136; on the acquisition by the underground of a regular printing press from the town of Mezhyrichya, Volhynia, in 1946, p. 768, n. 157. See also his article "Ukrainian Underground Publications in USSR," *Ukrainian Quarterly*, Vol. VIII (Summer, 1952), pp. 225–38.

27. See Stepan Khrin [pseud.], *Zymoyu v bunkri, 1947–48: Spohady-khronika* (A Winter in an Earth Fortress, 1947–48: Memoirs-Chronicle, Augsburg, West Germany: Do Zbroyi, 1950), *passim*. Allegedly the reminiscences of a UPA officer, published by a group of Ukrainians who are known to have had connections with the Ukrainian underground. A wealth of specific details has an authentic ring. The existence of very elaborate earth fortresses including underground hospitals has been confirmed by Polish General Staff officer Gerhard, *loc. cit.*, pp. 305ff.

28. See below, on the history of the OUN.

29. Shankowsky, "UPA," pp. 784–92.

30. Interview #73, with a former captain of the Soviet army, who expressed his indignation and disgust at seeing seventeen of his fellow-officers shot down in an ambush in a forest near Sarny, Volhynia, in 1944.

31. Shankowsky, "UPA," pp. 716, 747ff., esp. pp. 750 (dumping of arms), and 752 (refusal to help the MVD against the UPA, 1946).

32. The present writer has been supplied a copy of one of these. It is a well-written, handy pamphlet in Russian entitled *Slovo k boytsam i komandiram Krasnoy Armii* (A Word to the Soldiers and Officers of the Red Army). It is signed "Ukrainian Insurgents," dated October, 1944. Type resembles that used in the Soviet Union, may be assumed to be authentic.

33. Shankowsky, "UPA," pp. 789ff.; confirmed by Soviet historian I. Kh. Sas, ["The Presentation of Socialist Construction in the western provinces of the UkrSSR"], *Ukrayins'ky Istorychny Zhurnal* (Kiev), Vol. 1960, No. 4 (July-August), p. 105.

34. Bohodyst, *loc. cit.*, p. 66.

35. See also the previous discussion in Ch. III, above, pp. 94–95.

36. Shankowsky, "UPA," p. 802; Interview #74: The source was detailed to reindoctrinate one in the OUN spirit. He did this the more gladly because she happened to be a beautiful woman.

37. That number *excludes,* however, members of such temporary formations as the S.K.V., or Nationalist self-defense platoons. In other words, the 20,000 represented the hard core of UPA resistance. See Shankowsky, "UPA," p. 730n. Confirmed in a conversation with another prominent OUN member.

38. This is a logical inference from the more outspoken accounts by Blum and Gerhard. See this chapter, above, p. 115.

39. It was impossible to obtain the original text, but see the *New York Times*, May 13, 1947, p. 3 (per Associated Press): "WARSAW, May 12 (AP). A Government spokesman said today that Czechoslovakia and Russia had agreed, in recent accords with Poland, to assist in efforts to destroy Ukrainian Nationalist bands which have been reported terrorizing wide sections of south eastern Poland near the frontiers. The spokesman

said he did not know whether the Russians and Czechs were using troops against the Ukrainians, but that a policy of common action had been envisaged." Copyright by the New York Times. Reprinted by permission. Also by permission of the Associated Press.

See also the brief article by Hanson W. Baldwin, military correspondent of the *New York Times,* in which he states that two Soviet military divisions (in addition to police units) were engaged in operations against the UPA in 1949 (*ibid.,* May 15, 1949, p. 1).

40. E.g., Babiy, *op. cit.,* p. 157.

41. A very good, carefully checked account of the movement from its inception until about 1944 will be found in Armstrong, *op. cit.,* pp. 19ff., 142ff.

42. Petro Mirchuk in his *Ukrayins'ka povstans'ka armiya, 1942–52* (Ukrainian Insurgent Army, Munich, 1953), pp. 255ff., gives biographical sketches of six prominent leaders. E.g., the Commander in Chief of the Ukrainian Insurgent Army since 1943—Roman Shukhevych (alias Taras Chuprynka)—had joined the predecessor of the OUN, the Ukrainian Military Organization (UVO), already in 1923, when he was 16 years old. See pp. 313ff. for a reprint of an alleged underground "Declaration of the Supreme Command of the Ukrainian Insurgent Army," of September 25, 1947, in which the figure "more than 50 per cent" is given to characterize the membership of the OUN within UPA (p. 314).

43. On the genesis of the wartime UPA in 1943, which involved the forcible fusion of detachments of Bulba-Borovets and of the Melnyk faction of the OUN, see Armstrong, *loc. cit.*

44. Besides Armstrong, *loc. cit.,* see V. Martynets', *Ukrayins'ke pidpillya vid UVO do OUN: Spohady i materiyaly do peredistoriyi ta istoriyi ukrayins'koho organizovanoho natsionalizmu* (The Ukrainian Underground from the UVO to the OUN: Memoirs and Materials Concerning the Prehistory and the History of Organized Ukrainian Nationalism; Winnipeg, 1949)—a rather unsystematic, but voluminous collection of materials.

45. Martynets', *op. cit.,* pp. 37, 38. Italics in original. Kuchabsky is also the author of a very solid monograph on the struggle in West Ukraine, 1918–23: V. Kutschabsky, *Die Westukraine im Kampfe mit Polen und dem Bolschewismus* (Berlin, 1934).

46. See Chapter III, above.

47. Martynets', *op. cit.,* p. 171, says that for around one year and a half [1925–1926?], the UVO maintained the best espionage network in Poland. One may assume from the whole context that it worked for the German *Reichswehr.* Of greater relevance is the fact that Roman Shukhevych was allowed to complete professional military training abroad, after he had been discharged from a Polish officers' school as being politically unreliable. According to Mirchuk, he completed a course for higher officers abroad in 1930 (*op. cit.,* p. 256). According to a well-informed source, that was in Germany. This would explain to some extent why the UPA has been able to hold out for so many years.

48. "Decisions of the Grand Congress of the OUN, January 28-February 2, 1929," reprinted in *OUN v svitli postanov Velykykh Zboriv, Konferentsiy ta inshykh dokumentiv z borot'by 1929–1955 r.* (The OUN in the Light of the Decisions of the Grand Congresses, Conferences and Other Documents from the Struggle, 1929–1955, Munich: Foreign Divisions of the OUN, 1955), pp. 3ff. By "moral autonomy" is meant the rejection of the

Judeo-Christian moral code. The influence of "integral nationalism" (Hayes) is obvious; however toward the end of World War II the impact of those ideas started to wane and there would be no point in tracing them back to their West European prototypes in a study like this.

49. *Ibid.*, p. 16, capitalization as in original.

50. See Chapter III, above, pp. 86–87.

51. See on this Myroslav Prokop, *Ukrayina i ukrayins'ka polityka Moskvy; Chastyna I: Period pidhotovy do druhoyi svitovoyi viyny* (Ukraine and Moscow's Ukrainian Policy; Part I: The Preparation of World War II, Munich: Suchasna Ukrayina, 1956), pp. 129ff.

52. Mykola Lebed', *Ukrayins'ka Povstans'ka Armiya* (UPA, [Germany]: UHVR Press Service, 1946), Vol. I, p. 53.

53. The account has been deliberately simplified. See the warning on p. 118 and n. 43.

54. Shankowsky, "UPA," pp. 657ff. See also the reminiscences of S. Kosar, "Materials for the Study of Guerrilla Warfare in Volhynia," in *Orlyk* (Paris), Vol. 1947, No. 1, pp. 10–13 and No. 2, pp. 10–12.

55. See on this Mikołaj Kunicki, *Pamiętnik "Muchy"* (Diary of "The Fly," Warsaw, 1959). The author, a Pole, was commander of a Communist Polish partisan detachment which helped Soviet partisans to fight UPA from 1944–45.

56. Interview #12.

57. See on this the Soviet partisan leader Petro Vershyhora, *Lyudy z chystoyu sovistyu* (Men with a Clear Conscience, Kiev, 1946–47), Vol. II, pp. 95ff., esp. 102ff. (Chapter 16).

58. Official name given by German authorities to occupied rump Poland.

59. Armstrong, *op. cit.*, pp. 76ff., describes this action in detail.

60. See besides Lebed', *loc. cit.*, the remarkable, anonymous series of articles-memoirs in *Suchasna Ukrayina* (Munich) "Through German Eyes: Observations on the Emergence, the Structure, and the Actions of the Ukrainian Underground," in seven instalments (Nos. 1/26, 2/27, 4/29, 14/39, 16/41, 21/47 and 22/48; from January 7, 1952–October 19, 1952). The description of conditions in Galicia is in No. 1/26. The author is said to have been a high official in the German political police.

61. Shankowsky, "UPA," p. 686.

62. See the memoirs of Sydor Kovpak, *Ot Putivlya do Karpat* (From Putivlya to the Carpathians, Moscow, 1945), *passim*.

63. E.g., Major "Stepovy," a former instructor in a Soviet officers' school, continued to teach in the UPA officers' school "Oleni"; Dmytro Karpenko ("Yastrub"), an ex-Soviet Army major, organized the "national" detachments of the UPA (composed of Uzbeks and others)—Mirchuk, *op. cit.*, pp. 254–55.

64. E.g., Col. Leonid Stupnytsky, who had formerly served in the Army of the (Eastern) Ukrainian National Republic (UNR), 1917–1920, in 1943 became Chief of Staff of the UPA Group North. *Ibid.*, p. 239.

65. The young poet Joseph Pozychanyuk (b. ca. 1911, d. in battle in February, 1945). He had been on the editorial board of *Komsomols'ka Pravda* (Komsomol Truth [Kiev]); became a member of the OUN in 1940. He had been imprisoned by Soviets and Germans. See the sketch by B. Podolyak, "J.P.—Poet, Revolutionary, Member of the UHVR," *Suchasna Ukrayina*, February 18, 1951, pp. 9–10.

66. E.g., Drs. "Maksymovych" and "Kum," of the officers' school "Oleni" (Mirchuk, *op. cit.,* p. 254). See also Lebed', *op. cit.,* pp. 35ff.
67. An Eastern Ukrainian once told a Galician Nationalist: "Look here, I was born in Moscow but I am an Ukrainian. My wife is a Russian, but she was born here in Dniepropetrovsk. Are we Ukrainians, too?"
   On the activity of the OUN in Eastern Ukraine, see Armstrong, *op. cit.,* pp. 73ff. and *passim;* also Shankowsky, *Pokhidni hrupy OUN,* pp. 39ff., 102–03, 144, 169ff. and *passim.*
68. At the III Extraordinary Grand Congress of the OUN, August 21–25, 1943 —interview #12. There is no mention of those decisions in the reprinted materials of the Congress—see *OUN v svitli postanov . . . ,* pp. 90ff.
69. At that Congress, Roman Shukhevych was elected Head of the Bureau of the Leadership of the OUN; a month later he was appointed Commander in Chief of the UPA; in 1944 he became Head of the General Secretariat of the OUN. The creation of the UHVR is well analyzed in Armstrong, *op. cit.,* pp. 157–64. It was in July, 1944—interview #12.
70. So-called "Self-Defense Platoons."
71. Interview #1.
72. This problem is hinted at in Shankowsky, "UPA," pp. 793–94. On May 30, 1947, the UHVR decided to award UPA orders and decorations to all underground fighters of the OUN and meritorious civilians. On June 6, 1948, it decided to introduce in the security service ranks analogous to those of the UPA. It would appear that the security service, an integral part of the OUN, remained furthest removed from the UPA, for whatever reasons.
73. It should be stressed again that, a certain temptation notwithstanding, the military terminology of the UPA should be taken seriously. As the Germans and Soviets soon found out, General Roman Shukhevych and a few other Galician leaders, not to mention defectors from the officers corps of the Red Army, were professional soldiers, however unconventional their military training may have been.
74. They may have been right. Cf. Gerhard's comment that one of the greatest strengths of the OUN-UPA was its conspiratorial impenetrability—see this chapter, above, pp. 114–115.
75. Interview #12, with a high political officer of the UPA.
76. A description of the battle is contained in [Ukrainian SSR], *Kalendar-Dovidnyk na 1945 r.* (Calendar and Reference Book for 1945, Kiev), p. 171. The expression "new Stalingrad" is Stalin's. The battle took place in February, 1944.
77. Anonymous, *loc. cit.* (n. 60), No. 22/47, October 19, 1952.
78. *Ibid.*
79. It was signed by Khrushchev for the Communist Party of Ukraine (Bolshevik), Hrechukha for the Ukrainian Supreme Soviet, and D. S. Korotchenko for the Ukrainian People's Commissariat. Original of proclamation is kept in UHVR archives in New York City, where it was consulted by this writer. The document is referred to in Khrushchev's speech; its general appearance suggests authenticity.
80. See the abridged version in *Bol'shevik,* Vol. XX, No. 6 (March, 1944), pp. 7–35: ["Liberation of Ukrainian Lands from the German Aggressors and the Immediate Tasks of Reconstructing the National Economy of Soviet Ukraine"]. This should be assumed to be the most authoritative version. The section on Ukrainian nationalists comprises 3½ pages, immediately

following the compliments on the conduct of the Ukrainian people and Soviet Ukrainian partisans during the war (pp. 13–16).

81. On the plenum see *Pravda*, November 25, 1944, or Holubnychy, "Outline History of the Communist Party of the Ukraine," *The Ukrainian Review* (Institute for the Study of the USSR, Munich), Vol. 6 (1958), pp. 110–11. Henceforth abbreviated as Holubnychy, "Outline History." The second appeal was dated December 1, 1944—see Volodymyr P. Byelayev & Mykhaylo Rudnytsky, *Pid chuzhymy praporamy* (Under Foreign Flags, Kiev, 1956), pp. 194ff.

82. Andrew Melnyk is a prominent OUN leader, who during the war became a political rival of Stepan Bandera.

83. Section on German misdeeds in the Ukraine; Khrushchev, *loc. cit.*, p. 16.

84. In Soviet political protocol, the attribute "great" has normally been reserved to the Russians and, in the 1950's, for the Chinese, too. This is one of the rare instances where it has been applied to Ukrainians.

85. Concluding section, "The Ukrainian People Is Loyal to Its Fatherland—the Great Soviet Union," p. 32.

86. See also Robert Conquest, *The Soviet Deportation of Nationalities* (New York: St. Martin's, 1960).

87. Osyp Orlenko (pseud.), *Bol'shevyky v borot'bi z ukrayins'kym revolyut-siyno-vyzvol'nym rukhom v druhiy imperiyalistychniy viyni* (The Bolsheviks in the Struggle against the Ukrainian Revolutionary Liberation Movement in the Second Imperialist War, Kiev-Lviv, 1946), p. 27. (54 mimeographed pages.) Allegedly an underground publication: worn out, very badly done, appears authentic. Quotations from Soviet sources that are rather difficult to obtain in the West are generally reliable, though this particular appeal dated November 27, 1944.

88. See the abridged version in [UkrSSR], *Kalendar-dovidnyk na 1945 r.*, pp. 181–84, or the English translation in the Canadian Ukrainian pro-Communist newspaper *Ukrayins'ke Zhyttya* (Ukrainian Life, Toronto), December 20, 1945, p. 11.

89. Shankowsky, "UPA," p. 714.

90. Interviews #6, 33. Milovan Djilas writes in confirmation: *"After the expulsion of the Germans,* some two and a half million Ukrainians were drafted into the Red Army." *Conversations with Stalin* (New York: Harcourt, Brace & World, 1962), pp. 119–120; italics added.

91. See above, p. 88, on Stalin's attitude as related by Khrushchev and the Polish general Anders.

92. Shankowsky, "UPA," p. 742.

93. Interview #12. But see also the ["Declaration of the Leadership of the OUN after the conclusion of World War II in Europe"], dated May 1945, in *OUN v svitli* . . . , pp. 121ff., esp. Section IV on "Anglo-Soviet contradictions," pp. 128ff.

94. This reorganization is foreshadowed in a resolution in the cited declaration, Section IX, No. 2/ye, p. 140, but it appears to have been carried out in earnest after extensive Soviet counter-actions in the winter of 1945–46. See the extracts from the ["Resolutions of the Conference of the OUN Leadership in the Ukraine, . . . June 1946"], *ibid.*, pp. 143ff., and Shankowsky's analysis, "UPA," pp. 773ff. These resolutions show a hardheaded appraisal of the international situation and the situation in the Soviet Union; for example, the decline in British power is correctly evaluated.

95. Interview #62.
96. According to a Soviet account, some Ukrainian underground members went so far as the virgin lands in Central Asia. See G. Aksel'rod, ["With Sword and Knuckle-Duster"], *Yunost'* (Youth [Moscow]), Vol. 1959, No. 6, and Shankowsky's bibliographical article "Soviet and Satellite Sources on the Ukrainian Insurgent Army," *The Annals of the Ukrainian Academy of Arts and Sciences in the U.S.,* Vol. IX (1961), p. 258.
97. Shankowsky, "UPA," p. 755.
98. The author has been shown a typewritten copy of that order, the authenticity of which has been vouched for by Professor Shankowsky.
99. Orlenko, *op. cit.,* p. 16. Orlenko dates the appeal February 26, 1946, but such an appeal was published in the special sheet of *Rad. Ukrayina* intended for the Western provinces March 27, 1946, as announced in the table of contents of the available *Kiev* edition. It is possible either that (a) the reference in Orlenko is inaccurate, or (b) that the proclamation was reprinted with a month's delay.
100. Interview #12.
101. Peter Pirogov, *Why I Escaped,* p. 201. Reprinted with permission of Duell, Sloan & Pearce, Publishers.
102. For full citation and discussion, see Note IV-1, in the Appendix, pp. 419ff.
103. Byelayev & Rudnytsky, *op. cit.,* p. 203.
104. The New York *Times,* May 21, 1954, p. 5. See also the announcement of the execution of four Ukrainians convicted of spying on behalf of the U.S. *ibid.,* May 27, 1953, p. 1.
105. See the article by Stakhiv in *Suchasna Ukrayina,* June 6, 1954, p. 3.
106. "A Repentant Emigre—Nationalism in the Ukraine," *Manchester Guardian,* May 20, 1954, p. 7.
107. From an appeal published around February 10, 1956, in the Ukrainian provincial newspaper *Chervony Prapor* (Red Flag, Rivne, Volhynia), in an article entitled "The Motherland Forgives." See Ansel Talbert (military and aviation editor), "Behind Khrushchev's Co-existence Offer," New York *Herald Tribune,* February 16, 1956, p. 10, who quotes the expression cited in the text; also the Moscow correspondence of *Muenchener Merkur* (Mercury of Munich [Germany]), February 14, 1956. The appeal was later broadcast by Radio Moscow (present writer's interview with the monitor of an American radio station who picked it up himself). In short, though the original source is not available, the secondhand account should be regarded as reliable.
108. Shankowsky, "UPA," pp. 719, 734.
109. See Chapter III, above, p. 95.
110. Interview #74.
111. Interview #62.
112. Interviews #1, 12 and 64.
113. Shankowsky, "UPA," p. 736; interview #64.
114. The original was captured by the Ukrainian underground; a typewritten transcript is kept in the UHVR archives in New York. Professor Shankowsky vouches for its authenticity since he knows the hands through which it had passed. Instruction is undated.
115. Confirmed by interview #78: In Bukovina Red soldiers would go from house to house demanding, "Where are your menfolk?" Deportation of

families has been furthermore admitted in Kovalchuk's *Nakaz N. 312* (Order No. 312), of December, 1949. See Note IV-1, in the Appendix for full citation and discussion of authenticity.

116. Interview #69.
117. Interview #74.
118. Shankowsky, "UPA," pp. 734, 763.
119. Manuscript B.
120. Reprinted in *Pozytsiyi ukrayins'koho vyzvol'noho rukhu: Materiyaly z rid-nykh zemel' do pytan' borot'by za ukrayins'ku derzhavu* (Positions of the Ukrainian Liberation Movement: Materials from the Ukraine on Questions of the Struggle for a Ukrainian State, Munich: Prolog, 1948), pp. 25–81. The group who published it are known to have had contacts with the underground; materials should be regarded as authentic. The article was written in April, 1947.
121. *Ibid.*, p. 27.
122. For an extended scholarly discussion of the attitudes of former Soviet citizens on socio-economic issues see Alex Inkeles and Raymond R. Bauer, *The Soviet Citizen* (Cambridge, Mass.: Harvard University Press, 1959), *passim*, esp. pp. 242ff.
123. See V. P. Stakhiv, "The Program That Has Insured the Growth of the Underground," *Suchasna Ukrayina*, June 26, 1955. The two programs are usefully compared in *OUN v svitli postanov . . .*, pp. 103ff., the cited points being: 1(a)—on kolkhozes, p. 108; 11(b)—on political organization, p. 112.
124. E.g., the old program contained the following paragraph: "In the ranks of the OUN are fighting Ukrainian peasants, workers and intelligentsia against [our] oppressors—for an Independent and United Ukrainian State, for national and social liberation, for a new state order and a new social system." In 1949–1950, the non-committal attribute "new" was spelled out as follows: ". . . for a *democratic* state order and a just social system." *Ibid.*, p. 108.
125. [*Immediately for What Are We Fighting?*], printed in the underground, rather badly, on an exercise book stamped "Exercise Book of the State Paper Mills 'Hero of Labor,' Town of Dobrush, B[elorussian] SSR." Original kept in the UHVR archives in New York where consulted by author —should be regarded as authentic.
126. *Ibid.*, pp. 4ff.
127. *Ibid.*, p. 9.
128. "The Preparation of World War III and the Tasks of the Ukrainian People," in the underground *Byuleten' Byuro Informatsiyi UHVR* (Bulletin of the UHVR Information Bureau), No. 9 (May, 1951). Photostat consulted by author in UHVR archives in New York. Reprinted in *Suchasna Ukrayina*, November 29, 1953.
129. *Khrin, op. cit.*, pp. 84ff.
130. Besides Manuilsky's speech of January, 1945, and Khrushchev's in Kiev, March, 1944, see especially Khrushchev's speech in Kiev of October 13, 1945, on the first anniversary of the liberation, in *Kalendar dovidnyk na 1946 r.* (Calendar Almanac for 1946), pp. 192ff.; esp. 207ff.
131. Such lectures in Volhynia were ordered by Profatilov in his instruction.
132. E.g., a leaflet to be dropped from planes entitled "To the People of the Ukraine" and issued by the assembled at a meeting of the "intelligentsia

in Kiev," February 5, 1944. Original consulted in the UHVR archives in New York.

133. See *Pravda,* October 7, 1944 (editorial on "Mass Political Work in the Liberated Districts"). Also, the following important articles in *Rad. Ukrayina,* Kiev: O. Kasymenko, "Ukrainian-German Nationalists—the Most Heinous Enemy of the Ukrainian People," December 10, 1944; O. Bandura, "The End of the 'Grey Wolf,'" August 4, 1945; O. Vyshnya's feuilleton, *ibid.;* Ya. Halan, "Nationalist Vampires," August 14, 1946 (a very important article); L. Levchenko, "Off With You to the Garbage Heap of History," August 8, 1947 (a Ukrainian nationalist had written an anonymous letter to the editor); Ryaboklyach, *loc. cit.* (1951); Karmansky's series, *loc. cit.* (Chapter III, above; 1952). Among journal articles should be mentioned: O. Mstyslavets', "Branded Traitors," in *Radyans'ky Lviv* (Lviv), Vol. 1947, No. 1, pp. 56–61; S. Trofymyuk, "Forever Cursed by the People," in *Zhovten'* (October, Lviv), Vol. 1955, No. 5.

134. *Na vysokiy polonyni* (Up in the Mountain Pasture), staged in Lviv; see *Lvovskaya pravda* as cited by Havrylyuk, "Soviet Cinema and Theater in the Struggle Against the Ukrainian Underground," *Suchasna Ukrayina,* June 20, 1954, pp. 3ff.

135. *On the River Cheremosh,* reviewed in detail by L. Poltoratsky, "A Screenplay on the People from the Carpathians," *Iskusstvo kino* (Film Art [Moscow]), Vol. 1954, No. 5 (May), pp. 73–78; *This Must Not Be Forgotten,* reviewed by Mar'yanov in *Rad. Ukrayina,* July 17, 1954; the Czech film *Action B,* referred to in Byelayev & Rudnytsky, *op. cit.,* p. 210. The film was shown in the Soviet Ukraine.

136. O. Mstyslavets', *Roztlyteli svidomosty* (The Awakeners of Conscience, Lviv, 1950)—not available, mentioned in *Suchasna Ukrayina,* August 19, 1951; Yu. Smolych, *Vorohy lyudstva ta yikh naymantsi* (Enemies of Mankind and Their Hirelings), reviewed in *Rad. Ukrayina,* June 26, 1953; V. Rudnyev, *Ukrayins'ki burzhuazni natsionalisty—ahentura mizhnarodnoyi reaktsiyi* (Ukrainian Bourgeois Nationalists—Agents of the International Reactionary Movement, Kiev, 1955 [30,000 copies]); Byelayev & Rudnytsky, *op. cit.* (1956 [15,000 copies]). In the brief preface to the last work are listed other pamphlets and monographs on this subject that could not be identified, by M. Bazhan, O. Poltoratsky, V. Osechynsky; jointly by B. Dudykevych and Ya. Vitoshynsky.

137. Shankowsky, *loc. cit.* (1961).

138. The most interesting of those is the Ukrainian nationalist spy thriller by Vadim Peunov, *Poslednee delo Korshuna* (Korshun's Last Action, Stalino, 1955).

139. Mynko, "Chorny zmiy (Black Serpent)," *Dnipro* (Kiev), Vol. XXXII, No. 2 (February, 1958), p. 21, as cited by Shankowsky, *loc. cit.* (1961), p. 261.

140. See Bohodyst, as cited by Shankowsky, *ibid.,* p. 256.

141. On the Chervonoarmiys'k trial see Yu. Mel'nychuk, "When Blood Curdles in Your Veins," *Rad. Ukrayina,* June 5, 1959, pp. 3–4. For a brief account of similar trials, see Shankowsky, *ibid.,* p. 257.

142. See Ryaboklyach, *loc. cit.* (1951).

143. At the plenum of the Central Committee of CP of Ukraine which met December 12–14, 1945, Lytvyn, the Central Committee secretary in charge of propaganda, complained that the level of propaganda work in the Ukraine was deplorably low. It had to be increased if only to counteract

the talks of the new settlers from Poland. *Pravda,* July 14, 1946, per Holubnychy, "Outline History," p. 90.

144. Interview #73: source travelled from Eastern Germany to the Soviet Union, in October, 1945 and September, 1946.

Notes to Chapter V: Soviet Linguistic Policy . . .

1. Cf. especially the history of the peoples of the Hapsburg Empire. See, e.g., Oscar Jaszi, *The Dissolution of the Habsburg Monarchy* (Chicago: Univ. of Chicago Press, 1929), pp. 262ff. *et passim;* not so clearly in Robert A. Kann, *The Habsburg Empire: A Study in Integration and Disintegration* (New York: Praeger, 1957), pp. 107 *et passim.*

2. Royal Institute of International Affairs, *Nationalism* ("Study Group, [E. H. Carr, chmn."], [London: Oxford University Press, 1939]), p. 15. Cited by permission of Oxford University Press.

3. *Slavic and East European Journal,* Vol. XVII (1959), p. 17.

4. Reprinted from *Nationalism and Social Communication* (New York & Cambridge, Mass.: Wiley & M.I.T. Press, 1953), pp. 95–96, by Karl W. Deutsch, by permission of the M.I.T. Press. Copyright, 1953, the Massachusetts Institute of Technology. Italics added.

5. Cf. Vasyl Chaplenko, *Bil'shovyts'ka movna polityka* (Bolshevik Language Policy, Munich: Institute for the Study of the USSR, 1956), p. 5. (Mimeographed.)

6. In his "Critical Remarks on the Nationality Question," *Prosveshchenie* (Enlightenment), Vol. 1913, No. 10/12 (October-December), as cited by Chaplenko, *op. cit.,* p. 22.

7. As cited *ibid.* (Chaplenko), p. 18. Statement was made in 1914.

8. I. V. Stalin, *Marxism and Linguistics* (New York: International Publishers, 1951), p. 50. By permission of International Publishers Co., Inc.

9. *Ibid.,* pp. 55ff. By permission of International Publishers Co., Inc.

10. The material has been conveniently assembled and translated by John V. Murra *et al.* in *The Soviet Linguistic Controversy* (New York: King's Crown Press, 1951). For Stalin's statements alone, see also Stalin, *op. cit.* (n. 8, above).

11. Yu. Sherekh (Shevelov), "The Decline of Marrism," *Novi Dni* (New Days [Toronto]), Vol. 1950, No. 6 (June), p. 9. By author's permission.

12. Stalin, *op. cit.,* p. 12.

13. *Ibid.,* p. 28.

14. *Ibid.,* p. 45.

15. For a very clear and incisive analysis of the linguistic problems, as viewed by a political scientist, see Ch. IX in Elliot R. Goodman, *The Soviet Design for a World State* (New York: Columbia University Press, 1960), pp. 264–84, esp. pp. 276ff. A complicating factor, which does not, however, invalidate the main conclusion in the present work, is that some of Marr's followers have twisted his original class-oriented, a-national doctrine: ". . . the elements of Marr's theories, and the vagueness with which they were stated, lent themselves to easy perversion by his disciples, who, in the guise of following Marr's linguistic theories, joined other Soviet linguists in the systematic glorification of the Russian language" (Goodman, *op. cit.,* p. 277). Supreme tactician that he was Stalin in one breath laid the theoreti-

cal basis for the glorification of Russian and criticized linguists who Russified non-Russian languages too openly. For a different conclusion see Roman Smal-Stocki, *The Nationality Problem of the Soviet Union and Russian Communist Imperialism* (Milwaukee: Bruce, 1952), pp. 87-88. Professor Roman Smal Stocki, a philologist, writes: ". . . We can say that Marr made Russian a holy venerated language in the Communist church, like Greek or Old Church Slavic in the Christian Churches" (p. 88).

See also the discussion in Robert S. Sullivant, *Soviet Politics and the Ukraine, 1917–57* (New York: Columbia University Press, 1962), pp. 268–72. In my judgment, Professor Sullivant overemphasizes the importance of Stalin's tactical pseudo-concessions to the non-Russian peoples (". . . no language could be branded in Marxian terms as superior to any other," p. 270), does not sufficiently stress the official sanctioning of the actual, as contrasted with theoretical, predominance of Russian.

16. A convenient source is Charlotte Saikowski & Leo Gruliow, eds., *Current Soviet Policies IV: The Documentary Record of the 22nd Congress of the Communist Party of the Soviet Union* (New York: Columbia University Press, 1962), pp. 26–27. Henceforth cited as *Current Soviet Policies IV*.

17. *Ibid.*, pp. 103, 104; or *Pravda*, October 19, 1961, p. 7. Italics in first paragraph in original; others, added. Copyright 1962, the Joint Committee on Slavic Studies. Reprinted by permission.

18. See Note V-1, in the Appendix.

19. Arsen Khomenko, *Natsional'ny sklad lyudnosty USRR* (National Composition of the Population of UkrSSR, Kharkov, 1931), pp. 98ff.

20. Compiled from tables, *ibid.*, pp. 98, 132–34. The definition of nationality in the 1926 census has been cited in Note II-1, in the Appendix. On the relation of linguistic assimilation to nationality, see this chapter, below, and Chapter X.

21. The problem of the Jewish minority has been touched upon in Note I-3, in the Appendix. Other minorities have been ignored for simplicity's sake.

22. A possible explanation for the surprising assimilatory tendency among the Poles is that 200,000 of them (more than 55 per cent) live in the countryside (*Narodne hospodarstvo Ukrayins'koyi RSR v 1959 r.* [National Economy of the Ukrainian SSR]; Kiev, 1960, p. 14). But the number of Poles linguistically assimilated to Ukrainians exceeds 200,000, which means that Polish urban dwellers also fall prey to that tendency. Very possibly that tendency is caused by the discriminatory policy of the regime.

23. An attempt to do so has been made by Shankowsky, "The Effects of the Soviet Nationality Policy in the Light of the 1959 Census and Other Statistical Data," *Prologue* (New York), Vol. V, No. 1–2 (Spring-Summer, 1961), pp. 50ff. But the figures relate to the territory of the USSR as a whole, not the Ukrainian SSR, and cannot be used without further adjustments, which are likely to further impair the accuracy of the estimates.

24. P. H. Pod''yachikh, *Naselenie SSSR* (Population of the USSR, Moscow, 1961), p. 107.

25. Khomenko, *op. cit.*, p. 98. Khomenko always breaks the figures down into numbers of men and women. In the rural areas the figures for *Polessye* are 84.9% for men and 84.6% for women (average 84.7%); the national average is 96.5% for both men and women; the figures for the mining region are 89.7% for men and 89.9% for women.

26. Until 1934, Kharkov was the official capital of the Ukrainian SSR.

27. On intermarriages, see Chapter II, above, pp. 54–55.
28. See *Bol'shaya Sovetskaya Entsyklopediya* (2nd ed.), Vol. 44, p. 169A.
29. The following is based on a study of answers to the linguistic question, prepared by the writer for the Harvard Russian Research Center ("Findings of the Harvard Refugee Interview Project on the Extent of Ukrainian Spoken in the Ukrainian SSR," August 1959, MS).
30. Interview #33; also Yaroslava Surmach, "Sketches of Kiev," *Horizons* (Ukrainian Students' Review, New York), Vol. II, No. 1/2 (Fall, 1956/Spring, 1957), p. 56. Miss Surmach notes that in the Department of Folklore and Ethnography of the Kiev Academy of Sciences, "as in an oasis, Ukrainian was spoken exclusively."
31. The letter was reprinted in *Svoboda* (Liberty [Jersey City, N.J.]), January 8, 1958, p. 1.
32. Interview #6.
33. Interview #16.
34. Interview #79.
35. See, e.g., Surmach, *loc. cit.*, p. 61.
36. See also the excellent survey by Yosyp Hirnyak, "Birth and Death of the Modern Ukrainian Theater," in Martha Bradshaw (ed.), *Soviet Theaters, 1917–1947* (New York: Research Program on the USSR, 1954), pp. 250–338. Also the impression of an American scholar cited in the present work, pp. 200B–200C.
37. After the school reform started in 1959, which ostensibly left it up to parents to decide whether their children in Russian-language schools should study Ukrainian as a second subject, there may now (1962) be a few citizens who have not been taught Ukrainian at school; hence, the qualification "virtually all." See also below.
38. Vsevolod Holubnychy, "The Language of Instruction: An Aspect of the Problem of Nationalities in the Soviet Union," *Horizons, loc. cit.*, p. 27, quoting from *Visti* (News [Kiev]), September 24, 1939.
39. Decision No. 63, "Concerning the Realization of Compulsory Universal Education in the Schools of the Ukrainian SSR," *Zbirnyk nakaziv i rozporyadzhen' Narodnoho Komisariatu Osvity Ukrayins'koyi RSR* (Collection of Orders and Instructions of the People's Commissariat of Education of the UkrSSR), Vol. 1940, No. 27 (September), p. 4; italics added.
40. "Concerning the Approval of the UkrSSR Network of Schools for the School Year 1940–41 (July 4, 1940)," *ibid.*, Vol. 1940, No. 18 (June), pp. 14ff.
41. Interview #58. Respondent #33 stated that in the late 1940's, after attending a Ukrainian ten-year school, he transferred to a Russian one to perfect his knowledge of that language.
42. G. Yemel'yanenko, "In the Friendship of Peoples Lies Our Strength," *Pravda Ukrainy*, July 28, 1956, p. 3. See also the discussion in Chapter I, p. 26, above.
43. Oscar Jaszi, *op. cit.*, as quoted in Deutsch, *op. cit.*, p. 240. Reprinted from the latter work by permission of the M.I.T. Press. (Copyright 1953, The Massachusetts Institute of Technology.)
44. The number of hours of instruction for various disciplines in 1955–56 is given in E. N. Medynsky, *Prosveshchenie v SSSR* (Education in USSR, Moscow, 1955), pp. 88, 89. For more recent figures, after the 1958 school reform, see the instructions in *Radyans'ka Osvita* (Soviet Education [Kiev]),

June 6, 1959, p. 4. See also Table V-6, below, for the number of weekly hours devoted to Ukrainian and Russian in elementary and secondary schools of the Ukrainian SSR, 1959–1960.

45. As quoted by Holubnychy, "The Language of Instruction . . . ," *loc. cit.,* p. 36.

46. See also the more extensive discussion below, pp. 172ff.

47. Sullivant, *op. cit.,* p. 296.

48. See the figures in *Kul'turnoe stroitel'stvo SSSR* (Moscow, 1956), pp. 88–89.

49. Confirmed by a recent defector from Lviv in a public talk in New York, November 20, 1960: Russian-language schools tend to be better equipped. The informant was a director of a secondary school in Lviv.

50. S. Siropolko, *Narodnya osvita na sovyets'kiy Ukrayini* (Public Education in Soviet Ukraine, Warsaw: Ukrainian Scientific Institute, 1934), p. 48, citing the curriculum for rural schools in 1930–1931. The change was first made in 1938; see Sullivant, *op. cit.,* pp. 232–33.

51. Alexander C. Korol, *Soviet Education for Science and Technology* (Cambridge, Mass. & New York: M.I.T. Press & Wiley, 1957), p. 179.

52. "Persons who have graduated from schools whose language of instruction is other than Russian and who are entering the Russian-language sections [i.e., departments in which subjects are taught in Russian—Y.B.] of the higher schools *of the Republic,* in the language of which they have been taught, are allowed to take all their examinations in the native language. These persons are given only an oral control examination in Russian, the results of this examination not being considered if the student has [otherwise] obtained positive grades in the entrance competition." See Ministerstvo Vysshego Obrazovaniya SSSR (USSR Ministry of Higher Education), *Pravila priema i programmy priemnykh ekzamenov dlya postupayushchikh v vysshie uchebnye zavedeniya v 1957 g.* (Admission Rules and Programs of Entrance Examinations for Candidates for Admission to Higher Educational Institutions in 1957, Moscow, 1957), p. 6; italics added. The rules for 1959–60 were similar, except that it was not mentioned in what language the entrance examinations had to be taken by that particular group of secondary school graduates. (An oral examination in Russian was administered for control purposes only, as in 1957–58, except for applicants to the departments of philology, linguistics, journalism, and literary work who had to pass examinations in both their native language and Russian). See Note to Paragraph III (2), "Rules for Admission to Regular Higher Educational Establishments in the U.S.S.R. for the Academic Year 1959–60," as reproduced *in toto* in Nicholas De Witt, *Education and Professional Employment in the U.S.S.R.* (Washington, D.C.: National Science Foundation, 1961), p. 631.

In the academic year 1963–64, however, Russian language requirements for non-Russians were raised. When applying for admission to a higher school they were allowed to take a written examination in Russian the results of which were counted as additional points in the very complicated admissions procedure. See the explanation by Docent V. F. Nemtsov, Assistant Director of the Administration for Instructional Methods in Higher Educational Institutions of the USSR Ministry of Higher and Specialized Secondary Education, "Good New Replenishments for the Higher Educational Institutions," *Vestnik vysshey shkoly* (Bulletin for Higher Schools) , Vol. 1963, No. 4 (April), pp. 15–17; or *CDSP,* Vol. XV,

No. 19, p. 3. Some of the implications of this change are discussed in the present writer's forthcoming article in the *Comparative Education Review* (June or October, 1964), "Some Problems in the Education of the Non-Russian Peoples in the Soviet Union."

53. See the complaints by a teacher of Ukrainian in *Literaturna hazeta* (Literary Gazette [Kiev]), August 16, 1956, as cited by Ye. Shtendera in *Suchasna Ukrayina*, September 9, 1956, p. 4; also the editorial ["Urgent Tasks in the Teaching of Ukrainian"], in *Ukrayins'ka mova v shkoli* (Ukrainian Language at School [Kiev]), Vol. VII, No. 2 (March-April, 1957), p. 5.

54. DeWitt, *op. cit.*, pp. 25–26, 35–36, 138–39, 147–50.

55. See Chapter I, above, pp. 29ff.

56. See, e.g., the editorial in *Ukrayins'ka mova v shkoli*, Vol. 1959, No. 4 (April), p. 5: "This principle of being able to choose the language of instruction, in our opinion, must under no circumstances be left to take care of itself (*na samo plyv*). The press, the radio, the public must conduct insistent explanatory work among the parents and workers."

57. S. Chervonenko, ["Close Connection with Life is the Condition for Successful Ideological Work"], *Komunist Ukrayiny*, Vol. 1959, No. 7 (July), p. 38.

58. I. Bilodid, ["We Strengthen the Links of School with Life"], in *Ukrainskaya sovetskaya kul'tura: Sbornik statey* (Ukrainian Soviet Culture: Collected Articles, Kiev, 1961), p. 61.

59. R. Babiychuk, ["The Flourishing of Ukrainian Soviet Culture"], *ibid.*, p. 14.

60. *Ukrayins'ka Radyans'ka Entsyklopediya*, Vol. IX (Kiev, 1962), p. 514. See also Table V-4 (this book) for data on other than Ukrainian-language and Russian-language schools.

61. *Radyans'ka Ukrayina*, July 5, 1962, p. 1.

62. Interview #76, with a former University lecturer in Kiev.

63. See also the previous discussion, above, p. 159.

64. Incidentally, this makes it methodologically incorrect to base one's conclusions upon an analysis of catalogues. A catalogue is available listing all non-periodical publications in the Ukrainian SSR in 1955, but it is of little use for our present purpose. See UkrSSR Ministry of Culture, Main Administration of Publishing Houses and Polygraphic Industry, *Spysok literatury vypushchenoyi vydavnytsvamy Ukrayiny v 1955 r.* (Kiev, 1956).

65. Interview #80, referring to the time just before the German invasion. The respondent added that for this reason some parents were simply afraid to send their children to a Ukrainian-language school, because "the teaching of Russian in the Ukraine corrupts that language, and the teaching of it at a Ukrainian school corrupts it absolutely."

66. Bruno Kalnins, *Der sowjetische Propagandastaat* (The Soviet Propaganda State, Stockholm: Tiden, 1956), pp. 209ff. *Glavizdat* is apparently an abbreviation for "Main Administration for Book Publishing"; *Glavknigotorg*, "Main Administration for Book Sale."

67. The word "popular" has been put in quotation marks because it is ultimately the Party which decides what book should be made available to a large number of readers. Nevertheless, a comparison between the relative number of copies and that of titles is enlightening. (See these differences in both Tables V-8 and V-9.) It appears that the difference between copies and titles of Russian books is rather modest, but since 1938—a high water

mark of Russification—that difference has been very substantial in the case of *Ukrainian* books, showing that the relatively few Ukrainian titles are published in large editions.—See, however, the somewhat contrary impression by an American political scientist, above, p. 158.

68. See editorial "Urgent Tasks in the Teaching of Ukrainian Language," *loc. cit.* (note 53), p. 4. Blaming the Ukrainian *knigotorg* rather than the central agency in Moscow may imply either of two things; after 1955, the responsibility for certain decisions in this field may have been shifted downward, or it is still impolitic to criticize a Moscow agency.

69. *Kul'turnoe stroitel'stvo SSSR* (Moscow, 1956), p. 325.

70. *Sovetskaya Kul'tura*, of May 4, 1957, pp. 2–4, gave the following breakdown for the number of newspapers in the Ukraine: 8 Republican, or central papers, 45 provincial, and 820 city and district papers, plus 1,500 factory and *kolkhoz* papers appearing in large editions (i.e., not "wall newspapers"). But in 1956, only 1,273 newspapers were listed in central statistics (see Table V-10). In 1956, there were 26 provinces in the Ukraine, which means that not every province had two newspapers.

71. See V. Zatons'ky, *Natsional'na problema na Ukrayini; dopovid' na plenumi TsK LKSMU, cherven' 1926 r.* (National Problem in the Ukraine; address at a plenum of the Komsomol of Ukraine Central Committee, June 1926; Kharkov, 1926), pp. 4–5.

72. Heinz Kloss, as cited by Selig S. Harrison in *The Most Dangerous Decades: An Introduction to the Comparative Study of Language Policy in Multi-Lingual States* (New York: Language and Communications Research Center, Columbia University, 1957), p. 12. Harrison's introduction, with very comprehensive bibliographies compiled by several specialists, makes his book a most valuable study.

73. *Visnyk instytutu ukrayins'koyi naukovoyi movy* (Kiev), Vol. I, No. 1 (1928), pp. 5ff.

74. Ironic reference to a Ukrainian school of thought in the third quarter of the nineteenth century, associated with the name of Nicholas Kostomarov. Kostomarov, a well-known Ukrainian historian, wrote in 1862 an article in St. Petersburg's *Osnova* (Basis) "On the Teaching in the South Russian Language," in which he expressed doubt as to whether Humboldt's *Cosmos* and Mommsen's *History of Rome* could be taught in Ukrainian. See S. Yefremov, *Istoriya ukrayins'koho pys'menstva* (History of Ukrainian Literature, Kiev: Ukrainian Teacher, [pre-1917]), p. 23.

75. Quotation from a poem of Shevchenko's, preceded by the words: "I shall exalt those petty dumb slaves and . . ."

76. See, e.g., A. Khvylya, ["For Bolshevik Vigilance on the Front of the Creation of a Ukrainian Culture"], in *Movoznavstvo* (Linguistics [Kiev]), Vol. 1934, No. 1, pp. 8ff.; O. M. Finkel, ["Terminological Sabotage and Its Theoretical Roots"], *ibid.*, No. 2, pp. 66ff. as quoted in Uriel Weinreich, "The Russification of Soviet Minority Languages," *Problems of Communism*, Vol. II, No. 6 (1953), p. 53.

77. Cf. Stalin's letter to Kaganovich of 1926, as cited in Chapter I, above. See also the more extensive analysis in Sullivant, *op. cit.*, pp. 127–34.

78. Interview #75, with an ex-colonel of the Soviet army.

79. According to a well-informed British source, officials in Kiev were seen working with Ukrainian dictionaries propped up on their desks.

80. Roman Smal-Stocki, *Ukrayins'ka mova v sovyets'kiy Ukrayini* (Ukrainian

Language in Soviet Ukraine, Warsaw: Ukrainian Scientific Institute, Vol. 36, 1936), 271 pp.; also his *The Nationality Problem of the Soviet Union* . . . ; Yury Sherekh, "Principles and Stages of Bolshevik Linguistic Policy in the Ukraine," 3 installments, *Suchasna Ukrayina*, June 29, July 13 and 27, 1952; Uriel Weinreich, *loc. cit.*, pp. 46–57.

81. See, e.g., A. Khvylya, *Znyshchyty korinnya ukrayins'koho natsionalizmu na movnomu fronti* (Destroy the Roots of Ukrainian Nationalism on the Linguistic Front. Kharkov, 1933), p. 4; also the preface to the Ukrainian-Russian Dictionary published by the Academy of Sciences of the UkrSSR in 1953, Vol. I, pp. vff.

82. The policy might also have been used as a large-scale political provocation. Many of the officially backed protagonists of the Ukrainization later perished when the Party line changed.

83. *Istoricheskie zapiski* (Historical Notes [Moscow]), Vol. 48 (1954), p. 212. I am indebted for this note to Mr. Gregory Massell.

Notes to Chapter VI: Soviet Interpretation of Taras Shevchenko

1. Useful for general background are the very good studies by Ernest J. Simmons, "Introduction: Soviet Literature and Controls," and Robert M. Hankin, "Postwar Soviet Ideology and Literary Scholarship," in Ernest J. Simmons (ed.), *Through the Glass of Soviet Literature* (New York: Columbia University Press, 1953), pp. 3–26 and 244–89.

2. See Chapter V, above, p. 172, for those exceptions.

3. Ministerstvo Vysshego Obrazovaniya SSSR (USSR Ministry of Higher Education), *Pravila priema i programmy priemnykh ekzamenov dlya postupayushchikh v vysshie uchebnye zavedeniya v 1957 g.* (Admission Rules and Programs of Entrance Examinations for Candidates for Admission to Higher Educational Institutions in 1957, Moscow, 1957), pp. 25ff.

4. A. I. Bondarenko *et al.* (comps.), *Khrestomatiya z ukrayins'koyi literatury dlya 10 klasu seredn'oyi shkoly* (Reader in Ukrainian Literature for Grade X of Secondary Schools; Kiev, 1955), pp. 24–48. Another important statement reproduced is the resolution of the Central Committee of the Communist Party (Bolshevik) of Ukraine of August 24, 1946, "Concerning the Distortions and Errors in the Elucidation of the History of Ukrainian Literature Committed in the *Outline History of Ukrainian Literature*."

5. *Ibid.*, p. 37.

6. *Ibid.*, p. 13.

7. Bruno Kalnins, *Der sowjetische Propagandastaat*, pp. 210ff.

8. *Ibid.*, p. 211.

9. N. I. Karklina, ["Fundamental Questions of Library Work in the Decisions of the CPSU and the Soviet Government (1917–57)"], in [RSFSR Ministry of Culture], *Bibliotechnoe delo v SSSR* (Library Work in the USSR, Moscow, 1957), p. 108.

10. V. V. Serov, ["The Organization of Library Service for the Rural Population of the USSR"], *ibid.*, p. 236.

11. See Chapter V, above, p. 177.

12. Some 10 weekly hours out of 32–33 hours in Grade V, 9–10 (33) in Grade VI, 8–9 (34) in Grade VII, 8 (35–36) in Grade VIII and 7 out of 37 in

Grades IX and X, if lessons in Ukrainian and Russian grammar are included. See Table V-6 above.

13. I have looked over the readers in Ukrainian literature for Grades V–IX (1955 ed.).

14. DeWitt, *Education and Professional Employment in the USSR*, pp. 109–10.

15. L. F. Stetsenko, *Vyvchennya tvorchosti T. H. Shevchenka v shkoli* (The Study of the Works of T. H. Shevchenko at School, Kiev, 1955), p. 4, quoting Chernyshevsky as a motto for his teacher's handbook.

16. Marvin L. Kalb met a young girl in a Soviet library. She confided to him that she hated Soviet novels: "I read only Russian novels now. Russian novels of the nineteenth century. Those have no politics. They are pure art. We are all—me and my friends—sick and tired of politics in art. We want art again. Real art. . . ." See his *Eastern Exposure* (New York: Farrar, Straus, Cudahy, 1958), p. 125.—Quoted with the permission of the copyright holder, Farrar, Straus & Co.

17. Ministerstvo Vysshego Obrazovaniya SSSR, *loc. cit.* Required is an acquaintance with *Hamlet, Faust* (Part I) and two brief poems by Shevchenko: "Zapovit" (My Will) and "The Reaper."

18. And not only by Turgenev. Vovchok's *Marusya* (Mary) was rather popular in France, in French translation.

19. This episode is related, for example, in Akademiya nauk URSR, Instytut literatury im. T. H. Shevchenka (Ukrainian SSR Academy of Sciences, T. H. Shevchenko Institute of Literature), *Istoriya ukrayins'koyi literatury* (History of Ukrainian Literature, Kiev, 1954–1958), Vol. I, p. 267. Henceforth cited as *Istoriya ukr. lit.*

20. Serhiy Yefremov, *Istoriya ukrayins'koho pys'menstva* (Kiev, n.d. [pre-1917]), pp. 266, 267.

21. In my survey of the general Soviet interpretation of the poet's work I am in great debt to P. Odarchenko's article, "The Struggle for Shevchenko (Shevchenko in Soviet Interpretation)," *The Annals of the Ukrainian Academy of Arts and Sciences in the U.S.*, Vol. III (Spring, 1954), pp. 824–37. This article is based in turn upon Professor Odarchenko's 400 odd pp. MS.

22. As quoted by Odarchenko, *loc. cit.*, p. 827, from Richyts'ky's *Shevchenko v svitli epokhy* (Shevchenko in the Light of the Epoch).

23. Ye.S. Shablovsky, *Shevchenko ta yoho istorychne znachennya* (Shevchenko and His Historical Significance, Kiev, 1933), p. 252, partly cited by Odarchenko, *loc. cit.*, p. 828.

24. Shablovsky, *op. cit.*, p. 253.

25. As quoted by Odarchenko, *loc. cit.*, p. 827.

26. The text of the editorial has been reprinted with insignificant cuts in *Khrestomatiya z ukrayins'koyi literatury dlya 8 klasu* . . . (Reader in Ukrainian Literature for Grade VIII . . . , Kiev, 1955), pp. 273–75. Italics added.

27. As quoted by Odarchenko, *loc. cit.*, p. 834, from the unavailable *T. H. Shevchenko v dokumentakh i materialakh* (T. H. Shevchenko in Documents and Materials, Kiev, 1950), Part III. Cited by permission, the Ukrainian Academy of Arts and Sciences in the U.S., Inc.

28. As cited by Odarchenko, *loc. cit.*, p. 831.

29. See the Party decree of August 24, 1946, reprinted in *Khrestomatiya . . . dlya 10 klasu,* p. 21.
30. Odarchenko, *loc. cit.,* pp. 834–35. Cited by permission.
31. See Note VI-1, in the Appendix, for text and source.
32. The Praesidium members attending the session were L. I. Brezhnev, N. G. Ignatov, F. R. Kozlov, Kosygin, Mikoyan, Mukhitdinov, Suslov, Furtseva, Pospelov. See *Izvestiya,* March 12, 1961, p. 6.
33. See the chronicle ["Paying Tribute to the Memory of the Great Bard T. H. Shevchenko"], *Ukr. istorychny zhurnal,* Vol. 1961, No. 3 (May-June), pp. 149–50.
34. *Rad. Ukrayina,* March 10, 1961. An excerpt has been reproduced in Note VI-2, in the Appendix.
35. *Ibid.,* p. 2.
36. The two works involved were Dmyterko, *Obshchestvenno-politicheskie i filosofskie vzglyady T. G. Shevchenko* (Moscow, 1951) and I. Holovakha, *T. H. Shevchenko i rosiys'ki revolyutsiyni demokraty* (Kiev, 1953); the first on Shevchenko's socio-political and philosophical views, the second on his relationships with Russian revolutionary democrats. See the analysis in Petro Odarčenko (Odarchenko), "Ševčenko in Soviet Literary Criticism," in Volodymyr Mijakovs'kyj and George Y. Shevelov, eds., *Taras Ševčenko, 1814–1861: A Symposium* ('S-Gravenhage: Mouton & Co., 1962), pp. 294–95.
37. Odarchenko, *ibid.,* p. 297.
38. See, e.g., M. I. Marchenko's article directed to teachers of Ukrainian history in secondary schools, ["Shevchenko's Views on the Historical Past of the Ukrainian People"], *Ukr. istorychny zhurnal,* Vol. 1961, No. 1 (January-February), pp. 84–94. On p. 91 Marchenko asserts that Shevchenko evaluated Hetman Khmelnytsky positively for concluding a treaty of federation with Russia—a falsification (see below, this chapter). Also a recent work by Kyrylyuk, referred to by Odarchenko, *loc. cit.* (n. 36), p. 299.
39. O. I. Bilets'ky, ["Tasks and Perspectives of the Study of Shevchenko"], Akademiya nauk URSR, Instytut literatury im. T. H. Shevchenka (Ukr-SSR Academy of Sciences, T. H. Shevchenko Institute of Literature), *Zbirnyk prats' dev'yatoyi naukovoyi shevchenkivs'koyi konferentsiyi* (Collection of Papers of the Ninth Scholarly Shevchenko Conference, Kiev, 1961), pp. 14–15.
40. *Ibid.,* p. 38.
41. Stetsenko, *op. cit.,* pp. 153–54. In 1955, that search for Russian influences was subjected to incisive criticism by a Soviet Russian literary historian in his outstanding review of the "Academic" History of Ukrainian Literature, Vol. I. He found that approach "somewhat simplified," "one-sided," and in places "incorrectly exaggerated." "The reference to an influence does not explain anything by itself nor can it do so, because the very fact of influence calls for an explanation as well." See I. P. Eremin in *Vestnik Akademii Nauk SSSR* (Bulletin of the USSR Academy of Sciences, Moscow), Vol. 25, No. 10 (October, 1955), p. 106.
42. In Grade VIII. See *Khrestomatiya . . . dlya 8 klasu . . . ,* pp. 227–52.
43. Stetsenko, *op. cit.,* p. 128.
44. Letter to Hryhoriy Tarnavsky, of January 25, 1843—see Zaytsev (ed.), Shevchenko's *Tvory* (Works, Warsaw, Lviv: Ukrainian Scientific Institute, 1934–39), Vol. XI, pp. 23–25. Henceforth cited as *Tvory* (Zaytsev ed.).

45. September 30, 1842—*ibid.*, pp. 20–21.
46. See Ukrainian Free Academy of Sciences in Canada (L. Bilets'ky editor), Shevchenko's *Kobzar* (2nd rev. ed.; Winnipeg: Trident, 1952–54), Vol. II, pp. 322–24. Henceforth cited as *Kobzar* (L. Bilets'ky ed.).
47. See Note VI-3, in the Appendix, for references to Belinsky's argument.
48. Stetsenko, *op. cit.*, p. 147.
49. *Istoriya ukr. lit.*, Vol. I, p. 147.
50. Pavlo Zaytsev, *Zhyttya Tarasa Shevchenka* (Life of Taras Shevchenko, Paris, New York, Munich: Shevchenko Scientific Society, 1955), p. 322.
51. See his letter to M. Maksymovych, November 22, 1858, in Shevchenko's *Povna zbirka tvoriv v tr'okh tomakh* (Full Collected Works in 3 Vols., Kiev: State Publishers of Literature, 1949), Vol. III, p. 412. Henceforth cited as *Tvory* (1949).
52. Zaytsev, ["Shevchenko's Prose"], in *Tvory* (Zaytsev ed.), Vol. VII, pp. 299ff.
53. July 28–29, 1857. *Tvory* (1949), Vol. III, pp. 148ff.
54. See on this also Professor Shevelov's analysis, summarized in Note VI-4, in the Appendix.
55. Zaytsev, *op. cit.* (*Zhyttya . . .*), pp. 330, 367ff.; Biletsky in *Kobzar* (L. Biletsky ed.), Vol. IV, p. 61. In *Tvory* (1949), Vol. III, p. 422, Shevchenko's letter to Symyrenko of November 26, 1859, in which he accepted the financial offer, has been reprinted—but that fact has not been commented upon in his biography in the teachers handbook (Stetsenko, *op. cit.*), nor in the "academic" history.
56. In his diary, September 22, 1857. *Tvory* (1949), Vol. III, pp. 190–191.
57. Cf. *Tvory* (1949), Vol. I, pp. 257ff. In it the poet depicts three souls: one has been punished for auguring good luck when Khmelnytsky rode to Pereyaslav to conclude the treaty; the other for giving water to the horse of Peter I when he was riding home from the battle at Poltava at which he had defeated Mazeppa; the third for smiling at Catherine II. An English translation of the poem will be found in Clarence A. Manning, *Taras Shevchenko: Selected Poems* (Jersey City, N.J.: Ukrainian National Association, 1945), pp. 150ff.
58. *Ibid.* (*Tvory*), p. 550.
59. *Op. cit.*, Vol. I, pp. 235ff.: "Embodying in the present fate of the souls the position of the Ukrainian people under Tsar Nicholas I, Shevchenko expresses his indignation and wrath over the fact that Tsarism, the Cossack gentry, and the nobles have utilized the re-unification of the Ukraine with Russia and the defeat over the Swedes, for further increasing the oppression of the people. This idea has been expressed in an allegorical fashion: the 'souls' have been punished." This kind of reasoning has been called "highly dubious" even by a Soviet Russian reviewer; see Eremin, *loc. cit.*, p. 110.
60. Full text in *Tvory* (1949), Vol. I, pp. 292ff. Translation in Manning, *op. cit.*, pp. 171ff.
61. Stetsenko, *op. cit.*, pp. 104ff.; *Khrestomatiya . . . dlya 7 klasu . . .*, shortened text on pp. 42ff., with commentary; *Khrestomatiya . . . dlya 8 klasu . . .*, pp. 205ff. (abbreviated text). The cuts in the text do not seem to have been made for political reasons.
62. See p. 191 above.
63. Translated by Percy Paul Sever. Full Ukrainian text, *Tvory* (1949), Vol. I, p. 313. See also Manning, *op. cit.*, p. 179.

64. Stetsenko, *op. cit.*, p. 113. See also Note VI-5, in the Appendix.

65. Academician O. I. Bilets'ky, ["Shevchenko and World Literature"], in Aka-demiya nauk URSR (Ukrainian SSR Academy of Sciences), *Pam"yati T. H. Shevchenka: Zbirnyk stattey do 125-littya z dnya narodzhennya, 1814–1939* (In Memory of T. H. Shevchenko: Collected Articles on the 125th Anni-versary of His Birth, Kiev, 1939), pp. 207–26. The article by S. Shakhov-sky, ["Shevchenko and Russian Literature"] (pp. 261–96) is also much bet-ter documented than the post-1946 writings.

66. See the statement by Bilets'ky, cited above, p. 358. Likewise, P. Odar-chenko's valuable bibliographical article, "The Poetic Masterfulness of T. Shevchenko (In the Light of New Research, 1941–46," Ukrainian Acad-emy of Arts and Sciences in the U.S., *Shevchenkivsky richnyk* (Shevchenko Yearbook), No. 3 (1954), pp. 11–22.

67. E.g., in 1956, when the 100th anniversary of the birth of another Ukrain-ian classic, Ivan Franko, was celebrated O. Bilets'ky remarked that in view of the recently expanded cultural relations between the Soviet Union and India, the Indian element in Franko's poetry deserved renewed investiga-tion. See Ukrainian SSR Ministry of Higher Education, Kiev State Uni-versity, *XIII naukova sesiya; Tezy dopovidey; sektsiya filolohiyi* (13th Aca-demic Session; Theses of Delivered Papers, Philological Section; Kiev, 1956): O. I. Bilets'ky, "Franko and Indian Culture," pp. 3–6.

68. E.g., the size of the 1949 edition has not been indicated.

Notes to Chapter VII: Soviet Interpretation of Ukrainian History . . .

1. Cyril E. Black, "History and Politics in the Soviet Union," in Cyril E. Black (ed.), *Rewriting Russian History* (New York: Praeger, 1956), p. 3.

2. Mykhaylo Hrushevsky. *Istoriya Ukrayiny-Rusy* (2nd ed.; New York: Knyho-spilka, 1954–58), 10 vols. Henceforth, I shall refer to Hrushevsky's large history simply as "Hrushevsky," followed by a large Roman numeral to designate the volume.

3. See, e.g., William E. D. Allen, *The Ukraine: A History* (Cambridge [Eng-land] University Press, 1941), pp. 23, 30. It is not clear whether Allen has read the 1st volume of Hrushevsky's large history.

4. He wrote more than 2,000 works. See B. Krupnytskyj, "M. Hrushevsky and his Historical Work," in Hrushevsky, *op. cit.*, Vol. I, p. xviii. For an ob-jective appraisal of Hrushevsky's contribution to the history of East Slavs, see also Anatole G. Mazour, *An Outline of Modern Russian Historiogra-phy* (Berkeley: University of California Press, 1939), pp. 73ff. He writes: "Hrushevsky left a contribution to historical literature which, regardless of political feuds, will always have to be taken into consideration if Rus-sian [i.e., East European—Y.B.] history is to be seen in its entirety rather than as a series of episodic stages loosely revolving around the Muscovite state" (pp. 74–75).

5. S. Koval'ov "Correct the Mistakes in the Elucidation of some Problems in Ukrainian History," *Kul'tura i zhizn'* (Culture and Life, [organ of the Propaganda Section of the Central Committee of the All Union Commu-nist Party (Bolshevik)], Moscow), No. 3; reprinted in *Rad. Ukrayina*, July 24, 1946; M. Petrovsky, "Completely Unmask the Nationalist Distortions

in the History of the Ukraine (Concerning the Anti-Scientific Theories of Hrushevsky and his 'School')," *Rad. Ukrayina*, July 24, 26, 1946; K. Huslysty, "The Origins of East Slavic Peoples and the Kievan Rus," *ibid.*, September 14, 1946; "General Meeting of the Social Sciences Division of the Academy of Sciences of the UkrSSR," *ibid.*, September 20, 1946; "Create a Really Scientific, Marxist-Leninist History of the Ukraine," *ibid.*, October 3, 1947; M. Bazhan, "Against Nationalist Distortions in Current Scholarship concerning the History of the Ukraine," *ibid.*, December 13–14, 1947.

6. *Istoriya Ukrayiny: Korotky kurs* (Brief Course in Ukrainian History, Kiev, 1941); *Narys Istoriyi Ukrayiny* (Outline History of the Ukraine, Ufa, 1942); and *Istoriya Ukrayiny*, Vol. I (Ufa, 1943). I have read the 1942 outline.

7. The discussion was opened by S. Koval'ov. For a full list of ideological decrees in 1946–47, see Note I-2, in the Appendix.

8. Lytvyn's statement at the XVI Congress of the Communist Party (Bolshevik) of Ukraine in 1949: *XVI Z"yizd Komunistychnoyi Partiyi (bil'shovykiv) Ukrayiny, 25–28 sichnya [January], 1949 r.: Materiyaly z"yizdu* (Kiev, 1949), p. 142. The political controls over historians have been analyzed in Black, *loc. cit.*, pp. 16ff. On the control exercised by the Academy of Sciences of the USSR over the Academies of the republics, through semi-annual coordinating sessions, see also A. Nesmeyanov, "Scholarship in the Multi-national Soviet Country," *Izvestiya*, June 29, 1952 (as referred to by I. K-n., "What Do the Academies of Sciences Do in the USSR," *Suchasna Ukrayina*, July 27, 1952); and P. Krupnytskyj, *Ukrayins'ka istorychna nauka pid sovyetamy* (Ukrainian Historical Science under the Soviets, Munich: Institute for the Study of the USSR, 1957), pp. 38ff. (Mimeographed.)

9. Krupnytskyj, *op. cit.*, p. 60.

10. Akademiya nauk URSR, Instytut istoryi (Ukrainian SSR Academy of Sciences, Institute of History), *Istoriya Ukrayins'koyi RSR*, 2 Vols. (Kiev: Ukrainian SSR Academy of Sciences, 1953–1958).

11. Vol. I in its 2nd rev. ed. (1955) numbers 900 odd pages; Vol. II—almost 800.

12. Lytvyn in *Bol'shevik*, Vol. 1947, No. 7 (April), pp. 41–56. For Lytvyn's identification see *Rad. Ukrayina*, July 15, 1945, p. 3; and *XVI Z"yizd KP(b)U* . . . , p. 139.

13. Lytvyn, *loc. cit.*, p. 41.

14. *Ibid.*, pp. 43–44.

15. *Ibid.*, p. 55, my paraphrase. The exact phrasing of the second directive is worth quoting: "To an exhaustive criticism must be subjected the opinions of Hrushevsky and other Ukrainian bourgeois-nationalist historians who in spite of historical facts have tried to prove the timeless (*izvechnuyu*) estrangement (*otorvannost'*) and separate existence (*obosoblennost'*) of the Ukrainian people from the other peoples of our country; have tried to set the Ukrainian people against the Russian, to sow dissent between them."

16. "Undoubtedly [the histories of the Soviet Republics] were only substructures, on which was to rest the magnificent palace of the Soviet Union," Krupnytskyj, *op. cit.*, p. 59.

17. "Theses on the 300th Anniversary of the Reunification of the Ukraine and Russia (1654–1954), Approved by the Central Committee of the Communist Party of the Soviet Union," *Pravda* and *Izvestiya*, Jan. 12, 1954, pp.

2–3; complete text in *CDSP,* Vol. V, No. 51, pp. 3ff. Henceforth cited as "1654–1954 Theses."

18. Remnants of the pan-Slavic theme appear in Thesis V: Simultaneous struggle for liberation and reunification with Russia of the "fraternal Belorussian people"; Moldavian peasants taking part in the Ukrainian war for liberation; "widespread sympathy and response among the Polish peasants."

19. In a less prominent place the desire for reunification is asserted by Lytvyn, *loc. cit.,* p. 52. I. D. Nazarenko, a subordinate and later a successor of Lytvyn, in commenting upon the Party resolution "On Serious Inadequacies and Mistakes in the Section of Social Sciences of the Academy of Sciences of the Ukrainian SSR" (of August 1947), said: "The Ukrainian people has fought for its social and national liberation always together with and under the leadership of the Russian people." (*Rad. Ukrayina,* Sept. 20, 1946.) This is an exaggeration.

20. "The centralized Russian state played a tremendous role in the historic destinies of the Russian, Ukrainian, Belorussian and other peoples of our country. From its very beginning it was a lodestar and support to the fraternal peoples struggling against foreign enslavers" (from Thesis II). All translations from *Current Digest of Soviet Press.*

21. In a footnote to the *second* installment of ["Comrades-in-Arms (Popular form of armed struggle of the Russian and Ukrainian peoples)"], *Oktyabr'* (October, Moscow), Vol. 31 (1954), Nos. 3 (March), pp. 144–63; 4 (April), pp. 110–36; 5 (May), pp. 129–62; viz., *loc. cit.,* p. 118. See also Krupnytskyj, *op. cit.,* p. 63.

22. *Pravda,* February 18, 1956, pp. 4–6; or *Cur. Soviet Policies II,* p. 88.

23. An excellent introduction to his work is the special issue of the *Annals of the Ukrainian Academy of Arts and Sciences in the U.S.,* Vol. II (Spring 1952), exclusively devoted to Drahomanov. Editor of the issue is Ivan L. Rudnytsky.

24. See the article by M. Shch., "Ukrainian Historians in the Struggle for Historical Truth," in *Nashe Slovo* (Our Word, Warsaw), No. 16 (December 2, 1956), p. 2. *Nashe Slovo* is frequently more outspoken than the strictly censored Kiev press. The writer owes this excellent reference to Bohdan Wynar, *Ekonomichny koloniyalizm v Ukrayini* (Economic Colonialism in the Ukraine, Paris: [Ukrainian] Nationalist Publishers in Europe, 1958), pp. 164ff.

25. ["Raise the Ideological and Theoretical Level of Scholarly Works in History"], *Kommunist Ukrainy* (Rus. ed.), Vol. 1956, No. 6 (June), p. 70.

26. ["Change the Teaching of History in Ten-Year Schools in the Light of the Decisions of the 20th Congress of the CPSU"], *Radyans'ka shkola* (Soviet School, Kiev), Vol. 1956, No. 10 (October), p. 9.

27. ["On the Question of Studying the History of the Civil War in the Ukraine"], *Kommunist Ukrainy,* Vol. 1956, No. 10 (October), p. 28.

28. ["Pages about the Heroic Struggle of the Ukrainian People for Communism"], *Pravda,* July 25, 1962, pp. 2–3; or *CDSP,* Vol. XIV, No. 30, pp. 9–11. The work reviewed was: Institut Istorii Partii TsK KP Ukrainy (Institute of Party History of the Central Committee of Communist Party of Ukraine), *Ocherki istorii Kommunisticheskoy Partii Ukrainy* (Kiev, 1961).

29. Lysenko, *loc. cit.,* p. 15.

30. ["The Reconstruction of the Teaching of History in (Primary-Secondary)

Schools in the Light of the Perspectives of Communist Construction"],
Ukr. istorychny zhurnal, Vol. 1958, No. 6 (November-December), pp. 94–
102; quotation from p. 100.

31. V. O. Puns'ky ["Paths for Reforming the Teaching of History in Secondary Schools"], *ibid.,* Vol. 1959, No. 5 (September-October), pp. 107–10;
quotations from pp. 109–10; italics in the original.

32. I. F. Chernikov, ["Questions that Should Be Answered Now"], *ibid.,* pp.
113–14; quotation from p. 113.

33. Involved were a resolution of the Central Committee of the Communist
Party of the Soviet Union and the USSR Council of Ministers (of October 8, 1959?) and a resolution of the Central Committee of the Communist Party of Ukraine and the Ukrainian SSR Council of Ministers. Those
resolutions were being implemented in 1961. See M. M. Lysenko, ["Study
of the Topic 'Ukrainian Lands in the 14th-15th Centuries' in the Introductory Course in the History of the USSR and UkrSSR in Grade VII of
the Eight-Year-School"], *ibid.,* Vol. 1961, No. 5 (September-October), pp.
101–05. See also Nicholas DeWitt, *Education and Professional Employment in the USSR* (Washington, D.C.: National Science Foundation, 1961),
p. 110.

34. DeWitt, *ibid.* Also N. I. Barabash & A. V. Ivanchenko, ["From Our Ex-
perience of Reforming the Teaching of History in Grades 5 and 6 of the
Eight Year School"], *Ukr. istorychny zhurnal,* Vol. 1962, No. 1 (January-
February), pp. 84–90.

35. Lysenko, *loc. cit.* (1961), pp. 101–02.

36. I. O. Hurzhiy, ed., *Knyha dla chytannya z istoriyi URSR* (Reader in the
History of the Ukrainian SSR), 2 Vols. (Kiev, 1960–61).

37. V. Dyadychenko, F. Los', and V. Spyts'ky, *Istoriya URSR; pidruchnyk dlya
7–8 kl. 8-richnoyi shkoly* (History of the Ukrainian SSR: text for Grades
VII–VIII of an 8-Year School; Kiev, 1962). Unfortunately, I have not been
able to obtain that text, have cited it from Hurzhiy's review in *Ukr. istorychny zhurnal,* Vol. 1962, No. 3 (May-June), pp. 126–28.

38. See Yu. P. Lavrov, L. A. Shevchenko, ["Discussion of the Manuscript of
the Text in Ukrainian History for Secondary Schools"], *ibid.,* Vol. 1959,
No. 5 (September-October), pp. 114–16.

39. (1) O. D. Voyna, ["Some Contemporary Falsifications of the History of Soviet Ukraine in Bourgeois Historical Literature"], *ibid.,* Vol. 1957, No. 1
(July-August), pp. 137–42. Addresses himself to a series of books, concen-
trates on C. A. Manning's *Ukraine under the Soviets* (New York, 1953).
(2) A. L. Shlepakov, ["The Anglo-American Bourgeois Historiography on
the Reunification of the Ukrainian People in One Ukrainian Soviet
State"], *ibid.,* No. 2 (September-October), pp. 118–22. Attacks John A.
Armstrong's *Ukrainian Nationalism, 1939–1945,* among others. (3) V. S.
Savchenko, ["Ukrainian Bourgeois Nationalists in the Service of American
Imperialism"], *ibid.,* No. 3 (November-December), pp. 138–46; (4) I. F.
Yevsyeyev, ["Evil Slander Masquerading as a Scholarly Work"], *ibid.,* Vol.
1958, No. 4 (July-August), pp. 157–61; (5) L. O. Leshchenko, [" 'Prologue'
or Epilogue?"], *ibid.,* No. 6 (November-December), pp. 136–40; (6) V. H.
Symonenko, ["Against Bourgeois-Nationalist Falsifications of the History
of Ukraine"], *ibid.,* Vol. 1958, No. 3 (May-June), pp. 158–62; (7) I. I.
Slyn'ko ([""Unshakeable Unity of the Ukrainian People in Their Struggle

against the Germano-Fascist Robbers"], *ibid.*, Vol. 1959, No. 4 (July-Aug.), pp. 53–64) disputes, at length, the fact that Ukrainians at first supported the German occupation troops; (8) M. M. Bilousov & V. I. Klokov, ["Fal-sification of the Struggle of the Ukrainian People against Germano-Fascist Robbers"], *ibid.*, Vol. 1959, No. 1 (January-February), pp. 136–42. This has almost the same argument as in (7).

40. See Kol'chuk, "Much Ado About Nothing," *Ukr. istorychny zhurnal*, Vol. 1961, No. 3 (May-June), pp. 140–41.

41. See the Soviet bibliography: USSR Lenin Library, Moscow; State Public Library, Ukrainian SSR; and State Historical Public Library: *Nerushimaya druzhba bratskikh narodov SSSR* (Moscow, 1954), 72 pp. See also the brief interesting American study by A. Moskalenko, *Khmelnytskyj and the Treaty of Pereyaslav in Soviet Historiography* (New York: Research Program on the USSR, 1955). For an analysis of the propaganda campaign, see Chapter I above.

42. I have attempted to do so, in part, in my Ph.D. dissertation, *op. cit.*, pp. 364–81.

43. This is implied in a sentence in Thesis V: "October 1 (11), 1653, the Zem-sky Sobor in Moscow . . . consented to admit the Ukraine into the Rus-sian state."

44. I. P. Kryp"yakevych, *Bohdan Khmelnytsky* (Kiev, 1954), pp. 419–20. A work as scholarly as conditions allow.

45. P. P. Gudzenko *et al.* (eds.), *Vossoedinenie Ukrainy s Rossiey: Dokumenty i materialy v trekh tomakh* (Reunification of the Ukraine with Russia: Documents and Materials in 3 vols., Moscow, 1953), Vol. III, p. 413, docu-ment no. 197, l. 39. Henceforth abbreviated *Vossoedinenie III*.

46. O. Ohloblyn, *Ukrayins'ko-Moskovs'ka uhoda, 1654* (Ukrainian-Muscovite Agreement, 1654, New York, Toronto: Organization to Defend the Four Freedoms of Ukraine-League for the Liberation of the Ukraine, 1954), pp. 26ff. A valuable study, well documented.

47. *Vossoedinenie III*, pp. 560ff. (Doc. no. 245); 567ff. (Doc. no. 248). In his review article on the document collection, Andriy Yakovliv points out that the first document has been dated wrong. Its correct date is not March 21, as printed in the collection, but March 27 ("The Reunion of the Ukraine with Russia"), *The Annals of the Ukrainian Academy . . .*, Vol. VI, No. 3 (Winter-Spring 1955), pp. 1009–1010; and his book, *Dohovir Bohdana Khmelnyts'koho z moskovs'kym tsarem Oleksieym Mykhaylovy-chem 1654 r.* (Treaty of Bohdan Khmelnytsky with the Muscovite Tsar Alexey Mikhaylovich, 1654, New York: Tyszczenko & Bilous, 1954), pp. 105ff.). He also points out that the important draft of the treaty that was presented by the Ukrainian envoys in Moscow has been omitted in the collection ("The Reunion . . . ," *op. cit.*, p. 1005), its text is available in his book, *Dohovir . . .*, pp. 93–99. On the question of whether this doc-ument should be considered part of the treaty, see Ohloblyn, *op. cit.*, pp. 50ff.

48. *Vossoedinenie III*, p. 568, ll. 267–268.

49. The various viewpoints have been usefully enumerated in Ohloblyn, *op. cit.*, pp. 61ff. Allen in *op. cit.*, p. 135, speaks categorically of an "uncon-ditional union of the Ukraine with Muscovy, confirmed by the *Rada* of 8 January, 1654, and by the oath of allegiance sworn to the Tsar."

50. See also the section "Function and Methods of [Treaty] Interpretation,"

in Herbert W. Briggs (ed.), *The Law of Nations* (2nd ed.; New York: Appleton-Century-Crofts, 1952), pp. 897–99, and the literature there cited.

51. Yakovliv, "The Reunion . . . ," *loc. cit.*, pp. 1028ff.
52. *Vossoedinenie III,* p. 562: "Articles," l. 340.
53. *Ibid.*, p. 567: "Writ," l. 261.
54. In his essay on the "Unity and Indivisibility of Russia," in B. Nolde, *Ocherki russkogo gosudarstvennogo prava* (Essays in Russian State Law. St. Petersburg, 1911), as translated into English in *The Annals of the Ukrainian Academy* . . . , Vol. IV, No. 3, pp. 876–77. French translation available under the title *L'Ukraine sous le protectorat russe* (Paris: Payot, 1915).
55. B. Nolde, *loc. cit.* (*The Annals* . . .) , p. 876. Italics added.
56. *Ibid.*, pp. 875–76.
57. Vyacheslav Prokopovych, "The Problem of the Juridical Nature of the Ukraine's Union with Muscovy," *ibid.*, p. 964.
58. *Ibid.*, pp. 960ff. The exceptions were *aliens* in the service of the Tsar and the Muscovite people in the Valliessar Treaty with Sweden in 1658 (pp. 962–63). Prokovych thinks that the latter was a concession to *foreign* usage: in internal documents the Russian people are the "people of Muscovy." In addressing the Tsar Khmelnytsky never used the term *kholop* customary for Russians; he signed himself a "subject."
59. *Ibid.*, p. 964.
60. *Ibid.*, pp. 979–80. Reprinted with permission, the Ukrainian Academy of Arts and Sciences in the U.S., Inc. "Subjects" were called the emigre tsareviches (princes) of Georgia and Siberia who were ranking above the *boyars* at the Muscovite court. In some cases the Tsar had virtually incorporated their territories, in others, as in the case of the Georgian tsarevich who later ruled Georgia as Irakli I, Russian influence in their territories was purely nominal (pp. 970ff.). In other words there was a juridical difference between foreign "subjects" and Muscovite "servants" of the Tsar, and quite often this difference corresponded to the actual political situation.
61. *Istoriya Ukrayins'koyi RSR,* Vol. I (1955), p. 273. The statement is taken almost verbatim from the Fifth Party Thesis.
62. Ivan Tsyupa in *Izvestiya,* March 15, 1954, as cited by B. Krupnytskyj in "Bohdan Khmelnytsky and Soviet Historiography," Institute for the Study of the History and Culture of the USSR, *Ukrayins'ky zbirnyk* (Ukrainian Review, Munich, Vol. 3 (1955), p. 88. (Mimeographed.)
63. *Vossoedinenie III,* pp. 412–413, ("Decision of the *Zemsky Sobor*," l. 36), p. 414 (ll. 41–42: crucial, concluding argument for extending the protectorate). Allen, *op. cit.*, p. 132. On the Soviet side, see the acknowledgments in Kryp"yakevych, *op. cit.*, p. 450; the popular biography by K. Osipov, *Bogdan Khmel'nytsky* (2nd rev. ed.; Moscow, 1948), p. 359.
64. Ohloblyn, *op. cit.*, p. 17.
65. Krupnytskyj, "Bohdan Khmelnytsky . . . ," *loc. cit.*, p. 89.
66. Sketch based on Hrushevsky IX, pp. 1232ff.; Kryp"yakevych, *op. cit.*, pp. 504ff.; Osipov, *op. cit.* (1948), pp. 433ff.
67. Not identical with the envoy to Pereyaslav in 1654.
68. The fullest account of the conversation of June 19, 1657, is in Hrushevsky IX, pp. 1417ff. See also Kryp"yakevych, *op. cit.*, pp. 524ff.; Osipov, *op. cit.* (1948), pp. 442ff. From the context it appears clearly that the word

"merciless" has been used as an euphemism for "treacherous," see Hrushevsky and Osipov.

69. Allen, too, notices the independent behavior of Khmelnytsky after 1654 (*op. cit.*, p. 141), but fails to draw from this the appropriate conclusion as to the legal character of the Treaty.

70. A. M. Pankratova (ed.), *Istoriya SSSR: Uchebnik dlya VIII klassa sredney shkoly* (History of the USSR: Textbook for Grade VIII of Ten-Year Schools; 7th ed.; Moscow, 1949), p. 196.

71. B. D. Grekov, S. V. Bakhrushin, and V. I. Lebedev (eds.), *Istoriya SSSR; Tom I: S drevneyshikh vremen do kontsa XVIII v.* (History of the USSR; Vol. I: From the Earliest Times Until the End of the 18th Century; 2nd ed.; Moscow, 1947), pp. 502–03.

72. *Istoriya Ukrayins'koyi RSR* (1955), Vol. I, pp. 288, 289.

73. *Ibid.*, p. 290.

74. Kryp"yakevych, *op. cit.*, pp. 522, 526. K. Osipov, *op. cit.* (1st ed.: Moscow, 1939), pp. 388, 390; *op. cit.* (2nd ed.; Moscow, 1948), pp. 438–39.

75. Osipov, *op. cit.* (1939), p. 400.

76. Hrushevsky IX, p. 1501. See also Allen, *op. cit.*, pp. 137, 141.

77. *Vossoedinenie.* See Yakovliv, "The Reunion . . . ," *loc. cit.*, p. 1021.

78. Hrushevsky IX, pp. 1502–03.

79. Hrushevsky VIII, Pt. 2 (Kiev-Vienna, 1922), p. 78; as cited by Ohloblyn, *op. cit.*, p. 11.

80. Yakovliv, "The Reunion . . . ," *loc. cit.*, pp. 1017ff.

81. *Ibid.*, p. 1032. Cited by permission, the Ukrainian Academy of Arts and Sciences in the U.S., Inc.

82. See Konstantin F. Shteppa, "The 'Lesser Evil' Formula," in Black (ed.), *op. cit.*, pp. 107–20.

83. Krupnytskyj, *Ukrayins'ka istorychna nauka . . . ,* p. 18.

84. Hrushevsky IX, pp. 1479–1508.

85. Krupnytskyj, *Ukrayins'ka istorychna nauka . . . ,* p. 24.

86. *Bol'shaya Sovetskaya Entsyklopediya* (1st ed.; Moscow), Vol. 59 (1935), p. 818. Italics added.

87. Krupnytskyj, *Ukrayins'ka istorychna nauka . . . ,* pp. 27, 34.

88. "Decision of the Jury of the Official Commission in the Competition for the Textbook on USSR History for the 3rd and 4th Grades of Secondary Schools," in *K izucheniyu istorii: Sbornik* (Studying History: A Collection, Moscow, 1937), p. 38, or *Pravda*, August 22, 1937.

89. N. Yakovlev, "Teaching the History of the Fatherland," *Bol'shevik*, Vol. 24, No. 22 (November, 1947), pp. 28ff.

90. M. Nechkina, "On the Problem of the 'Lesser Evil' Formula," *V.I.*, Vol. 1951, No. 4, pp. 44ff.

91. See especially the editorial "For the further Improvement of Historical Scholarship in the USSR," *V.I.*, Vol. 1952, No. 9, pp. 11ff., or Shteppa, *loc. cit.*, pp. 118ff.

92. M. Nechkina, *loc. cit.*, p. 46.

93. See Shteppa, *loc. cit.*, p. 117.

94. A. Pankratova, "Urgent Tasks of Soviet Historical Scholarship," *Kommunist* [successor to *Bol'shevik*], Vol. 1953, No. 6 (April), p. 64.

95. Lysenko, *loc. cit.*, p. 9.

96. See A. V. Fadeev, "The Nature of the Foreign Policy of Tsarism in the Second Half of the 18th Century," *Prepodavanie istorii v shkole* (Teaching

History at School, Moscow), Vol. 1956, No. 3, pp. 36ff.; as cited in Lysenko, *loc. cit.,* p. 12.

97. *Ibid.* (Lysenko).
98. "Muslims of Soviet Central Asia: Trends and Prospects," *Middle East
Journal,* Vol. 9 (Summer 1955), pp. 306ff.
99. Krupnytskyj, *Ukrayins'ka istorychna nauka . . . ,* p. 43.
100. A postwar refugee said that a Ukrainian taxi-driver in the Donbas once
lent him a book published in Kiev in 1922, in which Hetman Mazepa was
favorably commented upon. See L. Ortynsky, "From behind the Barbed
Wire," *Suchasna Ukrayina,* March 21, 1954, p. 4.
101. In reviewing the second volume of the Academic History of the Ukrainian SSR (covering the Soviet Period), Gol'nev and Chernenko wrote in
Radyans'ka Ukrayina of Feb. 4, 1958, that "the general fault of the second
volume lay in too terse and too schematic a presentation" of individual
events. This applies even more to the literature of the early 1950's. See
Volodymyr P. Stakhiv, " 'The War with History' Continues," *Suchasna
Ukrayina,* March 2, 1958, p. 1.
102. "For a Deep Study of the History of the Ukrainian People," *V.I.,* Vol.
1955, No. 7, pp. 8, 10, as cited in Krupnytskyj, *Ukrayins'ka istorychna nauka . . . ,* p. 64.

Notes to Chapter VIII: The Communist Party of Ukraine and the Communist Party of the Soviet Union . . .

1. See his *Constitutional Government and Democracy* (New York: Ginn &
Co., 1946), p. 19. Cited with permission of the Blaisdell Publishing Company.
2. See John A. Armstrong, *The Soviet Bureaucratic Elite* (New York: Praeger, 1959), pp. 146–50, for a critical discussion, with many names; also
R. Conquest, *Power and Policy in the U.S.S.R.* (New York: St. Martin's
Press, 1961), pp. 68–69 *et passim;* and Lazar Pistrak, *The Grand Tactician: Khrushchev's Rise to Power* (New York: Praeger, 1961), *passim.*
Henceforth, Armstrong's 1959 work will be cited as Armstrong, *Elite.*
3. "Kommunisticheskaya partiya Ukrainy v tsifrakh" (The Communist Party
of Ukraine in Figures), *Partiynaya zhizn* (Party Life), Vol. 1958, No. 12
(June), pp. 57–59. Henceforth referred to as "KPU v tsifrakh."
4. Fainsod, *How Russia Is Ruled* (1963 ed.), p. 273n. and table on p. 272.
5. Membership figure from Melnikov's report to the Seventeenth CP of
Ukraine Congress: *Pravda Ukrainy,* September 24, 1952; or L. Gruliow
(ed.), *Current Soviet Policies: The Documentary Record of the Nineteenth
Communist Party Congress and the Reorganization after Stalin's Death*
(New York: Praeger, 1953), p. 56. Henceforth latter source cited as *Cur.
Sov. Policies I.* Population estimates by V. Holubnychy, "Statistics of the
Population of the Ukraine, 1940–1956," *Vpered* (Munich), No. 71 (October 1956), pp. 2ff.
6. See Fainsod, *loc. cit.* The discrepancy in the figures of Party members per
1,000 population between Fainsod (18.88) and myself (20.1) is explained
by my taking over a lower population figure from Holubnychy (38.1 million).
7. The official estimates for 1940 and 1956 are given as 191.7 and 200.2 mil-

lion (*Narodnoe khozaystvo SSSR v 1956 g.*, p. 17). I have assumed that the increase in population was the same each year (530,000). By withdrawing from the higher figure four times that amount (2.12 million) I have arrived at my estimate. Strictly speaking, the assumption is untenable owing to the war losses, but I have relied on it so as not to engage in complicated calculations to obtain a base figure for 1946. My mistake would lie in *overestimating* the population of 1952, rather than underestimating it.

8. Membership of CP of Ukraine announced at the Twenty-Second CP of Ukraine Congress; see *Radyans'ka Ukrayina*, September 28, 1961, p. 8. The All-Union Party figure (8,872,516) from Titov's credentials commission's report at the Twenty-Second CP of Soviet Union Congress (*ibid.*, October 22, 1961, p. 4). Population figures are based on official Soviet estimates as of January 1, 1961, adjusted for natural increase through September by using the 1960 average increase figure; see *Narodnoe khozaystvo SSSR v 1960 godu* (1961), pp. 8 and 60. The estimated population figures for October 1, 1961, are 43,668,000 for the Ukraine and 219,047,000 for the USSR.

9. In 1959 52 per cent of the population of the Russian Republic were living in urban areas compared with 46 per cent of that of the Ukrainian SSR—see *Nar. khoz. SSSR, 1960*, p. 10; but the differences in Party membership in leading Russian and Ukrainian industrial centers are much greater. See the figures for 1952 in Fainsod, *loc. cit.* and also pp. 279 and 282; for 1959 see also Herbert McClosky & John E. Turner, *The Soviet Dictatorship* (New York, etc.: McGraw-Hill, 1960), p. 246. In the latter book, apparently owing to a printing error, the absolute membership of the CP of Ukraine has been given as 1,180,000 (should have been 1,170,-000). The correct percentage figures are 27.9 and −8.6 (27.9 Party members in the Ukraine per 1,000 population; 8.6 points under the USSR average).

10. "KPU v tsifrakh," *loc. cit.*, p. 59. Refers to the year 1958, in which the CP of Ukraine had 1,095,250 members.

11. *Ibid.*, pp. 59, 57. For May, 1940, Holubnychy found a total membership of 636,914. See his "Outline History of the Communist Party of Ukraine," *Ukrainian Review* (Institute for the Study of the USSR, Munich), Vol. 6 (1958), p. 124; henceforth cited as Holubnychy, "Outline History." The difference in figures may be due to the fact that the 1958 statistics did not include candidate members as does Holubnychy.

12. Between the 1949 and 1952 Congresses 22,000 regular and candidate members were dropped from the rolls, see Holubnychy, *ibid.*, p. 119.

13. It nearly doubled between 1940 and 1958–59. In May 1940 there were about 353,000 Ukrainians in the CP of Ukraine (63.1% of 559,235); in 1958–645,075 (or 60.3% of 1,095,250). See pp. 229, 231, below. "KPU v tsifrakh," *loc. cit.*, p. 59, however, states that it "more than doubled."

14. *XVI z"yizd Komunistychnoyi Partiyi (bil'shovykiv) Ukrayiny, 25–28 sichnya 1949 r.: Materiyaly z"yizdu*, pp. 46–47.

15. "KPU v tsifrakh," *loc. cit.*, pp. 59, 58.

16. *Ibid.*, p. 58. It is also pointed out that more than 134,000 Party members had completed higher schools, and ca. 162,000 secondary schools. This means that by 1958 27 per cent had achieved professional and semi-professional status, about 8 per cent of whom are hidden in the category of "others."

17. *Ibid.*, p. 59, and *Nar. khoz. SSSR 1960*, p. 8.

18. Holubnychy, "Outline History," p. 124. See also Armstrong, *Elite*, p. 17. In theory, the Party Congress is the highest representative body, but it meets only infrequently.

19. Basil Dmytryshyn, *Moscow and the Ukraine, 1917–1953* (New York: Bookman Associates, 1956), pp. 247–48. "At no time did the delegates to the Party Congresses ever represent proportionately the national composition of the Party (p. 248)."

20. Armstrong, *Elite*, p. 16.

21. I. Ye. Kravtsev, *Marksysts'ko-lenins'ki pryntsypy proletars'koho internatsionalizmu* (Marxist-Leninist Principles of Proletarian Internationalism, Kiev, 1956), p. 51.

22. *Ibid.*

23. "The Party in Figures (1956–1961)," *Partiynaya zhizn,* Vol. 1962, No. 1 (January), pp. 44ff.; see *CDSP (Current Digest of the Soviet Press)*, Vol. XIV, No. 3, p. 5.

24. *Ibid.*

25. Cf. Holubnychy, "Outline History," p. 124.

26. See Khrushchev's statement on Stalin's alleged intention to deport all Ukrainians (Chapter I, above). Also the brief discussion in Armstrong, *Elite*, pp. 16–18.

27. Armstrong, *ibid.*, p. 17.

28. Holubnychy, "Outline History," p. 124.

29. See above, p. 231.

30. Armstrong, *Elite*, p. 17.

31. Borys Lewytzkyj, ["The Communist Party of the Ukraine in 1955"], Institute for the Study of the History and Culture of the USSR, *Ukrayins'ky zbirnyk,* Vol. 3 (Munich, 1955), p. 129. The documentation of this thesis would be a minor research project by itself, but Lewytzkyj is too careful a student of Soviet Ukrainian affairs to spread idle propositions. See also the discussion in Armstrong, *Elite*, p. 131. Professor Armstrong somewhat qualifies Lewytzkyj's thesis, but admits that the "[partisan] movement continued to be a proving ground for development of new elite members."

32. Panas Fedenko, *Ukrayina pislya smerty Stalina* (Ukraine after Stalin's Death, Munich: Institute for the Study of the USSR, 1956), p. 12. (Mimeographed.) Rakovsky appears to have been of Bulgarian descent, had Rumanian citizenship, and considered himself a Russian. A better parallel would have been that between Melnikov and Kviring. Kviring was dismissed as First Secretary of the Central Committee of the CP (Bolshevik) of Ukraine in May, 1925, under similar circumstances. See Holubnychy, "Outline History," p. 84.

33. See the editorial "Raise the Level of Ideological Work" in *Pravda Ukrainy,* March 4, 1953, p. 1. The plenum had met on February 27–28.

34. See Holubnychy, "Outline History," p. 104.

35. For Korotchenko's official biography, see *Entsyklopedicheskiy slovar'* (Encyclopedic Dictionary), Vol. II (went to press April 6, 1954), p. 159. Korotchenko was born in the Ukraine, but in the 1930's he is reported to have spelt his name with the Russian ending "-ov," i.e., *Korotchenkov* (Interview #83). He served as First Secretary of the Pervomaysk and Bauman District Committees in Moscow, then as a Secretary of the Moscow Province under Khrushchev, then as First Secretary of the Zaporozhe and Dnie-

propetrovsk Province Committees in the Ukraine. See also Armstrong, *Elite,* p. 54.

36. See the announcement in *Rad. Ukrayina,* March 4, 1947, p. 1.

37. *Pravda Ukrainy,* December 27, 1947, p. 1.

38. Late in 1961 Korotchenko was identified as Chairman of the Ukrainian SSR Supreme Soviet (*Rad. Ukrayina,* September 30, 1961, p. 1). His position has not changed to our knowledge.

39. First, the unpublished resolution of the All-Union Central Committee of July 26, 1946, dealing with the training, selection, and distribution of leading Party and Soviet personnel in the Ukrainian Party organization, which is referred to in the *Pravda* editorial of August 23, 1946; second, the criticisms of Ukrainian agricultural administration at the February, 1947, Central Committee Plenum in Moscow; see *Pravda,* February 28 and March 7, 1947.

40. On the fate of Postyshev and Kosior see Hryhory Kostiuk, *Stalinist Rule in the Ukraine: A Study of the Decade of Mass Terror (1929-39)* (Munich: Institute for the Study of the USSR, 1960), pp. 31ff., 93ff. *et passim.*

41. See Lazar Pistrak, *op. cit.,* pp. 228-33.

42. See *Kommunist* (Moscow), Vol. 1957, No. 12 (August), p. 26, as cited by Pistrak, *op. cit.,* p. 183. Pistrak refutes Khrushchev's accusations partly by proving that when Khrushchev regained power in December, 1947, he did nothing to rehabilitate Rylsky.

43. Institut Istorii Partii TsK KP Ukrainy (Institute of Party History of the Central Committee of CP of Ukraine), *Ocherki istorii Kommunisticheskoy Partii Ukrainy* (Kiev, 1961), p. 555. In his speech to the Twenty-Second CP of Soviet Union Congress Podgorny elaborated on this theme by saying that Kaganovich "lashed out (*izbival*) against cadres dedicated to the Party, persecuted (*travil*) and terrorized the leading workers of the Republic." Podgorny added, still in general terms that Kaganovich, "being a past master at intrigues and provocations, literally without the slightest basis, accused of nationalism the leading writers of the Republic and a series of leading Party workers as well." The only concrete detail added by Podgorny is that Kaganovich allegedly tried to convoke a plenary session of the Central Committee having on the agenda "The struggle against nationalism as the main danger in the CP of Ukraine." See *Pravda,* October 20, 1961, p. 3.

44. This is the argument of John A. Armstrong, *The Politics of Totalitarianism: The Communist Party of the Soviet Union from 1934 to the Present* (New York: Random House, 1961), pp. 204-05. Henceforth cited as Armstrong, *Politics.* An important hypothesis has been advanced by Borys Lewytzkyj in "Besonderheiten der sowjetukrainischen Entwicklung (Particularities of the Soviet Ukrainian Development)," *Osteuropa* (Eastern Europe), Vol. 1962, No. 10, p. 670. He found that the feeling of solidarity that had grown up among the Soviet Ukrainian leaders during World War II—between the "clan of partisans" and Khrushchev—helped those leaders to withstand the purges after 1945. Lewytzkyj's article is based on his forthcoming book on the Ukraine after World War II.

45. See Holubnychy, "Outline History," pp. 116-17, and Armstrong, *Elite,* p. 51.

46. See the report on the plenum of the Stalino obkom in *Pravda Ukrainy,* July 25, 1947, p. 1.

47. "There is some evidence, though it is far from conclusive, that both economic management and Party leadership in this area [Stalino and Voroshilovgrad] were linked to the Soviet power alignment headed by Georgi Malenkov." Armstrong, *Elite*, pp. 67–68. From 1940–44 Melnikov served as Deputy Minister of State Control of the USSR; see Armstrong, *Politics*, pp. 246 and 407.

48. *Pravda Ukrainy*, December 18, 1949, p. 1. Also Fainsod, *op. cit.* (1963 ed.), p. 321.

49. The followers of Andrey Zhdanov, Politbureau member, head of the Leningrad Party organization; see Fainsod, *ibid.*, pp. 321–2, for details.

50. See his official biographies in *Pravda*, Dec. 22, 1957, p. 1, or *Bol'shaya Sovetskaya Entsyklopediya*, 2nd ed., Vol. 51 (went to press April 28, 1958), p. 152.

51. April 13–15, 1950; see Holubnychy, "Outline History," p. 117.

52. Holubnychy, *ibid.*, p. 118, and *Pravda Ukrainy*, May 30, 1952, p. 1.

53. *Pravda Ukrainy*, September 25, 1952; condensed text in *Cur. Sov. Policies I*, pp. 56ff.; also Holubnychy, "Outline History," p. 118.

54. *Pravda*, June 13, 1953, p. 2; complete translation in *CDSP*, Vol. V, No. 21, p. 3.

55. See, e.g., Fedenko, *op. cit.*, pp. 13ff. Dmytryshyn, however, does not mention Beria in connection with Melnikov, characterizes the latter's ouster as "one of the conciliatory gestures" of the new leadership toward Ukrainian nationalism (*op. cit.*, p. 181). Among the later sources see esp.: Armstrong, *Politics*, pp. 242ff.; Conquest, *op. cit.*, pp. 211ff.; Robert S. Sullivant, *Soviet Politics and the Ukraine* (New York: Columbia Univ. Press, 1962), pp. 283–85.

56. Conquest, *op. cit.*, pp. 195ff., esp. 212ff.; Armstrong, *Politics*, pp. 239ff.

57. Armstrong, *ibid.*, p. 250ff.

58. June 28, 1953, four Moscow newspapers—*Pravda, Izvestiya, Trud* and *Komsomol'skaya Pravda*—carried on their first pages the notice that the second performance of the opera "Decembrists" had taken place in the *Bol'shoy Theatre*. Among the attending dignitaries were listed all members of the Party Presidium except Beria. See *CDSP*, Vol. V, No. 24, p. 5. On July 10, on p. 1, *Pravda* published the editorial condemning Beria: "Indestructible Unity of Party, Government and People."

59. *Pravda*, October 9, 1952; and *Cur. Sov. Policies I*, pp. 161ff.

60. Most of the doctors accused of plotting against the lives of Soviet dignitaries were Jews. See either Conquest, *op. cit.*, Chapter 8, or Armstrong, *Politics*, pp. 235ff., for a discussion of that episode.

61. *Pravda* and *Izvestiya*, March 28, 1953, p. 1; or *Cur. Sov. Policies I*, p. 259.

62. Translated in *Cur. Sov. Policies I, ibid.*, and in *CDSP*, Vol. V, No. 12, pp. 3ff.

63. *Pravda Ukrainy*, April 11, 1953; or *CDSP*, Vol. V, No. 17, p. 3.

64. Armstrong, *Politics*, p. 245.

65. *Zarya Vostoka* (Star of the East, Tbilisi), April 15, 16, 1953; and *CDSP*, Vol. V, No. 15, p. 3; also, Khrushchev's anti-Stalin speech in *Current Soviet Policies II*, p. 183A.

66. Armstrong, *Politics*, p. 245.

67. *Ibid.*, p. 244.

68. *Pravda*, June 13, 1953.

69. *Pravda*, July 10, 1953, editorial, as cited in n. 58, above.

70. *Pravda Ukrainy,* July 14, 1953, p. 1. Italics added.
71. Conquest, *op. cit.,* pp. 211ff.
72. Podgorny was born in 1903 into the family of a foundryworker in Kar-lovka, Poltava Province, Ukraine. He joined the Party as late as 1930, and in the 1930's he worked in various supervisory positions in the Ukrainian sugar industry, advancing to Deputy Minister of the USSR Food Indus-try by 1941. From 1946–50 he served as permanent representative of the Ukrainian Council of Ministers with the USSR Government in Moscow; from 1950 to August 1953, he was 1st Secretary of the Kharkov oblast Committe. See *Bol. Sov. Entsyklopediya,* 2nd ed., Vol. 51, pp. 224–25.
73. Lewytzkyj, *loc. cit.* (n. 31), p. 112.
74. *Pidhorny.* See *Rad. Ukrayina,* Oct. 1, 1961, p. 1.
75. Since February 20, 1960, the 2nd Secretary of the CP of Ukraine has been I. P. Kazanets. See *Cur. Sov. Policies IV* (The Documentary Record of the 22nd Congress of the CPSU; New York: Columbia Univ. Press, 1962), p. 230A.—When this book was already in press it was announced that a re-shuffle in the top Ukrainian Party leadership had taken place (July 2, 1963). M. V. Pidhorny (Podgorny) was relieved of his duties as First Secretary of the CPU Central Committee in connection with his election to Secretary-ship in the Central Committee of the All-Union Party. But his place was *not* taken by the former Second CPU Secretary Kazanets, it was merely announced that Kazanets had left the CPU Secretariat because of a trans-fer to another, unspecified position. The new First Secretary of the CPU is P. Yu. Shelest, the new Second CPU Secretary is M. O. Sobol'. Source as in the note immediately below (n. 76).
76. See the announcement in *Radyans'ka Ukrayina,* July 3, 1963, p. 1. Pod-gorny had been elected a Secretary of the All-Union Central Committee in June 1963. See *Pravda,* June 22, 1963, p. 1.
77. The Twenty-First Congress, being an extraordinary one, did not elect a new Central Committee.
78. By Zbigniew K. Brzezinski in his book *The Permanent Purge* (Cambridge, Mass.: Harvard University Press, 1956), p. 163. He appears in the list of full members of the Central Committee CP of Ukraine at its Sixteenth (1949) and Seventeenth (1952) Congresses: see *XVI z"yizd . . . ,* p. 232; and *Rad. Ukrayina,* Sept. 28, 1952. On his installation as First Secretary of the Georgian Communist Party see *Zarya Vostoka,* Sept. 27, 1953, or *CDSP,* Vol. V, No. 39, p. 44.
79. From 1944 until at least 1948, Serdyuk had been 1st Secretary of the Kiev Province Committee (*Rad. Ukrayina,* Nov. 6, 1944; June 21, 1946; March 7, 1948), in 1950—a Sec. of the Central Committee CP of Ukraine (*ibid.,* October 21, 1950), in 1952 he left the Central Committee to assume Sec-retaryship in the important Lviv *obkom* (*ibid.,* May 30, 1952). He was elected 1st Secretary of the Moldavian Party in 1954 (*Pravda,* Feb. 10, 1954). In 1949, the Moldavian Party had about 22,000 members; see Fain-sod, *op. cit.* (1963 ed.), p. 272. In May, 1960, Serdyuk was advanced to the not unimportant post of First-Vice Chairman of the Party Control Com-mittee, a body that may be used for the sanctioning and supervision of Party purges (see *Cur. Sov. Policies IV,* p. 231).
80. L. I. Brezhnev was born into the family of a steelworker in Dnieprodzer-zhinsk, Ukraine, in 1906. Since 1937 he had held administrative and Party posts in Dniepropetrovsk; in 1946 1st Secretary of Zaporozhe Province

Committee; in November, 1947, elected 1st Secretary Dniepropetrovsk Province Committee (machine building industry, with 60,000 Party members in 1952). In July 1950 he became 1st Secretary of Central Committee Moldavian Communist Party, was appointed alternate member of the Presidium and Central Committee Secretary at the Nineteenth Congress (1952), but dropped from both positions at the reorganization after Stalin's death, when he was made head of the Political Department of the Navy (see *Cur. Sov. Policies I*, p. 237). See also his official biography in *Pravda*, May 8, 1960, p. 1.

81. Second Secretary since February 1954, 1st Secretary since March 1956. *Pravda, ibid.*

82. In 1952, I. D. Yakovlev had been a Secretary of the Kiev Province Committee, became 2nd Secretary of the Kazakh Communist Party on August 10, 1955; see *Cur. Sov. Policies I*, p. 240, and *Cur. Sov. Policies II*, p. 199. Since 1958 Yakovlev served as 1st Secretary of the Ulyanovsk Province Committee in the RSFSR; see *Cur. Sov. Policies III* ([Leo Gruliow, (ed.)], Columbia Univ. Press, 1960), p. 220.

83. See Conquest, *op. cit.*, pp. 388–89. In July, 1960, Brezhnev left the Secretariat of the Central Committee, in which he had been a Secretary (*Pravda*, July 17, 1960).

84. *Pravda*, June 22, 1963, p. 1.

85. From at least 1945 until 1952 (?) Stakhursky was 1st Secretary of the agricultural Vinnitsa Province in the Ukraine (*Rad. Ukrayina*, January 21, 1945; March 3, 1946; August 24, 1948), then he headed the Party in the agricultural Poltava oblast (*ibid.*, Sept. 24, 1952). After serving as the head of the Khabarovsk organization he was transferred back into the Ukraine; was 1st Secretary of the Zhytomyr Province Committee after December, 1957; see *Cur. Sov. Policies III*, p. 219. Struev remained in his Russian post until 1958, then became a Vice-Chairman of the RSFSR Council of Ministers (*Cur. Sov. Policies III*, p. 220).

86. *Bol. Sov. Entsyklopediya*, 2nd ed., Vol. 51, p. 152.

87. *Pravda*, April 26, 1962, p. 1. In view of Kirilenko's prominence it might be worthwhile to briefly sketch his biography as presented in *Ukrayins'ka Radyans'ka Entsyklopediya* (Ukrainian Soviet Encyclopedia), Vol. VI (1961), p. 372. Kirilenko was born in 1906 in Alekseevka, Belgorod oblast, Russian SFSR. Belgorod is across the boundary of the Ukrainian Republic, about 70 miles north of Kharkov. That particular oblast is ethnically mixed so that Kirilenko may well have been born into a Ukrainian family. (Khrushchev was born not too far away but into a Russian family.) From 1925–29 Kirilenko worked in the Donbas mines. In 1939 he was a Secretary of the Zaporozhe *obkom* (Ukraine). After serving in the Red Army as a high political officer, like Khrushchev (1941–42) and a liaison officer with the aircraft industry (1942–44) he returned to Party work in the Ukraine: Second Secretary of Zaporozhe *obkom* (1944–47), First Secretary of Nikolaev *obkom* (1947–50), First Secretary of important industrial Dniepropetrovsk *obkom* (1950–55). Then transferred to head Sverdlovsk *obkom* in Russia (1955). Since 1957 has been rising in central (Moscow) Party organs as outlined in the main text.

88. See the biography in *Bol'shaya Sovetskaya Entsyklopediya* (2nd ed.), Vol. 51, p. 231. Also Fainsod, *op. cit.* (1963 ed.), p. 331.

89. Rumyantsev is identified as 1st Secretary of the Kharkov obkom in 1948 in *Cur. Sov. Policies I*, p. 239. See also Conquest, *op. cit.*, p. 410, and *Cur. Sov. Policies IV*, p. 231.

90. See Chapter 7 in Armstrong, *Elite*, in which he discusses the political power of professional ideologists.

91. *Pravda Ukrainy*, August 25, 1946.

92. Conquest, *op. cit.*, p. 288.

93. See the entries for Churaev and Titov in *Cur. Sov. Policies IV*, p. 232.

94. *Ibid.*, see also *Pravda*, March 3, 1961, p. 3.

95. See also Raymond L. Garthoff, *Soviet Strategy in the Nuclear Age* (rev. ed., New York: Praeger, 1962), pp. 27–28. His biography in *Ukrayins'ka Radyans'ka Entsyklopediya*, Vol. IX (1962), pp. 379–80, discloses that Moskalenko had been born into a peasant family (apparently Ukrainian) in the village of Grishino, Donetsk oblast, Ukrainian SSR, in 1902. He entered the Red Army in 1920, made it his life-time career. In 1948 he was appointed as one of the ranking military officers of the Moscow Military District (Khrushchev took over the leadership of the Moscow Party organization in 1949), in 1953, Moskalenko became the Commanding Officer of that District.

96. *Pravda*, October 26, 1960, p. 6.

97. See the *New York Times*, Nov. 8, 1962, p. 4.

98. *Krasnaya Zvezda* (Red Star [Soviet Army newspaper], Moscow), March 12, 1955.

99. See Boris Meissner, *Sowjetrussland zwischen Revolution und Restauration* (USSR between Revolution and Restoration, Cologne: Verlag fuer Politik und Wirtschaft, 1956), p. 138.

100. Garthoff, *op. cit.*, pp. 28, 42–43.

101. *Cur. Sov. Policies IV*, p. 229. Grechko was born in 1903 in the village Holodayevka, of the Rostov oblast, Russian SFSR. That area is ethnically mixed, too, so that Grechko may well have been born into a Ukrainian family. *Ukr. Rad. Entsyklopediya*, Vol. III (1960), p. 443.

102. *Bol. Sov. Entsyklopediya*, 2nd ed., Vol. 51, p. 152.

103. *Pravda*, July 13, 1955, p. 1.

104. *Pravda*, February 1, 1959, pp. 4–5; or *Cur. Sov. Policies III*, pp. 117–20.

105. *Pravda*, January 13, 1960, p. 2, and June 16, 1960, p. 2. An entry on Kirichenko, by the way, is missing from the *Ukr. Rad. Entsyklopediya*, Vol. VI (1961). This confirms our assumption that he had fallen from grace so deeply that he was made part of Soviet "un-history."

106. One of the most explicit denunciations of Babayev's was that by Karaev at the Twenty-First CP of Soviet Union Congress in Moscow. Complained Karaev: "Comrades Babaev and Durdiyeva, former Secretaries of the Turkmenistan Central Committee grossly ignored Leninist standards of Party life and the principles of Party leadership. They disregarded Bolshevist principles in the selection and advancement of personnel, *distorted the Party's sacrosanct principle of internationalism, were disdainful of personnel of other nationalities*, did everything they could to belittle Party organizational and political work, belittled the role of the intelligentsia and essentially debarred the intelligentsia from creative work." See *Pravda*, February 5, 1959, p. 3, or *Current Soviet Policies III*, p. 166.

107. Conquest, *op. cit.*, pp. 386–87.

108. See the biographical listing in Heinrich E. Schulz & Stephen S. Taylor, eds., *Who's Who in the USSR 1961–62* (New York: Scarecrow Press, 1962), p. 664.
109. See his speech in *Komsomolskaya Pravda*, October 30, 1958.
110. *Cur. Sov. Policies IV*, p. 234.
111. *Pravda*, November 14, 1961.
112. He is flatly identified as such by Conquest, *op. cit.*, p. 384.
113. At the Twentieth Party Congress (1956) Ekaterina Furtseva of the Moscow Party organization was elected candidate member of the Presidium, the first woman to have reached that circle. She was promoted to full membership in June, 1957, and served as a Secretary of the Central Committee from 1957 until May 4, 1960. For obscure reasons she was dropped from the Praesidium at the Twenty-Second Party Congress (October, 1961). Since May 4, 1960, she has served as Minister of Culture. See *Cur. Sov. Policies IV*, p. 232
114. Cf. the analysis in Fainsod, *op. cit.* (1963 ed.), pp. 235–37.
115. To obtain evidence, Party archives would have to be searched carefully with particular attention to the so-called *nomenklatura*, or the system of classifying Soviet cadres according to jurisdiction. Some indirect evidence has been obtained by Richard E. Pipes, who in his interviews with Soviet Asian refugees found that Party members of Central Asian nationalities were not prone to Russification and presumably helped each other rather than the Russians; see his "Muslims of Soviet Central Asia: Trends and Prospects," *Middle East Journal*, Vol. IX (Spring-Summer, 1955), p. 306.
116. The factor of youth is especially stressed in Harry Schwartz's commentary in the *New York Times*, December 30, 1957, p. 2.
117. Another interesting suggestion is that the Ukrainian Party cadres may be more accustomed to Khrushchev's oligarchic style of work. See Armstrong, *Elite*, pp. 149–50.
118. Lewytzkyj, *loc. cit.* (n. 31), pp. 101ff.
119. Chapter III, above.
120. See *Pravda Ukrainy*, June 18, 1953; also January 31, 1953. Also *Suchasna Ukrayina* (Munich), August 9, 1953, p. 4.
121. See this Chapter, above, p. 228.
122. Fainsod, *op. cit.* (1953 ed.), pp. 336ff., and n. 11 on p. 535.
123. That such a subdivision prevailed in enterprises of ferrous and non-ferrous metallurgy, and in coal mining, is clearly implied in the reorganization decrees cited below.
124. For a discussion, see e.g., Gregory Bienstock, Solomon M. Schwarz, and Aaron Yugow, *Management in Russian Industry and Agriculture* (London: Oxford University Press, 1944), pp. 58ff.
125. Editorial *Pravda*, January 5, 1956, p. 1, or *CDSP*, Vol. VIII, No. 1, pp. 20–21. Copyright 1956, the Joint Committee on Slavic Studies. Reprinted by permission.
126. *Izvestiya*, May 9, 1957, p. 6; or *CDSP*, Vol. IX, No. 19, p. 12. Copyright 1957, the Joint Committee on Slavic Studies. Reprinted by permission.
127. Admittedly, the federal government does support certain activities through grants-in-aid.
128. *Russia's Soviet Economy* (New York: Prentice Hall, 1950), p. 413. Cited by permission.
129. *Narodne hospodarstvo Ukrayins'koyi RSR* [1957], pp. 21, 488.

130. See *Izvestiya*, February 7, 1957, p. 4; or *CDSP*, Vol. IX, No. 7, p. 9. In 1955, the total of large and small enterprises of state industries in the Ukrainian SSR was 34,500 (*Nar. hosp. URSR* [1957], p. 21).

131. See the two ukases of the Presidium of the USSR Supreme Soviet: "No. 38: On Forming a Union-Republican Ministry of Ferrous Metallurgy of the USSR and a Union-Republican Ministry of Non-Ferrous Metallurgy of the USSR," of February 8, 1954, and "No. 185: On Reorganizing the USSR All-Union Ministry of Coal Industry into a Union-Republican Ministry of Coal Industry of the USSR and on Formation of a Union-Republican Ministry of Coal Industry of the Ukrainian SSR," of April 19, 1954; in *Vedomosti Verkovnogo Soveta SSSR* (USSR Supreme Soviet News), Vol. 1954, No. 3 & 9, pp. 119 and 316. Both ukases contain a provision that the enterprises involved are to be distributed according to a list "approved by the USSR Council of Ministers."

132. *Pravda* and *Izvestiya*, May 11, 1957, pp. 1–2; or *CDSP*, Vol. IX, No. 20, pp. 14ff. Copyright 1957, the Joint Committee on Slavic Studies. Reprinted by permission. See also (a) the Resolution of the Plenary Session of the Central Committee, following Khrushchev's Report, February 14, 1957 (*ibid.*, Feb. 16, or *CDSP*, Vol. IX, No. 7, pp. 27ff.) (b) the Theses of Khrushchev "On Further Improving the Organization and the Management of Industry and Construction" (*ibid.*, March 30, pp. 1–4; or *CDSP*, Vol. IX, No. 13, pp. 3ff.); and (c) his speech before the Supreme Soviet (*ibid.*, May 18, pp. 1–5, or *CDSP*, Vol. IX, No. 19, pp. 3ff.). A good factual account of the inefficiencies prevailing under the former system is given in the article by F. Khylyuk, ["Changes in the Administration of Industry and Problems of Productive Cooperation (Ukrainian SSR)"], *Planovoe Khozaystvo* (Planned Economy, Moscow), Vol. 1957, No. 9, pp. 73–79.

133. See M. A. Yasnov's speech in *Izvestiya*, May 10, p. 4 (*CDSP*, Vol. IX, No. 20, p. 4); N. T. Kalchenko's speech, *Izvestiya*, May 9, Vol. 1957, p. 3 (*CDSP*, Vol. IX, No. 19, p. 4).

134. Khrushchev, *loc. cit.* (Note 132, c above—*CDSP*), p. 13, Sec. IV. Copyright 1957, the Joint Committee on Slavic Studies. Reprinted by permission. See also the details in Alec Nove, *The Soviet Economy* (New York: Praeger, 1961), pp. 70–71. Nove's book henceforth cited as Nove, *Economy*.

135. See his Theses of March 30 (*loc. cit.* [*CDSP*], p. 7).

136. Khrushchev, *loc. cit.* (*CDSP*), p. 15.

137. They are conveniently summarized in Nove, *Economy*, pp. 68–69.

138. See also Nove's analysis "The Soviet Industrial Reorganization," in Abraham Brumberg (ed.), *Russia under Khrushchev* (New York: Praeger, 1962), pp. 189–204. Henceforth cited as Nove, "Reorganization."

139. Ye. Glowinsky, "Again on the Reorganization of Industrial Administration," *Suchasna Ukrayina* (Munich), June 2, 1957, p. 9.

140. Very revealing in this connection is the play by the Soviet Ukrainian playwright Alexander Kornyichuk "The Wings," in which the main hero is a very hard-working and competent *provincial* Party secretary, Romodan. The play appears to have been inspired by Khrushchev's new line, printed in *Novy mir* (New World, Moscow), Vol. 1954, No. 11 (November), pp. 2–50.

141. This episode is emphasized in Nove's thoughtful analysis, "Reorganization," p. 195.

142. Yu. Tarkovych, "Why the Large Textile Factory Is Not Built in Zhyto-myr," *Hovoryt' Radio Vyzvolennya: Zbirka materiyaliv ukrayins'koyi re-daktsiyi* (Radio "Liberation" Speaking: Selected Materials of the Ukrain-ian Desk, Munich, 1957), Vol. II, pp. 38ff. The materials are selective but based upon honest research. Incidentally, the textile factory was appar-ently not yet built as of late 1961, at the time of the Twenty-Second Ukrainian Party Congress. I have found no mention of it in the Congress materials (*Rad. Ukrayina*, September 29–October 1, 1961).

143. Glowinsky, *loc. cit.*

144. Belorussia has not been further subdivided into economic regions.

145. Nove, "Reorganization," pp. 197–98. Reprinted by permission.

146. *Ibid.*, p. 199, citing announcement by Kozlov in *Pravda*, January 31, 1958.

147. *Ibid.*

148. See Podgorny's report to the Congress of the CP of Ukraine, *Rad. Ukra-yina*, Sept. 29, 1961, p. 2.

149. "Law on Budget Rights of the USSR and the Union Republics," *Pravda*, October 31, 1959, p. 2; or *CDSP*, Vol. XI, No. 46, pp. 6–9.

150. "Law of the Ukrainian Soviet Socialist Republic on Budget Rights of the UkrSSR and Local Soviets of the Toilers' Deputies," *Rad. Ukrayina*, July 2, 1960, pp. 2–3. All those laws have been conveniently assembled in the series *Vazhneyshie zakonodatel'nye akty Soyuza SSR i Soyuznykh Respub-lik* (The Most Important Legislative Acts of the USSR and the Union Re-publics) under the title: *O byudzhetnykh pravakh Soyuza SSR, Soyuznykh Respublik i mestnykh Sovetov Deputatov Trudyashchikhsya* (On the Budg-etary Rights of the USSR, the Union Republics, and the Local Soviets of the Toilers' Deputies), Moscow, 1963. See pp. 22–30 on the All-Union, and pp. 72–85 on the corresponding Ukrainian Republican law.

151. See the remarks by USSR Supreme Soviet Deputy D. Rasulov in *Pravda*, October 31, 1959 (*CDSP*, Vol. XI, No. 45, pp. 6–8).

152. Nove, "Reorganization," pp. 200–01.

153. *Rad. Ukrayina*, July 8, 1960, p. 1. See also the more detailed legal refer-ences in I. M. Pakhomov, *Radyans'ke administratyvne pravo: Zahal'na chastyna* (Soviet Administrative Law, General Part; Lviv, Lviv University Publishers, 1962), pp. 128–29. This is a textbook for law students in the Ukrainian SSR.

154. Nove, "Reorganization," p. 201, citing *Pravda*, July 14, 1960.

155. Professor P. Alampiyev and V. Kistanov, "In the Interest of Integrated Development of the National Economy—New Network of Major Economic Regions," *Ekonomicheskaya gazeta* (Economical Gazette, Moscow), May 28, 1961, p. 2; or *CDSP*, Vol. XIII, No. 41, pp. 16–17.

156. Alampiyev & Kistanov, *loc. cit.* (*CDSP*), p. 17.

157. See Podgorny's speech in *Komsomolskaya Pravda*, Nov. 21, 1962, p. 1. See also Khrushchev's speech on the preceding day, *ibid.*, Nov. 20, 1962, p. 2.

158. Nove, in "Reorganization," pp. 202–03, makes the point that the planning function of the Gosplan, as it had existed before 1955, has now been divided between the Gosplan and the State Scientific and Economic Coun-cil: the former charged with current and the latter with long-term plan-ning. The Gosplan has also been further hedged in by a proliferation of economic committees, for example, the Scientific and Technical Commit-tee.

159. Nove, *Economy,* pp. 78–79. Italics supplied. Reprinted by permission of George Allen & Unwin, Ltd., the original publishers.
160. See this chapter, above.
161. *Rad. Ukrayina,* January 18, 1959, p. 4.
162. *Ibid.,* January 14, 1959.
163. See the Moscow despatch by Theodore Shabad, "Small Car Gains Despite Khrushchev Criticism," the *New York Times,* July 31, 1962, p. 7. Copyright by The New York Times. Reprinted with permission. See also an earlier Ukrainian write-up in *Rad. Ukrayina,* November 11, 1961, p. 3.
164. *Pravda,* January 31, 1959, pp. 3–4.
165. *Ibid.,* Nov. 20, 1962, p. 5.
166. Lysnyak and Dyadyk in *Pravda Ukrainy,* February 18, 1960, p. 5 and February 20, 1960, p. 5. Quotation from Dyadyk.
167. Lysnyak, *loc. cit.* See also a similar complaint by economist V. Men'shikov: A certain factory in Kiev was compelled to ship at great expense naval parts throughout the Soviet Union, though those parts could have been easily produced by similar plants on the spot. (["The Efficacy of Specialization and Cooperation in the Industry of the Kiev Economic Region"], *Ekonomika Radyans'koyi Ukrayiny* [Economics of Soviet Ukraine, Kiev], Vol. 1960, No. 6, p. 92.)
168. *Pravda,* July 14, 1960, pp. 2ff.; or *CDSP,* Vol. XII, No. 28, pp. 2off.
169. Italics added.
170. *Pravda,* January 12, 1961, pp. 4ff.; or *CDSP,* Vol. XIII, No. 2, pp. 3ff. (Quotation on pp. 9–10 in *CDSP.*) Copyright 1961, the Joint Committee on Slavic Studies. Reprinted by permission.
171. *Pravda,* October 20, 1961, p. 3.

Notes to Chapter IX: The Ukrainian SSR in International Affairs

1. United Nations Conference on International Organization (San Francisco), *Documents,* No. 30 (DC/5 [1]; April 27), p. 10ff., and No. 42 (P/10; April 30). See also Vsevolod Holub (Holubnychy), *Ukrayina v Ob"yednanykh Natsiyakh* (Ukraine in the UN, Munich: Suchasna Ukrayina, 1953), pp. 29ff.
2. On the international relations of the Ukraine from 1917 to 1923 see Roman Yakemtchouk, *L'Ukraine en droit international* (Louvain: Centre Ukrainien d'Etudes en Belgique, 1954), Vasyl Markus, *L'Ukraine soviétique dans les relations internationales et son statut en droit international, 1918–1923* (Paris: Les editions internationales, 1959), and John S. Reshetar, Jr., *Ukrainian Revolution, 1917–1920* (Princeton: Princeton University Press, 1952), *passim.* For a brief factual sketch see also Note IX-1, in the Appendix.
3. Harley A. Notter, *Postwar Foreign Policy Preparation, 1939–1945,* Department of State Publication 3580 (Washington, D.C., 1949), p. 318n., referring to a British aide-mémoire of December 30, 1943. The first quotation is apparently taken from the memorandum; the second is a paraphrase of Notter's.
4. See "The Conversion of the People's Commissariats of Defense and Foreign Affairs from All-Union into Union Republic Commissariats: A Re-

port by Comrade V. M. Molotov in the Supreme Soviet of the USSR, February 1, 1944," and "Law on Granting Powers to the Union Republics in the Realm of Foreign Relations and on the Conversion, in This Connection, of the People's Commissariat of Foreign Affairs from an All-Union to a Union-Republican Commissariat," in *Vneshnaya politika Sovetskogo Soyuza v period Otechestvennoy Voyny* (Foreign Policy of the USSR in the Period of the Fatherland War, Moscow, 1946), Vol. II, pp. 66ff.

5. *The Memoirs of Cordell Hull* (New York: Macmillan, 1948), Vol. II, pp. 1678–80; Notter, *op. cit.*, pp. 317ff.; also William H. McNeill, *America, Britain and Russia ("Royal Institute International Affairs Survey of International Affairs, 1939–1946";* London: Oxford University Press, 1953), p. 506.

6. Notter, *op. cit.*, p. 317.

7. Robert E. Sherwood, *Roosevelt and Hopkins* (New York: Harper, 1948), p. 854. Cited by permission, Harper & Row, Publishers, Inc.

8. On August 29, Gromyko indicated that his government would probably raise the subject again on another occasion; he mentioned it again, without discussing it, on September 27. Notter, *op. cit.*, pp. 318, 327.

9. See U.S. Department of State, *The Conferences at Malta and Yalta, 1945 ("Foreign Relations of the U.S.: Diplomatic Papers";* Washington, D.C., 1955), pp. 72–73, 75; henceforth cited as *U.S. Malta and Yalta Papers.* See also Vernon S. Aspaturian, *The Union Republics in Soviet Diplomacy: A Study of Soviet Federalism in the Service of Soviet Foreign Policy* (Geneva and Paris, 1960), pp. 102ff.

10. *U.S. Malta and Yalta Papers,* pp. 712 (Bohlen), 721 (Hiss).

11. On October 3, 1944, President Roosevelt had called Gromyko's proposal "absurd." See Notter, *op. cit.*, p. 333. See also the "Memorandum by the Acting Secretary of State (Stettinius)," of November 15, 1944, in *U.S. Malta and Yalta Papers,* pp. 48–49. For President Roosevelt's attempt to evade the issue at Yalta, see *ibid.*, pp. 712ff. and 722ff.

12. The main reason why Churchill supported Molotov appears to have been British reluctance to be the only country with a multiple representation. In his speech Molotov had adroitly harped on old American fears of being outvoted by the British Empire. See W. S. Churchill, *The Second World War: Triumph and Tragedy* (Boston: Houghton Mifflin, 1953), pp. 357ff.

13. A side aspect of the story which illuminates the nature of American politics is worth recounting here. Anticipating difficulties with "Congress and the American people" that might have arisen from granting the USSR three votes, President Roosevelt asked Churchill and Stalin for their support in case the United States would have to request two additional votes (February 10, 1945). Churchill and Stalin immediately agreed to do so (*U.S. Malta and Yalta Papers,* pp. 966ff.). On March 29 the secret agreements on (a) admitting the two Soviet Republics to the United Nations and (b) eventually giving the United States two additional votes for the sake of parity with the USSR were leaked to the *New York Herald Tribune*. The American public, thereupon, seems to have become indignant not at the admission of Belorussia and the Ukraine, but at the possibility of the United States asking for more votes. Sherwood, *op. cit.*, pp. 876–77.

14. *Yearbook* of the United Nations, 1947–48, p. 31.

15. See the "Appeal" of January 21, 1946, in *Vneshnaya politika Sovetskogo*

Soyuza, 1946 g. (USSR Foreign Policy in 1946, Moscow, 1952), p. 551; and the accounts of D. Z. Manuilsky's activities July 1, 1948, in *Vneshnaya politika . . . 1948* (Moscow, 1951), Vol. I, pp. 301–04), and December 3, 1949 (*Vneshnaya politika . . . 1949* [Moscow, 1953], pp. 621–26).

16. See Manuilsky's telegram to the Secretary-General of the United Nations, Trygve Lie, August 26, 1946 (*Vneshnaya politika . . . 1946*, pp. 601–02), and Manuilsky's speeches at the Security Council September 4, 1946 (*ibid.*, pp. 605–14), and November 10, 1946 (*ibid.*, pp. 614–23).

17. See, e.g., his speech at the Plenary Session of the United Nations General Assembly September 29, 1948 (*Vneshnaya politika . . . 1948*, Vol. II, pp. 225–30).

18. For a differing conclusion see Holubnychy (*op. cit.* in n. 1, above), who found that "quantitatively and qualitatively, elements stressing the *nationality question* predominate in the political speeches and actions of the representatives of the Ukrainian SSR." This question can only be settled by a more elaborate content analysis than the present writer has yet undertaken. See also the methodological Note IX-2, in the Appendix.

19. Holubnychy, *op. cit.*, pp. 73ff.

20. See Article I of both treaties.

21. *The History of the United Nations Relief and Rehabilitation Organization* (New York: Columbia University Press, 1950), Vol. I, p. 4; and Vol. II, p. 233; hereafter it will be cited as *History of UNRRA*). The experiences of the UNRRA missions to the Ukraine and Belorussia are sketched in Vol. II, pp. 231–56.

22. For the text of the agreement and explanatory letters see *ibid.*, Vol. III, pp. 332–37; also L. Kh. Palamarchuk, *Ukrayins'ka RSR v mizhnarodnykh vidnosynakh* (Ukrainian SSR in International Relations, Kiev, 1959), pp. 245ff. In Art. I(a); UNRRA agreed to supply to the Ukrainian SSR before July, 1946, goods and services valued at $189 million.

23. To be inferred from Art. V(a) of the agreement. See also John Fischer, *Why They Behave Like Russians* (New York: Harper, 1946), pp. 24–25. For a time, Mr. Fischer was a member of the UNRRA mission to the Ukraine.

24. Fischer, *op. cit.*, pp. 157–58, and *History of UNRRA*, Vol. II, p. 243.

25. See the incident reported by Fischer, *op. cit.*, pp. 157–58.

26. The total of UNRRA supply deliveries to the Ukraine was $188,199,300 (*History of UNRRA*, Vol. II, p. 250). An interesting detailed breakdown according to major categories (but excluding $2.4 million worth of medical and sanitation supplies) will be found *ibid.*, Vol. III, pp. 490–93. On co-operation, see *ibid.*, Vol. II, pp. 231–56; Fischer, *op. cit.*, *passim*, esp. Ch. 4 ("The Soviet Priesthood"), pp. 62–89; Marshall MacDuffie, *The Red Carpet* (New York: Norton, 1953), *passim*. MacDuffie, chief of the UNRRA mission in Kiev in 1946, revisited the Soviet Union in 1953.

27. Fischer, *op. cit.*, pp. 53–54.

28. See the reply by Minister of State Younger to a written question by Major Beamish, MP, in the House of Commons. The words are Younger's. Great Britain, *Hansard's Parliamentary Debates*, 5th Series, Vol. 472; House of Commons, Session 1950, March 1–24, written question No. 28.

29. U.S., Congress, House, Committee on Foreign Affairs, *Favoring Extension of Diplomatic Relations with the Republics of Ukraine and Byelorussia* (Hearing before the Special Subcommittee on H. Con. Res. 58, July 15,

1953), 83rd Congress: 1st Sess., 1953, pp. 77–78. Henceforth abbreviated as *Hearing on H. Con. Res. 58*.

Possibly as a consequence of the British diplomat's visit to Kiev, the Presidium of the USSR Supreme Soviet on December 16, 1947, passed a decree forbidding Soviet officials and agencies to have any contacts with foreigners, except through the USSR Ministry of Foreign Affairs. In the summer of 1953, however, A. Baranovsky, then Ukrainian Foreign Minister, requested the United Nations Secretariat to address any communications to the Soviet Ukrainian government not to Moscow, as had been the practice before, but directly to Kiev. See Holubnychy's article on the competence of the Ukrainian SSR Ministry of Foreign Affairs in *Vpered* (Munich), December 1955, pp. 5–6; and S. S. Studenikin *et al., Sovetskoe administrativnoe pravo* (Soviet Administrative Law; Moscow, 1950), p. 253.

30. "Certain preliminary inquiries" had been made by Senator Smith in June 1952. See *Hearing on H. Con. Res. 58*, pp. 76ff.

31. Two letters from the Department giving the reasons for its opposition will be found *ibid.* They are dated June 26, 1952, and March 13, 1953. The State Department gave four main reasons for its attitude: (a) the propaganda effects of U.S. diplomatic recognition could be negated by Soviet censorship and/or the two Republics rejecting the offer themselves; (b) the latter would reinforce the myth of their sovereignty; (c) the establishment of additional U.S. missions in the USSR would be expensive; and (d) the establishment of additional Soviet missions in the U.S. would arouse public hostility.

32. The resolution includes references to the "sovereignty of the Ukrainians and Belorussians, which is in harmony with the ideas expressed in the Declaration of Independence of the United States" and the American "policy of liberation." *Ibid.*, pp. 1ff.

33. Fischer, *op. cit.*, p. 121.

34. MacDuffie, *op. cit.*, p. 145.

35. In his foreword to the compilation *Ukrayins'ka RSR v mizhnarodnykh vidnosynakh* (1959), p. 13, Foreign Minister Palamarchuk says that the Ukraine has been visited by heads of state and outstanding political and non-official popular leaders from Albania, Afghanistan, Bulgaria, Czechoslovakia, Denmark, Hungary, India, Iran, Sweden, the United Kingdom, and Yugoslavia; and by parliamentary delegations from Ceylon, Czechoslovakia, Hungary, Indonesia, Norway, Rumania, and the United Arab Republic.

36. Aspaturian, *op. cit.*, pp. 166–67.

37. Borys Lewytzkyj, "Die Sowjetukraine und die europaeischen volksdemokratischen Laender (1958–60)," *The Annals of the Ukrainian Academy of Arts and Sciences in the United States*, Vol. IX (1961), pp. 189–200. The quotations are from p. 190. For a Soviet treatment of a very similar problem see I. F. Yevsyeyev, ["An Important Form of Cooperation between the Peoples of the Ukraine and Poland"], *Ukrayins'ky istorychny zhurnal* (Ukrainian Historical Journal, Kiev), Vol. 1961, No. 5 (October-November), pp. 87–96. This appears to be a summary of his later work *Sotrudnichestvo Ukrainskoy SSR i Pol'skoy Narodnoy Respubliki, 1944–1960 gg.* (Cooperation of the Ukrainian SSR and the Polish People's Republic, 1944–60; Kiev, 1962). The latter was not available to this writer.

38. The *New York Times*, February 3, 1944, pp. 1ff.

39. See also *U.S. Malta and Yalta Papers* and Sherwood, *op. cit.*

40. Fischer, *op. cit.*, p. 118.

41. Holubnychy, *op. cit.*, pp. 8ff., esp. pp. 15–16. Yakemtchouk, *op. cit.*, pp. 23ff., cites both considerations ("la question des nationalités et la politique internationale") without weighing their relative importance.

42. McNeill, *op. cit.*, p. 506. Reprinted by permission of Oxford University Press.

43. See Note 11, above.

44. Aspaturian, *op. cit.*, p. 113.

45. R. Emerson and I. L. Claude, Jr., "The Soviet Union and the United Nations: An Essay in Interpretation," *International Organization,* Vol. VI (February, 1952), p. 3. The authors state: "The Soviet Union, unlike some of its rivals, is wholly unencumbered by any illusion as to the possibility and even the desirability of realizing the concept of one world—unless, of course, it be a world dominated by Communism. . . . It is groundless Utopianism to think that the United Nations or any other international organization can now be utilized as the instrumentality to achieve world solidarity directed toward commonly shared goals and ideas" (*ibid.*). Reprinted by permission of the editor. A. Z. Rubinstein in his "Selected Bibliography of Soviet Works on the United Nations, 1946–1959," *American Political Science Review,* Vol. LIV (December 1960), pp. 985–91, briefly touches upon more recent attitudes of the regime, which have remained essentially the same.

46. Stalin, *O velikoy Otechestvennoy Voyne Sovetskogo Soyuza* (The Great Fatherland War of the USSR, 5th ed.; Moscow, 1947), pp. 164ff.

47. See above, p. 265.

48. Holubnychy, *Ukrayina* . . . , pp. 15–16. Aspaturian, *op. cit.*, p. 23, points out that Stalin knew it would have been politically risky, if not constitutionally impossible, for the United States to engage in "frivolous experimentation with multiple representation in foreign affairs." The present writer is not convinced that Stalin knew so much about American politics.

49. Aspaturian, *op. cit.*, p. 113.

50. *Ibid.*, p. 121.

51. I owe this suggestion to Professor Roman Smal-Stocki.

52. *Ibid.*, p. 65. By July 13, 1944, the USSR may have realized the farcical aspect of the negotiations between Korniychuk and Wasilewska, and Korniychuk was replaced by Dmitry Manuilsky, who had succeeded him as Foreign Commissar of the Ukrainian SSR.

53. In a private communication to this writer Professor Smal-Stocki has plausibly suggested the reason why at Yalta Lithuania had been chosen to represent the Baltic Republics in the United Nations. The Polish government-in-exile had territorial disputes not only with the Ukraine and Belorussia but with Lithuania as well. The admission of Lithuania to the United Nations would have allowed the USSR to have a third non-Russian spokesman in the United Nations against the claims of the strong Polish exile community.

54. *Ibid.*, pp. 78, 199.

55. Molotov's report of Feb. 1, 1944, in *Vneshnaya politika Sovetskogo Soyuza v period Otechestvennoy Voyny,* Vol. II, p. 74.

56. Quoted, *ibid.*, p. 76. The italics in the second sentence are mine, the following are Stalin's.

57. *Pravda* of June 28, 1946, as cited in Fainsod, *How Russia Is Ruled* (Cambridge, Mass.: Harvard University Press, 1953), p. 494. According to the calculations of R. Conquest (*The Soviet Deportation of Nationalities* [London: Macmillan, 1960], p. 54), more than 1,250,000 Soviet citizens were deported for suspected disloyalty, not counting any Ukrainians.

58. Cf. his "secret" speech at the Twentieth Party Congress in 1956 in Leo Gruliow (ed.), *Current Soviet Policies II* (New York: Praeger, 1957), p. 182.

59. A leaflet entitled "Narode Ukrayiny!" (People of the Ukraine!) which was to be dropped from planes. A copy is preserved in the archives of the Ukrainian Supreme Liberation Council in New York ("Prologue"). See also Chapter IV, above.

60. A large poster addressed "Do uchasnykiv tak zvanykh 'UPA' ta 'UNRA.' " A copy is kept in the same archives.

61. An abridged version of the speech was printed in Moscow's *Bol'shevik*, Vol. XX, No. 6 (March 1944), pp. 7–35, under the title ["The Liberation of the Ukrainian Lands from the German Conquerors and the New Tasks of Reconstructing the National Economy of Soviet Ukraine"]. Unfortunately, since the Kiev press was not available for the period, the companion speeches could not be consulted.

62. Academy of Sciences of the Ukrainian SSR, *Visnyk*, Vol. XXV, No. 5 (May 1954), p. 54.

63. E. R. Stettinius, *Roosevelt and the Russians: The Yalta Conference* (Garden City: Doubleday, 1949), p. 187. Reprinted by permission. See also Holubnychy, *Ukrayina* . . . , pp. 11ff.

64. See on this Chapter IV, above.

65. Cf. Aspaturian, *op. cit.*, p. 70. See Schulenburg's memo of July 11, 1940, in Germany, Auswaertiges Amt (Foreign Office), *Nazi-Soviet Relations, 1939–1941* (U.S. Department of State, 1948), p. 164.

66. Aspaturian, *op. cit.*, p. 71.

67. John A. Armstrong, *Ukrainian Nationalism, 1939–45*, esp. pp. 287–88.

68. See Chapter IV, above, pp. 123–24.

69. An excellent discussion of the problem in the American setting will be found in Gabriel A. Almond, *The American People and Foreign Policy* (New York: Harcourt, Brace, 1950).

70. Raymond A. Bauer, Alex Inkeles, and Clyde Kluckhohn, *How the Soviet System Works* (Cambridge: Harvard University Press, 1956), p. 214. Cited by permission of Harvard University Press.

71. In his article ["International Cultural Ties of Soviet Ukraine"], *Kommunist Ukrainy* (Rus. ed., Kiev), Vol. 1957, No. 12 (December), p. 72, K. Lytvyn gives the following figures: Ukrainian subscribers received 2,950 copies of foreign newspapers daily and 34,526 foreign journals and scientific periodicals a month.

72. Tsentral'ne statystychne upravlinnya pry Radi Ministriv URSR (Central Statistical Administration of the Ukrainian SSR Council of Ministers), *Narodne hospodarstvo Ukrayins'koyi RSR v 1960 rotsi; Statystychny shchorichnyk* (UkrSSR National Economy in 1960; Statistical Annual, Kiev, 1961), p. 312. Title also cited as *Nar. hosp. URSR, 1960*.

73. Figures on radio sets in *Nar. hosp. URSR (1957)*, pp. 506, 382. Approximate population figures for 1946, 1949, and 1952 in V. Holubnychy, "Statistics of the Population of the Ukraine, 1940–1956," *Vpered* (Munich), No. 71 (October 1956), pp. 2–3.

74. Leland M. Goodrich and Edvard Hambro say "no." Cf. their *Charter of the UN: Commentary and Documents* (Boston: World Peace Foundation, 1946), pp. 79ff.

75. On the reasons for admitting India to the League of Nations and her experience in that organization, cf. Sir J. C. Coyajee, *India and the League of Nations* (Waltor, 1932), and same title by V. Shiva Ram and Brij Mohan Sharma (Lucknow, 1932).

76. Kurishkov's cited article (n. 62, above) is a case in point. It is written in a propagandistic vein, making no attempt whatsoever to cover the subject in a scholarly fashion. Professor V. M. Koretsky "disposes" of recurrent expressions of doubt about the international status of the Ukraine by referring to her membership in the United Nations Security Council, etc. Cf. his "Growth of Sovereignty of the Ukr. Sov. Soc. Republic as part of the USSR," in Ukrainian SSR Academy of Sciences, *Visnyk*, Vol. XXV, No. 8 (August, 1954), pp. 3–13. Incidentally, late in 1960 Professor Koretsky was elected to a nine year term on the International Court of Justice, where he represents the USSR [sic].—For an authoritative exposition of the Soviet view of sovereignty, see I. Traynin's ["Problems of Sovereignty in the Soviet Federal (*soyuznom*) State"], *Bol'shevik*, Vol. XXI, No. 15 (August 1945), pp. 12–23. International lawyers interested in the subject should read Bohdan T. Halajczuk's "The Soviet Ukraine as a Subject of International Law," *The Annals of the Ukrainian Academy . . .* , Vol. IX (1961), pp. 167–88.

77. N. M. Ul'yanova, ["The Participation of the Ukrainian SSR in the International Labor Organization"], in Akademiya nauk URSR, Sektor derzhavy i prava (Ukrainian SSR Academy of Arts and Sciences, Political Science and Law Division), *Narysy z istoriyi derzhavy i prava Ukrayins'koyi RSR* (Papers on the History of State and Law of the Ukrainian SSR, Kiev, 1957), pp. 197–225.

78. V. I. Lisovskiy, *Ukrainskaya SSR i mezhdunarodnoe pravo* (Ukrainian SSR and International Law, Moscow: Legal Faculty of the Moscow Institute of Finances, 1960), 39 pp.

79. See his article, ["From the History of the Solution of the Danubian Problem"], *Ukrayins'ky istorychny zhurnal*, Vol. 1961, No. 6 (Nov.-Dec.), pp. 60–69.

80. And not only Ukrainian citizens. Professor Alexander Dallin in his book *The Soviet Union at the United Nations: An Inquiry into Soviet Motives and Objectives* (New York: Praeger, 1962), p. 91, found that all Soviet media played up Soviet successes at the United Nations, and played down or virtually ignored Soviet setbacks. He writes, "Even the most substantial accounts are curiously selective (*ibid.*)."

81. E.g., in Podgorny's speech in United Nations General Assembly on October 4, 1960, on which see below.

82. *Rad. Ukrayina*, November 16, 1952. Beria had said, among other things, that as of 1952 the Ukraine was producing more pig iron than France and Italy combined.

83. See *Pravda Ukrainy*, Feb. 28, 1957, pp. 3–4. On the rally see the *New York Times*, Dec. 31, 1956, p. 3.

84. The *New York Times*, September 24, 1960, pp. 6–9.

85. Excerpts from Prime Minister Diefenbaker's speech may be found in the

New York Times, September 27. Full text obtained from Permanent Mission of Canada to the United Nations: "Address by the Rt. Hon. John G. Diefenbaker, Q.C., M.P., Prime Minister of Canada, to the General Assembly of the United Nations, New York City, September 26, 1960."

86. See Note IX-3, in the Appendix, for excerpts from the Diefenbaker-Podgorny exchange.

87. The materials have been conveniently collected in *Digest of the Soviet Ukrainian Press,* November 1960. See also two remarkable articles in the *Neue Zuericher Zeitung:* "Colonialism in the Soviet Empire: Exile Political Figures Comment on Khrushchev's Speech" (September 28, 1960) and "Soviet Colonialism: The Unprotected Flank of Khrushchev's Political Offensive—The Effects of Diefenbaker's Speech" (November 20, 1960), as translated in *Problems of the Peoples of the USSR,* No. 8 (1961), pp. 15–19. Journal is published by the League for the Liberation of the Peoples of the USSR, Munich.

88. See the *New York Times,* October 9, 1962, p. 7, and October 10, 1962, p. 5; also *Time* Magazine, October 26, 1962, pp. 34+.

89. October 24, 1956, the eleventh anniversary of the United Nations was celebrated throughout the Soviet Union. The ceremonies in Kiev proved a small affair, with no member of the Soviet Ukrainian government in attendance. See *Pravda Ukrainy,* October 25, 1956, p. 4. This was the first time that the United Nations anniversary was celebrated at all.

90. MacDuffie complains that no Soviet citizen would spontaneously mention the United Nations in a conversation with him (*op. cit.,* p. 137). Interviewee #50 (an American scholar) found Soviet literature on the United Nations exceedingly meager; interviewee #33 (a recent defector) failed to show any interest in the international representation of the Ukraine. Ukrainian sovereignty was to him "a lie as transparent as limpid spring water." On the general problem of the political impact of Soviet representation in the United Nations see also Chapter VII, "The Domestic Image of the United Nations," in Dallin, *op. cit.* (n. 80), pp. 87–94.

91. November 12 (1949?), the British representative McNeill again raised the question of the United Kingdom establishing diplomatic relations with the Ukrainian SSR, in a speech in the United Nations Political Committee. Next day, Manuilsky replied that this was impossible so long as the United Kingdom continued to support the war criminals among the DPs. See *Rad. Ukrayina,* April 7, 1950 [sic]. On this occasion the offer of August, 1947, was mentioned.

92. Fischer remarks (*op. cit.,* p. 121) that the Ukrainians he met in 1946 were impressed with Manuilsky's speeches from the rostrum of the United Nations and assumed that he had great stature in world politics. To an observer who has access to impartial and complete media of information this might seem ridiculous, but it becomes quite plausible when we consider the particular character of Soviet news coverage.

93. It was discontinued around 1954.

94. Referred to in Holubnychy, *Ukrayina . . . ,* p. 66.

95. See above, p. 269.

96. Cf. the write-up by I. Tsyupa in *Dnipro* (Dnieper [Komsomol journal], Kiev), Vol. 1957, No. 10 (October), entitled "Thus Hearts Meet," reprinted in *Suchasna Ukrayina* (Munich), Nov. 17, 1957, p. 4.

97. See also Note IX-4, in the Appendix, on the way in which some teachers in Ukrainian secondary schools propose to discuss in class the participation of the Ukrainian SSR in international affairs.

Notes to Chapter X: Ukrainian Nationalism after the War: Conclusions

1. See V. Holubnychy, *The Industrial Output of the Ukraine, 1913–1956,* p. 4. On the composition of the sample and the methodological problems involved in the use of such data, see Note X-1, in the Appendix.
2. Interview #41. Less pronounced, but to the same effect are the statements of similar sources—#53, #54, and #73, the last a native Russian.
3. Interview #83.
4. *Russia Without Stalin* (New York: The Viking Press, 1956), p. 219. Cited by permission of the Viking Press.
5. See the "Nationalities Code Book" (unpublished material of the Project on the Soviet Social System, Russian Research Center, Harvard University, October 23, 1952), p. N 6. Used with permission of the Center.
6. *Ibid.,* and Sylvia Gilliam, "The Nationality Questionnaire" (unpublished report of the Harvard Project on the Soviet Social System, Russian Research Center, Harvard University, October, 1954), p. 35. "The Relation of Nationality to Experience and Attitude in the USSR," by Irving Rosow, and "The Nationality Problem in the Soviet Union," by John S. Reshetar, Jr., are two companion reports that have been combined with a summary and introduction by Frederick Wyle into Sylvia Gilliam *et al.,* "The Nationality Problem in the Soviet Union: The Ukrainian Case" (unpublished final report of the Project on the Soviet Social System, Russian Research Center, Harvard University, October, 1954). All these materials used with permission of the Center. In 1959 the material from the symposium went into Chapter XV of Alex A. Inkeles and Raymond A. Bauer, *The Soviet Citizen* (Cambridge, Mass.: Harvard University Press, 1959), pp. 338–73.
7. See on this our discussion in Chapter V, above.
8. See especially Gilliam, *loc. cit.,* p. 38. In this context, younger means those born after 1910; "rural" includes those "who were born and reared in the village and later moved to the city."
9. *Ibid.,* p. 34.
10. Interview #97.
11. Interview #60.
12. Interview #11.
13. Interview #70.
14. Interview #10.
15. Interview #40.
16. Interview #35.
17. Gilliam, *loc. cit.,* pp. 3–4.
18. U.S. Department of State, *The Soviet Union as Reported by Former Soviet Citizens: Interview Report No. 9* (1955), pp. 22–23. Similar opinions were expressed by my sources #7 and #73 (former Soviet officers). One of such officers interviewed by the State Department, a 41-year-old former lieutenant colonel, who had defected to the West, gave a very interesting

interview; see *ibid., Interview Report No. 15* (October, 1955), *passim,* esp. pp. 1, 15, 18.

19. (My) interview #44. A similar one of these illegal circles, which allegedly embraced several hundred students at the universities of Moscow, Leningrad, Kiev, and Odessa and called itself *Istinny Trud Lenina* (The True Work of Lenin's) is briefly sketched in Brigitte Gerland's Vorkuta labor camp memoirs, *Die Hoelle ist ganz anders* (Hell Is Altogether Different, Stuttgart: Steingrueben, n.d.), pp. 8ff. The reports might be exaggerated, but there are too many of them to be dismissed as wishful phantasies.

20. Interviews #13, and #59. Confirmed by an East Ukrainian who had served in the UPA: Ukrainians would infiltrate into Soviet institutions both in Western and Eastern Ukraine, destroy evidence incriminating Ukrainian patriots or, occasionally, kill Soviet agents who knew too much.

21. Interviews #33, and #2.

22. Interview #44.

23. Interview #35. See also Manuscript B—the memoirs of a former camp inmate.

24. Interview #44.

25. Interview #13.

26. [Ukraine, Communist Party of Ukraine], *XVI z"yizd komunistochnoyi partiyi . . . ,* p. 13.

27. R. A. Bauer, A. Inkeles, and C. Kluckhohn, *How the Soviet System Works: Cultural, Psychological, and Social Themes* (Cambridge, Mass.: Harvard University Press, 1956), p. 116; my interviews #11, #44, and #70.

28. Interview #11.

29. See also the extended critical discussion of university admission in Nicholas DeWitt, *Education and Professional Employment in the USSR* (Washington, D.C.: National Science Foundation, 1961), pp. 248ff., esp. p. 252 ("This policy is obviously discriminatory against academically qualified applicants"), and pp. 255B–256A.

30. Gilliam, *loc. cit.,* p. 13. The explanation may be that in the Ukraine there were more Ukrainian than Russian intellectuals to arrest.

31. *Ibid.,* p. 14.

32. See Chapter VIII, above, pp. 259ff.

33. Rosow, *loc. cit.,* pp. 10ff., 26, 31ff.

34. Gilliam, *loc. cit.,* p. 41.

35. *Ibid.,* p. 69.

36. *Ibid.*

37. Interviews #41 and #33. Respondent #41 said: "I have never hidden that I was a Ukrainian because nobody asked me that," meaning: it did not matter in my case.

38. See Chapter II, p. 73, above.

39. See p. 75, above.

40. In the academic year 1959–1960 62.3 per cent of all full time college students in the USSR were Russians, though the proportion of Russians among the total population was only 54.8 per cent (1959 census); see *Nar. khoz. SSSR, 1960,* pp. 780 and 14; also DeWitt, *op. cit.,* pp. 656–57. The percentage of Russians among the academic and scientific personnel in 1959 was 64.5. See *Narodnoe khozaystvo SSSR v 1960 godu: Statisticheskiy ezhegodnik* (USSR National Economy in 1960, A Statistical Annual; Moscow, 1961), p. 785.

41. Frank Lorimer, *The Population of the Soviet Union*, p. 50.
42. See Table II-22, above, p. 79.
43. See Chapter VIII, above, p. 259.
44. See Chapter V, above, p. 166.
45. The counter-assertion that the respondents to the Harvard nationality questionnaire might have hidden their nationality for reasons extraneous to career advancement does not appear plausible. The overwhelming impression from my interviews is that the battle for economic gains is a primary concern of every Soviet citizen, and I do not think that they would have misjudged their stakes.
46. See Garland, *op. cit., passim;* also Interview #31.
47. Gilliam, *loc. cit.*, pp. 124ff.
48. *Ibid.*, p. 26.
49. Interview #60.
50. Interview #31.
51. Manuscript B. See also M. Prokop, *Ukrayina i ukrayins'ka polityka Moskvy* . . . , pp. 127–128.
52. Manuscript B. Lesya is a fairly common Ukrainian name, which has been made famous by the great Ukrainian poetess Lesya Ukrayinka. The anecdote dates, of course, back to the period of the Stalinist "cult of personality."
53. I have used it in Chapter VII, above.
54. Interviews #12 and #61. See also Lev Shankowsky, *Pokhidni hrupy OUN,* pp. 169–172.
55. Interview #44.
56. Interview #72.
57. See Note I-3, in the Appendix.
58. See on this Pipes, "Muslims of Soviet Central Asia: Trends and Prospects," *Middle East Journal,* Vol. IX (Spring-Summer, 1955), pp. 155ff., 300ff.
59. See Chapter II, above, pp. 54–55.
60. Gilliam, *loc. cit.*, p. 7.
61. See Chapter V, above, p. 152.
62. Note the example of the two Galician girls in this chapter, above.
63. The best source on Western Ukrainians in Soviet labor camps is Garland, *op. cit., passim.* See also Joseph Scholmer, *Vorkuta* (London: Weidenfeld & Nicolson, 1954), pp. 113ff., 131. Dr. Scholmer, too, was imprisoned in the Vorkuta camps; he is a more perceptive observer than Brigitte Gerland. The original German version of his memoirs entitled *Die Toten kehren zurueck: Bericht eines Arztes aus Workuta* (The Dead Return: The Story of a Physician from Vorkuta, Cologne-Berlin: Kiepenheuer & Witsch, 1954), is preferred by those who have had the opportunity to compare the two. Two fascinating if very brief references to West Ukrainians in Siberian labor camps will also be found in Alexander Solzhenitsyn's semi-documentary novelette *One Day in the Life of Ivan Denisovich* (New York: Bantam, 1963). A young fellow crosses himself before starting to eat. He must be a Western Ukrainian for the Russians in the camps "didn't even remember which hand you cross yourself with" (p. 15). The adolescent Gopchik had been arrested for taking milk to the Ukrainian guerrillas in the woods. He had been given the same sentence an adult would have received—page 69.
64. Interviews #14, and #44.

65. Interview #71.
66. Manuscript B.
67. E.g., interviews #33, and #44.
68. Interview #11.
69. Interviews #13, and #10.
70. Interview #10.
71. Interview #35.
72. In Russian *khokhol* is a semi-pejorative nickname for Ukrainians.
73. Gilliam, *loc. cit.,* p. 47.
74. Reprinted from *Nationalism and Social Communication,* p. 152, by Karl W. Deutsch, by permission of The M.I.T. Press. Copyright 1953, The Massachusetts Institute of Technology.
75. *Ibid.,* pp. 130ff.
76. Gilliam, *loc. cit.,* pp. 94ff.
77. See on this Chapter I, above.
78. Interviews #6, #41, and #53.
79. Gilliam, *loc. cit.,* p. xiii *et passim.*
80. See Chapter III, p. 95n., above.
81. Point orally communicated by Professor Robert Feldmesser.
82. Interview #72. The statement refers to the 1930's; the situation might have changed now. Miss Gilliam found that the highly educated younger respondents to the nationality questionnaire, i.e., those who had already made a career in the Soviet Union or had stood at the threshold of it, tended to subscribe to the official version of Ukrainian history more "than any other age-education group and twice as frequently as the older well educated" (*loc. cit.,* p. 47).
83. Interviews #33, and #103.
84. See ["The Prose of 1957"], in *Literaturna Hazeta* (Kiev), Feb. 8, 1958, p. 2. Among the outstanding cultural events of recent years should be mentioned the publication of the multi-volume Soviet Ukrainian Encyclopedia (*Ukrayins'ka Radyans'ka Entsyklopediya;* 1959–   ). As of April 1963 it had been carried as far as the letter "P."
85. Interviews #71, and #11.
86. See his *Terror and Progress: USSR* (Cambridge, Mass.: Harvard University Press, 1954), p. 200.
87. According to interview #79, only Party members were admitted to graduate study of history in the Ukraine.
88. See, e.g., Yaroslav Halan, "Murderers in the Disguise of Political Emigres," *Rad. Ukrayina,* January 19, 1946; Bazhan's speech in the United Nations Committee No. 3, *ibid.,* February 5, 1946.
89. It is conveniently available in full English translation in the *Digest of the Soviet Ukrainian Press* (New York: Prolog), Vol. II, No. 5, pp. 8ff.
90. See Chapter IX, above, p. 281, also Note IX-3, in the Appendix.
91. See David Mitrany, *The Effect of War in Southeastern Europe* (New Haven: Yale University Press, 1936), p. 31, as quoted in Selig S. Harrison, *The Most Dangerous Decades* (1957), p. 8.
92. *Pravda,* February 1, 1959, pp. 4ff.
93. Royal Institute of International Affairs, London, *Nationalism,* p. 111.
94. See, e.g., the remarkable short story by Nikolay Zhdanov, "A Trip Home," *Literaturnaya Moskva* (Literary Moscow), Vol. 1956, No. 2 (translated in Edmund Stillman, *Bitter Harvest* [New York: Praeger, 1959], pp. 177–89),

and Crankshaw, *Russia After Stalin,* pp. 216–17. Zhdanov describes the experience of a Party functionary who travels home to his native village to settle a few matters arising from the death of his mother and finds that he is visiting an altogether different world. Crankshaw sketches the luxurious existence led by the Kiev elite. Even before he moved to Moscow, Kirichenko lived "the life of a potentate . . . , with an immense and luxurious establishment and a garage like a royal mews." (Quotation from p. 216.)

95. Interview #44.

96. Interview #13.

97. Interviews #10, #15, #18 and #33.

98. Interviews #33, #76, and #92. See also M. Sova, *Do istoriyi bol'shevyts'-koyi diysnosty: 25 rokiv zhyttya ukrayins'koho hromadyanyna SSSR* ([A Contribution] to the History of Soviet Reality: 25 Years of a Ukrainian Citizen's Life in the USSR, Munich: Institute for the Study of the History and Culture of the USSR, 1955), *passim.* (Mimeographed.)

99. Interview #61.

APPENDIX

Note I-1. The Terms "Nation" and "Nationalism"

The literature on "nationalism" is rather extensive but despite the efforts of many eminent scholars, the genesis of nations still remains shrouded in mystery. Overfacile generalizations about this process have been made frequently, and serious scholars had to spend time and effort to refute them—see, for example, the extensive but somewhat polemical argument in Rudolf Rocker, *Nationalism and Culture* (New York: Covici, Friede, 1937), and the more concise and balanced one by Rupert Emerson, "Paradoxes of Asian Nationalism," in *Far Eastern Quarterly*, Vol. 13 (February, 1954), pp. 131–42. But as soon as a body of people appears on the political stage that can be designated a "nation" or a "nationality," because, for one thing, it demands to be recognized as such and, for another, it succeeds in eliciting this recognition, it is possible for a student of nationalism to point out in retrospect several elements that have presumably been either responsible for the emergence of that group or have reinforced it during its development. In the words of Hans Kohn:

Nationalities come into existence only when certain objective bonds delimit a social group. A nationality generally has several of these attributes; very few have all of them. The most usual of them are common descent, language, territory, political entity, customs and traditions, and religion. . . . [But] none of them is essential to the existence or definition of nationality.—*The Idea of Nationalism* (New York: Macmillan, 1946), pp. 13–14. By permission of The Macmillan Company.

The most important of these factors is assumed to be a common political organization, the existence of a state, which in most cases precedes the formation of a nationality (*ibid.*, pp. 4, 15; also Emerson, *loc. cit.*, pp. 132–33). The latter process is said to result from the conscious will on the part of a decisive section of the people. As Professor Kohn puts it:

Nationality is formed by the decision to form a nationality. . . . Nationalities are created out of ethnographic and political elements when nationalism breathes life into the form built by preceding centuries. Nationalism is a state of mind, permeating a large majority of the people and claiming to permeate all its members; it recognizes the national state as the ideal form of political organization and the nationality as the source of all creative cultural energy and of economic well-being.—Kohn, *op. cit.*, pp. 15, 16. By permission of The Macmillan Company.

Sometimes this process of a more or less conscious formation of nationalities is also referred to as "nationalism" (see Carlton J. H. Hayes, *Essays on Nationalism* [New York: Macmillan, 1926], p. 5), while usually the term denotes the driving force behind this process.

Incidentally, it should be noted that the terminology in this field has not yet been firmly established. Professor Kohn, one of the foremost students of nationalism, uses the term "nationality" on par with what other scholars have called a "nation." Compare, e.g., the definition by Professor Emerson (orally communicated): "A nation is a large group of people shaped by a common historical tradition, inhabiting a particular territory and normally speaking a common language, who feel that they form a single and exclusive community destined to be an independent state." For a possible distinction between "nation" and "nationality" ("a people potentially but not actually a nation"), quite apart from the legal sense of the latter word, see also Royal Institute of International Affairs (E. H. Carr, chm. of study group), *Nationalism* (London: Oxford University Press, 1939), p. xvii. To my mind, the distinction between "actual" and "potential" nations is rather fine spun and liable to become a matter of fruitless controversy.

In a path-breaking study Professor Karl W. Deutsch has linked the development of nations to general so-cial mobilization. (See his *Nationalism and Social Communication* [New York & Cambridge: Wiley & M.I.T. Press, 1953]). Unfortunately, in my judgment, Professor Deutsch concentrates so much on the techniques of measuring national and social mobilization to the detriment of the development of his theory. Marxist-Stalinist theories relating to nationalism and national minorities have been commented on at length in numerous other sources: One of the best is Pipes's study *The Formation of the Soviet Union* (Cambridge: Harvard University Press, 1954), pp. 41ff.; one of the most recent, Sullivant's work *Soviet Politics and the Ukraine, 1917–1957* (New York: Columbia University Press, 1962), pp. 7–19, which the interested reader may want to consult.

Note I-2. Resolutions of the Central Committee of the Communist Party (Bolshevik) of Ukraine on the Cultural Struggle, 1946–48

During the reaction after World War II, which in professional literature is known as *zhdanovshchina* (Zhdanov's reign, after Stalin's chief ideological spokesman of the period, the late Andrey A. Zhdanov), Ukrainian Party authorities passed a series of decrees designed to regulate many aspects of cultural life. In some cases this was done under obvious prodding from the All-Union Party Central Committee in Moscow. There follows a list of the resolutions adopted by the Central Committee of the Communist Party (Bolshevik) of Ukraine, in roughly chronological order, with bibliographical references:

a) "Concerning the Distortions and Mistakes [Committed] in the In-

terpretation of the History of Ukrainian Literature in the 'Outline of the History of Ukrainian Literature,'" of August 24, 1946—text partly reprinted in *Radyans'ka Ukrayina,* September 11, 1946; relevant materials in *Kul'tura i zhizn',* organ of the propaganda section of the All-Union Party Central Committee, No. 3 (1946), by S. Kovalev; *Pravda Ukrainy,* June 30, by I. Stebun; *Rad. Ukrayina,* July 20, 21, 24, 26; August 11, 18, 27, 1946.

b) For resolution against the humoristic magazine *Perets'*—see attack in *Pravda,* August 24, 1946.

c) "Concerning the [Literary] Journal *Vitchyzna* (Fatherland),"—see

Rad. Ukrayina, August 17, October 4, 1946.

d) "Concerning the Repertoire of Amateur Circles in Cultural-Educational Establishments."

e) "Concerning the Repertoire of Drama and Opera Theatres in the UkrSSR and Ways of Improving It"—text printed in part, *ibid.,* October 12, 1946.

f) "Concerning Measures for the Further Improvement of the Work of Schools of the UkrSSR." Announcement of a Decision of the CC of CP(B)U of November 13, 1946 re bourgeois nationalist distortions in Ukrainian literature textbooks for classes IX and X.

g) "Concerning Political Mistakes and Inadequate Work of the Historical Institute of the Academy of Sciences, UkrSSR," of August 29, 1947—referred to *ibid.,* October 3, 1947; June 13, 1948.

h) "Concerning the Situation of and Measures for Improvement of Musical Arts in the Ukraine" (May 1948).

The first five resolutions are listed by *Literaturna Hazeta* (Kiev) October 12, 1946, as cited by Danylo Lobay, *Neperemozhna Ukrayina* (Invincible Ukraine, Winnipeg, Canada: Ukrainian Canadian Committee, 1950), p. 138, which is, by the way, a very useful secondary source. All those resolutions are also either referred to or reproduced in two Soviet Ukrainian sources: Ukraine, Ministerstvo kul'tury URSR (UkrSSR Ministry of Culture), *Kul'turne budivnytsvo v Ukrayins'kiy RSR* (Cultural Construction in UkrSSR), Vol. II (Kiev, 1961), pp. 142ff.; or Akademiya nauk URSR, Sektor derzhavy i prava (UkrSSR Academy of Sciences, Sector of State and Law), *Istoriya derzhavy i prava Ukrayins'koyi RSR, 1917–1960* (History of UkrSSR Public Law, Kiev, 1961), pp. 615ff.

On the purge of textbooks see Vovk and Bazylevsky in *Rad. Ukrayina,* August 20, 24, 1946; of libraries—Kalynovska, *ibid.,* September 20, 1946.

Note I-3. The Jewish Question in the Ukraine

The relationship between Soviet Ukrainians and Jews constitutes an important and controversial aspect of our main topic. A complete, exhaustive investigation of that aspect would call for a separate study. In view of its importance in this context, however, and rather than ignoring it altogether, I have decided to present it in sketchy form in order at least to raise some questions that ought to be raised, though leaving many of them unanswered.

There is no work on the Jewish question in the Ukraine which en-compasses all the postwar years. The work that most closely fulfills our requirements is Solomon M. Schwarz's standard study *The Jews in the Soviet Union* (Syracuse: Syracuse University Press, 1951), henceforth cited as Schwarz *I*. The second part of the book, a study of anti-Semitism in the Soviet Union, has been enlarged and published in Russian as *Antisemitizm v Sovetskom Soyuze* (New York: Chekhov, 1952), and will be referred to as Schwarz *II*. On the Ukraine in 1917–20 and 1939–45, the material in Schwarz *I* and *II* should be supplemented by the valuable survey article by Joseph L. Lichten, "A Study of Ukrainian-Jewish Relations," *The Annals of the Ukrainian Academy of Arts and Sciences in the U.S.,* Vol. V, No. 2/3 (Winter-Spring, 1956), pp. 1160–177. Dr. Lichten, formerly of the Polish diplomatic service, is the Director of the Foreign Languages Department of the Anti-Defamation League of B'nai Brith.

Nevertheless the following works deserve special mention. Those by Philip Friedman are all exceptionally well documented. They include the collection of memoirs edited by him under the title *Martyrs and Fighters: The Epic of the Warsaw Ghetto* (New York: Praeger, 1954)—hereafter, cited as Friedman *I;* his *Their Brothers' Keepers: The Christian Heroes and Heroines Who Helped the Oppressed Escape the Nazi Terror* (New York: Crown, 1957)—henceforth, Friedman *II;* and his splendid contribution "Ukrainian Jewish Relations during the Nazi Occupation," in the *YIVO Annual of Jewish Social Science* (New York: YIVO Institute for Jewish Research), Vol. XII (1958–59), pp. 259–96—henceforth, Friedman *III.* The late Dr. Friedman (d. in 1960), a native of Lviv (Western Ukraine), is regarded as one of the foremost historians of Jewish martyrology. A younger Jewish scholar, Erich Goldhagen (formerly of the Russian Research Center of Harvard University, now teaching at Hunter College, New York) is writing a book tentatively entitled *A Political and Cultural History of Soviet Jewry.* His article "Communism and Anti-Semitism," *Problems of Communism,* Vol. IX, No. 3 (May–June, 1960), pp. 35–43, is a concise but able summary of the subject. Lew Shankowsky's somewhat polemical but richly

documented "Russia, the Jews and the Ukrainian Liberation Movement," *The Ukrainian Quarterly,* Vol. XVI (Spring-Summer, 1960), pp. 11–25, 147–63, attempts to prove that anti-Semitism *organized by Ukrainians* did not exist in the Ukraine. On the general cultural policy of the regime throughout the Soviet Union there is an interesting book by B. Z. Goldberg, *The Jewish Problem in the Soviet Union* (New York: Crown, 1961). Goldberg is the son-in-law of the well-known Jewish writer Sholom Aleichem, and President of the American Committee of Jewish Writers and Artists. Very valuable in our context is Joseph B. Schechtman's account of his visit to the USSR in August, 1959, in *Star in Eclipse: Russian Jewry Revisited* (New York & London: Thomas Yoseloff, 1961). Schechtman is a prominent Zionist who had been born in Odessa. During the Ukrainian struggle for independence he was elected on a Zionist slate to the *Rada* and was a member of the Jewish National Secretariat. He frankly discusses many aspects of the Jewish problem in the USSR including some events in the Ukraine.

What is the number of Jews involved in our analysis? In 1897, 1.7 million Jews were living in the Eastern Ukraine, or 66.8 per cent of the total number of Jews in the territories later included in the Soviet Union (*within* pre-World War II boundaries). When the Pale of Settlement was abolished during the Revolution, their number fell to 1.6 million in 1926 (58.7 per cent) and 1.5 million (50.8 per cent) in January, 1939 (see Schwarz *I,* p. 15). A more recent estimate by Dr. Friedman puts the total number of Jews residing in *all* Ukrainian territories at the outbreak of World War II (that is, roughly within the area of the Ukrainian SSR in her 1945 boundaries) at 3.1 million, of whom 1.6 million lived in the Soviet Ukraine, 1.0 million in Galicia, then under Poland, and some 0.5 million in other regions under Czechoslovakia and Rumania. (Friedman *III*, p. 259.) According to Schwarz's estimate no fewer than 900,000 Jews were killed in the Ukraine between 1941–44 during the Nazi occupation (*ibid.*, p. 230). Partly as a result of this, the number of Jews even in the enlarged Ukrainian SSR was only 840,000 (according to the census of 1959), where they constituted only 2.0 per cent of the total population; in 1926 they numbered 5.4 per cent of the total in Eastern Ukraine alone and formed a consistently higher proportion in the West Ukrainian territories in 1930–31 (see Chapter II, p. 58, above, and Table II-7). Another important fact ought to be pointed out: In 1959, for the first time in the history of the Soviet Jewry, more Jews were living in the Russian Republic than in the Ukraine: 875,000 (38.1 per cent of all Jews in the USSR) compared with 840,000 (37.4 per cent in the Ukraine) and 150,000 (7.0 per cent in Belorussia) (see Schechtman, *op. cit.*, p. 28).

Nevertheless, despite the precipitant fall in the number of Jews in the Ukraine—perhaps best illustrated by the change in the share of Jews among the urban population of the Ukrainian SSR: 22.8 per cent in 1926 to 4.3 per cent in 1959 (see Table II-22, p. 79)—the role of the Jewish minority in the Ukraine is far from negligible. At the beginning of the academic year 1960–61, Jews made up 18,673 out of a total of 417,748 college students in the Ukraine, or about 4.5 per cent

(*Vysshee obrazovanie v SSSR: Statisticheskiy sbornik* [Higher Education in the USSR: Statistical Handbook, Moscow, 1961], p. 130). But among the professionals with higher education who were engaged in the national economy of the Ukrainian SSR on December 1, 1960, Jews numbered 83,689 persons or 12.2 per cent of the total (*ibid.*, pp. 70–71; or Table II-16, p. 70)—in the total population Jews number, as we have already seen, but 2.0 per cent. Because of the great contribution of the Jewish minority to Ukrainian economic and cultural life, it is important to consider their fate, though their total number may be declining over time.

To my mind, the Jewish question in the Ukraine has two main aspects: the preservation of a Jewish national community and the position of those Jews who do not join Jewish cultural and political organizations and many who want to assimilate themselves to the Russian or to the Ukrainian people. Both aspects are closely interrelated, but the second is the broader one. Both of them raise the double question: What has been the policy of the regime and what have been the attitudes of the population at large?

In the first part of his book *Jews in the Soviet Union*, Schwarz has proved conclusively that Communist ideology refused to accept the Jews as a separate nationality, that the regime has been very reluctant to permit separate Jewish organizations in the 1920's and 1930's, and that whatever success the Soviet Jews have achieved as a national group in various fields (for example, education, science, the press) was accomplished in spite of, rather than owing to, the regime. Summing up the situation as of 1949 Schwarz writes:

The suppression of the last Jewish newspaper of any importance, the dissolution of the only noteworthy Jewish publishing house in the Soviet Union, and the impenetrable official silence on all matters of Jewish interest, permit of only one interpretation. Sometime in 1948 it was decided to put an end to everything that in any way could stimulate or keep alive the national consciousness of Soviet Jews, so that they might ultimately disappear as a separate national group. Certainly, Jews will continue to live in the Soviet Union, and Jewish religious congregations may even exist, but there will be no "Jewry," no Jewish nationality, no Jewish community of culture.—I, p. 215. Cited by permission of Syracuse University Press.

Goldhagen writes with respect to official Party policy:

Anti-Semitism could not figure in any indictment drawn up against the Soviet dictatorship during the 1920's. But with the advent of the 1930's a new picture began to unfold itself.

The rich and indiscriminate armory of means wherewith bolshevism professed to pursue Utopia acquired a fresh instrument, time-honored and of proven efficacy; and the anti-Semitic spirits, which had been outlawed by bolshevism and driven to lead a repressed existence in the subterranean dwellings of Soviet society, were now emboldened to emerge and engage in their practice in the guise of a Communist *raison d'état.*—*op. cit.*, pp. 38, 39. Cited by permission of *Problems of Communism.*

According to the perhaps not unimpeachable source of the fanatic Adolf Hitler, who held forth on the topic of Soviet Jewry in one of his table talks:

Stalin made no secret before Ribbentrop that he was waiting only for the moment of maturation of a sufficiently large indigenous intelligentsia to make short shrift (*Schluss zu machen*) of Jews as a leadership stratum which he still needs today.—*Hitlers Tischgespraeche* (Bonn, 1951), p. 119, as cited by Goldhagen, p. 39n. Cited by permission.

Stalin's death has not reversed official policy in this respect. Dr. Morris N. Kertzer, the Secretary of the New York Board of Rabbis, who visited the Jewish communities in Moscow and Leningrad in the summer of 1956, found that the regime strictly limited their function to religious worship: educational activities were forbidden; there were not enough prayer books; and Sholom Aleichem was published in Russian, not in Yiddish (see his three articles in The *New York Times,* July 30, pp. 1ff.; July 31, p. 2; and August 1, 1956, p. 2). One of this writer's respondents told him that in the summer of 1957 he found the Jewish religious community in Kiev still very intimidated (interview #50); this has been confirmed by Schechtman, who visited Kiev two years later (*op. cit.*, p. 37). Suslov, a member of the Party Presidium, is reported to have told a Canadian Communist delegation: "We have no intention of calling back to life a dead culture (see the joint letter to the editor by Saul Bellow, Leslie Fiedler, Irving Howe, Alfred Kazin, Philip Rahv, Lionel Trilling, and Robert Penn Warren, in the *New York Times,* January 10, 1958, Henceforth, cited as Letter)."

In more recent years the anti-Semitic policy of the regime has been seemingly relaxed. Rowland Evans, Jr., for example, reported in the *New York Herald Tribune* of November 6, 1961, pp. 1, 10 that "since 1959, for example, five Jewish classics were published and some Jewish variety shows and amateur theatrical troupes permitted. A bi-monthly literary journal named *Soviet Homeland* started appearing in September of this year [1961] (p. 1)." But the occasion for Evans's survey was a sad one: the arrest, secret trial and sentencing to twelve years in jail of "one of the most prominent Jewish leaders in Leningrad," Gedalia Rubinovich Pechersky. In 1960, Soviet authorities also closed "up to a dozen synagogues in towns and cities off the beaten track of the tourist (p. 10)."

In this connection it is worth stressing that the Government of the Ukrainian National Republic in late 1917 passed a series of measures which were based on the recognition of the Jews as a separate nationality; they were to be carried out by its Minister for Jewish Affairs, Dr. Moisei Zilberfarb. Schwarz notes: "The Ukraine was the first country of the world to introduce extraterritorial cultural autonomy for minority nationalities (*I*, p. 88)." (See also *ibid.*, pp. 83, 92, 104; and Lichten, *op. cit.*, pp. 1164ff.). During the Soviet period, in the 1920's and early 1930's there existed in the Ukraine Jewish local administrative organs (*soviets*)—it would be interesting to find out to what extent the Ukrainian Communists, especially Skrypnyk, favored their existence and to what extent they were organized on direct orders from Moscow.

So much for the existence of the Jewish minority as a separate national group and government policies. What has been the attitude of the Ukrainian population toward the Jewish minority? The late Jewish historian Dr. Friedman admirably sums up the most important historical obstacles toward a rapprochement between the Ukrainians and Jews:

In the past Ukrainian Jewish relations were marked by social tension and conflicts. Although both peoples were oppressed by the same ruling nations there did not arise the desire for common solidary action against their oppressors. From around the 16th century some Jews served as managers or lessees of the estates of Polish owners. This function brought down upon them the wrath of the Ukrainian peasants and Cossacks and frightful massacres occurred in 1648–49, in the times of Bohdan Chmielnicki [Khmelnytsky], in 1768 (*Haidamaks*) and 1918–1921, in the period of Simon Petlura.

These events have had a powerful effect upon Ukrainian-Jewish relations in the 20th century, particularly in the Nazi period. They were exacerbated by the assassination of Simon Petlura, whom the Jews held responsible for the pogroms in 1918–21, in Paris, on May 25, 1926, by a Ukrainian Jew, Sholem Schwarzbart. The Ukrainians, both the extreme nationalists as well as the democratic and liberal elements, regarded Petlura as a national hero and martyr, and totally denied his complicity in the pogroms. (Friedman *III*, pp. 259–60.) Cited by permission of YIVO Institute.

In the minds of many people the progressive minority policy of the Ukrainian national government in 1917 has been overshadowed by the horrible pogroms that took place in the Ukraine from 1918–20. There is no need for examining the evidence in this note. I refer the reader to Elias Heifetz's *The Slaughter of Jews in the Ukraine in 1919* (New York, 1921) and Arnold D. Margolin's *Ukraina i politika Antanty* (The Ukraine and the Policy of the Entente, Berlin, 1921). That a Jewish leader of the stature of the late Dr. Margolin—he had been defense counsel in the Beiliss case—remained a friend of the Ukrainians despite the pogroms is a fact worth noting.

In the 1920's and 1930's there was a certain amount of anti-Semitism in the Soviet Ukraine. An elderly interviewee who had left the Soviet Union during World War II, an accountant by profession, told the author that when he was arrested a Jewish acquaintance intervened on his behalf with the NKVD (secret police). Nevertheless, he thought, "the whole trouble lay in the fact that the Jews would always take the side of the stronger (interview #3)." An interesting and, in my opinion, objective statement on the reasons for Soviet anti-Semitism was made in November, 1926, by Kalinin:

Why is the Russian intelligentsia perhaps more anti-semitic than it was under Tsarism? It is a natural development. In the first days of the revolution the mass of urban Jewish intellectuals and semi-intellectuals threw itself into the revolution. Members of an oppressed nation, a nation that never had any share in the government . . . they naturally flocked to the revolutionary work of construction, of which administration is a part. . . . At the very time when large sections of the Russian intelligentsia were breaking away, frightened by the revolution, at that very time the Jewish intelligentsia were pouring into the revolutionary stream, swelling it in a high proportion as compared with their numbers, and starting out to work in the revolutionary administrative organs.—As quoted in Schwarz I, p. 242. By permission.

Schwarz has proved (1) that until the pogroms of 1918–20 communism had virtually no influence whatsoever in *Jewish* political circles, because the Jews in the Bolshevik party, such as Trotsky, Zinoviev, and Bukharin, had renounced the nationality of their ancestors (*I*, pp. 92ff.); and (2) that after 1920, the proportion of Jews in the Communist Party of the Ukraine was much lower than that among the *urban* population (13.1 as compared to 22.7 per cent as of 1926–27 [*ibid.,* p. 261]), though it exceeded considerably that among the *total* population (5.4 per cent). Nevertheless, while taking these qualifications into account, the general state of affairs as described by Kalinin cannot be denied.

The misery in the Jewish ghettos in the Ukraine before 1917 was proverbial: one spoke of *luftmenshn,* or people living on thin air (Schwarz *I,* p. 19). At the same time, the Jews were characterized by resourcefulness coupled with a deep and genuine respect for learning. A Jewish artisan would starve, if he could only give his children the best education available, which made the average Ukrainian peasant wonder no end. When the Revolution opened the gates, the Jewish minority forged ahead to occupy important positions in government and society. The Ukrainians, however, a predominantly rural nation, were left behind: partly because they were more distrustful of the new regime and partly because they were ill-equipped to assume responsibilities in an urban-dominated society. The result was a certain degree of resentment at finding Jews in unaccustomed positions, and the prominence of certain assimilated Jews in the Communist party did not diminish that feeling of anti-Semitism.

On the positive side should be noted the cooperation between Jewish and Ukrainian intellectuals. The Jews in the Ukraine had the reputation of supporting the Russians in their attack on everything Ukrainian. Facts show that this opinion is, at the very least, vastly overdrawn. According to informed exile testimony, of the six best known

Yiddish writers in the Ukraine (L. Kvitko, Itsyk Fefer, Der Nister, David Feldman, Khaim Gildin, and A. Reyzin), the last three cooperated with the Soviet Ukrainian writers' organizations *Vaplite* (Free Academy of Proletarian Literature) and *Literary Market* that were suppressed in the late 1920's and early 1930's for alleged Ukrainian nationalist activity—see B. Podolyak, ["Facts Which Must Not Be Ignored"], *Suchasna Ukrayina* (Munich), September 16, 1951, pp. 9–10. Other Jews wrote in Ukrainian and became well-known either as Ukrainian poets and writers; for example, Ivan Kulyk, a translator of American and English verse into Ukrainian who was deported to a labor camp; Leonid Pervomaysky, who was attacked for "cosmopolitanism" in 1949 (see Schwarz *I*, p. 357); Natan Rybak; or well-known as literary critics and historians. One of the latter, Joseph Hermayze, was a defendant at the staged anti-nationalist trial of 1929 directed against the Ukrainian intelligentsia (the so-called SVU or "Union for the Liberation of the Ukraine" trial). He was sentenced to a labor camp. The Jewish-Ukrainian linguist Olena Kurylo was purged because she resisted the Russification of the Ukrainian language (Podolyak, *op. cit.;* and Yuriy Dyvnych [Lawrynenko], *Amerykans'ke malorosiystvo* [Neu Ulm, 1951], pp. 31ff.). This is confirmed by Friedman *III*, p. 260, who writes, "Toward the end of the 19th century and in the early years of the 20th century several Jews rose to prominence in the Ukrainian national movement and in the Ukrainian literary renaissance." Friedman then lists nine names. But most telling are the examples of Jewish-Ukrainian cooperation on the political plane. The Jew-

ish-born diplomat Polots'ky was executed for joining an anti-centralist opposition within the Communist Party (Bolshevik) of the Ukraine, known under the name "Shumskism." Furur Ven'yamin, a well-known figure in the Communist Party (Bolshevik) of the Ukraine and editor of the newspaper *Radyans'ke selo* (Soviet Village) devoted his energies to Ukrainizing the traditionally Russified Donets Basin—he committed suicide before being arrested (Dyvnych, *loc. cit.*).

The German occupation of the Ukraine in 1941–44 entailed the death of about 900,000 Jews. Schwarz has analyzed this period under the following relevant headings: "Popular Response to Nazi Incitation," "Civilian Efforts to Rescue Jews," and "The Underground's Reaction to Persecution of Jews (*I*, pp. 310ff.; *II*, pp. 126ff.)." On the basis of secret German reports Schwarz points out that German authorities tried to organize the first pogroms in the newly occupied territories as the action of indignant local inhabitants. But on the whole, they failed to incite the local population to open their carefully planned campaign against the Jews. He writes, ". . . the Nazi extermination policies evidently did not meet with the general assent of the White Russians"; then continues:

Matters were different in the Ukraine. Before the German invasion antisemitic feeling had run higher there than in the northwestern regions. Also, the German army was accompanied by exiled partisans of extreme nationalist Ukrainian groups that had always been violently antisemitic, and these reinforced, especially in the larger cities, the local antisemites. Here and there the local population, to judge from reports, did actually participate in the slaughter. Still there is no evidence of a general bloodlust.—*I*, p. 313. By permission. See also Lichten, *op. cit.*, p. 1169.

As far as civilian efforts to rescue the Jews are concerned, Schwarz finds that "On the whole, the number of Jews saved by non-Jews in the Nazi-occupied Soviet areas was appallingly low"; and he draws unfavorable comparisons with the numbers saved in France, Belgium, Holland, and even Poland (*II*, p. 141). But in the same work Schwarz explains the passivity of Soviet citizens in the face of Nazi mass executions as follows:

The Soviet people have grown so accustomed to subjecting themselves to authority; to keep silent while watching open violence; to suppress in themselves any manifestations of natural, sincere reactions to violence—that, taken as a whole, they proved to be even psychologically incapable of a healthy reaction to Hitler's policy of destroying the Jews.—*II*, p. 142. Cited with author's permission.

To the present writer it seems that a parallel could be drawn between the traumatic experience of the Ukrainian Jews in 1941–44 and that of Ukrainian peasants during the collectivization of 1928–33. A former Soviet citizen who had been born in a Ukrainian village assured this writer that large scale resistance against the collectivization did not exist: the peasants sadly but silently watched the NKVD troops round up the richer peasants for deportation; their only thought and hope was that they should escape that fate. Lichten, however, draws attention to an article by Major Ishak Lewin of the Israeli army: "Jewish Call for Friendship with Ukrainians—to whom it may concern. This is a plea for Friendship" (*Svoboda* [Jersey City, New Jersey], January, 1954, as cited

by Lichten, *op. cit.*, p. 1171). Major Lewin had been saved by Uniate Church authorities along with about 150 other Jews, including several rabbis. This had the appearance of a deliberately planned campaign. He confirms, moreover, the report (see Armstrong, *op. cit.*, p. 172) that the Uniate Metropolitan Sheptytsky wrote a letter to Himmler, protesting the employment of Ukrainian police units in campaigns against the Jews. Earlier in 1941, the Metropolitan had issued a pastoral letter condemning the participation of Ukrainians in the German inspired pogroms.

This and more recent evidence on Jewish-Ukrainian relations during World War II has been carefully assembled and very ably analyzed in Dr. Friedman's heavily documented, balanced account (*III*). Under the heading "The Attitude of the Collaborationist Elements to the Jews" (*op. cit.*, pp. 272–82) he documents at length the participation of many Ukrainians in pogroms, mostly in Western Ukraine (see, however, one reference to "a frightful account of the Ukrainian militia killing 213 Jews in the municipal park in Vinnitsa [Eastern Ukraine], in September, 1941, by an eyewitness, the German officer Erwing Binger"—at the end of footnote 46 on p. 279). After saying that it is impossible to give a complete answer to the question about the number of Ukrainians who collaborated with the Germans, Friedman summarizes his position as follows:

The collaborationist pro-Nazi actives consisted in part of elements that would in all probability not have attained to a position of power in Ukrainian society in normal times. The Ukrainian police was recruited mainly from among the rabble and the criminal elements. However, a large number of fellow travellers, particularly in the first years of the Russian-German war, when the military prestige of the Germans was very high, added weight to the collaborationists. And it was precisely in those years that the most extensive anti-Jewish operations took place. Apparently the pro-Nazi elements consciously exploited the "Jewish problem" in order to attract the largest possible number of adherents and fellow travellers, tempted by the prospect of getting rich quickly from Jewish plunder or appointment to positions vacated by Jews, or simply seeking compensation for an inferiority complex. Among the 35–40 million Ukrainians were many who remained indifferent to the catastrophic events. A handful secretly sympathized with the haunted Jews and discreetly expressed that sympathy. A still smaller group had the courage to risk life and limb in the attempt to rescue the Jews.— *III*, p. 282. By permission. (See also Friedman *I*, pp. 152, 156, and 175; *II*, pp. 131ff.)

Dr. Friedman also devotes special attention to the attitudes of the Ukrainian underground toward the Jews (in the section under that title, *III*, pp. 282–87, and an earlier section on the political setting). Thus on page 265 he reproduces a photostatic copy of Resolution No. 17 of the Second General Congress of the OUN (Organization of Ukrainian Nationalists), which met in Cracow in April, 1941, and was attended by followers of Bandera. That particular resolution on the one hand accepts the Nazi tenet that Jews "constitute the most faithful support of the ruling Bolshevik regime," on the other hand—diverging from the Nazi line—it warns the Ukrainian masses against forgetting "that the principal foe is Moscow" and taking out their frustrations on Jews. The

full resolution, as cited by Dr. Friedman from a contemporary document (*Postanowy II. welikoho zboru organizatsii ukrainskikh natsionalistiw* [Stryj, 1941], p. 14), reads:

The Jews in the U.S.S.R. constitute the most faithful support of the ruling Bolshevik regime and the vanguard of Muscovite imperialism in the Ukraine. The Muscovite-Bolshevik government exploits the anti-Jewish sentiments of the Ukrainian masses to divert their attention from the true cause of their misfortune and to channel them in time of frustration into pogroms on Jews. The OUN combats the Jews as the prop of the Muscovite-Bolshevik regime and simultaneously it renders the masses conscious of the fact that the principal foe is Moscow.—*III*, p. 265. By permission.

Particularly damaging to the cause of Ukrainian-Jewish collaboration would be the following document, whose authenticity, however, is not clearly proven. In the words of Dr. Friedman:

In October 1941 the German Secret Service in Lwow [Lviv] received a letter signed by the Bandera Group [a wing of the OUN—Y.B.], stating that Hitler had deceived the Ukrainians and demanding the release of imprisoned Ukrainian nationalists. The letter proclaimed the following watchwords: "Long live greater independent Ukraine without Jews, Poles, and Germans. Poles behind the San, Germans to Berlin, Jews to the gallows." Whether the letter was authentic or changes were introduced into the text by the German police or SS, who reported it on to Berlin, is unknown.—*III*, pp. 267–8. By permission. (The original source is *Ereignismeldung* No. 126 of the *Einsatzgruppen* in the Political Review of the German SP [Security Police] and SD [Secret Security Service], Berlin, October 29, 1941, document #4134 of the unpublished Nuremberg materials in the Ollendorf case.)

Whether that letter was authentic or had been "doctored" by the German political police, in the first two years of the German-Soviet war the Ukrainian Nationalist Underground made no attempts on behalf of the Jews (Friedman *III*, pp. 282ff.). It was only in the second half of 1943, when the German designs on the Ukraine had become brutally apparent, that the III Congress of the OUN dropped the anti-Jewish plank from its resolutions, repudiated the concept of an ethnic Ukraine, and declared that in an independent Ukraine all citizens would enjoy equal rights, regardless of creed and nationality. Friedman very briefly discusses the fact that at this stage (1943–44) the Ukrainian Nationalist Underground saved Jewish physicians and pharmacists on condition that they would work in their underground hospitals (see Chapter IV for sources). This is hardly an example of disinterested help, but it is nevertheless significant. A former officer of the underground told this writer that the relationship between some of the Jewish doctors and the underground fighters turned out to be much better than might have been expected from the fact that the Jews had been essentially impressed into performing a very dangerous task (interview #12). In view of this the attitudes of the Ukrainian Nationalist Underground toward the Jews may have undergone a considerable revision.

Finally, under the heading "Ukrainians Friendly to Jews" (*III*, pp. 287–94), Dr. Friedman discusses the evidence on Ukrainians helping Jews. He notes, for instance, that a prominent Ukrainian attorney and politician Kost Pankivsky of Lviv helped set up a co-ordinating body for aiding the imprisoned. Other members of the body were Madame Bartel, the widow of the Polish Prime Minister K. Bartel, who had been killed by the Nazis, and Dr. Max Schaff of the Jewish Relief Committee. "The committee saw to it that those held in German prisons received additional food, medicaments and underwear (*III*, p. 278)." He confirms the noble activities of Metropolitan Sheptytsky and several of his subordinates in hiding Jews in Greek Catholic monasteries (*ibid.*, pp. 290–4), adds that several Greek Orthodox priests, Ukrainian Baptists in Volhynia, and Seventh Day Adventists in Galicia also saved Jewish lives (*ibid.*). But the most telling evidence is perhaps that according to official German publications of the SS and the police of District Galicia, in the period from October, 1943, to June, 1944, alone, about one hundred Ukrainians were executed for so-called *Judenbeguenstigung*, that is for helping or concealing Jews. In the judgment of Dr. Friedman this is a substantial number for the following reasons. First, only part of such Ukrainians friendly to the Jews were apprehended and executed, some of those apprehended may have been given lighter sentences. Second, in many instances such persons were executed on the spot and do not figure in official statistics. Third, a limited time period is involved; and, finally, Galicia is only a small part of the Ukraine. (See *III*, p. 288; for other instances of Ukrainians collaborating with Jews see his *I*, p. 302, and *II*, p. 211.) Dr. Friedman himself regrets that material on Ukrainian-Jewish relations in Eastern Ukraine and in Transcarpathia, Bukovina and Bessarabia is lacking. But all in all, his is the fullest and best account on those relations during World War II.

In the postwar period the policy of the Soviet regime toward the Jews changed radically from that of the 1920's and *early* 1930's (Schwarz *II*, pp. 110ff.); he proves that the policy changed already with the Great Purges, but its systematic implementation was interrupted in the chaos of World War II. It has taken the form of insidiously ominous accusations during the last five years of Stalin's life. As is well known, those charges have been dropped in April, 1953. But another manifestation of official anti-Semitism has remained: "a policy of deliberate discrimination against the Jews in the professions, civil service and education. . . . The existence of an unofficial [not publicized?] but effective quota system for Jews was conceded by Nikita Khrushchev to a French Socialist delegation and a Canadian Communist delegation (cited letter to The *New York Times*)." For documentation, see Schwarz *II*, pp. 198ff., esp. 212ff.; also Goldberg, pp. 12, 298–99, 330; Schechtman, pp. 57ff.). Instead of analyzing this policy, of which good accounts are readily available I should like to refer to several important events: two from the immediate postwar period and two others from more recent years. It seems to me that all four shed some light on popular attitudes toward Jews.

Schechtman tells about the shock experienced by Maria Roza Hudes, a former underground Communist agent fighting the Nazis, when she was asked to relinquish a high Party post because she was a Jewess. In 1943, it appears, Hudes, who held a distinguished Communist record, joined Khrushchev's personal secretariat. She did not look like a Jewess so she was accepted without any question. But as soon as in the course of a routine inquiry Party

authorities learned of her Jewish background, she was asked to leave. In vain did she personally appeal to Khrushchev pointing to her battle record with the Soviet underground. Khrushchev replied to her:

Please do not exaggerate. We had no Jews in our Partisan detachments [*sic*]. Do you hear me? There were no Jews in our Partisans.

He continued:

. . . The Jews committed many sins against the Ukrainian people in the past. That is why this people hates them [*sic*]. We have no need for Jews in the Ukraine. . . . Here is the Ukraine and *it is not in our interest that the Ukrainians should associate the return of Soviet power with the return of Jews.*—As cited by Schechtman, *op. cit.*, p. 80. Reprinted by permission of A. S. Baines & Co.—Thomas Yoseloff, publishers. (Italics—Y.B.)

Khrushchev's statement may be misleading. He himself is a Russian and his credentials as a spokesman for the interests of the Ukraine are prone to be challenged on those grounds. Secondly, Stalin's hostile attitude toward the Jews in the 1940's is well known. Khrushchev, being then a subordinate of Stalin's, may have tried to rationalize the dictator's plans by an adroit reference to the wishes of the people— such things are not unknown in Soviet democracy. But there is evidence that some residents of Ukrainian cities did show hostility toward a certain category of Jews—those who were returning home from the eastern areas to which they had been evacuated during the war.

Schechtman complains only that "Jewish repatriates were manifestly unwelcome in the Ukraine (p. 71)"; Schwarz gives some details. In early 1944 many Jewish returnees were beaten up on the peasant markets in Kharkov, one was slain. The police arrested the murderer along with several other peasants who started fighting the police. In Kiev sixteen Jews were killed during a *pogrom*. It was set off by the murder of a Russian officer by a woman who was taken for a Jewess. The Jews returning to their apartments got only a part of their property back. They went to court but could not do anything against the Ukrainians that had taken their things because the latter were supported by their compatriots who gave false testimony (*II*, p. 196). Under normal circumstances such vicious attacks and outright thievery are inadmissible in any civilized state, but in wartime conditions, with the territory changing hands several times, pillaging is not unknown even in the most civilized countries. As an objective scholar Schwarz is, moreover, convinced that the hostile reception of the evacuees was partly the result of the privileged status of a few of them; as a rule, it was not the common people who were evacuated by the Soviet authorities in 1941–42 (*II*, p. 193). In other words, while there is this evidence of anti-Semitism in Ukrainian cities immediately after their reoccupation by Soviet troops it would seem that this particular evidence cannot be used to support charges of general hostility of the Ukrainians against the Jews.

Schechtman gives an account of a very important and not so well-known *pogrom*, which took place not immediately after the war but as late as October, 1959, and not in the Ukraine but in Malakhovka, a suburb of 30,000 inhabitants (3,500 of them Jews), only 15 miles southeast of Moscow. In the early morning hours of October 4, 1959, somebody set fire to the small wooden synagogue and to the nearby cottage of the caretaker of the Jewish cemetery. Firemen were able to save the synagogue, but the caretaker's hut perished in the blaze. Trapped inside was the caretaker's wife, the seventy-year-old Sarah Gordovskaya. Two viciously anti-Semitic leaflets were found near the place of arson. The most important aspect of the case may well be the strange attitude of Soviet authorities. Not only did it take the otherwise quite efficient Soviet police more than three months to apprehend the culprits, but a Soviet court also did not think the matter sufficiently grave to sentence them to more than ten to twelve years in prison. Western lawyers (for example, Maître André Blumel, a member of the National Presidium of the pro-Soviet "France-USSR") were not given frank and full accounts of the case by Soviet authorities who tried their best to hush the affair up (see Schechtman, pp. 46ff.). We have cited this case in our context not so much in order to show that outbursts of anti-Semitism are not limited to the Ukraine but to point out that the regime is evidently not interested in stamping them out and thus—either unwittingly or deliberately—abets them.

Our fourth case deals with the celebrated protest of the young Russian poet Evgeniy Evtushenko against the failure of Soviet authorities to erect a monument to the Jewish victims in Babiy Yar, near Kiev. On September 19, 1961, Evtushenko published in Moscow's *Literaturnaya Gazeta* a spirited poem in which he complained that no monument had as yet been erected to the Babiy Yar victims (translated in *CDSP*, Vol. XIII, No. 36, p. 18). Furthermore, he clearly implied that that was because of the existence of anti-Semites in leading positions.

The resulting controversy in the Soviet press is not our concern. We have to ask the question: What does the tragedy of Babiy Yar show about the popular attitude of the Ukrainians toward the Jews?

On September 24, 1941, a hidden bomb destroyed the Continental Hotel in Nazi-occupied Kiev in which German headquarters were stationed. Two days later the Nazis issued an order to the 30,000 Jewish inhabitants of Kiev to present themselves at a certain point in Kiev, on pain of death, for the purpose of "resettlement." Some 25,000 thousand did come. Under guard they were marched through the streets of Kiev, were led into the ravine of Babiy Yar, and there sadistically shot by German flying squads. Later the Germans executed and buried in the same ravine Soviet sailors and soldiers, railway employees, workers of the Bolshevik, Leninskaya, and Transsignal Kiev factories (Schechtman, *op. cit.*, pp. 88–94).

Two aspects of the tragedy are of particular importance in this study: What was the reaction of the Kievan population (Ukrainians and Russians) to the massacre in the Babiy Yar, and secondly, why have Soviet authorities still not built a monument in Babiy Yar? Leon Uris, the author of *Exodus* (New York: Bantam, 1958), has it that the massacre of Babiy Yar was carried out to the accompaniment of Ukrainian cheering (cited by Shankowsky, *op. cit.*, p. 20, in, referring to *Exodus*, pp. 80, 116). More responsible Jewish authors have refrained from making such accusations. Schechtman, for example, points out that it was not until September 21 that Kiev was finally taken by the Germans (p. 88). The massacre took place almost within a week after the occupation, and the

Jews themselves did not know what horrible fate awaited them. A clear implication of Schechtman's account is that the onlookers who saw the Jews being led out of the city suspected no more than the victims themselves. Schechtman then quotes the report of a Nazi official: "The population hardly knew that the Jews were liquidated, but recent experience suggests that they would not have objected (p. 93)." More credible is the verdict of a Ukrainian woman writer who lived in Kiev in those years. She is quoted in both Schechtman (p. 89) and Shankowsky (pp. 20–21). Dokiya Humenna writes: "There was not a person in Kiev who did not abhor, who inwardly did not shudder at Hitler's butchery of the Jews." (See her *Khreshchaty yar* [*The Cross-Shaped Ravine* (New York, 1956)], p. 203, as cited by Shankowsky.) It strains our credulity to believe that anybody among the Kievans applauded that massacre: the worst that the Kievans have been accused of by Soviet Ukrainian poets of Jewish origin is that they turned their backs upon Jews being led to execution (see Savva Golovanivsky and Leonid Pervomaysky, as referred to by Schechtman, pp. 97ff.).

But why has a memorial to the Jewish victims of Babiy Yar not yet been built, though there are two such memorials in the Lithuanian SSR, one in Latvia, and one in Belorussia (Schechtman, pp. 101ff.)? More than that, why did Soviet authorities in 1959 plan to fill in the ravine and construct in it a public park and stadium with amusement facilities [sic] (p. 102n). If it could be shown that that was a decision made in Kiev rather than Moscow and secondly, if so, that the city administration of

Kiev represented the will of the citizens of Ukraine's capital, that would be a shocking example of deep seated anti-Semitism in the heart of the Ukraine. But because of the gravity of the accusation it may be wiser to reserve our judgment, the more so because there is indirect evidence that the central authorities in Moscow are against singling out the Jews as victims of Nazi brutality; see the controversy after the publication of Evtushenko's poem; for example, Starikov's rejoinder "Concerning a Poem," in *Literatura i zhizn'* [a Stalinist organ called Literature and Life, Moscow], September 27, 1961, or *CDSP*, Vol. XIII, No. 37, pp. 14–17; Markov, *ibid.*, September 24, 1961, or *CDSP*, *ibid.*, p. 17. The Babiy Yar massacre and the history of the proposed monument are tragic and painful episodes, but until more evidence is found they cannot be used to substantially clarify Ukrainian-Jewish relations during and after World War II.

What prognoses could be made for future relations among those two peoples?

As hinted at by Schwarz, the crux of the Jewish question in the Ukraine in the 1920's and 1930's (and, for that matter, in Belorussia, too) lay in the socio-economic difference between the Ukrainians and the Jews. As he puts it: "Russians and Jews were ahead of the Ukrainian and White Russian majorities both economically and culturally (*I*, p. 81—in this context we may ignore the Russians)." Religious intolerance on the part of the peasantry contributed to the tension; Lichten (*op. cit.*, p. 1173) cites Reshetar (*op. cit.*, p. 253). Add to this, sweeping charges of Jewish collaboration with

the Soviet regime in general and the NKVD in particular, of Jews being more Russian than the Russians themselves in combating Ukrainian nationalism, and, on another plane, of their refusing to join the Red Army —and we obtain a picture of Ukrainian anti-Semitism before World War II. But in the 1940's and 1950's the situation changes. On the one hand, the Ukrainians have made considerable progress in socio-economic advancement (more on this in Chapter II). On the other hand, they seem to have realized that as far as the regime was concerned, the Jews are now "in the same boat," if not actually drifting outside. As put by a young Ukrainian student who defected to the West in the middle 1950's: "Now they [meaning the Jews] cannot dodge the draft any more (interview #33)." With a change in socio-economic and political fortunes, a change in attitudes of the Ukrainians toward the Jews appears inevitable. The evidence for this hypothesis is very slim indeed, but it is worth citing.

The same elder interviewee (#3) who complained that the Jews would take the position of the stronger, also pointed out that the Jews would be most likely to assimilate the Ukrainian language and customs if they were obliged to live among Ukrainians in a village. Least likely to do so were, in his opinion, Russians and Poles. He noted with approval that some Jews would learn to speak excellent Ukrainian, whereas the Russians in the Ukraine would never speak anything but Russian. The younger respondent (#33), who came from a small town in Eastern Ukraine, offered the following interesting comments on the attitudes of Ukrainians toward their national minorities. He found Ukrainian-Russian relations to be, on the whole, those of conflict. But how about the Jews? He said:

There was no distinct friction, you just felt an antipathy . . . in connection with the social position. A Jew would not be a collective farmer, but at the very least a vendor of mineral water, an employee in the commercial network, an official.

When asked to give an over-all characteristic of Ukrainian-Jewish relations, he answered:

[The interests of the two peoples] *tended rather to be common.* With Jews you could come to an agreement faster [than with the Russians]. With them it was easy and useful to be on good terms.

Admittedly, one cannot base one's conclusions on two interviews, however fascinating. But the respondents' answers conform so much with what one may assume from an analysis of the present situation of the Jewish minority in the Ukraine that they can serve for a hypothesis which may be formulated as follows: as the socio-economic difference between the Ukrainian majority and the Jewish minority will diminish by action of the regime, the Ukrainians will increasingly look upon the Jews as upon their comrades in suffering. That this is likely to happen despite some ugly doings, seems to be assured by the fact that there is no fundamental hostility between the two peoples. The pledge for this are two events of great importance which must not be forgotten in the West and in due time will again come to light in the Soviet Union: the far-sighted policy toward the Jewish community which

was decreed by the Ukrainian *Rada* in 1917, and the cooperation of numerous Jewish intellectuals and politicians in the cultural and political renascence of the Ukraine in the 1920's.*

* This conclusion is not invalidated by the fact that late in 1963 the Academy of Sciences of the Ukrainian SSR lent its name to the publication, in Ukrainian, of a crudely anti-Semitic book, with scurrilous cartoons, by Trofym K. Kychko (Kichko)—viz., *Yudayizm bez prykras* (Judaism Without Embellishment, Kiev, 1963; 191 pp., 1st printing of 12,000 copies). The present writer has not been able to obtain a copy of that book (under pressure from West European and American Communist Parties and on orders from Moscow it has reputedly been withdrawn from circulation). See, however, a brief editorial report on the book in the *New Leader*, Vol. XLVII, No. 6 (March 19, 1964), p. 3, entitled "Missing Voices," with reproductions of some of the cartoons on pp. 4–5. Also the editorial in the *New York Times*, March 30, 1964: "Anti-Semitism in the USSR." Ukrainian Americans have protested against the publication of such a propaganda piece by the Academy of Sciences of the Ukrainian SSR—see the excessively polemical editorial article "An Ugly Anti-Semitic and Anti-Ukrainian Provocation of Moscow," *Svoboda* (Jersey City, N.J.), April 4, 1964, Section II (English-language section), pp. 1–2; there is also available a more moderately worded declaration by the Foreign Representation of the Ukrainian Supreme Liberation Council (UHVR, or Prologue group) in New York, of March 31, 1964 (mimeographed press release in Ukrainian). The *Svoboda* article hints that the book encountered some criticism in the Soviet Ukraine herself (in the Kievan newspaper *Radyans'ka kul'tura* or Soviet Culture). In any case, it is my belief, that the book reflects more on its author and on the present directors of the Ukrainian SSR Academy of Sciences than on the Soviet Ukrainian intelligentsia or people as a whole.

Note I-4. Definitions of the Soviet Fatherland and Soviet Culture

There is no doubt that the regime tries to inculcate patriotic feelings for the whole Soviet Union. For instance, in the November 11, 1945, issue of *Radyans'ka Ukrayina,* a headline read: " 'Look at the Map of the USSR.' A factory talk on our Fatherland." See also its editorial on April 28, 1946: "Our Great Fatherland." To stress the unity of the USSR, sometimes, but not always, by any means, the expression "Soviet people" is used to designate all Soviet peoples collectively (for example, *ibid.,* May 9, 1946: "Glory Be to the Victorious [Soviet] People"). There is some evidence that the attempts of the regime to rear a Soviet patriotism do not always succeed. Witness the admonishing tone in which the following definition is offered:

For the Soviet people, Rodina [Fatherland] is not restricted to that village, town, *oblast,* or Republic where they were born and raised. . . . The interests of the entire Soviet government and of the Communist structure take precedence in their lives and work. . . . The Soviet people . . . understand that particularism, attempts to withdraw into a nationalist shell or efforts to set one people or republic against another, leads to bourgeois nationalism. This greatly weakens the material and spiritual strength of one's own people or republic. Only within a united *Otechestvo* [Fatherland, synonym of *Rodina*] have the peoples of the USSR become free and equal and attained successes impossible under capitalism (I. Ye. Kravtsev in the Russian language *Rabochaya Gazeta* [Workers Paper, Kiev], September 19, 1957).

In this connection, what should be chosen as the cultural basis of the So-

viet Fatherland? This has been discussed in a very revealing editorial article in *Bol'shevik,* Vol. XXI, No. 22 (November, 1946), pp. 1–8: "Concerning the Socialist Content and the National Forms of Soviet Culture." It is a beautiful rationalization of the concept of Russian supremacy and worth considering in some detail.

In the beginning of the article, *Bol'shevik* rebukes equally the deviation toward local bourgeois nationalism and Russian "great-power chauvinism" (p. 3). But then the keynote is sounded: national cultures in the USSR have been developed by mutual help among the various Soviet peoples (p. 3). Various facets of the development of Soviet nationalities are enumerated: new alphabets and literatures have been created; the native intelligentsia has grown; numerous cultural and scientific institutions established. This development has only been possible through Leninist-Stalinist nationality policy (an old theme from the 1930's) and *Russian help* (a postwar innovation). The Russian people have furnished material, cadres, the experience, and knowledge of its scholars, engineers, artists, leading workers, and war specialists. The leading role of Russian culture in the development of Socialist culture is explained by a paraphrase of Stalin's May 24, 1945, toast to the Russian people. Then we read the following passage:

The basis of Soviet culture is Leninist-Stalinist ideology, Leninism. Therefore, any attempts to remove and to alienate the national culture from the all-Soviet culture means an endeavor to tear apart the national form of a culture from its socialist contents, from Leninism. It is known that in their time the most rabid protagonists of Ukrainian nationalism, hiding under the title of members of the Communist Party [i.e., Khvylovy], declared that the "idea of the proletariat" they knew "without Muscovite art." This hostile theory, setting the Ukrainian culture in opposition to the Russian culture, led to an estrangement [*otryvu*] of Ukrainian culture from the all-Soviet culture [*sic*], from its socialist content, from the common tasks in building socialism. It led to an alienation of culture from the Bolshevik Leninist-Stalinist policy.—*ibid.*, p. 5.

The meaning of this paragraph becomes obvious at the point where Khvylovy is taken to task for his slogan "away from Moscow." Communism as such ("the idea of the proletariat") does not exist so far as the regime can help it: it is Communism as interpreted by the central authorities in Moscow, the leading role in which is played by Great Russians. For all practical purposes, all-Soviet culture becomes Russian culture as interpreted by the regime—the socialist content behind the facade of multi-national form. The proof lies in the following: All candidates of admission to Soviet institutions of higher learning must pass an entrance examination in Russian literature. Actually it is not Russian literature in the strict sense of the word but the literary heritage (including some pronouncements by Lenin and Stalin) which the regime wants to impart to every one of its better educated citizens. The list of works with which they must be acquainted comprises some thirty-odd authors, including Shakespeare ("Hamlet") and Goethe ("Faust," Part I). With the exception of these two and the Ukrainian poet Shevchenko, all of them are Russians. Had the regime really been concerned with creating a multi-national Soviet culture it might have included at least a sprinkling from the literary heritage of the other Soviet peoples: the Belorussians, the Georgians, Armenians, Uzbeks and others (USSR Ministry of Higher Education, *Pravila priema i programmy priemnykh ekzamenov dlya postupayushchikh v vysshie uchebnye zavedeniya v 1957 g.* [Admission rules and programs of entrance examinations for candidates for admission to higher educational institutions in 1957, Moscow, 1957], pp. 25ff.).

Note I-5. The Crimea

The Crimea is a peninsula of 25,600 square kilometers, and an estimated population of 1.1 million, 662,000 (or 59.2 per cent) of whom live in cities. The two main cities are the famous naval port Sevastopol (133,000 inhabitants) and the somewhat larger Simferopol, with 159,000 residents, which lies further inland. (Data as of April, 1956, from the *Ukrainian SSR Statistical Handbook* (1957), pp. 11, 7, 12.)

The peninsula is fairly rich in natural resources: near Kerch it possesses very abundant deposits of iron ore, though of inferior quality; lacking sources of energy it is dependent upon coal imports from the Donbas and upon water and winds to generate a certain amount of electricity; its soil is, however, fertile enough to sow grain crops, and the climate is so mild that tropical fruit and wine grapes can be grown. Thanks to its outstanding climate Crimea has developed into the major resort area of the Soviet Union (E. P. Maslov, *Krym* [Crimea, Moscow, 1954], *passim*).

Crimean history has been quite varied and, at times, very turbulent. In the sixth century B.C. Greek merchants settled in sections of the peninsula, from the fourth to the second centuries B.C., Crimea belonged to the Scythian kingdom. In the thirteenth century A.D. the whole of Eastern Europe was overrun by Turkic peoples, a branch of them remained in the peninsula and founded the Crimean Tatar Khanate (in 1428). In 1475 Turkey established a protectorate over the Crimean Tatars, which lasted until her defeat in the Turkish war with Catherine the Great. In the Treaty of Kuchuk Kainarji (1783) the peninsula was ceded to Russia. (See Maslov, *op. cit.*, pp. 41ff.; Edige Kirimal, *Der nationale Kampf der Krimtuerken* (mit besonderer Beruecksichtigung der Jahre 1917–18), Emsdetten (Westfalen); Lechte (1952), pp. 1ff.).

In the beginning of the last century there began a process which was to exert a decisive influence upon the fate of the Crimean Tatar population at the present time. On the one hand, the Russian Tsars directed Russian and Ukrainian settlers to take advantage of the fertile lands in the peninsula. On the other hand, Tatars would leave Crimea en masse to settle in Turkey proper. According to a contemporary estimate, there were about half a million Crimean Tatars in 1783 (Pipes, *The Formation of the Soviet Union,* p. 12). When the first all-Imperial census was taken in 1897, only 196,854 Tatars were counted in the Crimea, or 34.1 per cent of the total population, whereas Russians

and Ukrainians together formed 45.3 per cent of the total (*ibid.,* p. 80n. Figures are disputed by Kirimal, *op. cit.,* pp. 2–3).

In 1917–18, the Crimean Tatars attempted to organize their national life apart from the Russian center, but they proved no match for either the Communist sailors of Sevastopol or the (White) volunteers of General Wrangel. (See Pipes, *op. cit.,* pp. 79–81, 184–90, for details; Kirimal, *op. cit., passim.*) At that time, the total of Crimean Tatars and their descendants in the world amounted to more than two million, but only one-seventh of them lived in the Crimean peninsula. By December, 1926, when the next census was taken, the number of Tatars in the Crimea had further fallen to 179,094 as a result of war casualties and continued emigration. That was only 25.1 per cent of the total population of the peninsula (713,823), Russians, with 301 thousand, and Ukrainians, with 77 thousand inhabitants (42.2 per cent and 10.8 per cent) formed together the absolute majority (figures calculated from the [*All-Union Census of 1926*], Vol. V, p. 5).

During World War II, the Crimea was the site of protracted and fierce struggles. According to Maslov (*op. cit.,* p. 61) the Germans killed 130,-000 inhabitants and deported 80,000 others. According to *Pravda* (June 28, 1946), "Many . . . Crimean Tatars on instructions from German agents joined volunteer detachments organized by the Germans and together with German troops led an armed struggle against units of the Red Army; likewise, on instructions from the Germans, they would form subversive bands for fighting Soviet authority behind the front lines, while the bulk of the population of the Crimean Autonomous SSR would not offer resistance to these traitors to the Fatherland." On reoccupying the peninsula the Soviet government deported all Crimean Tatars in an unknown direction and called upon Russian and Ukrainian settlers to take their place. Kirimal (*op. cit.,* p. 325) points out that wartime disloyalty was only a welcome pretext; plans to deport all the Crimean Tatars into Kazakhstan had already been made in 1941.

In any case, the incorporation of the Crimea into the Ukrainian SSR in February, 1954, has given that Republic an economically valuable piece of land with a heavy political mortgage: Crimea is the only province in which the Ukrainians form a distinct minority. Moreover, it is claimed as

their rightful home by the Crimean Tatars, the majority of whom live outside the peninsula, mostly in Turkey, and who await the day when they will be able to return to their homeland (von Mende, as cited by Kirimal, p. 329, gives an illustration of the pressure for repatriation after World War I).

According to the census of 1959, the population of the Crimea has risen to 1.2 million people (71.4 per cent of them are Russians and 22.3 per cent Ukrainians, only 2.0 per cent *may,* but *need not* be Tatars [see Table II-7, below]). This is what has remained of the country of the proud Crimean Khans: a peninsula colonized by Russians and Ukrainians in the name of Leninist-Stalinist nationality policy.

Note II-1. The Definition of "Nationality" in the Censuses of 1926, 1939 and 1959

As the census of 1926 is the most complete, though not the most up-to-date on the national composition of the USSR, and as the definition of "nationality" in the 1939 census has been changed to "correct" the results of its predecessor, and as the 1959 census apparently adhered to the 1939 concept, considerable importance attaches to an understanding of the precise connotations of the terms used in the 1926 census.

In December, 1926, every resident of the Soviet Union was asked to fill out a questionnaire, in which question No. 4 referred to "nationality" (*narodnost'*) of the respondent. The accompanying instructions to the polltakers define the term as follows:

In this space is to be noted which nationality (*narodnost'*) the respondent considers

himself/herself to be a member of. *In case that the respondent should find it difficult to answer this question, greater weight should be attached to the mother's nationality.* Considering that the census aims at determining the ethnic (ethnographic) composition of the population, one should not substitute for nationality religion, citizenship or the fact that the respondent resides in the territory of some Republic. The answer to the question about nationality need not be the same as the answer to question No. 5 about the native language. (*Vsesoyuznaya perepis' naseleniya 1926 g.,* Vol. XVII [Moscow, 1929], p. 98. Italics in original.)

The term nationality (*narodnost'*) is furthermore defined as follows:

Though the term *narodnost'* has been chosen in connection with the necessity of obtaining data on the ethnic (ethnographic) composition of the population, *the determination of one's nationality has been left up to the respondent himself/ herself* and one should not change the statements of the respondent during the interview. Persons who have lost ties with the nationality of their ancestors may indicate the nationality which they consider themselves to be members of. (Instruction No. 10, *ibid.*, pp. 98, 101. Italics in original.)

From these instructions it appears that the term of the 1926 census has contradictory connotations. "Nationality" is defined in terms of both *ethnic descent* and *subjective allegiance;* apparently, it was left to the census taker and the respondent to settle between themselves which connotation should take precedence over the other. (See the analyses by V. Sadovsky and O. Chubenko in T. Olesievych *et al., op. cit.*, pp. 21ff. and 85ff.)

Nevertheless, despite some confusion in terms, the census of 1926 does not appear to have unduly discriminated against some nationalities at the expense of others, which is quite common if nationality is defined by a single criterion ("native language," for example). In the Soviet census of 1926 the objective characteristic of "native language," as determined by the census taker, was correlated to the subjectively declared characteristic of "nationality."

No comparable instructions are available for the 1939 census. But writing in *Pravda* shortly before the taking of the census, Professor Starovsky said:

The question about nationality every Soviet citizen will answer according to free self-determination. Nationality and native language are registered as told by the respondent. As far as the nationality and native language of children are concerned, the entries in the census questionnaire

will be made according to the statements of the parents. (V. Starovsky, ["The Sixteen Questions of the Census Sheet"], *Pravda*, Jan. 13, 1939, p. 2.)

More explicit is Sautin. He stated in 1940:

It is known that at the census of 1926 the census sheet did not include a question on nationality (*natsional'nost'*), ethnic membership being understood in the sense of ethnic (*plemennogo*) origin. In the instruction pamphlet issued by TsSU (Central Statistical Administration) before the 1926 census, it was specially emphasized, e.g., that the Russians resident in the Kuban Region [in North Caucasus— Y.B.], insofar as their ancestors had come from the Ukraine, should be counted not as Russians which they declared themselves to be, but as Ukrainians (according to the criterion of ethnic origin). (I. Sautin, "Naselenie strany sotsializma" [Population of the Country of Socialism], *Bol'shevik*, Vol. 1940, No. 10 [May], p. 17.)

Not having access to the instructions themselves we cannot state with assurance whether Sautin's sharp distinction between the concepts of *narodnost'*, of 1926, and *natsional'nost'*, of 1939, is justified or whether it has been overdrawn for political reasons. His categorical statement that residents of the Kuban area who were of Ukrainian descent declared themselves Russians is not wholly convincing. In the late 1920's Ukrainian schools were established in that province of the Russian Republic, only to be transformed into Russian schools in 1933. But a respondent of this writer who visited the Kuban province as late as 1937 encountered villages where Ukrainian was spoken exclusively (Interview #3). My impression from a careful reading of Sautin's ostensible exposition in the politico-theoretical journal *Bol'shevik* is that under the guise of change of concepts considerable pressure was exerted upon the respondents to change their national identification towards assimilation with larger nationalities, especially the Russians. (See also Lorimer, *op. cit.*, pp. 137ff.)

In 1959, in the judgment of a careful Western student of Soviet manpower, the 1939 concept of *natsional'nost'* was used again. (DeWitt, *op. cit.* (1961), p. 355.) This is very briefly and implicitly confirmed by a Soviet author, who says that the new nationality figures are based upon the declaration of the respondent. Significantly, he uses the 1939 term *natsional'nost'*, not the earlier one of *narodnost'*. (P. G. Pod'yachikh, *Naselenie SSSR* (Population of USSR, Moscow, 1961), p. 101.) A little more explicit are G. Maksimov and M. Marakhanov. They write that the program and the essential methodological characteristics of the 1959 census were those of the 1939 census. ("Vsesoyuznaya perepis' naseleniya 1959 g.," *Voprosy ekonomiki*, Vol. 1958, No. 9 (Sept.), p. 54.)

Note III-1. The Other Provinces of Western Ukraine— Transcarpathia, Northern Bukovina, Bessarabia

The Transcarpathian province of the Ukrainian SSR comprises an area of 12,800 square kilometers, with a population of ca. 920,000 (1959 census), only a quarter of whom (28.8 per cent) live in urban areas. It is a picturesque mountainous and wooded region (four-fifths of it are mountains and mountain slopes—see V. A. Anuchin, *Geografiya Sovetskogo Zakarpatiya* [Geography of Soviet Transcarpathia, Moscow, 1956], p. 9), with lumber industry, a little cattle raising, and a little agriculture. The province is important from the military point of view because troops stationed in it can easily control the Danubian plain; it provides them with ready access not only to Rumania and Hungary, but also to Czechoslovakia and Poland. The ethnic composition of its population is as follows: 74.6 per cent Ukrainians, 15.9 per cent Hungarians, 2.0 per cent Rumanians, 3.2 per cent Russians (there were none in 1930, when the Czech census was taken) and 1.3 per cent Jews (12.9 per cent in 1930!). (See Table II-7, for sources [1959 population census].)

Historically the province had been under Hungarian rule since the Middle Ages. After World War I Masaryk with the support of the majority of Carpatho-Ukrainian immigrants in the United States, persuaded the Allies to attach the province to the newly formed Czechoslovak Republic. That was legalized in the Treaty of Trianon. The Czechs had promised to grant its residents autonomy but kept postponing it until they were compelled to do so under German pressure after the Treaty of Munich (September 29, 1938). It must be stated, however, that on the whole the Czechs administered the province quite responsibly. Not knowing what to do with the emerging Ukrainian national movement, which was greatly aided by Ukrainian emigres from Eastern Ukraine and Galicia, the Czechs would now back Ukrainian nationalists and then support their opponents, the Russophiles; but they did not try to suppress everything Ukrainian as had been done by the Hungarians. (There is a good, objective sketch of that period by two

Czech authors, F. Nemec and V. Moudry, *The Soviet Seizure of Subcarpathian Ruthenia* [Toronto: Wm. B. Anderson, 1955], Chapter I; the "intransigence" of Hungarian nationalism is admitted by S. D. Kertesz, *Diplomacy in a Whirlpool: Hungary between Nazi Germany and Soviet Russia* [Notre Dame, Ind.: University of Notre Dame Press, 1953], p. 9.)

The role of Subcarpathian Ukraine in the prelude to World War II has already been mentioned (see Chapter I, above). International circles saw in Germany's attitude toward this little area an indication of her plans towards the Ukraine, and thus towards the USSR.

In 1944, the province was occupied by Soviet troops, and with due "democratic" paraphernalia the population expressed their desire to join the Soviet Union, which was promptly granted without any noticeable resistance on the part of the Czech government, which ceded that area in the Treaty of June 29, 1945. Hungary renounced her claims to the territory later in her peace treaty of 1947 (February 10). This phase has been well documented from the Soviet, the Czech, and the Ukrainian side as well. See besides Nemec-Moudry, I. F. Evseev, *Narodnye komitety Zakarpatskoy Ukrainy—organy gosudarstvennoy vlasti, 1944–1945* (People's Committees in Transcarpathian Ukraine—Organs of State Authority, 1944–1945, Moscow, 1954). I have read the preliminary draft of that book in Akademiya nauk UkrRSR, Sektor derzhavy i prava (Academy of Sciences of the Ukrainian SSR, Sector of "State" and Law), *Naukovi zapysky* (Scientific Notes), Vol. 1952, No. 1, pp. 206–67— it is legalism at its driest. See also Vasyl Markus, *L'Incorporation de l'Ukraine*

Subcarpatique à l'Ukraine soviétique, 1944–1945 (Louvain, Belgium: Centre Ukrainien d'Etudes en Belgique, 1956). A very brief but good treatment in English will be found in John A. Armstrong, *Soviet Bureaucratic Elite* (1959), pp. 108–10.

Soviet postwar policy in that area closely paralleled that in Galicia, with the difference that the Soviet government had more with which to impress the population in Transcarpathia than in Galicia. As a magnificent gesture, a university was established in Uzhhorod in December, 1944. A Ukrainian theater was formed there, too, and during the phase of Ukrainization schools were teaching in Ukrainian throughout that province. Industrialization, by no means as extensive as in Galicia, but noticeable, brought an influx of new people, mostly Russians, who are said to have taken away the best jobs (Interview #65). A comparison of the census data in Table II-7, above, reveals that some 30,000 Russians (3.2 per cent of 920,000) have settled in the province within ca. 15 years (1944–59). People who knew the province before the war say that it is one of the poorest of the Ukrainian SSR and the seat of abject poverty in comparison with the surrounding satellites: former bitter enemies of the Hungarian regime have come to the conclusion that now they are even worse off (Interviews #30 and #65). There have been rumors of strong troop concentration in that province, especially during the Hungarian Revolution of 1956. From the Soviet viewpoint, the changes in Transcarpathia have been authoritatively described in an article by a Secretary of the Province Party Organization, I. Vash, "Great Transformations," *Komunist*

Ukrayiny (Ukr. ed.), Vol. 1955, No. 6 (June), pp. 13–21.

The province of NORTH BUKO-VINA, officially known as CHER-NIVTSI province, after its capital Chernivtsi, is a small piece of land (8,000 square kilometers) to the east of the Transcarpathian province, with but 774,000 inhabitants as of 1959. There is some light industry (mostly food processing) in the town of Chernivtsi itself (146,000 residents); besides that there is only agriculture (almost three-quarters of the population, or 72.5 per cent live in villages). The ethnic composition is as follows (1959 census data): 66.9 per cent Ukrainians, 10.3 per cent Rumanians, 9.3 per cent Moldavians who are closely akin to Rumanians, 6.6 per cent Russians and 5.4 per cent Jews.

While being under Austrian rule, the province played a considerable role in the Ukrainian cultural development in the last decades of the nineteenth and the first decade of the twentieth century, producing the well-known Ukrainian writers Yu. Fed'-kovych and Olga Kobylans'ka and the philologists Stepan and Roman Smal-Stocki (father and son). After World War I Bukovina came under the rather inefficient and oppressive Rumanian rule. Ukrainian life was persecuted by the occupying power that wanted to Rumanianize the territory. On these and related aspects there is a magnificent, encyclopedic 965-page symposium by Ukrainian exiles: D. Kvitkovsky, et al., *Bukovyna, yiyi mynule i suchasne* (Bukovina—Her Past and Present, Paris, Philadelphia, Detroit, 1956).

During the Soviet-German maneuvering for the mastery of the Balkans (1940), Rumania was ordered to surrender to the USSR the formerly Austrian Northern Bukovina along with BESSARABIA, which from 1812–1917 had belonged to the Russian Empire (see Degras [ed.], *op. cit.*, Vol. III, pp. 458ff. for relevant documents). In 1944, the areas were occupied by Soviet troops again. The literature on Soviet pastwar policy is exceedingly slim, see, however, Jurij Fedynskyj, "Sovietization of an Occupied Area through the Medium of the Courts (Northern Bukovina)," *The American Slavic and East European Review*, Vol. XII (1953), pp. 44–56. It should be mentioned that by annexing Bessarabia (from 1944–1954 officially designated as IZMAIL province, then incorporated into Odessa province), the Soviet Union has established herself on the mouth of the Danube, thus strengthening her power in Balkan and Central European affairs.

Note IV-1. Sources on the Ukrainian Underground

The documentation of the account of armed resistance to the Soviet regime presents special difficulties because the regime is hardly interested in publicizing it abroad. Without any doubt, the best informed are Soviet and satellite security organs, certain incommunicative agencies of Western governments, and Ukrainian circles abroad which maintain contact with the underground, in that order.

Though relatively little is known about it, the subject lends itself particularly well to heated controversy. In the first place, it has been suggested by a Ukrainian exile writer that in the 1920's Soviet counterintelligence used to organize "resistance movements" with the aim of (a) luring important exiles into returning to their country where they would be liquidated in due time, and (b) of penetrating, with the unwitting help of the exile community, into non-Soviet intelligence networks. The accounts of Ukrainian armed resistance in the 1940's and 1950's, the argument runs, may ultimately be traced to the same source. See Zenon Yavorsky's letter of January 24, 1954, in *Nasha Derzhava* (Our State), which is a Ukrainian monarchist paper published in the United States.

The second argument for approaching the subject with circumspection is less elaborate: it usually appears in semipublic partisan polemics. It is alleged that a group of unscrupulous exiles has fabricated a saga of the underground in order to impress both the Ukrainian exile community and its sympathizers in the West with the strength of their particular group.

Working with both Communist and non-Communist material on the OUN-UPA this writer has become convinced that the Ukrainian Insurgent Army was neither a mere decoy for Soviet counterintelligence nor a figment in the imagination of certain Ukrainian exile groups, but did exist as a considerable force in the late 1940's and possibly early 1950's.

The best Communist sources on the movement—the only Communist sources that are on a professional, scholarly level—are those by Polish authors.

The franker and more analytical account is that by Brigadier General Ignacy Blum, "Udział wojska polskiego w walce o utrwalenie władzy ludowej: Walki z bandami UPA (Share of the Polish Army in the Struggle for

the Stabilization of People's Government: Actions against the UPA Bands)," *Wojskowy przegląd historyczny* (Review of Military History [Warsaw]), Vol. IV, No. 1 (January–March, 1959), pp. 3–29. Virtually the same material was incorporated in Blum's book *Z dziejów Wojska Polskiego w latach 1945–1948* (From the Actions of the Polish Army in 1945–1948. Warsaw: Ministry of People's Defense Publishers, 1960). The book does not deal exclusively with the UPA, but the struggle with the UPA occupies a prominent place in the book (Chapter III). In the Appendix to it the reader will find an ample selection of documents, some reproduced in facsimile. The book has obviously been written for a limited group of professional military officers. Its main purpose seems to be to give due credit to Polish troops fighting against Ukrainian and Polish anti-Communist guerrillas—hence it does not try to minimize the difficulties the regime had to face.

A valuable companion piece to Blum's article is that by Colonel of General Staff Jan Gerhard, "Dalsze szczegóły walk z bandami UPA i WIN na południowo wschodnim obszarze Polski (Further Details of the Struggle with the Bands of UPA and WIN in the Southeastern Area of Poland)," same journal, Vol. IV, No. 4 (October–December, 1959), pp. 304–35. Gerhard is a little critical of Blum's frank admission that the UPA enjoyed the support of the population, but he admits himself that UPA was very well organized. See also the announced article on a similar topic by J. Halaba and B. Szweijgert, same journal, Vol. V, No. 3, which I have not been able to consult, however. I have scanned the memoirs of Polish Communist partisan commander Mikołaj Kunicki, *Pamiętnik "Muchy"* ("Mucha's" Diary, Warsaw: Ministry of Defense Publishers, 1959)—found them less useful because more limited in scope than either Blum's or Gerhard's works. Shankowsky's bibliographical article, cited in this note, below, contains further references to Polish sources.

When the book was already in press I had been advised of the existence of two additional pieces of evidence, both by Polish Communist authors. The first is a paper by Ignacy Blum, on the topic of the struggle with the anti-Communist underground, which he delivered on October 5, 1958, at a session of the Division of Social Sciences of the Polish Academy of Sciences, Warsaw. The session was dedicated to the liberation war of the Polish people, 1939–1945. See "Udział Wojska Polskiego w obronie narodowych i społecznych interesów ludu polskiego oraz w umacnianiu władzy ludowej w latach 1945–1948 (The Share of the Polish Army in the Defense of the Democratic and Social Interests of the Polish People as well as in the Consolidation of the People's Government in the Years 1945–48)," in Polska Akademia Nauk, Wydział Nauk Społecznych, *Sesja naukowa poświęcona wojnie wyzwoleńczej narodu polskiego 1939–45: Materiały* (Warsaw: Ministry of People's Defense Publishers, 1959), pp. 241–65. In his earlier paper Blum gives a few interesting details that have not been incorporated in his article and book.

The second piece promises to be the best analytical treatment by far. It is by Major of the General Staff Wiesław Szota—see his "Zarys rozwoju Organizacji Ukraińskich Nacjonalis-

tów i Ukraińskiej Powstańczej Armii (Outline of the Development of the Organization of Ukrainian Nationalists and the Ukrainian Insurgent Army)," *Wojskowy przegląd historyczny,* Vol. VIII, No. 1 (January–March, 1963), pp. 163–218. This article was obtained too late for incorporation in this book.

Apart from the secondary, yet extremely valuable Polish sources, which may be supplemented by accounts of Western correspondents stationed in Poland (for example, a notice in *The Times* [London], June 20, 1947, and The *New York Times,* esp. in 1947), the writer has been forced to rely on

a) Soviet documents (amnesty proclamations, administrative instructions) that have been obtained by the Ukrainian underground and transmitted for publication in the West;

b) public speeches by Soviet dignitaries, comments that have appeared in the Soviet press—these sources usually denounce the underground in rather general terms;

c) a growing body of secondary Soviet sources, publicistic, and fictional, specifically devoted to combating the underground and hence hardly objective;

d) alleged underground publications (resolutions, instructions, propaganda leaflets);

e) printed testimony of, and personal interviews with, participants and first-hand witnesses; and, finally,

f) reports by correspondents of the most authoritative Western newspapers.

The most important single Soviet document is *Nakaz N. 312, 30 hrudnya 1949 r., m. Kyyiv, ministra Derzhav-*

*noyi Bezpeky URSR pro neprytyah-
nennya do kryminal'noyi vidpovidal'-
nosty uchasnykiv reshtok rozhromlenykh ukrayins'kykh natsionalistychnykh band u zakhidnikh oblastyakh
Ukrayins'koyi RSR, shcho dobrovil'no
z"yavylysya do orhaniv radyans'koyi
vlady z povynnoyu* (Order No. 312,
December 30, 1949, Kiev, of the Minister of State Security of the Ukrainian
SSR [M. Koval'chuk] Concerning a
Pardon to Be Granted to Those Guilty
of Crimes against the State as Remnants of Ukrainian Nationalist Bands
in the Western Provinces of the
Ukrainian SSR Who Voluntarily Surrender to the Proper Soviet Authorities). A photostat of it is kept in the
Archives of the Ukrainian Supreme
Council of Liberation (UHVR), Prologue Research Associates, New York
City.

From among Czechoslovak sources, I
have consulted "The End of a Criminal Career of a Bandera Chief," from
Prace (Labor, Prague), of September
7, 1947—typewritten translation courtesy of Professor Shankowsky.

There are two basic ways of establishing the authenticity of the sources
in question. By an elaborate expert
analysis one can determine the origin
of the document. But for an ordinary
student, an examination of the paper,
the ink, and the type is out of the
question. As indicated in the text, I
have been shown allegedly original
documents or copies made from them,
and whenever I have gained the impression that the documents or copies
were authentic have said so and have
said why.

The main objection against assuming the authenticity of the available
underground material, to wit, that
contact with the Ukrainian under-

ground did not exist, is disproved by
the following facts:

a) In 1947–49, fairly large groups of
Ukrainian guerrillas, totaling a few
hundred and coming from West
Ukrainian territories, crossed the
Czechoslovak - German - Austrian
frontier and surrendered to American authorities. See the *New York
Times,* September 12, 1947, p. 5;
September 15, 1947, p. 7.
Though it may be true, as claimed
by some of their political opponents, that a few among the groups
were impersonators (D.P.'s who
had gone over the Czechoslovak
frontier from Bavaria and come
back as "guerrillas") (Interview
#38), personal interviews with
some of the alleged underground
fighters have convinced the writer
that they had been members of
the UPA in the Ukraine.

b) As far as the period after 1949 is
concerned, claims of certain Ukrainian exiles to have contacts with
their fellow countrymen behind the
Iron Curtain must not be dismissed
lightly in view of the following
facts:

1. In May, 1953, Soviet authorities
announced the sentencing and
execution of four Ukrainians
who had allegedly been parachuted into the Ukraine to spy
for the U.S. (the *New York
Times,* May 27, 1953, p. 1; U.S.
denial, *ibid.,* p. 11).

2. A year later, the Soviet government made public the execution
of a certain Okhrymovych, a
well-known leader of the Ukrainian underground, who had likewise been parachuted into the
Ukraine (The *N.Y. Times,* May

21, 1954, p. 5, referring to *Krasnaya Zvezda,* Moscow, Soviet army newspaper, of May 20, 1954).

It is most probable that these men were equipped with wireless sets. Nor should we exclude the possibility of having secret couriers who might have smuggled a limited amount of both Soviet documents and Ukrainian underground publications.

Finally,

c) The Soviets have indirectly admitted the existence of Ukrainian underground publications in an article published in 1951. Ryaboklyach, in "The Indestructability of Friendship" (*Rad. Ukrayina,* August 12, 1951), complains that Ukrainian nationalists are using all means of struggle, including "ideological diversion."

Another way of establishing the authenticity of the documents in question would be to check them against independent evidence. Thus, for example, a particularly important document, the appeal to surrender of December 30, 1949, has been referred to in a paragraph in a Soviet book published in 1956 at sufficient length to permit identification. That document had been first made public by a group of Ukrainian exiles. See *Ukrainian Quarterly* (New York), Vol. VI, No. 4 (Autumn, 1950), pp. 296–97; and V. P. Byelayev and M. Rudnytsky, *Pid chuzhymy praporamy* (Under Foreign Flags, Kiev, 1956), p. 203.

Some details that have been given in the general denunciations of the movement in the Soviet press I have taken at their face value as highly se-

lective but substantially true descriptions of actions that have been presented in underground publications. I have done so especially if those details appeared unfavorable to the regime, according to the maxim that a totalitarian power frequently exaggerates its virtues, is more circumspect —and thus objective—in admitting weaknesses. Underground accounts have been interpolated into events documented by Soviet sources, whenever they appeared consistent with the latter.

Soviet secondary sources on the underground, unlike the Polish, are generally disappointing. The most useful of the group is a collection of bitter exposes by V. P. Byelayev and M. Rudnytsky, *op. cit.*

The most comprehensive histories of the UPA by Ukrainian exiles are those by Petro Mirchuk, *Ukrayins'ka povstans'ka armiya, 1942–1952* (Ukrainian Insurgent Army [Munich]: n.pub., 1953; 319 pp.), and Lew Shankowsky, "Ukrayins'ka povstans'ka armiya," in Myron Levyts'ky, ed., *Istoriya Ukrayins'koho Viys'ka* (History of the Ukrainian Armed Forces, 2nd rev. ed.; Winnipeg: Ivan Tyktor, 1953), pp. 635–832. Shankowsky's account is the better one: solid, documented, with an extensive bibliography. See *ibid.,* pp. 806, and 808, 810, for a tabulation of guerrilla actions, based on underground reports. Shankowsky has more recently published a comprehensive and careful bibliographical article in English, "Soviet and Satellite Sources on the Ukrainian Insurgent Army," *The Annals of the Ukrainian Academy of Arts and Sciences in the United States,* Vol. IX (1961), pp. 234–61—it is a most useful guide for independent research.

This writer has found most valuable interviews with former UPA members for adding, here and there, touches of pungent reality which is always in short supply in more formal printed sources, even good ones. The drawback of using such material in a serious study is that especially when the source of the interview is not clearly revealed the reader is asked to give his trust "at a com- pounded rate," so to speak, i.e., to trust the author who in turn has to trust his source of material.

To sum up, I have had to rely on my judgment as to veracity of the sources that are presently available. Whether this judgment has been a sound one will appear later, after the archives of Soviet security organs will, if ever, have been made public.

Note V-1. Definitions of "Native Language" in Soviet Censuses

The official instruction for census takers in the Ukrainian SSR in 1926 read:

As the native language of the respondent should be regarded that over which he/ she has a better command. If somebody does not usually speak the language over which he/she has a better command, one should regard as his/her native language that over which he/she has a better command. (See USSR Central Statistical Administration—Census Division, *Vsesoyuznaya perepis' naseleniya 1926 g.* (All-Union Population Census of 1926, Moscow, 1929), Vol. XIII, p. 451.)

We see that depending on the individual poll taker, the 1926 answers might fail to account for cases of recent and imperfect assimilation. For an incisive discussion of the problem with respect to the census of 1926 see Arsen Khomenko, *Natsional'ny sklad lyudnosty USRR* (National Composition of the Population of the UkrSSR, Kharkov, 1931), p. 14. His main point is that even the objective and valuable census of 1926 failed to distinguish between a true native language (*Muttersprache*, language spoken in the home into which respondent had been born) and conversational language (*Umgangssprache*).

Information on the "native language" question of the subsequent censuses is much less satisfactory. In 1937, the respondents were instructed to give as their native language "the one [they] used most naturally and freely"; they were to do the same in 1939. See Rose M. Somerville, "Counting Noses in the Soviet Union," *The American Quarterly on the Soviet Union,* No. 3 (November, 1940), p. 63, also referring to Professor V. Starovsky, "The Sixteen Questions of the Census Sheet," *Pravda,* January 13, 1939. Only in general terms have we learnt that the "essential methodological characteristics" of the 1959 census have been deliberately maintained the same as in 1939 (G. Maksimov & M. Marakhanov, "The All-Union Population Census of 1959," *Voprosy ekonomiki,* Vol. 1958, No. 9 (September), p. 54). This would imply, it seems, that as in 1939, the so-called native language should be interpreted as the language of conversation.

Note V-2. New Data from the 1959 Population Census on Ukrainian as a Means of Primary Communication in the Cities and in the Countryside and in the Different Provinces of the Ukrainian SSR

The newly released 1959 census data gives figures on the extent of Ukrainian being spoken by self-declared Ukrainians in the different provinces of the Ukrainian SSR, further broken down according to urban and rural residence and according to sex. Unlike after the 1926 census, no correlations have been made between all those factors and age. Nor have any figures been released on individual cities except those for Kiev—of great interest—and Sevastopol (Crimea), which is not particularly important. Age has been correlated with linguistic habits only for the entire Ukrainian group in the Soviet Union, of whom about 5.1 million (or 13.7 per cent) live outside the Ukrainian Republic, under conditions adverse to the preservation of their native language. (See Tsentral'noe statisticheskoe upravlenie pri Sovete Ministrov SSSR [Central Statistical Administration of the USSR Council of Ministers], *Itogi vsesoyznoy perepisi naseleniya 1959 goda: SSSR [Svodny tom]* [Results of the All-Union Population Census of 1959—Summary Volume, Moscow, 1962], Table 53, p. 184, and Table 54, p. 206.) For what they may be worth, here are the figures from the 1959 census comparable to those of the 1926 census.

The *All-Union* figures for 1959 show that in all residence categories more women among the self-declared Ukrainians gave Ukrainian as their native language than did men: 78.5 per cent of the women compared with 75.6 per cent of the men living in cities, and 95.2 per cent compared with 93.7 per cent in the countryside. This "edge" of women is retained in virtually all age groups. Are women, once they declare themselves Ukrainians, more strongly committed to the use of Ukrainian than men?

Furthermore, we observe that among the rural groups of self-declared Ukrainians there is little variation as to the use of Ukrainian between the different age groups. The sharpest difference in that category is among rural males between the age of 40 and 44: It is below the USSR rural male average by 3.1 percentage points (90.6 compared with 93.7 per cent). More variation is found among the urban Ukrainian males: It is 6.9 percentage points at the same age level (68.7 per cent compared with the All-Union average of 75.6). In the urban male group those of 55 years and older exceed the all-Union urban male average somewhat (that is, relatively more of them speak Ukrainian); those between 35 and 54 years fall below. Significantly, young male adults from 20 to 34 years are somewhat more prone to use the Ukrainian language (75.7–77.3 per cent); so are, to a somewhat lesser degree, the *male* children of theirs and of the middle-aged group (that is, the children between 0–19 years). The percentage points for those children fluctuate between 76.3 and 76.9. Curiously enough, the Ukrainian language is less favored for the Ukrainian urban *girls* (75.9–76.0 per cent compared with the All-Union female average of 78.5 per cent). The data has been derived from the same source, Table 54 (b), p. 212.

For those age variations, especially among the urban males, there might be two tentative explanations. The particularly restricted use of Ukrainian among those between 40 and 44 years might perhaps be traced back to the fact that the group received their secondary and higher education during the 1930's when so-called bourgeois nationalists were liquidated in large numbers in the Great Purge. The urban males might also be more mobile and thus more apt to leave the Ukraine than rural males, and females in both residence categories. From the Ukrainian viewpoint the fact that relatively more male children in the cities seem to speak Ukrainian is encouraging (apparently, the data is based on declarations by their parents). But why little Ukrainian city girls give up the Ukrainian language is both puzzling and somewhat disturbing, if one considers that one day they will rear children of their own.

In the *Ukraine,* among the *rural* population, the percentage of self-declared Ukrainians who in 1959 gave Ukrainian as their native language is in the high 90's, the national average being 98.6 per cent. The following exceptions may be noted: (1) only 64.8 per cent of the self-declared Ukrainians in the Crimea did so, (2) 94.2 per cent in the Sumy oblast, (3) 95.0 per cent in the Chernihiv, and (4) 95.5 per cent in the Donetsk oblast. (All these figures refer, of course, to rural dwellers only). These deviations might be perhaps explained as follows. In the Crimea,

where they constitute but 22.3 per cent of the *total* population, the Ukrainians have been strongly influenced by the strong Russian majority (71.4 per cent—see Table II-7, above), the more so since it was not until 1954 that the Crimea was annexed to the Ukrainian SSR. The Sumy and Chernihiv oblasts in northeastern Ukraine are both close to the Russian border. Most important is the figure for the Donetsk (formerly, Stalino) province. Traditionally the Donbas has been heavily Russified. In 1926, for example, only about 89.8 per cent of the self-declared rural Ukrainians in that area gave Ukrainian as their native language. The fact that in 1959 as many as 95.5 per cent of such Ukrainians in the Donetsk province spoke Ukrainian as their primary means of communication is a testimony to the efficacy of the Ukrainization policy of 1923–33 in that strategic area. Possibly some Ukrainians from other provinces settled in the Donetsk countryside, too, but most of them are likely to have taken residence in the cities.

Among the *urban* population in the Ukraine in 1959 (the national average of self-declared Ukrainians who gave Ukrainian as their native language was 84.7 per cent) we observe first that there is a small difference of one or two percentage points between the sexes, women being generally more prone to use the Ukrainian language. That difference is relatively small and we will henceforth consider only self-declared Ukrainian urban *males.* In the West Ukraine the percentage of such persons who gave Ukrainian as their native language is uniformly very high—from 92.7 in the Chernivtsi oblast (Northern Bukovina) to 98.0 in the Ternopil oblast in Galicia, with the Lviv province in between with 94.0 per cent. All these figures are high above the national average of 84.0 for males. High percentages will also be found in the prodominantly rural provinces of Eastern Ukraine, for example, Poltava with 95.0 per cent and Kirovograd with 93.8 per cent. On the other hand, apart from Crimea (only 40.1 per cent) lower than national averages will be found among the urban population of the ethnically mixed provinces on the Black Sea coast: Odessa—67.8 per cent, Nikolaev—73.9 per cent, and Kherson —83.3 per cent. In the industrial Kharkov province only 79.8 per cent of the urban males among self-declared Ukrainians gave Ukrainian as their native language, in the heavily industrialized Zaporozhe and Dniepropetrovsk oblasts the percentage is 80.3 and 89.2 respectively. The latter figure is somewhat higher than the national average and constitutes an interesting deviation from the pattern. What about the Ukrainian Ruhr, the Donetsk Basin? In the Donetsk oblast the percentage is rather low (73.9), in the Lugansk (formerly, Voroshilovgrad) oblast it is close to the national average (82.7). All the data in the last two paragraphs has been derived from Tsentral'noe statisticheskoe upravlenie pri Sovete Ministrov SSSR, *Itogi vsesoyznoy perepisi naseleniya 1959 goda: Ukrainskaya SSR* (Results etc.: Ukrainian SSR, Moscow, 1963), Table 53, p. 171, and Table 54, pp. 180–91.

What is the meaning of this data? A comparison with the results of the 1926 census shows that now more urban Ukrainians use Ukrainian as their primary means of communication than a generation ago. It is diffi-

cult to say to what extent this is due to the incorporation of the 1,500,102 (as of 1959) urban Ukrainians in the western provinces who are, on the whole, more committed to the Ukrainian language than their fellow-countrymen in the East. (The total of all urban Ukrainians in 1959 was 11,781,- 750 persons—see *ibid*.). On the other hand, the Ukrainization policy of the 1920's and early 1930's must have borne some fruit, too. It is particularly noteworthy that of the self-declared urban Ukrainians in the Donets Basin (Donbas) more now give Ukrainian as their native language (in 1926—54.3 per cent of the men in the Basin as a whole, in 1959—73.9 per cent in the more Russified Donetsk oblast). Is this the result of population exchange between the Donbas and the less Russified provinces of the Ukraine or that of the Ukrainization policy? Nor should another, third possibility be excluded. When we carefully look at the relative number of self-declared Ukrainians in 1926 and 1959 in our Table II-7 we notice a sharp drop in some provinces, notably in Lugansk (from 71.9 to 57.8 per cent) and Donetsk (60.2–55.6 per cent). It is entirely possible that with the shift in the concept of "nationality" between the 1926, and the 1939 and 1959 censuses (see on this Note II-1, in the Appendix) a considerable number of *ethnic* Ukrainians (Ukrainians by descent) who in 1926 were registered as Ukrainians in 1959 were counted as Russians. Thus the relative number of Ukrainians who in 1959 gave Ukrainian as their native language was artificially, that is, statistically increased without a real increase of Ukrainian-speaking people among

Ukrainians by descent. But this phenomenon is extremely difficult to evaluate.

Finally, subject to these and one additional qualification, here is some comparative data on the linguistic habits of the Ukrainian residents of the nation's capital, Kiev. In 1926, 66.4 per cent of the men and 62.4 per cent of the women gave Ukrainian as their native language. See on this Tsentral'noe statisticheskoe upravlenie SSSR, otdel perepisi (USSR Central Stat. Adm., Census Division), *Vsesoyuznaya perepis' naseleniya 1926 g.* (All-Union Population Census of 1926, Moscow, 1929), Vol. XII, p. 27. In 1959, the corresponding figures

were 72.1 per cent for men and 71.8 for women—a clear increase (*Itogi . . . : Ukrainskaya SSR,* p. 183). These figures ought to be interpreted with extra caution because we know that by 1959 Ukrainian city boundaries had been redrawn in such a way as to include within the city limits some suburbs and settlements inhabited predominantly by Ukrainians—see on this V. I. Naulko, "Sovremenny etnicheskiy sostav naseleniya Ukrainskoy SSR (Contemporary Ethnic Composition of the Population of the Ukrainian SSR)," *Sovetskaya etnografiya* (Soviet Ethnography, Moscow), Vol. 1963, No. 5 (September–October), p. 47.

Note VI-1. The 1954 Central Committee Theses on Shevchenko

In close union with Russian revolutionary democrats leading the struggle against Tsarism and serfdom was the great son of the Ukrainian people T. H. Shevchenko. With his works permeated with deep hatred against the oppressors, he has played an enormous role in the development of the national and social self-consciousness of the Ukrainian people. He saw the path to the liberation of the Ukrainian people above all in the revolutionary union of all Slavic peoples with the Russian people. Shevchenko

was an implacable fighter against Ukrainian bourgeois nationalism and liberalism.

From the "Theses on the 300th Anniversary of the Reunification of the Ukraine and Russia (1654–1954)," of the Central Committee of the Communist Party of the Soviet Union, as quoted by L. F. Stetsenko, *Vyvchennya tvorchosti T. H. Shevchenka v shkoli* (The Study of T. H. Shevchenko's Works at School, Kiev, 1955), p. 202. Full text in *Pravda* and *Izvestiya,* January 12, 1954, pp. 2–3, translated in *CDSP,* Vol. V, No. 51, pp. 3ff. This excerpt translated by the author.

Note VI-2. The Party Line During the Celebrations of the 100th Anniversary of Shevchenko's Death, March, 1961

The great son of the Ukrainian people T. H. Shevchenko was a protagonist and bard of the friendship of peoples, of the fraternal uniting of all toilers. His attitude toward the

Russian people was one of great love: his friendship with its progressive representatives was firm; he liked the Russian language, and wrote in it quite a few poems and works of prose,

The revolutionary struggle against Tsarism and serfdom Shevchenko led in close unity with Russian revolutionary democrats. Shevchenko was an implacable fighter against Ukrainian bourgeois nationalism, that wicked enemy of the people.

Excerpt from the editorial in *Radyans'ka Ukrayina*, March 10, 1961, p. 1—the issue dedicated to Shevchenko.

Note VI-3. Shevchenko's Attitude toward Prominent Russians and Ukrainians

Shevchenko's reverence for the Decembrists clearly appears from an entry in his diary on November 3, 1857, in which he calls them "the first noble Russian harbingers (*blagovestiteli*) of freedom, . . . our first apostle-martyrs." Complete text of this diary entry can be found in Shevchenko's *Povna zbirka tvoriv v tr'okh tomakh* (Full Collected Works in 3 Vols., Kiev, 1949), Vol. III, p. 207. (Henceforth cited as *Tvory* [1949].) Excerpt also in *Khrestomatiya z ukrayins'koyi literatury dlya 8 klasu* . . . (Reader in Ukrainian Literature for Grade VIII . . . , Kiev, 1955), p. 269; and stressed by L. F. Stetsenko, *Vyvchennya tvorchosti T. H. Shevchenka v shkoli* (The Study of T. H. Shevchenko's Works at School, Kiev, 1955), p. 138. One of the executed Decembrists, the poet Ryleev, wrote poems on the Ukrainian past ("Bohdan Khmelnytsky," "Nalyvayko"). But his attitude toward the Russian Radicals and Westerners of the 1840's and late 1850's is mixed, depending in part on their views on Ukrainian poetry and the Ukraine in general. See, for example, the following entry in Shevchenko's diary on November 10, 1857: "What a charming fellow that Mr. Zhemchuzhnikov must be. How delighted would I be to meet the man who has so sincerely and so entirely without hypocrisy become fond of my dear native tongue and my splendid, poor fatherland."

Leo Zhemchuzhnikov was a Russian painter who had painted 48 canvasses on Ukrainian subjects; he also gathered Ukrainian folklore (*Tvory* [1949], Vol. III, pp. 210, 465). In Petersburg he became one of Shevchenko's closest friends. Conversely, in the *History of Literature* published by the Academy of Sciences of the Ukrainian SSR, much emphasis is placed on favorable reviews which Shevchenko's first collection of poems is supposed to have received from the highly respected Russian critic Belinsky (*Istoriya ukrayins'koyi literatury* (Kiev, 1954), Vol. I, p. 223). This point is glossed over in Stetsenko's teacher's handbook *The Study of T. H. Shevchenko's Works at School;* nevertheless, Ukrainian pupils are encouraged to discuss the problem: "What was the attitude toward Shevchenko of progressive Russian cultural workers? How did Ukrainian liberals and nationalists receive him?" (See Stetsenko, *op. cit.,* p. 46. For other questions suggested by him see Note VI-4, p. 433.) From reading the so-called "academic" history which has been designed for college students and the interested public, one may get the impression that contemporary Ukrainian critics ignored Shevchenko's maiden work, for none of them is mentioned, while Russian critics, Belinsky in particular, seem to have praised it very warmly.

The first is simply not true, the

second is most contestable. There were favorable reviews from both Ukrainians and Russians. For example, the Ukrainian poet Hrebinka in the almanac *Lastovka* (Swallow; St. Petersburg, 1841). Notable reviews by Russian critics were published in the Petersburg journals *Sovremennik* (The Contemporary), which had once been edited by Pushkin, in Vol. XIX (1840); and in *Otechestvennye zapiski* (Fatherland Notes), Vol. X (1840). They are reprinted in Stetsenko, *op. cit.*, pp. 193–94. A useful survey of the entire subject will be found in Volodymyr Doroshenko's "How Were Shevchenko's Poems Received by the Ukrainians and the Muscovites," *Kyiv* (Kiev, Philadelphia), Vol. VI (March-August, 1955), pp. 58–64, 114–18, and 175–80. In the postwar years, one of the most favorable was attributed by Soviet scholars to Belinsky, that in *Otechestvennye zapiski*. It has been included in the new edition of his full collected works (*Polnoe sobranie sochineniy* [Moscow: USSR Academy of Sciences, 1954]), Vol. IV, pp. 171–72, with a very long note on pp. 625–27. For a recent scholarly defense of the attribution see F. Ya. Priyma, *Shevchenko i russkaya literatura XIX veka* (Shevchenko and Russian Literature of the 19th century, Moscow, 1961), pp. 69ff. Priyma is hard put to defend the attribution inasmuch as he himself is forced to admit that Belinsky was hostile to Ukrainian literature in the 1840's (p. 77). He explains this with a shift in the critic's attitudes. This study is valuable because the pros and cons are discussed with fairly ample quotations, allowing the reader to make up his own mind. But as late as 1939, when the collected works of Belinsky were published, the editors rejected the thesis of his authorship. So does Pavlo Zaytsev, the foremost living authority on Shevchenko in the West in *Zhyttya Tarasa Shevchenka* (Life of Taras Shevchenko, Paris-New York-Munich: Shevchenko Scientific Society, 1955), p. 79. (The book was ready to print in 1939; Soviet troops occupying Lviv seized the galley proofs. The author, Zaytsev, is the general editor of the excellent Warsaw-Lviv edition of the poet's works *Tvory* (1934–39), and a solid scholar. It is a shame that such a good work should suffer from the absence of basic scholarly apparatus such as footnotes and indices.) Dmitry Cizevsky, a highly respected historian of Slavic culture and literature, has called the arguments that have been adduced in support of that thesis "totally unconvincing"; see his stringent review of the "Academic History of Ukrainian Literature," Vol. I, in the *Annals of the Ukrainian Academy of Arts and Sciences in the U.S.*, Vol. IV (Winter-Spring 1955), pp. 1035ff. After reading two other reviews of Shevchenko's poems that were indubitably written by Belinsky in 1841 and 1842, this author finds it very implausible, to say the least, that the favorable review of 1840 could have been written by the same man. See his review of *Lastovka* in *Otech. zapiski*, reprinted in Belinsky, *op. cit.*, Vol. V, pp. 176–79 and nn. 798–800; likewise, his review of Shevchenko's "Haydamaky," from the same journal—see *ibid.*, Vol. VI, pp. 172–74, n. 731. *Lastovka* included a few poems by Shevchenko.

In 1841, Belinsky stated that Ukrainian was not a language, but a provincial dialect. He praised Gogol, a native Ukrainian, for writing in Russian, and in unmistakable terms ridiculed Shevchenko's Ukrainan fellow-writers explicitly and Shevchenko by implication. In his next review (of 1842), Belinsky in effect called the poem "Haydamaky" (one of Shevchenko's best) vulgar and not edifying. The poet reacted to Belinsky's strictures in a mordant way, perhaps already in the prologue to "Haydamaky" in 1841, but certainly in a letter to Hryhoriy Tarnavsky of January 25, 1843 (which has *not* been included in the 1949 Soviet edition of his works), and in the preface to the second planned edition of *Kobzar*, which is also missing from the 1949 edition. (For the former, see Zaytsev (ed.), Shevchenko's *Tvory* (Warsaw-Lviv: Ukrainian Scientific Institute, 1934–1939), Vol. XI, pp. 23–25—henceforth cited as *Tvory* [Zaytsev ed.]; for the 1847 preface see Ukrainian Free Academy of Sciences in Canada (L. Biletsky, ed.), Shevchenko's *Kobzar* (2nd rev. ed.; Winnipeg: Trident, 1952–1954), Vol. II, pp. 322–24—henceforth cited as *Kobzar* [L. Biletsky ed.].)

Significantly enough, in Stetsenko's teacher's handbook the sense of Belinsky's criticism of 1841 is completely distorted and the review of 1842 not mentioned at all (Stetsenko, *op. cit.,* pp. 167, 78). It is stated that in his 1841 review Belinsky criticized those works which idealized the life of the enslaved countryside. But this is not its main point. Instead, so as not to evoke any doubts in the pupils' minds that a Russian progressive critic could have given a bad review of a Ukrainian masterpiece, all of a sudden Dobrolyubov's favorable review of 1860 [sic] is substituted. At the same time, Dobrolyubov's warm reception of the "Haydamaky" is contrasted with the undocumented criticism of the "Ukrainian liberal, landowner and writer P. Kulish." In the "Academic"

History of Literature, which has been written for a more informed readership, Belinsky's critical review of 1841 is not mentioned in the chapter on Shevchenko, and that of 1842 is dismissed as a mistake which had nevertheless exerted a beneficent influence upon the poet. That latter proposition is buttressed by a quotation from a letter by Ivan Franko (*Istoriya ukr. lit.,* Vol. I, pp. 226–27). To sum up: after Belinsky in his reviews of 1841 and 1842 as much as questioned the right of Ukrainian authors to write their works in Ukrainian, there was little love lost between him and the talented and ambitious young poet. Postwar Soviet efforts to reconcile the two in the name of common "revolutionary democratic" goals seem to rest on shaky ground which is not solidified by attributing to Belinsky a piece which he never wrote. It is noteworthy that more recently those efforts have been abondoned; for example, Belinsky's name is nowhere mentioned in Ye. Kyrylyuk's long article "Immortality," in the centenary issue of *Rad. Ukrayina,* March 10, 1961, though the author refers to his Russian fellow-critics Dobrolyubov and Chernyshevsky.

The Soviet case rests on better foundations, as far as Shevchenko's admiration for Herzen is concerned. It is likely, as Stetsenko implies, that the poet became acquainted with Herzen's writings while he was still a student at the Academy (Stetsenko, *op. cit.,* p. 17); in any event, he expressed his respect for him in two entries in his diary on October 11, 1857, and February 6, 1858. (See the full text in *Tvory* [1949], Vol. III, pp. 198–99, 235–36; excerpt from the former, in which he called Herzen "our apostle, our only exile," is reprinted in the

Khrestomatiya . . . for Grade VIII, p. 269; both statements are stressed by Stetsenko, *op. cit.,* p. 138.) At the same time, with all due regard for Herzen's popularity, one need not accept the implicit Soviet thesis that it was under the influence of Russian radicals that the former serf Shevchenko, whose health had been broken in Tsarist exile, adopted in his late poems a sharp tone which might be interpreted as a call toward an armed peasant uprising. The typical Soviet method—collation of similar texts—shows with considerable plausibility that Shevchenko may have read the letter to the serfs that was printed in Herzen's *Kolokol* (Bell) on October 1, 1858, when he wrote his short poem *Ya ne nezduzhayu* . . . ("I am not ill . . .") November 22 of the same year (see Note VI-5, p. 433). This writer has found more convincing Zaytsev's remark that Shevchenko arrived at this radical conclusion by himself, after learning of the difficulties in which the promised emancipation of serfs threatened to bog down (it was finally proclaimed a few weeks after his death in February, 1861); see Zaytsev, *Zhyttya* . . . (1955), pp. 311ff. In short, even if he might have borrowed Herzen's words, the implication that Russian thinkers were his teachers should be accepted with a grain of salt.

But however clear might have been Shevchenko's admiration for Herzen, his relationship with Chernyshevsky who was fifteen years his junior stayed on a different plane. Their acquaintance was made the subject of careful scholarly investigation by the Soviet literary critic Marietta Shaginyan, which was submitted in 1944 as a "Doctor of Science" thesis, for an advanced academic degree in the USSR, higher than a Ph.D. in the United States or Europe. Apparently taking advantage of the relaxed censorship in 1945–46, she posed the question of the influence of Shevchenko on Chernyshevsky (*Taras Shevchenko* [Moscow, 1946], p. 309). She points out that Chernyshevsky, who had been born into the family of a prosperous town priest, did not know peasant life firsthand, though he would write a good deal about it. She says:

Shevchenko knew the real village, he understood the needs of the peasantry exceedingly well. With him stepped into *Chernyshevsky's life the very peasant revolutionary he had dreamed about throughout his career as a publicist.* Without committing an error one can, therefore, conclude that Chernyshevsky himself ardently thought to meet Shevchenko, that he counted on their meeting and that he should have profited much from it (as it turned out indeed!). *This is why one should trace the threads of mutual relations between those two great men of the 1850's not from Shevchenko to the "Sovremennik," but from Chernyshevsky to Shevchenko—Ibid.,* p. 313. First italics in the original, second added—Y.B.

As in July, 1862, Chernyshevsky was arrested by the Tsarist government, any letters by Shevchenko in which his name was mentioned were probably destroyed, if there had existed any such at all (Shevchenko's diary stops in July, 1858). Shaginyan's thesis of Chernyshevsky's initiative in meeting the Ukrainian poet is thus an inference from the slim accounts which mention both of them at Kostomarov's, and from a reconstruction of Shevchenko's call upon the Chernyshevskys. But considering the difference in age and Shevchenko's tremendous popularity upon his return from exile, her inference is far more plausible than any attempts to depict Chernyshevsky and his circle as "elder brothers." It is possible that in the person of Chernyshevsky the poet "first met the perfect type of a revolutionary materialist who knew very clearly where to go: a very clever and shrewd politician." (*Ibid.*, p. 329.) But from the evidence she presents it also appears that Shevchenko called at Chernyshevsky's in September, 1859, because the host was interested in the poet's impressions of the Ukraine from which the latter had just returned, while Shevchenko wanted to hear about Herzen and the life in London, where Chernyshevsky had gone in the summer. Moreover, in contrasting Shevchenko's warm relations with Chernyshevsky with a certain coolness that had crept into his meetings with his old Ukrainian friend Kostomarov, Shaginyan fails to consider the evidence on a later change in Shevchenko's attitude toward virtual Russophobia, which evidence has been presented by Zaytsev (*op. cit.* (1955), pp. 321ff. Shaginyan must have seen Zaytsev's biography in galley proofs).

On the whole, careful reading of Shevchenko's diary and his letters, enough of which have been included in the 1949 Soviet edition, will convince the student that Shevchenko's friends in the last years of his life were not only Russians, as the Soviet exposition would have us believe. One of the warmest, but platonic relationships existed between him and the young Ukrainian woman writer "Marko Vovchok" (Maria Markovych). This relationship is glossed over in Soviet accounts of his life, though it may have been more significant for his work than the encounter with Chernyshevsky. To commemorate their meeting on January 24, 1859, he wrote a beautiful short poem, "To Marko Vovchok" (*Tvory* [1949], Vol. I, p. 546). On the other hand, a certain friction in his relations with Kostomarov (1817–85) and Kulish (1819–97), which is stressed by all Soviet critics, appears to rest on a basis of fact. Shaginyan cites the memoirs of Catherine Tolstaya-Yunge, the daughter of Shevchenko's benefactor Count Fedor Tolstoy, to the effect that Shevchenko and Kostomarov would quarrel in her presence, often for hours, but it is not made clear what the issue between them was, nor does any major eruption seem to have taken place whose date has been recorded (Shaginyan, *op. cit.*, pp. 331ff.). In his biography Zaytsev, however, writes: "They often engaged in polemical disputes but they never quarrelled (*op. cit.* (1955), p. 345)." Shaginyan's hypothesis that in the last years of his life Shevchenko began to suspect Kostomarov's willingness to go over to the conservative camp (he did so after the poet's death), is not implausible. But the facts are that at least in 1857 Shevchenko greatly admired Kostomarov's book on Khmelnytsky (see his Diary, September 22–23, 1857—*Tvory* [1949], Vol. III, pp. 190–91); that throughout his life he met Kostomarov socially, and that Kostomarov was selected as one of the speakers at the poet's funeral.

There is more material on Shevchenko's relations with the writer and translator Panteleymón Kulish, who until recently was the *bête noire* of Soviet literary historians. His work has not been discussed in the "Academic" History of Ukrainian Literature, Vol. I (1954), but he made his reappearance in Vol. I of the four volume anthology of Ukrainian poetry (*Antolohiya ukrayins'koyi poeziyi*, Kiev, 1957). (See especially the introductory essay by Soviet Ukrainian poet Rylsky.) Both Zaytsev (*op. cit.*, pp. 317ff.) and Leonid Biletsky (*Kobzar* [L. Biletsky ed.], Vol. IV, pp. 19ff.) point out that the poet's relations with Kulish were sometimes rather strained, but the reasons for this were not political views, as implied in Soviet accounts—Kulish changed his rather frequently, but *after* the poet's death—but certain personality traits in his younger and very ambitious fellow-poet. Kulish found it very hard to reconcile himself to the fact that as a poet he was no match for Shevchenko. Finally he was ready to admit that at a certain price: Shevchenko would have to accept Kulish's somewhat patronizing criticism of his poems and submit them to his editing. On one occasion Shevchenko became angry and warned his friends not to let Kulish edit Vovchok's stories because he would "make them altogether prosaical." Kulish took this as a great personal insult, referred to the episode more than twenty-five years later.

But despite these occasional clashes, the friendship between Shevchenko and Kulish continued until Shevchenko's death. In Shevchenko's letters (see "To A. Markovych, April 22, 1857" in *Tvory* [1949], Vol. III, p. 368) we find an enthusiastic reference to a collection of poetry edited by Kulish called *Zapiski o Yuzhnoy Rossii* (Notes about South Russia); on December 10, 1857, he warmly praised Kulish's *Hramatka* (Reader): it had been put together "excellently, wisely and nobly (*ibid.*, p. 216)"; in a letter to Kulish of December 5, 1857, he praised the latter's masterpiece, the

historical novel *Chorna Rada* (Black Council); *ibid.*, p. 388. In Petersburg, Shevchenko showed great interest in a new anthology by Kulish—*Khata* (The Cottage). He also gave Kulish his Primary Reader (*Bukvar*) to print, but reclaimed it in the fall of 1860, because Kulish did not like Shevchenko's spelling and probably wanted to remake the work according to his own preconceptions (Zaytsev, *op. cit.* (1955), pp. 317, 372). Nevertheless, Soviet attempts to widen those personal differences between the two Ukrainian poets into a deep gulf separating the "revolutionary democrat" Shevchenko from the "Ukrainian bourgeois nationalist" Kulish are not supported by historical evidence.

In conclusion, we may say that the politically inspired attempts to isolate Shevchenko from other Ukrainian poets and place him in a very close relationship with Russian radicals that are currently hailed as predecessors of Bolshevism, may be recognized as such by any well educated Ukrainian who takes the trouble to look up the original sources, many of which have been published in the Soviet Union. Most objectionable has been the endeavor to make the ex-serf and former political prisoner Shevchenko an eager pupil of Russian revolutionaries. In the case of Chernyshevsky, who was fifteen years his junior, the proposition sounds ludicrous; in the case of Belinsky, who never had been a friend of Ukrainian literature, the proposition amounts to a scandalous falsification. No wonder that by 1961 Soviet critics had to retract from their extreme pro-Russian position: Belinsky's name has been dropped from the circle around and above Shevchenko, and we no longer hear any clear assertions that Chernyshevsky and others, *qua* Russians, were actually Shev- chenko's mentors—a common thesis of postwar Stalinist criticism.

Note VI-4. Recommended Questions for Discussing Shevchenko's Biography in Grade VIII of Soviet Ukrainian Schools

1. Characterize the epoch in which Shevchenko was living.
2. Tell about Shevchenko's childhood and youth.
3. What did Petersburg look like at the time; what significance had it in Shevchenko's life?
4. Who bought Shevchenko free and how?
5. Tell about Shevchenko's study at the Academy of Fine Arts and how he began to write poetry.
6. What significance for Shevchenko had his first journey to the Ukraine?
7. Tell how Shevchenko met peasants during his travels in the Ukraine.
8. What was the significance of progressive Russian literature for Shevchenko?
9. Tell about Shevchenko's activity in the Ukraine in 1845–47.
10. Tell of Shevchenko's life in exile.
11. What was the poet's attitude toward the Kazakh people?
12. How was Shevchenko received by Russian progressive intellectuals? How did Ukrainian liberals and nationalists receive him?
13. Characterize Shevchenko's activity after exile.
14. Tell about Shevchenko's third journey to the Ukraine (in 1859).
15. How were Shevchenko and his works received by the Tsarist government and the big landholders?
16. What did V. I. Lenin say about the prohibition to commemorate [the birthday] of Shevchenko?
17. How do the free peoples of the Soviet Union esteem the memory of the people's poet?

—Stetsenko, *op. cit.*, p. 46.

Note VI-5. A Letter in Herzen's *Kolokol* and Shevchenko's Appeal to "Sharpen the Axe"

In order to let the reader form his own opinion about the Soviet method of presenting Shevchenko, I shall quote extensively from three authoritative sources: Academician Korniychuk's introduction to Shevchenko's full collected works (1949), the History of Literature published by the Academy, Vol. I (1954), and Stetsenko's teachers handbook (*Vyvchennya . . . ,* 1955). All italics are mine. Writes Korniychuk:

In 1858 there was published in Herzen's *Kolokol* a letter to the serfs of Russia:

Do you hear, paupers, vain are the hopes you have placed in me, tells the Tsar. On whom shall we set our hopes now, on the landlords? But they, too, are with the Tsar, and the Tsar is clearly on their side. Rely only on yourselves, on the strength of your hands; sharpen your axes, and let's get on with it.

Having become acquainted with this letter, Shevchenko, too, calls upon the people to sharpen their axes against the Tsar:

. . . Do not wait for anything good,
Do not wait for the expected liberty—
She has fallen asleep; Tsar Nicholas
Has lulled her to sleep. To arouse
The blasted *(khyrennu)* liberty, one must steel
The club with the forces of the *mir*, the community,
And sharpen the axe well—
Then go about awakening her.
                              —Reprinted from *Tvory*
                              [1949], Vol. I, p. 15.

The "Academic" History of Literature gives the same two quotations, but dates the *Kolokol* letter, October 1, and prefaces Shevchenko's quotation with the significant remark: "November 22, of the same year, Shevchenko, *having already become acquainted with the preparations for the reform, wrote: . . .*" After citing another letter that had been written by a member of Chernyshevsky's circle in 1860, the History concludes:

This is only one example of the complete unity of thought that prevailed among the great revolutionary democrats in their stand on the then basic question of social order in Russia—the destruction of serfdom—p. 264.

In this particular statement the letter of truth has been observed. But throughout the work we find such stock phrases as those in the preface, for example:

The realistic Ukrainian literature has developed in the struggle against bourgeois nationalism, infatuation with decadence,

and abject bowing to everything foreign [sic]. In this it was supported by the leading workers of Russian literature, in particular by the revolutionary democrats Belinsky, Chernyshevsky, Dobrolyubov, whose socio-political and esthetical views have furthered the development of Ukrainian literature along the path of realism and concern for the people *(narodnosti)*. Revolutionary democratic ideals have been expressed with the greatest force in the works of Shevchenko (p. 12).

Quaere, would the former serf Shevchenko have become the poet of the oppressed without the help of Russian middle-class critic Belinsky?

Most interesting are the corresponding paragraphs from the teachers handbook. Stetsenko suggests the following interpretation of the cited poem of 1858:

In the poem "I am not ill . . ." *Tvory* [1949], Vol. I, p. 544. Shevchenko advanced the idea of a peasants' *revolution* as the only means for destroying the existing autocratic-serf-owning order and unmasks the *reform* for the emancipation of serfs that was then being prepared by landowners and the government. The poem has an *agitational-propagandistic character* and contains direct appeals to revolutionary struggle.

Note Stetsenko's effort to present Shevchenko as (1) a revolutionary, (2) an enemy of "reformism," and (3) as an agitator. In this writer's opinion, the poem is basically lyrical; it was written to record the mood of the poet at a certain moment; and unlike other poems of his, especially "The Message to My Fellow-Countrymen (1845)," makes no effort to capture a wide audience. Stetsenko continues:

After the poem "I am not ill . . ." has been read in class, *the teacher directs his pupils' attention to the image of the axe and stresses that the Ukrainian national poet had the same idea as the Russian revolutionary democrats,* who, too, called upon the people to take up their axes.— p. 123.

There follow concrete examples from Herzen's pamphlet *Khreshchennaya sobstvennost',* which Shevchenko read in 1857, and from the two letters in *Kolokol* that have already been mentioned. The quintessence of the suggested interpretation is:

That was a great meeting of minds, a union of ideas of the best sons of the two fraternal peoples—the Russian and the Ukrainian.—p. 124.

Nobody could quarrel with this particular statement, had it only been put in its proper perspective. The interpretation of that particular poem is touched upon in Professor Shevelov's scholarly analysis "The Year 1860 in Ševčenko's [Shevchenko's] Work," eds., Mijakovs'kyj & Shevelov, *op. cit.,* pp. 90–91. Shevelov's main point is that by the following year, 1860, the poet's

attitude significantly changed away from revolutionary violence to peaceful social and political reform, advancing as his hero "a peace loving man . . . with a good heart." (*Ibid.,* pp. 91ff.) That change of the poet's attitude has, of course, been ignored by Communist interpreters who would like to maintain the image of Shevchenko as a "revolutionary democrat."

The propaganda line is given without any qualification in the reader (*Khrestomatiya*) in Ukrainian literature for Grade VII (1955 ed.):

In the development of Ukrainian pre-October [i.e., pre-1917—Y.B.] literature a great role was played by T. H. Shevchenko. . . . While his predecessors criticized only separate negative aspects of the serf-owning order, Shevchenko, *following Russian revolutionary democrats,* posed the question of its destruction.

—Reprinted from *Khrestomatiya z ukrayins'koyi literatury dlya 7 klasu seredn'oyi shkoly* (1955), pp. 29–30.

Note VI-6. Evaluation of Shevchenko's Poems by Tsarist Police, 1847

In view of different Soviet interpretations, it might be refreshing to quote the opinion of the Deputy Chief of the Russian Tsarist gendarmerie Lieutenant-Gen. Dubelt, given by him at Shevchenko's trial in 1847:

[The poet] consistently proceeds in the direction he had mapped out: he inces-

santly complains about the suffering of the Ukraine in her present condition; he wants to arouse hatred against the rule of the Russians; and, by reminding [the present generation] of past liberty, exploits and glory of the Cossacks, he blames [them] for their indifference.

—As cited by Zaytsev in *Tvory* (Zaytsev, ed.), Vol. II, p. 249.

Note VIII-1. Chairmen of the Ukrainian Economic Regions as of July 1, 1957

1. VINNITSA: Yapaskurt, Vasiliy Vasil'evich
2. VOROSHILOVGRAD (LUGANS'K, DONBAS): Kuz'mych, Anton Savich
3. DNIEPROPETROVSK: Tikhonov, Nikita Alekseevich
4. ZAPOROZHE: Ivanovskiy, Georgiy Ivanovich
5. KIEV: Lysnyak, Pavel Yakovlevich

6. LVIV: Valuev, Vladimir Nikolae-
   vich
7. ODESSA: Rudnytsky, Peter Vasil'-
   evich
8. STALINO (DONETS'K, DON-
   BAS): Dyadyk, Ivan Ivanovich
9. STANYSLAVIV   (GALICIA):*

Yeremenko, Anatoliy Petrovich
10. KHARKOV: Skachkov,   Semen
    Andreevich
11. KHERSON: Prybyl'skiy, Ivan Se-
    menovich

Source: Pravda Ukrainy, June 1, 1957.

Note VIII-2. Chairmen of the Ukrainian Economic Regions as of December 26, 1962

1. DONETS'K (Donets'k [formerly
   Stalino], and Lugans'k [formerly
   Voroshilovgrad] Oblasts)—Khudo-
   sovtsev, Mykola Mykhailovych
2. KIEV (Kiev, Zhytomyr, Cherkassy
   and Chernihiv Oblasts)—Lisnyak,
   Pavlo Yakovlevych
3. LVIV (Lviv, Volhynia, Transcarpathia, Ivano-Frankivs'ka and
   Rovno Oblasts)—Yeremenko, Anatoliy Petrovych
4. PODDILLYA (Vinnitsa, Khmelnyts'ky, Ternopil' and Chernivtsi
   Oblasts)—Stepanenko, Ihor Dmy-
   trovych
5. DNIPRO (Dniepropetrovsk, Zaporozhe and Kirovohrad Oblasts)
   —Lukych, Leonid Yukhymovych

6. KHARKOV (Kharkov, Poltava,
   and Sumy Oblasts)—Soyich, Oleh
   Vladyslalovovych
7. BLACK SEA (Odessa, Crimea, Nikolaev and Kherson Oblasts)—Pry-
   bylsky, Ivan Stepanovych

Sources: Radyans'ka Ukrayina, December 27, 1962, p. 1, and January 11, 1963, p. 1. Translated
   in *Digest of the Soviet
   Ukrainian Press,* Vol. VII,
   No. 2 (February, 1963), pp.
   11–12. The spelling of the
   geographical names has been
   slightly changed, in order to
   make it consistent throughout the book.

Note IX-1. The Ukraine in International Affairs Before 1923

The international representation of
the Ukraine after World War II is not
without precedents. We leave aside
the relations of the semi-independent
Cossack state that existed in the
Ukraine from the sixteenth to the
eighteenth century, for they have been
touched upon in our discussion of the
Treaty of Pereyaslav in Chapter VII,
above. (Recently, they have been sum-

* In 1962 renamed the Ivano-Frankivs'ka oblast.

marized in a brief but scholarly pamphlet by V. I. Lisovskiy, *Ukrainskaya
SSR i mezhdunarodnoe pravo* (Ukrainian SSR and International Law, Moscow: Legal Faculty of the Moscow Institute of Finances, 1960), *passim.*)
After 1917 the Ukraine did participate
in international diplomacy, though on
a limited scale. Following the October
Revolution in Petrograd, the Ukrainian Central *Rada* in Kiev proclaimed
virtual independence by its Third Uni-

versal of November 20, 1917—see Romain Yakemtchouk, *L'Ukraine en Droit International* (Louvain: Centre Ukrainien d'Etudes en Belgique, 1954), p. 9. (For background see Reshetar, *The Ukrainian Revolution, 1917–1920, passim.* A more recent extensive analysis of those relations will be found in Vasyl Markus, *L'Ukraine soviétique dans les relations internationales et son statut en droit international, 1918–23* (Paris: Les éditions internationales, 1959).) On December 3, 1917, the Ukrainian democratic republic was recognized—for expediency's sake—by the Bolshevik Council of People's Commissars. In the same month, the French government entered into official relations with the Ukrainian National Republic, without quite recognizing it; Great Britain followed its example in January, 1918. In the treaty of Brest-Litovsk (February 7, 1918), however, which was signed by Soviet Russia, March 3, 1918, she was formally recognized by Soviet Russia and the Central Powers (Germany, Austria-Hungary, Bulgaria and Turkey). Recognition by the other successor states to the Russian Empire, to wit, Poland, Latvia, Lithuania, Estonia, and the Caucasian republics, followed later.—See Yakemtchouk, *op. cit.,* pp. 9ff.

When the Red Army finally conquered the Ukraine in the autumn of 1920, Lenin decided to leave the Soviet Ukrainian republic a modicum of formal independence. On December 28, 1920, an "independent and sovereign" Ukraine entered into a "military and economic union" with Soviet Russia—see the preamble and Art. 1 of the treaty between the Ukrainian SSR and the RSFSR, in Akademiya Nauk SSSR, Institut Istorii, *Obrazovanie SSSR: Sbornik dokumentov, 1917–1924* (Moscow-Leningrad, 1949), pp. 248–49; as cited by Yakemtchouk, *op. cit.,* pp. 13–14—and in the following years, until 1923, Soviet Ukraine concluded a number of treaties with several European powers. Some of these conventions were made directly, without the Russian Republic acting as formal intermediary—for example, the bilateral conventions with Estonia (November 25, 1921) and with Latvia (August 3, 1921), and the multilateral convention between Austria, Russia, and the Ukraine, signed in Vienna, December 7, 1921 (Yakemtchouk, *op. cit.,* pp. 14ff., with detailed references to League of Nations sources). In others, both the Ukraine and Russia appeared as a single contracting party—for example, the preliminary Peace Treaty of Riga between Poland, on the one hand, and the union of Russia and the Ukraine on the other hand, signed October 12, 1920. In still others, the Ukrainian government formally empowered the Russian delegation to enter into international agreements on its behalf: Thus the Ukraine was formally represented by Russia at the Conference of Genoa (1922) and Lausanne (1923)—*ibid.,* pp. 15ff. What this amounted to in practise was that several Bolshevik missions abroad included officials who were said to represent the Ukrainian Soviet Republic. When the Ukrainian SSR "joined" the Soviet Union in 1923, she relinquished her right to foreign representation.

Note IX-2. Use of Soviet Rather Than United Nations Sources in Chapter IX

It might be asked why the author has not consulted United Nations documents rather than Soviet sources. Though United Nations documents are more readily available in this country, reliance on Soviet material would seem to be more to the point in a work on Ukrainian nationalism. As Soviet media constitute practically the only source to which an ordinary Ukrainian in the USSR can go in search of foreign news, a careful analysis of United Nations records would not permit any conclusions as to the probable impact of any activity of the Ukraine in the United Nations, unless one finds out in each case how it has been reported to the Soviet public. As I am more concerned with the impact of the Ukrainian representation in the United Nations upon Ukrainian nationalism in the Soviet Union than with the nature of that representation as such, I have chosen that seemingly round-about method.

Note IX-3. Exchange on the Floor of the United Nations General Assembly Between Prime Minister Diefenbaker of Canada and Nikolay Podgorny, First Secretary of the Central Committee of the Communist Party of Ukraine (Excerpts)

DIEFENBAKER:

I turn now to a subject dealt with at great length by the Chairman of the Council of Ministers of the USSR, the subject of colonialism. He asked for and advocated a declaration at this session for "the complete and final elimination of colonial regimes".

I think it would be generally agreed that, whatever the experience of the past, there can no longer be a relationship of master and servant anywhere in the world. He has spoken of colonial bondage, of exploitation and of foreign yokes. Those views, uttered by the master of the major colonial Power in the world today, followed the admission of fourteen new Member nations to the United Nations—all of them former colonies. It seems that he forgot what had occurred on the opening day.

Since the last war seventeen colonial areas and territories, comprising more than 40 million people, have been brought to complete freedom by France. In the same period fourteen colonies and territories, comprising half a billion people, have achieved complete freedom within the Commonwealth. Taken together, some 600 million people in more than thirty countries, most of them now represented in this Assembly, have attained their freedom—this with the approval, the encouragement and the guidance of the United Kingdom, the Commonwealth and France.

There are few here that can speak with the authority of Canada on the subject of colonialism, for Canada was once a colony of both France and the United Kingdom. We were the first country which evolved over a hundred years ago by constitutional processes from colonial status to independence without severing the family connection.

I pause to ask this question: how many human beings have been liberated by the USSR? Do we forget how one of the postwar colonies of the Soviet Union sought to liberate itself four years ago, and with what results?

I say that because these facts of history in the Commonwealth and other countries invite comparison with the domination over people and territories, sometimes gained under the guise of liberation, but always accompanied by the loss of political freedom. How are we to reconcile the tragedy of the Hungarian uprising in 1956 with Chairman Khrushchev's confident assertion of a few days ago in this Assembly? Mr. Khrushchev said:

"It has been and always will be our stand that the peoples of Africa, like those of other continents striving for their liberation from the colonial yoke, should establish orders in their countries of their own will and choice". (A/PV.869, p. 51)

That I accept—and I hope that those words mean a change of attitude for the future on the part of those he represents.

What of Lithuania, Estonia, Latvia? What of the freedom-loving Ukrainians and many other Eastern European peoples which I shall not name for fear of omitting some of them? Mr. Khrushchev went further and said:

"Complete and final elimination of the colonial regime in all its forms and manifestations has been prompted by the entire course of world history in the last decades" . . . (*Ibid.*, p. 61).

There can be no double standard in international affairs.

I ask the Chairman of the Council of Ministers of the USSR to give to those nations under his domination the right of free election—to give them the opportunity to determine the kind of government they want under genuinely free conditions. If those conclusions were what his words meant, for they must apply universally, then indeed will there be new action to carry out the obligations of the United Nations Charter; then indeed will there be new hope for all mankind.

My hope is that those words of his will be universally acceptable and that he will give the lead towards their implementation here and now.

PODGORNY:

. . . The delegation of the Ukrainian Soviet Socialist Republic considers it its duty to state before the General Assembly that responsible representatives of the United States of America continue a policy of interference in the domestic affairs of the Ukrainian nation and of other nations of the socialist camp. Although Ukraine signed the United Nations Charter as an equal of the United States of America, a sovereign and free nation, the official organs of the United States of America, including the Congress, are engaging in a systematic campaign of slander against the Ukrainian state, utilizing the Hitlerite scum which committed crimes against the Ukrainian people. Some members of the United States Congress, apparently not too busy with affairs of state, make touching speeches after the same pattern on the occasion of the so-called "Captive Nations Week" * and "Ukrain-

* US Public Law 86-90, which was passed by Congress July 9, 1959, authorized the President to designate the third week in July 1959 and the following years as Captive Nations Week and to invite the people of the United States "to observe such week with appropriate ceremonies and activities." The history and the text of the law and President Eisenhower's

ian Independence Day," which means "independence" brought on the bayonets of the Kaiser's Germany.

This cheap masquerade rouses the indignation of the 42 million Ukrainian people. It also hurts the deep feelings of love for the mother-Ukraine among the Ukrainian toiling émigrés living in the United States of America and in Canada. It insults Ukrainian national dignity because Soviet Ukraine is to all of us, Ukrainians, the embodiment of free life and true independence.

The rude and slanderous address of the Prime Minister of Canada, Mr. Diefenbaker, at the session of the General Assembly, caused indignation among the Ukrainian people and among the broad masses of Ukrainian émigrés. Our delegation is getting many letters not only from Ukraine, but also from Ukrainian émigrés in the United States of America and Canada with resolute protests against this insulting attack.

Listening to Mr. Diefenbaker one might think that he must have obviously confused the audience of the high international forum of the United Nations with the dozen-odd brawlers who are picketing the delegations attending the Session, or that he confused it with NATO where anything can be said as long as it is anti-Soviet. No matter what, but the Canadian Premier picked the platform of the United Nations for an unworthy attack upon the peoples of a number of countries, members of the United Nations, including the Ukrainian people. He tried to present himself almost

as a "liberator" of the Ukrainian people, and this was not the first time he was doing it; but, excuse the expression: he looked simply ridiculous and foolish. What he resembled most is a person who had been asleep for the last 40 years, and now he is unable, as they say in Ukraine, to find either the gate or the fence. . . .

The economy of Ukraine probably exceeds the economies of several countries like Canada. By the yardstick of a developed industry and agriculture, Ukraine is among the most advanced countries in the world, and in production of steel, pig iron, iron ore mining and a number of other fields of industrial and agricultural production per capita we have overtaken the United States of America [sic]. Once a country of low literacy, it is now a land of high culture, and a leader in science and engineering. The number of students enrolled in institutions of higher education in Ukraine equals the number of students in Great Britain, France, Spain, Sweden and Austria put together, and it is ten times as large as in Canada. . . .

Sources: Address by the Rt. Hon. John G. Diefenbaker, Q.C., M.P., Prime Minister of Canada, to the General Assembly of the United Nations, New York City, September 26, 1960— full text courtesy of Permanent Mission of Canada to the United Nations.

Podgorny's speech in *Radyans'ka Ukrayina*, October 6, 1960, p. 2, as translated in *Digest of Soviet Ukrainian Press*, Vol. IV, No. 11 (November, 1960), pp. 1–2. The abbreviations have been spelled out by the author.

---

first proclamation is conveniently given in Roman Smal-Stocki, *The Captive Nations:* Nationalism of the Non-Russian Nations in the Soviet Union (New York: Bookman Associates, 1960), pp. 98–101.

Note IX-4. A Soviet Teacher Suggests How to Present the International Role of the Ukrainian SSR in Class Discussion, in the Last Grade of the Ten-Year (or, Eleven-Year) School in the Soviet Ukraine

The programs in the history of the USSR and modern history require teachers to demonstrate the contribution of the Ukrainian SSR to the solution of important international questions. Together with the Soviet Union the Ukrainian SSR is ardently defending (*vidstoyuye*) the rights of colonial and dependent countries. The Ukrainian SSR has played a meritorious role in history in being the first to draw the attention of world community to the events in Indonesia at the beginning of 1946. The Ukrainian delegation to the Security Council revealed the contemptible policy of Anglo-Dutch and American colonizers toward the young Republic of Indonesia. The firm (*rishucha*) stand which the Soviet Union, the Ukrainian SSR, and the Belorussian SSR took in the United Nations, the support given by all Socialist countries strengthened the confidence of the Indonesian people that they would achieve victory.

Elucidating the material on the collapse of imperialist aggression in Korea, in the Near and Middle East, I cite facts showing how the Ukrainian SSR actively participated in the United Nations to stop that aggression.

In the fall of 1956 the Government of Soviet Ukraine condemned in a special declaration the aggression of England, France, and Israel against Egypt. The Ukrainian delegation has constantly and consistently defended the rights of the People's Republic of China and her rightful place in the United Nations, and has come out for a recognition of the independence of the Algerian people.

The Soviet Union, the Ukrainian SSR and B [elorussian] SSR, showing a sincere feeling [of sympathy] toward and desire to help underdeveloped countries, participate in the UN Technical Assistance Commission. The USSR annually contributes 4 million rubles to the assistance fund, the Ukrainian SSR and Belorussian SSR annually contribute 500 thousand [sic], respectively 200 thousand rubles. The increase in the international prestige of the Ukrainian SSR is proved by the fact that in 1958 a permanent mission of the Ukrainian SSR to the UN was established.

A strong spirit of humanitarianism permeates the proposition of the Ukrainian SSR delegation which was moved at the last 13th session of the United Nations General Assembly in October 1958: "Be It Resolved to Designate a Year as the Year of Health Protection and Medical Research." That proposition was approved by world public opinion and was adopted unanimously by the General Assembly.

The study of basic questions of the foreign policy of the Soviet Union with a simultaneous elucidation of the activity of the Ukrainian SSR on the world stage, conducted while teaching the history of the USSR and modern history, has a great significance. It helps our studying youth to better find their way in international events.

The pupils will become convinced

that in the fraternal family of Soviet peoples under the leadership of the Communist Party the Soviet Ukraine has become transformed into a mighty agricultural-industrial sovereign socialist state, which firmly and consistently supports the Leninist foreign policy in the international arena.

Source: S. A. Kiperman, "From (Our) Experience of Studying the Foreign Policy of the Ukr-SSR in Lessons in the History of the USSR and Modern History," *Ukrayins'ky istorychny zhurnal,* Vol. 1959, No. 4 (July-August), p. 120.

Note X-1. Questionnaire and Interview Data Used Throughout the Work, with Particular Emphasis on Chapter X

In 1950 and 1951, the staff of the Harvard Project on the Soviet Social System administered general questionnaires to 948 Ukrainian refugees from the USSR, that is, 35 per cent out of a total sample of 2,718. Compare Gilliam, *loc. cit.,* p. i. A special questionnaire was filled out by 511 of them. This is the same sample we have encountered in our discussion of linguistic policy in Chapter V. Finally, 76 Ukrainians were given general interviews which were not, however, focused upon the problem of nationality.

As my concern differs in some respects from that of the Harvard Project, I set out to obtain a number of supplementary interviews between 1956 and 1959. (I have been concerned with evaluating—through direct observation and through inferences from Soviet policies—the strengths and weaknesses of Ukrainian nationalism *after* the war, not so much in the 1920's and 1930's, as have the Harvard studies; hence the attention I have paid to the integration of Western Ukraine, which has been neglected in the Harvard Project.) Altogether I have talked to 110 persons in this country and in Western Europe who have helped me out on various facets of the problem. To obtain a figure

comparable to that of the Harvard interviews, 44 persons should be subtracted from the total as scholars, clergymen, or men of affairs who have *not* been in the Soviet Union for an extended period of time either during or after the war, though some of them visited the country as tourists several years ago. By nationality these persons are either American or Ukrainian, all the "old émigrés" from the Eastern Ukraine (that is, those who left the country in 1919–20) and some wartime refugees from *Western* Ukraine have been included in this number. Of the remaining 66 persons, 32 may be called "postwar refugees," which means that they had extensive contacts with Soviet Ukrainians after 1945, lasting at least a month (several years, on the average), though not necessarily in the Soviet Ukraine itself. The others left the Ukraine during the war. Most of them are from Eastern Ukraine, and virtually all of them have been selected on the basis of special competence: professional skills, unusual life experiences, possession of otherwise inaccessible information.

Of the total "refugee" sample of 66 persons, 14 contributed firsthand information on the Insurgent Army and the Nationalist underground and eleven persons had returned from Soviet labor camps in Siberia and Central Asia where they met both Eastern and Western Ukrainians. The Eastern Ukrainians had been imprisoned for real and alleged collaboration with the Germans during the occupation of the Ukraine, 1941–44; most of the Western Ukrainians had been deported in connection with the struggle against the underground. By nationality, most of the 66 were Ukrainians, 3 of whom were anti-nationalist Russophiles. But I have also interviewed 4 Russians, 2 Americans, 2 Germans, 1 Pole, 1 Belorussian, and 1 Austrian. Finally, in addition to the Harvard samples and my own respondents I have drawn upon the interviews of postwar Soviet refugees made by the U.S. Department of State (see *The Soviet Union as Reported by Former Soviet Citizens,* a series of lithographed reports).

The utilization of interview data in such a study raises several methodological questions. In the first place, for legitimate reasons the sources cannot be precisely identified. It might have been better for scholarship if each particular statement could have been documented in detail, but sometimes scholarship has to defer to security demands. From the reader's viewpoint it is the old problem of trusting the integrity of the author, where he has dressed anonymous material in the conspicuously modern garb of numerical references. The second major problem is to what extent Soviet refugees constitute a representative sample of the entire Soviet population. Do they speak for contemporary Soviet citizens or are they akin to the French émigrés of the 1790's?

As far as the Harvard data are concerned, the various arguments for considering these refugees a peculiarly disaffected and hence rather limited minority of Soviet citizens, have been examined at some length by the authors of the published final report. They have found that only a minority of the respondents (about 40 per cent) claimed to have left the Soviet Union voluntarily; that the sample included an "unusual proportion of successful people"; and that about one third of the repondents "had once *favored* the Soviet regime." See Raymond A. Bauer, Alex Inkeles, and Clyde Kluckhohn's *How the Soviet System Works* (Cambridge: Harvard University Press, 1956), pp. 10ff. In short, if a bias is involved, it is not sufficiently large to disqualify the interview and questionnaire data for representing an unusually hostile minority.

Similar considerations apply to my own sample. In order to prove the acceptability of the data I shall now consider only the statements made by postwar defectors and former camp inmates, the group on whom I have mainly relied for my survey of political attitudes in Chapter X. Even the handful of former members of the underground speak for a wider population than may sometimes be supposed. In the discussion in Chapter IV we have seen that the Insurgent Army did enjoy broad popular support among Western Ukrainian peasants. More representative of the atttiudes of Eastern Ukrainians, however, are the postwar defectors from Red Army units stationed in Eastern Germany. In a way they are a particular sample for everyone of them had to be posted relatively near the Western border or West Berlin. Yet they need not be an unrepresentative sample so far as the Soviet population is concerned, for Soviet Army authorities, to the best of my knowledge, did not apply rigid political criteria in selecting troops for their German garrisons.

But are not the reports of former camp inmates grossly biased toward political disaffection? Even this view is not altogether tenable. The thousands of deported Western Ukrainian peasants whom the regime suspected of collaboration with the underground might perhaps be placed in this category. But not all Eastern Ukrainian "collaborators" were enemies of the regime in any sense but that ascribed by the ever suspicious MVD; see on this the valuable memoirs of H. Sova, *Do istoriyi bol'shevyts'koyi diysnosty— 25 rokiv zhyttya ukrayins'koho hromadyanyna v SSSR* ([A Contribution] to the History of Bolshevik Reality—25 Years of Ukrainian Citizen's Life in the USSR, Munich: Institute for the Study of the History and Culture of the USSR, 1955), pp. 73ff. (Mimeographed.) The interviews disclose that some of the Eastern Ukrainian inmates were common people who had unwittingly committed political indiscretions or minor felonies—in any but a police state they would have been left at large. For example, one person was sentenced to ten years of forced labor because he had said that collective farms "were not a good thing." The penalty for gleaning ears remaining on the fields after harvesting was ten years (under Stalin). One person was sentenced to seven years of forced labor because he had stolen state property consisting of—seven whole potatoes (Interview #11). Another person was sentenced to ten years of forced labor because he had said that the American harvesting combine was better than the Russian (Interview #15). To sum up, our postwar sample does not appear unduly biased toward anti-Soviet hostility.

Nevertheless, one problem should be kept in mind in evaluating the attitudes of postwar defectors from the Soviet Army. As a rule, scholars are not allowed to meet them until they have been screened through proper governmental agencies. A great number of them are not made available to scholarly interrogation at all. But those who are, attach themselves to established émigré groups of various political persuasions, because refugees find it exceedingly difficult to obtain non-manual jobs in Germany or Austria, where many of them are staying. If the choice of political affiliation in the free world were entirely voluntary, this would help to clarify the political attitudes of the Army defectors. But this is not quite the case. Certain émigré groups have various connections such that in the Western screening camps the defectors are exposed to only one type of reading, which by a reliable source is said to have been anti-Communist, but also Russian nationalist, that is, hostile to the aspirations of the non-Russian peoples in the USSR. In other words, academic researchers do not meet Soviet defectors "pure and fresh," but only after the latter have been submitted to lengthy interrogations and after they have been exposed—often one-sidedly—to the political views of established émigré groups.

This brings us to the third important objection against using such data. Depending upon one's contact channels it is possible to select respondents of different political presuasions all of whom are bona fide Soviet refugees. Unfortunately, the Harvard reports do not state anywhere with precision how the samples of 948, 511 or 76 Ukrainians were selected nor what the relationship between those three samples is. Note that besides Gilliam *et al.,* *op. cit.,* I have also consulted the methodological introductory chapters (I–III) in Alex Inkeles and Raymond A. Bauer, with Irving Rosow assisting, "Patterns of Life Experience and Attitudes under the Soviet System," unpublished final report of the Project on the Soviet Social System, Russian Research Center, Harvard University, October, 1954. Admittedly, the problem is most difficult because an exhaustive identification of the contacts would have jeopardized the anonymity of the respondents. Nor is there any reliable outside indication that a certain percentage of Soviet Ukrainians favor independence whereas a certain number of them do not, which would then have served as a guide for relying on certain channels of approach. In the absence of such information it is difficult to believe that data on certain political views can yield anything but imprecise results.

For my part, I have tried to personally interview every person who had extensive contacts with postwar Soviet Ukrainians. By working through the channels of the politically neutral Munich Institute, I have attempted to enlist the cooperation of anti-nationalist, Russophile Ukrainians and informed Russians, and I have also made a point of interviewing relatively uncommitted foreigners (two Americans, two Germans, and one Austrian) in order to obtain their observations on postwar Ukrainians. My postwar sample of 32 cases is too small to yield any meaningful quantitative data, but it may do for some qualitative propositions. (Nor would there have been any point in quantitatively analyzing the other 34 refugees, nor the total of 66, because of the smallness of the sample.)

Another danger of using interview data is that by selecting certain questions and suppressing others, a zealous interviewer may embark upon gathering footnotes for his own presuppositions. To forestall this temptation I have tried to follow as closely as possible the impartial Harvard nationality questionnaire. But only in very few cases did I succeed in orally administering all of its 35 questions: two test interviews in the United States revealed that this procedure would have lasted anywhere from two to three hours. The men I saw were frequently too busy to grant me more than an hour's time, in which case I had to ask those questions that I considered to be the most significant ones. As in selecting my sample, I have attempted, however, to be as impartial as possible in asking questions. In my endeavor I have been greatly helped by the previous work of the Harvard Project.

BIBLIOGRAPHY

Bibliographical Note

Originally it had been intended to scan every single issue of the Kiev press and of all relevant Soviet Ukrainian periodicals for the entire period, 1944–62. But the unevenness of library holdings in this country, where I did most of my research, caused me to modify my plans somewhat. The problem is that Soviet Ukrainian periodicals were not released to the United States in significant numbers until a few years after Stalin's death, sometime in 1955. As a result, there is a great scarcity of Republican periodicals for the earlier period (1944–55); after 1955, however, they provide an embarrassment of riches. In the earlier period I have had, therefore, to rely primarily on newspapers; for the later period I used more periodicals.

Before 1955, the relative paucity of sources, which are scattered between the Library of Congress, the New York Public Library, and the various libraries of Harvard University—to name only the three most outstanding collections in this country—did present some difficulties. For the years 1944–54 I have carefully scanned all the holdings of *Radyans'ka*

Ukrayina (Soviet Ukraine), a Kiev daily, in the Library of Congress. It has the most complete holdings in this country, although they too show large gaps in 1944 (first seven months are missing), 1945 (first half of the year missing), 1949 (last quarter missing), and 1953 (only several dozen issues available). To fill out the gap in the important year 1953, I have scanned through the first seven months of *Pravda Ukrainy* (Truth of Ukraine) a Kiev daily in Russian, of which there are very substantial holdings in the library of the Harvard Russian Research Center. For 1955 I have consulted the latter's files of *Pravda Ukrainy* merely to document specific events. There I also scanned the monthly *Komunist Ukrayiny* (Communist of Ukraine) published in Kiev for 1955. It is the Republican counterpart of Moscow's *Kommunist*—the authoritative Party theoretical journal. I read the Moscow press only in order to obtain material which was referred to in other sources, especially the eminently useful *Current Digest of the Soviet Press*. For 1944–55 I also checked the virtually complete Harvard sets of three important Moscow periodicals: *Bol'shevik* or (since 1952) *Kommunist, Voprosy istorii* (Problems of History), and *Voprosy ekonomiki* (Problems of Economics).

For the later period (1956–62), I have quickly scanned either *Radyans'ka Ukrayina* or *Pravda Ukrainy* from 1956–62, occasionally slowing down to carefully read every single issue in order to document, for example, the popular discussion of the 1958 school reform theses. Of great help in following both Soviet Ukrainian newspapers and periodicals has been the *Digest of the Soviet Ukrainian Press,* which has been published since the end of 1957 by Prologue Research Associates, of New York. From among the numerous periodicals I have found most useful *Komunist Ukrayiny,* published both in Ukrainian and Russian at Kiev (contents identical) and the two bi-monthlies *Ekonomika Radyans'koyi Ukrayiny* (Economics of Soviet Ukraine) available in Ukrainian and Russian and *Ukrayins'ky istorychny zhurnal* (Ukrainian Historical Journal). The last, established in 1957, was particularly worthwhile for my purpose; it is edited with college and secondary school teachers of history in mind and places heavy emphasis on recent or contemporary events. I have examined all issues of those periodicals with the greatest care. Occasionally valuable material could also be found in literary periodicals, such as *Vitchyzna* (Fatherland) or *Dnipro* (Dnieper) or in specialized sources such as *Radyans'ka shkola* (Soviet School). In summary, while my coverage of newspapers and periodicals is not exhaustive I believe it to be fully adequate for my purpose. The books that I have consulted with profit are all listed below; whether my monographic documentation is adequate can easily be judged from the text itself.

Finally, a few words on the manner in which the bibliographic items have been presented. While the divisions of the bibliography are based on the types of sources (documents, books, etc.) and not on their contents (Party history, literary interpretation, for example), all Soviet and Polish sources have been singled out in the appropriate divisions. Many of them are not primary sources in the strict sense of the word, but, with very few exceptions (for example, Pasternak's *Dr. Zhivago*), they have been approved by Soviet or Polish government censors, and they often present information which would otherwise not be available to Western researchers. Secondly, with the exception of some three items for which the originals were not available for rechecking, I have transliterated the titles of all Ukrainian and Russian articles. Thirdly, I have noticed that Soviet publishers attach little value to numbering the volumes of their periodicals consecutively starting with the year of appearance. Some Soviet periodicals give this information in an inconspicuous place, others do not, listing only the calendar year. For uniformity's sake, I have followed the Soviet system of citation, giving only the calendar year (e.g., *Bol'shevik*, Vol. 1945). Lastly, names of Soviet publishing houses have not been transliterated, but immediately translated into English.

I. State and Party Documents

A. SOVIET

Ukrainian SSR:

Do uchasnykiv tak zvanykh "UPA" ta "UNRA" (To the Members of so-called "UPA" and "UNRA" [Ukrainian National Revolutionary Army]). Kiev, February 12, 1944.

  Poster-size appeal to surrender, signed by Khrushchev, Hrechukha, and Korotchenko. Original consulted in UHVR archives in New York.

Ministerstvo kul'tury URSR (Ukrainian SSR Ministry of Culture). *Kul'turne budivnytstvo v Ukrayins'kiy RSR;* nayvazhlyvishi rishennya komunistychnoy partiyi i radyans'koho uryadu: Zbirnyk dokumentiv (Cultural Progress in the Ukrainian SSR; the most important decisions of the Communist Party and the Soviet government: A collection of documents). Vol. I (1917–41) and Vol. II (1941–60). Kiev: 1959–61.

Ministerstvo zakordonnykh sprav URSR (Ukrainian SSR Ministry of Foreign Affairs), Palamarchuk, L. Kh. (Minister of Foreign Affairs) (ed.). *Ukrayins'ka RSR v mizhnarodnykh vidnosynakh* (Ukrainian SSR in International Relations). Kiev, 1959.

  A useful collection of documents with introduction by Palamarchuk.

Nakaz N 312, 30 hrudnya 1949 r., m. Kyyiv, Ministra Derzhavnoyi Bezpeky URSR pro neprytyahnennya do kryminal'noyi vidpovidal'nosty uchasnykiv reshtok rozhromlenykh ukrayins'kykh natsionalistychnykh band u zakhidnikh oblastyakh Ukrayins'koyi RSR, shcho dobrovil'no z"yavylysya do orhaniv radyans'koyi vlady z povynnoyu (Order N. 312, December 30, 1949, Kiev, of the Minister of State Security of the Ukrainian SSR [M. Koval'chuk] Concerning a Pardon to be Granted to Those Guilty of Crimes against the State as Remnants of Ukrainian Nationalist Bands in the Western Provinces of the Ukrainian SSR Who Voluntarily Surrender to the Proper Soviet Authorities).

Extremely important document on armed resistance, a photostat of which is kept in the Archives of the Ukrainian Supreme Council of Liberation (UHVR) in New York.

Narode Ukrainy (To the People of Ukraine). Kiev, February 5, 1944.

The "intelligentsia" of Kiev appeals to Ukrainian Nationalist groups to surrender. Leaflets to be dropped from planes, original consulted in UHVR archives in New York. Signed by Hrechukha of the Ukrainian Supreme Soviet *et al.*

Narodny komisariat osvity URSR (Ukrainian SSR People's Commissariat of Education). *Zbirnyk nakaziv i rozporyadzhen' narodnoho komisariatu osvity Ukrayins'koyi RSR* (Collection of Orders and Instructions of the People's Commissariat of Education of the Ukrainian SSR). Kiev, Vol. 1940, Nos. 18 and 27 (June, September).

Vozz"yednannya ukrayins'koho narodu v yedyniy ukrains'kiy radyans'kiy derzhavi, 1939–49 rr.: Zbirnyk dokumentiv i materialiv (Reunification of the Ukrainian People into a Unified Ukrainian Soviet State: Collection of Documents and Materials). Kiev: Ukrainian SSR State Publishers of Political Works, 1949.

Ukrainian SSR, Communist Party (Bolshevik) of Ukraine:

Institut istorii partii TsK KP Ukrainy—Filial instituta marksizma leninizma pri TsK KPSS (Institute of Party History of the Central Committee of the Communist Party of Ukraine—Branch of the Institute of Marxism-Leninism at the Central Committee of the CP of the Soviet Union). *Kommunisticheskaya Partiya Ukrainy v rezolyutsiyakh i resheniyakh s"yezdov i konferentsiy, 1918–56* (The CP of Ukraine in Resolutions and Decisions of Congresses and Conferences, 1918–1956). Kiev: Ukrainian SSR State Publishers of Political Literature, 1958.

———. *Ocherki istorii Kommunisticheskoy Partii Ukrainy* (Outline History of the CPU). Kiev, 1961.

Once highly authoritative, now already criticized as outdated. See Mints's review in *Pravda*.

Profatilov, I. I. (First Secretary, Volhynian Province Committee). *Ocherednye zadachi po selakh* (Next Tasks in the Villages). Undated [issued before March 1945].

Top-secret instruction in Russian, captured by the Ukrainian underground. Typewritten transcript in UHVR archives, New York. Authenticity vouched for by informed source.

*Pytannya partiynoho budivnytstva. Zbirnyk materialiv i dokumentiv na
dopomohu partiynomu pratsivnykovi* (Problems in Party "Construction": A collection of materials and documents to help the Party
worker). Kiev, 1948.

Highly authoritative and useful collection.

*XVI Z"yizd Komunistychnoyi Partiyi (bil'shovykiv) Ukrayiny, 25–28 sich-
nya 1949 r.; Materiyaly z"yizdu* (16th Congress of the Communist
Party (Bolshevik) of Ukraine, January 25–28, 1949: Materials of the
Congress). Kiev: Ukrainian SSR State Publishers of the Political Literature, 1949.

Ukrainian SSR, Verkhovna Rada (Supreme Soviet):

"Zakon o zmitsnenni zv"yazku shkoly z zhyttyam i dal'shoho rozvytku
systemy narodnoyi osvity Ukrayins'koyi RSR (Law on the Strengthening of the Ties of School with Life and Further Development of the
System of Public Education in the Ukrainian SSR)," *Radyans'ka Ukrayina,* April 19, 1959, pp. 2ff.

Very important. See esp. Art. 9.

"Zakon Ukrayins'koyi Radyans'koyi Sotsialistychnoyi Respubliky pro
byudzhetni prava URSR i mistsevykh Rad deputativ trudyashchykh
(Law of the Ukrainian SSR on the Budgetary Rights of the Ukrainian SSR and Local Soviets of Toilers Deputies)," *Radyans'ka Ukrayina,* July 2, 1960, pp. 2–3.

Zasedanie Verkhovnogo Soveta USSR. Tret'ya, yubileynaya sessiya, 24. I.
1948 g. Stenograficheskiy otchet (Session of the Ukrainian SSR Supreme Soviet; 3rd Jubilee Session, January 24, 1948. Stenographic Report). Kiev: Ukrainian Publishers of Political Works, 1948. Russian
version.

Union of Soviet Socialist Republics:

Ministerstvo vysshego obrazovaniya SSSR (USSR Ministry of Higher Education). *Pravila priema i programmy priemnykh ekzamenov dlya postupayushchikh v vysshie uchebnye zavedeniya v 1957 g.* (Admission
Rules and Programs of Entrance Examinations for Candidates for Admission to Higher Educational Institutions in 1957). Moscow: Soviet
Science, 1957.

Very important.

*Vneshnaya politika Sovetskogo Soyuza v period Otechestvennoy Voyny:
Dokumenty i materialy* (Foreign Policy of the USSR during the Father-

land War: Documents and Materials). Vol. II (January 1–December 31, 1944). [Moscow]: State Publishers of Political Works, 1946.

Vneshnaya politika Sovetskogo Soyuza, 1945 g. (Foreign Policy of the USSR in 1945). [Covers period from end of the war only, September 4–December 31, 1945.] Moscow, 1949.

———. *Vneshnaya pol. S.S. 1946 g.* Moscow, 1952.

———. *Vneshnaya pol. S.S. 1947 g.* 2 Parts. Moscow, 1951.

———. *Vneshnaya pol. S.S. 1948 g.* 2 Parts. Moscow, 1951.

———. *Vneshnaya pol. S.S. 1949 g.* Moscow, 1953.

———. *Vneshnaya pol. S.S. 1950 g.* Moscow, 1953.

USSR, Communist Party of the Soviet Union (or All-Union CP [Bolshevik]), Central Committee:

"O zhurnalakh Zvezda i Leningrad (Concerning the Journals *Zvezda* and *Leningrad*)," *Bol'shevik*, Vol. 1946, No. 15 (August), pp. 11–14.

Excerpts from the essential decision of the All-Union Party Central Committee of August 14, 1946. Reprinted in numerous sources.

"Ob ukreplenii svyazi shkoly s zhyzn'yu i dal'neyshem razvitii sistemy narodnogo obrazovaniya v strane (On the Strengthening of the Relationship of the School with Life and on Further Development of the System of Public Education in the Country)," *Pravda*, November 14, 1958; or *Current Digest of the Soviet Press (CDSP)*, Vol. X, No. 46, pp. 7ff.

Important theses of the Central Committee of the Communist Party of the Soviet Union and the USSR Council of Ministers.

"Tezisy o 300-letii vossoedineniya Ukrainy s Rossiey (1654–1954 gg.): Odobreny TsK KPSS (Theses on the 300th Anniversary of the Reunification of the Ukraina with Russia [1654–1954]: Approved by the CC CPSU)," *Pravda* and *Izvestiya*, January 12, 1954, pp. 2–3.

Indispensable. Complete translation in *CDSP*, Vol. V, No. 51, pp. 3ff.

USSR, Verkhovny Sovet (Supreme Soviet):

Vedomosti Verkhovnogo Soveta SSSR (USSR Supreme Soviet News, Moscow; official journal).

"Zakon o byudzhetnykh pravakh SSSR i soyuznykh respublik (Law on the Budget Rights of the USSR and the Union Republics)," *Pravda*, October 31, 1959, p. 2; or *CDSP*, Vol. XI, No. 46, pp. 6–9.

"Zakon ob ukreplenii svyazi shkoly s zhyzn'yu i dal'neyshem razvitii sistemy narodnogo obrazovaniya v SSSR (Law on the Strengthening of the Relationship of School with Life and on Further Development of the System of Public Education in the USSR)," *Pravda*, December 25, 1958; or *CDSP*, Vol. XI, No. 4, pp. 13ff.

"Zakon o dal'neyshem sovershenstvovanii organizatsii upravleniya pro-myshlennost'yu i stroitel'stvom (Law on Further Improving the Organization of the Management of Industry and Construction)," of May 10, 1957. See *Pravda* and *Izvestiya*, May 11, 1957, pp. 1–2. Complete translation in *CDSP*, Vol. IX, No. 20, pp. 14ff.

Zasedaniya Verkhovnogo Soveta SSSR; 5 sozyva, vtoraya sessiya (22–25 dekabrya 1958 g.) Stenograficheskiy otchet (Sessions of the USSR Supreme Soviet; 5th Convocation, 2nd Session [Dec. 22–25, 1958]. Stenographic Report). Moscow: Publishers of the USSR Supreme Soviet, 1959.

Session passed the law on school reform.

B. OTHER

Canada. Address by the Rt. Hon. John G. Diefenbaker, Q.C., M.P., Prime Minister of Canada, to the General Assembly of the United Nations, New York City, September 26, 1960.

Full text courtesy of the Permanent Mission of Canada to the United Nations. A brief reference to the Ukraine provoked a series of official and semi-official protests by spokesmen for the Soviet regime.

Great Britain. *Hansard's Parliamentary Debates* (5th series). Vol. 472. House of Commons. March 1–24, 1950.

United Nations. *Treaty Series*. Vols. 10, 33, 37, 41, 42, 48, 49, 169.

United Nations, Department of Public Information. *Yearbook of the UN, 1946/47*.

———. *Yearbook of the UN, 1947/48*.

———. *Yearbook of the UN, 1950* through *Yearbook of the UN, 1960*.

United Nations Relief and Rehabilitation Organization (George Woodbridge, staff director). *The History of the United Nations Relief and Rehabilitation Organization*. 3 vols. New York: Columbia University Press, 1950.

U.S. *Congressional Record*. Vol. XCIX (83rd Congress, 1st Session—1953).

U.S. House of Representatives, Committee on Foreign Affairs. *Favoring Extension of Diplomatic Relations with the Republics of Ukraine and Belorussia*. Hearing before the Special Subcommittee on H. Con. Res. 58, July 15, 1953.

U.S. Department of State. *Foreign Relations of the United States. Diplomatic Papers. The Conference of Malta and Yalta, 1945*. Washington, D.C., 1955.

——— (Harley Notter, staff director). *Postwar Foreign Policy Preparation, 1939–45*. Washington, D.C., 1949. Department of State Publication No. 3580. General foreign policy.

Valuable.

II. BOOKS AND PAMPHLETS

A. SOVIET AND POLISH

Akademiya nauk URSR (Ukrainian SSR Academy of Science). S. M. Byelousov (responsible ed.). *Pam''yati T. H. Shevchenka: Zbirnyk stattey do 125-littya z dnya narodzhennya, 1814–1939* (In Memory of T. H. Shevchenko: Collected Articles on the 125th Anniversary of His Birth, 1814–1939). Kiev: Ukrainian SSR Academy of Sciences, 1939.

Quality of articles much higher than in 1946–54.

———. Instytut ekonomiky (Institute of Economics). *Narysy ekonomichnoyi heohrafiyi URSR* (Outline of the Economic Geography of the Ukrainian SSR). 2 vols. Kiev: Ukrainian SSR Academy of Sciences, 1949–54.

Largely descriptive.

———. Instytut ekonomiky. A. A. Nestorenko, I. N. Romanenko, and D. F. Virnyk (eds.). *Ocherki razvitiya narodnogo khozaystva Ukrainskoy SSR* (Outline of the Development of the National Economy of the Ukrainian SSR). Moscow: USSR Academy of Sciences, 1954.

Pretty good.

———. Instytut istoriyi i arkheolohiyi Ukrainy (Institute of the History and Archeology of the Ukraine). K. Huslysty, L. Slavin, and F. Yastrebov (eds.). *Narys istoriyi Ukrainy* (Outline History of the Ukraine). [Ufa:] Ukrainian SSR Academy of Sciences, 1942.

———. Instytut istoriyi (Institute of History). A. K. Kasymenko *et al.* (eds.). *Istoriya Ukrayins'koyi RSR* (History of the Ukrainian SSR). Vol. I, 2nd ed. revised. Kiev: Ukrainian SSR Academy of Sciences, 1955.

———, ———. *Istoriya Ukrayins'koyi RSR*. Vol. II. Kiev: Ukrainian SSR Academy of Sciences, 1958.

Shows some of the effects of policy after the 1956 Congress, in that some weaknesses of the Bolshevik organization in the Ukraine in 1917–20 are frankly admitted.

———. Instytut literatury im. T. H. Shevchenka (T. H. Shevchenko Institute of Literature). O. I. Bilets'ky (ed. in chief). *Istoriya ukrains'koyi literatury* (History of Ukrainian Literature). Vol. I. Kiev: Ukrainian SSR Academy of Sciences, 1954.

Compare the reviews by Cizevsky and Eremin.

———, ———. *Istoriya ukrayins'koyi literatury*. Vol. II. Kiev: Ukrainian SSR Academy of Sciences, 1958.

Deals with the Soviet period, shows some signs of the more liberal policy after the 20th Party Congress.

———, ———. *Zbirnyk prats' vos'moyi naukovoyi shevchenkivs'koyi konfe-rentsiyi* (Collected Papers of the Eighth Scholarly Shevchenko Confer-ence [in 1959]). Kiev: Ukrainian SSR Academy of Sciences, 1960.
    See the article by Ye P. Kyrylyuk.

———, ———. *Zbirnyk prats' dev"yatoyi naukovoyi shevchenkivs'koyi kon-ferentsiyi* (Collected Papers of the Ninth . . . Conference [in 1960]). Kiev: Ukrainian SSR Academy of Sciences, 1961.
    See the article by O. Bilets'ky.

———. Instytut movoznavstva im. O. O. Potebni (O. O. Potebnya Institute of Linguistics). I. M. Kyrychenko (ed. in chief). *Ukrayins'ko-rosiys'ky slovnyk* (Ukrainian-Russian Dictionary). Vol. I. Kiev: Ukrainian SSR Academy of Sciences, 1953.
    Preface contains useful data on Soviet linguistic policy.

———. Sektor derzhavy i prava (Division of State and Law). *Narysy z istoriyi derzhavy i prava Ukrayins'koyi RSR* (Sketches from the History of State and Law of the Ukrainian SSR). Kiev: Ukrainian SSR Acad-emy of Sciences, 1957.
    Some interesting materials. See esp. the article by Ul'yanova.

———, ———. *Istoriya derzhavy i prava Ukrayins'koyi RSR, 1917–1960* (History of State and Law of the Ukrainian SSR, 1917–60). Kiev: Ukrainian SSR Academy of Sciences, 1961.
    Less useful than its title would imply.

Anonymous. *K izucheniyu istorii: Sbornik* (Studying History: A Collec-tion). Moscow: Party Publishers of the Central Committee of the All-Union Communist Party (Bolshevik), 1937.
    Contains the important "Decision of the Jury of the Official Com-mission in the Competition for the Textbook on USSR History for the 3rd and 4th Grades of Secondary Schools."

Anuchin, V. A., and Spiridonov, A. I. *Zakarpatskaya oblast'* (The Trans-carpathian Province). Moscow: State Publishers of Geographical Works, 1947.
    Useful.

Anuchin, V. A. *Geografiya Sovetskogo Zakarpat'ya* (Geography of Soviet Transcarpathia). Moscow: State Publishers of Geographical Works, 1956.
    Scholarly.

Babiy, V. M. *Vozz"yednannya Zakhidnoyi Ukrayiny z Ukrayins'koyu RSR* (Re-unification of Western Ukraine with the Ukrainian SSR). Kiev: Ukrainian SSR Academy of Sciences, 1954.
    Weak.

Babiychuk, I. [Ukrainian SSR Minister of Culture] (ed.). *Ukrainskaya sovetskaya kul'tura: Sbornik statey* (Ukrainian Soviet Culture: A Col-lection of Articles). Kiev: State Publishers of Political Literature, 1961.

Some fairly interesting up-to-date articles. See those by Babiychuk and Bilodid, Section III, A, below.

Belinsky, V. G. *Polnoe sobranie sochineniy* (Complete Works). Vols. IV–VI. Moscow: USSR Academy of Sciences, 1954–55.

Blum, Brigadier General Ignacy. *Z dziejów wojska polskiego w latakh 1945–1948* (From the Actions of the Polish Army in 1945–48). Warsaw: Ministry of Defense Publishers, 1960.

Excellent analysis with extensive documentation (documents are reprinted on pp. 191–330 of the appendix). Chapter III embodies author's earlier article on UPA.

Byelayev, Volodymyr P., and Rudnytsky, Mykhaylo. *Pid chuzhymy praporamy* (Under Foreign Flags). Kiev: Soviet Writer, 1956.

Very important polemics against Ukrainian nationalists.

Dibrova, Prof. O. T. *Heohrafiya Ukrayins'koyi RSR;* Pidruchnyk dlya 8 klasu vos'myrichnoyi shkoly (Geography of the Ukrainian SSR: Textbook for Grade VIII of an Eight-Grade School). Kiev: *Radyans'ka shkola* (Soviet School), 1961.

Dubrova, Aleksey T. *USSR: kratkaya ekonomiko-geograficheskaya spravka* (Ukrainian SSR: A Short Economico-geographical Outline). Moscow: Publishers of Geographical Works, 1954.

Useful figures and map.

[Greek-Catholic Church, Initiative Group for the Reunification with the Orthodox Church.] *Diyannya soboru hreko-katolyts'koyi tserkvy 8–10 bereznya 1946 r. u L'vovi* (Proceedings of the Synod of the Greek-Catholic Church in Lviv, March 8–10, 1946). Lviv: Presidium of the Synod, 1946.

Indispensable.

Grekov, B. D., Bakhrushin, S. V., and Lebedev, V. I. (eds.). *Istoriya SSSR: Tom I: S drevneyshikh vremen do kontsa XVIII v.* (History of the USSR: Vol. I: From the Early Times until the End of the Eighteenth Century). 2nd ed.; Moscow: State Publishers of Political Works, 1947.

College textbook.

Gudzenko, P. P., *et al.* (eds.). *Vossoedinenie Ukrainy s Rossiey: Dokumenty i materialy v trekh tomakh* (Reunification of the Ukraine with Russia: Documents and Materials in 3 vols.). 3 vols. Moscow: USSR Academy of Sciences Publishers, 1953.

See the review article by Yakovliv.

Harasymenko, M., and Dudykevych, B. *Borot'ba trudyashchykh Zakhidnoyi Ukrainy za vozz''yednannya z Radyans'koyu Ukrayinoyu, 1921–39 rr.* (Struggle for the Toilers of Western Ukraine for Re-unification with Soviet Ukraine, 1921–39). Kiev: Ukrainian SSR State Publishers of Political Works, 1955.

Fairly well documented.

Hirshfeld, A. *Migratsiyni protsesy na Ukrayini* (Migration Processes in the Ukraine). Kharkov: State Publishers on the National Economy, 1930.

> Penetrating scholarly analysis on the basis of the 1897 and 1926 population censuses.

Kaliteevskaya, A. V., Nikolaeva, N. A., and Polenina, S. V. (comps.). *O byudzhetnykh pravakh Soyuza SSR, soyuznykh respublik i mestnykh sovetov deputatov trudyashchikhsya* (On the Budgetary Rights of the USSR, the Union Republics, and the Local Soviets of the Toilers' Deputies). Moscow: State Publishers of Legal Literature, 1963.

> A useful compilation of the 1959–60 budgetary laws in the series *Vazhneyshie zakonodatel'nye akty Soyuza SSR i soyuznykh respublik* (The Most Important Legislative Acts of the USSR and the Union Republics).

Kasymenko, O. K. *Istoriya Ukrayins'koyi RSR.* Populyarny narys (History of the UkrSSR: A Popular Outline). Kiev: Ukrainian SSR Academy of Sciences, 1960.

> Interesting.

[Kharkov.] *Khar'kov: Spravochnaya kniga* (Kharkov: A Reference Book). Kharkov: Kharkov Provincial Publishers, 1957.

> Contains important data on schools.

Khomenko, Arsen. *Natsional'ny sklad lyudnosty USRR* (National Composition of the Population of the Ukrainian SSR). Kharkov: State Publishers on the Economy of the Ukraine, 1931.

> Very useful evaluation of the 1926 census results by a Soviet Ukrainian statistician. See also the work by T. Olesiyevych *et al.* [Bib. II, B.] (Warsaw, 1931).

Khrestomatiya z ukrayins'koyi literatury dlya 5 klasu seredn'oyi shkoly (Anthology of Ukrainian Literature for the 5th Grade of Ten-Year Schools). Compiled by N. I. Zhuk. 4th ed. Kiev: *Radyans'ka shkola,* 1955.

Khrestomatiya . . . dlya 6 klasu seredn'oyi shkoly (Anthology . . . for the 6th Grade of Ten-Year Schools). Compiled by P. K. Volyns'ky, Kanyuka, S. M., and N. I. Padalka. 9th ed. Kiev: *Radyans'ka shkola,* 1955.

Khrestomatiya . . . dlya 7 klasu seredn'oyi shkoly (Anthology . . . for the 7th Grade of Ten-Year Schools). Compiled by P. Padalko, *et al.* 3rd ed. Kiev: *Radyans'ka shkola,* 1955.

Khrestomatiya . . . dlya 8 klasu seredn'oyi shkoly (Anthology . . . for the 8th Grade of Ten-Year Schools). Compiled by O. K. Babyshkin, *et al.* Kiev: *Radyans'ka shkola,* 1955.

Khrestomatiya . . . dlya 10 klasu seredn'oyi shkoly (Anthology . . . for the 10th Grade of Ten-Year Schools). Compiled by A. I. Bondarenko, M. F. Kashuba, and S. M. Shakhovs'ky. 12th ed. Kiev: *Radyans'ka shkola*, 1955.

Khvylya Andriy. *Znyshchyty korinnya ukrayins'koho natsionalizmu na movnomu fronti*. Kharkov: *Radyans'ka shkola*, 1933.

[Komsomol: Communist Union of Leninist Youth]. *Spravochnik komsomol'skogo propagandista i agitatora* (Reference Book for Komsomol Propagandists and Agitators). Moscow: "Young Guards," 1957.

Kovpak, Sydor A. *Ot Putivlya do Karpat* (From Putivl' to the Carpathians). Moscow: State Publishers of Political Works, 1945.

Soviet partisan memoirs.

Kravtsev, I. Ye. *Marksysts'ko-lenins'ki pryntsypy proletars'koho internatsionalizmu* (Marxist-Leninist Principles of Proletarian Internationalism). Kiev: Society for the Spreading of Political and Scientific Knowledge, 1956.

Extremely important information.

———. *Razvitie natsional'nykh otnosheniy v SSSR* (Development of Nationality Relations in the USSR). Kiev: Ukrainian SSR Academy of Sciences, 1962.

One of the propaganda pamphlets elucidating the decisions of the Twenty-second Party Congress of 1961. A change from 1956.

Kryp"yakevych, I. P., *Bohdan Khmelnyts'ky*. Kiev: Ukrainian SSR Academy of Sciences, 1954.

A biography as scholarly as Soviet conditions allow.

Kryven', P. V. (ed.). *Ukrayins'ka RSR;* Ekonomichno-heohrafichna kharakterystyka (Ukrainian SSR: An Economico-Geographical Characteristic). Kiev: Kiev University Press, 1960.

A college textbook of economic geography.

Kunicki, Mikołaj. *Pamiętnik "Muchy"* (Diary of the "Fly"). Warsaw: Ministry of Defense Publishers, 1959.

Memoirs of a Polish Communist partisan leader in the Western Ukraine.

Lenin, V. I. *Izbrannye stat'i po natsional'nomu voprosu* (Selected Articles on the Nationality Question). 2nd ed. Moscow, 1925.

———. *Sobranie sochineniy* (Collected Works). Vol. XIV. 2nd ed. Moscow, 1923.

Lisovskiy, V. I. *Ukrainskaya SSR i mezhdunarodnoe pravo* (Ukrainian SSR and International Law). Moscow: Legal Faculty of the Moscow Institute of Finances, 1960.

A thin pamphlet of 39 small pp.: schematic but suggestive.

[Lviv]. *L'viv: Dovidnyk* (Lviv: A Reference Book). Lviv: Publishers of Books and Journals, 1955.

Contains important data on schools.

Lyalikov, Nikolay. *Sovetskaya Ukraina: Ocherk economicheskoy geografii* (Soviet Ukraine: Outline of Economic Geography). Moscow: State Publishers of Geographical Works, 1954.

   Valuable.

Maslov, E. P. *Krym: Economiko-geograficheskaya kharakteristika* (Crimea: A Characterization in Terms of Economic Geography). Moscow: State Publishers of Geographic Works, 1954.

Medynsky, E. N. *Prosveshchenie v SSSR* (Education in USSR). 3rd ed. revised. Moscow: State Publishers of Textbooks and Pedagogical Works, 1955.

   This edition contains valuable data on curricula in Soviet Ukrainian schools. Earlier editions (1947 and 1952) are not so good.

[Odessa]. *Odessa: Spravochnik* (Odessa: A Handbook). Odessa: Odessa Province Publishers, 1957.

   Valuable details.

Orlenko [pseud.], Osyp. *Bol'shevyky u borot'bi z ukrayins'kym revolyutsiyno vyzvol'nym rukhom v druhiy imperiyalistychniy viyni* (The Bolsheviks in the Struggle against the Ukrainian Revolutionary Liberation Movement in the Second Imperialist War). Kiev-Lviv, no publisher, 1946. (Mimeographed.)

   Appears an authentic underground pamphlet.

Osipov, K. *Bogdan Khmel'nitskiy* ("Zhizn' zamechatel'nykh lyudey: Seriya biografiy [Life of Remarkable Men: Series of biographies]," Vols. IV–V.) Moscow: Publishers of the Central Committee of the Komsomol "Young Guards," 1939.

   A remarkably objective popularization.

———. *Bogdan Khmel'nitskiy*. 2nd ed. revised. Moscow: "Young Guards," 1948.

   In this case, "revised" is a synonym for "purged."

Pakhomov, I. M. *Radyans'ke administratyvne pravo* (Soviet Administrative Law). Lviv: Lviv University Press, 1962.

   Brief but up-to-date legal text.

Palamarchuk, L. Kh. (ed.)—see Section I A, Ukrainian SSR, Ministerstvo zakordonnykh sprav.

Pankratova, A. M. (ed.). *Istoriya SSSR: Uchebnik dlya VIII klasa sredney shkoly* (History of the USSR: Textbook for Grade VIII of Ten-Year Schools). 7th ed. Moscow: State Publishers of the RSFSR Ministry of Education of Textbooks and Pedagogical Works, 1948.

Pasternak, Boris. *Doktor Zhivago*. Ann Arbor: University of Michigan Press, 1959. In Russian.

   The novel by the late Nobel prize winner; written, but not published, in the USSR.

Peunov, Vadim. *Poslednee delo Korshuna* (Korshun's Last Action). Stalino, 1955.

　　Fascinating "spy thriller": the hero is a Ukrainian nationalist working underground. Fiction with an authentic ring.

Pod'yachikh, P. G. *Naselenie SSSR* (Population of the USSR). Moscow: State Publishers of Political Literature, 1961.

　　Popular brochure explaining the results of the 1959 census.

Polska Akademia Nauk, Wydział Nauk Społecznych (Polish Academy of Sciences, Division of Social Sciences). *Sesja naukowa poświęcona wojnie wyzwoleńczej narodu polskiego 1939–1945: Materiały* (Scientific Session Devoted to the Liberation War of the Polish People, 1939–45). Warsaw: Ministry of People's Defence Publishers, 1959.

　　Valuable papers delivered in the fall of 1958. See esp. that by Blum, this bibliography, Section III, A.

Poltava (pseud.), P. *Bezposeredn'o za shcho my vedemo nash biy?* (Directly for What Are We Fighting?). [Western Ukraine: Ukrainian Insurgent Army], 1949.

　　Small propaganda pamphlet printed on an exercise book stamped "Exercise book of the State Paper Mill 'Hero of Labor,' town of Dobruch, B[elorussian] SSR." Author shown original from the UHVR archives in New York, convinced of its authenticity.

Priyma, F. Ya. *Shevchenko i russkaya literatura XIX veka* (Shevchenko and Russian Literature of the Nineteenth Century). Moscow: USSR Academy of Sciences Press, 1961.

　　As scholarly as circumstances allow.

RSFSR, Ministerstvo Kul'tury (Russian SFSR, Ministry of Culture). *Bibliotechnoe delo v SSSR: Sbornik statey* (Library Work in the USSR: Collection of Articles). Moscow, 1957.

Rudnyev, V. *Ukrayins'ki burzhuazni natsionalisty—ahentura mizhnarodnoyi reaktsiy* (Ukrainian Bourgeois Nationalists—Agents of the International Reactionary Movement). Kiev: Ukrainian SSR Publishers of Political Works, 1955.

Rybak, Natan. *Pereyaslavs'ka Rada* (The Council of Pereyaslav). Kiev: Soviet Writer, 1948.

　　A novel which expresses the Party line.

Shablovsky, Ye. S. *Shevchenko ta yoho istorychne znachennya* (Shevchenko and his Historical Significance). Kiev: All-Ukrainian Academy of Sciences Publishers, 1933.

　　Revealing; author was later arrested as a Ukrainian nationalist.

Shaginyan, Marietta. *Taras Shevchenko.* Moscow: 2nd ed. revised. State Publishers of Literature, 1946.

　　Remarkably good, objective book.

Shevchenko, Taras H. *Povna zbirka tvoriv v tr'okh tomakh* (Full Collected Works in 3 vols.). Edited by Korniychuk. Kiev: State Publishers of Literature, 1949.

Some letters missing.

Solzhenitsyn, Aleksander. *One Day in the Life of Ivan Denisovich.* Translated by Ronald Hingley & Max Hayward. New York: Bantam, 1963.

Original appeared in *Novy mir* (Moscow), Vol. 1962, No. 11 (November). Powerful, semi-documentary novel by a former inmate of Soviet labor camps. Two sidelights on imprisoned Western Ukrainians (pp. 15, 69ff.).

Stalin, Iosif V. *O velikoy Otechestvennoy voyne Sovetskogo Soyuza* (Great Fatherland War of the USSR). 5th ed. Moscow: State Publishers of Political Works, 1952.

———. *Voprosy leninizma* (Problems of Leninism). 11th ed. Moscow: State Publishers of Political Works, 1940.

Stetsenko, L. F. *Vyvchennya tvorchosti T. H. Shevchenka v shkoli: Posibnyk dlya vchyteliv serednikh shkil* (The Study of the Works of T. H. Shevchenko at School: Manual for Teachers). 2nd ed. revised. Kiev: *Radyans'ka shkola,* 1955.

Very important.

Sul'kevich, S. *Territoriya i naselenie SSSR* (Territory and Population of the USSR). Moscow: Political Publishers of the Central Committee of the All-Union Communist Party (Bolshevik), 1940.

Slim booklet on the 1939 census.

[Ukrainian Insurgent Army]. *Slovo k boytsam i komandiram Krasnoy Armii* (A "Word" to the Soldiers and Officers of the Red Army). [Soviet Ukraine], October, 1944.

Interesting propaganda leaflet, should be assumed to be authentic.

[Ukrainian SSR]. *Kalendar dovidnyk na 1945 rik* (Calendar-Almanac for 1945). Kiev: no publisher.

———. *Kalendar dovidnyk na 1946 rik* (Calendar-Almanac for 1946). Kiev: no publisher.

Both volumes contain useful material.

———. Ministerstvo Vyshchoyi Osvity URSR, Kyivs'ky Derzhavny Universytet (Ukrainian SSR Ministry of Higher Education-Kiev State University). *XIII naukova sesiya; Tezy dopovidey; Sektsiya filolohiyi* (XIII Academic Session: Theses of Papers Read; Philological Section). Kiev, 1956.

———. ———. (Ukrainian SSR Ministry of Higher Education). *Naukovi pratsi kafedr suspil'nykh nauk vuziv m. Kyyeva,* vypusk 2: "Z istoriyi KPU" (Scholarly Papers of the Departments of Social Sciences of Higher Schools in Kiev City. Issue #2: "From the History of the Communist Party of Ukraine"). Kiev, 1959.

See Slipchenko's article.

Vershyhora, Petro. *Lyudy z chystoyu sovistyu* (Men with a Clear Conscience). 2 vols. Kiev: Ukrainian Publishers of Political Works, 1946–1947.

Stalin Prize winning memoirs of a Soviet partisan leader; important.

Wobly, Konstantin (ed.). *Die Sowjet-Ukraine.* Berlin: SWA Verlag (Publishers of the Soviet Military Administration), 1948.

Popular survey, a few interesting figures.

Zatons'ky Volodymyr P. *Natsional'na problema na Ukrayini; dopovid' na plenumi TsK LKSMU, cherven' 1926 r.* (National Problem in the Ukraine; address at the plenum of the Komsomol of Ukraine Central Committee, June 1926). Kharkov: Youth Sector of the State Publishers of the Ukraine, 1926.

———. *Natsional'na problema na Ukrayini* (The Nationality Problem in the Ukraine). Kharkov: State Publishers of the Ukraine, 1927.

Useful figures on the late 1920's. The second item is a second and enlarged edition of Zatonsky's 1926 booklet.

———. *Pro vchyteliv ta shkolu: Promovy* (On Teachers and Schools: Speeches). Kharkov: *Radyans'ka shkola,* 1935.

Useful statistics from the de-Ukrainization period.

B. OTHER

Allen, William E. D. *The Ukraine: A History.* Cambridge (England) University Press, 1941.

Almond, Gabriel A. *The American People and Foreign Policy.* New York: Harcourt, Brace, 1950.

Excellent contribution to the general subject of the interrelationship between foreign policy and public opinion.

Ammende, Ewald (ed.). *Die Nationalitaeten in den Staaten Europas* (National Minorities in the States of Europe). Vienna: Braumueller, 1931.

Collection of useful reports.

Anonymous. *Hovoryt' Radio Vyzvolennya: Zbirka materiyaliv ukrayins'koyi redaktsiyi* (Radio "Liberation" Speaking: Selected Materials of the Ukrainian Division). Vol. II. Munich: no publisher, 1957.

Useful.

Armstrong, John A. *Ukrainian Nationalism, 1939–1945.* New York: Columbia University Press, 1955.

Penetrating study of the activities of Ukrainian Nationalists in German occupied Ukraine, and their reception by the Eastern Ukrainian population.

———. *The Soviet Bureaucratic Elite: A Case Study of the Ukrainian Apparatus.* New York: Praeger, 1959.

Excellent monograph, based in part on unpublished Soviet sources.

————. *The Politics of Totalitarianism: The Communist Party of the Soviet Union from 1934 to the Present.* New York: Random House, 1961.

Indispensable.

————. *Ukrainian Nationalism.* New York: Columbia University Press, 1963.

Second, somewhat enlarged edition of author's *Ukrainian Nationalism, 1939–1945.*

Aspaturian, Vernon S. *The Union Republics in Soviet Diplomacy. A Study of Soviet Federalism in the Service of Soviet Foreign Policy.* Geneva & Paris: E. Droz, 1960.

Indispensable study of a neglected subject.

Barghoorn, Frederick C. *Soviet Russian Nationalism.* New York: Oxford University Press, 1956.

Comprehensive.

Bauer, Raymond A., Inkeles, Alex, and Kluckhohn, Clyde. *How the Soviet System Works: Cultural, Psychological, and Social Themes.* Cambridge: Harvard University Press, 1956.

Final report of the Harvard Project on the Soviet Social System.

Bauer, Raymond A., co-author (1959)—see Inkeles, Alex.

Bienstock, Gregory, Schwarz, Solomon M., and Aaron Yugow. *Management in Russian Industry and Agriculture.* London: Oxford University Press, 1944.

Still useful.

Black, Cyril E. (ed.). *Rewriting Russian History: Soviet Interpretations of Russia's Past.* New York: Praeger, 1956. (Published for the Research Program on the USSR.)

Borys, Jurij. *The Russian Communist Party and the Sovietization of Ukraine: A Study in the Communist Doctrine of the Self-Determination of Nations.* Stockholm, 1960.

Indispensable scholarly study of the 1917–1921 period.

Bradshaw, Martha (ed.). *Soviet Theaters, 1917–1947.* New York: Research Program on the USSR, 1954.

Valuable collection of articles by competent exiles. See that by Hirnyak, cited below.

Briggs, Herbert W. (ed.). *The Law of Nations.* 2nd ed. New York: Appleton-Century-Crofts, 1952.

Brumberg, Abraham (ed.). *Russia under Khrushchev: An Anthology from Problems of Communism.* New York: Praeger, 1962.

Some articles are extremely good.

Brzezinski, Zbigniew K. *The Permanent Purge.* Cambridge: Harvard University Press, 1956.

Penetrating analysis with useful data on Soviet personalities.

Buell, Raymond Leslie. *Poland: Key to Europe*. New York & London: Knopf, 1939.

Valuable for background.

Carr, Edward H. *The Bolshevik Revolution, 1917–1923*. Vol. I. New York: Macmillan, 1951.

Chaplenko, Vasyl. *Bil'shovyts'ka movna polityka* (Bolshevik Linguistic Policy). Munich: Institute for the Study of the USSR, 1956. (Mimeographed.)

Useful, especially on theory.

Churchill, Sir Winston. *The Second World War: Triumph and Tragedy*. Boston: Houghton Mifflin, 1953. Vol. IV of his memoirs.

Cohen, Elliott E. (ed.). *The New Red Anti-Semitism: A Symposium*. Boston: Beacon Press, 1953.

Useful.

Conquest, R. *The Soviet Deportation of Nationalities*. New York: St. Martin's, 1960.

Though the book does not deal with the deportation of Ukrainians it is a highly valuable study on a little publicized aspect of Soviet nationality policy.

———. *Power and Policy in the U.S.S.R.: The Study of Soviet Dynastics*. New York: St. Martin's, 1961.

A difficult work but indispensable for an understanding of the struggle for power in Moscow.

Counts, George S. *Khrushchev and the Central Committee Speak on Education*. Pittsburgh: University of Pittsburgh Press, 1959.

Useful translation of the Central Committee of the Communist Party of the Soviet Union and USSR Council of Ministers theses on educational reform of 1958, with little commentary.

Coyajee, Sir J. C. *India and the League of Nations*. Waltor, 1932.

India's admission to the LN created a precedent for the admission of the Ukraine to the UN.

Crankshaw, Edward. *Russia without Stalin*. New York: The Viking Press, 1956.

Perceptive observations of a well-known British traveller and student of the USSR.

Dallin, Alexander. *German Rule in Russia, 1941–1945: A Study of Occupation Policies*. New York: St. Martin's, 1957.

Standard work, attacked several times in Ukrainian Soviet periodicals.

———. *The Soviet Union at the United Nations: An Inquiry into Soviet Motives and Objectives*. New York: Praeger, 1962.

First full-length inquiry into an important subject. Valuable.

Degras, Jane (ed.). *Soviet Documents on Foreign Policy.* Vol. III. London and New York: Oxford University Press, 1953. Published under auspices of the Royal Institute of International Affairs.

Deutsch, Karl W. *Nationalism and Social Communication.* New York & Cambridge: Wiley and M.I.T. Press, 1953.
Indispensable for methodology.

DeWitt, Nicholas. *Education and Professional Employment in the USSR.* Washington, D.C.: National Science Foundation, 1961.
Most valuable statistically oriented study.

Djilas, Milovan. *Conversations with Stalin.* New York: Harcourt, Brace & World, 1962.
Well-known book contains some interesting sidelights on Ukrainian nationalism immediately after the end of World War II.

Dmytryshyn, Basil. *Moscow and the Ukraine, 1917–1953.* New York: Bookman Associates, 1956.
Valuable scholarly survey.

Doroshenko, Dmytro. *History of the Ukraine.* Edmonton [Canada]: Institute Press, 1939.

Dushnyck, Walter. *Martyrdom in Ukraine: Russia Denies Religious Freedom.* New York: The American Press, n.d.

Dyvnych [Lawrynenko], Jurij. *Amerykans'ke malorossiystvo* (American Little-Russianism). New Ulm, Germany: Ukraina, 1951.
Polemical booklet with useful facts.

Fainsod, Merle. *How Russia Is Ruled.* Cambridge: Harvard University Press, 1953. 2nd revised and enlarged edition published in 1963.

Fedenko, Panas. *Ukrayina pislya smerty Stalina* (Ukraine after Stalin's Death). Munich: Institute for the Study of the USSR, 1956. (Mimeographed.)
Useful survey of the Soviet press.

Felinski, M. *The Ukrainian in Poland.* London: author, 1931.
Polish point of view; useful.

Fischer, George. *Soviet Opposition to Stalin.* Cambridge, Mass.: Harvard University Press, 1952.
An analysis that would have been even more valuable had more space been devoted to the opposition of the non-Russian peoples.

Fischer, John. *Why They Behave like Russians.* New York & London: Harper and Bros., 1946.
Some interesting observations by a former member of the UNRRA mission to the Ukraine.

Friedman, Philip. *Their Brothers' Keepers: The Christian Heroes and Heroines Who Helped the Oppressed Escape the Nazi Terror.* New York: Crown, 1957.

——— (ed.). *Martyrs and Fighters: The Epic of the Warsaw Ghetto.* New York: Praeger, 1954.

Fully documented studies by an eminent Jewish historian.

Friedrich, Carl J. *Constitutional Government and Democracy.* New York: Ginn & Co., 1946.

Garthoff, Raymond L. *Soviet Strategy in the Nuclear Age.* Revised ed. New York: Praeger, 1962.

Most valuable for an understanding of the role of the military in Soviet politics.

Gerland, Brigitte. *Die Hoelle ist ganz anders* (Hell is Quite Different). Stuttgart: Steingrueben, n.d.

Memoirs of a former inmate of the Vorkuta labor camps; useful on attitudes of Western Ukrainians only.

Goldberg, B. Z. *The Jewish Problem in the Soviet Union.* New York: Crown, 1961.

A useful book by the son-in-law of Sholom Aleichem, and President of the American Committee of Jewish Writers and Artists.

Goodman, Elliot R. *The Soviet Design for a World State.* New York: Columbia University Press, 1960.

Excellent, thought-provoking study.

Goodrich, Leland M., and Edvard Hambro. *Charter of the UN: Commentary and Documents.* Boston: World Peace Foundation, 1946.

Thorough.

Gruliow, Leo (ed.). *Current Soviet Policies: The Documentary Record of the Nineteenth Party Congress and the Reorganization after Stalin's Death.* New York: Praeger, 1953.

———. *Current Soviet Policies II: The Documentary Record of the Twentieth Communist Party Congress and Its Aftermath.* New York: Praeger, 1957.

———. *Current Soviet Policies III: The Documentary Record of the Extraordinary Twenty-First Communist Party Congress.* New York: Columbia University Press, 1960.

All these volumes are extremely useful.

Gruliow, Leo, co-editor—see Saikowski, Charlotte.

Harrison, Selig S. *The Most Dangerous Decades: An Introduction to the Comparative Study of Language Policy in Multi-Lingual States.* New York: Language and Communications Research Center, Columbia University, 1957.

Comprehensive bibliographies with a very good introduction.

Hayes, Carlton J. H. *Essays on Nationalism.* New York: Macmillan, 1926.

Heifetz, Elias. *The Slaughter of Jews in the Ukraine in 1919.* New York: Th. Seltzer, 1921.

Report blaming Petlyura and his Government for the pogroms. See, however, Margolin's book.

Holubnychy, Vsevolod. *Ukrayina v Ob''yednanykh Natsiyakh* (The Ukraine in the UN). Munich: *Suchasna Ukrayina* (The Ukraine Today), 1953.

Most valuable historical study.

Hrushevsky, Mykhaylo (Michael). *A History of Ukraine.* Edited by O. J. Frederiksen. New Haven: Yale University Press, 1941.

Good for introduction.

——. *Istoriya Ukrayiny-Rusy* (History of the Ukraine-*Rus'*). 10 vols. 2nd ed. New York: Knyhospilka, 1954–58.

Standard work on Ukrainian history from the earliest times until the second half of the seventeenth century.

Hull, Cordell. *Memoirs.* 2 vols. New York: Macmillan, 1948.

Inkeles, Alex, and Raymond A. Bauer. *The Soviet Citizen: Daily Life in a Totalitarian Society.* Cambridge, Mass.: Harvard University Press, 1959.

A considerably expanded final report of the Harvard Project on the Soviet Social System. See their *How the Soviet System Works* (1956).

Institute for the Study of the USSR, Munich. Nikolai K. Deker and Andrei Lebed (eds.). *Genocide in the USSR: Studies in Group Destruction.* New York: The Scarecrow Press, 1958.

A useful collection of brief but documented papers. See the article by Yurchenko, this bibliography, section III, B.

——, Research Section. *XXII Party Congress and Personnel Changes among the Top Staff of the Communist Party of the Soviet Union and the Communist Parties of the Union Republics.* Munich, 1961.

Handy lists of names.

Kalb, Marvin L. *Eastern Exposure.* New York: Farrar, Straus, Cudahy, 1958.

Perceptive journalistic account of the post-Stalinist "thaw."

Kalnins, Bruno. *Der sowjetische Propaganda Staat: Das System und die Mittel der Massenbeeinflussung in der Sowjetunion* (The Soviet Propaganda State: The System and the Means of Mass Manipulation in the Soviet Union). Stockholm: Tiden, 1956.

Useful scholarly study.

Kann, Robert A. *The Multinational Empire: Nationalism and National Reform in the Hapsburg Monarchy.* 2 vols. New York: Columbia University Press, 1950.

Useful for background.

Kertesz, Stephen D. *Diplomacy in a Whirlpool: Hungary between Nazi*

Germany and Soviet Russia. Notre Dame, Ind.: University of Notre Dame Press, 1953.
    Valuable analysis.

Khrin (pseud.), Stepan. *Zymoyu v bunkri, 1947–48: Spohady-Khronika* (A Winter in an Earth-Fortress, 1947–1948: Memoirs-Chronicle). Augsburg, Germany: Do Zbroyi (To Arms), 1950.
    Reminiscences of an UPA (Ukrainian Insurgent Army) Officer, probably authentic.

Kirimal, Edige. *Der nationale Kampf der Krimtuerken, mit besonderer Beruecksichtigung der Jahre 1917–1918* (National Struggle of the Crimean Turks, with Special Consideration of the Years 1917–18). Emsdetten (Westfalen), Germany: Lechte, 1952.
    Valuable.

Kleist, Peter. *Zwischen Hitler und Stalin, 1939–1945* (Between Hitler and Stalin, 1939–1945). Bonn: Athenaeum, 1950.
    Memoirs of an official of the German Foreign Office.

Kluchevsky, V. O. *A History of Russia.* Vol. V. London: Dent, 1931.

Kohn, Hans. *The Idea of Nationalism.* New York: Macmillan, 1946.

Konovalov, S. (ed.). *Russo-Polish Relations: A Historical Survey.* Princeton: Princeton University Press, 1945.
    Extensive quotations from primary sources.

Korol, Alexander C. *Soviet Education for Science and Technology.* New York: Wiley & M.I.T. Press, 1957.

Kostiuk, Hryhory. *Stalinist Rule in the Ukraine: A Study of the Decade of Mass Terror (1929–1939).* Munich: Institute for the Study of the USSR, 1960.
    An indispensable monograph that has been simultaneously published in Munich, London, and New York.

Krupnytskyj, Borys. *Ukrayins'ka istorychna nauka pid sovyetamy* (Ukrainian Historical Science under the Soviets). Munich: Institute for the Study of the USSR, 1957. (Mimeographed.)
    Most valuable survey by an eminent Ukrainian historian.

Kubijovyč (Kubiyovych), Volodymyr. *Western Ukraine within Poland, 1920–39: Ethnic Relationships.* Chicago: Ukrainian Research and Information Institute, Inc., 1963.
    A brief but valuable statistical analysis by the well-known Ukrainian demographer.

Kulischer, Eugen N. *Europe on the Move: War and Population Changes, 1917–47.* New York: Columbia University Press, 1948.
    Valuable.

Kvitkovsky, D., et al. *Bukovyna, yiyi mynule i suchasne* (Bukovina—Her Past and Present). Paris, Philadelphia, Detroit, 1956.
    Magnificent encyclopedic work of 965 pp.

Lebed', Mykola. *Ukrayins'ka Povstans'ka Armiya: Yiyi geneza, rist i diyi u vyzvol'niy borot'bi ukrayins'koho narodu za ukrayins'ku samostiynu sobornu derzhavu* (UPA: Its Genesis, Development and Actions in the Liberation Struggle of the Ukrainian People for an Independent and United Ukrainian State). Vol. I. [Germany]: UHVR Press Service, 1946.

Descriptive account.

Levyts'ky, Myron (ed.). *Istoriya Ukrayins'koho Viys'ka* (History of the Ukrainian Armed Forces). 2nd ed. revised. Winnipeg: Ivan Tyktor, 1953.

Lobay, Danylo. *Neperemozhna Ukrayina: Fakty pro borot'bu Moskvy z ukrayins'kym natsionalizmom na kul'turnomu fronti po druhiy svitoviy viyni* (Invincible Ukraine: Facts on Moscow's Struggle with Ukrainian Nationalism on the Cultural Front after World War II). Winnipeg: Ukrainian Canadian Committee, 1950.

Extremely useful survey; extensive quotations from the Soviet Ukrainian Press.

Lorimer, Frank. *The Population of the Soviet Union: History and Prospects.* Geneva: League of Nations, 1946.

Standard work.

Luckyj, George S. N. *Literary Politics in the Soviet Ukraine, 1917–34.* New York: Columbia University Press, 1956.

Indispensable for period covered.

Macartney, C. A. *National State and National Minorities.* London: Oxford University Press, 1934.

Valuable.

MacDuffie, Marshall. *The Red Carpet.* New York: Norton, 1953.

Account of a trip through the USSR in 1953 by the former head of the UNRRA mission to the Ukraine.

McNeill, William Hardy. *America, Britain, and Russia: Their Cooperation and Conflict, 1941–46,* in [Royal Institute of International Affairs], *Survey of International Affairs, 1939–46.* London, etc.: Oxford University Press, 1953.

Valuable.

Majstrenko, Iwan. *Borot'bism—A Chapter in the History of Ukrainian Communism.* New York: Research Program on the USSR, 1954.

Margolin, Arnold D. *Ukraina i politika Antanty* (Ukraine and the Policy of the Entente). Berlin: Efron, 1921.

A pro-Ukrainian analysis by the late Jewish leader and defense counsel in the Beiliss case. In Russian. See, however, Heifetz's book.

Markus, Vasyl. *L'Incorporation de l'Ukraine Subcarpatique a l'Ukraine soviétique, 1944–45.* (Incorporation of the Subcarpathian Ukraine into

Soviet Ukraine, 1944–45.) Louvain: Centre Ukrainien d'Etudes en Belgique, 1956.

Able short study.

———. *L'Ukraine soviétique dans les relations internationales et son statut en droit international, 1918–1923* (The Soviet Ukraine in International Relations and Her Status in International Law, 1918–23). Paris: Les éditions internationales, 1959.

Comprehensive (326 pp.) analysis by a Western educated Ukrainian international lawyer.

Martschenko, Basilius. *Soviet Population Trends, 1926–39.* New York: Research Program on the USSR, 1953. (Mimeographed.)

Valuable, if somewhat technical discussion by a former employee of Soviet census authorities.

Martynets', V. *Ukrayins'ke pidpillya vid UVO do OUN: Spohady i materialy do peredistoriyi ta istoriyi ukrayins'koho organizovanoho natsionalizmu* (The Ukrainian Underground from the UVO to OUN: Memoirs and Materials Concerning the Prehistory and the History of Organized Ukrainian Nationalism). Winnipeg: no publisher, 1949.

A rather unsystematic but voluminous collection of materials.

Mazour, Anatole G. *An Outline of Modern Russian Historiography.* Berkeley: University of California Press, 1939.

Good on the contribution of Hrushevsky.

Meissner, Boris. *Sowjetrussland zwischen Revolution und Restauration* (Soviet Russia between Revolution and Restoration). Cologne: Verlag fuer Politik und Wirtschaft, 1956.

Useful sketches on Soviet personalities.

Mijakovs'kyj, Volodymyr, and George Y. Shevelov (eds.). *Taras Ševčenko, 1814–1861: A Symposium.* 'S-Gravenhage (Netherlands): Mouton, 1962.

Very valuable.

Mirchuk, Petro. *Ukrayins'ka povstans'ka armiya, 1942–52* (Ukrainian Insurgent Army, 1942–52). Munich: no publisher, 1952.

Useful, especially on personalities.

Moore, Barrington, Jr. *Terror and Progress—USSR.* Cambridge: Harvard University Press, 1954.

Suggestive interpretation.

Moskalenko, A. *Khmelnytskyj and the Treaty of Pereyaslav in Soviet Historiography.* New York: Research Program on the USSR, 1955. (Mimeographed.)

Fairly interesting brochure, with some excellent comments by Yaresh.

Murra, John V. *et al.* (comps.). *The Soviet Linguistic Controversy.* New York: King's Crown Press, 1951.

Useful translations.

Nemec, F. [Former Czechoslovak Government Delegate in Ruthenia] and Moudry, V. *The Soviet Seizure of Subcarpathian Ruthenia.* Toronto: Wm. B. Anderson, 1955.
A valuable collection of documents with memoirs and an objective introduction.

Nove, Alec. *The Soviet Economy: An Introduction.* New York: Praeger, 1961.
An excellent and reasonably up-to-date introduction by the well-known British economist and public servant.

Nykolyshyn, S. *Kul'turna polityka bol'shevykiv i ukrayins'ky kul'turny protses* (Cultural Policy of the Bolsheviks and the Ukrainian Cultural Process). No publisher, 1947.
Valuable analysis of the Soviet press, with extensive quotations.

Ohloblyn, O. *Ukrayins'ko-Moskovs'ka uhoda, 1654* (Ukrainian-Muscovite Agreement, 1654). New York-Toronto: Organization to Defend the Four Freedoms of the Ukraine—League for the Liberation of the Ukraine, 1954.
Valuable historical study.

Olesiyevych, T., *et al. Ukrayins'ka lyudnist' SSSR* (Ukrainian Population of the USSR). Warsaw: Ukrainian Scientific Institute, 1931.
Vol. I of its works. Valuable appraisal of the 1926 census data by a group of Ukrainian exile scholars. See also the book by Khomenko (Kharkov, 1931).

[Organization of Ukrainian Nationalists, Foreign Divisions, i.e., Bandera group]. *OUN v svitli postanov Velykykh Zboriv, Konferentsiy ta inshykh dokumentiv z borot'by 1929–1955 r.* (The OUN in the Light of the Decisions of Grand Congresses, Conferences, and other Documents from the Struggle of 1929–55). [Munich]: Foreign Divisions of the OUN, 1955.
A useful, if incomplete collection of documents.

Pennar, Jaan (ed.). *Islam and Communism.* [A Conference Sponsored by the Institute for the Study of the USSR at the Carnegie International Center, New York City, June 25, 1960.] New York: 1960.
Valuable papers, but uneven in documentation.

Petlyura, Symon. *Statti, lysty, dokumenty* (Articles, Letters, Documents). New York: Ukrainian Academy of Arts and Sciences in the U.S., 1956.
Indispensable for an understanding of the events in 1917–20.

Pipes, Richard E. *The Formation of the Soviet Union: Communism and Nationalism, 1917–23.* Cambridge: Harvard University Press, 1954.
Indispensable for background and analysis.

Pirogov, Peter. *Why I Escaped.* New York: Sloan & Pearce, 1950.
Perceptive account by a former Soviet pilot.

Pistrak, Lazar. *The Grand Tactician. Khrushchev's Rise to Power*. New York: Praeger, 1961.

Best biography of Khrushchev to date, especially good on the Stalinist years.

Polons'ka-Vasylenko, N. D. *The Settlement of the Southern Ukraine (1750–75)* [Special issue of] *The Annals of the Ukrainian Academy of Arts and Sciences in the U.S.*, New York, Nos. 14–15 (Summer–Fall, 1955).

Pozytsyi ukrayins'koho vyzvol'noho rukhu: Materialy z ridnykh zemel' do pytan' borot'by za ukrayins'ku derzhavu (Positions of the Ukrainian Liberation Movement: Materials from the Ukraine on Questions of the Struggle for a Ukrainian State). Munich: Prolog, 1948.

Reprints of underground materials by UHVR circles in contact with the underground.

Prokop, Myroslav. *Ukrayina i ukrayins'ka polityka Moskvy; Chastyna I: Period pidhotovy do druhoyi svitovoyi viyny* (Ukraine and Moscow's Ukrainian Policy; Part I: The Preparation of World War II). Munich: *Suchasna Ukrayina* (The Ukraine Today), 1956.

Well-documented study with a useful bibliography.

Ram, V. Shiva, and Brij Mohan Sharma. *India and the League of Nations*. Lucknow, 1932.

Radkey, Oliver S. *The Election to the Russian Constituent Assembly of 1917*. Cambridge, Mass.: Harvard University Press, 1950.

Essential.

Reshetar, John S., Jr. *The Ukrainian Revolution, 1917–20*. Princeton: Princeton University Press, 1952.

Pioneering scholarly study.

Ritvo, Herbert, annotator. *The New Soviet Society. Final Text of the Program of the Communist Party of the Soviet Union*. [New York]: New Leader, 1962.

One of the most useful numerous editions of the Program, lavishly annotated, with incisive comments.

Rocker, Rudolf. *Nationalism and Culture*. New York: Covici, Friede, 1937.

Royal Institute of International Affairs, Study Group (E. H. Carr, chm.). *Nationalism*. London, etc.: Oxford University Press, 1939.

Indispensable.

Rubinstein, Alvin Z. *The Foreign Policy of the Soviet Union*. New York: Random House, 1960.

Saikowski, Charlotte, and Leo Gruliow (eds.). *Current Soviet Policies IV: The Documentary Record of the Twenty-Second Congress of the Communist Party of the Soviet Union*. New York: Columbia University Press, 1962.

Extremely useful. See also the preceding volumes edited by Gruliow alone.

Schechtman, Joseph B. *Star in Eclipse: Russian Jewry Revisited.* New York & London: Thomas Yoseloff, 1961.

A prominent Zionist and former deputy to the Ukrainian *Rada* shares his valuable experiences from, and reflections on, his trip to the USSR in August, 1959.

Scholmer, Joseph. *Die Toten kehren zurueck (Bericht eines Arztes aus Vorkuta)* (The Dead Return: The Account of a Physician from Vorkuta). Cologne-Berlin: Kiepenheuer & Witsch, 1954.

———. *Vorkuta.* London: Weidenfeld & Nicolson, 1954.

Memoirs by a perceptive former inmate. German version is better. More comprehensive in coverage than Gerland's book.

Schulz, Heinrich E., and Dr. Stephen S. Taylor (eds.). *Who's Who in the USSR, 1961/62.* New York: Scarecrow Press, 1962.

Useful, up-to-date.

Schwartz, Harry. *Russia's Soviet Economy.* 1st ed. New York: Prentice-Hall, 1950.

Schwarz, Solomon M. *The Jews in the Soviet Union.* [Syracuse, N.Y.]: Syracuse University Press, 1951.

Standard work.

———. *Antisemitizm v Sovetskom Soyuze* (Anti-Semitism in the USSR). New York: Chekhov, 1952.

An enlarged version of the second part of the English work.

Shankowsky, Lew. *Pokhidni hrupy OUN. Prychynky do istoriyi pokhidnykh hrup OUN na tsentral'nykh i skhidnikh zemlyakh Ukrayiny v 1941–43 rr.* (The OUN Raiding Groups: Materials for the history of the OUN raiding groups in the central and eastern regions of the Ukraine from 1941–43). Munich: *Ukrayins'ky Samostiynyk,* 1958.

A very important study that supplements and occasionally corrects Armstrong's work of 1955.

Sherwood, Robert E. *Roosevelt and Hopkins: An Intimate History.* New York: Harper and Bros., 1948.

Shevchenko, Taras. *Kobzar* (The Bard). Edited by Leonid Biletsky. 4 vols. 2nd ed. revised. Winnipeg: Trident, 1952–54.

Published under the auspices of the Ukrainian Free Academy of Sciences in Canada, Institute of Shevchenkology. Best edition of Shevchenko's masterpiece with extensive commentaries by the editor.

———. *Selected Poems.* Edited by Clarence Manning. Jersey City, N.J.: Ukrainian National Association, 1945.

Translations of Shevchenko's main poems, with an introduction.

———. *Tvory* (Works). Edited by Pavlo Zaytsev. 13 vols. Warsaw-Lviv: Ukrainian Scientific Institute, 1934–39.

Best scholarly edition.

Shevelov, George Y., co-editor—see Mijakovs'kyj, Volodymyr.

Shimkin, Demitri B. *Minerals—A Key to Soviet Power.* Cambridge: Harvard University Press, 1953.

Siropolko, S. *Narodnya osvita na sovyets'kiy Ukrayini* (Popular Education in Soviet Ukraine). Warsaw: Ukrainian Scientific Institute, 1934.

> Vol. XXII in the series. Solid scholarly work based exclusively on Soviet sources.

Smal-Stocki, Roman. *Ukrayinska mova v sovyets'kiy Ukrayini* (Ukrainian Language in Soviet Ukraine). Warsaw: Ukrainian Scientific Institute, 1936.

> Vol. XXXVI in its series. Comprehensive survey of Soviet material that is now little accessible.

——. *The Nationality Problem in the Soviet Union and Russian Communist Imperialism.* Milwaukee: Bruce, 1952.

——. *The Captive Nations: Nationalism of the Non-Russian Nations in the Soviet Union.* New York: Bookman Associates, 1960.

Solovey, Dmytro. *Lyudnist' Ukrayiny za sorok rokiv vlady TsK KPSS u svitli perepysiv* (The Population of the Ukraine for the Last Forty Years under the Rule of the Communist Party of the Soviet Union). Detroit: Ukrainian Free Society of America, 1961.

> Valuable reprint from *Vil'na Ukrayina* (Free Ukraine) #24–#27.

Sova, H. *Do istoriyi bol'shevyts'koyi diysnosty.* 25 rokiv zhyttya ukrayins'koho hromadyanyna SSSR ([A Contribution] to the History of Bolshevik Reality: Twenty-five years of a Ukrainian Citizen's Life in the USSR). Munich: Institute for the Study of the History and Culture of the USSR, 1955. (Mimeographed.)

> Valuable memoirs.

Stalin, I. V. *Marxism and Linguistics.* New York: International Publishers, 1951.

> Useful compilation.

Stettinius, Edward H., Jr. *Roosevelt and the Russians: The Yalta Conference.* Garden City, New York: Doubleday, 1949.

> Important.

Stillman, Edmund (ed.). *Bitter Harvest: Intellectual Revolt Behind the Iron Curtain.* New York: Praeger, 1959.

> Excellent collection of translations from Soviet and East European works that appeared during the post-Stalinist thaw.

Sullivant, Robert S. *Soviet Politics and the Ukraine, 1917–57.* New York: Columbia University Press, 1962.

> Valuable scholarly survey.

Temperley, Harold W. (ed.). *A History of the Peace Conference.* Vol. VI. London: Frowde, Hodher & Stoughton, 1924.

> Useful on the background of the Curzon line.

Ukrainian Association of Victims of Russian Communist Terror. *The Black Deeds of the Kremlin—A White Book.* 2 vols. Toronto (Canada), 1953–56.

[Ukrainian Catholic Church]. *First Victims of Communism: White Book on the Religious Persecution in Ukraine.* Rome: no publisher, 1953.
Indispensable.

Ukrayins'ka Vil'na Akademiya Nauk v SShA (Ukrainian Academy of Arts and Sciences in the United States). *Shevchenkivs'ky richnyk* (Shevchenko Yearbook). No. 3 (1954).
Valuable collection.

Vynar, Bohdan. *Rozvytok ukrayins'koyi lehkoyi promyslovosty* (Development of Ukrainian Light Industry). Denver, Colo.: Zarevo, 1955.
Valuable little study.

———. *Ekonomichny koloniyalizm v Ukrayini* (Economic Colonialism in the Ukraine). Paris: [Ukrainian] Nationalist Publishers in Europe, 1958.
Not a full treatment, but contains some valuable data.

Winch, Michael. *Republic for a Day: An Eye-Witness Account of the Carpatho-Ukraine Incident.* London: Robert Hale, 1939.

Wlasowsky, Ivan. *Outline History of the Ukrainian Orthodox Church.* Vol. I. New York & Bound Brook, N.J.: Ukrainian Orthodox Church of USA.
Valuable.

Yakemtchouk, Romain. *L'Ukraine en Droit International* (The Ukraine in International Law). Louvain: Centre Ukrainien d'Etudes en Belgique, 1954.
Able legal study from the Ukrainian point of view.

Yakovliv, Andriy. *Dohovir Het'mana Bohdana Khmel'nyts'koho z moskovs'kym tsarem Oleksiyem Mykhaylovychem 1654 r.* (Treaty of Pereyaslav Between Hetman Bohdan Khmelnytsky and the Moscovite Tsar Alexey Mikhaylovich, 1654). New York: Tyszczenko & Bilous, 1954.
Good legal study.

Yefremov, Serhiy. *Istoriya ukrayins'koho pys'menstva* (History of Ukrainian Literature). Kiev: Ukrainian Teacher [pre-1917].
An early edition of the standard work.

Zaytsev, Pavlo. *Zhyttya Tarasa Shevchenka* (The Life of Taras Shevchenko). New York-Paris-Munich: Shevchenko Scientific Society, 1955.
Very good biography.

III. Articles in Journals and Symposia

A. soviet and polish

Anonymous. "Konferentsiya z pytan' kul'tury movy (Conference on the Problems of the Culture of [Ukrainian] Language)," *Ukrayins'ka mova i literatura v shkoli* (Ukrainian Language and Literature at School), Vol. 1963, No. 2 (April), pp. 91–93.

Chronicle of a very important conference in February 1963, published in the professional journal of the teachers of Ukrainian language and literature. See also the report under *Nashe slovo,* this Bibliography, Section IV, A, below.

———. "Mizhrespublikans'ky seminar z pytan' druzhby narodiv (Inter-Republican Seminar on Questions of Friendship of Peoples)," *Ukrayins'ky istorychny zhurnal* (Ukrainian Historical Journal, Kiev—henceforth abbreviated *Ukr. ist. zhurnal*), Vol. 1961, No. 5 (October–November), pp. 165–66.

A reasonably full account of the proceedings of an important conference.

———. "Vshanuvannya pam''yati velykoho kobzarya T. H. Shevchenka (Paying Tribute to the Memory of the Great Bard T. H. Shevchenko)," *Ukr. ist. zhurnal,* Vol. 1961, No. 3 (May–June), pp. 149–50.

Antonenko-Davydovych, Borys. "Tonny i hram (Tons and [One] Gram)," *Dnipro* (Dnieper, Kiev), Vol. 1961, No. 11 (November), pp. 135–45.

Spirited defense of the use of the Ukrainian language by a writer who had been imprisoned by Stalin, released under Khrushchev.

Babiychuk, I. [Ukrainian SSR Minister of Culture]. "Rastsvet ukrainskoy sovetskoy kul'tury (Flowering of the Ukrainian Soviet Culture)," in *Ukrainskaya sovetskaya kul'tura:* Sbornik statey (Ukrainian Soviet Culture: A Collection of Articles, Kiev, 1961), pp. 3–46.

Barabash, N. I., and A. V. Ivanchenko. "Z dosvidu perebudovy vykladannya istoriyi u 5–6 klasakh vos'myrichnoyi shkoly (From [Our] Experience of Reorganizing the Teaching of History in Grades V–VI of an Eight-Year School)," *Ukr. ist. zhurnal,* Vol. 1962, No. 1 (January–February), pp. 84–90.

Bilets'ky, O. I. "Shevchenko i svitova literatura (Shevchenko and the World Literature)," in Akademiya nauk URSR, *Pam''yati T. H. Shevchenka . . .* (1939), pp. 207–26.

Stimulating scholarly piece. See Bibliography, Section II, A, above, for full citation of symposium.

———. "Franko ta indiys'ka kul'tura (Franko and Indian Culture)," in Ukrainian SSR, Ministerstvo Vyshchoyi Osvity URSR-Kyivs'ky Derzhavny Universytet, *XIII naukova sesiya; Tezy dopovidey; Sektsiya filolohiyi* (Kiev, 1956), pp. 3–6.

See Bibliography, Section II, A, above.

———. "Zavdannya i perspektyvy vyvchennya Shevchenka (Tasks and Perspectives for the Study of Shevchenko)," in Akademiya nauk URSR, Instytut literatury im. T. H. Shevchenka, *Zbirnyk prats' dev''yatoyi naukovoyi shevchenkivs'koyi konferentsiyi* (Collected Papers of the Ninth Scholarly Shevchenko Conference), pp. 13–25.

A frank and courageous address by the late dean of Ukrainian literary historians.

Bilodid (Beloded), I. (Ukrainian SSR Minister of Education). "Ukreplyaem svyazi shkoly s zhyznyu (We Strengthen the Ties of School with Life)," in *Ukrainskaya sovetskaya kul'tura;* sbornik statey, pp. 47–78.

———. "Ukrayins'ka mova sered mov sotsialistychnykh natsiy SRSR (The Ukrainian Language among the Languages of the Socialist Nations of the USSR)," *Vitchyzna* (Fatherland, Kiev), Vol. 1962, No. 2 (February), pp. 185–96.

Bilousov, M. M., and V. I. Klokov. "Fal'syfikatsiya borot'by ukrayins'koho narodu proty nimets'ko-fashysts'kykh zaharbnykiv (Falsification of the Struggle of the Ukrainian People against the Germano-Fascist Aggressors)," *Ukr. ist. zhurnal,* Vol. 1959, No. 1 (January–February), pp. 136–42.

Polemics against Western historians.

Blum, Brigadier General Ignacy. "Udział Wojska Polskiego w obronie narodowych i społecznych interesów ludu polskiego oraz w umacnianiu władzy ludowej w latach 1945–1948 (The Share of the Polish Army in the Defence of the Democratic and Social Interests of the Polish People as well as in the Consolidation of the People's Government in the Years 1945–48)," in Polska Akademia Nauk, Wydzial Nauk Społecznych, *Sesja naukowa poswięcona wojnie wyzwoleńczej narodu polskiego 1939–45: Materiały* (Warsaw: Ministry of People's Defence Publishers, 1959), pp. 241–65.

Excellent scholarly paper by a high Polish officer. Includes details not contained in his other article, cited immediately below. For full citation of symposium see this Bibliography, Section II, A, above.

———. "Udział Wojska Polskiego w walce o utrwalenie władzy ludowej: Walki z bandami UPA (Share of the Polish Army in the Struggle for the Stabilization of People's Government: Actions Against the UPA Bands)," *Wojskowy przegląd historyczny* (Review of Military History, Warsaw), Vol. IV, No. 1 (January–March, 1959), pp. 3–29.

Excellent analysis. Embodied in his book (see above). See also the article by Gerhard, below.

Bohodyst, I. P. "Sotsialistychna perebudova zakhidno-ukrayins'koho sela (Socialist Reconstruction of the West Ukrainian Village)," *Ukr. ist. zhurnal,* Vol. 1957, No. 2 (September–October), pp. 69–82.

———. "Pidnesennya politychnoyi aktyvnosti trudyashchykh u borot'bi za zmitsnennya radyans'koho ladu v zakhidnikh oblastyakh URSR (1944–1950) (Raising the Political Activity of the Toilers in the Struggle for Strengthening Soviet Authority in the Western Provinces of UkrSSR,

1944–1950)," *Ukr. ist. zhurnal,* Vol. 1959, No. 6 (November–December), pp. 56–66.

Fairly frank and enlightening.

Boyko, I. "Pidvyshchuvaty ideyny i teoretychny riven' naukovykh prats' z istoriyi (Raise the Ideological and Theoretical Level of Scholarly Works in History)," *Komunist Ukrayiny* (Communist Ukraine, Kiev), Vol. 1956, No. 6 (June), pp. 60–70. Appears also in parallel Russian edition (*Kommunist Ukrainy,* Kiev).

The Party line in historiography after the Twentieth Party Congress.

Burlin, V., Darahan, M., and Ye. Dolhopolov. "Pereotsinka osnovnykh fondiv URSR ta yiyi znachennya (Re-Evaluation of the Basic [Capital] Funds of the Ukrainian SSR and Its Meaning)," *Ekonomika Radyans'koyi Ukrayiny* (Economics of Soviet Ukraine), Vol. 1960, No. 6 (November–December), pp. 3–10.

Buts'ko, M. O., and V. T. Poznyak. "Naukova konferentsiya z pytan' internatsional'noho vykhovannya trudyashchykh (A Scientific Conference on Problems of an Internationalist Education of the Toilers)," *Ukr. ist. zhurnal,* Vol. 1961, No. 1 (January–February), pp. 154–55.

Valuable information on the inter-university conference of September, 1960.

Chervonenko, S. "Tisny zv"yazok z zhyttyam—umova uspikhu ideolohichnoyi roboty (Close Connection with Life Is the Condition for Successful Ideological Work)," *Komunist Ukrayiny* (Ukr. ed.), Vol. 1959, No. 7 (July), pp. 24–40.

Important article by the then Secretary of the Central Committee of the Communist Party of Ukraine in charge of ideological affairs.

Chernikov, I. F. "Nazrili pytannya (Questions That Are Ripe [for an Answer])," *Ukr. ist. zhurnal,* Vol. 1959, No. 5 (September–October), pp. 113–14.

An interesting contribution to the discussion of how Ukrainian history ought to be taught in secondary schools. Polemizes with Puns'ky, below.

Daniyalov, G. D. "O dvizhenii bortsev pod rukovodstvom Shamilya (On the Movement of Mountaineers under the Leadership of Shamil)," *Voprosy istorii* (Historical Problems, Moscow), Vol. 1956, No. 7 (July), pp. 67–72.

Shamil's rehabilitation.

Darahan, M., co-author—see Burlin, V.

Dement'ev, A., co-author—see Metchenko, A.

Denysenko, P. I., *et al.* "Materialy do istoriyi KPU (Materials for the History of CPU)," *Ukr. ist. zhurnal,* Vol. 1958, No. 3 (May–June), pp. 121–34.

Useful chronology of Central Committee plenums, congresses.

Dolhopolov, Ye., co-author—see Burlin, V.

Dudnyk, P. T. [Ukrainian SSR Deputy Minister of Education]. "Pidnesty na vyshchy riven' robotu shkil zakhidnykh oblastey URSR (Raise onto a Higher Level the Work of Schools in the Western Provinces of the Ukrainian SSR)," *Radyans'ka shkola* (Soviet School, Kiev), Vol. 1947, No. 2 (March–April), pp. 1–7.

Dyachenko, Oleksandr. "Rozdumy nad lyuds'kymy kharakteramy (Vidtvorennya v khudozhniy literaturi natsional'noho kharakteru ta yoho evolyutsiyi) (Reflections on Human Character: The Representation in Belles-Lettres of National Character and Its Evolution)," *Vitchyzna*, Vol. 1962, No. 11 (November), pp. 139–52.

Later printed as a pamphlet. A well-thought out defense of national character in a period of "fusion of nations."

Editorial, "Do kontsa preodolet' posledstviya kul'ta lichnosti (Overcome the Last Consequences of the Cult of Personality)," *Kommunist Ukrainy* (Rus. ed.), Vol. 1956, No. 8 (August), pp. 1–9.

A good example of the "thaw" after the Twentieth Party Congress.

Editorial. "Kommunisticheskaya Partiya Ukrainy v tsifrakh (Communist Party of Ukraine in Figures)," *Partiynaya zhizn'* (Party Life, Moscow), Vol. 1958, No. 12 (June), pp. 57–59.

Extremely important Party statistics.

Editorial. "Nevidkladni zavdannya u vykladanni ukrayins'koi movy (Urgent Tasks in the Teaching of Ukrainian)," *Ukrayins'ka mova v shkoli* (Ukrainian Language at School, Kiev), Vol. 1957, No. 2 (March–April), pp. 3–5.

Editorial. "O sotsialisticheskom soderzhanii i natsional'nykh formakh sovetskoy kul'tury (Concerning the Socialist Content and the National Forms of Soviet Culture)," *Bol'shevik*, Vol. 1946, No. 22 (November), pp. 1–8.

Editorial. "Ob ideynosti kommunista (On the Ideological Firmness of a Communist)," *Kommunist* (Moscow), Vol. 1956, No. 9 (June), pp. 3–14.

Summary of the decisions made at the Twentieth Party Congress.

Editorial. "Partiya v tsifrakh (1956–1961) (Party in Figures, 1956–61)," *Partiynaya zhizn'*, Vol. 1962, No. 1 (January), pp. 44–54.

Interesting figures. Complete translation in *CDSP*, Vol. XIV, No. 3, pp. 3ff.

Editorial. "Pid znakom lenins'koyi yednosty (Under the Sign of Leninist Unity)," *Komunist Ukrayiny* (Ukr. ed.), Vol. 1957, No. 7 (July), pp. 1–6.

Repeats accusation against Malenkov, Kaganovich and Co. that they were unfriendly to the aspirations of the non-Russian Republics.

Editorial. "Povnishe vykorystovuvaty perevahy novoyi formy upravlinnya (Utilize to a Fuller Extent the Advantages of the New Form of Administration)," *Komunist Ukrayiny* (Ukr. ed.), Vol. 1958, No. 3 (March), pp. 11–22.

Editorial. "Usilit' ideyno-politicheskuyu rabotu partiynykh organizatsiy (Strengthen the ideological-political work of Party organizations)," *Bol'shevik,* Vol. 1944, No. 17/18 (September), pp. 1–8.
Very important.

Editorial. "Velichie i moguchestvo sovetskoy derzhavy (Greatness and Power of the Soviet State)," *Bol'shevik,* Vol. 1944, No. 2 (dated January), pp. 1–6.
Comment on the Constitutional amendment of February 1, 1944.

Editorial. *Visnyk Instytutu Ukrayins'koyi Naukovoyi Movy* (Bulletin of the Institute of a Ukrainian Scientific Language, Kiev), Vol. I, No. 1 (1928), pp. 5–8.
Excellent example of the atmosphere in some Ukrainian circles during the Ukrainization.

Editorial. "Za dal'neyshee uluchshenie rukovodstva narodnym khozaystvom SSSR (For a Further Improvement of the Management of the USSR National Economy)," *Voprosy ekonomiki* (Problems of Economics, Moscow), Vol. 1957, No. 4 (April), pp. 3–11.
Important statement on the impending plan to reorganize the administration of industry.

Editorial. "Za dal'neyshiy pod''em istoricheskoy nauki v SSSR (For a Further Improvement of Historical Scholarship in the USSR)," *Voprosy istorii,* Vol. 1952, No. 9 (dated September, published in October), pp. 3–16.
Among other things, Soviet historians confess their mistakes in the light of Bagirov's criticism at the Nineteenth Party Congress.

Editorial. "Za glubokoe nauchnoe izuchenie istorii ukrainskogo naroda (For a Deep Scholarly Study of the History of the Ukrainian People)," *Voprosy istorii,* Vol. 1955, No. 7 (July), pp. 3–10.
Important; reveals some changes in atmosphere after Stalin's death.

Editorial. "Za tisny zv''yazok ideolohichnoyi i orhanizators'koyi roboty (For a Close Link between Ideological and Organizational Work)," *Komunist Ukrayiny* (Ukr. ed.), Vol. 1962, No. 8 (August), pp. 7–14.
Report on the Central Committee of the Communist Party of Ukraine plenum of August 1962.

Editorial. "Zadachi Gosplana SSSR v novykh usloviyakh upravleniya promyshlennost'yu i stroitel'stvom (The Tasks of the USSR Gosplan in the New Conditions of Administering Industry and Construction)," *Planovoe Khozaystvo* (Planned Economy, Moscow), Vol. 1957, No. 7 (July), pp. 3–11.
Important details.

Enevich, F. "Ser'eznye nedostatki zhurnala 'Kommunist Ukrainy' (Serious Deficiencies of the Journal *Kommunist Ukrainy*)," *Kommunist* (Moscow), Vol. 1952, No. 20 (November), pp. 108–13.

Good illustration of the anti-Ukrainian course in late 1952, early 1953.

Eremin, I. P. Review of *Istoriya ukrayins'koyi literatury*, Vol. I, by Akademiya nauk URSR, Institut literatury im. T. H. Shevchenka. *Vestnik Akademii Nauk SSSR* (Bulletin of the USSR Academy of Sciences, Moscow), Vol. 1955, No. 10 (October), pp. 105–06.

Outstanding.

Evseev, I. F.—see Yevsyeyev, I. F.

Fadeev, A. "O literaturnoy kritike (On Literary Criticism)," *Bol'shevik*, Vol. 1947, No. 13 (July), pp. 20–35.

"Zhdanovshchina" applied.

Gafurov, B. "Uspekhy natsional'noy politiki KPSS i nekotorye voprosy internatsional'nogo vospitaniya (Successes of the Communist Party of the Soviet Union Nationality Policy and Some Questions of Internationalist Education)," *Kommunist* (Moscow), Vol. 1958, No. 11 (August), pp. 10–24.

Extremely important programmatical piece signifying a radical change in Soviet nationality policy. Later re-issued as a pamphlet.

Gerhard, Jan [Col. of General Staff]. "Dalsze szczegóły walk z bandami UPA i WIN na południowo wschodnim obszarze Polski (Further Details on Actions against the UPA and WIN Bands in the Southeastern Area of Poland)," *Wojskowy przegląd historyczny*, Vol. IV, No. 4 (November–December, 1959), pp. 304–35.

Very important analytical study.

Il'ichev, L. "K novomu pod"emu ideologicheskoy raboty (Towards a Higher Level of Ideological Work)," *Kommunist* (Moscow), Vol. 1960, No. 14 (September), pp. 22–40.

An important statement by the Central Committee of Communist Party of the Soviet Union Secretary for ideology (in 1961).

Ivanchenko, A. V., co-author—see Barabash, N. I.

Ivasyuta, M. K. "Sotsialistychna perebudova sil's'koho hospodarstva v zakhidnykh oblastyakh Ukrayins'koyi RSR (Socialist Reconstruction of Agriculture in the Western Provinces of the Ukrainian SSR)," *Ukr. ist. zhurnal*, Vol. 1959, No. 4 (July–August), pp. 3–13.

Some valuable figures.

Kalnberzin, Ya. [Secretary of the Central Committee of the Communist Party of Latvia]. "Vospitanie trudyashchykhsya v dukhe druzhby narodov (Educating the Toilers in the Spirit of Friendship of Peoples)," *Kommunist* (Moscow), Vol. 1955, No. 15 (October), pp. 26–41.

Contains strictures against Russian chauvinism in such a form as to reveal a slight shift in nationality policy.

Karklina, N. I. "Osnovnye voprosy bibliotechnoy raboty v resheniyakh Kommunisticheskoy partii Sovetskogo Soyuza i Sovetskogo pravitel'stva 1917–1957 (Fundamental Questions of Library Work in the Decisions of the CPSU and Soviet Government, 1917–1957)," in RSFSR [Russian Republic] Ministry of Culture, *Bibliotechnoe delo v SSSR* . . . , pp. 25–68.

Some interesting figures on Soviet reading habits. See also Bibliography, Section II, A, above.

Khrushchev, Nikita S. "Osvobodezhdenie ukrainskykh zemel' ot nemetskikh zakhvatchikov i vosstanovlenie narodnogo khozaystva Sovetskoy Ukrainy (Liberation of Ukrainian Lands from German Aggressors and the Immediate Tasks of Reconstructing the National Economy of Soviet Ukraine)," *Bol'shevik,* Vol. 1944, No. 6 (March), pp. 7–35.

Abridged stenographic report of a very important speech.

Khylyuk, F. "Perestroyka upravleniya promyshlennost'yu i voprosy kooperirovaniya proizvodstva (Ukrainskaya SSR) (Changes in the Administration of Industry and Problems of Productive Cooperation: UkrSSR)," *Planovoe khozaystvo* (Planned Economy, Moscow), Vol. 1957, No. 9 (September), pp. 73–79.

Good factual account of the inefficiencies prevailing under the former system.

Kiperman, S. A. "Z dosvidu vyvchennya zovnishn'oyi polityky Ukrayins'koyi RSR na urokakh istoriyi SRSR i novitn'oyi istoriyi (From [Our] Experience of Studying the Foreign Policy of the UkrSSR in Lessons of USSR History and Modern History)," *Ukr. ist. zhurnal,* Vol. 1959, No. 4 (September–October), pp. 116–20.

Interesting suggestions on an unusual subject.

Klokov, V. I., co-author—see Bilousov, M. M.

Kol'chuk, A. M. "Bahato halasy daremno (Much Ado About Nothing)," *Ukr. ist. zhurnal,* Vol. 1961, No. 3 (May–June), pp. 140–41.

Bitter detailed polemics with Ukrainian historians now living in the West who attended the International Historical Congress in Stockholm.

Korets'ky, V. M. "Rozkvit suverenitetu ukrayins'koyi radyans'koyi sotsialistychnoyi derzhavy v skladi SSSR (Growth of the Sovereignty of the Ukr. Socialist Republic as a Part of the USSR)," in Akademiya nauk URSR (Ukrainian SSR Academy of Sciences), *Visnyk* (Bulletin), Vol. 1954, No. 8 (August), pp. 3–13.

Legalistic argument by a prominent international lawyer, since 1961 a member of the International Court of Justice.

Korniychuk, Aleksander. "Kryl'ya" (The Wings), *Novy mir* (New World, Moscow), Vol. 1954, No. 11 (November), pp. 3–50.

A play on the Party after Stalin's death.

———. "Chomu khvylyuyet'sya Vatykan (What Is the Vatican So Excited About)," *Suchasne i maybutnye* (Present and Future, Kiev), Vol. 1946, No. 1 (January), pp. 4–5.

Korotchenko, D. "V bratskoy sem'e sovetskikh narodov—k kommunizmu (In the Fraternal Family of Soviet Nations—Towards Communism)," *Kommunist Ukrainy* (Rus. ed.), Vol. 1962, No. 12 (December), pp. 26–36.

Koval'chak, H. I. "Industrializatsiya Zakhidnykh Oblastey Ukrayins'koyi RSR (Industrialization of the Western Provinces of the UkrSSR)," *Ukr. ist. zhurnal*, Vol. 1959, No. 6 (November–December), pp. 3–12.
  Some interesting figures.

Kravtsev, I. " 'Natsional'ny komunizm'—ideolohichna dyversiya imperializmu ta yoho ahentury v robitnychomu rusi ("National Communism" Is an Ideological Diversion of Imperialism and Its Agents in the Workers Movement)," *Komunist Ukrayiny* (Ukr. ed.), Vol. 1957, No. 7 (July), pp. 26–36.
  While the bulk of the article decries the "revisionist" heresy in Eastern Europe, the last pages contain a warning to Ukrainian Communists.

Kuchkin, A. P. "Korenizatsiya sovetskogo apparata v Kazakhstane v pervoe desyatiletie sushchestvovaniya respubliki, 1920–1930 gg. (Rooting of the Soviet Apparatus in Kazakhstan in the First Decade of the Existence of the Republic, 1920–1930)," *Istoricheskie zapiski* (Historical Notes, Moscow), Vol. 48 (1954), pp. 202–27.
  Rationalizes so-called functional *korenizatsiya*.

Kurishkov, E. (Ye.) L. "Pro mizhnarodne predstavnytsvo Ukrayins'koyi RSR (International Representation of the UkrSSR)," in Akademiya nauk URSR, *Visnyk,* Vol. 1954, No. 5 (May), pp. 46–56.
  Important.

Kyrylyuk, Ye. P. "Zavdannya radyans'koho shevchenkoznavstva v pidhotovtsi do 150-richchya vid dnya narodzhennya velykoho poeta (Tasks of Soviet Shevchenko Studies in Preparation for the 150th Anniversary of the Great Poet's Birth)," in Akademiya nauk URSR, Instytut literatury im. T. H. Shevchenka, *Zbirnyk prats' vos'moyi naukovoyi shevchenkivs'koyi konferentsiyi,* pp. 9–32.
  Important paper delivered in 1959. See also Bibliography, Section II, A, above.

Lavrov, Yu. P., and L. A. Shevchenko. "Obhovorennya rukopysu pidruchnyka z istoriyi Ukrayiny dlya seredn'oyi shkoly (Discussion on the Manuscript of the Secondary School Textbook in Ukrainian History)," *Ukr. ist. zhurnal*, Vol. 1959, No. 5 (September–October), pp. 114–16.
  The book was published as late as 1962.

Lenin, V. I. "K voprosy o natsional'nostyakh ili ob 'avtonomizatsii' (On the Nationality Question or on "Autonomization")," *Kommunist*, Vol. 1956, No. 9 (June), pp. 22–26; or *Kommunist Ukrainy* (Rus. ed.), Vol. 1956, No. 7 (July), pp. 19–23.

Publication of Lenin's notes of December 30–31, 1922, was intended as a demonstration that in changing the nationality policy in 1954–56 Khrushchev followed in the footsteps of Lenin. Notes are directed against Stalin. See also the commentary in Prosyanyk, below.

Leshchenko, L. O. "Z istoriyi rozvyazannya dunays'koyi problemy (From the History of the Solution of the Danube Question)," *Ukr. ist. zhurnal*, Vol. 1961, No. 6 (November–December), pp. 60–69.

Solid research article on the participation by the Ukrainian SSR at the Danube Conference of 1948.

———. " 'Proloh' chy epiloh?" ("Prologue" or Epilogue), *Ukr. ist. zhurnal*, Vol. 1958, No. 6 (November–December), pp. 136–40.

Polemics with *Prologue*, of New York.

Lomidze, G., co-author—see Metchenko, A.

Lysenko, M. M. [Director in Charge of the Section of Historical Methodology of the Ukrainian SSR Scientific Research Institute of Pedagogy]. "Perebuduvaty vykladannya istoriyi v seredniy shkoli u svitli rishen' XX z"yizdu KPRS (Change the Teaching of History in Ten-Year-Schools in the Light of the Decisions of the Twentieth Party Congress)," *Radyans'ka shkola*, Vol. 1956, No. 10 (October), pp. 8–16.

Very important article.

———. "Vyvchennya temy 'Ukrayins'ki zemli v XIV–XV st.' v elementarnomu kursi istoriyi SRSR i URSR v VII klasi vos'myrichnoyi shkoly (Studying the Topic "Ukrainian Lands in the XIV–XV Centuries" during the Basic Course of USSR and Ukrainian SSR History in Grade VII of the Eight-Year School)," *Ukr. ist. zhurnal*, Vol. 1961, No. 5 (September–October), pp. 101–05.

A significant retreat from his 1956 demands.

——— and I. M. Skrypkin. "Perebuduvaty vykladannya istoriyi v shkoli v svitli perspektyv komunistychnoho budivnytsva (Change the Teaching of History at School in the Light of the Perspectives of Communist Construction)," *Ukr. ist. zhurnal*, Vol. 1958, No. 6 (November–December), pp. 94–102.

Demands of 1956 toned down a little.

Lytvyn, K. "Ob istorii ukrainskogo naroda (On the History of the Ukrainian People)," *Bol'shevik*, Vol. 1947, No. 7 (April), pp. 41–56.

Indispensable programmatic article. Lytvyn was then Secretary of the Central Committee of the Communist Party (Bolshevik) of Ukraine in charge of ideology.

———. "Mezhdunarodnye kul'turnye svyazi Sovetskoy Ukrainy (International Cultural Ties of Soviet Ukraine)," *Kommunist Ukrainy* (Rus. ed.), Vol. 1957, No. 12 (December), pp. 67–77.

Informative.

Maksimov, H., and M. Marakhanov. "Vsesoyuznaya perepis' naseleniya 1959 g. (The All-Union Population Census of 1959)," *Voprosy ekonomiki* (Problems of Economics, Moscow), Vol. 1958, No. 9 (September), pp. 49–59.

Relatively little information.

Manuil's'ky, D. Z. "Ukrayins'ko-nimets'ki natsionalisty na sluzhbi u fashysts'koyi Nimechchyny (Ukrainian-German Nationalists in the Service of Fascist Germany)," in [Ukrainian SSR], *Kalendar dovidnyk na 1945 r.*, pp. 181–84.

Important speech to West Ukrainian teachers, of January 6, 1945. See also Section II, A, for full citation of book.

Marakhanov, M., co-author—see Maksimov, H.

Marchenko, M. I. "Pohlyady T. H. Shevchenka na istorychne mynule ukrayins'koho narodu (Shevchenko's Views on the Historical Past of the Ukrainian People)," *Ukr. ist. zhurnal,* Vol. 1961, No. 1 (January–February), pp. 84–94.

Continuing falsification on the popular level.

Men'shykov, V. "Efektyvnist' spetsializatsiyi ta kooperuvannya v promyslovosti kyyivs'koho ekonomichnoho rayonu (The Efficacy of Specialization and Cooperation in the Industry of the Kiev Economic Region)," *Ekonomika Radyans'koyi Ukrayiny* (The Economy of Soviet Ukraine, Kiev), Vol. 1960, No. 6 (November–December), pp. 89–92.

Enlightening details.

Metchenko, A., Dement'ev, A., and G. Lomidze. "Za glubokuyu razrabotku istorii sovetskoyi literatury (For a Deep Working Out of the History of Soviet Literature)," *Kommunist,* Vol. 1956, No. 12 (August), pp. 86–100.

Among other things, rehabilitation of Sosyura's "Love the Ukraine."

Mstyslavets', O. "Tavrovani zradnyky (Branded Traitors)," *Radyans'ky Lviv* (Soviet Lviv), Vol. 1947, No. 1, pp. 56–61.

Polemics with the underground.

Naulko, V. I. "Sovremenny etnicheskiy sostav naseleniya Ukrainskoy SSR (Contemporary Ethnic Composition of the Population of the Ukrainian SSR)," *Sovetskaya etnografiya* (Soviet Ethnography, Moscow), Vol. 1963, No. 5 (September–October), pp. 46–59.

Solid professional article, obtained while this book was in print.

Nechkina, M. "K voprosu o formule 'naymen'shee zlo': Pis'mo v redaktsiyu (On the Problem of the "Lesser Evil" Formula: Letter to the Editor)," *Voprosy istorii,* Vol. 1951, No. 4 (April), pp. 44–48.

Very important.

Nesterenko, A. "Rol' Ukrainskoy SSR v sozdanii material'no-tekhniche-skoy bazy kommunizma (Role of the UkrSSR in Establishing the Material-Technological Base of Communism)," *Ekonomika Sovetskoy Ukrainy* (The Economy of Soviet Ukraine, Kiev), Vol. 1961, No. 6 (November–December), pp. 19–24.

An interesting prognosis.

Nikolayenko, V. Yu. "Shlyakhom zdiysnennya lenins'kykh pryntsypiv narodnoyi osvity (Fulfilling the Leninist Principles of Popular Education)," *Radyans'ka shkola,* Vol. 1957, No. 4 (April), pp. 5ff.

Novichenko, L. " 'Nash sovremennik': K 100-letiyu so dnya smerti T. H. Shevchenko ('Our Contemporary': On the Occasion of the 100th Anniversary of the Death of T. H. Shevchenko)," *Kommunist,* Vol. 1961, No. 4 (March), pp. 61–67.

Novykov, A. I. "Vykhovannya trudyashchykh u dusi druzhby narodiv i sotsialistychnoho internatsionalizmu na suchasnomu etapi (Education of Toilers in the Spirit of Friendship of Peoples and Socialist Internationalism at the Present Stage [of Communist Construction])," *Ukr. ist. zhurnal,* Vol. 1961, No. 5 (November–December), pp. 21–28.

Apparently a report on the activity of the Ukrainian Association for the Dissemination of Political and Scientific Subjects.

Pankratova, A. "Nasushchnye voprosy sovetskoy istoricheskoy nauki (Urgent Tasks of Soviet Historical Science)," *Kommunist,* Vol. 1953, No. 6 (April), pp. 55–69.

Revealing programmatical article.

Pidluts'ky, H. I. "Vyvchennya pytan' istoriyi Ukrayiny XVIII st. u 7 klasi vos'myrichnoyi shkoly (Teaching Problems in the History of the Ukraine in the Eighteenth Century in Grade VII of the Eight-Year School)," *Ukr. ist. zhurnal,* Vol. 1961, No. 6 (November–December), pp. 88–93.

Pisarev, I. "Naselenie strany sotsializma: K itogam perepisi 1939 g. (Population of the Country of Socialism: The Results of the 1939 Census)," *Planovoe khozaystvo,* Vol. 1940, No. 5 (May), pp. 12–21.

Poltoratskiy, L. "Stsenariy o lyudyakh Karpat (A Screenplay on the People from the Carpathians)," *Iskusstvo kino* (Film Art, Moscow), Vol. 1954, No. 5 (May), pp. 73–78.

A fairly detailed review of a film depicting the "socialist transformations" in Western Ukraine, including the fight with the underground.

Ponarovs'ka, H. I. "Pro vykladannya rosiys'koyi movy v pochatkoviy shkoli z ukrayins'koyu movoyu navchannya (Teaching Russian in Elementary Schools with Ukrainian as the Language of Instruction)," *Radyans'ka shkola,* Vol. 1947, No. 1 (January–February), pp. 32–36.

Some figures not available elsewhere.

Prosyanyk, O. "V. I. Lenin pro yednist' diy i bratnyu druzhbu ukrayins'koho i rosiys'koho narodiv (V. I. Lenin on the Unity of Action and the Fraternal Friendship of the Ukrainian and Russian Peoples)," *Komunist Ukrayiny* (Ukr. ed.), Vol. 1957, No. 10 (October), pp. 14–24.

Re-issuing of a work of Lenin's taken as a vantage point for a discussion of nationality policy.

Puns'ky, V. O. "Pro shlyakhy perebudovy vykladannya istoriyi v seredniy shkoli (On the Paths of Reorganizing the Teaching of History in Ten-Year Schools)," *Ukr. ist. zhurnal*, Vol. 1959, No. 5 (September–October), pp. 107–10.

Compare the rejoinder by I. F. Chernikov, above.

Poznyak, V. T., co-author—see Buts'ko, M. O.

Pustokhod, P. I. "Z istoriyi perepysiv naselennya v SRSR (From the History of Population Censuses in the USSR)," *Ukr. ist. zhurnal*, Vol. 1959, No. 1 (January–February), pp. 51–62.

A brief historical survey skirting controversial problems.

Ryl's'ky, Maksym. "Poeticheskoe mirovozzrenie Shevchenka (Shevchenko's Poetical *Weltanschauung*)," *Kommunist Ukrainy* (Rus. ed.), Vol. 1961, No. 2 (February), pp. 57–64.

Important article by Soviet Ukraine's foremost poet.

———. "V sem'e vol'noy, novoy (In a Free and New Family [of Nations])," *Kommunist Ukrainy* (Rus. ed.), Vol. 1962, No. 12 (December), pp. 45–47.

Fairly outspoken polemics with assimilationists, esp. A. Agaev's "V sem'e vol'noy, novoy," *Izvestiya*, Dec. 5, 1961, p. 4.

Ryzhkov, I., and O. Shkuratov. "Pytannya rozvytku lehkoyi promyslovosty (Problems of the Development of Light Industry)," *Ekonomika radyans'koyi Ukrayiny*, Vol. 1962, No. 1 (January–February), pp. 33–39.

Good article on a neglected aspect of industrial development.

Sanov, Lazar. "Suchasny heroy i pochuttya novoho (The Contemporary Hero and the Feeling of the New)," *Vitchyzna*, Vol. 1946, No. 7/8 (July/August), pp. 255–65.

Useful on the ideological purge of literature.

Sas, I. Kh. "Vysvitlennya sotsialistychnoho budivnytstva v zakhidnykh oblastyakh Ukrayins'koyi RSR (Presentation of Socialist Construction in the Western Provinces of the UkrSSR)," *Ukr. ist. zhurnal*, Vol. 1960, No. 4 (July–August), pp. 102–09.

Sautin, I. "Naselenie strany sotsializma (Population of the Country of Socialism)," *Bol'shevik*, Vol. 1940, No. 10 (May), pp. 12–22.

Savchenko, V. S. "Ukrayins'ki burzhuazni natsionalisty na sluzhbi amerykans'koho imperializmu (Ukrainian Bourgeois Nationalists in the Service of American Imperialism)," *Ukr. ist. zhurnal*, Vol. 1957, No. 3 (November–December), pp. 138–46.

Polemic with Ukrainian-American publications (*Ukr. Quarterly*).

Serov, V. V. "Organizatsiya bibliotechnogo obsluzhyvaniya sel'skogo naseleniya SSSR (The Organization of Library Service for the Rural Population of the USSR)," in RSFSR, Ministerstvo kul'tury, *Bibliotechnoe delo v SSSR*, pp. 201–37.

See Section II, A, above, for full citation of book.

Shakhovs'ky, S. "Shevchenko i rosiys'ka literatura (Sh. and Russian Literature)," in Akademiya nauk URSR, *Pam"yati T. H. Shevchenka* . . . , pp. 261–96.

Fairly well documented. See also Section II, A, above.

Sherstyuk, F. Yu. "Vykryttya i rozhrom komunistychnoyu partiyeyu Ukrayiny natsionalistychnoho ukhylu v 1926–1928 rr. (Discovery and Destruction by the Communist Party of Ukraine of the Nationalist Deviation in 1926–28)," *Ukr. ist. zhurnal*, Vol. 1958, No. 3 (May–June), pp. 73–82.

Shevchenko, L. A., co-author—see Lavrov, Yu. P.

Shkuratov, O., co-author—see Ryzhkov, I.

Shlepakov, A. M. "Anhlo-amerykans'ka burzhuazna istoriohrafiya pro vozz"yednannya ukrayins'koho narodu v yedyniy ukrayins'kiy radyans'kiy derzhavi (Anglo-American Bourgeois Historiography on the Reunification of the Ukrainian People in a Single Ukrainian Soviet State)," *Ukr. ist. zhurnal*, Vol. 1957, No. 2 (September–October), pp. 118–22.

Skaba, A. "Zadachi ideologicheskoy raboty v svete resheniy XXII s"yezda KPSS (Tasks of Ideological Work in the Light of the Decisions of the Twenty-Second Congress of the Communist Party of the Soviet Union), *Kommunist Ukrainy* (Rus. ed.), Vol. 1962, No. 3 (March), pp. 10–22.

Important article by the Secretary of the Central Committee of the Communist Party of Ukraine in charge of ideology.

Skrypkin, I. M., co-author—see Lysenko, M. M.

Skrypnychenko, Yu. "Reaktsiyni pidstupy Vatykana proty slovyans'kykh narodiv (Reactionary Wiles of the Vatican against Slavic Peoples)," *Suchasne i maybutnye* (Present and Future, Kiev), Vol. 1945, No. 10 (December), pp. 21–29.

Slipchenko, V. A. "KP(b)U—orhanizator rozhromu kurkul's'ko-natsionalistychnoyi kontrrevolyutsiyi v 1921–23 rr (Communist Party (Bolshevik) of Ukraine—the Organizer of the Destruction of the *Kulak*-Nationalist Counterrevolution in 1921–23)," in Ukrainian SSR, Ministerstvo vyshchoyi osvity, *Naukovi pratsi kafedr suspil'nykh nauk vuziv m. Kyyeva*, vypusk 2, pp. 73–90.

Fairly well-documented article on an important subject. See Section II, A, above, for full citation of symposium.

Slyn'ko, I. I. "Nepokhytna yednist' ukrayins'koho narodu v borot'bi proty nimets'ko-fashysts'kykh zaharbnykiv (Unshakeable Unity of the

Ukrainian People in the Struggle against the Germano-Fascist Aggressors)," *Ukr. ist. zhurnal,* Vol. 1959, No. 4 (July–August), pp. 53–64.

Lengthy polemics with Western historians who found that Ukrainians temporarily favored the Nazis over the Communists in World War II.

Strel'skiy, V. "Ideynoe vospitanie naroda i sovetskaya istoricheskaya nauka: Zametki prepodavatelya istorii (The Ideological Education of the People and Soviet Historical Science: Notes of a History Teacher)," *Kommunist Ukrainy* (Rus. ed.), Vol. 1962, No. 3 (March), pp. 41–49.

Suprunenko, N. "K voprosu ob izuchenii istorii grazhdanskoy voyny na Ukraine (On the Question of Studying the History of the Civil War in the Ukraine)," *Kommunist Ukrainy* (Rus. ed.), Vol. 1956, No. 10 (October), pp. 23–31.

Very important article charging that under Stalin distortions had been committed.

Symonenko, P. "Kto zhe nuzhdaetsya v osvobodezhdenii? (Who Does Need Liberation?)," *Kommunist Ukrainy* (Rus. ed.), Vol. 1961, No. 2 (February), pp. 82–88.

Contra Prime Minister Diefenbaker of Canada and Ukrainian exiles.

Symonenko, R. H. "Proty burzhuazno-natsionalistychnykh fal'syfikatsiy istoriyi Ukrayiny (Against Bourgeois-Nationalist Falsifications of the History of the Ukraine)," *Ukr. ist. zhurnal,* Vol. 1958, No. 3 (May–June), pp. 158–62.

———. "Fal'sifikatorskie uprazhneniya zaokeanskikh istorikov (Falsification Exercises of Historians from Behind the [Atlantic] Ocean)," *Kommunist Ukrainy* (Rus. ed.), Vol. 1961, No. 1 (January), pp. 55–66.

Taranenko, V. M. "Uchast' trudyashchykh Ukrayiny v osvoyenni tsilynnykh ta perelohovykh zemel' (1954–1956) (Participation of the Toilers of Ukraine in the Cultivation of Virgin and Fallow Lands, 1954–1956)," *Ukr. ist. zhurnal,* Vol. 1959, No. 6 (November–December), pp. 46–55.

Shuns total figures like the plague.

Traynin, I. "Voprosy suvereniteta v sovetskom soyuznom gosudarstve (The Problem of Sovereignty in the Soviet Federal State)," *Bol'shevik,* Vol. 1945, No. 15 (August), pp. 12–23.

Useful.

Ul'yanova, N. M. "Uchast' Ukrayins'koyi RSR v Mizhnarodniy Orhanizatsiyi Pratsi (Participation of the Ukrainian SSR in ILO)," in Akademiya nauk URSR, Sektor derzhavy i prava, (Ukrainian SSR Academy of Sciences, Division of Political Science and Law), *Narysy z istoriyi derzhavy i prava Ukrayins'koyi RSR,* pp. 197–225.

Solidly documented research article. See Section II, A, above, for full citation of symposium.

Vash, I. (Secy. of the Transcarpathian Province Party Committee). "Ve-
lyki peretvorennya (Great Transformations)," *Komunist Ukrayiny*
(Ukr. ed.), Vol. 1955, No. 6 (June), pp. 13–21.

Vershyhora (Vershigora), P. "Brat'ya po oruzhiyu: O narodnykh formakh
vooruzhennoy bor'by russkogo i ukrainskogo narodov (Comrades in
Arms: Popular Forms of Armed Struggle of the Russian and Ukrainian Peoples)," *Oktyabr'* (October, Moscow), Vol. 1954, No. 3 (March),
pp. 144–63; No. 4 (April), pp. 110–36; No. 5 (May), pp. 129–62.

   A usual article with a single unusual footnote (No. 4, p. 118).

Vorob'ev, I. "Razvitie natsional'nykh otnosheniy v period stroitel'stva
kommunizma (Development of Nationality Relations in the Period of
the Construction of Communism)," *Kommunist Ukrainy* (Rus. ed.),
Vol. 1962, No. 1 (January), pp. 33–42.

   Useful.

Voyna, O. D. "Pro deyaki suchasni fal'syfikatsiyi istoriyi radyans'koyi
Ukrayiny v burzhuazniy istorychniy literaturi (About Some Contemporary Falsifications of the History of Soviet Ukraine in Bourgeois Historical Literature)," *Ukr. ist. zhurnal*, Vol. 1957, No. 1 (July–August),
pp. 137–42.

Yakovlev, N. "O prepodavanii otechestvennoy istorii (Teaching the History of the Fatherland)," *Bol'shevik*, Vol. 1947, No. 22 (November), pp.
26–37.

   Very important programmatical article.

Yemel'yanenko (Emel'yanenko), G. "Leninskie printsipy natsional'noy
politiki KPSS (Leninist Principles of the Communist Party of the Soviet Union Nationality Policy)," *Kommunist Ukrainy* (Rus. ed.), Vol.
1956, No. 10 (October), pp. 49–61.

   Representative illustration of the policy immediately after the Twentieth Party Congress.

Yevsyeyev, I. F. "Narodni komitety Zakarpats'koyi Ukrayiny (People's
Committees of Transcarpathian Ukraine)," in Akademiya nauk URSR,
Sektor derzhavy i prava (Ukrainian SSR Academy of Sciences, Division
of Political Science and Law), *Naukovi zapysky* (Learned Notes), Vol.
1952, No. 1, pp. 206–67.

   Later published as *Narodnye komitety Zakarpatskoy Ukrainy—organy gosudarstvennoy vlasti, 1944–1945* (Moscow, 1954). Legalism at its
driest.

———. "Zliysny naklep pid vyhlyadom naukovoyi pratsi (Evil Slander
Masquerading as Scholarly Work)," *Ukr. ist. zhurnal*, Vol. 1958, No. 4
(July–August), pp. 157–61.

   An unbalanced mixture of praise and criticism of Markus' French
book on the Transcarpathian Ukraine.

———. "Vazhlyva forma spivrobitnytstva narodiv Ukrayiny i Pol'shchi (An Important Form of Cooperation between the Ukrainian and Polish Peoples)," *Ukr. ist. zhurnal,* Vol. 1961, No. 5 (September–October), pp. 87–96.

Cultural cooperation. In 1962 published in book form.

Zalyevs'ky, A. D. "Rozhrom kurkul's'ko-natsionalistychnoho bandytyzmu na Ukrayini (1921–1922 rr.) (Destruction of the *Kurkul*-Nationalist Bands in the Ukraine, 1921–22)," *Ukr. ist. zhurnal,* Vol. 1959, No. 4 (July–August), pp. 90–98.

Rather outspoken analysis, well documented.

Zhdanov, Andrey A. "O zhurnalakh *Zvezda* i *Leningrad* (Concerning the Journals *Zvezda* i *Leningrad*)," *Bol'shevik,* Vol. 1946, No. 17/18 (September), pp. 4–19.

Essential.

Zhdanov, Nikolay. "A Trip Home," *Literaturnaya Moskva* (Literary Moscow), Vol. 1956, No. 2.

A very revealing short story, which has been subsequently condemned. I have read it only in translation—see Edmund Stillman (ed.), *Bitter Harvest,* pp. 177–89.

B. OTHER

Bilinsky, Yaroslav. "The Ukrainian SSR in International Affairs after World War II," *The Annals of the Ukrainian Academy of Arts and Sciences in United States,* Vol. IX, No. 1–2 (1961), pp. 147–66.

———. "The Soviet Education Laws of 1958–9 and Soviet Nationality Policy," *Soviet Studies,* Vol. XIV (October, 1962), pp. 138–57.

Black, Cyril E. "History and Politics in the Soviet Union," in Black (ed.), *Rewriting Russian History . . . ,* pp. 3–31.

———. Review of *Istoriya SSR: Ukazatel' sovetskoy literatury za 1917–52 gg. . . . ,* by Akademiya nauk SSSR—Fundamental'naya biblioteka obshchestvennykh nauk, *The American Historical Review,* Vol. LXIII (October, 1957), p. 129.

Chubenko, O. "Reyestratsiya movnoyi i natsional'noyi oznaky v perepysi 1926 r. (Registration of Language and Nationality in the 1926 Census)," in T. Olesiyevych *et al., Ukrains'ka lyudnist' SSSR* [See Bib. II, B], pp. 85–105.

Useful.

Cizevsky, Dmitry. Review of Vol. I of the *Istoriya ukrayins'koyi literatury* (History of Ukrainian Literature), by Akademiya nauk URSR, Instytut literatury im. T. H. Shevchenka, in *The Annals of the Ukrainian Academy of Arts and Sciences in the US,* Vol. IV (Winter–Spring, 1955), pp. 1035–40.

Stringent, but just.

Claude, Inis L., co-author—see Emerson, Rupert.

Doroshenko, Dmytro. "Mykhailo Dragomanov and the Ukrainian National Movement." *Slavonic and East European Review*, Vol. XVI (April, 1938), pp. 654–66.

    Essential for an understanding of the Eastern Ukrainian movement.

Doroshenko, Volodymyr. "Yak strinuly Shevchenkovi poeziyi ukrayintsi i moskali (How Were Shevchenko's Poems Received by the Ukrainians and the Muscovites)," *Kyiw* (Kiev, Philadelphia), Vol. VI (March–August, 1955), pp. 58–64; 114–18; and 175–80.

    Useful.

Dovhal, S. "A Fight for the Language," *Problems of the Peoples of the USSR* (Munich), No. 18 (June, 1963), p. 47.

    Brief but valuable survey based on little accessible sources.

Emerson, Rupert. "Paradoxes of Asian Nationalism," *Far Eastern Quarterly*, Vol. XIII (February, 1954), pp. 131–42.

    Important for methodology: criticism of some oversimplifications.

———, and Claude, I. L., Jr. "The Soviet Union and the United Nations: An Essay in Interpretation," *International Organization*, Vol. VI (February, 1952), pp. 1–26.

    Valuable.

Fainsod, Merle. "The Communist Party since Stalin," *The Annals of the American Academy of Political and Social Science*, Vol. 303 ([Russia since Stalin: Old Trends and New Problems] January, 1956), pp. 23–36.

    Excellent analytical survey.

Fedynskyj, Jurij. "Sovietization of an Occupied Area through the Medium of the Courts (Northern Bukovina)," *The American Slavic and East European Review*, Vol. XII (February, 1953), pp. 44–56.

Friedman, Philip. "Ukrainian Jewish Relations during the Nazi Occupation," in *YIVO Annual of Jewish Social Science* (YIVO Institute for Jewish Research, New York), Vol. XII (1958/59), pp. 259–96.

    Fully documented study by an eminent Jewish historian.

Goldhagen, Erich. "Communism and Anti-Semitism," *Problems of Communism*, Vol. IX, No. 3 (May–June, 1960), pp. 35–43.

    Valuable scholarly survey article.

Halajczuk, Bohdan T. "The Soviet Ukraine as a Subject of International Law," *The Annals of the Ukrainian Academy of Arts and Sciences in the United States*, Vol. IX, No. 1–2 (1961), pp. 167–88.

    Scholarly discussion.

Hirnyak, Yosyp. "Birth and Death of the Modern Ukrainian Theater," in Martha Bradshaw (ed.), *Soviet Theaters, 1917–47*, pp. 250–338.

Holubnychy, Vsevolod. "The Language of Instruction: An Aspect of the Problems of Nationalities in the Soviet Union," *Horizon* (New York,

Ukrainian Students Review), Vol. II, No. 1/2 (Fall 1956/Spring 1957), pp. 26–37.

Well-documented analytical article.

———. "Inzhenery v Ukrayini (Engineers in Ukraine)," *Visti Ukrayins'kykh Inzheneriv* (Ukrainian Engineering News, New York), Vol. VIII, No. 3–4 (May–August, 1957), pp. 55–59.

Interesting statistical data.

———. "Outline History of the Communist Party of the Ukraine," *The Ukrainian Review* (Munich: Institute for the Study of the USSR), Vol. VI (1958), pp. 68–125.

Extremely useful well-documented survey.

———. "O neopublikovannykh dannykh perepisey naseleniya SSSR (Unpublished Data of Soviet Population Censuses)," *Vestnik instituta po izucheniyu SSSR* (Bulletin of the Institute for the Study of the USSR, Munich), Vol. 1960, No. 2 (34) (April–June), pp. 66–72.

Hrushevsky, Mykhaylo. "The Traditional Scheme of 'Russian' History and Problem of Rational Organization of the History of the Eastern Slavs," *The Annals of the Ukrainian Academy of Art and Sciences in the United States,* Vol. II (Winter, 1952), pp. 355–64.

Extremely important article translated from the *Sbornik statey po slavyanovedeniyu* (Slavic Symposium), Vol. I (St. Petersburg: Imperial Academy of Sciences, 1904).

Hrynioch, Rev. Dr. Ivan. "The Destruction of the Ukrainian Catholic Church in the Soviet Union," *Prologue* (New York), Vol. IV, No. 1–2 (Spring–Summer, 1960), pp. 5–51.

An excellent article by a prominent Catholic authority.

Kosar, S. "Prychynky do istoriyi volyns'koyi partyzanky (Materials for the History of Guerrilla Warfare in Volhynia)," *Orlyk* (Paris), Vol. 1947: No. 1, pp. 10–13; No. 2, pp. 10–12.

Useful detailed account.

Krupnytskyj, Borys. "Bohdan Khmel'nyts'ky i sovyets'ka istoriohrafiya (B. Kh. and Soviet Historiography)," *Ukrayins'ky zbirnyk* (Ukrainian Review, Munich: Institute for the Study of the USSR, 1955), No. 3, pp. 82–99. (Mimeographed.)

Valuable survey.

———. "M. Hrushevsky i yoho istorychna pratsya (M. Hrushevsky and His Historical Work)," in Hrushevsky, *Istoriya Ukrainy-Rusy,* Vol. I (2nd ed., New York: Knyhospilka, 1954–58), pp. 1–30.

Valuable appraisal.

Kubiyovych, Volodymyr. "Natsional'ny sklad naselennya radyans'koyi Ukrayiny v svitli sovyets'kykh perepysiv z 17.12.1926 i 15.1.1959 (National Composition of the Population of Soviet Ukraine in the Light of Soviet Censuses of 12/17/1926 and 1/15/1959)," in *Zapysky NTSh*

(Shevchenko Scientific Society Notes), Vol. CLXIX (1962), pp. 1–16 (in reprint).

Analysis by a well-known Ukrainian demographer now living in the West. See also his article in *Ukrayins'ka Literaturna Hazeta.*

Kucera, Jindrich. "Soviet Nationality Policy: The Linguistic Controversy," *Problems of Communism,* Vol. III, No. 2 (March–April, 1954), pp. 24–29.

Valuable article by a professional linguist.

Lavrinenko (Lawrynenko), Ju[rij]. "Moscow Centralism on the Defensive: Stages in Most Recent Developments," *Prologue* (published by Ukrainian exiles in Munich-New York-Cairo), Vol. I, No. 3 (Summer, 1957), pp. 82–101.

Suggestive.

Lewytzkyj, B. "Komunistychna Partiya Ukrainy—1955 rik (Communist Party of Ukraine, 1955)," *Ukrayins'ky zbirnyk* (Ukrainian Review, Munich: Institute for the Study of the USSR), No. 3 (1955), pp. 100–31. (Mimeographed.)

Valuable survey.

——. "Die Sowjetukraine und die europaeischen volksdemokratischen Laender (1958–1960) (Soviet Ukraine and the European People's Democracies, 1958–1960)," *The Annals of the Ukrainian Academy of Arts and Sciences in the United States,* Vol. IX (1961), No. 1–2, pp. 189–200.

An important informative article.

——. "Besonderheiten der sowjetukrainischen Entwicklung (Particular Features of the Soviet Ukrainian Development)," *Osteuropa,* Vol. XI (Oct. 1962), pp. 669–75.

Thought-provoking summary of a major work to be soon published in West Germany.

Lichten, Joseph L. "A Study of Ukrainian-Jewish Relations," *The Annals of the Ukrainian Academy of Arts and Sciences in the United States,* Vol. V (Winter–Spring, 1956), pp. 1160–77.

Essential to supplement Solomon M. Schwarz's book.

Meyer, Peter. "Stalin Follows in Hitler's Footsteps," in Elliott E. Cohen (ed.), *The New Red Anti-Semitism: A Symposium,* pp. 1–18.

Good analysis of the Slansky trial.

Nolde, Boris. "Essays in Russian State Law," *The Annals of the Ukrainian Academy of Arts and Sciences in the United States,* Vol. IV (Winter–Spring, 1955), pp. 873–903.

Excerpt from the third essay entitled "The Unity and Indivisibility of Russia," which originally appeared in his *Ocherki russkogo gosudarstvennogo prava* (St. Petersburg, 1911), was translated into French

under the title *L'Ukraine sous le protectorat russe* (Paris: Payol, 1915).
Outstanding.

Nove, Alec. "The Soviet Industrial Reorganization," in Brumberg (ed.),
Russia under Khrushchev, pp. 189–204.
Valuable.

Odarchenko, Petro. "Poetychna maysternist' T. Shevchenka: v svitli
novykh doslidiv, 1941–1946 rr. (The Poetic Masterfulness of T. Shevchenko: In the Light of New Research, 1941–46)," in Ukrayins'ka
Vil'na Akademiya Nauk v SShA (Ukrainian Academy of Arts and Sciences in the United States), *Shevchenkivs'ky richnyk* (Shevchenko Yearbook), No. 3 (1954), pp. 11–22.
Valuable bibliographical article.

———. "The Struggle for Shevchenko (Shevchenko in Soviet interpretation)," *The Annals of the Ukrainian Academy of Arts and Sciences in
the United States*, Vol. III (Spring, 1954), pp. 824–37.
Excellent survey, based on a 400 pp. MS.

Odarčenko (Odarchenko), Petro. "Ševčenko in Soviet Literary Criticism,"
in Mijakovs'kyj & Shevelov (eds.), *Taras Ševčenko, 1814–1861*, pp. 259–
302.
Indispensable bibliographical article, brings the earlier one up to
date.

Ornstein, Jacob. "Soviet Language Policy: Theory and Practice," *The
Slavic and East European Journal*, Vol. XVII (1959), pp. 1–24.

Pap, Michael. "Soviet Difficulties in the Ukraine," *Review of Politics*,
Vol. XIV (April, 1952), pp. 204–32.
Valuable.

Pipes, Richard. "Muslims of Soviet Central Asia: Trends and Prospects,"
Middle East Journal, Vol. IX (Spring–Summer, 1955), pp. 147–62, 295–
308.
Excellent.

Poltava (pseud.), P. "Kontseptsiya samostiynoyi Ukrayiny i osnovna ten-
dentsiya politychnoho rozvytku suchasnoho svitu (The Conception of
an Independent Ukraine and the Basic Tendency of Political Development in the Present World)," in *Pozytsiyi ukrayins'koho vyzvol'noho
rukhu . . .* , pp. 25–81.
Revealing and apparently authentic statement by a Nationalist Underground leader.

Prokopovych, Vyacheslav. "The Problem of the Juridical Nature of the
Ukraine's Union with Muscovy," *The Annals of the Ukrainian Academy of Arts and Sciences in the United States*, Vol. IV (Winter–Spring,
1955), pp. 917–80.
Essential detailed study of the terms employed in the Treaty.

Pytel', Oleksander. "Natsional'ni vidnosyny na Ukrayini v svitli staty-styky (Relations between the Nationalities in the Ukraine in the Light of Statistics)," in O. T. Olesiyevych *et al., Ukrayins'ka lyudnist' SSSR,* pp. 43–84.
Most valuable.

Reshetar, John A., Jr. "Ukrainian Nationalism and the Orthodox Church," *The American Slavic and East European Review,* Vol. X (February, 1951), pp. 38–49.
Valuable.

———. "National Deviation in the Soviet Union," *The American Slavic and East European Review,* Vol. XII (April, 1953), pp. 162–74.

———. "The Significance of the Soviet Tercentenary of the Pereyaslav Treaty," *The Annals of the Ukrainian Academy of Arts and Sciences in the United States,* Vol. IV (Winter–Spring, 1955), pp. 981–94.
Essential.

Rubinstein, A. Z. "Selected Bibliography of Soviet Works on the United Nations," *American Political Science Review,* Vol. LIV (December, 1960), pp. 985–91.

Rudnytsky, Ivan L. "Two Studies of the Sovietization of Carpatho-Ukraine [Review of *The Soviet Seizure of Subcarpathian Ruthenia,* by F. Nemec & V. Moudry, and *L'Incorporation de l'Ukraine subcar-patique à l'Ukraine soviétique, 1944–1945,* by V. Markus]," *Canadian Slavonic Papers,* Vol. II (1957), pp. 111–17.
Stimulating review article.

Sadovsky, V. "Ohlyad literatury pro ukrayins'ku demohrafiyu (Survey of Literature on Ukrainian Demography)," in T. Olesiyevych *et al., Ukrayins'ka lyudnist' SSSR,* pp. 9–29.
Solid.

Shankowsky, Lew. "Ukrainian Underground Publications in USSR," *Ukrainian Quarterly* (New York), Vol. VIII (Summer, 1952), pp. 225–38.

———. "Ukrayins'ka povstancha armiya (Ukrainian Insurgent Army)," in *Istoriya Ukrayins'koho Viys'ka,* edited by Myron Levyts'ky, pp. 635–832.
Best analytical account on the UPA available, well-documented.

———. "Russia, the Jews and the Ukrainian Liberation Movement," *The Ukrainian Quarterly,* Vol. XVI (Spring & Summer, 1960), pp. 11–25 & 147–63.
Somewhat polemical, but richly documented.

———. "The Effects of the Soviet Nationality Policy in the Light of the 1959 Census and Other Statistical Data," *Prologue* (New York), Vol. V, No. 1–2 (Spring–Summer, 1961), pp. 27–87.
Valuable.

———. "Soviet and Satellite Sources on the Ukrainian Insurgent Army," *The Annals of the Ukrainian Academy of Arts and Sciences in United States,* Vol. IX (1961), No. 1–2, pp. 234–61.

Bibliographical article, indispensable for serious study.

Sherekh (pseud.), Yu. "Prysmerk marryzmu" (The Decline of Marrism), *Novi Dni* (New Days, Toronto), Vol. 1950, No. 6 (July), pp. 8–12.

Scholarly article in popular form by an eminent linguist.

Shevelov, George Y. "The Year 1860 in Ševčenko's Work," in *Taras Ševčenko, 1814–61.* Edited by Mijakovs'kyj, V. & Shevelov, G. Y., pp. 68–106.

Very valuable for the interpretation of the poet's last years.

Shteppa, Konstantin F. "The 'Lesser Evil' Formula," in *Rewriting Russian History* . . . . Edited by Black, C. E., pp. 107–120.

Good survey by a professional historian.

Somerville, Rose M. "Counting Noses in the Soviet Union," *The American Quarterly on the Soviet Union,* No. 3 (November, 1940), pp. 51–73.

Surmach, Yaroslava. "Sketches of Kiev," *Horizon* (New York, Ukrainian Students Review), Vol. II, No. 1/2 (Fall 1956/Spring 1957), pp. 56–64.

Notes by a perceptive visitor to the Ukraine in the summer of 1956.

Weinreich, Uriel. "The Russification of Soviet Minority Languages," *Problems of Communism,* Vol. II (1953), No. 6, pp. 46–57.

Valuable.

Weinstein, Harold B. "Language and Education in the Soviet Ukraine," *Slavonic and East European Review,* Vol. XX (1941), pp. 124–48.

Yakovliv, Andriy. "Bohdan Khmelnyts'ky's Treaty with the Tsar of Muscovy in 1654," *The Annals of the Ukrainian Academy* . . . , Vol. IV (Winter–Spring, 1955), pp. 904–16.

Especially valuable to those to whom Yakovliv's Ukrainian book is not available.

———. "The Reunion of the Ukraine with Russia [Review of *Vossoedinenie Ukrainy s Rossiey* . . . edited by P. P. Gudzenko *et al.*]," *ibid.,* pp. 1002–034.

Excellent.

Zaytsev, Pavlo. "Prozova tvorchist' Shevchenka (Shevchenko's Prose)," in *Tvory,* by T. Shevchenko. Edited by P. Zaytsev. Vol. VII, pp. 297–310.

Valuable article, with bibliography.

———. "Zhandarms'ka otsinka politychnoho znachinnya pershoho 'Kobzarya' (The First *Kobzar* as Evaluated by [Russian] Gendarmes)," *Tvory* (Zaytsev edition), Vol. II, pp. 247–49.

Particularly interesting as a contrast to official Soviet interpretation.

IV. Newspapers

A. SOVIET AND POLISH

Izvestiya (Moscow):

Akhed Agaev. "V sem'e vol'noy, novoy: Zametki o vzaimobogashchenii natsional'nykh kul'tur (In a Free, New Family: Remarks on the Mutual Enrichment of National Cultures)," December 5, 1961, p. 4.

A Daghestani writer praises non-Russians who write their works in Russian. See the veiled critique by Ryl'sky (Section III, A).

Literaturna Hazeta (Literary Gazette, Kiev [semi-weekly organ of the Presidium of the Union of Soviet Writers of Ukraine; renamed *Literaturna Ukrayina* in 1962]):

Pryhara, Maria, and Zabila, Natalia. "Polipshyty Prodazh Knyzhok (To Improve Book Sales)," December 5, 1958, p. 2.

Excellent example of shortage of Ukrainian books (for children).

Literaturna Ukrayina:

Buryak, Borys. "Kharakter i abstraktsiyi (Character and Abstractions)," January 29, 1963, pp. 2, 4.

Spirited and witty polemics with assimilationists.

Nasha kul'tura (Our Culture, Warsaw [a monthly supplement to *Nashe slovo,* immediately below]):

Porkhun, D. "Dolya ridnoyi movy (The Fate of [Our] Native Language)," No. 3 (59) (March 1963), pp. 5–6.

Most revealing.

Nashe slovo (Our Word, Warsaw [organ of the Ukrainians in Poland]).

Shch. M., "Ukrayins'ki istoryky v borot'bi za istorychnu pravdu (Ukrainian Historians in the Struggle for Historical Truth)," No. 16, December 2, 1956, p. 2.

Very revealing article.

Pravda (Moscow):

Editorial. "Protiv ideologicheskikh izvrashcheniy v literature (Against Ideological Distortions in Literature)," July 2, 1951.

Sosyura was not to love the Ukraine as such but only the Soviet Ukraine.

Khrushchev, Nikita S. "Tezisy doklada tov. N. S. Khrushcheva o dal'neyshem sovershenstvovanii organizatsii upravleniya promyshlennost'yu i stroitel'stvom (Comrade Khrushchev's Theses from His Report on Further Improving Organization of the Management of Industry and Construction)," March 30, 1957, pp. 1–4.

For a complete translation see *CDSP,* Vol. IX, No. 13, pp. 3ff.

————. "O dal'neyshem sovershenstvovanii organizatsii upravleniya promyshlennost'yu i stroitel'stvom (On Further Improving Organization of the Management of Industry and Construction)," May 8, 1957, pp. 1–5.

Kosior, S. "Torzhestvo leninsko-stalinskoy natsional'noy politiki (Triumph of the Leninist-Stalinist Nationality Policy)," December 24, 1937.

> Information on the Ukraine in the 1930's.

Mints, I., Academician. "Stranitsy geroicheskoy bor'by ukrainskogo naroda za kommunizm (Pages about the Heroic Struggle of the Ukrainian People for Communism)," July 25, 1962, pp. 2–3; or *CDSP*, Vol. XIV, No. 30, pp. 9–11.

> Review of the outline history of the Communist Party of Ukraine.

Ryl'skiy, Maksim, Sosyura, Vladimir, and Gnat Yura. "Zaupokoynye torzhestva (Memorial Services)," Feb. 25, 1958, p. 4.

> Reprinted from *Radyans'ka Ukrayina*, Feb. 22. A good example of Soviet polemics with Ukrainian "bourgeois nationalists" abroad. Translated in *Digest of the Soviet Ukrainian Press*, Vol. II, No. 5 (March, 1958), pp. 8ff.

Ryl'skiy, M., and M. Bazhan. "Vo imya cheloveka (In the Name of Man)," December 22, 1958, p. 3.

> Among other things, a spirited defense of the Ukrainian language.

Pravda Ukrainy (Truth of Ukraine, Kiev [Russian language daily of the Central Committee of the Communist Party of Ukraine, the Government and Supreme Soviet of the Ukrainian SSR]):

Editorial. "Uluchshit' rukovodstvo razvitiem ekonomiki i kul'tury v zapadnykh oblastyakh Ukrainy (Improve Guidance over the Development of the Economy and Culture in Western Ukraine)," June 26, 1953; p. 1.

> A good example of post-Melnikov "revelations." Complete translation in *CDSP*, Vol. V, No. 24, pp. 17ff.

Shiraev, Yu. "Puti dal'neyshego sblizheniya natsiy v SSSR: besedy o XXI s"yezde KPSS (Paths [Leading to] a Further Rapprochement of the Nations in the USSR: Talks about the Twenty-First Communist Party of the Soviet Union Congress)," July 25, 1959, pp. 2–3.

> Gives the new Party line, decries opposition thereto.

Yemel'yanenko, G. "V druzhbe narodov—nasha sila (In the Friendship of Peoples Lies Our Strength)," July 28, 1956, pp. 2–3.

> See his later article in *Rad. Ukrayina*.

Radyans'ka Ukrayina (Soviet Ukraine, Kiev [Ukrainian daily of the Central Committee of the Communist Party of Ukraine, the Ukrainian SSR Government and Supreme Soviet]):

Halan, Yaroslav. "Natsionalistychni upyri (Nationalist Vampires)," August 14, 1946.

Important polemics against the Ukrainian Insurgent Army.

Karmans'ky, Petro. "Vatykan—natkhnennyk mryakobissya i svitovoyi reaktsiyi (The Vatican Is the Inspirer of Frenzied Obscurantism and of the World Reactionary Movement)," December 9–13, 1952.

Reprint of a pamphlet by the octogenarian poet, extending over several issues.

Koval'ov, S. "Vypravyty pomylky v osvitlenni deyakykh pytan' istoriyi Ukrayiny (Correct the Mistakes in the Elucidation of Some Problems in Ukrainian History)," July 24, 1946; reprinted from *Kul'tura i zhizn'* (Culture and Life, organ of the Propaganda Section of the All-Union Central Party Committee, Moscow), No. 3.

Started the drive against "bourgeois nationalism" in Ukrainian historiography in 1946.

Kravtsev, I. "Komunistychne vykhovannya trudyashchykh (Communist Education of the Toilers)," December 11, 1958, pp. 3–4.

———. "V. I. Lenin pro rosiys'ku i natsional'ni movy nashoyi krayiny (V. I. Lenin on the Russian and the National [i.e., non-Russian] Languages of our Country)," April 13, 1960, pp. 3–4.

Exposition of the new Soviet nationality policy, polemics with its opponents, including those in the Ukraine.

Kyrylyuk, Ye. "Bezsmertya (Immortality)," March 10, 1961, p. 2.

An evaluation of Shevchenko's work, not devoid of clumsy distortions.

Yemel'yanenko, H. "Shlyakhom lenins'koyi druzhby narodiv (Along the Path of Leninist Friendship of Peoples)," March 27, 1959, pp. 3–4.

See his earlier article in *Pravda Ukrainy* for revealing contrast.

Robitnycha Hazeta (Workers Gazette, Kiev [organ of the Ukrainian SSR Trade Unions]):

Kravtsev, I. "Podolannya natsionalistychnykh perezhytkiv—vazhlyve zavdannya internatsional'noho vykhovannya trudyashchykh (Overcoming the Nationalist Survivals Is an Important Task of the Internationalist Education of Toilers)," December 17, 1958, pp. 3–4.

Sovetskaya kul'tura (Soviet Culture, Moscow [Ministry of Culture tri-weekly]).

B. OTHER

Current Digest of the Soviet Press (CDSP).

Digest of the Soviet Ukrainian Press (New York: Prologue; monthly).

A valuable supplement to the *CDSP*.

The Manchester Guardian.

The New York Herald Tribune.

The New York Times.

Suchasna Ukrayina (Ukraine To-day, Munich [bi-weekly published through 1960 by the UHVR (Ukrainian Supreme Liberation Council) group of Ukrainian Nationalists]):

Anonymous. "Nimets'kymy ochyma: sposterezhennya pro povstannya, strukturu i diyi ukrayins'koho pidpillya (Through German Eyes: Observations on the Emergence, the Structure and the Actions of the Ukrainian Underground)," seven installments in Nos. 1/26, 2/27, 4/29, 14/39, 16/41, 21/47, and 22/48 (January 7–October 19, 1952).
    Very important memoirs of a German who had been a high official of the political police in Galicia during the war.

Glowins'ky, Yevhen. "Kryza plyanovoho hospodarstva v SSSR (Crisis of the Planned Economy in the USSR)," May 7, 1957, pp. 5–6.

———. "Shche pro reorhanizatsiyu upravlinnya promyslovistyu (More on the Reorganization of Industrial Administration)," June 2, 1957, pp. 9ff.
    Sober and able analyses.

Ortyns'ky, Lyubomyr. "Zza kolyuchykh zadrotovan' (From Behind the Barbed Wire)," March 21, 1954, p. 4.
    The experiences of a former Soviet prisoner of war, good on postwar Donbas.

Prirva, Yevhen. "V p"yatu richnytsyu likvidatsiyi ukrayins'koyi hreko-katolyts'koyi tserkvy (The Fifth Anniversary of the Liquidation of the Ukrainian Greek Catholic Church)," March 18, 1951, pp. 6–8.

Sherekh (pseud.), Yuriy. "Pryntsypy i etapy bol'shevyts'koyi movnoyi polityky na Ukrayini (Principles and Stages of Bolshevik Linguistic Policy in the Ukraine)," June 29; July 13, 27, 1952.
    Excellent analytical survey.

Stakhiv, Volodymyr P. " 'Viyna z istoriyeyu' tryvaye dali ("The War with History" Continues)," March 2, 1958, p. 1.

Svoboda (Liberty, Jersey City, N.J., daily; Ukrainian nationalist orientation).

The Times (London).

Ukrayins'ka Literaturna Hazeta (Ukrainian Literary Gazette, Munich; monthly supplement to *Suchasna Ukrayina*):

Kubiyovych, Volodymyr. "Natsional'ny sklad naselennya URSR i chyslo ukrayintsiv u svitli perepysu 15.1.1959 (National Composition of the Population of the Ukrainian SSR and the Number of Ukrainians in the Light of the Census of January 15, 1959)," Vol. VI, No. 3 (March, 1960), pp. 1–2.

Valuable. See also author's later symposium article (Section III, B).

Ukrayins'ke zhyttya (Ukrainian Life, Toronto; pro-Communist, reprints Soviet materials).

Ukrayins'ki visti (Ukrainian News, pro-Communist weekly published in New York):

Palamarchuk, L. Kh. (Ukrainian SSR Minister of Foreign Affairs). "Ukrayina v borot'bi za myr (Ukraine in the Struggle for Peace)," December 19, 1957, p. 2.

Vil'ny ukrayins'ky robitnyk (Free Ukrainian Worker, Paris; mimeographed monthly newssheet of the Ukrainian Section of *Force Ouvrière*).

Vpered (Forward, Munich; left socialist monthly that was published by Ukrainian exiles, ceased publication):

Holub[nychy], Vsevolod. "Pro kompetentsiyi ministerstva zakordonnykh sprav USSR (The Competence of the Ministry of Foreign Affairs of the UkrSSR)," December, 1955, pp. 5–6.

———. "Statystyka naselennya Ukrayiny v 1940–1956 rr. (Statistics of the Population of the Ukraine, 1940–1956)," October, 1956, pp. 2–3.

Able scholarly analyses.

M-ko, I. "Yak treba rozumity zakon Verkhovnoyi Rady URSR (How to Understand the Law of the Supreme Soviet of the Ukrainian SSR)," July, 1959, p. 4.

An able interpretation by a former Soviet editor.

V. Encyclopedias

A. soviet

Bol'shaya Sovetskaya Entsyklopediya (Large Soviet Encyclopedia). 65 Vols. 1st ed. Moscow, 1926–1939. See esp.:

V. K., "Khmelnytsky," Vol. 59 (1935), pp. 816–18.

Bol'shaya Sovetskaya Entsyklopediya. 51 vols. 2nd ed. Moscow, 1949–1958. See esp.:

"Ukrainskaya Sovetskaya Sotsialisticheskaya Respublika" (Ukrainian SSR), Vol. 44 (1956), pp. 67–167.

"Ukrainsky yazyk" (Ukrainian Language), *ibid.*, pp. 169–72.

"Ukraintsy" (Ukrainians), *ibid.*, pp. 172–75.

Entire Vol. 51 (1958) for biographical sketches of Khrushchev's lieutenants.

Entsyklopedicheskiy slovar' (Encyclopedic Dictionary). 3 vols. Moscow, 1953–55.

Ukrayins'ka radyans'ka entsyklopediya (Ukrainian Soviet Encyclopedia). Kiev, 1959– .

Incomplete to date.

B. OTHER

Entsyklopediya Ukrayinoznavstva (Encyclopedia of Ukrainian Studies). Munich & New York: Molode Zhyttya (Young Life), 1949. Vol. I, arranged according to broad subject areas (archeology of Ukraine, history, geography, etc.).

Indispensable reference work published by the Shevchenko Scientific Society. The *Ukrayins'ka radyans'ka entsyklopediya* appears to be a belated response to it. Vol. II (Ukrainian—small topics alphabetically arranged) is being completed; an updated English version of Vol. I is being published by Toronto University Press.—See esp.

Polons'ka-Vasylenko, N., and M. Chubaty, "Istoriya tserkvy" (History of the Church), Vol. I, pp. 601–21.

Pologne, 1919–1939 (Poland, 1919–1939). 3 vols. Neuchatel, Switzerland: Editions de la Baconnière, 1946–47.

Polish Encyclopedia; valuable.

VI. STATISTICAL HANDBOOKS

A. SOVIET

Russian SFSR (Soviet Federated Socialist Republic)

Tsentral'noe statisticheskoe upravlenie RSFSR (RSFSR Central Statistical Administration). *Narodnoe khozaystvo RSFSR. Statisticheskiy sbornik* (Russian SFSR National Economy: A Statistical Handbook). Moscow: State Publishers of Statistics, 1957.

Tsentral'noe statisticheskoe upravlenie pri Sovete Ministrov RSFSR (RSFSR Council of Ministers Central Stat. Adm.). *Narodnoe khozaystvo RSFSR v 1960 g. Statisticheskiy ezhegodnik* (RSFSR National Economy in 1960: A Statistical Annual). Moscow: State Publishers of Statistics, 1961.

Ukrainian SSR

Tsentral'ne statystychne upravlinnya pry Radi Ministriv SRSR—Statystychne upravlinnya Ukrayins'koyi RSR (Central Statistical Administration of the USSR Council of Ministers—Ukrainian SSR Statistical Administration). *Narodne hospodarstvo Ukrayins'koyi RSR. Statystychny zbirnyk* (Ukrainian SSR National Economy: A Statistical Handbook). Kiev: State Publishers of Statistics, 1957.

———. *Dosyahnennya Radyans'koyi Ukrayiny za sorok rokiv. Statystychny* zbirnyk (Achievements of Soviet Ukraine in 40 Years: A Statistical Handbook). Kiev: State Publishers of Statistics, 1957.

Tsentral'ne statystychne upravlinnya pry Radi Ministriv URSR (Central Statistical Administration of the Ukrainian SSR Council of Ministers). *Radyans'ka Ukrayina v tsyfrakh* (Soviet Ukraine in Figures). Kiev: State Publishers of Statistics, 1960.

An abridged version of the more comprehensive statistical handbooks, not so useful.

Tsentral'ne statystychne upravlinnya pry Radi Ministriv URSR (Central Statistical Administration of the Ukrainian SSR Council of Ministers). *Narodne hospodarstvo Ukrayins'koyi RSR v 1959 rotsi;* Statystychny shchorichnyk (Ukrainian SSR National Economy in 1959; Statistical Annual). Kiev: State Publishers of Statistics, 1960.

Contains very valuable data on the distribution of nationalities in the Ukraine (from the 1959 census).

——. *Narodne hospodarstvo Ukrayins'koyi RSR v 1960 rotsi;* Statystychny shchorichnyk (Ukrainian SSR National Economy in 1960; . . .). Kiev: State Publishers of Statistics, 1961.

Detailed data on occupations from the 1959 census.

——. *Narodne hosp. . . . v 1961 r.* . . . (Ukrainian SSR National Economy in 1961). Kiev: State Publishers of Statistics, 1962.

Less useful than preceding volumes, but has interesting comparative data on college enrollments in the Ukrainian SSR.

USSR

Ministerstvo Finansov SSSR; Byudzhetnoe upravlenie (USSR Ministry of Finances; Budget Administration). *Gosudarstvenny byudzhet SSSR i byudzhety soyuznykh respublik;* Statisticheskiy sbornik (State Budget of the USSR and Budgets of the Union Republics: A Statistical Handbook). Moscow: State Financial Publishers, 1962.

Some very important data in a rare publication.

Ministerstvo Kul'tury SSSR, Glavizdat, Vsesoyuznaya Knizhnaya Palata (USSR Ministry of Culture, Main Administration of Publishing, All-Union Book House). *Pechat' SSSR za sorok let, 1917–1957* (USSR Publications in 40 Years, 1917–1957). Moscow, 1957.

Tsentral'noe statisticheskoe upravlenie pri Sovete Ministrov SSSR (Central Statistical Administration of the USSR Council of Ministers). *Dostizheniya sovetskoy vlasti za sorok let v tsifrakh* (Achievements of the Soviet State in 40 Years in Figures). Moscow: State Publishers of Statistics, 1957.

Tsentral'noe statisticheskoe upravlenie pri Sovete Ministrov SSSR (Central Statistical Administration of the USSR Council of Ministers). *Kul'-*

turnoe stroitel'stvo SSSR (Cultural Construction in the USSR). Moscow: State Publishers of Statistics, 1956.

See also the volume for 1940, below.

——. *Itogi vsesoyuznoy perepisi naseleniya 1959 goda: SSSR (Svodny tom)* (Results of the All-Union Population Census of 1959: USSR [Summary volume]). Moscow: State Publishers of Statistics, 1962.

——. *Itogi vsesoyuznoy perepisi naseleniya 1959 goda: Ukrainskaya SSR* (Results of the All-Union Population Census of 1959: Ukrainian SSR). Moscow: State Publishers of Statistics, 1963.

The two volumes, obtained while this book was in print, contain very important data from the 1959 population census. The entire series (one volume for each Republic and a summary volume for the Soviet Union) apparently are supposed to present the final evaluation of the census. If so, they compare rather unfavorably with the 56 larger volumes on the 1926 census (see this section, below).

——. *Narodnoe khozaystvo SSSR;* Statisticheskiy sbornik (USSR National Economy: A Statistical Handbook). Moscow: State Publishers of Statistics, 1956.

——. *Narodnoe khozaystvo SSSR v 1956 godu;* Statisticheskiy ezhegodnik (USSR National Economy in 1956: A Statistical Annual). Moscow: State Publishers of Statistics, 1957.

——. *Narodnoe khozaystvo SSSR v 1958 g.;* Statisticheskiy ezhegodnik (USSR National Economy in 1958; . . .). Moscow: State Publishers of Statistics, 1959.

——. *Narodnoe khozaystvo SSSR v 1960 g.;* . . . (USSR National Economy in 1960; . . .). Moscow: State Publishers of Statistics, 1961.

Contains valuable nationality data from the 1959 census.

——. *Promyshlennost' SSSR* (USSR Industry). Moscow: State Publishers of Statistics, 1957.

——. *Sovetskaya Torgovlya* (USSR Trade). Moscow: State Publishers of Statistics, 1956.

——. *Vysshee obrazovanie v SSSR* (Higher Education in the USSR). Moscow: State Publishers of Statistics, 1961.

Contains invaluable data on the distribution of college students and college graduates of different nationalities.

Tsentral'noe statisticheskoe upravlenie SSSR, otdel perepisi (USSR Central Statistical Administration, Census Division). *Vsesoyuznaya perepis' naseleniya 1926 g.* (All-Union Population Census of 1926). 56 Vols. Moscow: Central Statistical Administration Publishers, 1926–33.

Relevant materials in Vols. V, XI–XIII, XVII.

Tsentral'noe upravlenie narodno-khozaystvennoho ucheta Gosplana SSSR (Main Administration of National Economic Accounting of the

USSR Gosplan). *Kul'turnoe stroitel'stvo SSSR* (Cultural Construction in the USSR). Moscow: Gosplan Publishers, 1940.

See the corresponding volume for 1956, above.

B. OTHER

Holub[nychy], Vsevolod. *The Industrial Output of the Ukraine: A Statistical Analysis.* Munich: Institute for the Study of the USSR, 1957.

Valuable statistics collected before the Soviet government started publishing its handbooks.

VII. BIBLIOGRAPHIES

A. SOVIET

Akademiya nauk SSSR—Fundamental'naya biblioteka obshchestvennykh nauk (USSR Academy of Sciences—Basic Library of Social Sciences). *Istoriya SSSR: Ukazatel' sovetskoy literatury za 1917–1952 gg.* [*Tom I:*] *Istoriya SSSR s drevneyshikh vremen do vstupleniya Rossii v period kapitalizma* (History of USSR: List of Soviet Literature from 1917–52. [Vol. I:] History of USSR from the Earliest Times until Russia's Entering into Capitalism). Moscow: USSR Academy of Sciences Publishers, 1956.

———. ———. *Prilozhenie; Skhema klassifikatsii; Vspomagatel'nye ukazateli* (Appendix; Classification Scheme; Helpful Indices). USSR Academy of Sciences Publishers, 1956.

Most useful for establishing the Party line in historiography. Main volume has 725 pp. Reviewed by C. E. Black.

Gosudarstvennaya ordena Lenina biblioteka SSSR im. V. I. Lenina; Gos. publichnaya biblioteka USSR; Gos. publichnaya istoricheskaya biblioteka (USSR State . . . Lenin Library [Moscow]; Ukrainian SSR State Public Library; State Public Historical Library). *Nerushimaya druzhba bratskikh narodov SSSR.* Sbornik bibliograficheskikh i metodicheskikh materialov dlya massovykh bibliotek (Unshakeable Friendship of Fraternal Peoples; Collection of Bibliographical and Methodological Materials for Mass Libraries). Moscow, 1954.

Most authoritative Soviet bibliography on Pereyaslav.

Ministerstvo Kul'tury Ukrayins'koyi RSR, Holovvydav, Knyzhkova palata URSR (Ukrainian SSR Ministry of Culture, Main Administration of Publishing, Ukrainian SSR House of Books). *Periodychni vydannya URSR, 1918–1950: Zhurnaly—bibliohrafichny dovidnyk* (Periodicals in the Ukrainian SSR, 1918–50: Journals—Bibliographical Guide). Kharkov: Publishers of the Ukrainian SSR House of Books, 1956.

Ministerstvo Kul'tury URSR, Holovne upravlinnya vydavnytsv ta poli-
hrafichnoyi promyslovosti (Ukrainian SSR Ministry of Culture, Main
Administration of Publishing and Polygraphical Industry). *Spysok literatury, vypushchenoyi vydavnytstvamy Ukrayiny v 1955 r.* (List of
Works published in the Ukraine in 1955). Kiev, 1956.

B. OTHER

Kravtsiv, Bohdan. "Zhurnaly i hazety v Ukrayins'kiy SSR (Journals and
Newspapers in the Ukrainian SSR)," in Svoboda, *Al'manakh na rik
1963* (Almanac for 1963, Jersey City, N.J., 1963), pp. 77–84.
Valuable bibliographical article.

Lawrynenko, Jurij. *Ukrainian Communism and Soviet Russian Policy
toward the Ukraine: An Annotated Bibliography, 1917–53.* New York:
Research Program on the USSR, 1953.
Indispensable; 454 pp.

U.S. Library of Congress. *Monthly List of Russian Accessions.*
Now title changed to *Monthly Index of Russian Accessions.*

VIII. Unpublished Materials

Bilinsky, Yaroslav. 66 personal interviews with former Soviet citizens, or
persons who came into extensive contact with Soviet Ukrainians (32
of them left the USSR after 1945), plus 44 personal interviews with
scholars and other competent persons.

———. "Findings of the Harvard Refugee Interview Project on the Extent of Ukrainian Spoken in the Ukrainian SSR." Brief unpublished
study prepared for the Harvard Russian Research Center in August,
1959.

Gilliam, Sylvia. "The Nationality Questionnaire," unpublished report of
the Project on the Soviet Social System, Russian Research Center, Harvard University, October, 1954. (Mimeographed.)

———, *et al.* "The Nationality Problem in the Soviet Union: The Ukrainian Case." Unpublished final report of the Project on the Soviet Social System, Russian Research Center, Harvard University, October,
1954.
Includes the reports by Gilliam, Reshetar, and Rosow, with a summary and introduction by Frederick Wyle.

Kucera, Jindrich. "Language Policy in the Soviet Union." Unpublished
Ph.D. dissertation, Harvard University, 1952.

Manuscript A: On the liquidation of the Greek Catholic Church.

Manuscript B: Memoirs of a former inmate of Soviet labor camps.

"The Nationalities Code Book." Unpublished material of the Project on the Soviet Social System, Russian Research Center, Harvard University, October 23, 1952.

Reshetar, John S., Jr. "The Nationality Problem in the Soviet Union." Unpublished report of the Project on the Soviet Social System, Russian Research Center, Harvard University. (Mimeographed.)

Rosow, Irving. "The Relation of Nationality to Experience and Attitude in the USSR." Unpublished report of the Project on the Soviet Social System, Russian Research Center, Harvard University, October, 1954. (Mimeographed.)

GLOSSARY OF UNFAMILIAR TERMS

AND ABBREVIATIONS

CP—Communist Party.

CP(B)U—Communist Party (Bolshevik) of Ukraine.

Central *Rada*—Central Council, the Ukrainian democratic Parliament in 1917–18.

KGB—Committee of State Security of the USSR Council of Ministers. From March, 1954, to date has controlled the secret police, the border guards, and the internal-security troops. See also MVD, below.

kolkhoz—collective farm.

kolkhoznik—collective farm peasants.

korenizatsiya—"taking roots," or the Soviet policy in the 1920's which had as objective the rooting of the Soviet and Party apparatus in the non-Russian Republics.

MVD—Ministry of Internal Affairs, successor to NKVD (see below). From 1946 to 1949 it was left in charge only of the border guards and internal-security troops, the other political functions of the old NKVD being exercised by its sister ministry, the MGB, or Ministry of Internal Security. From Stalin's death in March, 1953, until March, 1954, the MVD again exercised all the functions of the old NKVD. See also KGB, above.

NKVD—People's Commissariat of Internal Affairs: From 1934 until 1946 it was in charge of border guards, internal-security troops, and secret (political) police. See also MVD and KGB, above.

OUN—Organization of Ukrainian Nationalists.

obkom—oblast or Province Party Committee.

oblast—Province.

Russian SFSR—Russian Soviet Federated Socialist Republic.

SSR (when preceded by name of nationality, Kazakh SSR, e.g.)—Soviet Socialist Republic.

UHVR—Ukrainian Supreme Council of Liberation, the government-like body set up by the OUN (see above) and the UPA (see below) in late 1943.

UPA—Ukrainian Insurgent Army.

UVO—Ukrainian Military Organization, the predecessor of the OUN (see above) in the 1920's.

Ukrainian SSR—Ukrainian Soviet Socialist Republic.

WIN—Liberty and Independence. Name of a group of Polish anticommunist guerrillas operating after World War II.

INDEX

Author's note: Throughout the index, the capital letters refer to the left (A) and the right (B) columns in the Appendix; the abbreviation CP stands for the Communist Party; the term "Russian" refers exclusively to the Russian Socialist Federated Republic (SFSR), not to the Soviet Union as a whole.

Postyshev, P. P., 235; and influx of Russian officials into the Ukraine, 293; and persecution of Ukrainian nationalists, 158

Power, political, relative character of, 226

Pravda, 14, 15, 16, 26, 30, 191, 208, 220, 225, 238, 239, 251, 257

Prisoners of war, from German camps, 50; join UPA (Ukrainian Insurgent Army), 121

Professionals, 83, 298; among CP of Ukraine members, 229, 367n16; and identification as Ukrainians, 285; nationality of, 63, 69–71, 77–78; number of, 63–66, 71, 76–77; number of Jews among, 397B; number of Ukrainians among, 76. *See also* College graduates; Elite

Propaganda: and the tercentenary of the Treaty of Pereyaslav, 18–19, 210; by falsification, 203, 208, 432B, Chapters VI and VII, *passim;* by lectures, 12–13, 24, 25–26, 137; by motion pictures, 26, 137; by oversimplification, 434A–435B; by theater plays, 137; falsification detectable in, 223; neo-scholastic methods of, 195; weaknesses of, 348–49n143

Public administration, 59; language of, 6, 8, 34; Russification of, 156. *See also* Budget; Agricultural policy; Collectivization; Industrial administration; Industrialization

Purges: and Serdyuk's position in the CP of Soviet Union, 371n79; in non-Russian Communist Parties, *1958–59,* 318n93; of libraries, 395B; of textbooks, 395B

Radio receivers, data on availability of, 279

Rashidov, Sh. R., 247n, 248

Rebet, Lev, 281

Red Army, 18, 103, 125, 127, 130, 132, 372n87; and Beria, 238; as instrument of Russification, 182; draft into, 50, 129–30; exposes Soviet citizens to the West, 10; national detachments in, 314n30; patterns of friendship in, 295; position of Ukrainians in, 286–87; relations

Red Army (cont.) with UPA (Ukrainian Insurgent Army) of, 117; UPA includes former officers of, 123, 126

Repatriates to USSR: not all of them allowed to return to Ukraine, 50–51

Republics, Soviet, *see* Councils of Ministers, Soviet Republics

Research personnel, 291; academic qualifications of, 73; nationality of, 73–74, 76–77; number of, 62, 71–74; number of Russians among, 290, 386n40; number of Ukrainians among, 76, 290, 292

Resettlement: of different peoples approved by Lenin, 143; of national minorities across the Curzon Line, 116; of Western Ukrainians, 93–94, 139

Retail turnovers, relative, 67–69

Riga, Polish-Soviet Treaty of, 85

Right Bank Ukraine, 295; number of Poles in, 58–59; Russification in, 150

Roman Catholic Church, *see* Holy See

Romzha, Bishop Theodore, 105

Roosevelt, Franklin D.: accepts in principle Stalin's claim to Western Ukraine, 88; and admission of the Ukraine to the United Nations, 265, 271, 272, 273, 275–76, 378n13; attitude toward the United Nations of, 271

Rostov Province (Russia), 245

Rovno: German occupation authorities located in, 121; textile mills promised in, 259

Rovno Province: anti-Soviet guerrillas reported in, 132; CP of Ukraine strength in, 249; number of Russians in, 330n98

Rumania, 3, 142; and claims to Northern Bukovina, 59, 84; peace treaty with, 266n, 267; Ukrainian irredenta and Soviet policy, 7; UPA (Ukrainian Insurgent Army) raids into, 116, 130; visitors from, 380n35

Rumanians, number in Ukraine, 54

Rumyantsev, A. M., 243

Rural population: higher birth rate among, 56; overall decrease of, 47;

* This entry refers exclusively to the Russian Republic